"汉学与当代中国"座谈会文集 2016

THE COLLECTED WORKS
AT THE SYMPOSIUM ON CHINA STUDIES 2016

文化部对外文化联络局
中外文化交流中心
编

中国社会科学出版社

图书在版编目(CIP)数据

“汉学与当代中国”座谈会文集.2016 / 文化部对外文化联络局，中外文化交流中心编.—北京：中国社会科学出版社，2017.7

ISBN 978 - 7 - 5203 - 0661 - 4

Ⅰ.①汉… Ⅱ.①文… ②中… Ⅲ.①汉学—文集
Ⅳ.①K207.8-53

中国版本图书馆CIP数据核字(2017)第147382号

出 版 人 赵剑英
责任编辑 夏 侠
责任校对 周晓燕
责任印制 王 超

出 版 中国社会科学出版社
社 址 北京鼓楼西大街甲158号
邮 编 100720
网 址 http://www.csspw.cn
发 行 部 010 - 84083685
门 市 部 010 - 84029450
经 销 新华书店及其他书店

印刷装订 北京君升印刷有限公司
版 次 2017年7月第1版
印 次 2017年7月第1次印刷

开 本 710×1000 1/16
印 张 36.25
字 数 629千字
定 价 298.00元

2016 年 10 月 24 日，中宣部副部长景俊海出席“汉学与当代中国”座谈会开幕式

On October 24, 2016, Jing Junhai, Vice-Minister of the Publicity Department of the CPC Central Committee, attending the opening ceremony of the Symposium on China Studies

2016 年 10 月 24 日，文化部党组成员、副部长丁伟出席“汉学与当代中国”座谈会开幕式

On October 24, 2016, Ding Wei, Member of the Leading Party Members’ Group and Vice-Minister, the Ministry of Culture, attending the opening ceremony of the Symposium on China Studies

2016 年 10 月 24 日，文化部对外文化联络局局长谢金英出席“汉学与当代中国”座谈会开幕式

On October 24, 2016, Xie Jinying, Director of the Bureau for External Cultural Relations of the Ministry of Culture, attending the opening ceremony of the Symposium on China Studies

2016 年 10 月 24 日，文化部对外文化联络局副局长朱琦在“汉学与当代中国”座谈会开幕式后接受媒体采访

On October 24, 2016, Zhu Qi, Deputy Director of the Bureau for External Cultural Relations of the Ministry of Culture, interviewed by CCTV after the opening ceremony of the Symposium on China Studies

“汉学与当代中国”座谈会开幕式前并行圆桌会议

The round table meeting held before the opening ceremony of the Symposium on China Studies

2016 年 10 月 24 日，“汉学与当代中国”座谈会开幕式后嘉宾与汉学家合影

Group photo of distinguished guests and sinologists at the opening ceremony on October 24, 2016

“汉学与当代中国”座谈会开幕式现场

At the opening ceremony of the Symposium on China Studies

座谈会现场

At the Symposium on China Studies

座谈会现场

At the Symposium on China Studies

座谈会现场

At the Symposium on China Studies

座谈会现场

At the Symposium on China Studies

座谈会现场

At the Symposium on China Studies

座谈会现场

At the Symposium on China Studies

2016 年 10 月 26 日至 29 日，汉学家在四川省成都市开展有关“一带一路”的文化交流与考察

Sinologists on a visit to Chengdu, Sichuan Province for cultural exchange on the theme of the “Belt and Road” initiative from October 26 to 29, 2016

主办：中华人民共和国文化部　中国社会科学院

承办：中外文化交流中心

Hosts：Ministry of Culture of the People's Republic of China
Chinese Academy of Social Sciences

Organizer: Network of International Culturalink Entities

目 录

“一带一路”与国际格局

文化认同与共同遗产

CONTENTS

China's Route and Common Value

Interconnection and Mutual Development

『一带一路』与国际格局

The Belt and Road and International Structure

从“一带一路”到全球治理：哲学社会科学的桥梁作用

阿尔布劳 【英国】

英国社会学学会 荣誉副会长 / 英国社会科学院 院士 / 荣休教授

不论哪位学者，在受邀来到中国、并针对“一带一路”这一主题发表讲话时，内心都是充满敬畏之情的。因为“一带一路倡议”的发起者——当代的中国，是迄今为止世界上最具实力的、为人类集体而代言的机构，与中国的呼声相比，我个人的见解委实微不足道。

有人曾做过这样的争论——究竟该把中国称作一个国家，还是一种文明？在我看来，中国既是一个国家，一种文明，也是一个整体，这种将中国、中国人民仅仅凝聚在一起的力量，是西方世界闻所未闻的。中国实现目标的能力早已得到证实，在世界的其他地区，能够拥有这种能力的，除军事力量之外，便只有企业的力量，但这两者能够利用的人力资源仅仅是中国的一小部分。

正是因为拥有这种能力，中国的领导层才能够以“一带一路”倡议对西方的全球化做出回应，中国才能够采取另外一种方式影响全球事务，才能够与其他国家一道，构建一个更加美好的世界。由于“一带一路”倡议的核心在于国家之间的互联互通，因而共同的文化基础是十分必要的。很显然，哲学社会科学需要尽早地的参与进来，才能更好地探讨如何构建这种基础。

中国对自身国力充满信心的同时，也邀请国外学者一道，为创建一个更好的世界而共同努力。习近平主席在今年 5 月 17 日哲学社会科学工作座谈会上讲道：“要向外看、积极探索关系人类前途命运的重大问题”。

1. " 一带一路 "是迄今为止最具雄心壮志的一项工程，它把中国的和平发展与整个世界的繁荣与幸福联结在一起

2013 年 10 月 3 日，习近平在印度尼西亚首次提出共同建设 21 世纪海上丝绸之路的建议，并指出中国与东盟国家之间的互动交流为"……相互学习、相互借鉴……提供了重要的文化基础"

然而在西方，为国家间的和平互动构建基础的问题，常被纳入全球治理的范畴。如果从最广义的视角出发，可以这样来看待全球治理：所谓的全球治理是指，为应对国际挑战、为保持全球社会秩序而形成的过程或机制。从狭义角度来看，国际货币基金组织、世界银行、世贸组织等国际经济组织，往往被视作全球治理机制的核心。但是西方认为正是这些经济组织促成并推进着全球化向前发展。许多人，包括我自己在内，都对这种观点持批判态度。因为这种观点将全球化的理念十分不必要地限制在了经济过程上，将全球治理局限于经济组织上。

至少应在联合国各个机构内，在维和问题、卫生问题、移民问题、气候变化问题的干预上，对这种观点进行平衡和抵消。新的可持续发展目标就是要超越经济的藩篱来审视问题。

2. " 一带一路 "面临的风险在于，它容易被人误解为中国版的" 美式全球化 "

在孕育成全球化问题的解决方案之前，"一带一路"面临着被误解的风险，容易被误解为一种经济战略，更糟的是，容易被世界其他国家视作是国家霸权主义的延伸，认为"一带一路"只不过打着为各国带来利益的幌子而已。这些国家会用看待美国的角度来解读中国。

"一带一路"若想取得长期的成就，则有必要强调其非经济层面的特征，从而将"一带一路"与全球化区别开来。由于"一带一路"倡议具有深厚的文化内涵，因此中国的文化实力、对哲学社会科学重要性的认识等，都能促成对全球治理的整体的认识，而这种认识恰恰是当今世界所需要的。

***

首先，我要探讨全球化和"一带一路"的区别。总体而言，这样的对比太过宽泛，因此这里只能勾勒出一个大体框架，以示两者间的区别。

在过去三十年中，全球化在西方话语中占据支配地位，但在它的内涵中，似

乎很少包括国际交流、全球市场、共同命运的意识、国家主权的丧失以及国家间愈发强烈的相互依赖等主题。

3. 西方全球化作为一种话语，融合了“故事”、战略以及意识形态

当然，所有这些问题都有待进行实证研究，而相关的研究正不断取得更大的成果。尽管如此，全球化一直都是一种话语，涉及政治内容、演讲、评论以及辩论。由于“一带一路”正处于愿景形成和政策形成的初期阶段，因此在这两个方面，可以与全球化进行比较。

在这里，我要对全球化的三种话语进行区分：故事、战略、意识形态。这三种形式经历了连续的发展阶段，但每种形式都在同化前一种形式的同时，避免了对前一种形式的替代。

首先，全球化是一种“故事”。这一点至少可以追溯到20世纪70年代，最明显地体现在乔治·莫德尔斯基关于世界政治的教科书中的一章中。在这部作品中，莫德尔斯基提倡一种“跨国视角”，将全球化看作“将世界融为一体”的历史过程中的高潮阶段。在这个版本中，全球化的根源已经消失在时间中，当下则被视作历史过程的高潮阶段，这个过程可以追溯到历史的开始。

在社会学领域，罗兰德·罗伯特森的早期作品阐释了世界是如何随着区域性的多元化而变为统一事件的这个“故事”。1990年，国际社会学协会在马德里举办世界社会学大会，会上对这一观点给予了公开认可，并将会议主题确定为：“统一与多元：适合整个世界的社会学”，在会议文集中，一信息被传播开来，并传达给来自世界各个地区的4000多名与会代表。

其次，全球化是一种战略。这种观点曾在20世纪80年代初步引起了学术界的热议，随后这一理念被纳入到商业领域。跨国公司发现这个理念能很好地融入其背景叙事，有助于跨国公司在全球范围内的扩展。

有关这一理念的参照性文本出现在《哈佛商业评论》上，作者为西奥多·列维特，文章题目为《市场的全球化》(1983)。在文章中，他认为全球化意味着消费者选择的同质化，这为企业制定全球战略提供了基础。“全球战略”已经成为企业计划的标准特征。

第三，全球化是一种意识形态。在西方民主体制中，凡是企图赢得多数选民支持的话语，其中总能找到资本利益的政治表达。自苏联解体后，在新自由主义

必胜信念的激励下，20 世纪 90 年代出现了一系列的说法——这些说法预言民族国家最终将灭亡，民族文化最终将变得同质化。

4. 西方全球化话语：故事—文明的进步；战略—走向全球；意识形态—自由主义民主

对于许多美国人而言，这种新的全球化明显符合其国家利益。最流行的一种观点体现在托马斯·弗里德曼的畅销作品《雷克萨斯与橄榄树》（1999）中。作者将全球化看作一种体制，而美国则是这一体制中"唯一且占据支配地位的超级大国"，从"文化角度来看，全球化在很大程度上（并非完全）都可以看作是美国化的一种扩张"。此时，故事、战略、意识形态已经融为一体。克林顿总统将全球化定义为一种不可逆转的历史趋势，美国政坛的领导层开始积极地制定一套激进的、社会民主主义政策，这些政策被称作"第三种道路"。

当美国总统克林顿及副总统艾尔·戈尔在将民主党派的选举方案中，朝着更加开放的市场、改革公共服务的方向进行重新定位时，全球化成为了选举方案中的关键词。英国的新工党追随了美国的新民主党的步伐，20 世纪 90 年代的一段时期内，欧洲的左翼政治领导人也曾掀起过一场较为松散的运动，在认同"第三种道路"理念的西方国家中，这种运动的规模更加广泛。

然而人们对于全球化的信心因为两个事件而发生动摇。第一个事件是反全球化运动在国际范围内的迅速蔓延。1999 年 12 月，世贸组织在西雅图的会议不得不因为抗议活动而取消。抵抗全球化运动、反全球化运动，以及随后的另类全球化运动成为当时全球意识形态冲突的象征性标志。

导致对全球化信心减弱的另外一个事件是 2001 年 9 月 11 日，世贸中心双塔的倒塌。对于中国以及其他国家而言，全球化至今仍然是美国推行的一项策略，人国际金融机构则为这项策略的执行奠定了基础，为推行新自由主义经济政策提供便利。尽管美国对这一意识形态已经失去信心，但它的全球影响力仍然在持续。

5. " 一带一路 " 要求中国学习西方对待全球化的态度——积极鼓励思想界的参与。

那么，对于全球化给思想界造成的混乱，我们是否应该选择忘记？这种做法显然是错误的。在全球化进程中，思想界曾爆发过激烈的理论辩论，这种辩论既涉及国内公共政策，也涉及国际公共政策。一些最著名的西方学者，如乌尔里希·贝克、阿米塔伊·埃茨奥尼、安东尼·吉登斯、罗伯特·帕特南等人，均对“改造政府、社会资本、民间社会”等理念的提出做出过重要贡献，而这些变化正是通过全球化来推动的。

我这里想要强调的是，中国需要学习西方对待全球化的态度，积极鼓励思想界的参与，但这一次是为“一带一路”构建更为饱满的理论框架，指出“一带一路”对于全球社会秩序的潜在贡献、对全球治理的潜在贡献。因而要在西方对全球化失去信心时，填补“一带一路”的理论空白。但这一次，应该把文化问题，而不是经济问题放在理论的中心位置。

***

为了更好地区别“一带一路”与西方经济全球之间的区别，我依次从历史、战略、意识形态等几个角度进行了分析。很明显，“一带一路”将在“历史”上留下浓墨重彩的一笔。2013 年 9 月 7 日，习近平主席首次提出“丝绸之路经济带”的倡议。在 2014 年 6 月 15 日，第六届中阿合作论坛上，习近平主席在文明交流史的语境中提到了郑和下西洋。

西方的全球化叙事采用了世界–历史模式，而“一带一路”倡议的叙事则以发展国家间、文化间、文明间的交流为主，并不是描述“西方现代性、先进性”的“故事”。

从战略方面讲，“一带一路”与中国的两个百年目标——2021 年全面建成小康社会、2049 年，建成富强、民主、文明、和谐的社会主义现代化国家——是相契合的。通过“一带一路倡议”习近平主席将两个百年目标与每个中国人的“民族复兴”梦紧密联系在一起。

当然，这两个百年目标在所有目标、计划、日程中处于首位，在西方观察者的眼里，这两个目标不仅极具雄心壮志，而且十分具体、非常全面，通过标语、街道标牌以及媒体的宣传，具有极强的可见度以及对公众的震撼力。

因此，“一带一路”作为国家战略的延伸，能够号召并凝聚国家、企业的资源以及人民的能量。然而西方人对于国家实力和企业实力的看法并不一致，对西方而言，全球化的方向作为一种战略，主要依靠的是全球企业的商业计划，把国际金融组织当作一种支持者，而不是目标的制定者。因此，政府时常在商业需求和选民的需求之间左右为难，对于社会民主主义而言，这更是一个难以逾越的困境。

在意识形态方面，“一带一路”的理念基础十分明显——中国特色的社会主义，因此与西方全球化的理念有着根本的差别。不论是新自由主义，还是社会民主对经济原则的修正，西方理论往往会中和文化差异，鼓吹文化的普遍性。

6. 中国的“一带一路”话语：故事，2000 年的文化碰触；中国梦；意识形态：中国特色的社会主义

中国的“一带一路倡议”不仅能够调动市场来支持社会主义建设，而且能够在中国文明的文化基础上建设社会主义，这有助于“一带一路”的参与国保持各自的文化和经验。中国并非借此推广社会主义。

中国不仅需求沿线（64 个）国家的理解和合作，同时还确保这些伙伴国在参与“一带一路”建设的过程中，能够保证各自的文化主权。这里我要提出的问题是：西方全球化未能创造出一个令各国相互尊重、平等分享利益的世界，那么中国的一带一路是否能够完成西方的未竟之业？

***

2014 年 4 月，习近平在布鲁日的欧洲学院发表讲话，从他轻松幽默的言辞中，我们看到了他对未来工作的形象表达。在提到自己喜欢中国茶但也喜欢欧洲啤酒时，习近平主席将中国“和而不同”的信仰与欧盟“统一而多元”的理念进行了对比。

他指出，两种信仰分别代表着两种伟大的文明，两者对于“共同的文化繁荣”都是十分必要的。随后习近平主席呼吁：“让我们同心协力，让人类文明的花朵共同开放。”这番言辞正是全球治理的优雅表达，它指出了实现文化间相互理解的一个重要前提——那就是通过合作来实现共同目标。

从这个角度来看，在过去二十年中，西方对于文化的展望，与中国务实的文化实践的确发生了交汇。不论是千年发展目标还是可持续发展目标，都为中国的五年计划、更为国际合作打下了基础。

对于全球化的影响，历来存在两种不同的说法：一种说法看到了全球化、全球化时代给世界带来的同质化影响，另一种说法看到了各国通过采取不同的措施来应对共同的全球挑战，看到了共同的全球时代。正如乌尔里希·贝克在《风险社会》（1986）以及我本人在《全球时代》（1996）中强调的一样，对共同威胁的意识是我们这个时代无处不在的特征，也正是因为这个特征，我们这个时代的现

代性才能与传统的现代性区别开来。

7. 每个国家都从自身的文化出发，应对全球时代特有的统统挑战

在分享这种共同挑战的意识的同时，我们也要认识到中国和西方在于全球治理方法上的差异。西方全球化和欧盟都具有这样几个同样的特点：建立体制框架，将各国变为大的整体的组成部分，这种做法会带来摩擦，忽视文化差异带来的风险。最近英国通过全民公决离开欧盟的事件便是对这种风险的最好的阐释。

当然，中国的方法也具有一定的危险性，这一点，王义桅教授在解读“一带一路倡议”的文章中已经做出了十分清晰的描述。王教授列举了“一带一路”在政治、安全、经济、法律以及道德层面所面临的一系列风险。共同体的构建是用来控制这些风险的一种战略，欧洲经济共同体的成立便是很好第一个例子。对于英国观察者而言，这点与英国脱欧的语境极为契合，因为英国脱欧的一个主要的理由便是——欧盟已经偏离了共同体的最初精神。

中国认识到了共同体这一理念所蕴含的力量，因此在 18 大上提出了“命运共同体”的概念，以此作为实现全球一体化的方案。这一概念唤起了共同体特有的共同理解，以及命运一词中所隐含的方向感和目标感。想要找到一种能够引起所有文化共鸣的有效方案，最大的挑战在于不同语言之间的互译，不过在这一点上，我们取得了进步，至少在英语语言上取得了进步。

8. 命运共同体必须成为一个跨文化概念，其含义是：并非一方独有，而是多方共享

不论是东方模式还是西方模式，中国和欧洲在全球治理上采取的措施必须相互交流和借鉴，寻求共同语言的重要性并不亚于共同承担任务。“命运共同体”这一概念必将成为人类文化遗产中一个十分关键的概念。我们有必要注意这一概念是如何形成的——它是在与东盟国家、非洲国家、拉丁美洲国家、加勒比国家的对话这个语境中脱颖而出，而不是在欧洲经验的框架下形成。

因而，它是一个跨文化概念，并不独属于某个特定的民族文化，而属于多个文化。跨文化主义这一理念来自古巴社会科学家、人类学家费南多·沃提兹——他在探索一种全新的、独特的、从本土中脱颖而出的音乐文化时提出了这一概念。

马克思主义从最初发展至今，特别是在中国的发展，一直都是一个巨大的跨文化资源。在当今时代，可持续性已经变成最成功的一个跨文化概念，这一概念源自于不同文化之间的对话，与我们的共同命运息息相关。

跨文化再生性指代的是一个过程，需要我们开展实证研究、社会科学研究和历史研究。从中国社会学家余硕的文章中，我们可以读到他对于十七、十八世纪中欧文化触碰的解读，作者本人也在文中表示，希望中国梦能够成为世界各国共生的梦想。

9. 哲学社会科学与实证社会研究必须携手并力，为提高"新全球治理"的普适性和务实性做出贡献

针对全球文互动的实证研究和哲学分析正是"一带一路"这一影响力深远的工程所带来的丰硕成果。推动全球治理所需要的语言，不再适用于以国家间竞争为主的历史时期。对于我们的新时代而言，理念的发展是必要的，从社会科学专业的角度来看，更是必要的，所有这些理念的发展都会对我们所谓的哲学社会科学的发展做出贡献。

中国具有的独特优势能够为"新全球治理"提供源源不断的理念。我曾在中国的《国际交流》刊物上发表过一篇文章，其中列举了中国文化遗产的8项属性，这8项属性对于领导我们这个日渐破碎的世界极为适用。而在全球治理方面，中国文化贡献最大的几个属性为：尊重、敬畏、互惠。

遗产是一方面，抓住时代的机遇又是另外一方面。中国具有强大的领导力，对于理论的理解和阐述都具有十分广泛的吸引力，这无异于一笔丰富的遗产。我之前曾提到过，《习近平谈治国理政》中收录了些习主席的讲话，这些讲话都有着明确原则作基础，并且对这些原则进行了详尽地阐述。

10. 从《习近平谈治国理政》一书中，我们能够发现一个应用理论的模式，而这个模式恰好为阐释全球治理树立了榜样

这些原则都是关于公共政策的一些看法，这些看法统一而连贯，面向广大群众。近年来，西方领导人中很少有哪位能够对这些原则做出明确阐释。目前，中国社会科学家也应像习主席一样，为全球治理寻求具有同样意义的原则。中国与他国的对话过程，正是验证这些原则的绝好机会。

不论是在过去还是在将来，各国都会捍卫本国的文化自主权，没有什么能够

限制他们推广自身理念的权利、限制他们将这些理念强加给全人类的权利。然而在命运共同体当中，各国都能找到一种安全感，能够做到相互尊重，能够找到成功合作的共同基础。命运共同体的务实性和普适性，决定了它必然排斥独断性，因而能够通过经验和论辩不断地进行修正和改进。

Philosophical Social Science as a Bridge from "Belt and Road" to Global Governance

Martin Albrow / United Kingdom of Great Britain and Northern Ireland

Honorary Vice-President of the British Sociological Association /Fellow of the Academy of Social Sciences/Emeritus Professor

It is only with awe that any individual scholar can respond to an invitation to speak on the theme of 'Belt and Road' in the country of its origin.For what is one voice compared with the initiative launched by the most powerful collective human agency our world has ever seen, namely contemporary China?

Some have debated whether to call China a nation state or a civilization. I would say it is both, and additionally also a corporate entity. The bonds that hold it and its people together are more intimate than any known to Western states. Its proven capacity to deliver its goals is matched elsewhere in the world only by corporations or military forces and they can draw on a mere fraction of the population that China possesses.

It is this capacity that enables the Chinese leadership to advance the 'Belt and Road' initiative as a response to Western globalization, as an alternative way of extendingits national influence in world affairs, but also of joining with other countries to build a better world. Since interaction with other countries is at the core of the initiative, philosophical social science clearly needs to be involved at the earliest stage to enquire how that necessary common cultural foundation can be built.

Confident in its power, China invites foreign scholars to contribute to the collective efforts to create a better world. President Xi Jinping said in his speech to the Symposium of Philosophical Social Sciences this year on May 17th, 'We should look to foreign countries and explore those key issues that are related to human prospects and destiny.'

1. 'Belt and Road' is the most ambitious project yet to link the peaceful development of China with the prosperity and well-being of the world as a whole.

Announcing the Maritime Silk Road in Indonesia on October 3rd, 2013 President Xi spoke of the way the ASEAN countries and China had interacted and built a 'cultural foundation … to gain from each other's experience'.[1]

Very frequently in the West the question of the foundations for peaceful interaction between nations is viewed as the problem of global governance.In its broadest sense this may be seen as all those processes and institutions that respond to challenges that extend beyond national boundaries and maintain social order on a global scale.

In a narrower sense economic institutions like the IMF, World Bank and WTO have at times been regarded as the institutional core of global governance.But in the West they have also been seen as enabling and carrying globalization forward. Many, including myself, have criticised this outlook as an unnecessary limitation of the idea of globalization to economic processes and a fatal restriction of global governance to economic institutions.

At the very least it is necessary to counterbalance this view with the huge variety

1 Xi Jinping, 2014, *The Governance of China*, Foreign Languages Press, Beijing, p. 323.

of United Nations agencies and interventions in peacekeeping, health, migration and climate change. The new Sustainable Development Goals for instance go far beyond economic considerations.

2. 'Belt and Road' runs the risk of being regarded as the Chinese equivalent to American globalization

Conceived as an answer to globalization therefore 'Belt and Road' runs the risk of being regarded as an economic strategy only, and, still worse, being regarded by the rest of the world as so much of it has viewed globalization, namely as an extension of national hegemony under the pretence of benefiting all nations. For the United States they will read China.

For the long-term success of 'Belt and Road' it is therefore necessary to emphasize those non-economic features that make it different from globalization. It is also a project with profound cultural implications where the cultural strengths of China and its awareness of the role of philosophical social science can lead to the holistic view of global governance that the world requires today.

***

My argument will build in the first place on a comparison between globalization and 'Belt and Road'. Vast though that task could be in principle,I will seek to reduce it to broad outlines that highlight the differences.

Globalization has been such a dominant component of Western political discourse for the last thirty years that its scope seems to exclude very little – world-wide communication, a global market, consciousness of a common fate, loss of national sovereignty, growing interdependence and so on.

3. Western globalization as discourse combines story, strategy and ideology

All of these are of course open to empirical research and the findings continue to mount. But paralleling all these developments globalization has been *discourse*, the stuff of policies, speeches, commentaries, and debate. Since 'Belt and Road' is at that early stage of vision and policy formulation it is in this respect we can compare it with globalization.

I want to distinguish three versions of the discourse of globalization: as *story*, as *strategy* and as *ideology*. They happen to have developed as successive phases, each assimilating the previous one, without replacing it.

First, globalization as *story*. We can trace this back at least to the 1970s, most notably marked by a chapter in George Modelski's textbook on world politics that advocated a transnational view and saw globalization as the culmination of a historicprocess that had brought the world to be one place.[1] The roots of globalization in this version are lost in time and the present is seen as the culmination of a process that stretches back to the beginning of history

In sociology Roland Robertson's early work represented this story of the world becoming singular even as localities became ever more diverse.[2] In 1990 the Madrid World Congress of the International Sociological Association gave this view a public endorsement with its chosen conference theme: "Sociology for One World: Unity and Diversity." In its Congress volume it disseminated the message to 4000 delegates from that single, diverse world.[3]

Second, globalization as *strategy*. Following hot on the heels of the early academic discussion in the 1980s the idea was leveraged into the business world, multinational corporations finding it well adapted to be the background narrative for their ambition to extend their reach worldwide.

The bench mark text appropriately was published in the *Harvard Business*

1 George Modelski, 1972, *The Principles of World Politics,* Free Press, New York

2 Roland Robertson, 1992, *Globalization: Social Theory and Global Culture,* Sage, London.

3 Martin Albrow and Elizabeth King (eds.), 1990, *Globalization, Knowledge and Society,* Sage, London.

Review by Theodore Levitt "The Globalization of Markets" (1983)where he argued that globalization meant the homogenization of consumer choice providing the basis for firms to develop global strategies. 'Going global' became a standard feature of the corporate plan.

Third, globalization as *ideology*.In the Western democracies the interests of capital will always find political expression in a discourse aimed to win the support of the majority of the electorate. Prompted by the neo-liberal triumphalism that followed on from the collapse of the Soviet Union a series of accounts appeared in the 1990s that predicted the end of the nation-state and the homogenization of national cultures.

4. Western globalization discourse: *story*, the advance of civilization; *strategy*, going global; *ideology*, liberal democracy

For many Americans this new globalization was clearly in their own national interest. The prevailing view was that of Thomas Friedman whose bestseller *The Lexus and the Olive Tree*(1999)saw globalization as a system with the United States as 'the sole and dominant superpower', where 'culturally speaking, globalization is largely, though not entirely, the spread of Americanization'.[1]

The story, the strategy, the ideology merged. President Clinton spoke of globalization as the direction of history that could not be turned back and American political leadership set about energetically to forge a progressive, social democratic set of policies, generally known as the Third Way.

Clinton and his Vice-President Al Gore adopted globalization as the keyword in a re-orientation of the Democratic Party's electoral programme towards more open markets and reform of public services. The New Democrats in the United States were followed by New Labour in the United Kingdom and for a period in the 1990s there was a loose movement of leftist political leaders in Europe and more widely in

1 Thomas L. Friedman, op. cit. p. 5.

the West signed up to the social democratic ideas of the Third Way.[1]

Two events shook that confidence in the benefits of globalization. The first was the rapid international growth of the anti-globalization movement, signalled by its protests leading to the cancellation of the World Trade Organization meeting in Seattle in December 1999. At that point the opposition of globalization and anti-globalization, later alter-globalization,became the symbolic marker of the ideological conflict of the global age.

The second event undermining confidence in globalization was the destruction of the twin towers of the World Trade Center on the 11th September, 2001. However, for the rest of the world, China included, globalization to this day remains an American project, underpinned by the international financial institutions, promoting neo-liberal economic policies. Its global power and influence persists even as the United States itself has lost faith in the ideology.

5. 'Belt and Road' will require the equivalent intellectual creativity to that which built the response to globalization in the West

Should we then also forget the intellectual ferment of the Third Way years as a matter of mere historical interest? That I think would be a mistake. This was a period of intense theoretical debate that informed both domestic and international public policies. Some of the most prominent Western academics, including Ulrich Beck, Amitai Etzioni, Anthony Giddens, and Robert Putnam contributed to a ferment of ideas about reinventing government, social capital, and civil society, with globalization as the underlying driver of change.

What I suggest here is that China needs too to aim for the same kind of intellectual engagement that the West devoted to globalization, but this time to develop a fuller theoretical account of 'Belt and Road' for its potential contribution to the world's social order, or, as it is best conceived, to global governance. Indeed I hold it would be of immense value to the world if you seek to fill the theoretical

1 Anthony Giddens, 1998, *The Third Way*, Polity, Cambridge.

vacuum in the West arising from the loss of faith in globalization. But this time cultural issues, rather than economic ones, should be the centre of attention.

***

To highlight the differences between 'Belt and Road' and Western economic globalization I take history, strategy and ideology in turn.Plainly 'Belt and Road' also has a profound anchorage in *history*, specifically in China's explorations and exchanges with the world beyond the Middle Kingdom. President Xi Jinpingon September 7th 2013 began his very first speech proposing the Silk Road Economic Belt by recalling two missions more than 2100 years ago made by an envoy of the Han dynasty to Central Asia. When speaking at the 6th China-Arab States co-operation forum on June 15th, 2014 he referenced the voyages of Zheng He in the context of the history of exchanges between the two civilizations.

Compared then with the Western world-historical narrative of globalization, the Chinese 'Belt and Road' initiative depends on a narrative of developing exchanges between countries, cultures and civilizations, not on a story of advancing Western modernity.

In respect of *strategy* Belt and Road fits within the Two Centenary Goals of 2021 when the full *Xiaokang,* moderately well off society, will have been achieved and 2049 by which point China will have become a 'strong, democratic, civilized, harmonious and modern socialist society'. Xi links those goals repeatedly to the Chinese Dream of national rejuvenation, a dream for the country and also for 'every ordinary Chinese' (*Realize Youthful Dreams*, 4th May 2013).

These goals are of course only the apex of an architecture of goals, targets, plans and timetables, that for Western observers are not only extraordinary in their ambition, detail and comprehensiveness, but also in their visibility and public penetration through banners, street signs and the media. Even more impressive is their record of demonstrated success over nearly 40 years of the great opening-up policy.

'Belt and Road' therefore is the extension of a national strategy that can call on the combined resources and energies of the state, businesses and people. For the West, however, always conflicted over the respective powers of the state and business, the direction of globalization as a strategy depended on the business plans of the global corporations, with the international financial institutions serving as enablers rather than goal setters. Governments then are torn between the demands of business and those of their electorates. This is the intractable dilemma of social democracy.

In respect of *ideology* Belt and Road is founded clearly on socialism with Chinese characteristics and therein lies a fundamental difference from Western ideas of globalization. Whether as neo-liberalism or in the social democratic corrections to those economic doctrines, Western theories neutralised cultural difference and promoted them as universally applicable.

6. China's 'Belt and Road' discourse: *story*, 2000 years of cultural encounters; *strategy*, the Chinese dream; *ideology*, socialism with Chinese characteristics

The Chinese Belt and Road initiative not only calls on markets to help socialism, but it explicitly builds socialism on the cultural traditions of Chinese civilization and therefore directly allows for other countries to join the Belt and Road initiative from their own cultural experience. Chinese socialism is not for export.

Even as China seeks greater understanding and co-operation with the 64 other partner countries, it is inviting them to join on the basis of their cultural autonomy. The question I ask here is: Can this succeed where Western globalization has largely failed in creating a world where countries can enjoy equal respect and a rightful share in its benefits?

***

The task ahead has a vivid expression in a profound yet apparently light hearted passage in the speech President Xi made to the College of Europe in Bruges in April 2014. In referring to his equal enjoyment of Chinese tea and European beer he contrasted China's belief in "harmony without uniformity" with the EU's stress on being "united in diversity".

He pointed to each as representative of two great civilizations and both as being necessary for a "common cultural prosperity". He then appealed: "Let us work together allowing for all flowers of human civilization to blossom together".[1] That is a more eloquent way of speaking of global governance and points directly to a basis as vital as understanding between cultures, namely co-operation for common goals.

In this respect there has been in the last twenty years a definite convergence between the Western outlook and Chinese cultural practices in goal setting and pragmatic programmes. The Millennium Development Goals and now the Sustainable Development Goals provide the same basis for co-operation internationally as the five year plans do in China.

These are markers for our time that highlight the difference between an account that sees the world homogenized by globalization, the age of globalization, and one that sees countries responding variously to common global challenges, the global age. As Ulrich Beck recognised in his *Risk Society*(1986) and I emphasized in my book *The Global Age* (1996) the sense of common threat is the pervasive feature of our time that marks it off from an old modernity.

7. Every country responds from its own culture to the common challenges that mark out the Global Age

While sharing this sense of common challenges we also need to face up to the differences that exist within both the Western and Chinese approaches when it comes to global governance. Building institutional frameworks for large entities where countries are the constituent parts that characterises both Western globalization and the EU, brings with it the risk of overriding and neglecting cultural difference. I

1 Xi Jinping, op. cit., p. 310.

need only mention the recent British vote to leave the European Union to illustrate the dangers of ignoring this.

The Chinese approach however also brings its own risks, very clearly outlined in the recent account of the 'Belt and Road' initiative by Professor Wang Yiwei.[1] He lists a series of risks, political, security, economic, legal and moral. The construction of community is one strategy for containing them that he highlights and he cites the establishment of the European Economic Community in 1965 as an example at the regional level. For the British observer that is an exceptionally relevant point in the context of the British exit from the European Union, because a main complaint has been that the Union has departed from the original spirit of a community.

Recognizing the power of the idea of community the 18th CPC National Congress advanced the concept of a "community of common destiny" as a formula for global integration. This certainly evokes both the common understanding that characterises community and the sense of purpose and direction conveyed by the idea of destiny. Finding a formula that resonates effectively across all cultures is of course the translation challenge that exceeds all translation challenges, but this does takes us forward, at least in the English language.

8. A community of common destiny must become a transcultural concept, belonging to none, shared by all

Eastern and Western, Chinese and European approaches to global governance have to engage with each other. Finding a common language is as important as sharing a common task. 'Community of common destiny' may well succeed in becoming a key concept in a cultural heritage that belongs to all humankind. But let us note how it arises. It does so in the context of dialogues with ASEAN, Africa, Latin America and Caribbean countries, as well as out of the experience of Europe.

It is then a *transcultural* concept, belonging to no national culture in particular,

1 Wang Yiwei, 2016, *The Belt and Road Initiative. What Will China Offer the World in its Rise.* New World Press, Beijing.

but crossing many. It was probably a Cuban social scientist, the anthropologist Fernando Ortiz who first employed the idea of transculturalism when exploring the emergence of a new and distinctive musical culture arising out of native, African and Spanish roots in Cuba.[1]

Marxism from its beginning and in its development to this day, in particular in China, has been a huge transcultural resource. In my own time sustainability has become one of the most successful transcultural concepts, arising out of dialogue between cultures, linked so closely to our common destiny.

Transcultural generativity as a process is also much in need of empirical, social scientific and historical research. For a recent example we can read the account of European and Chinese seventeenth and eighteenth century encounters by the Chinese sociologist Yu Shou who also looks forward to a transition from the China dream to a world symbiotic dream.[2]

9. Philosophical social science and empirical social research must join together in contributing to the pragmatic universalism of the new global governance

Empirical research and philosophical analysis of global interactions between cultures are essential accompaniments of a programme as far reaching as 'Belt and Road'. The language which is necessary to promote global governance has to develop beyond that which was the medium for understanding in an older modern period of competition between nation states. The development of concepts for our new age is a necessary professional concern for social scientists and they can all contribute to what we may properly call philosophical social science.

China has particular strengths that make it an ideal source for contributions

1 Fernando Ortiz, 1951, *Los Bailes y l Teatro de los Negros en el Folklore de Cuba,* Cardenas y Cia, Havana.

2 Yu Shou, 2015, "Universal dream, national dreams and symbiotic dream: reflections on transcultural generativity in China-Europe encounters" , *Journal of China in Comparative Perspective*, Vol 1, No 1, pp. 44-81, 201-227.

to the new global field of concepts. In a paper in your new journal *International Communication* I highlighted 8 qualities in China's cultural heritage that represent a uniquely appropriate set for a leadership role in our fragmenting world.[1] Of these I would single out respect, reverence and reciprocity as obvious contributions to a recasting of global governance.

Heritage is one thing, capturing the moment of our time is another, and here you have the huge asset of a leadership that both understands and speaks theory in a way that has a popular appeal. As I have pointed out elsewhere, President Xi's speeches collected in his *The Governance of China* are grounded in and elaborate a set of explicit principles.

10. In President Xi's *The Governance of China* we find a model of applied theory that can serve as an example of what is needed for an account of global governance

They offer the kind of coherent view of public policy for a general public that Western leaders have been unable to articulate in recent years. Now is the moment for Chinese social scientists to seek principles of equivalent value for the governance of the globe. These you will test in dialogue with other nations.

The cultural autonomy of nations will be as jealously guarded in the future as it has been in the past, and there can be no restriction on their right to profess values for themselves and to commend them to all human beings. Yet in a community of common destiny they will only find security for themselves and respect from others when they find a common basis for working together successfully, in a pragmatic universalism that denies dogmatism and is open to correction through experience and debate.

1 Martin Albrow, forthcoming, (in Chinese) "Bridging the divides – China's role in a fragmenting world" , *International Communication.*

“一带一路”倡议与中国大外交

郑永年 【新加坡】
新加坡国立大学东亚研究所　所长、教授

2015 年 3 月 28 日，国家主席习近平出席亚洲博鳌论坛，在本次论坛上，习主席详细展示了丝绸之路经济带及 21 世纪海上丝绸之路经济带的愿景，赢得了全世界的关注。“一带一路”倡议从此得到沿线国家广泛而热烈的响应，一系列合作项目已经陆续上马。“一带一路”倡议涉及 60 多个国家，覆盖人口超过全球总人口数的一半，所占经济总量约为全世界的 1/3。在过去几年里，习近平主席和李克强总理在外事访问过程中不断推进“一带一路倡议”的实施进程。

然而中国在实施“一带一路”战略的过程中，并非始终一帆风顺。这点最明显的体现在美日两个大国对于刚刚成立的亚洲基础设施投资银行（AIIB）的态度上。作为实施“一带一路”倡议的主要保障，亚洲基础设施投资银行的创始成员国包括英国、法国、德国等西方国家，但美日两国尚未参与。尽管一些国家对“一带一路”倡议依然存有疑虑，但全世界都已经意识到，中国提出的这一倡议是不容忽视的。从根本上讲，“一带一路”属于经济工程，但它会对外交、政治乃至安全等多个领域造成影响。

中国希望通过“一带一路”倡议来展现她所代表的和平、尊重、开放以及包容的代精神。对中国而言，这一倡议的国际战略意义在于，它有助于打破中美之间关于安全问题的困境，有利于中国以崛起大国的身份承担起区域责任和国际责任，增强中国在世界舞台上的软实力。

中国的“大外交”

自改革开放以来，中国一直奉行由邓小平确立的“韬光养晦”的外交政策。在邓小平的领导下，中国实现了与世界接轨。随着中国国际地位的不断提高，国际社会开始期望中国能在国际事务中扮演更加重要的角色。当然，这种领导方式偶尔也会遭到苛责，认为中国缺乏大方向上的外交战略，在变幻莫测的国际环境中，这种外交政策过于低调。自步入新世纪以来，特别是在中共十八大之后，中国领导人逐渐勾勒出“大外交”的战略蓝图。

中国“大外交”战略的主要特色可以概括为“两条腿，一个圈”。“两条腿”包括与美国、俄罗斯、印度以及欧洲主要国家建立的新型大国关系，而“一个圈”则主要指针对亚洲邻国的周边外交，三者互相交接、相辅相成。

新型大国关系

新型大国关系是当前中国发展同大国关系的外交。尽管新型大国关系这个理念是针对中美关系提出的，但它同样适用于中国同俄罗斯、印度以及欧洲等主要国家的双边关系，而这些国家也大都是“一带一路”的沿线大国。从地缘政治上看，能够对中国的发展和“一带一路”构成致命的外在威胁和挑战的也正是这些大国。只有处理好同这些大国的关系，才能确保“一带一路”顺利实施。自邓小平执政的后期开始，国际和平环境一直被视为中国可持续发展的前提。中国必须根据国际环境的变化随时调整自身的外交政策，如此才能保证国际和平和国内的发展。今天，对于中国而言，同美、俄、印、欧构建新型大国关系对于维持国际和平至关重要。

在中美关系上，随着中国崛起和美国全球主导地位的相对衰落，中美之间的博弈有所升温。虽然双方都希望博弈能够导致双赢而非“零和”的结果，但从国际政治的角度看，大国之间的博弈很容易受非理性因素影响，其结果不见得就是博弈者所预期的，甚至可能相反。根据西方国际关系理论和经验，崛起中的大国经常挑战守成大国，而后者往往对前者产生恐惧和戒备，从而陷入“修昔底德陷阱”。这个隐喻的意义在于警示我们，要注意到崛起大国与守城大国对抗而带来的危险——例如，在古希腊时代，雅典城邦曾挑战斯巴达城邦、一个世纪之前，德国曾挑战英国等。哈佛大学贝尔弗尔科学及国际事务研究中心的葛莱汉姆·艾莉森曾领导团队做过一个实验，针对过去500年中16起案例中的12起进行分析，最终得出的结论是，每当陷入这种困境时，最终必然会引发战争。

在中国主席习近平看来，“修昔底德陷阱”并非无可避免。早在2013年，中国就提出构建中美新型大国关系的倡议，目的就在于避免历史上一再上演的新兴大国与守成大国之间争霸而导致战争的悲剧。2015年，中国国家主席习近平在访美期间提出，同美方一道构建新型大国关系，实现双方不冲突不对抗、相互尊重、合作共赢，是中国外交政策的优先方向。美国总统奥巴马也提出，美中两国都有能力管控分歧，避免陷入“修昔底德陷阱”。多年来，尽管中美两国在诸多领域存在分歧，但在多数情况下，都能够以国家环境和全球趋势为基础，努力构建这种新型大国关系。虽然美国表示不会参与亚洲基础设施银行——“一带一路”倡议的重要保障，但中国却表示，大门永远向美国敞开。

在中俄关系上，“一带一路”经过中亚、东欧的广大地区通往欧洲，而这一带是俄罗斯地缘政治利益的核心。因此，中国必须在与中亚国家合作的同时，注重与俄罗斯的合作。在这方面已经存在一个有效的国际机制，即上海合作组织。上合组织是针对有关国家共同面临的问题，如恐怖主义，而不是针对第三方的。它可以为“一带一路”提供助力。2015年5月，习近平主席出访俄罗斯，两国政府发表联合声明，正式确认“欧亚经济联盟”与“一带一路”对接，这将更加有利于中国与中亚国家拓展合作。

在中印关系上，“一带一路”经过东南亚，到达印度洋和非洲，因而也涉及印度的地缘政治利益。近年来，无论在中东还是非洲，印度已在扮演重要角色。中国的快速崛起和“走出去”已经引起印度高度关注。中印之间还存在领土主权纠纷，但如果处理得好，两国就能够克服地缘政治利益纠纷，实现合作。毕竟，中印相处数千年都没有大的冲突，今天两国间的纠纷是西方帝国主义遗留的问题。中国在实施“一带一路”过程中，如果能考量到印度的地缘政治利益，两国就可以找到巨大的合作空间。

在中国与欧盟的关系上，“一带一路”将从亚洲出发一直联通欧洲。中国与欧洲并不存在直接的地缘政治冲突，双方都能从互惠互利的经贸关系中实现发展。目前，欧洲国家正陷入经济衰退的困境，因此对中欧关系给予了高度重视，至少在经济层面如此。因此，中国的“一带一路”在欧洲才会受到如此热捧。2015年3月，17个欧洲国家，包括英国、法国、德国、意大利，均加入了中国亚洲基础设施投资银行的建设。2015 年 9 月 28 日，欧盟委员会发表声明，欢迎中国的“一带一路”与欧洲的投资计划接轨。一个月后，即同年 10 月，习近平主席在访问英国时，两国同意携手构建“面向 21 世纪全球全面战略伙伴关系”2015 年 10 月末至 11 月初，欧洲多位重要领导人，包括荷兰国王威廉–亚历山大・克劳斯・乔治・费迪南德、德国总理默克尔、法国总统弗朗索瓦・奥朗德等人，相继访问中国。在默克尔和奥朗德访华前夕，德法两国驻华大使在中国《人民日报》上联合发表文章，宣布德法两国是“中国在欧盟的核心伙伴”。同年 11 月，中国外交部表示，中国已经申请加入欧洲复兴开发银行。12 月 14 日，欧洲复兴开发银行委员会通过决议，接受中国的申请。与此同时，欧洲复兴开发银行宣布已经准备好与亚洲基础设施投资银行开展合作。对于中国领导人而言，这真是中国与欧盟关系的“黄金时期”。尽管双方在中国的市场经济地位、人权等很多政治问题上仍然存在较大的分歧，但中国目前已经有足够的实力与欧盟中的大国深化双边关系。

“一带一路”

“一带一路”的主要目标是发展中国家。尽管它也延伸至欧洲一些发达国家，但沿线的 60 多个国家大都是中小发展中国家。这些国家相对于中国而言经济较为落后，因此经济发展始终被放在首位。“一带一路”倡议包括经贸、金融、基础设施、文化等多个方面的内容。中国与沿线国家的经济发展要素呈现很强的互补性，如果能够有效结合，就可以释放出巨大的生产力。“一带一路”可以看作中国主要面向发展中国家的外交，沿线国家多半拥有丰沛的自然资源与人力资源，但普遍缺乏资金、人才、技术，且面临基础设施不足、市场规模过小、治理能力不佳等瓶颈。而中国所具备的三大优势可以协助这些国家克服瓶颈，激发经济发展动力。 在过去几十年中，中国经历了世界上最大规模的基础设施建设。自改革开放以来，中国的经济发展一直以大规模基础设施建设为特征。

一是基建优势。今天，中国从事基础设施建设的能力堪称世界第一，有能力同时在多国承建水库、电厂、超高压输电网、深水港、机场、工业区、传统铁路、高速公路、高速铁路、移动通信网络等项目。中国也有能力协助整个地区（如东南亚）建设跨国基础设施网络，让各国克服国内市场规模过小的障碍，并能够在地区内发展产业分工，形成跨国产业集群。很显然，基础设施建设是每个国家实现工业化、城市化、经济腾飞的前提。

二是发展经验优势。中国在改革开放过程中，在经济发展、公共治理、城市规划等领域积累了丰富的经验，中国可以与沿线国家分享这些经验。中国在改革开放过程中取得的发展成就说明，经验是具有普适性的。与此同时，中国能够从自身的学习过程中获益，通过不断摸索，最终找到一条适合中国国情的治理模式。因此，不论是中国经验还是中国的教训，对于国情和需求与中国类似的发展中国家而言，都是具有借鉴意义的。在所谓的中国模式遭到西方批判时，许多发展中国家却从中发现了可以学习和借鉴的共性。

三是金融优势。若没有金融支持，历史上没有任何一个国家能够顺利地推行大外交战略或“走出去”战略。中国同时拥有庞大的外汇储备和丰沛的国内储蓄，并已建立独立的全球支付系统，中国和许多国家都签订了本币互换协议，人民币作为国际贸易结算货币日益普及。随着人民币即将正式纳入国际货币基金组织特别提款权货币篮子，并占 10.92% 的权重，人民币将加快成为可自由兑换货币，并位列美元（41.73%）、欧元（30.93%）之后，成为世界第三大货币。因此，中国有能力为广大发展中国家提供低成本的融资平台与信贷机制。

周边外交

周边外交是中国大外交战略的核心和前沿，这是由中国特殊的地缘政治环境所决定的；而“一带一路”的起点就是中国周边地区。

在世界大国中，中国的地缘政治环境非常特殊。同英国相比，英伦三岛孤悬于大西洋，英国是典型的海洋国家；而中国既是陆地大国又是海洋大国。同美国相比，美国周边只有两个国家，即北面的加拿大和南面的墨西哥，地缘环境非常简单，且这两个国家的实力与美国不可相提并论，并都需依赖美国发展；而中国则不同，周边有十几个海陆国家，且包括俄、日、印等强国。所以，中国外交不能机械地模仿英美，必须根据自己所处地缘政治环境，制定务实可行的外交战略。

当今国际安全领域的多数热点问题都发生在中国周边，其中很多是和中国直接相关的，包括朝鲜核问题、东海主权纠纷、台湾问题、南海主权纠纷、缅甸问题、中印边界问题、阿富汗问题等。近年来，旧的问题和矛盾依然存在甚至加剧，新的问题也正在出现，如果中国不能很好地进行处理，随时都可能转化成重大危机。

周边地区是中国国际秩序的基础。中国要塑造有利于己的国际秩序，就必须把战略重点放在周边。未来中国要面对的危机更可能直接来自周边的中小国家。

而如果周边发生重大危机或中国同周边国家关系出现重大危机，就会对中国国际秩序造成直接和严重的冲击，甚至可能导致中国崛起的根基不稳。

几乎所有周边国家都是"一带一路"的沿线国家。过去几年里，中国政府提出了"睦邻、安邻、富邻"及"亲、诚、惠、容"的周边外交理念和目标，而"一带一路"则是将这些理念付诸行动、实现这些目标的最好途径。

此外，在今后很长的历史时期里，中国面临的主要地缘政治压力仍然来自美国，尽管中美之间没有直接的地缘政治纠纷，且两国在经济上高度相互依赖、相互补充。但中美之间的摩擦和冲突，更可能是中国和周边美国盟友之间的摩擦和冲突。这就意味着建设新型大国关系和周边外交也是密不可分的，两者必须统筹兼顾，不可偏废其一。

"一带一路"倡议与中国追求的"时代精神"

任何大国的崛起，都需要一种"时代精神"作为前提，中国也不例外。在世界政治领域，外界向来批评中国缺乏"软实力"。在西方国家严重，中国的外交政策，特别是对发展中国家的外交政策，是毫无道德原则可言的。例如，西方鼓吹中国为发展中国家的独裁政权提供无条件贷款和投资。然而中国的"一带一路"倡议不仅是对古丝绸之路文化精神的一种传承，更将这种精神注入了现代元素，强调了当代和平、尊重、开放、包容等时代精神。从中国的视角来看，构建一种增强时代精神的机制，是成功实施"一带一路"倡议的关键因素之一。

"时代精神"是德国哲学家黑格尔于19世纪提出的一个概念，认为国家要么有意识地去顺应时代精神，要么主动地去创造时代精神。对于18、19世纪的大英帝国而言，当时的时代精神是自由贸易，之所以自由贸易是"时代精神"，是因为自由贸易符合那个时代的世界经济发展大趋势。英国靠自由贸易立国，也通过自由贸易建立了全球性的帝国。不过，在建立大英帝国的过程中，自由贸易的话语背后，往往是赤裸裸的大炮和武力政策。商船在前，炮舰随后是英国崛起的主要特征。东印度公司、鸦片战争、殖民地等，也是"自由贸易"的内在部分。

对于19至20世纪的美国而言，当时的时代精神是自由与民主。在大英帝国衰落之后，崛起的美国成为世界霸主。在自由贸易方面，美国远不如英国。英国是经济自由主义的故乡，其根深蒂固的经济自由意识形态，使得人们相信自由贸易是一场双赢游戏，因此英国往往奉行主动的、单边开放政策，即使另一个国家不对英国开放，英国也可以向那个国家开放。但美国在自由贸易上实行的对等政策，只有另一个国家向美国开放的时候，美国才向那个国家开放。

美国的“时代精神”不是自由贸易，而是“自由民主”。自由民主曾经使得美国具有无限的吸引力，“美国梦”不仅仅是美国人的梦，也是很多落后国家的梦。不过，和大英帝国一样，在美国向世界各国推行自由民主的背后也是大炮和暴力，制裁他国、用武力解决国与国之间的矛盾、占领他国等也都是美国“自由民主”的一部分。这种方式直到今天仍然延续着，同时也促使着美国的相对衰落。

大英帝国和美国的兴衰说明了，“时代精神”能够成为一个国家崛起的基础，也可以为这个国家带来莫大的利益。不过，当这个国家在向外推广其“时代精神”的过程中，如果方法使用不当，甚至诉诸武力，造成“己所不欲而加于人”的局面，就很难可持续发展，避免不了最终的衰落。

对 21 世纪的中国来说，这个时代精神又是什么呢？人们可以说，这是中国文明的自信和复兴。丝绸之路既是中国古老文明的一部分，也可以成为当代中国文明在国际政治舞台上自信和复兴的有效方法。 当然，今天人们说丝绸之路，并不是要对古老文明的简单重复，更不是要去步早先大英帝国和美国的后尘；相反，中国必须既超越自己的传统，更需要努力超越英美早先帝国主义式的崛起模式。

中国文明是世界上唯一的世俗文明，其文化的开放性和包容性，非其他基于宗教之上的排他性文明所能比拟。从秦始皇帝统一国家到汉唐盛世，中国是世界上最开放的帝国。直到明清才开始变得封闭起来。中国开放传统的宝贵经验需要总结。在开放的状态下，中国如何组织自己的外部关系呢？主要是两部分组成。就其他国家和中华帝国的关系来说，就是“朝贡体系”；就中国“走出去”来说，就是“丝绸之路”。

朝贡体系存在了数千年，直到西方帝国主义入侵中国之后才衰落。从本质上讲，朝贡体系是一种贸易体系，贸易是实的一面，朝贡只是形式。朝贡国定期地送“礼物”给天朝，向中国皇帝叩几个头。但通过朝贡这一形式，朝贡国不仅从中国皇帝那里得到了比其送的礼物要贵重得多的礼物，而且更是取得了和中国的通商贸易的权利。尽管这种体系带有浓厚的封建色彩，但仍不失为一种低成本的自由贸易模式。当西方依靠大炮武力来打开中国的贸易大门时，朝贡体系已经几乎名存实亡。叩头的仪式在当时是无可非议的，是符合当时的做法的，为所有朝贡国所接受，这是中国和朝贡国之间的外交均衡，否则很难解释为什么这个体制能够生存数千年。自 19 世纪西方列强入侵中国后，清朝再也跟不上“时代精神”，朝贡体系也走到了尽头。

和朝贡体系相比较，人们对丝绸之路并没有什么大的异议。今天中国提出的“丝绸之路经济带”包括陆地和海上丝绸之路，而古代的丝绸之路从也是由海陆两条线路组成。陆地丝绸之路从中国向西，通过中亚、中东的广大地区和欧洲连接起来。提到海上丝绸之路，大多数人能够想起的就是明朝郑和下西洋。但实际上，中国从秦汉开始就进行海上贸易，尤其是和东南亚国家的贸易，并且这种贸易从来就没有中断过。秦汉、唐宋开放时期，海上贸易是合法的。尤其在宋朝，中国和东南亚国家的贸易非常兴盛。反而在郑和下西洋中断之后，明朝实行海禁，海上贸易变成了民间的贸易，并且是非法的。

这里要强调的一点就是，通过朝贡体系和丝绸之路，中国形成了一个自然的区域国际秩序。这种区域秩序体现着中国热爱和平的传统文化精神。这里所说的自然区域国际关系秩序，区别于人为的、通过国家力量尤其是武力来组织的国际关系秩序。在历史上，无论是帝国时代的国际关系，还是帝国解体之后所形成的基于民族国家之上的近现代国际关系，都是基于暴力之上的。 大英帝国、苏联、美国在确立以自身为中心的区域国际关系时，往往用武力开路，武力也是这个秩序的基础。中国所确立的这个自然区域国家秩序体系，是在西方基于民族国家之上的国际体系产生之后才解体的。

作为大国的中国，历史上并没有像西方国家那样，有计划地去打造以自己为中心的国际关系，尽管中国自称为“中间王国”。中国古代国际关系的形成，是中国和周边国家根据互相需要而打交道、互动过程中形成的自然秩序。中国所考量的只是如何治理这个自然形成的秩序。从这个角度来说，中国可以说始终是“韬光养晦”，外交的核心始终是贸易，很少用得上国家武力和征服。朝贡体系的核心是贸易，丝绸之路的核心也是贸易；或者说，中国国际关系的核心是经济贸易。而经济贸易，用今天的话说，是一种双赢和互惠的关系。“一带一路”倡议正是复兴古丝绸之路的精神，并在其中融入现代元素。

如今，随着全球化进程的快速演进，在国际竞争中脱颖而出的国家，大多都具有开放和包容的精神，而不是那些民族主义情节较为严重的国家。从经济学角度来讲，前者能够有效地调动和配置国际生产要素。中国在过去三十年中之所以能在经济上取得伟大成就，一个关键因素便在于他的开放精神。简言之，中国的和平崛起可以看作是顺应时代精神——即开放精神的崛起。

这种时代的新精神中既包含着西方哲学中“文化多元性”的概念，也包含着中国“和而不同”、“己所不欲勿施于人”的传统精神，更包含着当代中国外交政策中“和平共处五项原则”所秉持的精神。这种新的价值观与大英帝国的“自由贸易”或是美国的“自由民主”等概念截然不同。

如今，“一带一路”倡议的提出、“丝路基金”和“亚洲基础设施投资银行”成立等，都为区域经济和国际经济的发展提供了平台和工具。这恰好凸出了中国对促进区域经济和全球经济发展所做出的贡献，在自身崛起的同时，也能让伙伴国从中受益。这种发展战略正是时代精神的体现。

此外，中国可以通过两种方式来开展合作式发展、践行“和平、尊重、开放、包容”的时代精神。第一，允许丝绸之路沿线国家的人们大众通过多种渠道参与到“一带一路”倡议，并分享经济发展带来的成果。例如，可以在规划阶段参考当地政府、社会、非政府组织的意见。第二，尽管中国在“一带一路”倡议中扮演主要角色，但同时也要鼓励其他国家参与，以此向外界宣示——中国并不会垄断所有项目。重点要放在中立性和专业性上。为确保项目成功，可以邀请具有实力、掌握高新技术的国外企业一同参与。由于中国的文化精神中自古便包含着着开放和包容的元素，因此中国具备协调各方利益、开启双赢局面的能力。

与此同时，作为起步较晚的发展中国家，中国具有一定的优势，可以借鉴其他国家的发展经验，特别是在亚洲基础设施投资银行和丝路基金的运营方面，可以借鉴西方发达国家的经验。通过发展绿色产业、控制国内污染、构建低碳城市等方式，中国可以有效推动国内经济发展。与此同时，中国可以吸引来自美国和日本的外商进行直接投资，提供技术和设备，这样美日两国不仅能从中国的经济增长和城市化中分享红利，同时也有助于促进中国经济的产业升级。

“一带一路”倡议的国际意义

对于中国而言，“一带一路”的国际意义主要包括三方面：一是有助于突破中国与有关国家之间的安全困境；二是与广大发展中国家实现双赢，更好地承担大国责任；三是形成中国在国际上的软实力。

突破安全困境

“一带一路”通过发展和强化中国与广大发展中国家的关系，将有助于突破国家间的安全困境，并为深化区域经济合作提供新的动力。

第一，美国在中东、非洲以及中亚等地区出现权力真空，而“一带一路”为恰好为中国提供了一个填补真空的机会。美国的“重返亚太”战略一方面有效地挤压了中国的外交空间，但同时也迫使其把战略资源从其他地区调动至东亚，这必将导致美国的战略能力在这些地区相对下降，北京大学国际关系学院院长王缉思认为，而“一带一路”倡议恰好为中国提供了一个填补空缺的机会。“一带一路”倡议一方面将促进经贸发展作为首要目标，但在另一方面也反映出中国针对美国“重返亚太”战略做出的回应。

第二，“一带一路”可以为突破中日在东亚的安全困境创造条件。“一带一路”的实施可以把中日之间的竞争延伸到沿线的众多发展中国家去，从而降低中日在东亚竞争的激烈程度。在发展中国家，中国具有一定优势。实际上，一国在海外的竞争优势就是其内部优势的延续。当前，日本国内的经济发展优势已基本用尽，很难再如往日那样在国际社会扮演经济发展的“领头雁”角色。在今后相当长的时间里，中国国内的经济发展优势决定了中国有能力在发展中国家中扮演这种领导角色。

第三，“一带一路”能够产生更多的共同利益，在地区国家间催生更多的合作的可能性，从而缓解南海问题的紧张局势。

第四，“一带一路”有助于突破中国与西方在贸易和投资上的安全困境。西方国家经常以所谓“威胁国家安全”等理由将中国的资本和产品拒之门外。“一带一路”有助于中国在发展中国家找到这些新的投资和贸易空间，从而减少中国与西方国家之间的经贸摩擦及其引发的其他问题。

承担大国责任

作为世界上最大的发展中国家，中国将通过“一带一路”全面发掘与沿线众多发展中国家的互补互利机会，与这些国家实现双赢，从而承担更多大国责任。从这个意义上讲，“一带一路”是中国走向国际、承担国际责任之路。

一方面，“一带一路”有助于中国实现可持续发展。当前，中国经济结构亟待调整。对此，国内的深化改革自然是至关重要的；同时，也可以充分发挥外部经济要素的作用。这样既可以促进国内改革，又可以在一定程度上减轻改革的压力。历史上，西方发达国家在成长为经济大国的过程中，无一不充分利用了外部经济要素。它们的经济发展往往伴随着对外殖民主义和帝国主义的政策。中国当然不能走西方的老路，但必须找到一条和广大发展中国家相互尊重、共同发展、合作共赢的道路。“一带一路”就是这样一条道路。

今天，中国已经从资本短缺国家变为资本过剩国家，具备了庞大的资本积累，如此庞大的资本大都存在银行，不仅没有增值，而且面临贬值的风险。但同时，中国资本在加快“走出去”，对外投资规模越来越大。在“一带一路”实施过程中，中国要做的就是把大量资本积累转化为投资，从而实现保值增值；而沿线发展中国家要做的就是利用中国的资本来加快国内建设、推动经济发展。

此外，“一带一路”不仅有助于为中国企业成熟的产品找到广阔的海外新市场，而且有助于将中国国内富余的产能有秩序地向外移转，转化为沿线发展中国家经济发展的要素，在促进这些国家经济发展的同时，推动中国国内的产业结构调整。在这一过程中，中国企业的跨国经营能力也可以得到全面提高。

另一方面，“一带一路”通过将外部经济要素（资本和技术）引入发展中国家，同其内部要素（廉价的劳动力和丰富的资源）相结合，从而大大激发它们的经济发展动力，并带动中国与东南亚、南亚、中亚、中东、非洲等地区国家经济伙伴关系的升级，促进区域经济发展。

今天，西方国家虽然发达，但也面临继续发展的瓶颈，在相当程度上缺乏发展动力，更无力帮助发展中国家。即使那些具备援助能力的国家，也往往对援助和投资附加了民主、人权等政治和意识形态上的前提条件，使很多发展中国家难以接受，反而严重制约了发展中国家的发展。相比之下，中国的投资和援助并不附带任何前提条件。中国已经明确表示，“一带一路”的原则是实现共同发展。只有广大发展中国家都富裕起来，中国自身的发展才是可持续的。

形成在国际上的软实力

“一带一路”为中国在国际上建设软实力提供了一个契机和平台。它有助于把中国发展的宝贵经验传播到其他发展中国家，尤其是改革开放以来形成的市场与政府两手并用的独特发展经验。

今天，广大发展中国家在推动经济发展上仍面临巨大压力。这些发展中国家在实现独立后继续依赖西方。这主要是由于之前的宗主国继续通过各种方式影响着新独立国家的发展。很显然，这种模式即便没有失败，也并没有取得成功。20

世纪 80 年代以来，西方开始在发展中国家推行“华盛顿共识”或西方发展经验，但这些经验并不适合发展中国家。

中国在短短三十多年里从一个非常贫困的国家跃升为世界第二大经济体这一事实本身，就使得许多发展中国家对中国经验深感兴趣。与此同时，中国通过发展来减少贫困、通过融入世界经济来实现发展，这些都为中国赢得了赞誉。中国经验是在不断修正西方经验的基础上积累而成，而这正是很多发展中国家所需要的。

结语

改革开放三十多年来，中国正逐渐成为世界强国。今天中国所面临的地缘政治和国际形势，要求中国既要“走出去”，在国际舞台上维护国家利益，同时也要承担起作为大国的国际责任。在这个过程中，中国将面临巨大挑战，这就必然需要大外交战略来解决。“一带一路”可以成为当代中国全面走向世界的开端，也是中国崛起必须通过的重要“考试”。

The "Belt and Road" Initiative: China's Grand Diplomacy

Yongnian Zheng / Singapore

Professor and Director of the East Asian Institute at the National University of Singapore

On 28 March 2015, Chinese President Xi Jinping caught world attention when he detailed his vision for the Silk Road Economic Belt and the 21st Century Maritime Silk Road (the OBOR Initiative) at the Boao Forum for Asia.[1] This Initiative has since received wide and enthusiastic responses from countries along the routes and a number of cooperation projects have already been underway. The OBOR Initiative involves more than 60 countries, covering over half of the global population and economic aggregates of about one third of the world. In the past few years, President Xi Jinping and Premier Li Keqiang have been busy promoting the implementation of the Initiative in their visits abroad.

China's promotion of the OBOR Initiative has not been all smooth sailing though. Notably, the US and Japan, two major powers in the region, have yet to become a

1 Thereafter, China's National Development and Reform Commission, Ministry of Foreign Affairs and Ministry of Commerce jointly issued a document, *Vision and Actions on Jointly Building Silk Road Economic Belt and 21st Century Maritime Silk Road*, a sign that the Belt and Road Initiative promoted by China as a foreign cooperation platform had entered its first year of implementation.

member of the newly established AIIB (Asian Infrastructure Investment Bank), a major pillar of the OBOR Initiative, even though it has the participation of Western powers such as the UK, Germany and France. While some countries are still suspicious of China's real objectives, the region and the world are aware that they cannot afford to ignore China's initiative. Although the OBOR is fundamentally an economic project, it will impact on other realms such as diplomacy, politics and even security.

With the OBOR Initiative, China hopes to demonstrate that it represents the spirit of the age of world peace, endorses mutual respect among nations, and strives for openness and inclusiveness. For China, the international strategic significance of this initiative is to facilitate a breakthrough in the security dilemma between China and the US, assume China's regional and international responsibilities as a rising great power and build China's soft power on the world stage.

China's Grand Diplomacy

Since China announced its reform and open-door policy, the country had adopted a low profile foreign policy established by the late Deng Xiaoping. Under the leadership of Deng Xiaoping, China joined the world; with its continuous rise, it is expected by the world community to play a more important role in world affairs. Indeed, from time to time, the leadership has been criticised for not having an overall foreign policy strategy and for adopting a foreign policy which was too reactive to changing international environments. In response, in the new millennium, particularly, since the 18th Congress of the Chinese Communist Party, the Chinese leadership has gradually formulated a grand strategy.

China's grand diplomacy is featured by the so-called "two fronts and one circle" strategy. The "two fronts" include a new type of great powers relationship with countries such as the US, Russia, India and major European countries, and the OBOR Initiative which mainly deals with developing countries; the "one circle" refers to peripheral diplomacy that is mainly related to China's Asian neighbors.

These three aspects connect with and reinforce each other.

A New Type of Great Powers Relationship

The new type of great powers relationship is China's foreign policy initiative for developing relations with big powers.[1] While the idea was initially raised for China-US relations, it is also applied to China's relations with Russia, India, and other major powers in Europe and other regions, most of which are also countries along the Belt and Road. From a geopolitical point of view, these great powers could pose serious and vital external threats and challenges to the development of China and the Belt and Road Initiative. Careful handling of these relationships in terms of not only the economy and trade, but also war and peace is thus critical for the implementation of the OBOR Initiative. Since the late Deng Xiaoping, international peace has been regarded as the prerequisite for China's sustainable development. China has to adjust its foreign policy to every change in the international environment in order to maintain international peace and domestic development. For China today, building a new type of great powers relationship with the US, Russia, India and major European countries is essential for achieving a peaceful international environment.

With the rise of China and the relative decline of the US's global dominance, the competition between China and the US has intensified. Despite the interdependence and the hope for arriving at a win-win situation instead of a zero-sum game, historical experiences show that competition among major countries can easily be affected by irrational factors, with unexpected and even adverse results. According to Western theories and experiences of international relations, rising powers often challenge established ones, and the latter often fear and take precautions against the former, leading to a situation known as the Thucydides trap, a term coined by a Greek historian. The metaphor warns of the attendant dangers when a rising

1 In China, since the Western notion of "great powers" has negative connotations, implying great power politics in world affairs, the official expression is "a new type of major countries relationship." In this paper, for the convenience of understanding, the conventional term of "great powers" was used.

power rivals a ruling power—as Athens challenged Sparta in ancient Greece, or as Germany did Britain a century ago. A research team helmed by Graham Allison of the Harvard Belfer Center for Science and International Affairs has concluded after analyzing 12 of 16 cases over the past 500 years that the result of such a situation was war.[1]

To Chinese President Xi Jinping, the Thucydides trap between China and the US is not inevitable, and he does not want this to happen. As early as in 2013, China put forward the initiative of a new type of great powers relationship with the US to avoid the Thucydides trap. In September 2015, during his visit to the US, President Xi declared that establishing a new type of great powers relationship with the US, which features non-conflict, non-confrontation, mutual respect and win-win cooperation, is a priority of China's foreign policy. US President Barack Obama, while not accepting President Xi's notion directly, also expressed that both the US and China are capable of managing disagreements and avoiding the Thucydides trap. Over the years, the two countries have largely strived for such a new type of great powers relationship based on their national conditions and global trends, despite their disagreements in various realms. While the US has not joined the AIIB, a major tool of the "Belt and Road" initiative, China has indicated that the door is always wide open for the US.

With Russia, the Belt and Road connects with Western Europe through Central Asia and Eastern Europe, the core of Russia's geopolitical interests.[2] Therefore, while cooperating with Central Asian countries, China has emphasized its

1 Graham Allison, "The Thucydides Trap: Are the U.S. and China Headed for War?" *The Atlantic*, September 24, 2015.

2 Over 100 years ago, British geographer Sir Halford John Mackinder regarded Central Asia as the world's geopolitical centre and held that controlling Central Asia was the key to controlling the world. The British Empire and the US firmly believed in this theory. After the collapse of the Soviet Union, the US and its European allies extended their geopolitical influence to the doorstep of Russia by quickly incorporating several former Soviet republics into Central Asia and Eastern Europe. Although this has greatly affected Russia's geopolitical interests, a weakened Russia was hapless to such infringements after the collapse of the Soviet Union. A recovered Russia now is set to regain its lost geopolitical interests, a root cause of the Ukraine crisis today.

cooperation with Russia.[1] One effective multilateral mechanism, the Shanghai Cooperation Organization (SCO), is already in place in this realm. The SCO is to address the common problems faced by the member countries, such as terrorism, rather than targeting at a third party. It can thus offer some assistance to the OBOR Initiative. In May 2015, during President Xi's visit to Russia, the Chinese and Russian governments issued a joint statement, formally endorsing the synergy between Russia's "Eurasian Economic Union" (EEU) and China's "Silk Road Economic Belt (SREB)",[2] which is favorable for China to expand cooperation with Russia and Central Asian countries.

With India, the Belt and Road covers Southeast Asia, the Indian Ocean and Africa and impacting on the geopolitical interests of India. In recent years, India has played an important role in the Middle East and Africa, and paid close attention to China's rapid rise and aggressive "going global" approach.[3] The amicable settlement of the territorial disputes between China and India can address divergence in their geopolitical interests and facilitate cooperation. Two facts add weight to such a scenario: China and India have been neighbors for thousands of years without major

1 Russia sees much of this region as its own backyard, and has been promoting its own plans for a Eurasian Economic Union. At the moment, though, Chinese and Russian leaders have seemingly reached an understanding on aligning and coordinating their respective strategies, no doubt boosted by their broader strategic relationship at a time when both are experiencing unease, of different sorts, in their ties with the West. For further information, see Tim Summers, "Roadmap to a Wider Market," *The World Today,* October and November 2015, pp. 18-20. Available at https://www.chathamhouse.org/sites/files/chathamhouse/publications/twt/What%20exactly%20is%20%27one%20belt%2C%20one%20road%27%20Summers.pdf. Accessed December 6, 2015.

2 *Xinhua*, "Zhonghua renmin gongheguo yu eluosi lianbang guanyu sichou zhilu jingjidai jianshe he ouya jingji lianmeng jianshe duijie hezuo d lianhe shengming (quanwen)" (Joint Statement Between the People's Republic of China and the Russian Federation on Cooperation of Connection Between the Silk Road Economic Belt and the Eurasian Economic Union (full text)), May 9, 2015. Available at http://news.xinhuanet.com/world/2015-05/09/c_127780866.htm. Accessed January 5, 2016.

3 Some scholars have pointed out that "India's suspicions of China's '21st century Maritime Silk Road' is more serious and New Delhi has hinted at various options to counter it, through its own initiatives and collaboration with the United States and Japan." For further information, see C. Raja Mohan, "New Silk Road: Delhi View," *The Word Today*, September 2015, Volume 71, Number 5. Available at at https://www.chathamhouse.org/sites/files/chathamhouse/publications/twt/New%20Silk%20Road%20Delhi%20View%20RajaMohan.pdf. Accessed December 6, 2015.

conflicts, and from a Chinese perspective, the territorial disputes are issues left by Western imperialism. China is likely to take India's geopolitical interests into account when implementing the Belt and Road Initiative. There is thus huge room for cooperation between the two countries.

On China-EU relations, the Belt and Road Initiative extends from Asia to Europe. China and European countries have no direct geopolitical conflict and thrive on mutually beneficial economic and trade relations. Currently, European countries are plagued by weak economic recovery and have attached much importance to China-EU relations at least in economic terms. China's Belt and Road Initiative has thus been warmly received. In March 2015, 17 European states, including the United Kingdom (UK), France, Germany and Italy, joined the AIIB initiated by China. On September 28, 2015 the European Commission issued a statement to welcome the connection or integration of the Belt and Road Initiative and the European Investment Plan.[1] A month later in October, during President Xi's state visit to the UK, the two countries agreed to jointly build a "global comprehensive strategic partnership oriented toward the 21st century." Thereafter from late October to early November 2015, a number of key European leaders including the King of the Netherlands Willem-Alexander Claus George Ferdinand, German Chancellor Angela Merkel and French President François Hollande visited China in succession. On the eve of Merkel's and Hollande's visits, German and French ambassadors to China jointly published an article in China's *Renmin Ribao* (*People's Daily*) stating

1 The European Investment Plan was proposed in November 2014 by Jean-Claude Juncker, chairman of the European Commission, with the European Union and the European Investment Bank offering 21 billion euros as a seed fund. The Plan aims to attract around 315 billion euros from the private and public sectors with 15 times leverage investment in the coming three years. The investment priorities of the Plan include infrastructure, emerging strategic industries (new energy, information technology, aeronautics and astronautics, and high-end equipment manufacturing) and other fields, which are aimed at revitalizing investment within the European Union, promoting economic growth and increasing employment. For more information, see *Xinhua*, "Oumeng weiyuanhui huanying 'yidai yilu' duijie 'ouzhou touzi jihua'" (European Commission Welcomes the Connection of the Belt and Road Initiative and the European Investment Plan), September 29, 2015. Available at http://news.xinhuanet.com/world/2015-09/29/c_1116708073.htm. Accessed January 5, 2016.

that the two countries are "China's core partners in the EU."[1] In November, China's Ministry of Foreign Affairs confirmed that China had applied to join the European Bank for Reconstruction and Development (EBRD).[2] Subsequently on December 14, the EBRD Commission adopted a resolution, accepting China's accession to the bank. Meanwhile, the EBRD stated its readiness to cooperate with the AIIB.[3] For the Chinese leadership, this is a "golden age" for China-EU cooperation. While differences prevail between China and the EU over a wide range of policy areas

1 Ke Muxian and Gu Shan (Michael Clauss and Maurice Gourdault-Montagne), "Defa shi zhongguo zai oumeng dd hexin huoban" (Germany and France Are China's Core Partners in the EU), *Renmin Ribao* (*People's Daily*), October 26, 2015, p. 21.

2 *Xinhua*, "Caijing guancha: shenru ouzhou fuxing kaifa yinhang, zhongou duijie youjin yibu" (Finance Observation: China's Application for Membership of the EBRD Has Advanced the Connection Between China and Europe), November 9, 2015. Available at http://news.xinhuanet.com/fortune/2015-11/09/c_1117083390.htm. Accessed January 5, 2016.

3 The EBRD, founded in 1991 and headquartered in London, is one of the most important financial institutions in Europe for development. The original intention of establishing the EBRD was to help achieve economic transition in Central and Eastern European (CEE) countries. At present, the bank's business scope covers Central and Eastern Europe, Eastern and Southern Mediterranean, Central Asia and other regions, providing investment and financing support for the economic transformation and development of these regions. China will join the EBRD as a non-borrowing member, but the EBRD will not carry out businesses in China. China-invested companies and financial institutions may conduct project and financing cooperation with the bank in countries with EBRD borrowing membership. China's central bank, the People's Bank of China, enthused that China's entry to the EBRD would vigorously promote the connection of the Belt and Road Initiative and the European Investment Plan, and provide more room for China and the EBRD to conduct various forms of project investment and cooperation in Central and Eastern Europe, Eastern and Southern Mediterranean, Central Asia and other regions; it also stated that China's accession to the EBRD is in the interests of all parties and is a win-win situation. The EBRD on the other hand said that China's participation in the bank would further promote Chinese enterprises to invest in areas covered by the EBRD. At present, the cooperation projects, about which China and the EBRD have been discussing, focus on infrastructure and energy, including financing credit to the railway project for the connection of Kazakhstan and China. For more information, see *Xinhua*, "Ouzhou fuxing kaifa yinhang zhengshi tongyi zhongguo jiaru" (The European Bank for Reconstruction and Development Formally Accepted China's Accession), December 15, 2015. Available at http://news.xinhuanet.com/world/2015-12/15/c_128530165.htm. Accessed January 6, 2016; *Xinhua*, "Zhongguo zhengshi jiaru ouzhou fuxing kaifa yinhang" (China Formally Joins the European Bank for Reconstruction and Development), December 16, 2015. Available at http://www.bj.xinhuanet.com/hbpd/jrpd/jrpd/2015-12/16/c_1117483137.htm. Accessed January 6, 2016; Xinhua, "Zhongguo jiaru ouzhou fuxing kaifa yinhang youhe yiyi?" (What Is the Significance of China's Entry into the European Bank for Reconstruction and Development?), December 15, 2015. Available at http://news.xinhuanet.com/world/2015-12/15/c_128532002.htm. Accessed January 6, 2016.

such as the recognition of China's market status and human rights issue, China has been able to deepen its relationship with major EU powers.

The Belt and Road Initiative

The Belt and Road Initiative is mainly targeted at developing countries. Although it extends to some developed countries in Europe, most of the over 60 countries along the Silk Road Economic Belt and the 21st Century Maritime Silk Road are small and medium-sized developing countries. These countries are mostly more backward than China, and economic development tops their agenda. The Belt and Road Initiative covers multiple areas including trade, finance, infrastructure and culture. China and countries along the routes are in complementarity especially in terms of the drive for economic development. Huge productivity can be released if efforts are effectively combined. Most Belt and Road countries are blessed with rich natural and human resources; they need capital, development experience and technology to fully explore their own resources and overcome such bottlenecks as inadequate infrastructure, small market size, and poor governance. Specifically, China has three major advantages that these countries could tap on.

The first is infrastructure. In the past decades, China has experienced the largest scale of infrastructure building in the world. Indeed, since the reform and opening up, China's development has been marked by large scale of infrastructure construction. Today, China's capability in infrastructure construction is second to none in the world. China is undertaking infrastructure projects such as reservoirs, power plants, ultra high voltage (UHV) grid, deep water ports, airports, industrial parks, traditional railways, high-speed railways, highways and telecommunications networks simultaneously in many countries. It also has the capacity to build transnational infrastructure networks, overcome the obstacle of small domestic market size, and develop intraregional division of labor to form transnational industrial clusters for an entire region (such as Southeast Asia). Evidently, infrastructure construction is the precondition of every country's industrialization, urbanization and economic take-off.

The second is development experience. During its process of reform and opening-up, China has accumulated rich experience in the areas of economic development, public governance and urban planning to share with countries along the Belt and Road. The fact that China's economic development has been achieved during the reform and opening up in an age of globalization indicates the universality of its experience. China has also benefited from its own learning process, making relevant adjustment and gradually developing its own model of governance suitable for its national conditions. China's experience and lessons learned hence have reference values for many developing countries with similar needs and conditions. While the so-called China model has met with critics from the West, many developing countries have found similarities that they could draw on.

The third is financial advantage. No country in history can promote its grand diplomacy smoothly or "go global" without financial backing. China boasts huge foreign exchange reserves and domestic savings, and has established an independent global payment system. As China has signed currency swap agreements with many countries, the renminbi (RMB) has increasingly become popular as a trade settlement currency.[1] With the impending inclusion of the RMB in the International Monetary Fund's special drawing rights (SDR) basket at a share of 10.92 percent, it will accelerate the process of the RMB becoming a freely convertible currency and the world's third-largest currency after the US dollar (41.73 percent) and the euro

1 In 2009, China kick-started the pilot project of using the RMB as its foreign trade settlement currency. Cross-border trade settlement of the RMB in that year amounted to only 3.5 billion yuan, covering mainly Hong Kong, Macao and Southeast Asia, and cross-border commodities trade settlement of the RMB accounted for less than 1% of China's customs import and export. Six years thereafter, from January to November in 2015, cross-border settlement of the RMB exceeded more than 10 trillion yuan, involving 192 countries and regions in the world, while cross-border commodities trade settlement of the RMB skyrocketed to 27% of China's customs import and export.

(30.93 percent).[1] China hence has the ability to provide developing countries with low-cost financing and credit.

Peripheral diplomacy

Peripheral diplomacy is the core of China's grand diplomacy, which is determined by the special geopolitical environment of the country. The Belt and Road initiative has thus to first connect with China's neighboring areas.

The geopolitical environment of China is unique. Unlike the UK, a maritime state with the British Isles isolated in the Atlantic Ocean, China is both a land power and a maritime power. Compared to the US, which adjoins two much weaker countries, namely, Canada in the north and Mexico in the south, that have to largely rely on the US for their development, China has over 10 neighbors, both land and maritime. China's neighbors include strong powers such as Russia, Japan and India. China's diplomacy has to consider these factors and be both practical and flexible to suit its own geopolitical environment.

Today, most of the hot-spot issues in the realm of international security are in the neighborhood of mainland China. Many of them are directly related to China, including the nuclear issue of North Korea, the Taiwan independence movement, sovereignty disputes over the East and South China Seas, the China-India border dispute, and Afghanistan. In recent years, while old problems and disputes remain unresolved or have even intensified, new ones such as the South China Sea disputes have emerged. These issues may translate into major crises for China if not handled cautiously.

China's periphery is undoubtedly the basis of the Chinese world order. It will

1 The IMF's recent move is an official recognition of the RMB's importance in the global trade and monetary systems; RMB has already become the main currency for transactions between China and the rest of the Asia-Pacific, and the fourth most-used currency for payments globally (albeit at less than 3% of the total transactions). For more information, see Giri Rajendran, "IMF Puts China's Yuan RMB into Its Currency Basket," December 2, 2015.) Available at http://www.iiss.org/en/iiss%20voices/blogsections/iiss-voices-2015-dda3/december-5c5a/imf-puts-chinas-yuan-rmb-into-its-currency-basket-f998. Accessed December 6, 2015.

have to give strategic priority to its neighboring areas if it is to shape a favorable regional and international order for itself. The crises China has to face in the future are more likely to stem directly from its neighboring small and medium–sized countries, crises that will have a direct and serious impact on the Chinese world order and possibly shake the foundations of China's rise.

Almost all the surrounding countries are countries along the Belt and Road. In the past few years, the Chinese government has strived to maintain good neighborly diplomacy with "amity, sincerity, mutual benefit and inclusiveness" and an "amicable, secure and prosperous neighborhood." However, translating these ideas and goals into reality has been a herculean task. The Belt and Road Initiative is considered the best approach to materializing these ideas and achieving these goals.

Indeed, for a long time in the past and in the likely future, most of the geopolitical pressures China faces will continue to come from the US even though the two have no direct geopolitical disputes and the two economies are highly interdependent and complementary. Frictions and conflicts between the two countries are more likely to be those between China and US allies that are China's neighbors. This means that building a new type of great powers relationship with the US is inextricably linked to peripheral diplomacy, and China must make progress on both fronts simultaneously.

The Belt and Road Initiative and China's Pursuit of the "Spirit of the Age"

Conforming to the "spirit of the age" is the premise of the rise of a great power, China included. China has been criticized for lacking in "soft power" in world politics. To many in the West, China's diplomacy, particularly in the developing world, is without moral principles. For example, it has been alleged that China has provided unconditional loans and investment to developing countries with authoritarian regimes. With the Belt and Road Initiative, China hopes to not only inherit but also modernize the cultural spirit of the ancient Silk Road, highlight the spirit of the present age featuring peace, mutual respect, openness and inclusiveness. From a Chinese perspective, this spirit-enhancing mechanism is also an essential factor for the successful implementation of the Belt and Road Initiative.

"The spirit of the age" was coined by German philosopher Georg Wilhelm Friedrich Hegel in the nineteenth century. The country either consciously complies with the spirit of the age, or takes the initiative to create the spirit of the age. For the British Empire in the 18th and 19th centuries, the spirit of the age was free trade which was in line with the megatrends of global economic development at that time. The British Empire relied on free trade to establish a global empire. However, in the process of building the British Empire, what was behind the rhetoric of free trade tended to be blatant conquests by force. The main characteristic of the rise of the British Empire is "merchant ships in front, and gunboats behind"; the East India Company, Opium Wars and colonies were very much part of the British "free trade".

For the US from the late 19th century to the 20th century, the spirit of the age was freedom and democracy. After the fall of the British Empire, the US rose to become the world's superpower. It was left far behind by the UK in free trade. Britain was home to economic liberalism and had a deep-rooted awareness of economic liberalism, believing firmly that free trade can lead to a win-win situation. Consequently, the UK often pursued an active and unilateral open-door policy. By contrast, US emphasis was reciprocity; it would not open itself to a country which was closed to the US.[1]

"The spirit of the age" for the US was "freedom and democracy" rather than free trade. Freedom and democracy once endowed America with infinite appeal. The "American dream" was not only the dream of Americans, but also the dream of many poor countries. Nevertheless, like the British Empire, America also used gunboats and violence to bolster its promotion of freedom and democracy to the rest of the world. It imposes sanctions against other countries, solves disputes between

1 Deepak Lal, *Reviving the Invisible Hand: The Case for Classical Liberalism in the Twenty-First Century* (Princeton, NJ: Princeton University Press, 2006).

countries by force and occupies countries in the name of "freedom and democracy". The US continues to use this approach today, much burdened by its promise to spread democracy to the rest of the world, a possible reason for in its relative decline.

The rise and fall of the British Empire and the US indicate that "the spirit of the age" is the foundation of the rise of a great power and brings great benefits to the country. However, "the spirit of the age" could not be imposed on others by force as it is not sustainable and would ultimately lead to its decline.

To be a great power, China in the 21st century would need to acquire a spirit of the age possibly from its long history of civilization and to modernize it to meet the demands of the time. Specifically, the OBOR Initiative attempts to draw on the valuable experience of the ancient Silk Road and inherit its peace-loving cultural spirit of respecting other countries, reciprocating to realize a win-win situation, and adopting an open and inclusive approach. However, China would not simply duplicate its ancient civilization, or follow the footsteps of the British Empire and the US. It looks to the OBOR Initiative to help it go beyond its own traditions toward a new path of rise while avoiding the Anglo-American model.

Among great civilizations in the past, the Chinese civilization was the only secular civilization known for its openness and inclusiveness. From China's first emperor Qin Shi Huang, who unified the country, to the prosperity of the Han and Tang dynasties, China had been the most open country in the world. China did not avoid contacts with other countries until the Ming and Qing dynasties. Ancient China built its diplomatic relations in two ways. One was its relationship with neighboring countries, via the tributary system. The other was its approach to engage the world, via the ancient Silk Road.

The tributary system had been in existence for thousands of years before China's encounter with the West in modern times. It began to decline after modern Western imperialist powers penetrated China. In essence, the tributary system was a trading system,[1] with trade being practical and tribute being merely a form. Tributary states regularly sent "gifts" to China and performed the feudal style of kowtowing to the Chinese emperor. In return, tributary states not only received much larger gifts from China, but also obtained the rights to trade with China. Despite its feudal nature, this was in fact a kind of low-cost model of free trade. While Western imperialist powers used gunboats to force China to trade with them, the tributary system was largely symbolic. The kowtow ritual was above criticism at the time as it conformed with ancient practices and was well accepted by all the tributary states. The thousand-year tributary system was reflective of a balance of power situation between ancient China and its tributary states. After Western powers invaded China in the 19th century, the Qing dynasty did not keep pace with "the spirit of the age" and the tributary system came to an end.

By contrast, the ancient Silk Road has not evoked as much debate. At present, the Belt and Road Initiative includes the overland "Silk Road Economic Belt" and the "21st-Century Maritime Silk Road." Likewise, the ancient Silk Road also consisted of both overland and maritime routes. The overland Silk Road started from China through the expansive areas of Central Asia and the Middle East to Europe. The maritime Silk Road has often been associated with Zheng He's voyages to the Western Seas during the Ming Dynasty. In reality, China began to undertake maritime trade, particularly with Southeast Asian countries, as early as in the Qin and Han dynasties, and such trade links had never been interrupted. During the opening periods of the Qin and Han dynasties, and of the Tang and Song dynasties, maritime trade was legal; especially in the Song Dynasty, trade between China and Southeast Asia was even booming. Maritime trade was made illegal and unofficial

---

1 Since modern times, the tributary system has been constantly demonized as the embodiment of ancient Chinese power chauvinism. This view, however, has no historical basis as it judges the past in today's viewpoint and looks at Chinese culture from the perspective of Western culture. The elements of inequality in the tributary system, such as kowtow rites, could not be accepted by the West, which worship the concept of equality. In reality, the tributary system was an embodiment of "reciprocity" in ancient Chinese culture.

after the Ming Dynasty implemented maritime prohibition and after Zheng He's voyages to the Western Seas.

The tributary system and the Silk Road enabled ancient China to naturally form a regional order, if not international. The way such a regional order was organized embodied China's traditional peace-loving cultural spirit.[1] Regional order was naturally achieved, unlike those achieved through national power or violence. In history, both international relations in the Age of Empires and modern international relations based on nation states after the collapse of empires were predicated on violence. Great powers such as the British Empire, the US and the former Soviet Union, usually resorted to force to establish self-centered regional and international orders, with force playing a fundamental role in these orders. After the establishment of modern Western international order based on nation states, ancient China's naturally formed regional order finally disintegrated.

As a great power, ancient China did not build a self-centered regional order in the same planned manner as did the Western powers even though China called itself a Middle Kingdom (*Zhongguo*). Ancient China's international order was naturally formed between China and its neighboring countries in accordance with each other's needs. Ancient China only needed to concern itself with how best to govern this naturally formed order. It had always been "keeping a low profile," considering trade as the core of its foreign policy and refraining from the use force to subdue its tributary states. Trade was the core of both the tributary system and the ancient Silk Road. The core of the Chinese world order was thus economy and trade. In today's terms, the economic and trade relationship can be explained as a kind of win-win and mutually beneficial relationship. The Belt and Road Initiative hopes to revive the spirit of the ancient Silk Road and build a modern version around it.

---

1 In history, only when China was conquered by northern ethnic minorities and became the "colony" of these minorities did China adopt temporary expansionist policies. What needs to emphasized is that these minority "conquerors" were eventually "conquered" by the Chinese culture, not only accepting the Chinese culture, but also becoming its intrinsic components.

Today, with rapid globalization, countries that are more likely to win in international competition are those who are more open and inclusive than those who are more nationalistic. Economically, the former are able to mobilize and efficiently allocate international productive factors for better development. A critical factor for China's great achievements in economic development during the past three decades is its openness. Simply put, China's peaceful rise can be viewed as a rise with openness, one of the spirits of the current age.

Such a new spirit of the age embodies Western philosophies like cultural pluralism and echoes the Chinese traditional ideas of "harmony in diversity" (*he'er butong*), "never do to others what you do not want them to do to you" (*jisuo buyu, wushi yuren*), and contemporary Chinese foreign policy of "Five Principles of Peaceful Coexistence." It is a kind of new value unlike the British Empire's "free trade" idea and America's "freedom and democracy" concept.

At present, the Belt and Road Initiative, the Silk Road Fund (SRF), and the AIIB are all platforms and tools of regional and international economic development. This is indicative of China's commitment to promoting regional and global economic development, and allowing participating countries to jointly benefit from its rise. This is a strategic move to highlight the spirit of the age.

In addition, China could adopt participatory development and practice the current age's spirit of peace, respect, openness and inclusiveness in two ways. First, by allowing both society and the public in countries along the Belt and Road to participate in the Initiative in various ways and share the gains of economic development. while the opinions of local governments, society, non-governmental organizations, among others would be consulted during the planning stage. Second, by welcoming the participation of other countries, albeit with China playing a lead role, it shows its willingness to share and its disinterest in monopolizing all of the projects. Neutrality and the emphasis on expertise will be the central focus. Foreign companies with strong capabilities and high technological know-how would be invited to ensure the success of the projects. As openness and inclusiveness has traditionally been part of the Chinese cultural spirit, China has the ability to accommodate and coordinate different interests for mutual benefit and win-win situations.

Meanwhile, China enjoys the advantage of being a late developing country, drawing from the experience of other countries, especially those of Western developed countries in the operation of the AIIB and SRF. By promoting domestic development such as developing green industries, controlling environmental pollution, building low-carbon cities, and so forth, China also promote foreign direct investment from the US and Japan and provide technologies and equipment, so that they can continue sharing the dividends of China's economic growth and urbanization. This can also help promote industrial upgrade of the Chinese economy.

International Implications of the Belt and Road Initiative

For China, the Belt and Road Initiative helps it break the security dilemma between China and related countries; achieve a win-win situation for China and other developing countries and fulfill its responsibilities as a great power; and promote China's soft power to the world.

Breaking the Security Dilemma

By developing and strengthening relations between China and other developing countries, the Belt and Road Initiative will help break China's security dilemma, and provide a new driving force for deepening regional economic cooperation.

First, the Initiative provides China with the opportunity to fill a vacuum left by the US in the Middle East, Africa, and Central Asia. While the US has effectively squeezed China's diplomatic space with its "pivot to Asia" strategy, it has also forced the US to direct its strategic resources to East Asia, leading to a relative decline of its strategic capability in areas such as the Middle East, Africa, and Central Asia. China is poised to move in to take its place via the Belt and Road

Initiative according to Wang Jisi, dean of School of International Relations at China's Beijing University. While enhancing the economy and trade are its primary objectives, OBOR largely reflects China's foreign policy considerations as a countermeasure for US's pivot to Asia.[1]

Second, the implementation of the Belt and Road Initiative will extend China-Japan competition to many developing countries along the routes, alleviating their competition in East Asia, and hence the security dilemma between the two countries. Even with the keen competition, from a Chinese perspective, China has an edge over Japan where developing countries are concerned. At present, the advantages of Japan's domestic economic development have largely been exhausted and it could no longer act as the "leading goose" of economic development in the region. Conversely, China's remarkable domestic economic development has boosted its capacity to play such a leading role.

Third, the Belt and Road Initiative will ease tensions in the South China Sea as it generates common interests and the necessity for cooperation among claimant states. Fourth, the initiative is also expected to help solve China's security dilemma with the West. Western nations prefer not to accept Chinese capital and products with the excuse that it "threatens national security." The Belt and Road Initiative will divert China's trade and investment focus to the developing countries, filling the vacuum caused by the economic and trade frictions with the West.[2]

Assuming Responsibilities as a Great Power

As the world's largest developing country, China will fully explore the opportunities of its complementarities with developing countries along the Belt and

1 Wang Jisi, "Xijin: Zhongguo diyuan zhanlue de zai pingheng" (Looking West: China's Geostrategic Rebalancing), *Huanqiu Shibao* (*The Global Times*), October 17, 2012.

2 On the other hand, most developing countries over-rely on Western markets, and they also need to "walk with two legs", with one "leg" kept in the West, and the other in China. Realistically, the maintenance of steady growth of the global economy requires the developing countries to comprehensively explore their economic growth potential, expand their domestic demand, and deepen economic cooperation among them in order to boost transnational investment and trade.

Road and realize mutually beneficial and win-win outcomes, while shouldering more responsibilities as a great power. In this sense, the Belt and Road Initiative is an approach for China to go international and assume more regional and global responsibilities.[1]

The Initiative is also crucial for China's sustainable development. While China needs to adjust its economic structure, the country can also give full play to the role of external economic factors. Historically, in the transformation to become economic powers, developed countries in the West had capitalized on external economic factors, often resorting to policies of colonialism and imperialism, Current circumstances have dictated that China pursue a new path, such as the Belt and Road Initiative, that features mutual respect, common development, and win-win cooperation with other developing countries.

With the huge amount of capital surplus that it has accumulated over the years, China is looking for areas to further grow its financial resources which are currently saved in banks and at risk of devaluation. While it will continue to invest domestically, it will accelerate its pace of "going global," with the scale of the country's overseas investment becoming larger. As it implements the Belt and Road Initiative, China wants to translate its huge capital into investment in order to increase its value; on the other hand, countries along the routes could utilize China's capital to accelerate their domestic construction and promote economic development.

The Belt and Road Initiative will also pave the way for mature Chinese products to enter overseas markets and transfer surplus capacity in China to where it is most needed. A win-win situation as it will promote the adjustment of China's industrial

---

1 Some scholars believe that the Belt and Road is a global concept, comparable with China's "*Zouchuqu*" (Going global) policy of 2001 or even the Reform and Opening up Policy of 1979. For more information, see François Godement, "Europe Scrambles to Benefit from China's 21st-Century Silk Road," *Global Asia*, September 26, 2015. Available at http://carnegieendowment.org/2015/09/26/europe-scrambles-to-benefit-from-china-s-21st-century-silk-road/iife. Accessed December 6, 2015.

structure while helping the economic development of these countries.[1] In this process, the transnational operation capacity of Chinese enterprises can also be comprehensively increased.

For developing countries, the introduction of external economic factors (capital and technology) could work in combination with internal factors (cheap labor and rich natural resources) to greatly stimulate their economic development, and upgrade China's economic ties with Southeast Asia, South Asia, Central Asia, the Middle East, and Africa, and promote regional economic development.

Despite their advanced economies, Western countries today are facing development bottlenecks. Even for those with the capacity to offer assistance, their foreign aid and investment often come attached with political and ideological conditions, which more often than not seriously restrict the development of developing countries. China's foreign investment and assistance are offered with no strings attached. China has made it clear that the principle of its foreign investment in the Belt and Road Initiative is joint development. It believes that China's development would only be sustainable if other developing countries are prospering as well.

Building China's Soft Power

The Belt and Road Initiative offers an opportunity and platform for China to extend its soft power to the world. It strives to share its experience of development to other developing countries, especially its experience of utilizing both market and government power in its reform and opening-up.

Many developing countries, especially former colonies, are under huge pressure

1 "As China rebalances its domestic economy, it can deploy what has become excess industrial and infrastructure capacity to neighboring countries...this will facilitate deeper market integration between China and its neighbors and greater interdependence." For more information, see Douglas H. Paal, "China's Counterbalance to the American Rebalance," November 1, 2015.) Available at http://carnegieendowment.org/2015/11/01/china-s-counterbalance-to-american-rebalance/ikv8. Accessed December 6, 2015.

to promote economic development. After gaining independence, they continued to rely on the developed economies of the West. This is because former colonizers continue to affect the development of the newly independent states. This model has not been successful, if not failed. Since the 1980s, the West has started to promote the "Washington Consensus", or chiefly Western development experience, among developing countries, which is more often than not unsuitable for developing countries.

China's experience offers an alternative development model. Its transformation from an extremely poor country to the second-largest economy in the world within just over three decades is nothing short of remarkable. Its feat in poverty reduction through development and integration with the world economy has also won praises from the World Bank. Developing countries found relevance in China's experience which is modified from lessons learnt from the West.

Concluding remarks

After more than three decades of reform and opening-up, China has emerged as a world power. The geopolitical and international situation facing China today requires the country to "go global" and safeguard its national interests on the world stage, while it shoulders responsibilities as a great power. In the process, China has met with huge challenges, which need to be tackled by grand diplomatic strategies. The Belt and Road Initiative is China's first major and extensive foray into the world. China considers this huge venture as a "test" of its diplomatic skills as it rises.

认识与了解中国是有效参与“一带一路”的必要条件

托济克　【白俄罗斯】
白中友好协会　主席

首先我要向“2016汉学与当代中国座谈会”的主办方表示衷心的感谢，他们使我有机会在此见到这么多非常杰出的政治家和汉学家。我很高兴自己能借助此次会议的机会再次造访这个我所喜爱的国家，并就白俄罗斯中国学的发展问题，以及白俄罗斯参与“一带一路”建设——尤其是参与“丝绸之路经济带”建设问题，发表自己的观点。

2017年1月20日，是白俄罗斯共和国与中华人民共和国建交25周年纪念日。中国是世界上率先承认白俄罗斯为独立主权国家的国家之一，在这25年中，两国共同谱写辉煌篇章：两国从初步接触到相互了解，再到建立“全面战略伙伴”和“互利合作”关系。2016年9月29日，白俄罗斯总统卢卡申科和中国国家主席习近平共同签署了关于建立“全面战略伙伴关系”、发展“全天候友谊”的联合声明，将白中两国关系的发展提升至新的高度。

我认为，白中两国关系的未来发展应注意以下几个方面：多年来在互惠互利原则基础上，白俄罗斯–中国两国合作呈阶梯状和系统化发展，中方从未向我们提出过任何条件。两国关系中从未出现任何冲突。因此，不仅仅是白中两国领导人，而且还包括很多专家都指出，白中两国的友好关系堪称现代国际关系体系之典范。

白俄罗斯的领导者和普通民众普遍认为，与中方发展全面战略伙伴关系完全符合白俄罗斯的国家战略利益。而我本人认为，建立在这一高度上的两国合作，也符合中国和中国人民的利益。

中国是我们在联合国及其他国际组织中的可靠盟友及伙伴。在中国的支持下，白俄罗斯在上海合作组织中，先后获得了“对话伙伴国”和“观察员国”的地位。中国对我们开放了他们非常广阔的市场，并为落实两国重要合作项目，以及那些对于发展白俄罗斯经济来说非常迫切的项目，提供政府和商业贷款的支持。

以白俄罗斯在经济、交通、科技、文教等领域的潜力，最大限度地全面参与和实现中国国家主席习近平所提出的“一带一路”倡议，也符合白俄罗斯的国家利益。我们认为这一构想的提出非常及时，且为国际社会打造了一种经济合作的新模式，以抗衡或缓解在当今世界经济关系体系中表现得越来越明显的那些危险的、令人不安的倾向。

我们相信，“一带一路”倡议是非常切合实际的。这首先是因为它的基础性原则是使所有参与国都互利互惠。“一带一路”不仅有助于参与国——尤其是丝路沿线国家，实现本国经济在众多领域中的现代化发展，同时也将切实提高当地居民的生活水平。其次，这一倡议有充足的资金作为保障 —— 这里首先指的就是丝路基金和亚洲基础设施投资银行的资金保障。作为丝路经济带沿线国家，白俄罗斯愿意最大限度地利用这一机遇所带来的可能性。

我们希望，中国—白俄罗斯工业园区（ “伟石”工业园），能成为丝绸之路经济带上的一个重要环节。2015 年 5 月，卢卡申科总统和习近平主席曾共同考察该园区，并了解其施工建设情况。习主席称这一正在建设中的园区为“丝路明珠”。

关于建设这一工业园区的政府间协议，签订于 2011 年。其建设用地，位于白俄罗斯的中心位置（同时也是欧洲的中心位置），占地 90 平方公里（合 13.5 万亩）。园区临近国际机场，交通十分便利，不仅有柏林—莫斯科跨国公路穿越其间，还毗邻一条连接西欧、中欧和东北欧（通过俄罗斯）以及中国西部省份（通过俄罗斯和哈萨克斯坦）的铁路干线。工业园区距波罗的海东岸不冻港——克来彼达港 500 公里。

白俄罗斯国家立法机构为园区制定了特殊的法律制度体系，以确保园区内的各项经营活动能顺利开展。目前，园区正在进行工程、交通和生产等基础设施建设，预计 2017 年首批进驻企业将能正式投入运营。

然而令人遗憾的是，白俄罗斯有意拓展和深化其与中国合作的客观需求和愿望，因缺乏科学方法和信息交流等方面的保障，而受到抑制。中国的快速发展，让世界有目共睹；然而，我国很多企业和领域的领导者们，他们对现代中国的了解，却至少要落后十至十五年。

俄罗斯仍然保留着非常强大的、拥有几百年传统的苏联中国学流派。而我们白俄罗斯几乎只能从头开始。曾经，我国国内只有几个人精通汉语；无论大学还是中学，都不教授汉语；因为既没有教科书，也没有老师。时至今日，国内已经有 9 个大学和 10 个中学开设了汉语教学，同时也编写了不少中文教科书。

在 2006 年 11 月白俄罗斯教育部和中国汉办共同签署了关于汉语教学的合作协议。受益于中国汉办的理解与支持，2007 年 1 月在白俄罗斯国立大学，白俄罗斯国内首家以孔子命名的中国学学院正式开始工作。如今，在白俄罗斯已建有三所孔子学院，它们在全国各级教育机构内已开设了近十个班级。

在白俄罗斯中学、大学，以及孔子学院各班级里学习汉语的人数约有 3500 人。有意学习者人数更多，但缺乏好的老师、好的课本以及教学法上的保障。

与此同时，白俄罗斯的中国学正处于起步阶段。因此，我有必要再次指出：我们非常缺乏对于现代中国的了解。我们既不了解中国经济各领域发展的技术方法与技术水平，也不了解中国人的习俗与传统，以及他们在集体协作与个体交往间的特点。不了解这些，我们就很难发挥双边互惠合作的巨大潜力，尤其是在区域间合作以及企业间合作的层面。

对我们而言最有益的是中国在改革开放政策方面所取得的成功经验。受益于这一经验，中国正在大踏步地向世界最具影响力和最完善国家方向迈进。中国的发展，并非依靠军事和政治力量，而是通过发展热爱和平与仁爱之潜力，这为世界其他国家的发展提供了互利合作伙伴关系的新样本。

对于正处于系统性现代化发展初级阶段的白俄罗斯经济而言，总结中国的发展经验是其现阶段最迫切任务，其中包括国企改革、国有和非国有经济成分的权限分配、税收和关税政策对于具体领域及生产的促进（或抑制）作用、对各级管理人员的物质和精神奖励机制、执法机关针对企业和公司财务—经济活动所颁布的各项规章制度、银行在保障经济持续快速发展和以信贷形式支持出口方面所扮演的角色，以及用于吸引外资和先进技术及管理人才的一系列特别措施体系等。

我相信，在不远的将来，我们会清晰地看到：作为改革开放政策的实施结果而在中国形成的生产和社会政治关系，并非是由一种形态向另一种形态，由一种

“主义”向另一种“主义”转换的过渡性事物，而是一种对于 21 世纪来说最为先进也最为乐观的社会经济体系。而这一新生事物也正在引发白俄罗斯的极大关注。

这就是为什么白俄罗斯将会对那些在深层研究上述问题中给予我们协助的中国朋友表示感谢的原因。在我看来，对上述问题最合理的解决方式就是大力加强在白俄罗斯国立大学里的孔子学院的建设。我们必须在中白双方的共同努力下，将其建设成为一个强大的区域性的科研中心，该中心应致力于中国研究，并为在中国同白俄罗斯及区域内其他国家建立起更有效的合作形式献计献策。

这一科研中心的主要职能和研究领域将包括以下几个方面：研究白俄罗斯和区域内其他国家参与实现“一带一路”构想的可能性；为中白两国经贸和投资合作提供咨询和信息服务；为两国在教育、文化、卫生、体育、旅游和其他人文领域的合作提供必要协助；协调科研和教育机构、专家学者个人为建立白俄罗斯的中国学学派所进行的各种活动。

上述问题解决的前提是：需要委派至少五至六名中国学者和专家到这一中心来，与白俄罗斯同事一起工作；保证此中心有开展工作所需立法证明、科研证明、分析证明和其他材料证明；为白俄罗斯学者和专家提供学习中国改革开放政策的经验和成果的机会，包括让其到中国的相关部委、企业及各类组织中见习等。

我相信，实现上述提议将有助于两国经济的协同发展，促进“一带一路”沿线国家间的多边合作，以及白中两国经贸投资领域的双边合作。

Understanding China Is the Essential Condition for Effectively Participating in the Construction of the Belt and Road

Anatoli Tozik / Belarus

Chairman of the Belarus-China Friendship Society

First of all, I would like to express heartfelt thanks to the organizers of the 2016 Symposium on China Studies; they give me the opportunity to meet with so many outstanding politicians and sinologists. I am very pleased to revisit this country, which I like, through this symposium, and express my views on the development of Chinese studies in Belarus, and Belarus' participation in the construction of the Belt and Road, especially the construction of the Silk Road Economic Belt.

January 20, 2017 marked the 25th anniversary of the establishment of diplomatic relations between the Republic of Belarus and the People's Republic of China. China is one of the countries which became the first countries in the world to recognize Belarus as an independent sovereign country. In a very short period of time, the two countries jointly created a brilliant chapter: From an initial engagement and mutual understanding between the two countries to the establishment of a comprehensive strategic partnership and a mutually-beneficial relationship of cooperation. On

September 29, 2016, the President of Belarus, Alexander Lukashenko, and Chinese President Xi Jinping signed a joint declaration on establishing a comprehensive strategic partnership and developing an all-weather friendship, upgrading the relations between the two countries to a new height.

In my view, the following considerations should be given in the future development of the relations between our countries: Over the years, the cooperation between the two countries featured step-like and systematic development on the basis of reciprocity and mutual benefit; China never imposed any conditions on Belarus; no conflicts occurred in the relations between the two countries. Therefore, the leaders of the two countries and many experts believe that the friendly relationship between them should be hailed as a model in the modern system of international relations.

The leaders and the ordinary people of Belarus generally believe that Belarus' development of a comprehensive strategic partnership with China fully meets the national strategic interests of Belarus. In my opinion, the bilateral cooperation at this level also conforms to the interests of China and of the Chinese people.

China is a reliable ally and partner for us in the United Nations and other international organizations. With the support of China, Belarus obtained the status of dialogue partner and observer country in the Shanghai Cooperation Organization. China has opened its very vast market to us and has provided government support and commercial loans for carrying out the important cooperation projects between our two countries as well as the projects which are very urgent for the development of Belarus' economy.

It is our national interest to tap Belarus' potential in economy, transportation, science and technology, culture and education to fully participate, to the greatest extent, in and achieve the great strategic conception of the Belt and Road Initiative put forward by Chinese President Xi Jinping. We think that this conception is very well-timed and offers a new model of economic cooperation for the international community to counteract or mitigate the increasingly obvious risky and disturbing tendencies in today's system of worldwide economic relations.

In our opinion, the Belt and Road Initiative is very realistic. The reasons are as follows: First, its basic principle lies in ensuring mutual benefit and reciprocity among all of the participating countries. The Belt and Road not only helps the participating countries, especially the countries along the Silk Road, achieve their economic modernization in many fields, but it will also truly improve the living standards of local residents. Second, this initiative is supported by sufficient funds, which first refer to the fund guarantee from the Silk Road Fund and the Asian Infrastructure Investment Bank. As one of the countries along the Silk Road Economic Belt, Belarus is willing to utilize the possibilities that this opportunity offers to the greatest extent.

We hope that the China-Belarus Industrial Park can serve as an important segment of the Silk Road Economic Belt. In May, 2015, the President of Belarus, Alexander Lukashenko, and Chinese President Xi Jinping visited this park together to learn about its construction. President Xi hailed the park under construction as a pearl on the Silk Road.

The intergovernmental agreement on the construction of this industrial park was signed in 2011. Covering an area of 90 sq.km., its construction site is located at the center of Belarus, also the center of Europe. Being adjacent to an international airport, this park enjoys very convenient transportation, and it can get access to the Berlin-Moscow transnational highway and is close to a trunk railway connecting Western Europe, Central Europe and Northeastern Europe (via Russia) and Western China (via Russia and Kazakhstan). This industrial park is 500km away from the Port of Klaipeda, an ice-free port on the eastern coast of the Baltic Sea.

Belarus' state legislature has developed a special legal system for this park to ensure that the operating activities in it can be smoothly carried out. At present, the park's infrastructure is under construction, including engineering, transportation and production facilities. The first batch of enterprises are expected to officially begin operating in this park by 2017.

However, unfortunately, Belarus' objective needs and desire to expand and intensify its cooperation with China are inhibited due to a lack of scientific methods and information exchanges. China's rapid development impresses the world. However, with respect to the leaders of many enterprises and fields in Belarus, their understanding of modern China lags behind by at least 10—15 years.

Russia still preserves the very powerful Soviet school of China studies with several hundred years of traditions, while we almost have to start from scratch. In the past, there were only a few people proficient in Chinese in Belarus; Chinese was not taught in our universities and middle schools because no textbooks or teachers were available. At present, nine universities and ten middle schools teach Chinese and have compiled Chinese textbooks in Belarus.

In November, 2006, the Belarus Ministry of Education and China's Office of the International Chinese Language Council ("Hanban") signed a cooperation agreement on Chinese teaching. Thanks to Hanban's understanding and support, the first Institute of China Studies, which is named after Confucius, in Belarus was officially put into operation at Belarusian State University in January, 2007. Now three Confucius Institutes have been founded in Belarus and they have established nearly ten classes at educational institutions nationwide.

About 3,500 students are learning Chinese in the classes of middle schools, universities and Confucius Institutes in Belarus. There are more people who have the desire to learn Chinese, but no good teachers, textbooks and teaching methods are available.

Meanwhile, China studies are at the initial stage in Belarus. Thus, it is necessary for me to stress again that we know little about modern China. We do not know China's technological methods and levels in various fields, the customs and traditions of the Chinese people nor are we familiar with the characteristics of the Chinese people through collective collaboration and individual contacts. Without an understanding of these aspects, it is very difficult for us to tap the enormous potential of the two parties in mutually-beneficial cooperation, especially interregional and inter-enterprise cooperation.

The most beneficial thing for us is China's successful experience in reform and opening up. Thanks to this experience, China is advancing in leaps and bounds to become the most influential and a perfect country in the world. China's development relies on tapping the potential of its love of peace and its kindheartedness rather than its military and political forces. This offers a new sample of a mutually-beneficial partnership for the development of other countries around the world.

As Belarus' economy is at the initial stages of systematic modernization, the urgent task for Belarus during the current stage consists in summarizing China's developmental experience; this experience covers the reform of state-owned enterprises, the distribution of authority and powers in state-owned and non-state-owned economic sectors, the roles of the policies of taxation and customs tariffs in promoting (or inhibiting) specific fields and production activities, the mechanism of material and spiritual rewards for management personnel at various levels, the regulations and systems developed by law enforcement agencies for the financial and economic activities of enterprises and companies, the roles of banks in guaranteeing sustained and rapid economic development and supporting exports with credit, as well as a series of systems with special measures for attracting foreign capital, advanced technologies and management talents.

I believe that in the near future, we will clearly see that the production and social political relations formed in China as a result of the reform and opening up do not entail the transition from one form to another form, from one "-ism" to another "-ism"; instead, these relations represent the most advanced and most optimistic social economic system for the 21st century. This new thing is attracting a great amount of attention from us.

This is the reason why we will thank our Chinese friends for assisting us in in-depth studies of the above issues. In my view, the most rational way to address these issues lies in vigorously building a Confucius Institute at Belarusian State University. We must turn it, with concerted efforts from both sides, into a powerful regional scientific research center dedicated to China studies and offering ideas and suggestions on establishing more effective methods of cooperation between China and Belarus and other countries in the region.

The main functions and research fields of this center will cover the following aspects: studying the possibility that Belarus and other countries in the region can participate in and realize the conception of the Belt and Road Initiative; providing consulting and information services for the economic, trade and investment cooperation between China and Belarus; providing necessary assistance for the cooperation between the two countries in the fields of education, culture, health, sports, tourism and other humanistic fields; assisting scientific research and educational institutions, experts and scholars in carrying out the activities for establishing the school of China studies in Belarus.

The preconditions for addressing the above issues are as follows: send 5–6 Chinese scholars and experts to this center for working with Belarusian colleagues; guarantee the legislative, scientific research and analysis certificates and other evidentiary materials necessary for this center's work; provide Belarusian scholars and experts with the opportunities for learning about the experiences and achievements of China's reform and opening up, including sending them to Chinese ministries, enterprises and organizations where they can learn first-hand.

I believe that the realization of the above proposals will be conducive to the coordinated economic development of both countries, multilateral cooperation among the countries along the Belt and Road, and bilateral cooperation between the two countries in the fields of the economy, trade and investment.

“一带一路”对国际贸易的潜在影响

爱丽莎　【意大利】

经济学副教授 / 意大利国际政治研究所 (ISPI)　高级研究员

“一带一路”倡议，是指习近平主席于 2013 年提出的。“一带一路”致力于在中国古代丝绸之路的基础之上，分别打通海陆两条国际化经济带，并在沿线构建互通互联网络，以此缓解跨境贸易中存在的诸多瓶颈。海陆两条经济带均以中国国内多个区域为起点，横穿中亚、南亚，并最终抵达欧洲。

“一带一路”的前身为中国古代丝绸贸易的交通道路（包括海路陆路两条），最早可以追溯到汉代（公元前 206 年至公元后 220 年）。直到十九世纪中期，德国地质学家斐迪南·冯·李希霍芬男爵才将这两条通路命名为“丝绸之路”，这一名称随后在 20 世纪 90 年代末中国政府开展的“走出去”战略中得以沿用。古代丝绸之路包括陆上通路和海上通路，两者均以中国和欧洲为起点和终点，途经南方走廊、伊朗、土耳其，最终将西安与罗马连接在一起。而“一带一路”则途经中亚、俄罗斯及东欧，分别从欧洲南部和北部穿过，最终抵达北欧主要港口鹿特丹，辐射地域远比古代丝绸之路广阔。此外，古代丝绸之路的形成主要受到中国及其伙伴国的贸易活动影响，并无计划性可言。相比之下，“一带一路”则是由中国政府设计的全面的国家发展战略，对国际发展具有重大影响。

稳固与重要伙伴国之间的商业关系和商业交流，向来是国际关系中的主要目标，因此，在“一带一路”倡议的启迪下，全世界范围内的商界、政界、学术界纷纷就该战略对国际政治经济可能造成的影响展开了热烈的讨论。尽管在该战略中，贸易始终处于关键性的支柱地位，但“一带一路”并非仅仅是复兴古代欧亚联系的一种手段。它更是一项宏伟的工程，具有更深远的意义，将对亚欧乃至非洲各地的经济、地缘政治产生巨大影响。通过兴建交通基础设施、促进互通互联等措施，该工程旨在刺激广大欠发达地区——如国内陆地区、中国西部，以及中亚“斯坦国”等地区的经济发展。上述区域也是未来几十年内最具发展前景的区域。

具体而言，“一带一路”包括“丝绸之路经济带”和“海上丝绸之路”两条线路，每条线路都覆盖无数条交通走廊，旨在促进中国与欧洲间的跨境联通。这种连通性具体表现在政策协调、基础设施建设（包括铁路及公路）、贸易便利化、金融一体化、国民交流等五个领域。由于基础设施建设在新丝绸之路战略中占据支配性地位，因此，中国与贸易伙伴国间的国际贸易线路将会受到最直接、最明显的影响。另外，海陆丝绸之路沿线地区大多由于基础设施薄弱而面临贸易流通受阻的问题，因此，“一带一路”倡议的另外一个影响将体现在沿线国家贸易量的增长上。

根据中国社会科学院发布的《“一带一路”沿线国家工业化进程报告》显示，“一带一路”沿线将覆盖65个国家、世界总人口的2/3、全球GDP总量的1/3。目前，由于铁路运输成本相对较高，且中亚地区的陆路运输基础设施薄弱，中国60%的贸易（以价值衡量）都是经由海路实现（贸易量所占比重更高）。因此，“一带一路”倡议将对中国的贸易线路、欧亚地区的区域联通性、国际联通性产生重大影响。与此同时，“一带一路”倡议还具有这样一种潜质——它能够在很大程度上重绘世界贸易地图，使中国在国际贸易关系中成为游戏规则的改变者。

基础设施投资对于提高海上联通效率具有至关重要的作用，因而在当前国际贸易线路的格局中，“一带一路”倡议必将极为有效地促进贸易增长。诚然，基础设施投资需要具备一定的金融实力，许多国家无法独立承担，但参与“一带一路”工程的金融机构能够促进国际合作和国际伙伴关系的建立，从而克服财力上的限制。同时，国际合作能够出台种种奖励机制，诱导船运公司为盈利状况欠佳的区域提供货运服务。

“一带一路”沿线国家的贸易增长主要通过两个途径来实现。第一，对于关系紧密的贸易伙伴国，可以在原有的贸易关系基础上，扩大贸易范围，降低运输成本，减少贸易阻碍。尽管许多人士曾针对“一带一路”对于贸易的影响做出种种估计，但此类评估终非易事，因为最重要的影响取决于——贸易线路要从当前处于支配地位的海运转向铁路运输。第二，开辟新的贸易线路有助于发掘潜在的贸易机会、建立新的贸易伙伴关系，对中亚地区的“斯坦国”而言尤其如此。该区各国市场前景广阔，具有强劲的增长潜力，且与中国和欧洲的贸易。

The likely Impact of Belt and Road on International Trade[*]

Alessia Amighini / Italy

Associate Professor of Economics /Senior Associate Research Fellow at the Italian Institute for International Political Studies (ISPI)

The so-called New Silk Roads proposed by Xi Jinping in 2013 is a commitment to ease bottlenecks to cross-border trade by building networks of connectivity along the existing and planned international routes from various regions of China across Central and South Asia to Europe as a terminal point. Under the label of 'One Belt, One Road' (OBOR), or 'Belt-and-Road Initiative' (BRI), the project has since become the centrepiece of China's economic diplomacy.

The BRI is much broader in scope than its predecessors, i.e. the ancient Silk Road(s) dating back to the Han Dynasty (206 BC –220 AD), labelled in that way by German geologist Baron Ferdinand von Richthofen only in the mid-nineteenth century, and the "Go Out" policy introduced by the Chinese government back in the late 1990s. Unlike the old Silk Roads between China and Europe, which included

* This comment is part of a longer chapter forthcoming in the next Nomos and Khaos report edited by Nomisma.

land routes and sea-lanes connecting Xian to Rome mainly through southern corridors crossing Iran and Turkey, the Belt and Road project should travel through Central Asia, Russia and Eastern Europe, with the aim to reach the main Northern European port of Rotterdam both from Southern and Central Europe. Unlike the ancient Silk Road, which was largely an unplanned outcome of the trading activities between China and its partner countries, the Belt and Road project is a comprehensive national development strategy designed by the government, with massive international development impact.

As securing commercial ties and flows with important partner countries has always been a major goal of international relations, the Belt and Road project has inspired lively debates in business, policy and scholarly circles all over the world about its impact on current international economic and political affairs. In fact, although trade is a key pillar of the project, the BRI is not just a way of reviving ancient trade links between Asia and Europe, but an ambitious programme with massive economic and geo-political impact on various regions in Asia, Europe and also Africa. By providing transport infrastructure and increasing connectivity, the Belt and Road project aims to stimulate economic development over vast areas of land from the least developed inner and western provinces of China to the so-called STAN countries in Central Asia, the region with the most promising development prospects in the next few decades.

The BRI specifically includes a 'Silk Road Economic Belt' and a 'Maritime Silk Road', both encompassing a number of corridors with the main aim to promote cross-border connectivity between China and Europe. Connectivity covers the five major areas of policy coordination, infrastructure construction (including railways and highways), trade facilitation, financial integration and people-to-people exchanges. As infrastructure construction is the dominant feature of the New Silk Road, its most evident and direct impact is likely to be on the *routes* of international trade between China and its trading partners. Moreover, because insufficient infrastructure acts as a major barrier to trade flows precisely along the land routes and sea-lanes where the BRI should develop, an additional impact will be on the *volume* of trade among the countries covered by the initiative.

According to the *Industrialization of the Belt and Road Countries Report* published by the Chinese Academy of Social Sciences, BRI will extend across up to 65 countries, accounting for over nearly two-thirds of the world's population, one-third of global GDP. Currently, 60% of China's trade (in value) travels by sea (and a much higher share in volume), due to the lower transport costs associated with international shipments compared to railway transport and to the lack of infrastructure for land transport across Central Asia. Therefore, the BRI is likely to have major implications on the routes of China's trade to the extent that it will improve regional and international land connectivity across Eurasia. BRI has the potential to significantly alter world trade routes and to become a game changer in international trade relations.

Under the current pattern of international trade routes, the Belt and Road initiative will have major trade-creating effects, to the extent that investment in infrastructure will be vital to increase the efficiency of maritime connectivity. Moreover, international cooperation and partnerships through the financing institutions related to BRI will allow overcoming the difficulties faced by individual countries who are not able to bear alone the financial effort required by infrastructure investment. International cooperation is also required to create incentives for shipping companies to serve destinations that are not profitable (Fugazza, 2015).

Trade creation along the Belt and Road will work through two major channels. On the one hand, one type of trade creating effect will work through the expansion of existing trade ties between pairs of countries that are already important trade partners, through the decrease of transport costs and trade barriers. Although some estimates exist, assessing the impact of BRI on trade is not an easy task because the most important impact will arise from the switch of trade routes from the current predominance of seaborne trade to railway trade. An additional type of trade creating effect will work through new trade routes that will unlock potential trade ties with new trading partners, most notably in the so-called STAN countries in Central Asia, large and growing markets where both China and Europe currently hold good trade relations, which could further improve based on the complementarities of their economic structures.

“一带一路”和中国的大开放战略

阮宗泽 【中国】
中国国际问题研究院　常务副院长

我的发言是着重于“一带一路”和中国的大开放战略。我主要讲三个问题：

一，世界对中国是有期待的。怎么理解世界对中国有期待？我觉得中国的身份在发生一个大的转变。中国改革开放以来，特别是用了很长的时间一直在融入国际体系，或者可以说中国逐渐从局外、体系外的力量成为体系内的力量，当然，中国也有一种责任来维护现在国际体系的稳定和它的发展。

二，中国从消费者到生产者的转变。因为中国过去很多时候在学习和融入国际体系，现在中国的身份转变了，我们要逐渐向社会、世界提供公共产品。我特别想指出，有的人批评中国，说中国过去是“搭便车”，现在中国不再搭便车，中国要开始学着驾驶。

三，中国身份的转变也在于中国面临一个平衡，我们从事的是要独善其身还要兼济天下的关联发展。中国的发展是近年来国际政治当中最深刻的变化之一。但同时大家又在想，中国的发展跟世界是什么关系？中国能不能对世界的和平与繁荣带来更大的发展？提供更大的发展条件？

习近平主席在 2016 年的新年贺词当中讲道：“世界这么大，问题这么多，国际社会期待听到中国的声音，看到中国的方案，中国不能缺席。”所以中国一定要有我们自己的想法。而且习近平主席又强调，世界应该是一个百花园，不是一花独放，而是百花齐放。

正是在这种情况下，中国倡导“一带一路”。当然，我们还有很多的一些外交方面的倡议，我认为“一带一路”是其中最具有代表性的倡议。

中国提出“一带一路”和中国自身未来的发展也密切相关。“一带一路”象征着中国更大的开放，前所未有的开放。这种开放会对中国自身内部的进一步改革提供一种动力。从20世纪70年代末开始，中国推行改革开放以来，开放和改革总是一个硬币的两面，是相互作用的。更大的开放就意味着中国自身要有更大的改革。

习近平主席讲，现在是中国要深化改革的时期，而且是“伤筋动骨”的时候。过去容易的地方我们已经改了，接下来的“改”将更加艰难、更加考验着我们。这时候需要用更大的开放为中国下一步的改革注入动力。

我认为这就是“一带一路”在其中扮演着不可或缺的重要角色，它特别强调中国和世界的连接，这种连接体现在政策、设施、贸易、资金、民心等方方面面。而这样一种连接会对中国进一步的国内改革以及更大的开放、向世界提供更多的公共产品。

“一带一路”实际上是中国参与全球治理一个有效的路径或者新的路径，我认为现在的全球治理面临两大瓶颈：

一，公共产品提供不足。现在出现了一系列新的全球性问题，但是存在一种全球治理的赤字。从国际机制上讲，它不足以提供这么多，或者还没来得及提供这么多的机制，存在供给短缺。

二，我认为现在全球治理当中也出现一些现象，这个现象就是最近的“反全球化”现象，比如我们经常看到的对全球化的批判或者对区域化的反动。英国脱欧、美国出现的“特朗普现象”都说明，全球化一方面在发展，另一方面出现一些抵制的声音和势力。

在这种情况下，中国要参与全球化，中国要进一步推动全球化的发展。我认为“一带一路”就是一个推动全球化发展的最好的工具和最好的路径。现在出现越来越多全球性的跨境问题，网络安全、气候变化、环境等等问题，这些问题靠陈旧的传统的联盟体制是不能解决的，必须要靠全球性的伙伴关系才能有效应对。这就是“一带一路”所倡导的一种精神，就是一种伙伴、开放、合作、共赢的精神。

最近我们看到，从去年以来，联合国通过《2030可持续发展计划》，我认为中国“一带一路”对推动《2030可持续发展计划》具有不可替代的作用。2016

年 9 月份在杭州 G20 峰会上《2030 可持续发展计划》已经成为杭州峰会的共识。在联合国，中国又提出落实《2030 可持续发展的中国行动计划》，在这一点我非常有感受。因为我自己还担任联合国国际开发署人类发展报告咨询委员会的中方专家，我们在联合国讨论人类发展时，特别是发展中国家对中国这些年的发展尤其感兴趣和着迷。他们这样跟我讲，在 30 年前，中国跟我们国家发展水平差不多，但 30 年以后，已经判若两人。实际上中国的发展对广大发展中国家是一个激励，我们从你们的发展当中看到希望、看到信心。所以说，你们能做到，我们也能做到。实际上“一带一路”所推动的理念就是要共同发展、共同进步。

最后要提到两点挑战：

一，“一带一路”并不是一蹴而就的，它是一次长征。中国现在正在纪念长征 80 周年，“一带一路”也将是一场长征，所以说不会是一蹴而就、一帆风顺的。

二，可能还有一些误解需要消除。在与一些人和朋友交流时，他们对“一带一路”有一些误解。我想正是有这些不了解或者误解，更加增加了我们要相互沟通、相互交流的必要。

像今天这样一个会议，就有助于我们的交流，我认为恰逢其时。谢谢！

The Belt and Road Initiative and China's Great Opening-up

Ruan Zongze / China

Executive Vice-President of China Institute of International Studies

My speech will focus on the Belt and Road Initiative and China's Great Opening Up Strategy. I will mainly discuss three issues:

1. The world has expectations regarding China. How should we interpret these expectations? I think China's status has greatly changed. Since China's reform and opening up, China has striven to become part of the international system; in particular, it took a very long time for China to make this effort. China has gradually changed from an outsider and a force outside the system to a force within the system. Of course, China is obligated to safeguard the stability and development of the existing international system.

2. China has changed from a consumer to a producer. In the past, China often learned from and endeavored to become part of the international system. Now China's status has changed. China should gradually provide public goods to society and to the world. I would like to point out that some people have criticized China and have believed that China was a free rider in the past; now China should no

longer be a free rider, China should start to learn how to drive.

3. The change in China's status calls for a balance for China. China should independently seek vigorous development and also benefit the world. China's development has witnessed one of the most profound changes in the international political arena in recent years. However, people may wonder: What is the relationship between China's development and the world? Can China further promote e world peace and prosperity? Can China provide greater conditions for development?

In his 2016 New Year's Speech, Chinese President Xi Jinping said:"The world is too big, and challenges are too many, to go without the voice from China being heard, without solution ideas from China being shared, without the involvement of China being needed." Thus, China must have its own ideas. President Xi Jinping also stressed that the world should be a garden where all of the flowers rather than one flower bloom together.

Against such a background, China advocates the Belt and Road Initiative. Of course, China has put forward many other initiatives concerning diplomatic affairs. I believe that the Belt and Road Initiative is the most representative.

The Belt and Road Initiative put forward by China is also closely related to China's future development. The Belt and Road symbolizes China's wider and unprecedented opening up. This opening up will provide impetus for further reforms within China. China has carried out reforms and opening up since the late 1970s. Similar to the two sides of a coin, reform and opening up interact with each other. Greater opening up means that China needs greater reforms.

According to Chinese President Xi Jinping, China needs to intensify its reforms and tackle the more knotty problems in the current period. In the past, we launched reforms in the fields which were easy to reform; hereafter, reforms will become more difficult and they will be subject to more tests. Thus a greater opening up is required to inject vitality into China's next reforms.

In my opinion, the Belt and Road Initiative will play an important and indispensable role in this process. It especially stresses the connectivity between China and the world. Such connectivity is reflected in various aspects including policy, facilities, trade, capital and public mind. Such connectivity will further push forward domestic reforms and China's opening up and help provide more public goods to the world.

In fact, the Belt and Road Initiative is an effective and new way for China to participate in global governance. I believe that the current global governance is subject to two major bottlenecks:

1. Public goods are inadequate. Now a series of global problems are occurring; however, there is a deficit in global governance. The international mechanisms are not sufficiently available, or there is not enough time to provide so many mechanisms; there is a supply shortage.

2. In my view, there are some phenomena in global governance, one of which is the recent wave of anti-globalization, such as the commoncriticism of globalization or the counteractionagainstregionalization. Brexit and Donald have Trump's election as US President show that globalization is developing on the one hand, some voices and forces boycotted globalization on the other hand.

Under such a circumstance, China should participate in and further promote globalization. I think the Belt and Road Initiative is the best tool and way to boosting globalization. The global cross-border issues are on the rise, including network security, climate change and the environment. These issues cannot be addressed by the outdated traditional alliance system. In order to effectively deal with these issues, it is necessary to rely on global partnership. This is a spirit advocated by the Belt and Road Initiative, namely, a spirit of partnership, opening up, cooperation and win-win outcome.

Last year, the United Nations adopted the *2030 Agenda for Sustainable Development*. I believe that the Belt and Road Initiative put forward by China is playing an irreplaceable role in promoting this agenda. The *2030 Agenda for Sustainable Development* became the consensus at the G20 Hangzhou Summit held in September, 2016. In UN, China has proposed to carry out *China's National Plan on Implementation of the 2030 Agenda for Sustainable Development*. I have a deep experience on this aspect because I am a Chinese expert onthe UNDP Human Development Report Advisory Committee. When we discussed human development in the United Nations, the experts from other countries, especially the developing countries, were particularly interested in China's development over the years. They said to me that, 30 years ago, China's development level was similar to that in their countries, but 30 years later, China has totally changed; in fact, China's development has inspired the developing countries; they can see hopes and confidence from China's development;so China can make it, they can also make it. Actually, the philosophy promoted by the Belt and Road Initiative is common development and progress.

Finally, I want to emphasize two challenges:

1. The Belt and Road Initiative cannot be achieved overnight. It is a long march. Now China is commemorating the 80th anniversary of the victory of the Long March. The Belt and Road Initiative will be a long march, so it cannot be smoothly accomplished in one action.

2. It may be necessary to dispel some misunderstandings. Communication with some people and friends shows that they have some misunderstandings about the Belt and Road Initiative. I think these misunderstandings make more necessary enhance our communication and exchanges.

Today's meeting is conducive to our communication. It is the right time for communication. Thank you!

“一带一路”与中国的“天下”观

巴得胜　【比利时】
比利时根特大学　汉学系教授

2013 年 9 月 7 日，习近平主席在访问纳扎尔巴耶夫大学时宣布开展“一带一路”工程，后于 2013 年 10 月 3 日，在印度尼西亚国会发表重要讲话时，重申了这一倡议。自此之后，这一重大经济及地缘政治计划引起了热烈反响，但同时也引发了一些疑虑。香港的《南华早报》于 2014 年 4 月 2 日发表的一篇社论中称，这一倡议“是中国有史以来提出的，意义最为重大、影响最为广泛的工程，它在国内政策和外交政策上的意义将对经济、战略以及外交关系产生重大影响。”在接下来的内容里，我并不想过多的谈论世界对中国提出的这一重要倡议的反响。相反，我打算仔细地讨论一下，中国作为世界大国，在她寻求自我认同的历史上，“一带一路”所扮演的角色，以及中国接下来将会以何种视角来审视国际关系的性质和作用。

正如“一带一路”倡议的名称所示，该倡议包含两个要素：连接中国与欧亚地区的陆上新丝绸之路（一带），连接中国东南沿海城市与欧洲和非洲的海上新丝绸之路（一路）。据估计，这一倡议将覆盖 65 个国家，影响近 44 亿人口。“一带一路”的名称会让我们立刻联想到中国历史上的“丝绸之路”——自汉代起形成的，一张横跨欧亚、连接当时国都长安（如今的西安）与罗马帝国的交通网络。中国历史上的“丝绸之路”在很长时间内，并非中国直通欧洲的一条通路，而是指横跨欧亚大陆、连接城市与国都的多条道路。此外，经由这条路径的商品并非仅仅局限于丝绸，因此“丝绸之路”和“21世纪丝绸之路”的说法可能会引起歧义。故而，“一带一路”这一名称的含义为：陆上联通欧亚，海上联结亚非欧。中国领导人在很多场合常都曾强调，新丝绸之路“是中国为实现亚非欧互通互联这一目标而绘制的宏伟蓝图”很显然，“一带一路”倡议的提出，是中国经济实力、政治实力增强所带来的逻辑结果。从这个角度来看，该倡议表现出“自改革开放以来，经过数十年的适应和融入国际体制，中国正采取一种积极而全面的战略来应对不断变换的国际形势。”从这个角度讲，“一带一路”也包括“统一”的因素。从这里，我们能够读出中国传统的“天下”观的影子。

早在中国的秦朝（公元前221—206年）统一六国时，天下的概念便首次在中国政治史上引起了重视，后来由于汉朝（公元前206—220年）推行“独尊儒术”的政策，这一概念变得愈发重要。受到地域统一和政治统一的启发，中国史学早在公元前11世纪便出现了“中华民族”的概念。公元前221年建立的秦朝代表着至高无上的文明，其国民是在神的干预下才出生在这个国家，秦朝四周的地域被视作蛮夷之地。正如塞巴斯蒂安·哈尼斯所说，“‘天下’与‘蛮夷’两个概念是互构的：天下所指代的，并不是地理概念，而是一个文化共同体，这一共同体的边界是由中国儒家思想的哲学和道德传统的知识与实践来界定。凡是不尊奉中国传统者，均被视作蛮夷。”因此，在实现“天下”统一的过程中，中国文化领域的统一和国民的统一被视为非常重要的一个逻辑步骤。“天下统一”被作为一项神圣的使命，是真正统治的最终目的。故而在中国，政治问题在某种程度上都被视作内政。

据最早的史料记载，1700年之前，亚洲经济大约占世界经济的三分之二，而中印两国又是当时世界上最大的经济体，这一事实使得将世界视为天下做法沿袭下来。当然，这并不意味着历史事件对中国没有造成任何影响，只是当时的政治并不允许对“天下”的概念进行重新解读。后来，公元618年李氏家族夺取政权，取代了隋朝，天下的概念发生了重大变化。李氏家族建立唐朝后，中华民族后裔与鲜卑族和突厥族的后裔发生融合，加之唐朝青睐外来佛教，汉代形成的、以“自我—他者”二元对立为特征的“天下”概念已经变为“多元化”的代名词。唐朝建立后，中国与周边国家的文化交流为彼此都带来了十分重要的影响，因此自我—他者的二元对立已经变得无关紧要。随着中国的传统文化被纳入到元朝（1279—1368）和清朝（1644—1911）体系中，中国已经不再是一个单一的统一体，因此天下的概念再次发生了根本性的变化。为了实现统治的合法化，清朝选择尊奉儒家“德”的概念，即大清王朝各族群之间的和谐共存。这一选择具有重大意义，它强化了“儒家具有普适性”的信念，也就是说，尽管中国文化的中心地带被外族所统治，但这并没有导致“天下”理念的崩坍，相反，儒家思想特有的转化性，使外族统治者发生了转变，这为“天下”统一的最终实现提供了可能。这种“中国—非（纯粹的）中国”的二元对立并不意味着两者间存在消极或对抗的关系。“蛮夷”的他者性使得外族能够和平地融入中华民族中来。

对于19世纪中叶的中古历史而言，有一点必须要引起注意：1700年左右，亚洲和中国的优势主要在于广阔的疆域和众多的人口，在西方的工业革命之前，国家的经济规模与人口数量的关系更加紧密。然而从18世纪开始，西方经济开始迅速增长，并超过亚洲诸国。欧洲在19、20世纪崛起的同时，中国的经济正陷入停滞状态。20世纪初期，亚洲经济所占的全球份额跌至28%，20世纪中期继续降至19%。中国在世界经济和世界政治领域地位的下降，对中国的自体感知造成了重要的影响。

随着中国重拾在世界政治经济领域的地位，“天下”的文化概念仍然强调着其一贯的“民族国家”的身份，中国的经济发展方式和政治发展方式被视为恢复传统国际身份的两种手段。关于这一点，倪宁灵曾评论说：“对国家地位这个概念进行重新节点，能够塑造一个国家在国际环境中的战略定位，并与其自我定义的国家行为者的身份相适应。中国不仅将其身份定义为‘民族国家’，同时也定义为现代意义上的‘天下’。”由于中国在历史上便获得了“文明国家”的身份，许多哲学作品中也论及“天下”这一概念，因此，当代中国学者将中国在世界舞台上的再次崛起描述为“和平崛起”或“和平发展”。从“天下”或“世界主义”的视角来看，国家不该强调其文明的优越性，而应该对所有文化、宗教以及政治体制保持开放态度。传统儒家思想中的“天下”观——如果重新解读——实则为世界提供了一条代替“西方体系”的道路，同时仍然对新儒家“儒家思想能够为新型世界文化提供基础”的理念进行强调。“一带一路”倡议便被视为中国用来恢复国际地位的这样一种手段，因为这一倡议给予了中国“复兴中的[负责任的]大国”的形象，因为“崛起”、“发展”等语汇，也是当代领导层创造出的表达方式。

对于直接参与“一带一路”工程的国家而言，中国为其扭转经济停滞或经济下降的困境提供了绝好的机会，欧洲国家也不例外。在2015年6月29日召开的第 7 届中欧峰会上，中国与欧盟宣布，中国的"一带一路倡议"将与欧盟委员会主席容克提出的投资计划进行对接（基础设施投资在中国和欧洲的计划中均占有重要地位）。在 2015 年 9 月 28 日于北京举行的中欧经贸高层对话中，欧盟宣布，中国是唯一一个参与容克计划的非欧盟成员国。当然，由于"一带一路"倡议注重基础设施投资，欧洲多国决定参与"亚洲基础设施投资银行"的建设，并于 2014 年在北京签约。中国与全世界愈发紧密的经济和金融联系无疑将成为中国最大的优势，中国在整个欧亚地区的政治影响力必然得到提升。也可以看作是邓小平 20 世纪 70 年代提出的"改革开放"政策在当代取得的成就。

对中国而言，继 2001 年加入世贸组织、2008 年举办北京奥运会、2010 年举办上海世博会之后，"一带一路"倡议更加强调了中国的新地位，这恰好是习近平主席所谓"百年屈辱后民族复兴的"具体表现，"天下"的概念也因此获得了新的内涵。这一点在穆春山就"一带一路"倡议发表的评论中得到充分的诠释："一些中欧、东欧国家甚至也被纳入到 [中国]'周边外交'的重要战略框架内。"复旦大学经济学院教授王健也表示："'新丝绸之路经济带'建设会给当前的国际格局带来复杂的变化，有利于中方与国外伙伴一道，构建一个以合作、和平、和谐为特色的大环境，为东亚、南亚等地区创造有利条件 ...... 对于'新丝绸之路经济带'所覆盖的国家和地区而言，'一带一路'倡议与欧亚非以及拉丁美洲国家的大方向是一致的，而朝着这个方向继续前进，会给全世界四分之三的人口带来利益。"对于中亚地区而言，通过"一带一路"倡议促进经济发展，自然而然会对多边区域安全、发展、合作带来有利的影响（上海合作组织——中国打造的第一个全球治理组织便是绝佳的例证），同时，"21 世纪海上丝绸之路"的建设有利于中国南海问题的解决。"一带一路"倡议给予我们这样一个美好的愿景：增长、经贸、投资、区域一体化等，最终能够改善中亚以及中国南海区域的安全环境，提高稳定性。目前的一些紧张形势似乎会对新丝绸之路的整体战略思想造成威胁或危害，但最终都会成为有利于"一带一路"实施的优势。

The Belt and Road and China's "Tianxia" Concept

Bart Dessein / Belgium

Professor of the Department of Chinese Language and Culture at Ghent University

Ever since Chinese President Xi Jinping announced the 'One-Belt-One-Road' project on the occasion of a visit to Nazerbajev University in Kazakhstan on 7 September 2013, and reiterated this initiative in a speech delivered on 3 October 2013 in the Indonesian parliament,[1] this major economic and geostrategic plan has at times met with enthusiasm, and at other times with skepticism, doubt, and suspicion. In the following pages, I will not primarily deal with the world's reaction to this important Chinese initiative that was in an editorial in the Hong Kong *South China Morning Post* of 2 April 2015 called "the most significant and far-reaching project the nation has ever put forward, having domestic and foreign policy implications that impact the economy and strategic and diplomatic relations".[2] Rather, I will reflect on the way the Belt and Road initiative figures in the larger history of Chinese self-identity as a world nation and her concomitant perspective

1 J. Wang, "Shanghai Luntanzhengcejianyibaogao – Sichouzhiluyuanzhuohuiyi" , *Zhongguo guan*, vol.42, No.7, 2015, p.1.

2 http://www.scmp.com/comment/insight-oinion/article/1753773/one-belt-one-road-initiative-will-define-chinas-role-world (last accessed: 25 September 2016).

on the nature and role of international relations.

As the name suggests, the Belt and Road initiative comprises two elements: a new terrestrial Silk Road (One Belt) that is to connect China with the rest of Eurasia, and a new maritime Silk Road (One Road) that is to connect China's south-eastern coastal cities with Europe and Africa. Obviously, this initiative of which it is estimated that it will eventually reach 4.4 billion people in more than 65 countries,[1]immediately brings to mind the historic 'Silk Road,' which was, actually, a network of roads that, starting in the Han dynasty, crossed the Eurasian continent, eventually linking the then capital Chang'an (present-day Xi'an) with the Roman empire. As the historical 'Silk Road' was, for the majority of its long existence, nota single road that directly connected China and Europe, but a multitude of road connections between local cities and capitals across the Eurasian continent, and as, moreover, silk was only one of the many commodities traded along the road, the terms 'Silk Road' and 'Twenty-first-Century Silk Road' may be misleading.[2]It is, therefore, more the general concept of (re)connecting Asia and Europe over land and connecting Asia, Europe and Africa over water that underlies the name Belt and Road. Chinese leadership has on several occasions underlined that the new Silk Road indeed "should be seen as a grand blueprint for China's ambitions to connect three different continents, namely Asia, Europe, and Africa".[3]

It is clear that this Belt and Road initiative is concomitant with and a logical outcome of China's growing economic and political clout. In this sense, the initiative demonstrates that "after decades of adaptation and integration into the international system since the launch of the reform policy at the end of the 1970s, the Chinese government is now developing a proactive and comprehensive strategy

1 See J. Verlare and F. P. van der Putten, " 'One Belt, One Road' : An Opportunity for the EU's Security Strategy" , *Clingendael Policy Brief*, December 2015, p.2.

2 The name 'Silk Road' is a translation of the German 'Seidenstrasse,' coined by Baron Ferdinand von Richthofen in the 19th century.

3 See A.K. Stahl, "China's New Silk Road Diplomacy: Implications for China's Relations with Europe and Africa" , *EU-China Observer*, Vol.1, No.15, 2015, p.17.

to deal with the changing situation in the world".[1]The name 'One-Belt-One-Road' in this respect further also comprises an element of unification. It is here that we touch upon the historical reminiscence of the traditional Chinese concept *tianxia* (all under heaven).

The concept *tianxia* has first attained importance in China's political history with the unification of the empire in the Qin dynasty (221–206 BCE) and the subsequent ascent of Confucianism as political doctrine in the Han dynasty (206 BCE–220 CE).Inspired by the territorial and the political unification of the then China, historiography has projected the coming into existence of a Chinese state back in time to the 11th century BCE, and has identified the state that was established in 221 BCE as a realm of supreme civilization, the citizens of which were born through divine intervention and who are surrounded by non-Chinese (*i.e.*, the so-called *yi*). As Sebastian Harnisch stated: "The concepts '*tianxia*' and '*yi*' are co-constitutive: the former does not depict a geographical, but a cultural community, whose boundaries are determined by knowledge and practices of China's Confucian philosophical and moral traditions. '*Yi*' describes those who do not follow the 'Chinese way'".[2]A logical outcome of the perception that the unification of the Chinese cultural realm and its inhabitants were interpreted as a logical step in the unification of the known world (*tianxia*) and that such a unification of 'all under heaven' was seen as a divine enterprise and as the ultimate goal of true rulership, has been that, in China, politics were always in some sense regarded to be internal

1 J. Men, "China's New Silk Road and EU-China Relations" , *EU-China Observer*, Vol.1, No.15, 2015, p.12.

2 Sebastian Harnisch, "China's historical self and its international role" , in *China's International Roles. Challenging or supporting international order?* Role theory and international relations. Edited by S. Harnisch, S. Bersick and J.-C. Gottwald. New York and London: Routledge, 2016, pp.39-40. See also J. Townsend, "Chinese Nationalism" , in *Chinese Nationalism.* Edited by J. Unger. Armonk NY: M. E. Sharpe, 1996.

politics.[1]

The fact that from earliest records and until about 1700, Asia accounted for roughly two-thirds of the world's economy, and that China and India were the largest economies in the world by a large margin, sustained this *tianxia* perception of the world. This does not mean that historical occurrences that affected China's body politic would not have necessitated a reinterpretation of the 'all under heaven' concept. A first major such historical development occurred when the Li family took over the Sui throne and established the Tang dynasty in 618 CE. When, with the Tang, political power came in the hands of the Li family which was of mixed Chinese/Xianbei/Turkic descent and favored non-Chinese Buddhism, the earlier Han *tianxia* concept that had been characterized by a 'self'-'other' dichotomy developed to be an expression of benign pluralism.[2]Indeed, cultural exchange between China and her neighboring territories in the period preceding the installment of the Tang dynasty had influenced China as much as China had influenced others, and the self-other dichotomy had become irrelevant. When China's traditional cultural sphere was incorporated in the Mongolian empire (1279–1368) and in the Manchu Qing empire (1644–1911), it stopped to be an independent unity. This, again, fundamentally changed the *tianxia* concept. It has been of major importance that the Manchus chose to legitimize their rule through accentuating the Confucian concept 'virtue' (*de*), understood as the harmonious co-existence of the different ethnic groups in their empire.[3]This choice strengthened the conviction that Confucianism had a 'universalizing' capacity, that is to say, the conviction

---

1 See Y. Pines, "Imagining the Empire? Concepts of 'Primeval Unity' in Pre-imperial Historiographic Tradition" , in *Conceiving the Empire. China and Rome Compared.* Edited by Fritz-HeinerMutschler and AchimMittag. Oxford: Oxford University Press, [2008] 2009, p. 81. This is significantly different from the Roman case. For the Romans of the period of expansion, history was a progressive phenomenon, moving towards their domination of the world through expansion. See A. Mittag and F.-H. Mutschler. "Epilogue" , in *Conceiving the Empire. China and Rome Compared.* Edited by F.-H. Mutschler and AchimMittag. Oxford: Oxford University Press, [2008] 2009, p.440.

2 For some theoretical reflections: see C. Kinnvall, "Globalization and Religious Nationalism: Self, Identity, and the Search for Ontological Security" , *Political Psychology* 25/5, 2004, pp.747-748.

3 See H. Harrison, *China. Inventing the Nation.* London: Arnold, 2001, pp.36-38.

grew that political authority over the Chinese cultural heartland exerted by non-Chinese did not necessarily lead to a collapse of 'all under heaven,' but that, on the contrary, the transformative influence of Confucianism was able to 'transform' non-Chinese, making it possible that 'all under heaven' would, eventually, be unified.[1] This 'Chinese'—'not yet (fully) Chinese' dichotomy does not necessarily imply a negative or confrontational relationship; the others of '*yi*' allowed for a peaceful incorporation of a foreign people into the Chinese.[2]

It is, for the history of China since the middle of the 19th century important to note that Asia's and China's strength until around 1700 had basically been the result of the region's massive size and population as, before the industrial revolution, the size of a country's economy more closely followed the number of its people. Starting from the 18th century, however, Western economies started to grow much faster than their Asian counterparts. The rise of Europe in the 19th and 20th century was concomitant with a stagnation of the Chinese economy. As a result, Asia's global share had fallen by half to 28 per cent by the early 20th century, and by the middle of the 20th century, it had further fallen to 19 per cent.[3]This decline of China's role in the world economy and politics has had an important impact on the country's self-perception.

In the process of regaining its traditional position in world politics and economy, the culturalistic *tianxia* concept has continued to inform the way China has identified – and still identifies – itself as a nation-state, and the way her economic

1 For a more detailed discussion: see B. Dessein, "Historical narrative, remembrance, and the ordering of the world: a historical assessment of China's international relations" , in *China's International Roles. Challenging or supporting international order?* Role theory and international relations. Edited by S. Harnisch, S. Bersick and J.-C. Gottwald. New York and London: Routledge, 2016, pp.22-37.

2 See S.Harnisch, "China's historical self and its international role" , in *China's International Roles. Challenging or supporting international order?* Role theory and international relations. Edited by S. Harnisch, S. Bersick and J.-C. Gottwald. New York and London: Routledge, 2016, p.40; Z. Wang, Never Forget National Humiliation: Historical Memory in Chinese Politics and Foreign Policy. New York: Columbia University Press, 2012, p.41.

3 H. S. Kohli, A. Sharma and A. Sood, *Asia 2050. Realizing the Asian Century*. Los Angeles, London, New Delhi, Singapore, Washington DC: Sage, 2011, p.20.

and political development are seen as instruments to restore this traditional international role. Nele Noesselt in this respect remarked that "[t]he configuration of national role conceptions shapes a state's strategic positioning in the international system and corresponds to its self-defined national actor identity," and that "China defines itself not only as a nation-state (*guojia*) but also as a modern *tianxia*".[1] Based on its historical identity as a 'civilization state,'[2] and influenced by the philosophical writings on *tianxia*, contemporary Chinese scholars portray China's new ascent on the world stage as a 'peaceful rise' (*hepingjueqi*) or a 'peaceful development' (*heping fazhan*). From the perspective of *tianxia* or worldism, rather than insisting on the superiority of one's civilization, nations are expected to maintain open attitudes toward all cultures, religions, and political systems.[3]The traditional Confucian concept 'all under heaven' is – in a new interpretation – suggested as an alternative for the West phalian world system,[4] and lingers on in the New Confucian claim that Confucianism provides the basis for a new 'world culture'.[5]The 'Belt and Road' initiative can be seen as one such instrument in the restoration of China's international position, as this initiative allows China to present itself as a '[responsible] great power' (*daguo*) in its 'revival' (*fuxing*) –as this 'rise' or 'development' is also termed by, among

1 N. Noesselt, "China and socialist countries. Role change and role continuity" , in *China's International Roles. Challenging or supporting international order?* Role theory and international relations. Edited by S. Harnisch, S. Bersick and J.-C. Gottwald. New York and London: Routledge, 2016, pp.175-176. See also T. Zhao, "Tianxiatixi: Diguoyushijiezhidu" (Tianxia: Empire and world institution), *ShijieZhexue* 5, 2003, pp.2-33; T. Zhao, *Tianxiatixi: Shijiezhiduzhexuedaolun* (The tianxia system: An introduction to the philosophy of a world institution), Nanjing: Jiangsu Education Press, 2005).

2 See W. Zhang, *The China Wave: The Rise of a Civilizational State*. Hackensack NJ: World Century Publishing Cooperation, 2012.

3 See T. Zhao, *The Tianxia System: An Introduction to the Philosophy of a World Institution*. Nanjing: Jiuzhou Publisher, 2005, pp.280-292.

4 See W. A. Callahan, "Chinese Visions of World Order: Post-hegemonic or a New Hegemony?" , *International Studies Review* 10/4, 2008, pp.750, 752-753, 759.

5 See T. Zhao, "Rethinking Empire from a Chinese Concept 'All-under-Heaven' (Tian-xia)" , *Social Identities* 12/2, 2006, pp.29-41.

others, contemporary leadership.[1]

Many countries that are directly involved in the 'One Belt One Road' project may perceive China as providing them with an opportunity to reverse economic stagnation or decline. This is also true for Europe. During the seventeenth China-EU summit of 29 June 2015, China and the European Union have declared synergies between the 'One-Belt-One-Road' initiative and the European Commission President Jean-Claude Juncker's investment plan (infrastructure investments being a major part of both plans). During the EU-China high-level economic dialogue held in Beijing on 28 September 2015, Brussels announced that China became the first non-EU country to announce contribution to the Juncker Plan.[2]And, of course, with the focus on infrastructure, the Belt and Road initiative is also connected to Beijing's launching in 2014 of the 'Asian Infrastructure Investment Bank' in which all major European countries have decided to participate.[3]

Increased economic and financial links between China and the world will undoubtedly mean greater leverage of Beijing, and an increased political clout of China in the whole of Eurasia and Africa.[4]This can be seen as the contemporary result of the policies of 'opening up to the world,' initiated by Deng Xiaoping at the end of the 1970s.[5]

For China, after the global world acknowledged its membership of the World

---

1 See J. Wang, "Shijiedaguoyuzhanlüehanjing: Zhongguoguojijuese de xinketi" (Great powers and their strategic environment: new issues of China's international role), *XiandaiGuojiGuanxi* (Contemporary International Relations) 4, 2010, pp.38-44.

2 L. Liang, "China vows win-win cooperation between OBOR, Juncker plan" . Xinhua, 2016/02/18. http://news.xinhuanet.com/english/2016-02/18/c_135107691.htm (last accessed 24 September 2016).

3 See "Three major nations absent as China launches World Bank rival in Asia" (http://www.reuters.com/article/2014/11/05/us-china-aiib-idUSKCN01D08U20141105) Reuters, 5 November 2014. (last accessed 25 September 2015). See alsohttp://www.scmp.com/comment/insight-oinion/article/1753773/one-belt-one-road-initiative-will-define-chinas-role-world (last accessed: 25 September 2016).

4 A. Vangeli, "China's New Silk Road and its Impact on Sino-European Relations" , *EU-China Observer*, Vol.1, No.15, 2015, p.26.

5 D. Shambaugh, *China goes global. The partial power*. Oxford: Oxford University Press, 2013.

Trade Organization in 2001, or granted China the organization of the 2008 Beijing Olympic Games and the 2010 Shanghai World Exposition, the 'One-Belt-One-Road' initiative underscores the country's new position, and incarnates President Xi Jinping's *fuxing* after the century of humiliation that set in the middle of the 19th century, and that gave the traditional *tianxia* concept a fundamental blow. That China's new role indeed reintroduces the traditional '*tianxia*' concept is illustrated by Mu Chunshan's comment on the Belt and Road initiative that: "Some Central and Eastern European countries are even included in the important diplomatic scope of [China's] 'greater neighborhood'.[1] Also Wang Jian of the Faculty of Economics of Fudan University, Shanghai, witnessed of this when claiming that "Through establishing the 'New Silk Road Economic Belt', China can, at present, create complex changes in global structures, and initiate an environment of cooperation with external partners that is characterized by collaboration, peace and harmony, and is creating beneficial circumstances that conform to East Asia and South Asia. [...] Seen from the countries and regions that are included in the 'New Silk Road Economic Belt', it is obvious that this [project] is in accordance with the larger direction [of development] of Europe, Asia, Africa and the Latin American continent. Going ahead along this direction, will bring benefit to nearly three quarter of the world's population".[2]For Central Asia, the economic development through the 'Belt and Road' initiative will naturally also have its impact on the advancement of multilateral regional security and development cooperation (as in the 'Shanghai Cooperation Organization,' the first ever structure for global governance initiated by China), and also the issue of the South China Sea is in the same way related to the 'Twenty-first-Century Maritime Silk Road' project. These initiatives may foster the hope that favoring growth, trade, investment and regional integration could eventually also lead to the improvement of the overall stability and security

1 C. Mu, "How Does Europe Rank in China's Diplomacy?" , *The Diplomat*, 5 April 2014.

2 J. Wang, "Shanghai Luntanzhengcejianyibaogao – Sichouzhiluyuanzhuohuiyi" , *Zhongguo guan*, vol.42, No.7, 2015, p.2.

situation in Central Asia as well as in the region of the South China See.[1] Existing tensions that may appear to be elements that threaten to jeopardize the entire strategic idea of the New Silk Road may therefore also precisely prove to be strength.[2]

1 H.D. Schweisgut, "EU-China 40th Anniversary: Expectations for Expanding Connections" , *EU-China Observer*, Vol.1, No.15, 2015, p.10.

2 B. Dessein, "New China: New Power or Revisiting the Old?" , in *Power in the 21st Century. Determinants and Contours.* Edited by T. Struye de Swielande and D. Vandamme. UCL Presses Universitaires de Louvain. Scène Internationale, 2015, p.165.

“一带一路”：引发社会变革的连锁反应

费尔南多 【墨西哥】
墨西哥众议院政治协调委员会　政党协调员

核聚变是从两个原子的碰撞开始，通过爆炸引发的一系列连锁反应，释放巨大的能量，随着无数个原子两两相碰，能量不断地被释放、增强，以至于无穷。

在我们寄予厚望的人类身上也发生着同样的连锁反应：当人类的男男女女在统一愿景下进行有意识的互动时，定然会造成一系列的变化，引发威力巨大的社会连锁反应。这种连锁反应会为互动双方带来变革，最终为各方带来利益，形成双赢局面。

我们必须找到一种智慧的方式，促进政治和社会上的交流互动，这样才接近力量之源——人民大众。通过自觉和相互理解，通过群体的反思和承担社会责任，我们才得以共同应对未来的挑战。

目前已经到了我们对人类整体的未来进行讨论的时刻，我们应该有意识地去想象、去创造一个最可靠、最真实的未来，一个属于这个星球上每一个个体的未来。

现在，已经到了我们改变视角、改变价值观、让我们的意识彼此相连的时刻。

我们可以在恐惧和茫然构成的围城中祈愿这一理想的实现，也可以满怀希望和信念，在阳光的普照下迎接这一天的到来，两种方式是截然不同的。

如果我们把自身局限在本就不甚殷实的传统遗产中，一味只求获取更多，不思变革进取，整个人类的命运和结局亦会截然不同。达尔文在提出进化论之初便已经断言，世界上的所有物种都要倚靠进化才得以生存。

我们必须走出放任造成的狭隘，下定决心促成变革，为所有人类创造最好的环境。我们要定义这样一条将人类命运连为一体的路线，这条路线的起点，便是相互间的理解和人类的团结。这有助于促进文明之间的共情、推进爱的全球化、实现自然环境与人类之间的平衡、对我们的共同价值观进行诠释、有助于定义和践行公平正义、实现价值平衡。

在我看来，中国恰恰是这方面的典范，她具有坚毅的品质，具备转换现实的力量，她向全世界展示了这一点，她是人类未来的主要缔造者。

中国在世界政治和世界经济上的影响力告诉我们，如果没有中国，我们是看不到未来的。

目前，中国已经成为世界大国，在国力提升的同时，不断地借助全球化带来的包容、通过人类的互通互联寻求互利互惠。

“一带一路”的意义在于，它为经济交流、政治和文化交流树立了一个开放且整体化的模型。

“一带一路”倡议为开放合作、建立多边金融合作机制构建了政策框架，有助于奠定产业基础和基础设施建设，同时能够强化与沿线国家的关系，推动现代化步伐，减少贫困。

本次会议恰好见证了中国在与全世界交流互通、分享彼此的经验和智慧、共享发展和繁荣、分享经历和经验等方面做出的贡献。正是这些交流和共享，让所有人类构成一个紧密的整体，不论性别的差异、国别的差异，所有人都是这个独一无二、无可媲美的共同体的一员，我们共同决定着——在第三个千禧年中，我们将如何实现世界的一体化发展，如何以真诚、和谐、智慧的方式共存；我们共同决定着如何为人类的未来制定一份明晰的最佳方案。

“一带一路”的根本价值观是“和平共处五项原则”，即：相互尊重领土和主权完整、互不侵犯、互不干涉内政、平等互利、和平共处。

身为一个墨西哥公民，我是自豪的。但同时，作为一个世界公民，我既关注着南极圈，又同样关注着中国的喜马拉雅山，关注阿拉斯加的同时，也同样关注着阿拉伯、印度、乌拉尔山、中东地区的沙漠，当然，我还关注着墨西哥、澳大利亚、俄罗斯、荷兰等地区。但我特别关注的，是世界范围内贫富差距的迅速扩大、不平等现象的不断增多、环境的恶化、有利于人类的共同价值观的丧失。但我更担心的是，政治的去人性化，只有人性化、敏感的政治才能为所有人类创造一个更好的世界。

全世界共有 75 亿人口，我们通过各种方式进行着互通互联。我们在知识领域不断取得伟大的成就，人均寿命从一个世纪前的 48 岁已经延长至如今的 71 岁。

但与此同时，我们面临着全球性的重大挑战：全球环境危机、给养危机等等，每年有 300 多万儿童因为缺乏食物而饿死，贫富差距每天都在拉大，99% 的财富集中在 1% 的人手中，流离失所的难民（650 万人）带来了人道主义危机，海洋污染、河流污染、土壤沙化、南北极冰盖的融化等，都是我们不得不面对的危机。

我们获取的知识每天都在更新，只需点几下鼠标即可。从纳米技术到人工智能，成千上万种技术塑造者我们的未来。在新千年里，我们正更积极、更快地实现着发展，如今的 80 后、90 后，最终将抛弃崇尚消费主义、快乐主义、相对主义等“轻浮”的行为模式，成为弘扬新的人类精神和共存方式的积极分子。世界上所有地区都拥抱生活的变化和变革。“践行自由理念的人学会行走，然后像雄鹰一样展翅高飞”。

与中国积极开展合作交流会带来积极的成果，这些成果体现在国际秩序方面、全球治理方面、经济发展方面和践行正义等方面。始终坚持人性的原则，始终尊重各国的自主权，这些都是全球发展和变革不可或缺的因素。这种新的外交语言、新的贸易方式，有助于我们在这个不断进化的星球上共存。

我今天的建议是：

1. 推进爱的全球化。我们所爱的事物是值得为之奋斗的，我们要去追求它、改善它。

2. 不论从个人角度还是国际关系的全球化角度来看，我们都应该一致承认相互依赖的原则。

3. 使政治和经济变得人性化。

4. 拆除仇恨的壁垒。

5. 构建“一带一路”所宣扬的互通互联的理念。

不论是国际关系、文化与文化之间的关系还是人类与人类的关系，若想创造一个公平、负责的世界，其关键因素均是为世界公民谋求福祉。国际关系在“一带一路”倡议中占据重要位置，因为中国能够很好地利用外交手段来进行协商和谈判，因而“一带一路”必然能够取得世界公认的成就。中国和其他国家行为者采取的外交手段和战略合作不仅能够为一个大洲带来利益，更能够令每一个世界公民获益。

然而外交中往往面临着这样一个难题：许多国家尚未意识到彼此间文化交流和文化联通的重要意义。

在这一点上，中国为我们提供了一个绝佳平台，借助这个平台，我们便能够实现我们的共同目标。

我深深地相信，本次会议的举办，定然能够给我们带来希望，让我们共同去创造一个人人共享、更好的世界！感谢贵方邀请，感谢贵方的盛情，更感谢贵方的良苦用心。

对我个人而言，中国总能给我带来灵感，从古代老子的《道德经》、孙子兵法，到近代的中国经验，中国人的勤劳、坚毅，以及中国艺术家作品中浓缩的千年历史等等，都像音乐、雕塑等艺术形式一样，不断地丰富着我们的灵魂。从封建王朝到新中国的成立，再到代邓小平提出一国两制构想，中国实现了极大的跨越式发展。

邓小平思想和改革开放政策证明，中国是一个顽强不屈、锐意进取的国家，中国正日渐走向更美好的未来。

今天，就让我们彼此的意识相连，引发一场连锁反应，从而发挥我们的才华，释放人类的潜力，让我们以负责的态度去构建一个人人共享的美好世界。

愿人性永存！

The Belt and Road: "Reaction to the Chain for the Social Transformation"

Fernando García Cuevas / Mexico

Coordinator of the Federal Deputies of the Parliamentary Group of the PRI (Institutional Revolutionary Party) of the State of Mexico

The nuclear fusion starts with the collision of two atoms that explode causing a chain reaction/ that releases all of his power and energy, expanding two by two to the infinity.

In the human is where my hope grows, in the same way that the chain reaction happens because of the two atoms collapsing, men and women, when they produce conscious interaction, sharing the same vision, detonating changes that produce a powerful social chain reaction, that causes bursts of interactive transformation, giving place to the molecular game of rewards for everyone, in a point of win-win.

We require to find smart ways of interactive politic and social communication just to get to he population as well as to the original source of power so it can be discovered, one in awareness and understanding, one in group reflection and social responsibility, in a way that we can overcome the future challenges.

Its time to talk about the integral future of the humanity, take it in our hands and further, in our consciences to imagine and create the most solid and real future for every single living /being of our planetary community.

Its time to change the perspective and values, its time to connect our awareness.

It is not the same to see the day through a wall full of fear and uncertainties, that see it to the light of the sun, full of hope and faith in ourselves.

It is not the same to live anchored to the heritage of poor conviction, to the belief of insufficiency, to the conviction of not being able to change, that permanently inspired /because of the certainty of the beginning of the evolution that Darwin enacted with his sentence to all living creatures of survive and breed.

We must come out of the alley of resignation and take part with determination the conviction to do, so we can create the best circumstances for all the humanity.

We need to integrate and define the line of the route that starts with the development of comprehension and the human solidarity.

That helps to boost the civilization of empathy, that stimulates love globalization that pays attention to the balance between the nature of our planet and our human specie, that defines the universal values, that defines and execute the justice, equity and balance values.

China in my opinion is an example of character, determination and transforming force of reality. They have shown to the world, they know it. They are the main character in the design of the new humanity.

Their influence in the politics and global economy shows us that the future can't be seen without China.

In the present China have placed it self as one of the stronger countries in the world and it search for mutual benefit From the human interconnection that is active in the inclusive globalization.

The analysis / of "The belt and road initiative" / in order to achieve an effective model in a open and integrator model of economic interchange, politic and cultural / that is based in the meaning / of the Silk routes.

The initiative of the belt and road implies the creation of a frame for a open cooperation, new mechanisms of multilateral financing designed to set the industrial basis and infrastructure with the objective of ensure and strengthen the relationships with countries involved in the silk routes and to enlarge the march of the modernization and the reduction of the poverty.

This global meeting confirms/ the permanent commitment of China to interact with the world, to share reciprocal knowledge and wisdom, development and prosperity, stories and experiences that bonds us as humanity, between men and women, towns and nations of this unique and incomparable planetary community of the third millennium, to determine the formulas that give a solid and integral global development, honest, harmonic and smart.

coexistence between all the nations in the world, as a unequivocally formula of the best future for humanity.

The "Five principles of pacific coexistence"; as fundamental values of One belt, One road:

(1) mutual respect to the territorial sovereignty and integrity; (2) mutual agreement of no aggression; (3) mutual agreement of non-intervention in internal issues; (4) equality and mutual benefit; (5) pacific coexistence.

I'm Mexican, proudly Mexican, I am a citizen of the world that is concerned directly what happens in Antarctica that in the Himalayas, in China as in Alaska, in the desert of Arabia as in India, in the Urals, in Middle east, of course in Mexico as in Australia, Russia or Netherlands. Specially I have to say it, I am really concerned about the growing inequality and poverty in the world, the environmental deterioration, the loss of universal values that protects and make good to men. But the thing that I worry more about the politic dehumanization, because nothing that is alive is estrange for me and the sensitive politic and human /is and will be, the thing that facilitates a better world for all humanity.

We are seven thousand five hundred million people, we experience an intensive process of interconnection in all ways. We have reached extraordinary achievements in our knowledge society. The hope of life in the world is 71 years when a century ago was of 48 years.

We face globally big challenges as: environmental global crisis, alimentary crisis that lets die more than 3 million children every year for lack of food, a terrible crisis because of the inequality that grows up every day the belt of poor and rich letting as a consequence/ that one percent of the rich concentrates more of the wealthy of the 99%, humanitarian crisis because of the displaced of the world, plus 65 million people, contamination of the oceans and rivers, desertification of the earth and melting of the poles.

Our access to the knowledge we develop day by day, we have it one click away. Thousands of new prototypes in processes marks the profile of our new future, since the nanotechnology until the artificial intelligence. The millennials generation push us in a positive and fast way, they are the ones who were born in the 80's and 90's, that eventually.

will leave behind the behavioral molds of the *light man* that privileges the consumerism, the hedonism and the relativism to be activists that promote new humanized and productive ways of planetary coexistence. Without a place to doubts the life transforms and evolves in every second. "The man in the exercise of his freedom learn to walk and then like the eagles to fly in the heights". The humanity wont loose off sight the life.

The interchange of cooperation with China in a positive way can generate positive results, the international structure, the global government, the economy and the justice with the principle of the conscious humanity and the auto determination of the countries, they are a indispensable for the global development and transformation, so it is indispensable to apply the new diplomatic language and of business with a human sense that appears as a powerful tool of evolutive global coexisting. They are worth to assume consciously.

My proposals today are:

- Boost love globalization, because just what you love is what you fight for, you improve it, you seek for it.
- Recognize overwhelmingly the principle of the interdependency from the individual to the globalization of our international relations.
- Humanize politics and economy.
- Bring down walls of hate.
- Build bridges that bring us in all senses as the The Belt and road initiative promotes.

Build a equitable world, fair, responsible, where international. intercultural and humans relations by excellence be the key to build vital agreements for integral benefit of the citizens od the world. The international relations have an important paper and primordial in "The belt and road initiative", because knowing how to use diplomacy as the best tool of negotiation can generate positive results internationally recognized. We know that the diplomatic tools and strategic associations established in China and other international actors, will be the key piece to achieve big benefits no just for a continent but for everyone.

A diplomacy that will have the challenge to communicate the importance of cultural links between nations.

China, with this purposes, it turns into a powerful platform to get out to the meeting of our universal goals.

I have the absolute conviction that this world meeting organized by our hosts, will work to boost the hope of a better world for everyone. Thank you for summoning us, thank you for your hospitality, thank you for the purpose.

For me China has always been an inspiration, the teaching that comes with antiquity with Lao Tse and Taoteching with art of war, the experiences, the hard work, the implacable perseverance and the millenary history condensed in the large colorful and magic of the Chinese artists, that produce sensations like music and plastic arts that enrich our soul, with this transforming the character of the popular revolution that caused a big jump from the dynasties to the transforming time of the seventies, when Deng Xiaoping defended China as a nation with two systems.

His radical thinking and transforming what will show that China was one of the nations with more tenacity and willing of reinvention. Capacity to reinvent and build day by day the best future.

Let today begin the merging of consciences that detonates the chain reaction that cultivate our talents and human capacities to generate responsibly and naturally a better world for every one.

Long live humanity!

“一带一路”推进与中国战略思维方式

黄仁伟　【中国】
上海社会科学院　副院长 / 世界中国学论坛　秘书长

古代中国有两个伟大案例，一个是万里长城，是当时国家安全的基础设施；另一个是南北大运河，是当时经济流通动脉的基础设施，它们影响了上千年的中国历史走向。一带一路就是当代中国与当代世界发展的基础设施网络，它和中国历史与现实的发展经验一脉相承的，也可能影响数百年甚至更长时间的世界历史走向。为此，需要了解中国战略文化的思维方式，有助于理解中国提出和推进一带一路倡议的动机和行为方式。

“要想富，先修路”，是当代中国的一句流行语。基础设施是发展的先决条件，尤其是交通基础设施网络，更是市场联结和产业经济带的纽带。中国经济和社会的发展变化，是与全国范围的基础设施革命紧密结合的。仅仅 15 年左右的时间，中国就基本形成了覆盖各省的高速公路、高速铁路、远距离输变电、无线通信、油气管线、港口机场、全球定位等立体交叉网络体系。在此过程中，中国逐渐形成和具备了为整个欧亚大陆提供基础设施网络的经验和能力。在 2 至 3 倍于中国的时间里，可能实现欧亚大陆的全面联结即“五通”，这不是一句空话。

“积小胜为大胜”，这是中国战略文化的重要思想方法。这么一个巨大工程并不是在短时期内可以完成的，它需要 30 年至 50 年时间来实现其宏伟目标。同时，它又分解为一个又一个具体项目，由一个个地区和不同阶段组合而成的。这就是当代中国的“渐进主义”方法，中国改革开放和现代化的重要成果都是采取渐进方式取得的。中国老百姓的俗语说“一口吃不成胖子”，就是这个道理。

“量力而行”是中国人在工作中一贯倡导的稳健务实、实事求是的方法。一带一路倡议的目标非常宏大，不可能由中国一家来“包打天下”。要根据中国的能力、实力和东道国的可接受度，来逐步推进一带一路的具体项目。例如，中东欧国家非常欢迎一带一路项目到他们的国家落地，于是形成“16+1”模式。但是16个国家一起上有困难，只能从捷克、匈牙利、塞尔维亚等几个国家开始，从改造陈旧铁路系统入手，见效后可以形成更大范围、更多领域的项目。

“有所为而有所不为”，就是抓住重点、兼顾一般。一带一路倡议的空间范围覆盖60多个国家，与中国的距离远近不同，合作伙伴的密切程度也不同。这需要选择一批国家作为战略支点，重点建设一带一路项目。目前的重点地区主要是东南亚、中亚等地区；重点国家主要有俄罗斯、巴基斯坦、印尼和哈萨克斯坦等。如果我们不分轻重、一哄而上，势必出现项目成功率很低的混乱局面。

“两相情愿”原意是指男女之间谈恋爱需要双方都有内心的倾慕。在一带一路的项目合作中更是需要双方、甚至是多方自愿，绝不能出现强加于人的单边主义甚至强权主义的做法。中国方面要根据当地的实际需要选择项目，东道国也要根据中国的能力和利益相关度来进行选择。目前中国与一些国家本身的基础设施战略规划结合，形成良好的互动关系，为重大项目落地奠定了基础。

“预则立，不预则废”，是指对重大事件的战略前景要进行预测和预判，做好预案，才能确定其取得成功的路径。毋庸讳言，一带一路在其实现过程中将面对各种风险，包括安全风险、政治风险、经济风险、社会风险、文化风险、生态风险等等。每一个大类下面，还可以细分若干专项风险。而且每种风险都不会单独存在，而是集中风险交织共生、相互作用。中国应和东道国合作伙伴共同分析预测大项目可能遇到的各种风险，制定防范措施和危机反应机制。一个重大项目的建设周期长达几年甚至十几年，使用周期长达几十年甚至几百年，进行战略预测是保证重大工程取得长期效应的前提条件。

“由乱而治”是中国政治文化理念的一个总结，讲的是“乱”与“治”的辩证关系。一带一路沿线地区不乏动乱甚至局部战争，他们对一带一路的推进肯定有消极影响。动乱需要治理，一带一路沿线地区恰恰可以成为国际合作进行全球治理或地区治理的实验区。例如，国际合作共同打击恐怖主义，在一带一路沿线地区必然是一个不可回避的课题。它不是一带一路倡议的直接内容，却是其中的必要条件。打击毒品、非法移民、洗钱等跨国犯罪活动，都可能在一带一路推进过程中形成必要的国际合作机制。

“自上而下”与“自下而上”，这是政府与民众、政府与市场、国企与民企等几种互动关系的概括。在一带一路倡议提出以来，国外朋友总是有人问起，一带一路究竟是市场行为还是政府行为，国内学者也有人质疑这是政府大包干。我认为是政府倡导和推动的市场和产业一体化进程，其最终主体是企业。因为一个巨大的基础设施网络，需要极大的协调组织机制，在这方面中国政府的能力是举世公认的。一带一路倡议要在几十个国家中落实，更需要政府间的合作机制。然而，项目竞标、投资建设、经营管理等微观主体是企业，依据的是市场规则，政府不可能充当主体。因此，自上而下和自下而上，二者缺一不可。

“有容乃大”、“兼容并蓄”，这是中国文化形成过程的主要特征，在“一带一路”推进过程中就体现为“开放、包容”。中国倡导“一带一路”，不等于中国一家单干，更不是排挤其他大国或制度、价值观不同的国家。中国不主张搞排他性的盟国体系，也不会在一带一路进程中扩张势力范围。中国文化提倡“己所勿欲，勿施于人”。中国长期受到超级大国及其盟国体系的排挤，深受其害，不会再去重复那一套。相反，我们欢迎西方国家包括美国、日本在内参与一带一路进程，成为亚投行成员，具体投入有关项目。

“海内存知己”、“四海之内皆兄弟”，中国古代把世界看作“天下”，把周围地区看作“海内”，天下和海内构成了中国文化的空间概念。一带一路继承和发扬这种空间观，在一带一路沿线实行“早期收获计划”，结成各种类型的战略伙伴关系，构建长期稳定的战略支点。这种战略支点，不是传统意义上的军事基地或盟国关系，而是利益结合点、网络枢纽点、金融中心点、文化汇集点、产业链接点、资源交换点、安全保障点。这些战略支点撑起整个一带一路网络，是各国共享的公共产品。

“欲取之，必先予之”，“多与少取、只与不取”，这是中国的传统义利观，前提是“取之有道”。在此基础上，通过共同利益、合作共赢而建构的新义利观，是一带一路利益结构形成的伦理基础。君子并非只讲“义”而不讲“利”，关键在于讲“道”。这个道就是共同利益，越是深厚的共同利益，则越符合道义，就越有持续生命力。中国企业要警惕自己的行为过于把盈利作为第一考虑，造成“竭泽而渔”的后果。但是，中国和各国政府也要防止把“一带一路”看作是政府援助项目，对成本、盈利等基本核算手段置之不顾，造成另一种“竭泽而渔”。二者都是不可持续的。

简言之，“以天下为己任”是中国历代志士仁人的最高价值追求。一带一路是以人类命运为己任的当代中国责任体现和价值追求。我们要通过一带一路的推进，把利益共同体、责任共同体和命运共同体落到实处，从抽象概念转化为沿线地区实现共同发展、共同安全、共同治理的实践平台，使中国文化的精神价值内涵就在一带一路项目上得到物质体现和社会体验。

Promotion of the Belt and Road Initiative and China's Strategic Thought

Huang Renwei / China

Vice-President of the Shanghai Academy of Social Sciences/Secretary General of the Institute of China studies

There were two great cases in ancient China: First, the Great Wall which was the infrastructure for safeguarding national security at that time; second, the North-South Grand Canal which was the infrastructure serving as the artery of economic circulation at that time. They influenced China's historical orientation for one thousand years. The Belt and Road will be the network of infrastructures for the development of contemporary China and the contemporary world. It inherits the developmental experience from China's history and reality and it may influence the historical orientation of the world for several hundred years to come, even for a longer time. Therefore, it is necessary to understand the line of thought of China's strategic culture, which helps understand China's motive and behavioral pattern for putting forward and promoting the Belt and Road Initiative.

"In order to become rich, it is necessary to build roads first" is a catch phrase in contemporary China. Infrastructure is the precondition for development; in particular, transportation infrastructure is the bond for the connection among the markets and the economic industrial belt. The development changes in China's economy and society are closely related to the revolution in infrastructure across China. In only 15 years, China has basically built a three-dimensional cross network system covering various provinces, including highways, high-speed railways, long-distance power transmission and transformation, wireless communications, oil and gas pipelines, ports and airports and global positioning. In this process, China has gradually acquired and developed the experience and capability for providing the entire Eurasia with a network of infrastructures. It is possible to realize an all-round connectivity, namely the "five-way connectivity", in Eurasia within a period 2—3 times longer than the one in China. This is not empty talk.

"Many small victories add up to one big one". This is an important way of thinking in China's strategic culture. Such a giant project cannot be completed within a short period of time; it will take 30—50 years to achieve this ambitious goal. The project is divided into specific subprojects and is a combination of different areas and different stages. This is a gradualism-based method in contemporary China. The important achievements in China's reform, opening up and modernization have been made in a gradual way. As a Chinese saying goes, one meal will not make a fat man. This saying reveals the reason that is behind the above-mentioned situation.

"One should act according to his or her ability". This is the sound, pragmatic and realistic way advocated by the Chinese people in their work. The goal of the Belt and Road Initiative is very ambitious and cannot be achieved merely by China alone. Concrete projects involving the Belt and Road Initiative should be gradually carried out according to China's ability, strength and the acceptable level of the host country. For example, the central and eastern European countries greatly welcome the implementation of the Belt and Road projects, so the "16+1" mode is taking shape. However, it is difficult to bring together 16 countries in one step, so actions have to be started from the Czech Republic, Hungary and Serbia to renovate the old railway system; after the effects are produced, projects will be launched on a wider scope and in more fields.

"It is necessary to take actions in certain fields while refraining from acting in other fields". It is essential to focus on key points and also consider the general condition. The Belt and Road Initiative covers more than 60 countries which are at different distances from China and have different levels of partnership with China. This calls for choosing a number of countries as the strategic pivots, which will be the key to carrying out the Belt and Road projects. At present, the key regions include Southeast Asia and Central Asia; the key countries are Russia, Pakistan, Indonesia and Kazakhstan. If we do not consider the priorities and rush headlong into action, the following chaos will certainly occur: the rate of success of the project will be very low.

"Both sides are willing to do the thing". The original meaning of this saying is that two lovers should adore each other from the bottom of their heart when falling in love. Regarding cooperation on the Belt and Road projects, it should be based on the willingness of both parties, even multiple parties rather than unilateralism or hegemony characterized by forcing the unwilling party or parties to engage in the cooperation. China should choose projects in line with the actual local needs, and the host country should also make selections according to China's ability and the relevancy of interests. Currently, China has coordinated with the strategic plans of some countries regarding infrastructures and interacts well with these countries, thus laying the foundation for carrying out major projects.

"Preparedness ensures success and unpreparedness spells failure". This saying means that, only when the strategic prospects of major events are forecast and pre-judged and plans are developed accordingly can the route to achieving success be determined. Undoubtedly, the process of realizing the Belt and Road will be subject to various risks, including risks involving security, politics, economics, the society, culture and ecology. Each major category of risks includes a number of special risks. No risk exists alone; risks intertwine and interact with each other. China should work with the host country partners to analyze and forecast possible risks for major projects, and develop precautionary measures and crisis response mechanisms. The construction of a major project takes several years, even more than a decade, while the use of the finished project may last for several decades, even several hundred years. Strategic forecasting is the precondition for guaranteeing long-term effects of major projects.

"Governance comes out of turmoil". This saying partially summarizes China's political and cultural philosophies and touches upon the dialectical relationship between turmoil and governance. The regions along the Belt and Road are vulnerable to turmoil, even local wars, so they certainly exert a negative impact on pushing the Belt and Road Initiative forward. Turmoil calls for governance. The regions along the Belt and Road can definitely become the experimental regions for international cooperation on global governance or regional governance. For example, international cooperation in combating terrorism is unavoidable for the regions along the Belt and Road. This is not directly incorporated into the Belt and Road Initiative, but it is the necessary condition for carrying it out. With respect to combating transnational criminal activities including drugs, illegal immigrants and money laundering, necessary international cooperation mechanisms may be developed in the process of promoting the Belt and Road Initiative.

"From top to bottom" and "from bottom to top" summarizes several methods of interaction between the government and the people, between the government and the market, and between state-owned enterprises and private enterprises. Since the Belt and Road Initiative was put forward, some foreign friends have often wondered: Is the Belt and Road a market activity or a governmental activity? Some domestic scholars have doubted whether the government should take on everything. In my opinion, in the process of integration of the market and industry that has been advocated and promoted by the government, the final principal players are the enterprises. This is because a huge network of infrastructures needs an important coordinated, organized mechanism, and the capability of the Chinese Government regarding this aspect is universally acknowledged. In order to ensure that the Belt and Road Initiative is carried out in dozens of countries, it is quite necessary to develop an intergovernmental cooperation mechanism. However, the main micro players involved in project bidding, investment construction and operation management are the enterprises, and the market rules govern, so it is impossible for the government to be the key player. Therefore, both "from top to bottom" and "from bottom to top" are indispensable.

"Greatness lies in inclusiveness", "all outstanding elements are absorbed". This is the main characteristic of China's process of cultural formation. This is reflected as openness and inclusiveness in the process of promoting the Belt and Road Initiative. China advocates the Belt and Road, but such advocacy does not mean that China acts alone and squeezes out other large countries or the countries with different systems and value outlooks. China does not uphold an exclusive system of allied countries and it will not expand the sphere of its influence during this process. Chinese culture advocates the following saying: Do not do to others what you would not have them do to you. China has been pushed aside and greatly harmed by the superpowers and their system of allied countries for a long time, so China does not repeat such an activity. On the contrary, we welcome Western countries, including the USA and Japan, to participate in the Belt and Road process, to join the Asian Infrastructure Investment Bank, and to take part in relevant projects.

"Bosom friends exist within the four seas", "within the four seas all men are brothers". In ancient times, China regarded the world as "the land under heaven", and the surrounding areas as "within the four seas". "The land under heaven" and "within the four seas" constitutes the spatial concept in Chinese culture. The Belt and Road Initiative inherits and carries forward the spatial concept. The Early Harvest Program will be implemented along the Belt and Road; various types of strategic partnerships will be established; long-term stable strategic pivots will be built. These strategic pivots are not traditional military bases or allied country relations, but the common grounds of interests, network hub points, central financial points, cultural aggregation points, industrial connection points, resource exchange points and security guarantee points. These strategic pivots will support the entire network of the Belt and Road and will be the public goods shared by the various countries involved in the project.

"In order to take, one must first give", "we should give more and ask for less, even only give something and ask for nothing". This is China's traditional view of righteousness and benefit. The precondition is that "something is obtained in a virtuous way". The new view of righteousness and benefit developed through common interests and win-win cooperation on this basis is the ethical basis for forming the structure of interest in the Belt and Road. A gentleman does not merely emphasize righteousness and without paying attention to benefits; the key lies in stressing virtuousness. This virtuousness refers to common interests—if common interests are more profound, they are more consistent with virtuousness and show more continued vitality. The Chinese enterprises should be vigilant against their behaviors of putting gains first and thus making excessive demands on others in disregard of their hardships. However, China and the governments of various countries should also avoid the following situations: The Belt and Road is considered as a series of government-assisted projects; no considerations are given to the basic means of financial calculation such as costs and profits, which leads to a dead end. Both situations are unsustainable.

In a word, "including the improvement of the well-being of all of the people in the scope of one's own duty" has been the highest value pursued by the people of all ages with high ideals in China. The Belt and Road Initiative is the embodiment of responsibilities and the pursuit of values of contemporary China for the destiny of humankind. We should, through efforts in promoting the Belt and Road Initiative, put into place the community of common interests, the community of shared responsibilities and the community of a common destiny, and turn the abstract concept into the practical platform for achieving joint development, common security and joint governance in the regions along the Belt and Road, so that the spiritual value connotation of Chinese culture appears in the material embodiment and social experience in the Belt and Road projects.

“一带一路”：中国的共赢倡议

贾维德　【巴基斯坦】
巴基斯坦国立科技大学中国研究中心　主任

尊敬的大会主持、各位学者、女士们、先生们：

能够出席本次座谈会，与来自世界各地的杰出汉学家就“一带一路”与世界格局这一主题分享我的观点，本人深感荣幸。

2016 年，整个世界正处于面临重大抉择的十字路口。不论是过去还是将来，我们都曾、都将面临选择，但长期陷入选择的困境是不可取的。在“霸权、仇恨、偏执、不公、仇外、创造性破坏”等意识形态的影响下，我们的世界经历了世界大战以及冷战的时代，但这个时代的阴影尚未褪去。这便是所谓“零和博弈”的反映，即一方的获胜必然造成另一方的损失，其最终结果是混乱、无政府主义、种族隔离、经济停滞、秩序失调、系统性的崩溃、环境灾难，以及全球性的领导危机。贪欲、欺骗、道德破产大行其道，社会团结和国际理解面临危机，这一切都给这个 70 亿灵魂共同居住的“孤独”的星球带来了浩劫。

有人说，人类是永远不会吸取教训的。我们寄希望于当代的领导人和各国政府，希望他们能够迅速从过去的经历中汲取教训，因为众所周知，十字路口恰恰是事故的高发地段。目前是当代历史中最具决定性意义的时代，在这个时代里，中国的崛起为我们带来了一丝乐观、一份希望，让我们认识到，或许这个世界的“自杀”倾向有可能发生逆转，或许，“全天下”能够统一起来，构建起一个“命运共同体”。 如此一来，专门从死亡、毁坏、仇恨以及战争中获利的商人必将破产。我们不需要第二次冷战，也不再需要任何一场热战。从这个角度来看，中国的“一带一路”倡议为我们提供了另外一条道路，为创造“双赢局面”塑造了典范。就个人而言，我更喜欢称之为“双喜”局面。“一带一路”倡议旨在促进区域间和社会间的互通互联、赢得全球社会的民心与民意、促进文化的交融、确保共存、构建共同体，以及提高整个世界的“多极性”。“一带一路”倡议致力于复兴几百年来便已存在的海陆两条商贸路径。目前，陆上丝绸之路的建设已经展开，届时，六条走廊将把中国以及欧亚非、中东、海湾地区、南非、东亚等地区的65国紧紧联系在一起。

“一带一路”将促进欧亚大陆的腹地开放，有助于稳定西亚和中东局势、缓和南亚地区冲突，通过赢得民心、民意来推动命运共同体的构建。“一带一路”将确保这个由各国共建的共同体始终处于赢者地位，因为只有和平、繁荣、公正以及和谐才最终能够带来共赢的局面。中巴经济走廊是“一带一路”倡议中的旗舰工程。在高达460亿美元（目前已增至515亿美元）的经济保障下，这项工程将通过能源通道、高速公路、基础设施、铁路、工业区以及油气管道等，将中国的喀什与世界上最深的温水港——巴基斯坦的瓜达尔港连接在一起，惠及沿线30亿民众。目前，中巴经济走廊中近150亿美元的早期收获项目已经接近完工。

世界各国与巴基斯坦一样，正不断加深与中国的合作和联通，在中国崛起的带动下，“中国梦”将变为各国的梦想，中国取得的成就，将为世界各国带来利益。可以说，当今世界的游戏规则正在发生改变。

The Belt and Road: China's Win-Win Initiative

Syed Hasan Javed / Pakistan

Director of Chinese Studies Center of Excellence at the National University of Science and Technology

Honorable Chair, Distinguished Scholars Ladies and Gentlemen

It is a great honor for me to present my views at this illustrious gathering of eminent Sinologists from all over the world on the theme 'Belt and Road' Initiative and International Structure".

The world in 2016 is at a crossroad. It may have remained at crossroad before, or many remain at crossroad in future. But being at a crossroad for long, is never advised or recommended. The era of perpetual Wars and Cold Wars inspired by the ideology of domination, hate, bigotry, injustice, xenophobia, creative destruction continues unabated. This is the reflection of what is known as "Zero Sum Paradigm" i.e heads I lose, tails you gain and vice versa. The resulting consequences have been chaos, anarchy, social apartheid, economic stagnation, governance dis-functionality, systemic failures, environmental disasters and above all, leadership crisis globally. The dominating culture of greed, deception, moral bankrupcy, erosion in community solidarity, international understanding are all playing havoc with the "lonely " planet inhabited by 7 million souls.

It is said humanity never learns. Let us hope the contemporary generation of leaders and governments learn from the past experiences soon, because the crossroads are places where most accidents take place. At this defining time in contemporary history, the rise of China offers as a hope of optimism and possibility that the suicidal course of the world could be reversed and "a community of shared destiny" could be constructed under the heavens. The merchants of death, destruction, hate and war would however be rendered jobless. There would be "no need for Cold War II" or any hot war. China's initiative of "Yi Dai Yi Lu" or "Belt and Road" is an alternative diplomatic paradigm of "Double Win" or "Shuang Ying". I would also term it as "Shuang Xi" or "Double Happiness". The strategy aims to connect regions, societies and win hearts and minds of the global community, build convergence, co-existence, community and multi-polarity. The Belt and Road aims to construct "Silk Road Economic Belt and the 21st Century Maritime Silk Route" to revive centuries old land and sea based commerce and trade exchanges The land connectivity is being built by constructing six corridors linking China with 65 countries in the Euro-Asia, Africa, Middle East, Gulf, South Asia and South East Asia.

The Belt and Road will open up the interior of Euro Asiatic Continent, help stabilize West Asia and Middle East, contribute to lessening in tension in South Asia and build a Community of shared destiny by winning hearts and minds. The Belt and Road is a "Winning Coalition of States" because only peace, prosperity and justice and harmony will eventually win. China Pakistan Economic Corridor (CPEC) is a flagship project of the Belt and Road. The US$ 46 billion (now US 51.5) PEC aims to build Energy, Motorways, Infrastructure, Railways, Industrial Zones and Oil and Gas Pipelines from Kashgar to World's deepest Warm water port, city of Gwadar. The CPEC will benefit a total of 3 billion people in the region. Almost US$15 billion of Projects of CPEC are nearing completion under "Early Harvest Program".

Like Pakistan, other countries in the world are also translating the "Chinese dream" for their own deeper engagement and interaction with China in order to benefit from its rise. New rules of game are evolving.

“一带一路”与国际格局

雅克 【英国】

英国剑桥大学政治和国际研究系　高级研究员 / 清华大学　客座教授

中国最显著的一个特征在于思想永远不会止步，时刻处在发展变化之中。在最初的二十年里，中国孕育了无数的新思想，这些思想大多着重于东部沿海地区的发展。如今在“一带一路”倡议的背景下，中国的注意力逐渐转向西方。可以说，目前的中国已经成为一个具有高度创造性、永远在不停进取、影响力不断扩大且始终面向未来的一个国家。相比之下，西方国家的状况已经糟糕到令人吃惊的程度：长期陷入零增长的困境、观念愈发保守、活力和创造力正逐渐消失。在中国加入世贸组织后的十年里，美国频繁地指责中国免费搭乘全球经济的快车，一味从全球化进程中活力，却很少为国际公共事业做出应有的贡献。然而从当前的状况来看，美国当初真该保留这份言论——时代已经发生变化，中国已经摆脱了过去的保守，正逐渐摸索出适合于自身发展的道路。自 2013 年以来，中国已经成为全球经济中高度活跃的经济体，亚洲基础设施投资银行的成立以及“一带一路”倡议的实施，标志着中国对世界经济的掌控力已经达到了惊叹的程度。在短短五年不到的时间里，中国已经从当初的“坐享其成”转变为全球化的缔造者和塑造者，其地位已经取代了当初苛责她的美国。

本次座谈会上，诸位已经谈到了中式全球化和美式全球化的区别。我打算从一个稍微不同的角度来探讨这个问题，将马歇尔计划放在“一带一路”的框架内进行审视。当然，两者间的区别是多方面的，但我只想重点谈一个方面——文化差异。马歇尔计划是第二次世界大战结束后，美国对西欧各国进行经济援助、协助重建的计划，其本质是发达国家之间的互助计划。而“一带一路”所秉持的理念却是：中国作为发展中国家，如何能够帮助欧亚地区的多数发展中国家实现发展。尽管欧洲也参与了“一带一路”工程，但却并不是整个工程的核心舞台。“一带一路”倡议的关键参与者是东亚、中亚、南亚以及西亚诸国。

我们不妨停下来思考一下，美国对于“一带一路”倡议作何反应。美国的沉默反而显得更加刺耳，显然认为中国提出的倡议不值得回应，认为中国的倡议没有任何重大意义当然，有一些国家选择附和美国，对亚洲基础设施投资银行不屑一顾，因而错失良机。目前为止，国际上明显地出现了两种截然不同的话语：自西方金融危机之始，国际货币基金组织便持续不断地将多数资源分配给欧洲，从这点便能看出——美国仍然以发达国家作为主要导向，至于发展中国家，美国的兴趣主要在军事和安全两个方面，美国军队介入伊拉克战争和阿富汗战争便是很好的例子。因此，美国对发展中国家的援助大多是军事援助，而不是发展方面的援助。相比之下，中国对于发展中世界的高度关注和贡献主要体现在发展方面。这并不令人感到惊讶。作为发展中国家的一员，中国与发展中世界的关系自然远比美国紧密：中国与美国不同，她能够切实地认识到发展中国家所面临的首要问题——而对于美国而言，发展中国家只是一个空泛的概念，并非一种切实的体验。因此，美国在将自身价值观强加给发展中国家时，并没有认为这样做有和不妥之处。此外，在向发展中国家提供贷款时，美国始终强调“附加条件”，对于发展中国家而言，这些条件并不具备任何实用性。相比之下，“一带一路”倡议却彰显出中国以自身经验帮助亚洲发展中国家实现发展的义举。

中美之间的区别具体表现在对待基础设施的态度上。基础设施建设在中国的转型具有重大意义，从亚洲基础设施投资银行的名称上便能看出，中国将亚洲未来发展的重点放在了基础设施建设上。相比之下，美国从不重视发展中国家的基础设施，这一点，在美国的传统盟友——埃及和菲律宾两国破败的基础设施中便能得到很好的诠释。当然，美国自身对于基础设施也不够重视，机场、铁路、桥梁等，大多比较陈旧，但最主要的还是意识形态上的原因，是否承认一国基础设施的重要性，主要取决于该国是否具有举足轻重的地位，在涉及资助问题时尤其如此。但根据盛行于20世纪80年代的新自由主义经济的观点来看，国家的地位应该被缩减到最低程度，就连针对发展中国家而提出的华盛顿共识中也秉持同样的理念。全球化带来的影响是不均衡的。在全球化进程中，成就最大者在东亚，南亚展现出的前景也十分光明，但最明显的消退出现在西方，而最大的失败者要属中东、非洲以及中亚地区。“一带一路”正是为应对这些失败而寻求解决措施。中国的发展方式向来强调包容和平衡，如果“一带一路”取得成功——帮助占有世界人口 60% 的欧亚大陆实现发展——或者仅仅取得百分之五十的成功，则中国定然会改变整个世界。尽管“中国式全球化”采取的模式有所不同，但它能够促使世界由发展不均走向普遍获益，由少数国家的现代化走向形式多样的现代化。可以说，中国经验将变成一种极具普适性的经验。与此同时，“一带一路”会促进国际格局的再建和重构，推动国际格局的民主化，让整个世界格局不再取决于生活在发达国家的 15% 的世界人口，而是取决于生活在发展中国家的 85% 的国际大众。

The Belt and Road and International Structure

Martin Jacques / United Kingdom of Great Britain and Northern Ireland

Senior Fellow at the Department of Politics and International Studies at the University of Cambridge /Visiting Professor of Tsinghua University

One of China's most striking features is the way in which thinking doesn't stand still but is constantly in movement. For the first two decades the new thinking was overwhelmingly preoccupied with China, with the primary focus being the eastern seaboard. Contrast that with today where attention is increasingly concerned with the western regions in the context of Belt and Road. China has become a highly creative, restless and expansionary force, single-mindedly orientated to the future. The contrast with the West is startling: becalmed in a state of almost zero growth and increasingly inward looking, the West is sapped of energy and creativity. For a decade after China joined the WTO, the United States frequently criticised it for being a free rider on the global economy, a beneficiary of globalisation without paying its dues for global public goods. Perhaps the US now wishes that it had kept its own counsel: how times have changed. China was not in the business of passivity but rather it was busy learning the ropes. Since 2013 it has become hyper-active as regards the global economy. The formation of the AIIB and the launch of One

Belt One Road together marked a breathtaking intervention. No longer the passive beneficiary, China in less than half a decade has become the maker and shaper of globalisation, displacing its critic the United States.

This morning we have been discussing some of the differences between Chinese-style and US-style globalisation. I want to think about this in a slightly different way. There have been several references to Marshall Aid in the context of Belt and Road. The differences between them, of course, are manifold, but here I want to focus on one in particular, which is perhaps the *critical* difference. Marshall Aid was America's scheme to rescue its developed partner, namely Western Europe, from wartime devastation. One arm of the developed world was assisting another. In complete contrast, the idea of Belt and Road is about how China, itself a developing country, can assist the development of numerous other developing countries on the Eurasian land mass. True Europe is also involved, but it can hardly be regarded as centre stage in the project. The key players, certainly in the Belt, are East Asia, Central Asia, South Asia and West Asia.

Let us pause for a moment and reflect on the response of the United States to Belt and Road. The silence has been deafening. It has largely been ignored by the US, on the grounds that it is of no great consequence, a Chinese initiative which should be left as such. There are echoes here of the manner in which the US, to its considerable cost, similarly dismissed the AIIB. What is emerging more and more clearly is that there are two very different discourses. The orientation of the United States is towards the developed world as its primary concern. By way of illustration, since the onset of the Western financial crisis, the IMF has allocated most of its resources to Europe. The US may be heavily involved with the developing world but its interest is largely military and security, as illustrated by the American military engagement in the wars in Iraq and Afghanistan. Its typical form of aid to developing countries is military rather than developmental. In contrast, China's overwhelming preoccupation and commitment to the developing world concerns their development. This is not surprising. As a developing country, China has an affinity with the developing world that the US does not have: it understands the priorities and problems of a developing country in a way that the US does not – for the latter the developing world is a construct not a lived experience. It thus sees nothing wrong in projecting onto the developing countries its own values – hence the insistence on conditionality– even though as a rule they are of little relevance or utility to a developing country. Compare this with China. Belt and Road is clearly an attempt by China to extrapolate from its own experience as a developing country and apply the lessons it has learnt to other developing countries in Asia.

A concrete example of the difference between China and the US concerns infrastructure. The latter has been fundamental to China's transformation and the very name of the AIIB – the Asian Infrastructure Investment Bank – testifies to the importance China attaches to the role of infrastructure in Asia's future development. The United States, on the other hand, gives little importance to infrastructure in developing countries, as illustrated by the dilapidated state of the infrastructure in traditional allies like Egypt and the Philippines. America's neglect of infrastructure, of course, extends to itself, where the airports, railway infrastructure and bridges are generally antiquated. The reason not least is ideological, namely a refusal to recognise that major infrastructural projects as a rule depend on the state playing a pivotal role, not least when it comes to funding. But the neo-liberal orthodoxy that has reigned since 1980 believed that the role of the state should be belittled and shrunken. The same thinking extended to the Washington Consensus, America's doctrine for the developing world.

The record of globalisation is very patchy. Its greatest success has been in East Asia. South Asia shows some promise. In the West a major backlash is underway. The regions of greatest failure are the Middle East, Africa and Central Asia. One Belt One Road seeks to address those failures. Its approach is informed by inclusivity rather than exclusivity and balanced rather than imbalanced development. If the project is successful – or even half successful – in transforming the Eurasian land mass, home to over 60 per cent of the world's population, it will transform the world. From being patchy, globalisation – albeit a rather different China-inspired globalisation – will become a universal benefit, and modernity – in the form of diverse modernities – will become a universal experience. And in time OBOR will lead to the reinvention and reconstitution – and democratisation – of the international system based not on the 15 per cent of the world's population who live in the developed world but based on the 85 per cent who live in the developing world.

“一带一路”与新型发展合作

张蕴岭 【中国】

中国社会科学院　研究员 / 国际研究学部　主任

“一带一路”倡议提出后，受到国内外越来越大的关注。究其原因，一是因为提出了新的发展合作理念，为大家所接受；二是因为见之于行动，不是空谈，有了看得见的成效。如今，“一带一路”不仅仅是一种区域合作倡议，更是一种扩及世界的广义合作理念与平台。[1]

一　创新发展动能

“一带一路”是通过陆、海网络把亚洲、欧洲和非洲广大地区连接起来，以推动基础设施建设、产业园建设、港口经济区和港口物流网建设为重点，实现大区域间的互联互通，促进投资、商品、服务、资金、技术和人员的便利化流动，以此创建新的发展动能，形成经济发展的新局面。

中国提出倡议，当然有自己的战略性考虑，其中首要的是为经济的转型拓展新的发展空间。改革开放以来，中国的东部沿海地区成为经济发展的中心，由于其地理优势成为最具活力的地区，越来越多的资源和劳动力流向东部沿海地区。其结果，西部的发展缺乏活力，国内发展的区域不平衡加剧，而区域发展失衡反过来成为影响整个社会经济稳定与可持续的重要因素。中国政府一直为纠正失衡

1　2016 年以来，联合国亚太经社理事会、联合国开发署，联合国工发组织与世界卫生组织等都签署了一带一路共建协议或者合作备忘录，联合国第 71 届大会通过决议，支持“一带一路”的建设。

做出努力，最具影响的当属“西部大开发战略”，涵盖了12个省、区、市，中央为基础设施建设（包括公路、高速公路、铁路、电力和天然气项目等）提供大力支持，并制定优惠政策鼓励东部资源向西部流动。尽管西部大开发战略取得了明显的进展，但西部地区的竞争优势并没有得到显著的提高，东部和西部地区之间的发展不平衡也没有得到显著的降低，其中一个重要的原因是西部受到地缘“内部制约”。与西部大开发战略的国内导向相比，“一带一路”突出了西部发展的向内和向外发展战略结合，让西部有了更为开放的市场空间。

丝绸之路经济带通过陆地网络把中国—中亚—西亚—俄罗斯—欧洲以及中国—东南亚—南亚连接起来，建设开放的新发展带；而海上丝绸之路通过海上网络把中国—东南亚—印度洋—非洲—欧洲以及中国—大洋洲连接起来，构建跨海合作区，实现共同发展。[1]将中国与“一带一路”倡议沿线国家相连接，有助于建立一个新的经济空间，不仅为中国的西部地区拓展出新的延伸带，而且也为整个中国提供了新的发展合作空间。

中国有众多的接邻和近邻国家，从地区上来说，本身就是一个巨大的地缘带，实现中国与周边国家之间的互联互通需要跨境基础设施网络的支持，包括公路、铁路和航空，但现在所有这些跨境基础设施无论是在硬件上还是在软件上都很落后。“一带一路”有助于改善陆地跨境基础设施网络，提高现代化港口的连接，发展港口区经济，构建海上物流网络。显然，“一带一路”建设将会大大改善中国与外部链接的环境，让周边地区成为一个中国与邻国共享的开放发展空间。

经过了三十多年的高速增长，中国经济转向了“新常态”的局面，即从高速增长转变为中等速度的增长。为了创造新的增长引擎，需要建立内需拉动的增长动力，同时拓展外部市场机会。尽管发展中国家能够提供全球经济的新空间，但落后的基础设施和产业供应链形成发展的瓶颈，如果通过参与“一带一路”倡议得到改善其综合经济环境，不仅有利于当地经济的发展，而且会为中国企业走出去和扩大贸易提供机会。

“一带一路”倡议是以发展合作为导向的，它使得中国能够在沿线区域和国家通过发展基础设施网络、建立工业园区等许多项目来寻找新的经济发展机会。中国的制造业需要重新寻找生产场所以降低成本，提升技术水平，保持竞争优势，亚洲、非洲的发展中国家具有巨大的发展空间和可利用的成本优势。当然，“一

1 参看“一带一路”文件，http://news.xinhuanet.com/english/china/2015-03/28/c_134105858_2.htm

带一路”合作机制下的产能建设，不同于以往的简单的产能转移，不是把过时的和污染的生产转移出去，而是与当地国家共同协商、设计、建造新的产业，从这个角度来说，是产业的扩展与提升。中国推动“一带一路”下的产能合作，是一种新型的合作发展方式。不同于传统意义上的援助，也不同于基于市场成本型落后产能的转移。

二　创新发展思路

“一带一路”倡议提出依靠创新推动发展的新思路。在“一带一路”机制下的创新是合作创新，不同于一般的技术创新，它是通过学习经验，分享资源，共享利益来建构新的综合发展环境，培育新的经济增长引擎，实现包容与平衡的可持续发展。

“一带一路”的创新也包括构建新的合作机制，如建立亚投行、新开发银行等，它们不是要取代现有的机制，如世界银行（世行，WB）、亚洲开发银行（亚行，ADB）等国际机构，而是做增量，推动合作，与原有的机制合作互补。像亚投行支持的基础设施项目，就是与亚行、世行联合开展融资业务的。[1]

世界经济的发展处在一个新的调整期，需要新的思路和新的倡议，“一带一路”就是诸多新思路、新倡议中最有影响力的，得到的支持多，参加的国家多。“一带一路”不仅推动合作，也推动开放，通过实现互联互通，促进经济要素的跨国流动，实现资源的高效配置和市场的深度融合，通过开放合作，凝聚共同利益，因此会推动沿线国家实现经济政策协调、开展更加深入和广泛的高标准区域合作，共同营造一个开放、包容、均衡的区域经济合作架构。

“一带一路”不搞“区域第一主义”，遵行“开放的区域主义”，“对所有国家、国际和地区组织开放和参与”[2]。也就是说，“一带一路”建设，不仅沿线国家可以参与，也欢迎世界上其他国家参与建设。以亚投行为例，其成员资格对真正有兴趣并愿意做出贡献的所有国家开放。[3] 互联互通并不仅仅局限于这些路线，涵盖了横跨欧亚大陆的多种多样的连接。[4]

1　参看新闻“AIIB and ADB provide loan together on the project”, http://bank.jrj.com.cn/2016/03/22102320721783.shtml

2　Vision document, http://english.mofcom.gov.cn/article/zt_beltandroad/

3　亚投行成立于 12 月 25 日，最初的成员 57 个，其中 37 个来自亚洲，20 个来自其他地区。

4　Summers,Tim: “China’s ‘New Silk Roads’ : sub-national regionsand networks of global political economy”, *Third World Quarterly*, 2016, 37(9), pp.1628-1643.

“一带一路”倡议推进的重点为：（1）政策协调，通过协调经济发展战略和政策，制定计划和措施，为合作伙伴的实施计划提供政策支持；（2）通过建设基础设施网络实现互联互通，包括了建设计划和技术标准系统的整合；（3）通过改善投资和贸易便利化促进贸易和投资，消除投资和贸易壁垒，创造良好的营商环境；（4）通过建立货币稳定体系的金融合作、投融资体系和信用信息系统，实现货币互换结算，发展债券市场，建立新的金融机构，如亚投行（AIIB）、新开发银行（NDB）以及上海合作组织（SCO）融资机构；（5）通过促进文化交流和学术交流、人员交流与合作、媒体合作、青年和妇女的交流和志愿服务，以赢得公众的支持。中国作为一个发展中的大国，可以在上述实践中扮演特殊的角色，作为倡导者和主要参与者，提供关键的资本投入和技术支持[1]。

互联互通是“一带一路”建设的优先领域。互联互通包括基础设施建设，法规、规则和标准一致或者连接，以及人员方面的流动与交流。基础设施建设的重点是建立现代化的交通网络，法规、规则与标准的一致，重点在实现便利化，取消或者大幅度减少交通运输、贸易和投资的限制；人员的流通便利，重点在有利于工程技术人员、商务人员的出行，教育、文化人员的交流和公民的旅行。为此，将推动建立“一带一路”框架下的各种合作机制，制定合作规则。

投资和贸易合作是“一带一路”建设的关键领域，旨在通过促进投资和贸易便利化，消除贸易和投资壁垒，在沿线国家之间构建自由贸易区。“一带一路”倡议下的合作将有助于扩大贸易和投资，提高贸易和投资结构，通过改善基础设施、建立工业区、港口网络、发展筹资以及能力建设等创造新的发展领域。

金融合作是“一带一路”建设的关键支撑。金融合作涵盖了广泛的跨境金融议程，其中包括货币稳定、项目融资、双边货币互换、结算、债券市场、人民币计价债券等。亚投行、新开发银行、丝路基金以及中国—东盟银行间协会和上合组织银行间协会等都将发挥各自作用。“一带一路”建设中要加强金融监管合作，建立有效的监管协调机制，提高风险应对和危机管控的能力，建立区域金融风险预警系统，创建交流与合作的机制应对跨境风险和危机。通过这些协同努力，有助于促进货币的稳定，增强信用体系的能力，鼓励商业性股权投资基金和民间资金参与重点项目的建设。

民心相通为“一带一路”建设提供了公共支持。“一带一路”建设不仅包括

1 The B&R document,http://english.mofcom.gov.cn/article/zt_beltandroad/。

了促进经济的议程，也包括文化、学术交流、培训、媒体合作、人才，以及青年和妇女交往，从而“赢得公众对深化双边和多边合作”的支持，在各种合作机制下，促进人才交流，旅游、体育交流，疫情信息共享、预防治疗技术和医务人员的培训交流，提高科学和技术合作，以及对青年就业、创业培训实践合作、职业技能开发、社会保障管理和非政府组织之间的交流与城市之间的合作。

考虑到“一带一路”沿线国家经济的多样性，“一带一路”不可能制定与实行单一的规划，各个方面的建设都与东道国的发展规划对接，实现双赢，让各方从参与中收益。[1]现实中，“一带一路”沿线的大多数国家的经济发展水平都不高，基础设施投入不足。通过参与“一带一路”建设，把本国的发展融入大区域的合作网络中，就有利于突破本国能力的限制、跨国链接的限制，以及物流网络的限制。

中国在建设基础设施网络方面积累了丰富的经验，既有设备技术能力，也有管理经验，中国可以在改善基础设施方面发挥重要作用。鉴于“一带一路”涉及的地域广，由中国出面协调、推动，许多跨国的项目就可以成行，才有可能构建连接跨国基础设施网络，包括铁路、公路、港口网络，以及石油、天然气管道，电信和电力网络。在融资方面，除了从丝路基金、亚投行等机构直接融资，其他金融机构也将会积极参与“一带一路”建设。更重要的是，企业作为主要参与者，可以在 PPP 的合作框架下，突破自身的融资限制，规避单打独斗的风险。

从未来发展的前景看，丝绸之路经济带建设、海上丝绸之路沿途的建设，会逐步完善亚洲、欧洲和非洲之间的互联互通，通过建设基础设施网络，会为发展新工业区、金融中心、自由贸易和投资区，以及其他综合项目，如油气管道、电网、互联网络、输电线路和通信网络等提供新的环境，这将会催生一个巨大的亚欧非大市场。[2]

三 创新发展合作

“一带一路”建设采取共同参与、共同规划、共同建设和共享成果的合作方式，不同于传统的开发援助，参与方作为平等的伙伴。从地缘范围看，“一带一路”

1 Wang, Yong: “Offensive for defensive: the belt and roadinitiative and China’s new grand strategy”, *The Pacific Review*, 2016, 29(3), pp.455-463.

2 Summers, Tim: “China’s ‘New Silk Roads’ : sub-national regionsand networks of global political economy”, *Third World Quarterly*, 2016, 37(9), pp.1628-1643.

建设覆盖了 60 多个国家的广大地区，它需要所有相关合作伙伴的积极参与和密切合作。“一带一路”建设遵循的原则是“在满足所有参与者利益的基础上通过协商共同建设，努力整合所有参与者的国家发展战略”[1]。大多数“一带一路”沿线国家和地区都是发展中经济体，人均 GDP 水平仍然很低，不到世界平均水平的一半，任何单独的国家都难以建立一个良好的基础设施网络。由于基础设施的发展需要长期的投资，公共资金和金融机构的合作支持至关重要。亚投行是基础设施发展合作融资的新型模式，有助于解决长期投资的瓶颈约束。亚投行的运作将严格遵循国际公认的原则，由其成员共同做出决策。既要适应新的需求，又面临着新的挑战，既要改革现有的国际机构，又要建立新的国际机构。亚投行旨在为世界经济带来新的动力，尽管美国和日本目前拒绝参与亚投行，但来自亚洲、非洲和欧洲的许多国家都积极加入亚投行并成为其创始成员国。亚投行能够提供投资资金、技术帮助，充分考虑其伙伴国家项目的需求。事实上，由于基础设施投资额大，预计在未来几年还会进一步增加，所有的发展中国家在满足自己的基础设施需求方面都面临着巨大的压力。联合国贸易和发展会议估计为实现 2030 年可持续发展目标（SDGs），发展中国家每年需要投资 3.3~4.5 万亿美元，这些投资主要集中在基础设施项目（电力、电信、交通、水、卫生）以及与基础设施相关的具体项目（如食品安全、减缓和适应气候变化、健康和教育）。实施 2030 年可持续发展议程，对一些国家运用全球资源有重要意义，包括公共和私人基础设施投资。[2]

在资金来源方面，发展合作传统上是通过双边和多边捐赠者的资助。但研究表明，发展援助的份额在基础设施融资中仅占 6—7 %。[3] 这表明需要创新发展合作方式。“一带一路”倡议中的共同参与，公私伙伴关系（PPP）模式提供了新的发展合作框架。过去的经验表明，在电力、电信、运输和供水等领域，发展中国家的外商直接投资份额较少，现有的投资相对于满足可持续发展议程所需要的有效资源而言仍只占一小部分。亚投行是以推动基础设施建设为出发点建立的。尽管大家都知道，经济的可持续发展需要良好的基础设施来支持，但是，长期以来，

1 参看“一带一路”文件，http://news.xinhuanet.com/english/china/2015-03/28/c_134105858_2.htm

2 UNCTAD: *World Investment Report*, 2016, United Nations Publications.

3 Miyamoto, Kaori and Emilio Chiofalo, “Official Development Finance for Infrastructure:Support by Multilateral and Bilateral Development Partners” , 2015, *OECD Development CooperationWorking Papers*, No. 25, OECD Publishing.

基础设施投资的融资问题一直是一个瓶颈。通过亚投行的自身融资，国际市场融资，以及调动国内公私部门融资的潜力，将为基础设施的建设注入新的活力。“金砖国家”建立的“新发展银行”也是如此，功能主要是有助于解决发展融资的瓶颈限制，通过提供贷款、担保、参股或其他金融工具支持，以合作的方式实现社会、环境和经济的可持续发展。从未来的角度来看，成立更多地以发展为导向的新型机构是必要的，它能为包容性发展带来新的活力。

目前，世界经济正处于困难的调整期。由于收入分配差距加大，发展的不平衡加剧，贸易和投资增速放慢，保护主义盛行。“一带一路”带来的是开放、合作、发展的新风。由于政府支持，又有国际机构的参与，会对公共和私人投资具有吸引力，这会有助于改善内部和外部的贸易与投资环境，进而调动经济增长的潜能。

当然，由于国情复杂和各国利益的不同，形成共建“一带一路”的合力并非易事，各种风险都有，如国家政局风险、投资风险、恐怖主义威胁风险等等，需要认真研究，需要综合把握，需要利弊权衡。同时，“一带一路”建设基于长期的发展，不是短期行为，是“百年工程”，在推进和建设上要考虑轻重缓急，不能急功近利，急于求成。

中国作为“一带一路”建设的倡导者，需要协调各方利益，评估不同商业项目风险，加强双边经济贸易协定和规则，促进和推广成功的合作模式，构建关键的创业项目，寻找与各国之间关于发展经济、政治合作、安全保障和人员交流的契合点。由于“一带一路”涉及几十个国家，各国之间需要有效的合作协调机制，同时，对“一带一路”建设的五个优先领域，需要一个有效的协调机制，安排好轻重缓急，做好不同国家的利益平衡和共同受益。特别是，许多沿线国家是经济不发达国家，相互之间联系不畅，道路条件差，铁路技术标准多样化，增加了运输周转环节而导致低效率。在所有国家沿跨境高速铁路以确保具有相同的标准程序、效率和安全性是困难的。由于海上运输信息共享有限，在一些国家频繁发生海上安全事故，为了改善这种状况，需要大量的投资，但这些项目不可避免地要等待相当长时间才能实现投资利润。

“一带一路”倡议有助于推动合作共赢的地区与国际新秩序的构建，特别是在全球经济经历深刻变化的背景下，“一带一路”倡议可以提供一种新的理念，一种新的方式，通过激发参与热情，动员资源投入，改善发展中国家的综合发展环境，创建新的发展动能，才有助于世界经济走出低迷，进入新的发展阶段。[1] 面对世界发展中的问题，各种反应和对策都有可能发生。在当前美国新政府推行“美国第一”的保护主义政策的形势下，中国基于开放合作与共同发展的“一带一路”倡议具有特别的意义。“一带一路”是合作倡议，不是战略竞争，它有助于培养合作精神，增强命运共同体意识，从而也助于推动构建一个合作与和平的地区与世界。

1 Feng, Zhongping and Jing Huang: “Sino-European Cooperation on the Belt and Road Initiative: Drive, Dynamics, and Prospect” , *Contemporary International Relations*(现代国际关系), 2016, 2, pp.9-15.

The Belt and Road Initiative and New-type Development Cooperation

Zhang Yunling / China

Fellow and Director of International Studies, CASS

The Belt and Road Initiative has attracted increasing attention at home and abroad since it was put forward. This is attributable to the following factors: First, the new philosophy of development cooperation has been presented and accepted by the people; second, there are concrete actions rather than empty talk; some actions have produced tangible effects. At present, the Belt and Road Initiative is not only a regional initiative of cooperation, but also an extensive cooperation philosophy and platform across the world.[1]

1. Impetus for Innovative Development

Connecting the vast areas of Asia, Europe and Africa through land and marine networks, the Belt and Road Initiative focuses on promoting the construction of

1 Since 2016, U.N. Economic and Social Commission for Asia and the Pacific, the United Nations Development Programme, the United Nations Industrial Development Organization and the World Health Organization have signed agreements or memoranda on understanding for the joint construction of the Belt and Road; the 71st Session of the United Nations General Assembly adopted a resolution supporting the construction of the Belt and Road.

infrastructures, industrial parks, port economic zones and port logistics networks to enable connectivity among large regions and boost the facilitated flow of investments, goods, services, capital, technologies and personnel, so as to create new impetus for development and form a new pattern of economic development.

Of course, China has its own long-term considerations in putting forward the initiative. The primary consideration lies in seeking a new space for the development of economic transformation. Since the reform and opening up, China's eastern coastal areas have become the center of economic development; they have developed into the most vibrant areas thanks to their geographical advantages, so more and more resources and labor have flowed into those areas. As a result, the western region has suffered a lack of vigor for development, and a regional imbalance in domestic development has increased; this imbalance in regional development has become an important factor which affects the stability and the sustainable development of the whole society and economy. The Chinese Government has made efforts to correct this imbalance. The most influential move made by the Chinese Government was the Great Western Development project. The project covers 12 provinces, autonomous regions and municipalities. Under the project, the Central Government has provided vigorous support to the construction of infrastructures including roads, highways, railways, electric power and natural gas projects, and it has developed preferential policies for encouraging the flow of resources from the eastern region to the western region. Noticeable progress has been made through the project, but the competitive advantages of the western region have not been significantly improved, and the imbalance between the development of the eastern and western areas has not been greatly decreased. One of the important causes is that the western region is subject to "internal restrictions" at a geographical level. Compared with the Great Western Development project which focuses on domestic development, the Belt and Road Initiative combines the inward development project with the outward one in western development so that there is a more open market space for the western region.

The Silk Road Economic Belt connects China-Central Asia-Western Asia-Russia-Europe and China-Southeast Asia-Southern Asia through a land network in order to build a new open developmental belt, while the Maritime Silk Road connects China-Southeast Asia-the Indian Ocean-Africa-Europe and China-Oceania through a maritime network in order to build a trans-sea cooperative zone for common development.[1] Connecting China with the countries along the Belt and Road is conducive to establishing a new economic space, developing a new extension belt for Western China and providing new space for development cooperation for the whole of China.

China has a number of contiguous and neighboring countries. Regionally, it is a vast geographical belt. The connectivity between China and the surrounding countries needs the support of cross-border infrastructure networks, including highways, railways and aviation routes. However, all of these cross-border infrastructures are highly underdeveloped in terms of both hardware and software. The Belt and Road helps improve the cross-border terrestrial infrastructure network, increase the connections of modern ports, develop the economy of port zones and build a maritime logistics network. Obviously, the Belt and Road Initiative will tremendously improve the environment for the external connection of China, and make the surrounding region become an open developmental space shared by China and its neighboring countries.

With more than three decades of rapid growth, China's economy has shifted to the new normal—from high-speed growth to medium-speed growth. In order to create a new growth engine, it is necessary to build the driving forces for domestic demand-led economic growth while expanding the external market opportunities. The developing countries can provide the new space for the world's economy, but the underdevelopment of the infrastructures and the industry supply chain is the bottleneck for development. If their comprehensive economic environment is

1 See the Belt and Road document, http://news.xinhuanet.com/english/china/2015-03/28/c_134105858_2.htm.

improved by their participation in the Belt and Road Initiative, this will be beneficial for developing the local economy, and can provide the opportunities to Chinese enterprises to go global and expand trade.

With a focus on development cooperation, the Belt and Road Initiative enables China to seek new economic development opportunities by carrying out a number of projects, such as developing the infrastructure network and building industrial parks in the regions and countries along the Belt and Road. China's manufacturing industry needs to find other places of production for reducing costs, increasing the technical level and sharpening the competitive edge, while there are enormous spaces for development and cost advantages for its utilization in the developing countries in Asia and Africa. Of course, the development of production capacity under the Belt and Road cooperation mechanism is different from the previous simple transfer of production capacity—outward transfer of outdated and polluting production; on the contrary, there are consultations with the countries involved in order to design and build new industries. From this perspective, it represents industrial expansion and improvement. Cooperation regarding production capacity under the Belt and Road Initiative as promoted by China is a new-type method of cooperative development. It is different from the traditional assistance and transfer of production capacity based on market costs.

2. Thinking of Innovative Development

The Belt and Road Initiative brings about a new line of thought regarding innovation-driven development. The innovation under the Belt and Road mechanism is cooperation innovation and is different from general technical innovation. It means that a new comprehensive development environment is built, a new economic growth engine is fostered, an inclusive and balanced kind of sustainable development is achieved through learning experiences, sharing resources and interests.

Innovation under the Belt and Road Initiative also includes the building of a new cooperation mechanism such as the establishment of the Asian Infrastructure Investment Bank and the New Development Bank. They do not replace the existing mechanisms such as the World Bank (WB), the Asian Development Bank (ADB) and other international institutions; on the contrary, they generate growth, promote cooperation and complement the original mechanisms. The Asian Infrastructure Investment Bank supports infrastructure projects by performing financing operations along with the Asian Development Bank and the World Bank.[1]

The development of the world's economy is in a new period of adjustment, so new ways of thinking and new initiatives are needed. The Belt and Road Initiative is the most influential one among a number of new lines of thought and new initiatives, and receives the most support and witnesses the largest number of participating countries. The Belt and Road Initiative propels cooperation and opening up; with the Belt and Road Initiative, connectivity is achieved so as to promote the transnational flow of economic elements which enables an efficient allocation of resources and deep integration of markets; opening up and cooperation shape common interests; therefore, it can stimulate the countries along the Belt and Road to achieve coordination in economic policies, engage in deeper and more extensive high-standard regional cooperation and jointly create an open, inclusive and balanced regional framework for economic cooperation.

Instead of giving the top priority to a certain region, the Belt and Road Initiative follows an open regionalism; it is open to all countries, international and regional organizations and welcomes their participation[2]. This means that not only the countries along the Belt and Road but also other countries around the world are welcome to participate in building the Belt and Road. Take the Asian Infrastructure Investment Bank as an example: its membership is open to all countries which

1 See "AIIB and ADB provide loan together on the project" , http://bank.jrj.com.cn/2016/03/22102320721783.shtml

2 Vision document, http://english.mofcom.gov.cn/article/zt_beltandroad/

show interest and are willing to make contributions.[1] Not limited to these routes, the connectivity diversely covers Eurasia.[2]

The priorities of the Belt and Road Initiative include: (1) there is coordination in policy-making—the economic development strategies and policies are coordinated to develop plans and measures for providing partners with policy support of implementation plans; (2) the infrastructure network is built to achieve connectivity, including the integration of construction plans and systems of technical standards; (3) investment and trade facilitation are improved to promote trade and investment, remove the barriers to them and create a good business environment; (4) the financial cooperation for systems of monetary stability, the investment and financing system and the credit information system are established to make currency swap settlements, develop the bond market and build new financial institutions such as the Asian Infrastructure Investment Bank (AIIB), the New Development Bank (NDB), the Shanghai Cooperation Organization (SCO)'s financing institution; (5) cultural and academic exchanges, personnel exchanges and cooperation, media cooperation, youth and women's communication and volunteer services are promoted to win the support of the general public. As a large developing country, China can play a special role in the practical activities mentioned above. As the advocate and main participant, China provides the key capital input and technical support.[3]

Connectivity is the priority in the development of the Belt and Road Initiative. Connectivity covers the building of infrastructures, the consistency or connection of laws, regulations, rules and standards, and the personnel flow and exchange. The priority in the building of infrastructures consists of building a modern transportation network, while that in the consistency of laws, regulations, rules and standards consists of realizing facilitations, removing or greatly reducing the

1 The Asian Infrastructure Investment Bank was established on December 25th, 2015. There are 57 initial members, including 37 members from Asia and 20 members from other regions.

2 Summers, Tim: "China's 'New Silk Roads' : sub-national regions and networks of global political economy" , *Third World Quarterly*, 2016, 37(9):1628-1643.

3 See "The B&R document" , http://english.mofcom.gov.cn/article/zt_beltandroad/.

restrictions on transportation, trade and investment, and that in the personnel flow lies in facilitating the movement of technical engineering personnel and commercial personnel, the exchange of educational and cultural personnel and the movement of citizens. For this purpose, actions will be taken to build various cooperation mechanisms under the Belt and Road framework and develop rules of cooperation.

Investment and trade cooperation is the key field in the development of the Belt and Road Initiative and aims at building free trade zones in the countries along the Belt and Road by promoting investment and trade facilitation and removing the barriers to trade and investment. The cooperation under the Belt and Road Initiative will help expand trade and investments, increase the trade and investment structure, and create new development fields by improving infrastructures, building industrial zones and port networks, developing financing and strengthening capacity building.

Financial cooperation is the key support for the construction of the Belt and Road Initiative. Financial cooperation covers extensive cross-border financial agendas, including monetary stability, project financing, bilateral currency swap, settlements, a bond market, RMB-denominated bonds. The Asian Infrastructure Investment Bank, the New Development Bank, the Silk Road Fund, the China-ASEAN Inter-bank Association and the Shanghai Cooperation Organization's Inter-bank Association will play their roles. In the construction of the Belt and Road, it is necessary to reinforce cooperation on financial supervision, build an effective mechanism to coordinate supervision, enhance the capability for addressing risks and controlling crises, establish a regional early-warning system for financial risk, and create an exchange and cooperation mechanism for coping with cross-border risks and crises. These concerted efforts are conducive to increasing monetary stability, enhancing the capability of the credit system and encouraging commercial equity investment funds and private funds to participate in the construction of major projects.

Common aspirations shared by the people in different countries provide public support for the construction of the Belt and Road Initiative. The construction of the Belt and Road Initiative covers not only the agendas for promoting economic development, but also cultural and academic exchanges, training, media cooperation, and contacts among talents, young people and women, so that the support for deepening bilateral and multilateral cooperation is won from the general public. Under various cooperation mechanisms, efforts are made to boost talent, tourist and sports exchanges, the sharing of epidemic information, training and exchanges involving prevention and treatment technologies and medical personnel, and to enhance scientific and technological cooperation, practical cooperation in youth employment and entrepreneurial training, vocational skills development, social security management, exchanges among non-governmental organizations and cooperation among cities.

Given the economic diversity in the countries along the Belt and Road, it is impossible to develop and carry out unitary plans for it; the construction concerning various aspects should be linked to the developmental plans of the host countries so that a win-win outcome can be achieved and various participants can benefit from their participation.[1] In reality, the level of economic development is not high and infrastructure input is not sufficient in most of the countries along the Belt and Road. Participation in the construction of the Belt and Road Initiative incorporates the development of the participating countries into the cooperation network of a large region, so as to break through the restrictions in the capability of the participating countries, transnational connections and logistics networks.

China has acquired rich experience in building an infrastructure network. With equipment and technical capacity as well as managerial experience, China can play an important role in improving the infrastructures. Given that the Belt and Road Initiative involves vast areas, the coordination and impetus from China make it possible to achieve success in many transnational projects and build transnational

1 Wang, Yong: "Offensive for defensive: the belt and road initiative and China's new grand strategy" , *The Pacific Review*, 2016, 29(3):455-463.

infrastructure networks, including railways, highways and port networks, oil and gas pipelines, telecommunications and electric power networks. With respect to financing, besides the direct financing from such institutions as the Silk Road Fund and the Asian Infrastructure Investment Bank, other financial institutions will also actively participate in the construction of the Belt and Road Initiative. More importantly, as main participants, enterprises can, under the PPP cooperation framework, go beyond the financing restrictions on them and avoid the risks from acting alone.

For the future developmental prospects, the construction of the Silk Road Economic Belt and that along the Maritime Silk Road will gradually improve the connectivity among Asia, Europe and Africa. The construction of infrastructure networks will provide a new environment for developing new industrial zones, financial centers, free trade and investment zones, other comprehensive projects such as oil and gas pipelines, electric power networks, internetworks, power transmission lines and communication networks; this will give birth to a huge market covering Asia, Europe and Africa.[1]

3. Innovative Development Cooperation

The construction of the Belt and Road is carried out under the cooperation mode of joint participation, joint planning, joint construction and the sharing of achievements. It is different from traditional development assistance; participants are equal partners under such a cooperation mode. Geographically, the construction of the Belt and Road covers vast areas in more than 60 countries. It requires active participation by and close cooperation among all of the relevant partners. The development of the Belt and Road follows the principle that consultation and joint construction are carried out on the basis of addressing the interests of all of the participants and efforts are made to integrate the national developmental

1 Summers, Tim: “China’s ‘New Silk Roads’ : sub-national regions and networks of global political economy” , *Third World Quarterly*, 2016, 37(9):1628-1643.

strategies of all of them.[1] Most of the countries and territories along the Belt and Road are the developing economies where the per capita GDP level is very low and is less than half of the world's average level, so it is difficult for a single country to build a good network of infrastructures. The development of infrastructures calls for long-term investments, thus the cooperation and support from public funds and financial institutions are crucial. The Asian Infrastructure Investment Bank represents a new way to achieve cooperative financing for the development of infrastructures and is conducive to coping with the bottleneck constraints in long-term investments. The Asian Infrastructure Investment Bank will be strictly operated under the internationally recognized principle that its members jointly make decisions. It adapts to the new needs and faces new challenges; it should reform the existing international institutions and build new international institutions. The Asian Infrastructure Investment Bank is designed to bring new power to the world's economy. The USA and Japan have refused to join the Asian Infrastructure Investment Bank at present, but many countries from Asia, Africa and Europe have actively joined it and have become its founding members. The Asian Infrastructure Investment Bank can provide investment funds and technical assistance, and fully take into account the requirements of the projects of its partner countries. In fact, infrastructure investment is massive and is expected to increase further in the next years; all developing countries are subject to huge pressure in meeting their infrastructural needs. As estimated by the United Nations Conference on Trade and Development, in order to reach the Sustainable Development Goals (SDGs) of 2030, the developing countries need an annual invest of 3.3–4.5 trillion USD. These investments are mainly concentrated in infrastructure projects—electric power, telecommunications, transportation, water and health—and infrastructure-related projects such as those involving food safety, climate change mitigation and adaptation, health and education. The implementation of the sustainable development agenda of 2030 is of great significance for some countries to utilize

1 See "The B&R document" , http://news.xinhuanet.com/english/china/2015-03/28/c_134105858_2.htm.

global resources, including public and private infrastructure investments.[1]

Regarding the source of the funds, traditionally, development cooperation is funded by bilateral and multilateral donors. However, according to research, development assistance accounts for only 6%—7% of infrastructure financing.[2] This shows that it is necessary to innovate on the development cooperation mode. Regarding the common participation in the Belt and Road Initiative, the public-private partnership (PPP) mode offers a new framework of development cooperation. According to past experience, the foreign direct investments in the developing countries only make up a small share of such fields as electric power, telecommunications, transportation and water supply, while the existing investments only constitute a small part with respect to the effective resources necessary for carrying out the sustainable development agenda. The Asian Infrastructure Investment Bank is designed to push forward the development of infrastructures. As we know, sustainable economic development needs to be supported by excellent infrastructures; however, the financing problem concerning investment in infrastructures has been a bottleneck for a long time. The financing from the Asian Infrastructure Investment Bank and the international market, and the tapping of the financial potential of domestic, public and private sectors will inject new vigor into the building of infrastructures. The New Development Bank established by the BRICS countries works in this way and is mainly aimed at resolving the bottleneck constraints on development financing; it provides support by means of loans, guarantees, equity participation or other financial instruments, and helps foster sustainable social, environmental and economic development through cooperation. Regarding future prospects, it is necessary to establish more new-type development-oriented institutions so that they can bring new vigor to inclusive development.

At present, the world's economy is in the middle of a difficult period of

1 UNCTAD: "*World Investment Report*" , 2016, United Nations Publications.

2 Miyamoto, Kaori and Emilio Chiofalo, "Official Development Finance for Infrastructure:Support by Multilateral and Bilateral Development Partners" , 2015, *OECD Development Cooperation Working Papers*, No. 25, OECD Publishing.

adjustment. As the income distribution gap is widening and the levels of development are becoming increasingly unbalanced, there is a slowdown in trade and investment, and protectionism is rife. The Belt and Road Initiative brings new elements: opening up, cooperation and development. Thanks to governmental support and the participation of international institutions, there will be attraction for public and private investments and this will help improve internal and external trade and investment environments and thus this will arouse the potential for economic growth.

Of course, the national conditions are complicated and interests are different, so it is difficult to make concerted efforts in the Belt and Road Initiative and so various risks, such as national political risks, investment risks and terrorist threat risks, will emerge; it is necessary to conduct a careful study, give overall considerations, and weigh the advantages and disadvantages. Meanwhile, the construction of the Belt and Road Initiative is based on long-term development rather than short-term behavior and it is a long-lasting project, therefore, the order of priorities should be considered in making progress and performing the construction, and it is unwise to seek quick success and instant benefits.

As the advocate of the construction of the Belt and Road Initiative, China should coordinate the interests of various stakeholders, evaluate the risks of different commercial projects, strengthen the bilateral economic and trade agreements and rules, promote and apply successful cooperation modes, build key start-up projects, seek the common points among countries during economic development, political cooperation, security guarantee and personnel exchange. The Belt and Road Initiative involves dozens of countries, so it is imperative to establish an effective mechanism to coordinate the cooperation among the countries; meanwhile, in order to address the five priorities in the development of the Belt and Road Initiative, it is necessary to build up an effective mechanism of coordination to properly arrange the order of priorities and ensure that the interests of different countries are balanced and benefits are shared by them. In particular, many countries along the Belt and

Road are economically underdeveloped; the contacts among them are not smooth; their road conditions are poor; diverse technical standards for railways increase the intermediate steps in transportation and thus decrease the efficiency. It is difficult to ensure the same standard procedure, efficiency and safety in the cross-border high-speed railways across all of the countries. The sharing of maritime transportation information is limited; maritime accidents are frequent in some countries. In order to improve the situation, heavy investments are required, but it inevitably takes a long time for these projects to deliver investment profits.

The Belt and Road Initiative helps build up the areas with win-win cooperation and a new international order; in particular, amidst the profound changes in the world's economy, the Belt and Road Initiative can provide a new philosophy and a new mode, under which the enthusiasm for participation is aroused and resources are mobilized to improve the environment of comprehensive development of the developing countries and generate a new impetus for development, thus moving the world's economy out of recession and into a new stage of development.[1] There are many responses and countermeasures before the problems in world development. Currently, the new US administration is applying a protectionist policy of putting America first; against such a background, the Belt and Road Initiative put forward by China on the basis of open cooperation and joint development is of special significance. The Belt and Road Initiative is an initiative of cooperation rather than one of strategic competition. It contributes to developing a spirit of cooperation, enhancing the awareness of a community with a common destiny, thus helping build up a cooperative and peaceful region and world.

1 Feng, Zhongping and Jing Huang: “Sino-European Cooperation on the Belt and Road Initiative: Drive, Dynamics, and Prospect” , *Contemporary International Relations*, 2016, (2):9-15.

2016 汉学与当代中国座谈会

奎恩 【爱尔兰】

国际与欧洲事务研究中心 主任 / 爱尔兰前财政部长与教育部长

首先，我要向中国社会科学院表示感谢，感谢贵方邀请我代表都柏林国际与欧洲事务研究所参加今天的这次活动。本次座谈会的主题是中国与 2013 年提出的“一带一路”倡议。尽管许多批评人士曾对此表示出忧虑，但“一带一路”是一项开放式的工程，时间跨度也远比一般的政府项目或政府工程更长。

由于我最初的专业是建筑和城市规划，因而我把“一带一路”倡议看作是中国为构建交通路径和沟通路径而做出的努力，这两条路径定然会与 21 世纪的全球化现象构成互补。“一带一路”是一项开放性的工程，旨在促进世界各个地区的一体化，让全球的各个体系融为一个连贯的整体。它并不是一个详细的总体方案，而是中国向世界各国发出的一份邀请，邀请全世界一同探讨——在 21 世纪，我们如何重新规划这条连接古代中西方的商贸通路和文化通路。

“岛国心态”的概念对我们而言并不陌生，它并非仅仅体现在地理和交通的闭塞上。这种孤立主义往往表现为——为巩固岛内群体的统一性而在情绪上做出的一种反应。通过与外来者的对比，它能够帮助我们对“差异”的概念进行界定。几个世纪以来，地理环境的差异、自然风光的不同、语言和种族的差别等，都在强化着我们关于“此”和“彼”的意识。然而，全球化对科学技术、社会现状、交通状况、政治现实等方面带来的影响，正从根本上改变着我们的世界，这也是人类历史上第一次发生这样的改变。有些人或许不喜欢这种改变，但没有人能够阻止它的发生。

作为一名爱尔兰公民，我可以告诉诸位，当你生活在一个岛屿上，而这个岛屿恰好处在欧洲西海岸，且与另外一个岛屿隔海相望，你会时常感受到交通闭塞带来的局促感，每当我们不得不外出时，往往是通过海陆或空陆出行。然而地理位置的闭塞并没遏止我们对于出行的渴望，当我们不得不移民海外、谋求生计时，地理的局限并没有阻挡我们的步伐。

仅仅在一百五十年前，当爱尔兰岛仍属于大不列颠及爱尔兰联合王国的一部分时，爱尔兰遭遇了一场被称为“马铃薯饥荒”的灾难与悲剧，八百万人口中，有两百万人死于饥荒，两百万人移民海外。这场悲剧发生在当时最富有、最庞大的帝国的中心，对此，爱尔兰人的记忆是刻骨铭心的。想到那些流亡在外、被迫到澳大利亚、新西兰、加拿大、美国等地求生的爱尔兰人，我们的哀痛之情是真挚而深切的。

然而，我们在 19 世纪经历的悲剧，却促成了我们在 21 世纪的转变。如今，爱尔兰境内仅有 600 万人口，但世界各地却有 7300 人自称是爱尔兰后裔。相对于欧洲各国而言，爱尔兰人是在全球范围内分部最广、最为成功的族裔。从这个角度来看，爱尔兰人并不是自我孤立的。与此同时，我们的凝聚力变得更强，我们对自我的意识更为清晰，与那些人口数量和国土面积远远超过爱尔兰的国家和民族相比，我们更具影响力。任何一个国家的酒馆都无法与爱尔兰的酒馆相媲美、都无法赶超它在社交网络中的中心地位，也没有哪个国家在欢庆节日时，能像爱尔兰人庆祝圣帕特里克节一样隆重。

这一切并非人为的规划所致，甚至是我们不曾奢望的。自 1922 年取得政治独立后，几十年以来，这场移民浪潮都被视作一场爱尔兰的悲剧。当初，一代又一代贫苦而缺乏教育的男男女女从爱尔兰海岸出发，在异国他乡开启了美好的生活。如今，我们的年轻人接受了良好的教育，他们仍然渴望着到外面的世界去探索，去开阔眼界。与前几代的爱尔兰移民相比，他们更加自信，在未来的生活中会更加的自信。他们会带着满满的热诚响应“一带一路”倡议，紧紧抓住这一倡议所带来的重大机遇。

谈到这里，则不能不对东西方之间的海陆联通做一番审视。总体而言，“一带一路”倡议是受到各国热烈响应的，但诸多细节问题仍然有待探讨。比如，许多人建议将“一带一路”的终点设定在鹿特丹。诚然，作为荷兰和欧洲的重要港口，鹿特丹的重要性自然不会减弱，但却不适合作为“一带一路”的终点。

绝佳的终点在欧洲西海岸的爱尔兰——香浓河河口。香浓河是爱尔兰及英国境内最长的河流，河口处建有世界上第一个跨大西洋机场，是连接北美、南美的绝佳纽带。这里具有无穷的潜力和可能性，因此更适合作为“一带一路”的终点，作为全球互通互联的结点。

从近期欧洲乃至世界的政治形势来看，全球化进程成就了赢家、但也导致输家的出现。正确与否暂且不论，这种说法反映了大众对于全球化所持的态度。这也是政治家和决策者必须面对的一个问题。英国脱欧、欧洲大陆涌现的狭隘的民族主义等，都是很好的例证。美国总统大选中的言行不一、唐纳德·特朗普的最终获胜等，都是欧洲经历过的灾难在新世界的表现。

我们要如何帮助民众恢复曾经那份对于开放和包容的热忱？如何才能使民众认识到，作为国家公民，他们的生活已经得到了极大的改善？在这个方面，中国取得的成就远远超过其他国家。目前为止，中国已经帮助 5 亿人口摆脱了长期贫困的状态。发达国家如何才能像中国一样，取得如此巨大的成就？

中国提出的“一带一路”倡议并不是一份既定的方案。在我看来，它是一封来自中国的邀请函，它正邀请世界各国一同踏上 21 世纪的旅程，去探索各种潜在的可能——尽管东西方早在几千年前便已经为踏上这次旅程迈出了第一步。

现代世界步入 21 世纪尚不足 20 年，从科学的角度来看，全球化现象已经产生，而且必将持续下去、愈演愈烈。目前为止，我们已经观察到那些自认赢家或输家的人做出了何种反应。事实上，不论是赢家还是输家，不论在世界哪个区域，人类显然是最大的赢家，而在我看来，人类的赢家地位必将保持下去。但若想做到这一点并不容易，除非我们能打破“岛国心态”，让所有人都意识到，这个世界上存在所有人共有的一片区域。“一带一路”倡议恰恰认清了我们所面临的新现实，所以才会受到热烈的响应。让我们携手同心，为“一带一路”的成功共同奋斗。

The Symposium on China Studies 2016

Ruairí Quinn / Ireland

Chairman of the Institute of International and European Affairs/Former Minister for Finance and Former Minister for Education and Skills of Ireland

I want to start by thanking the Chinese Academy of Social Sciences for inviting me, on behalf of the Institute of International and European Affairs, Dublin, to participate in this three-day event. The theme of this Symposium is the "Belt and Road" initiative proposed by China in 2013. Despite the concerns expressed by some critics, this is an open ended project, with a much longer time span than the usual governmental programmes or projects.

Having trained originally as an architect and town planner, I view it as an attempt to create a physical and communications pathway, which can/will complement the 21st century phenomenon of globalization. It is an open attempt to provide for the integration of large parts of the worlds global systems into a coherent entity. It does not propose to be a precise master plan. Rather, it is an invitation to explore, how an ancient East/West roadway of trade, commerce and culture, can be reimagined for the 21st century.

The concept of an "island mentality" is not new, nor is it purely physical. Isolationism can be an emotional response to consolidate the island groups. It also helps define difference by contrast with the strange outsider. For centuries across the globe, nature, landscape, language and race reinforced the sense of us and them. But the technical, and now social, physical and political realities of globalisation are fundamentally changing our world for the first time in our human history. Some people may not like it, but none of us can stop it.

As an Irish citizen, I can tell you, that when you live on an island, off another island, which is itself off the western coast of Europe, you are constantly aware of the basic physical constraints. Consequently, travel of necessity begins with a sea or an air journey. But Ireland's location has not stopped our desire to travel or indeed the imperative to emigrate simply to survive.

Just over a hundred and fifty years ago, the island of Ireland, then an integral part of the United Kingdom of Great Britain and Ireland, was confronted with a disaster/tragedy of a potato famine. The population of eight million, lost two million to starvation and another two million to emigration. The memory of this tragedy, which happened at the centre of the richest/largest empire of the time, is still strong among Irish people. However the lament for Irish exiles, forced to find new lives in many different countries in the modern world, such as Australia, New Zealand, Canada, and the United States, as well of course within Europe, including the island of Britain, was real and heartfelt.

But our 19th century tragedy has become a 21st century transformation. While there are 6 million people on the island of Ireland today, more than 73 million people, across the world self-describe themselves as being of Irish descent. The Irish have become Europe's most widespread and successful global tribe. While we are not alone in this regard, we have become more cohesive, more self conscious and consequentially more influential than nationalities and peoples much bigger than us. No other nation has the equivalent of the Irish pub, and its central role for contact and networking. No other country's national holiday gets as celebrated and respected as St Patricks Day.

This was not consciously planned, or even wished for. For decades after winning political independence in 1922, emigration was seen as a national tragedy. Generations of poor, and scarcely educated men and women left the shores of Ireland. Many, but not all, made great new lives for themselves and their children. Today, by contrast, our young migrants, anxious to see and explore the world are very well educated and much more self confident than previous generations. They have been, and will become even more so in the future, enthusiastic explorers of the "Belt and Road" and all the opportunities which it will have to offer.

At this point, let me examine the connections between East and West, land and sea. The "Belt and Road" proposal is welcomed in principle, but must be explored in detail. For example, there are many suggestions that the route would end in Rotterdam, at the North Sea of Europe, combining maritime and road routes. While the Dutch port of Rotterdam will remain important, it is not suited to be the end stop of "One Belt, One Road".

That point in Europe is located on the West coast of Ireland, at the mouth of the River Shannon, the longest river in Ireland and Britain. It is also the location of the first transatlantic airport, with superb links to the New Worlds of North and South America. There are endless possibilities surrounding its location, as it completes the connection of the "Belt and Road" and links a truly global system of structured interconnection.

It is clear from recent political events, across Europe and beyond, that the process of globalization has produced losers as well as winners. True or not, it is the public's perception of outcomes that are what politicians and policy workers must address. The British decision on Brexit is one example. The rise of narrow-minded nationalism in Continental Europe is another. The tone and tenor of the United States Presidential Election, and the victory of President-elect Donald Trump, is a

New World manifestation of Europe's old woes.

How can we help people to reconnect with their previous enthusiasm for openness and inclusion? How can we enable more people to perceive themselves as citizens whose lives have really improved? China, more than any country, has lifted 500 million people out of what was continuous poverty. How does the developed world start again to do the same thing?

The "Belt and Road" initiative is not put forward as a completed solution. Rather, I see it as an invitation to commence a journey to travel a path in the 21st century, to explore the potential that still exists, even if the first steps were taken thousands of years ago, between people of East and West.

Our modern world is less than twenty years into the 21st century. The phenomenon of globalization, from a scientific point of view is here, both to stay and to intensify. We are already seeing the reactions of people who perceive themselves to be either losers or winners. In fact, across the globe, humanity is clearly the winner, and that must, in my mind continue. But it will not do so easily until the "island mentality" is recognized and reassured that there is a place in our shared world for all of us. The "Belt and Road" initiative is a welcome recognition of our new reality. We should work together to make it happen.

“一带一路”与中欧关系：认知，互动与可能性

程卫东　【中国】
中国社会科学院欧洲研究所　副所长

“一带一路”倡议及其实施对沿线各国的经济与社会发展以及国家间关系，将不可避免地将产生某种影响。但是，“一带一路”对国际格局到底产生什么样的影响，以及多大程度的影响，则充满着不确定性。这种不确定性是由多种因素造成的。特别是，“一带一路”只是中国提出的一个倡议，虽然倡议中包括了建设“一带一路”的目标、原则、方法与重点，但是沿线国家之间还没有形成一个达成广泛共识的规划与路线图，因此，它并不必然导致一种具有明确性、确定性的结局，“一带一路”实施本身具有诸多不确定性，因此，它对国际格局的影响也具有不确定性。

中国与欧洲分别是“一带一路”的两端，都是“一带一路”建设的重要组成部分，同时对于中国与欧洲之间的广大区域，中欧也都能够发挥巨大的影响力。因此，“一带一路”对于中国与欧洲本身，对于中欧关系，以及对于中欧与亚欧大陆及非洲国家之间的关系，都将产生不可忽视的影响。“一带一路”对中欧关系的影响，在某种程度上也可反映出它对国际格局的可能影响。

“一带一路”对中欧关系的影响，显然不只是在于“一带一路”倡议本身。一个倡议对现实的影响，取决于很多因素，是各种因素综合作用的结果。除了客观上的因素，如沿线各国的经济状况、地理因素、基础设施现状等之外，中欧双方关于“一带一路”的认知，以及围绕“一带一路”的互动，将直接影响“一带

一路”作用的发挥，以及中欧关系的可能走向。

一 认知与“一带一路”对中欧关系的影响

认知对于国际关系的影响，早已为人们所知悉。正确的认知与共识，能推动国际关系向正确的方向发展，错误的认知与分歧，则有可能导致国际关系向负面的方向发展。

中国政府关于“一带一路”建设的目标、内容、原则与合作机制，一直都是很清晰的，体现在中国政府公布的关于“一带一路”的官方文件以及领导人讲话中。其核心要点，概而言之，包括四个方面：（1）目标：共同打造开放、包容、均衡、普惠的区域经济合作架构；（2）合作内容：以五通为核心的亚欧非大陆及附近海洋的互联互通，实现沿线各国的多元、自主、平衡、可持续发展；（3）建设原则：在遵守联合国宪章的前提下，坚持开放合作，和谐包容，市场运作，互利共赢的原则，坚持共商，共建与共享；（4）合作机制，利用各种多双边合作机制，中国愿意承担更多的责任，推动“一带一路”建设。

从中国政府关于“一带一路”倡议的内容中，可以看出，“一带一路”建设将为中欧合作提供新的机遇与合作空间，有利于进一步推动中欧关系的发展。一方面，“一带一路”的目标在于通过合作推动整个区域的发展，而区域经济的发展符合中国与欧洲的利益；另一方面，“一带一路”建设也有助于推动欧洲，特别是中东欧地区的基础设施建设，这也是欧洲急需的建设重点。

但从到目前为止的欧洲的反应来看，并不是所有欧洲人都认同中国关于“一带一路”建设的倡议。欧洲对“一带一路”倡议的认知，既有积极的一面，也有消极的一面。

从积极面看，一部分人认同“一带一路”对沿线国家的发展以及对中欧的重要性，认同区域合作对于区域经济发展与地区和平与稳定的重要性（欧洲一体化本身就是区域合作的典范），认同基础设施对于经济发展的重要性（“容克计划”很大一部分也是投资于欧洲基础设施）。

从消极面看，有一些欧洲人对于中国倡导的“一带一路”存在着疑虑，主要表现在：（1）认为“一带一路”是以中国利益为核心的经济外交的体现；（2）“一带一路”具有地缘政治意义，并将会引发地缘政治冲突；（3）“一带一路”将破坏欧盟的统一机制；（4）“一带一路”机制缺乏透明性；（5）“一带一路”建设面临着诸多困难，不具有成功的可能性。

上述不同观点不仅反映了欧洲智库对“一带一路”认知上的差异，也反映了欧洲不同机构、不同国家对于“一带一路”的认知差异。从整体上看，欧盟对“一带一路”表现出一定程度的支持，主要表现在欧盟希望中国的“一带一路”倡议与欧盟的“容克计划”对接上，但总体上反应比较谨慎。从欧盟成员国角度看，对“一带一路”表示支持与参与的主要是中东欧国家，但也主要将“一带一路”理解为是服务于中国外交战略的倡议，并因此认为，中国将愿意为自己的外交战略支付对价，将为沿线国家的基础设施联通及其他设施建设提供基金，与此同时，他们对于中国“一带一路”的地缘政治影响也表现出一定程度的怀疑。

认知在很大程度上将决定欧洲关于“一带一路”的行动。如果欧洲将“一带一路”理解为以中国利益为核心的战略，欧洲将不可能全力支持“一带一路”建设。要发挥“一带一路”推动中欧关系进一步发展，双方在加强对“一带一路”共同认知方面，还需做进一步的沟通。

二 中欧在“一带一路”建设上的互动

认知只是事物的一方面，正确的认知，只是推动国际关系向良性方向发展的第一步。国际关系在实践上是否能够向良性方向发展，还取决于很多因素。正如约瑟夫·奈所提出的，虽然大家都认识合作有利，为什么国家之间经常不合作？这涉及复杂的哲学上的问题即知与行的关系。但总体上来看，知有利于行，而行的结果有利于进一步认知。在存在多种认知或认知不确定的情况下，行动有利于引导、确认或强化认知的方向。

“一带一路”是一个涉及多个区域、数十个国家的倡议，它不仅对区域、对沿线国家，甚至对全球关系都会产生重大影响。“一带一路”建设及其对国家关系的影响，不是哪一个国家能够左右，能够决定的。除了“一带一路”倡议内容本身的影响外，国际行为体之间围绕“一带一路”的互动，对于双方之间的关系以及更广泛的国际关系，将具有重要影响。中欧的互动不仅对“一带一路”建设将会产生重大影响，而且对中欧关系的未来也是如此。

互动的方式很多，合作，旁观，竞争，反对，破坏等。从到目前为止的欧洲反应来看，中欧围绕“一带一路”开展了一定的互动，总体来看，是积极的，但是，并没有达到紧密型合作的程度，而且在不同事项上欧洲不同的国际行为体，与中国在“一带一路”建设的互动上，也表现出了不同的特点。大体来看，有以下几种：

1. 在欧盟层面上，中欧未就一带一路建设形成综合型的、整体性的合作机制。但是，中欧双方均表示，愿意就“容克计划”与“一带一路”倡议进行对接与合作。合作的重点在于对欧洲的投资，包括基础设施、长期投资等方面。但是，中欧的合作并不包括欧洲之外其他区域的合作，而是限于欧盟范围内。

2. 欧盟部分成员国加入了亚投行，共同致力于投资并改善亚洲基础设施。这表明，中欧双方在亚洲基础设施的需求与前景存在着一定的共识。

3. 部分欧盟成员国及其他欧洲国家与中国签署了关于“一带一路”的合作备忘录或合作框架协议，并积极开展了项目合作及其他相关合作。这些国家主要是中东欧国家，表明中东欧国家相对来说比较认同中国的“一带一路”倡议，并积极参与到具体的建设中来。不过，还应注意的是，中东欧国家与中国的合作，也主要是限于与这些国家的双边合作，以及部分情况下涉及中东欧地区的合作。

总体来看，中欧关于“一带一路”倡议的互动是良性的，积极的，但互动主要限于中国与部分中东欧国家的双边合作，以及在有限事项上与欧盟整体开展了互动。

三 “一带一路”对中欧关系未来影响的可能性

如上所述，由于在认知方面存在着多样性与差异性，在互动上存在多种可选的模式，以及在现实中存在着不同的互动模式，“一带一路”对中欧关系的未来走向的影响，也存在着不确定性，并不必然导致中欧关系的更进一步发展，也不必然导致中欧关系退步，而是存在着多种可能性。哪种可能性成为现实，在很大程度上取决于中欧双方的选择，同时也受“一带一路”建设的现实效果的影响。外部因素过于复杂，这里仅就认知与互动的组合探讨可能性问题。

几种可能性：

1. 积极认知＋合作型互动：“一带一路”为中欧关系的进一步发展提供一个合作的平台与契机，进一步充实并促进中欧全面战略伙伴关系的发展。

如果中欧就“一带一路”倡议的目标、内容、积极影响等内容上达成某种共识，欧洲认同中国“一带一路”建设对区域发展及其带来的互利共赢的积极效果，并愿意共同致力于“一带一路”建设，则“一带一路”倡议将是中欧发展的一个新的契机，一个重要的平台。它将几个方面实现双方共赢的成就：（1）促进中欧双方各自建设与发展目标的实现，如促进中东欧基础设施建设，加强中欧间产能合作；（2）加强欧亚大陆及非洲的发展，通过区域经济发展与繁荣，促进地区的稳定，并为区域经济合作提供基础与强劲的推动力；（3）通过“一带一路”建设，促进亚欧非广大区域的交流与互鉴，促进命运共同体建设，从而推进地区的和平与稳定，并在此基础上解决目前国际社会面临的很多重大危机，包括恐怖主义，难民问题，地区冲突等；（4）进一步推动中欧双方共同倡导的多边主义、多极化的国际格局的形成。如果这些成就能够实现，中欧全面战略伙伴关系将进一步实至名归。

2. 消极认知与对抗性互动：“一带一路”倡议将导致中欧关系向消极方向发展。

在这种情形中，欧洲将“一带一路”视为实现中国某种对欧洲产生不利影响的地缘政治战略，从而在行动上采取消极甚至对抗性措施，以抵销其所认为的中国地缘战略目标。这是“一带一路”倡议对中欧关系影响的最坏的可能性。在这种情形下，中欧之间不仅不可能围绕“一带一路”开展合作，而且，还会影响到中欧合作已经取得的成就，中国“一带一路”倡议的目标也难以实现，而且有可能加剧区域之间的不信任与对抗，从而导致亚欧非大陆问题的进一步加剧。

3. 上述两种情形之外的其他认知与互动的组合。在完全认同与完全不认同中国“一带一路”倡议之间，与完全合作与对抗性互动之间，充满着多种可能性，不同组合对中欧关系未来的影响也不尽相同。

总体来看，在认知上中欧越趋于一致，在互动上双方越给予配合、支持、合作，中欧关系就越有可能向进一步深入、扩大的方向发展，双方的关系就将越紧密。但是，在这些情形中，由于存在着认知上的差异，在互动上既有合作也有消极互动，中欧关系将是既有发展的一面，也有摩擦的一面，发展与摩擦的具体情形将取决于认知差异的程度与性质，以及互动方面合作性与对抗性的程度、范围与性质。

从到目前为止欧洲的反应来看，“一带一路”对中欧关系的影响处在第三种可能性之中。由于“一带一路”倡议涉及内容本身的复杂性与未来实践的不确定性，同样的事，从不同角度看，会有不同的观点，因此，在可预见的将来，欧洲完全认同中国“一带一路”提议，并开展全方位的合作，可能性不大，但是，“一带一路”倡议重点在于建设联通性，在于促进区域合作与发展，符合国际社会发展与合作的大趋势，欧洲也没有特别理由反对“一带一路”倡议，因此，总体来看，“一带一路”倡议对中欧关系的影响，将是积极的，正面的。它将为中欧合作提供新的机遇与可能性。

但是，要想“一带一路”倡议成为中欧合作的新平台，成为推动中欧关系发展的新机遇，还要很多事要做。特别是：

（1）进一步加强沟通，扩大中欧关于“一带一路”的共识，使双方在认知上寻找更多的共同点，通过认知上的交流与趋同，消除欧洲对“一带一路”的疑虑，减少或避免因认知上的差异与误解，而对双方政策与行动上产生负面影响。在“一带一路”起步阶段，最重要的是不要让认知上的差异成为双方合作的障碍，中欧双方的关系不能建立在对“一带一路”歧见与错误认知基础之上。在双方认知不一致的情况下，至少不能因此全面否定“一带一路”，应该给“一带一路”建设与中欧在“一带一路”合作中留有足够的合作空间。认知问题，留给实践逐步解决。

（2）在行动与政策上逐步寻找共同点，逐步扩大双方在“一带一路”建设中的合作。合作不只是局限于中欧双方之间，而且也应逐步扩大到整个“一带一路”建设之中，并从合作中加深对“一带一路”的认知，共同推动“一带一路”在整个区域发展中发挥积极作用。

（3）通过实践逐步消除双方认知上的不一致，从而进一步扩大双方在“一带一路”建设中的合作，从而使认知与合作形成一个良性的循环。在双方认知存在差异的情况下，仅靠认知上的交流与对话是不够的，因为不确定性总是存在，只有通过实践与实践的结果，才能消除对“一带一路”的疑虑与歧见。认知推动合作，合作进一步推动认知。

总体来看，中欧在“一带一路”建设上，还是保留了巨大的合作空间。欧洲虽然对“一带一路”有这样那样的疑虑，但是，还是在朝合作的方向上前进。

我相信，随着“一带一路”建设的逐步推进，中国“一带一路”倡议对区域发展的贡献将会逐步显现，中国推动区域合作与发展的诚意与“一带一路”的有效性也会逐步展现，而欧洲对“一带一路”的各种疑虑也会逐步得到澄清。在此过程中，中欧双方都会认识到，合作对中欧，以及对亚欧非整个地区的发展，并进而推动全球经济发展，都是有益的。因此，从长远地看，我认为，中欧关系的未来将前景光明。

The Belt and Road Initiative and China-Europe Relations: Cognition, Interaction and Possibility

Cheng Weidong / China

Deputy Director of the Institute of European Studies, CASS

The Belt and Road Initiative and its implementation will inevitably exert a certain impact on the economic and social development of the countries along the Belt and Road and the relations among countries. However, there is uncertainty regarding the impact of the Belt and Road Initiative on the international pattern and the extent of that impact. Such uncertainty is caused by a number of factors. In particular, the Belt and Road is only an initiative put forward by China. The initiative covers the goal, principles, methods and priorities for the construction of the Belt and Road, but the countries along the Belt and Road have not yet reached a broad consensus on a plan and roadmap; therefore, it does not necessarily lead to a definite outcome. The implementation of the Belt and Road Initiative is subject to many uncertainties, so its impact on the international pattern is uncertain.

China and Europe are both ends of the Belt and Road. Both China and Europe are important parts of the construction of the Belt and Road and they can exert a huge influence on the vast areas between China and Europe. Therefore, the Belt and Road

Initiative will exert a non-negligible impact on China and Europe themselves, China-Europe relations, the relations among China, Europe and the countries of Eurasia and Africa. The impact of the Belt and Road Initiative on China-Europe relations can, to some extent, reflect its possible impact on the international pattern.

Obviously, the impact of the Belt and Road Initiative on China-Europe relations does not consist in the Belt and Road Initiative itself. The impact of an initiative on reality depends on many factors and results from the interaction among various factors. Besides objective factors (such as the economic conditions of the countries along the Belt and Road, their geographical factors and the current situation of their infrastructures), China's and Europe's perception of the Belt and Road, and their interaction involving the Belt and Road Initiative will have a direct bearing on the roles of the Belt and Road and the possible directions of China-Europe relations.

1. Cognition and the Impact of the Belt and Road Initiative on China-Europe Relations

The impact of cognition on the international relations was familiar to people long ago. Correct knowledge and consensus can promote the development of international relations in the right direction, while incorrect knowledge and differences may cause the international relations to develop in the wrong direction.

The Chinese Government has clearly specified the goal, contents, principles and cooperation mechanisms for the construction of the Belt and Road.They are embodied in the official documents of the Chinese Government concerning the Belt and Road Initiative and the speeches of Chinese leaders.Key points are summarized as follows: (1) goal: jointly develop an open, inclusive, balanced and universal regional economic cooperation framework; (2) cooperation contents: build the connectivity of Eurasia, the African Continent and the nearby seas mainly including connectivity concerning five aspects, and achieve a diversified, independent, balanced and sustainable development of the countries along the Belt and Road;

(3) construction principles: subject to complying with the United Nations Charter, uphold open cooperation, harmony and inclusiveness, market operations, mutual benefit and win-win results, and uphold consultation, joint construction and sharing; (4) cooperation mechanisms: utilize various bilateral and multilateral cooperation mechanisms—China is willing to take more responsibilities to push forward the construction of the Belt and Road.

As shown by the Belt and Road Initiative put forward by the Chinese Government, the construction of the Belt and Road will offer new opportunities and space for China-Europe cooperation, and is conducive to further boosting the development of China-Europe relations. On the one hand, the Belt and Road Initiative is designed to promote the development of the whole region through cooperation, while regional economic development meets the interests of both China and Europe; on the other hand, the construction of the Belt and Road also helps propel the construction of infrastructures of Europe, especially in Central Europe and in Eastern Europe, which is also an urgent priority for Europe.

However, Europe's reaction so far indicates that not all of the European people are familiar with the Belt and Road construction initiative put forward by China. Europe's perception of the Belt and Road Initiative is both positive and negative. The analysis of the perception of well-known European think tanks of the Belt and Road Initiative carried out by a Shanghai scholar, Associate Professor Mao Xinya, also supports this judgment.

Regarding the positive perception, some people recognize the importance of the Belt and Road Initiative for the development of China, Europe and the countries along the Belt and Road, as well as the importance of regional cooperation for regional economic development and regional peace and stability—European integration itself is the model of regional cooperation, and they recognize the importance of infrastructures for economic development—Juncker's Plan largely calls for investments in European infrastructures.

Concerning the negative perception, some European people cast doubts on the Belt and Road Initiative advocated by China, mainly because: (1) they believe that the Belt and Road Initiative is the embodiment of economic diplomacy focusing on China's interests; (2) the Belt and Road Initiative is of geopolitical significance, and will trigger geopolitical conflicts; (3) the Belt and Road Initiative will destroy the unified mechanism of the EU; (4) the mechanism of the Belt and Road Initiative is non-transparent; (5) the construction of the Belt and Road will be subject to many difficulties and it is impossible to achieve success in its construction.

The above views reflect not only the differences in European think tanks' perception of the Belt and Road Initiative, but also the different perception of the Belt and Road by different European institutions and countries. Overall, the EU shows a certain amount of support for the Belt and Road Initiative, as mainly evidenced by the fact that the EU hopes that this Initiative can be connected to Juncker's European Plan; however, the EU is relatively cautious about the Belt and Road Initiative. For the EU member states, the support for and participation in the Belt and Road Initiative mainly comes from central and eastern European countries;however, they mainly maintain that the Belt and Road is an initiative for serving China's diplomatic strategy, thus they believe that China is willing to pay the price for its own diplomatic strategy and will provide funds for infrastructure connectivity and other infrastructure construction in the countries along the Belt and Road. Meanwhile, they also cast certain doubts on the geopolitical impact of the Belt and Road Initiative put forward by China.

Knowledge and perception will largely determine Europe's actions regarding the Belt and Road Initiative. If Europe considers it as a strategy focusing on China's interests, it will be impossible for Europe to fully support its construction. In order to further develop China-Europe relations through the Belt and Road, the two sides need to communicate more in order to strengthen a common understanding and perception of the Belt and Road Initiative.

2. China and Europe's Interaction in the Construction of the Belt and Road

Cognition is merely one aspect of the matter. A correct understanding is only the first step of promoting favorable development of international relations. The beneficial development of international relations also depends upon many other factors. As mentioned by Joseph Nye, why do countries often choose not to cooperate even though they all recognize that cooperation is beneficial? This involves a complicated philosophical issue: The relationship between cognition and action. However, cognition is generally favorable to action, while the result of action is beneficial for further cognition. In the case of various perceptions or cognitive uncertainties, action helps guide, confirm or reinforce the direction of cognition.

The Belt and Road is an initiative involving a number of areas and tens of countries. It exerts a major impact on the regions involved, the countries along the Belt and Road,and even on global relations. The construction of the Belt and Road and its impact on national relations cannot be determined by one country. Besides the impact of the Belt and Road Initiative itself, the interactions involving the Belt and Road among the international players exert a great influence on bilateral relations and, more extensively,on international relations. China-Europe interactions will have great effects on the construction of the Belt and Road and future China-Europe relations.

The interactions take various forms, including cooperation, observing, competition, objection and destruction. As indicated by Europe's reaction till now, China and Europe have engaged in a certain amount of interactionregarding the Belt and Road Initiative. Overall, thoseinteractionshave been positive, but close cooperation has not yet been achieved, and different internationalEuropean players show differentcharacteristicswhen interacting with China on the construction of the Belt and Road with respect to different matters. For example, there are the following differences:

1. At the EU level, China and Europe have not yet developed a comprehensive and integrated mechanism for cooperation on the construction of the Belt and Road. However, both China and Europe have expressed the willingness to enable some kind of connection and cooperation between Juncker's Plan and the Belt and Road Initiative. The priority of cooperation lies in investments in Europe, including infrastructures and long-term investments. However, China-Europe cooperation does not include the cooperation involving other regions other than Europe;it is limited to EU.

2. Some EU member states have joined the AIIB (Asian Infrastructure Investment Bank) and are jointly committed to investing and improving Asia's infrastructures. This shows that China and Europe have reached some consensus on the demand and prospects of Asia's infrastructure.

3. Some EU member states and other European countries have signed memoranda of cooperation or cooperation framework agreements for the Belt and Road Initiative with China, and have actively engaged in cooperation on projects and other relevant cooperation activities. These countries are mainly central and eastern European countries, suggesting that they recognize the Belt and Road Initiative advocated by China to some extent, and they have actively participated in its concrete construction. However, it should also be noted that thecooperationbetweencentral and eastern European countries and China mainly includes bilateral cooperation with these countries, and sometimes it involves regional cooperation in the central and eastern Europe.

Overall, the interactions between China and Europe on the Belt and Road Initiative are beneficial and active; they mainly involve bilateral cooperation between China and some central and eastern European countries, and there are interactions with the EU as a whole on limited matters.

3. Possibilities of the Future Impact of the Belt and Road Initiative on China-Europe Relations

As mentioned above, there are diversities and differences in cognition, so many methods of interaction are available. There are different interaction modes in reality.The impact of the Belt and Road Initiative on the future China-Europe relations is uncertain—it will not necessarily lead to further development nor to the deterioration of China-Europe relations; there are many possibilities. Which possibility will become reality? This largely hinges on the choices made by China and Europe, and it is affected by the practical results of the construction of the Belt and Road. External factors are too complicated, so those possibilities discussed here are by only considering the combination of cognition and interaction.

Several possibilities are as follows:

1. Active cognition + cooperative interaction: the Belt and Road Initiative provides a platform for cooperation and an opportunity for the further development of China-Europe relations; it further reinforces and boosts the development of a comprehensive strategic partnership between China and Europe.

If China and Europe reach a certain consensus regarding the goal, contents and active impact of the Belt and Road Initiative, and Europe recognizes the active effect from its construction as advocated by China on regional development,the mutual benefits and win-win results from that construction, and Europe is willing to be jointly dedicated to the construction of the Belt and Road, the Belt and Road Initiative will offer a new opportunity and an important platform for the development of both China and Europe. It will deliver win-win outcomes concerning the following aspects: (1) promoting the achievement of the construction and developmental goals of China and Europe throughconstructingthe infrastructures in central and eastern Europe and intensifying the production capacity cooperation between China and Europe; (2) reinforcing the development of Eurasia and Africa, promoting regional stability through regional economic development and prosperity, and providing the foundation and strong impetus for regional economic cooperation; (3) boosting communication and mutual learning among vast areas in Asia, Europe and Africa, the construction of a community with a common destiny through the construction of the Belt and Road so as to push forward regional peace and stability, and on this basis, cope with many major crises in the current international community, such as terrorism, the refugee problem and regional conflicts; (4) further stimulating the formation of multilateral and multipolar international patterns jointly advocated by China and Europe. If these achievements can be made, a comprehensive strategic partnership between China and Europe will be further developed.

2. A negative perception and confrontational interaction: The Belt and Road Initiative will lead to the development of negative relations between China and Europe.

In this case, Europe considers the Belt and Road Initiative as a geopolitical strategy of China for exerting a negative impact on Europe, thus Europe takes negative, even confrontational, measures to offset China's geo-strategic goal;this exists in the opinion of Europe. This is the worst case scenario regarding the impact of the Belt and Road Initiative on China-Europe relations. In this case, China and Europe cannot cooperate on the Belt and Road Initiative; the achievements which have been made through the cooperation of China and Europe will be affected;the goal of the Belt and Road Initiative advocated by China is difficult to achieve; the distrust and confrontation among regions might be exacerbated, thus aggravating the problems in Eurasia and on the African Continent.

3. Other combinations of perception and interaction besides the above two cases: There are many possibilities between complete recognition of and complete refusal to recognize the Belt and Road Initiative advocated by China, between complete cooperation and confrontational interaction. The future impact on China-Europe relations varies according to the different combinations.

Overall, if China and Europe become more consistent in their knowledge and perception, show more coordination, support and cooperation in interaction, it will be more likely that China-Europe relations will be further deepened and expanded, and the relations between the two sides will become closer. However, in these cases, there are differences in cognition, and both cooperation and negative interaction exist, and China-Europe relations will witness a mixture of development and friction. The specific cases involving development and friction will depend upon the extent and nature of the differences in cognition, the extent, scope and nature of cooperation and confrontation in interaction.

The reaction from Europe up until now shows that the scenario belongs to the third possibility regarding the impact of the Belt and Road on China-Europe relations. The contents of the Belt and Road Initiative are complicated and the future operation is uncertain, thus there may be different perspectives and views about the same things; it is unlikely that Europe will completely recognize the Belt and Road Initiative advocated by China and engage in all-round cooperation in the foreseeable future. However, the priority of the Belt and Road Initiative consists in building connectivity and promoting regional cooperation and development, which conforms to the general trend of the development and cooperation within the international community, and Europe has no special reason to oppose the Belt and Road Initiative; therefore, in general, the impact of the Belt and Road Initiative on China-Europe relations should be positive and active. It should provide new opportunities and possibilities for China-Europe cooperation.

However, in order to turn the Belt and Road Initiative into a new platform for China-Europe cooperation and a new opportunity for boosting the development of China-Europe relations, many things still need to be done. In particular:

(1) Communication must be further enhanced, and China and Europe's consensus on the Belt and Road must be expanded so that both sides seek more common points in perception.Communication and agreement on cognition must be made possible in order to dispel Europe's misgivings about the Belt and Road Initiative, and the negative impact, from the differences in and misunderstandings of cognition, must be reduced or avoided in the policies and actions of both sides. The most important

thing during the initial stage of the construction of the Belt and Road is to ensure that the differences in cognition do not become barriers to bilateral cooperation since the relations between the two sides cannot be based on disagreements in and incorrect cognition of the Belt and Road. If there are differences between the two sides regarding cognition, at least the Belt and Road must not be completely denied because of those differences, and enough room for cooperation should be reserved for the construction of the Belt and Road and for China-Europe cooperation on it. The issue of cognition should be gradually addressed in practice.

(2) Common points in action and policy must be gradually sought after, and the cooperation between the two sides must be progressively expanded in the construction of the Belt and Road. Cooperation must not be limited to that between China and Europe and should be gradually extended to the whole construction of the Belt and Road;moreover, it is necessary to deepen the cognition of the Belt and Road during cooperation, as well as to jointly promote the active roles of the Belt and Road in all aspects of regional development.

(3) The differences in the cognition of the two sides must be gradually eliminated through practice so as to further expand the cooperation between the two sides in the construction of the Belt and Road, so that cognition and cooperation give rise to a virtuous cycle. If there are differences between the two sides regarding cognition, merely relying on communication and dialogue concerning cognition is not enough because uncertainties will always exist. Only practice and the result of practice can dispel the misgivings about and disagreements on the Belt and Road Initiative. Cognition promotes cooperation, while cooperation further boosts cognition.

Overall, there is a huge space for cooperation between China and Europe on the construction of the Belt and Road. Europe has misgivings about the Belt and Road, but Europe is advancing in the direction of cooperation.

I believe that, with the gradual construction of the Belt and Road, the contributions from the Belt and Road Initiative put forward by China to regional development will gradually emerge, and China's sincerity in pushing forward regional cooperation and development and the effectiveness of the Belt and Road will also gradually become evident, while Europe's misgivings about the Belt and Road will be gradually removed. In this process, China and Europe will realize that cooperation is beneficial for developing China, Europe and the whole region of Asia, Europe and Africa, and thus for promoting the development of the global economy. Therefore, I believe that China-Europe relations will have a bright future in the long term.

西班牙与“一带一路”

维克多　【西班牙】
马德里弗朗西斯科德维多利亚大学中西关系中心　主任 / “知华讲堂”副主席

西班牙人对于“一带一路”倡议的理解略有不同。我们对“一带一路”的看法是，中国希望欧洲积极参与“一带一路”，西班牙有自己的特征，同时也是作为欧洲有自己的特征，对我们来说“一带一路”将改变世界地缘政治，我想对我们来说是有很多的含义的。“一带一路”意味着欧洲和中国又有了一个共同的文化的项目或者是共同的目标。如果一切顺利的话，我们有机会改变历史。

在西班牙，我们非常重视“一带一路”。在推进中，我们各个部门加强合作，包括经济领域、学术界和政界。在政界，我们跟各个党派合作，不管哪个政党当权都要落实这个项目。我们的政体决定执政的政府是期限不长，但是“一带一路”合作却是一个长期项目。我们不能够把这个项目只看作关于中国的项目，应该看作造福所有人的项目，我们持开放的态度，我们也需要跟年轻人加强沟通。因为年轻人是中坚力量，我们也准备召开一些国际的会议，在会议上来探讨这些问题。

“一带一路”是一个全球性的项目，它不光会影响沿线国家的商业经济，同时也将带来社会和文化方面的影响。我觉得第二点影响可能更加重要，更长久，也就是说文化的影响比经济的影响更重。所以我想，面对这样的现实，大家都应该积极地参与。那么现在已经提出很多与此相关的项目。一开始，它是经济的影响，但是也是一个发展友谊和促进合作的项目。

习主席说过这是一个伟大的项目，在“一带一路”沿路国家将会产生重大积极影响。古时候的“丝绸之路”，如今全新的“一带一路”，这对于任何想参与的人都是一个巨大的机遇，未来的几年我们将看到这个历史性项目再次振兴，在经济投资、基础设施建设方面将带来巨大影响。对所有的参与人都会带来积极的影响，增加社会的正义，同时还可以打造一个合作的环境。“合作”、“福祉”、“和平”，所以西班牙希望参加这个项目。

我们领导人非常重视中国的作用，他们希望能够和中国加强合作和友谊，我们的合作友谊可以说40年前就开始了。

西班牙在传统的“丝绸之路”是目的地之一，或者说是“丝绸之路”最后的一个目的地。西班牙有很多的城市受到“丝绸之路”的影响，使西班牙同中国直接进行合作，和整个亚洲大陆进行合作。同时中国也希望当有公司到西班牙来投资时，能得到西班牙的支持。比如说在财务、电讯和可持续能源使用方面，西班牙有自己独特的优势。而且中国领导人说“我们可以通过铁路运输，源源不断地把义乌的商品运送到西班牙马德里的市场”。有关瓦伦西亚开始的海上丝绸之路，它们保持得很好，而且保持古老丝绸的市场，这个港口一直在开放，它不光是丝绸之路的最末端的目的地，同时也是一个很好的桥梁。

我们讲到大西洋之路也很近。因为西班牙是通往拉丁美洲一个重要的枢纽。

我们讲到地面交通和铁路运输的时候，马德里就是很好的枢纽，中国和西班牙首都之间的飞机航班数量增加了很多。我们举办研讨会来促成中西之间的贸易合作，像马德里一样，瓦伦西亚举办了许多国际会议，抓住机会，因为瓦伦西亚是非常重要的城市。在5、6个月之后，瓦伦西亚的负责人会访问中国来协商双方的合作开展。

因此西班牙不仅是“丝绸之路”的目的地，同时也是一个桥梁，是通向欧洲其他地方的桥梁，也是通向北非和南美的一个桥梁。

为什么呢？因为我们处于一个重大的战略和地缘政治上的重要地位。我们跟拉丁美洲和北非有着很强的文化联系，也是有很多方便游客的线路，还有商务方面的活动、国际交流等。西班牙是世界上较早同中国建立外交关系的西方国家之一，并且在国际交流方面非常活跃。而且我们需要进一步加大这种交流的力度，让更多的人知道“一带一路”。有必要让老师和年轻人更多地了解“一带一路”，增加有关出版物方面的交流，交流不光是学术界的事情，而是使更多人贴近“一带一路”这个项目。

Spain and the Belt Road Initiative

Víctor Cortizo Rodríguez / Spain

Director of the Center for China-Spain Relations at the Francisco de Vitoria University in Madrid /Vice-president of "Cátedra China"

The vision that we have in Spain of this initiative is a bit different. Those of us who are friends of China want and encourage the participation in this project. Spain has its own, unique identity but it is European as well.

For us, the new vision of the silk route, which was once something of the past and has now become a new project that will change the geopolitical vision of the world, is more difficult.

This initiative means that for the first time Europe and China can share a common project, a common objective. Our countries need to work together and we have an opportunity to change history…

In Spain we are busy with the aim of creating interest in this initiative, as well as discovering our role in it. To do this we are working with all important sectors regarding this project: economic, academic and also political. In the political sector we work with all parties to ensure that this project is for all and does not depend on any current political party in power.

Our democracy, as all Western Democracies, thinks short term and this project is long term. We have ensured that the political and economic leaders consider this initiative not as a strategy of China but also a proposal of mutual benefits. We want this proposal to be open to everyone in our countries and be valued positively by the entire society. This project needs to communicate with the young people for they are going to experience & live its development in a natural way in a world where the young are clearly living globalization.

We are beginning the preparations for an international congress about this initiative and we want to talk about all this issues.

The increase in commercial transactions by sea and air from the Indian Ocean to Europe via Mediterranean or Africa, causes a shift of investments in infrastructures to the south bound. In this sense, it shows a scenario of strengthening of new routes in detriment of the old ones and with an additional reinforcement of intra-Asian infrastructures toward AIIB.

In addition to the expansion of Chinese enterprises in the world under this scheme, another essential fact is the extension of renminbi-denominated trade (RMB). Its inclusion in the International Monetary Fund (IMF) under the Special Drawing Rights (its global reserve asset) sets the stage for gaining more share of the global payments market, currently at 2.79% according to SWIFT and the second largest currency used after the Japanese Yen. For Chinese companies, paying and investing in RMB is key to proper treasury management and reserve control.

Finally, one of the most controversial macroeconomic impacts of the Belt and Road is the decrease of Chinese foreign currency reserves. The "New Silk Road" finances its projects against internal reserves, which causes balance of payments reserves to suffer, and thus the RMB exchange rate against the USD depreciates. The financing via own resources causes confusion among investors and analysts, who pay attention to the possible costs of the People's Bank of China defence of the exchange rate.

In fact, the PBOC does not defend the exchange rate. By contrast, internationalization increases the demand for foreign currency against the national currency in relative terms. Therefore, the PBOC drains yuan in the form of domestic credit, increasing money supply via reserves. As international demand for RMB increases, the PBOC adjusts the pace of money creation to nominal demand.

The Belt and Road initiative is a world-wide dimension project, which is called to modified not only commercial routes but social and cultural movements too.There is not a nation who can stay off this reality and it is more necessary than ever to be present in an active way, proposing and acting.The initial vocation is economic, but it is also friendship and cooperation between nations, and as President Xi Jinping defined it at the end of 2013, “It is an extraordinary work of well-being creation in favour of people along their way.”

Even if the origin has been Central Asian, since the very beginning it has been understood as a huge possibility to anyone who wants to be a part of it.In the following years we will be able to see the construction of this historical project, which has in the economic investment and the infrastructure the most visible aspects. But it is also remarkable the all kind of exchanges, that will mean a positive influence from all the participants, an increase in social justice and above all a peaceful environment of cooperation.

Development, well-being, cooperation and Peace. Spain wants to be in this world-wide range project.Our leaders are concerned about the importance of China and they want to increase friendship and cooperation that began 40 years ago.Spain has been a destiny in the traditional silk route, the end of the journey, and there are still many cities around the country which proof their role in it. But we want Spain to be in the new route.This project will allow Spain a direct connection with China and the whole Asian continent. China also wants Spanish support to the Strip and Route Initiative and encourages their companies to invest in Spain, Xi said. He added that both parts may continue cooperating in fields as finances, telecommunications and sustainable energies, using their respective advantages to complement each other. In addition, the Chinese leader pointed out that both parts must increase their commerce by railway connection of merchandises that connects the city of Yiwu, in the oriental province of Zhejiang in China, with Madrid.

China also wants Spanish support to the Strip and Route Initiative and encourages their companies to invest in Spain, Xi said. He added that both parts may continue cooperating in fields as finances, telecommunications and sustainable energies, using their respective advantages to complement each other.

Relative to the ground and railway transport, Madrid already has a good communication, even if it is still reduced. Flights have grown a lot, like general communication relationships between China and the capital of Spain.

The great role of Spain in this is to be not only the destiny, but a bridge to the rest of Europe, to North Africa and to South America.

Why is Spain so important in the silk route? It is because Spain is in strategic geographic and geopolitical position and has influential cultural relationships with other countries in Latin America and North Africa. In addition, Spain is high level tourist receiver with growing importance. business and international communication dynamic, a country with a lot of exchanges and large diplomatic links.

It is necessary to increase swaps and group reflections, giving the chance to know about this initiative to more and more people and how far it can goes. Exchanges between young people and college teachers must be favoured, increase documentaries and publications, so they are not only available for high academy level, and they can be set closer to every country involved in this project.

Spain wants to be part of this great project and many initiatives are being developed to become an active part of this global project.

“一带一路”与国际格局

颂蓬　【泰国】
兰实大学外交与国际问题研究院　院长

引言

自中国国家主席习近平于2013年年底提出共建“一带一路”的合作倡议后，外界对中国动机的分析不外有两种：一种探讨地缘政治，分析作为崛起的中国与当前世界唯一的超级大国美国之间的势力平衡。中美两国间的竞争在亚太地区的表现最为明显。另外一种则着重中国国内的经济问题——中国正努力实现经济软着陆，同时缩小东部沿海城市与西部内陆城市间的差距，从而提高全国各地区人民的生活水平。

本文从国际政策和内部经济因素入手，指出在某些语境下，两个因素相互关联，通过分析20世纪80年代至21世纪10年代之间国际、区际发生的重大事件、中美及东南亚国家等关键参与方的发展情况，阐述这一时期内势力平衡的发展过程，以及对国际秩序造成的影响。

全球大事年表

20世纪80年代是冷战时期的最后十年，当时并没有人预计到冷战会在不远的将来结束。随着伊朗掀起革命浪潮，中东地区的冲突开始爆发。由于中苏冲突仍在持续，苏联的军队仍然驻扎阿富汗。然而，这一时期东亚国家的经济发展情况较为平稳，亚太经合组织的成立反映出各成员国协同合作、发展经济的决心。

当时美国的经济状势头良好，而中国则在邓小平的领导下，拉开了改革开放的序幕。在东南亚地区，越南侵略柬埔寨的问题引发周边各国高度关注，这促成了东盟国家与中国之间的紧密关系。

20世纪90年代，冷战结束，苏联解体，东欧及中亚地区多国实现了独立，世界格局的发展进入了一个新的阶段。随着海湾战争的爆发，美国对海湾地区进行的干预愈发深入。在经济方面，由最初的12个环太平洋国家成立的亚太经合组织逐步引起了一些重要经济体的兴趣，因而成员数量也增长至21个，其中包括三个观察员。由于东南亚国家从亚洲金融危机中汲取了教训，因此在2008年金融危机来袭时，各国在抵抗危机方面所做的准备更为充分。虽然美国在冷战后成为世界上唯一的超级大国，但仍然不断插手中东事务。

在江泽民主政期间，中国进行了体制改革，经济得以快速发展，城市化不断加深，中国人民解放军开启了现代化的进程。在这一时期内，中国成为东盟的全面对话伙伴。越南从柬埔寨（后改名为柬埔寨王国）撤军后，东南亚局势逐渐平稳。外商直接投资源源不断地涌入，在部分程度上促进了东南亚地区的经济发展。随着越南、老挝、缅甸、柬埔寨等国家先后加入，东盟的力量得到进一步增强。

进入21世纪后，世界格局的发展翻开了新的篇章。911恐怖袭击拉开了反恐战争及阿富汗战争的序幕（2001—2014）。非传统安全威胁不断增加。中俄在签署《中俄睦邻友好合作条约》后，两国关系变得更为紧密，但台海局势趋紧。

在胡锦涛主政期间，中国在外商直接投资、网络与空间、科学技术、经济以及外交等领域的实力均有提升。在这一时期内，中国加入了世贸组织，更于2001年成立了上海合作组织。同一年还发生了中国战斗机与美国侦察机相撞事件。解放军的现代化进程仍在持续，民族主义情绪开始在中国复苏。新疆发生的暴恐事件引起中国政府高度关注。中国与东盟国家签署《自由贸易协定》，双方成为战略合作伙伴。2002年，非典爆发，并扩散至整个亚洲。在这一时期内，中国通过对非投资和援助扩大了影响力。

与此同时，东盟的外交实力有所提升，经济一体化程度进一步提高，与非东盟国家的关系也不断加强。

21世纪的第一个十年里，世界面临着新的挑战：中国崛起、美国“重返亚太”、美俄在乌克兰问题上的冲突等，均引起世界各国的关注和忧虑。此外，欧盟的金融危机、移民危机以及英国脱欧等问题，从长远来看必将在全世界范围内引发忧虑。与此同时，伊斯兰国的恐怖势力已经蔓延到中东多个国家，这是全人类所面临的一个重大问题。

美国正面临总统选举、伊斯兰国问题、与俄罗斯的潜在冲突以及中国的崛起等严峻的挑战。

在习近平主席的领导下，中国在世界政治和经济领域的地位不断提升。中国的 GDP 已经超过美国，成为世界第二大经济体。中国在非洲和中东欧地区的影响更加明显。

尽管东盟对中国南海问题早有心理准备，但在中国南海问题上，依然面临着严峻的考验。2015 年底，东盟共同体正式成立。

自然格局

从以上列举的事件中可以看出，在国际体制中，区域间各个层级发生的事件以及世界政治主要参与者之间发生的事件，都是行为与反应所造成的自然结果，这种自然国际格局的背后是结果逻辑和适当性逻辑。在国际地位和外交政策的形成过程中，国家利益是至关重要的。

过去四十年中的大事反映出全球各国、各国人民之间的理解和合作得到进一步增强，彼此间的交流不断增多。目前为止，全世界大多地区都沉浸在这种合作的氛围之中，尽管仍有少数区域仍然处于战乱之中。总体而言，各国的生活水平得到了全面提高，消灭贫困的斗争取得了进一步的胜利。

泰国与中国的关系也不例外。两国的关系主要受到外部和内部因素的影响。近年来，中泰两国的合作关系和相互理解一直不断增强，贸易额大幅提升，各级交流访问也愈发频繁，总体而言，两国的关系得到了大幅度的提升。

“一带一路”与东盟互联互通

2009 年，《东盟互联互通总体规划》出台，对 2011 至 2015 年期间的具体工作进行了部署。对于泰国而言，这一规划使得湄公河次区域的联通工程得到了广泛的关注。尽管泰国与东盟多年前便开始了这项工程的实施，但进展始终非常缓慢，主要原因在于，大部分精力都放在了缩小贫富差距上。为了进一步推进东盟成员国之间的互联互通，东盟刚刚制定并发布了《东盟互联互通总体规划 2025》，对 2016 年至 2025 年的实施工作进行了部署和安排。

“一带一路”倡议与“东盟互联互通”之间具有绝佳的互补性，从总体上来说，东盟绝大多数国家对中国“一带一路”倡议的反应都非常积极。东盟国家深深地了解“一带一路”工程的伟大之处。简单地说，经济发展需要基础设施，更需要双边经贸，但从更深层的角度来看，几千年来，东南亚国家和中国在文化、信仰、价值观等层面都具有相当程度的共通性。精神层面的因素能够促进双方更好的相互理解，加强东盟与中国的双边合作。经过仔细研究后会发现，“一带一路”与“东盟互联互通”不仅在形式——基础设施方面，在原则和理念层面更也存在着诸多共性。两者都具备相当程度的灵活性、包容性、开放性，都注重磋商和对话，注重彼此的国家利益、注重国家应该承担的责任。因此，东盟与中国必须在这种共通性的基础上开展合作，进一步推进相关工程和项目。在双方努力下取得的成果有助于保障区域安全、优化经济结构，更有助于提高人类的生活水平，构建人与自然的和谐。

结语

相关各方之间应彼此增进理解，为实现最终共同的目标而努力。可以说本次座谈会便是为相互理解而做出的榜样和示范。因此，我要向中国政府及相关部门，特别是中国文化部和社会科学院表示感谢，预祝各方做出的努力最终取得圆满成功。

The Belt and Road and International Structure

Sompong Sanguanbun / Thailand

Dean of the Institute of Diplomacy and International Studies at Rangsit University

Introduction

When the Belt and Road Initiative initially launched in late 2013, there were two analyses of China's motivation behind this idea. One is concerning geopolitics, the balance of power between China, as a rising power, and the U.S., the existing sole dominant power. Such a rivalry between the two has apparently been felt in the Asia-Pacific region. The other is concerning Chinese domestic economic problems as China has been trying to bring its economy to a soft landing manner as well as to narrow the gap between eastern coast cities and inner cities in the western part, and hence elevate a better living standard for the unfortunate throughout the country.

This paper focuses on two elements mentioned above, namely international politics and internal economic reasons, which are interrelated under certain contexts, by introducing significant events that occurred at both global and regional levels, including developments in key players, namely the U.S., China and Southeast Asian nations, from the 1980s to 2010s, with a view to demonstrating the developments of the balance of power and their impact on the international structure during the said period.

Timelines of Global Events

In the 1980s the world witnessed the final decade of the Cold War, without knowing in advance that it would end in a not-too-long future. The conflict in the Middle East flared-up because of the Iranian Revolution. Sino-Soviet Conflict continued. Soviet troops remained in Afghanistan. However, East Asian countries had done well with their economies, and the Asia-Pacific Economic Cooperation emerged, reflecting the determination of member states to advance their economies by working together.The U.S. was doing well with her economy. China, under the guidance of Deng Xiaoping, was at the beginning of reform process, which, partly, led to the Tiananmen Square protests in 1989. In Southeast Asia, issue of Vietnamese occupation of Kampuchea was high on the agenda of countries in the region. This led to a close relationship between ASEAN and China.

The 1990s witnessed a new era because of the end of Cold War and the collapse of the Soviet Union, which consequently brought about independence to several countries in Eastern Europe and Central Asia. The incident of the Gulf War did tie the U.S. involvement in the region deeper. On the economic front, the Asia-Pacific Economic Cooperation (APEC), a prominent economic cooperation forum among Pacific rim countries which was established in 1989 by twelve members initially, had increasingly drawn interest from important economies and therefore expanded its membership to more than twenty economies. The lessons of the Asian Financial Crisis had taught Southeast Asia countries to be more prepared and able to withstand against the 2008 financial crisis.The U.S. has become a single dominant power, but continued to be preoccupied with problems in the Middle East.

China, under Jiang Zemin, was underwent institutional reform and enjoying fast growing economy. Urbanization has increased, while public protests expanded in rural areas. The modernization of the PLA began. China became a full Dialogue

Partner of ASEAN. The situation in Southeast Asia was stabilized as a result of the withdrawal of Vietnamese troops from Kampuchea (later renamed the Kingdom of Cambodia). Foreign Direct Investment continued to pour into the region which partly helped develop their economies. ASEAN position has been strengthened with new members, Vietnam, Laos, Myanmar and Cambodia joined in respectively.

In 2000s the world witnessed another chapter because of the incident of the 9 September terrorist attack on New York which led to the beginning of the War on Terror, the Afghanistan War (2001-2014). Non-traditional security threats have been intensified. Sino-Russian relations become closer as the two signed an important document, Twenty Years Treaty of Friendship and Cooperation. Tension across the Taiwan Strait occurred.

China, under Hu Jintao's leadership, witnessed strength in several areas, including FDI, internet and space science, economy and foreign affairs. China became a member of WTO. Shanghai Cooperation Organization was founded in 2001. The U.S.-China mid-air collision took place in 2001. Modernization of the PLA continued. The revival of nationalism emerged across the country. Xinjiang violence caused a major concern to the Chinese authorities. China signed an agreement on FTA with ASEAN, and both sides become Strategic Partnership. SARS epidemic spread throughout Asia. China expanded its influence, through investment and assistance, in Africa.

ASEAN's diplomacy performance has been enhanced. Its economic integration has been strengthened further, including connection with non-ASEAN nations.

The 2010s is experiencing a new challenging scenarios, namely the rise of China and the U.S. pivot toward Asia-Pacific. The U.S.-Russia confrontation over Ukraine also concerned the world. Another crisis that caused concern around the globe in the long run is the European Union crisis of financial and migration issues as well as the Brexit. The ISIS fighting has spread into several countries in the Middle East. This is another major concern for humankind.

The U.S. is also facing vital challenging moment. The presidential election, ISIS issues, potential further conflict with Russia, and China's rise.

China, under Xi Jinping's leadership, seems to enjoy increasing status both politically and economically. Her GDP surpassed of the U.S. and become the second largest world economy. Chinese presence in Africa and Central/Eastern Europe are more apparent.

ASEAN faced a challenging issue of South China Sea, even thought it was expected and therefore prepared for it to happen. The ASEAN Community has officially commenced at the end of 2015.

Natural Developments

The above scenarios have demonstrated that, under the international system, the interconnection between events in various regions at different levels and interactions among significant players in world politics occurred according to natural course of actions and reactions. Natural patterns in the international system are the logic of consequences and the logic of appropriateness. National domestic interests are also vital to the process of shaping one's foreign positions/policies.

The situations during the past four decades mentioned above reflect a better understanding, a growing cooperation as well as a more exchanges amongst countries/peoples around the globe. So far the world, except in certain areas, has enjoyed cooperation atmosphere, as there are a small number of war between states and more integration in various forms regionally. Living conditions have improved all over, poverty eradication has been advanced.

The relationship between Thailand and China is no exception. The level of the relationship depends on both external and internal factors. Thailand and China have enjoyed a closer cooperation atmosphere, a better mutual understanding, volume of trade has increased tremendously, the exchanges of visit have increased at all levels. The relationship of the two is improving substantially.

Belt and Road and ASEAN Connectivity

The Master Plan of ASEAN Connectivity was first officially inaugurated in 2009 covering the period between 2011 and 2015. In addition, as far as Thailand is concerned, it has also given attention to connectivity projects in a smaller area, the so-called Mekong sub-region. Although Thailand and ASEAN have taken this Connectivity Plan into action for many years, the progress has been moving slowly, due to the fact that they have paid much attention to the objective of narrowing the gap between the haves and haves not. However, in order to advance the connectivity among member states further, ASEAN has just commenced a Master Plan of ASEAN Connectivity 2025 covering the period between 2016 and 2025.

The Belt and Road Initiative is a perfect complement to the said ASEAN Connectivity. Generally speaking, the majority of ASEAN members welcome China's Belt and Road Initiative. ASEAN understands this grand strategy very well. The simple reason is that economic development needs infrastructure and trading with each other. In addition , there are more profound reasons that explain better, namely culture, belief, faith, and values that Southeast Asian nations and China have commonly upheld in their societies for thousands years. This spiritual elements that help promote a better mutual understanding and enhance mutual cooperation between ASEAN and China. And when study deeper, there are similarities of the Belt and Road Initiative and ASEAN Connectivity not only in the form of physical infrastructure, but also in their principles. There are elements of flexibility, inclusiveness, openness, consultations, dialogue, caring and sharing both interests and responsibilities.

Both ASEAN and China must, therefore, cooperate in this connection to advance all projects concerned. Tangible results of these efforts will help secure or even advance our security and economic structures that conducive to a better living standards for human beings as well as a harmonious situation between humans and nature.

Conclusion

We need to promote cooperation and mutual understanding among all concerned parties, with a view to achieving our common ultimate goals. This kind of exercise we are conducting at this Symposium is the case in point. I, therefore, commend the Chinese government and concerned authorities, in particular Ministry of Culture and the Chinese Academy of Social Sciences and wish them all the success in their endeavors.

理解“一带一路”

任琳 【中国】
中国社会科学院世界经济与政治研究所国际战略研究室　副主任

杭州峰会为大家提供了一个了解“一带一路”重要性的机会。杭州 20 国峰会的平台使“一带一路”得到很好的宣传，使互通互联的概念得到很好的阐述。通过杭州 20 国峰会，中国展示了落实“一带一路”的坚强决心。而且 20 国峰会宣布了很多实际的措施。比如说衡量基础投资指数，每三年会有一个评估，之后对基础设施建设做一个评估和检查等。落实措施中最关键的是经济合作。

理解“一带一路”，我想与大家分享三个关键词

关键词一：互通互联

目前全球经济出现衰退，世界需要处理诸如经济发展和增长等中长期问题。现在世界关注的不是经济放缓，因为世界经济发展速度还没有到最低的时候，关键是我们一定要制定适当的战略，比如说短期的政策。有些发达国家喜欢用短期赤字措施，但这一措施已经被证明效果不好，而且还产生了一些负面效果。在这种情况下，中国提出“一带一路”倡议，我认为非常好。这一倡议不一定是唯一解决困境的方法，但我觉得是一个选项，能够帮助我们解决问题。

“一带一路”意味着不仅是基础设施的互通互联，同时是文化和社会的互通互联，互通互联强调了命运共同体，因为我们现在面临的是全球的问题，需要全球的战略来解决这个问题。没有一个国家能够单打独斗来解决某个全球性的问题。

互通互联也意味着通过资源的优化来分享中国产业产出方面的最佳实践，来推动文明的建设。

“一带一路”倡议是长期的一个战略。多长？这可能需要一代、两代甚至三代人的努力。为了提高资源配置效率、促进经济发展，“一带一路”更关注结构改革，国内外、跨区域的发展。

关键词二：活力再振兴

首先是通过技术革新带来新的活力。历史上每一项进步都离不开科技的进步，尤其是每一次工业革命之后。现在世界经济比较虚弱，最新技术的推动力削弱了，而且这方面已经失去了动力。但是我觉得科技作为一个世界经济的推手是不可替代的。

其次，我们不仅要寻找新的活力源泉，要建设一个健康、充满活力、可持续发展的世界经济，更要发挥贸易和投资（特别是基础设施投资）的潜力，使其成为经济增长的发动机，为寻找合作模式创新带来经济增长。我们需要找到新的经济增长驱动力，不仅是在“一带一路”的地区，同时在别的地区也要推动经济的发展。

第三，在每一个层次上激活地方经济增长活力，而不是单纯依靠等待模式。“一带一路”需要政府与市场之间的平衡。它鼓励市场力量的创新，如PPP要求公众和私营部门的智慧。“一带一路”是主动的（而不是一个完成的计划），目标在一个包容、相互连接的解决方案，以结构改革的战略，对我们面临的全球性问题和挑战。一项倡议意味着它不是最终计划和单向方式，而是一个开放项目，欢迎更多支持性的想法和经验。

最后，激活世界经济需要更好的制度环境，一个开放的、公平的、中立的全球治理秩序或机制，而不是保护主义，排他性和非中性。英国脱欧提醒我们，贸易保护主义存在反全球化的事实。

关键词三：包含、包容

关键词包容在这里有两层含义。一是包容性发展，二是机构参与的包容性。

“一带一路”倡议实现了两个目标，“一带一路”增加了信息经济的重要性，通过国内地区间和全球的互通互联，目的之一是消除贫困，目的之二是包容性的参与。

“一带一路”也是促进包容性在制度中的超越之路。伴随着“一带一路”倡议，中国2013年提出亚投行并于2016年初正式运行，成员国包括来自亚洲、欧洲、非洲、美洲和大洋洲的57个创始成员国。它致力于进一步完善现有的全球金融治理机制，并考虑发展中国家等的融资需要。

我们有个良好的希望，希望“一带一路”有良好的预期，有光明的未来。

Understanding the Belt and Road

Ren Lin / China

Deputy Director of the Research Section of International Strategy of the Institute of World Economy and Politics, CASS

1ST Key Word: transformation

At this moment, the global economic downturn appears, the world needs to deal with mid-long term issues, such as economic development and growth. The world wide cautious of the global economy is not due to the low growth rate (since it does not hit the lowest point in history), but because the global policy basket has been unable to find any strategies to cope with the given situation, since the short-term monetary stimulation preferred by the U.S. and Japan turns out to be helpless and even have side effects. In this given situation, the Belt and Road is a correspondent coping strategy initiated by China, which transforms from short-term stimulation to long-term structural reform. It is also the China scheme or pharmacy of global economic governance. the Belt and Road is an initiated and long-term approach. How long? While, It may take 1,2,3 generations. the Belt and Road concerns structure reform, domestic, cross-regional, and international, in order to enhance efficiency of resource allocation and promote economic development.

2nd Key Word: Invigorative

1stly, ask for vitality from technology innovation. Every leap of the world economy in the human history cannot be separated from the great progress of science and technology after each industrial revolution.

Current world economy is weak. One of the important reasons is driving force of the latest technological innovation has been losing effectiveness and invalid, but not there is no timely manner to replace it as a new drive. Therefore, in order to achieve the goal of reviving the world economy, we need to get started with technological innovation.

2ndly, seek for growth from the innovation of growth and cooperation mode. we not only need to find new sources of vitality, to build a healthy and vibrant and sustainable growth of the world economy, to stimulate the potential of trade and investment (especially infrastructure investment) as the engine of economic growth. But also, we need to seek for the innovation of cooperation model and growth mode. For example, trade deficit sometimes prohibits cooperation, since it is not an even division of a cake model in the classical game theory. Establishing special economic zones (SEZ) locally at the target country is a way out of the trap. It shares experience of SEZ operation, which serves as one of multiple ways to reduce trade deficit, since the products producing in SEZ could export to China and the world.

3rdly, activate the local vitality of economic growth at each level, rather than solely relying on the wait on to model. the Belt and Road needs to balance between market and government. It encourages innovation of market force, such as PPP calls for the wisdom both from the public and the private sectors. the Belt and Road is an initiative (instead of a finalized project) that targets at an inclusive and inter-connective solution, with the idea of structure reform, to the global issues and challenges that we are confronting with. An initiative means that it is not a finalized plan and one-side manner, but an open project that welcomes more supportive ideas and experience.

Last but not the least, invigorative world economy requires preferable institutional environment, which is an open, fair and neutral order or institutions of global governance, instead of protectionism, exclusiveness and non-neutrality. Brexit reminds the world of the fact that protectionism exists as one anti-globalization forces. G20 Hangzhou summits expresses that G20 is against protectionism.

3rd Key Word: Inclusiveness

G20 promotes Inclusiveness. Inclusiveness has two meanings. The 1st one is inclusive development; while the 2nd one is inclusive institutions. the Belt and Road fulfills these two meanings.

1stly, Belt and Road increases focus on emerging and developing countries; tends to enhance their ability to resist risks; wants to restart trade and investment as the new engine of global economic growth; pays attention to inclusive and inter-connective development domestically and regionally, eliminates poverty. The content bears the spirit of interconnection and inclusivity.

2ndly, the Belt and Road promotes inclusive institution among and beyond the road. Accompanying the Belt and Road, Asia infrastructure investment bank proposed by China in 2013, officially opened in early 2016, includes 57 intention founding member countries from Asia, Europe, Africa, America and Oceania. It devotes to further improve the existing global financial governance mechanism, and taking into account the financing needs of countries, such as developing countries.

中国道路与共同价值

China's Route and Common Value

西方的政治学与中国传统政治思想：从忽略到认同

尤锐　【以色列】
以色列希伯来大学人文学院　副院长

我从 20 世纪 90 年代初开始涉及中国思想史的研究，但在很长一段时期内都感到很困惑，不知道自己归属于什么学术专业。先秦思想史在西方学术界基本上属于“中国哲学”的范围，研究者主要从西方哲学角度来对其进行分析，但我本身对西方哲学并不感兴趣，所以也不太愿意自称是在研究“中国哲学史”。1994 年我在南开大学留学时见到刘泽华先生及先生的弟子们，第一次听说还有“中国政治思想史”这个题目，如醍醐灌顶，从此以后我就以“中国政治思想史”为自己的学术专业了。1996 年我到美国洛杉矶加州大学留学，之后参加了许多在欧美举办的学术会议，跟欧美的各位同仁的关系都很密切，在接触中发现他们大多对“中国传统政治思想”（traditional Chinese political thought）、“中国传统政治文化”（traditional Chinese political culture）都不感兴趣，而在那个时候甚至这些概念在欧美学术界都是极为罕见的。

西方学者对中国古代思想的政治内涵的忽略是令人费解的。其实无论我们如何去理解中国古代思想，其中明显的政治趋向都是难以否认的。中国古代思想家所讨论的题目——如君权的本质、国家的起源及其必然性、君臣关系、统治者与老百姓之间的关系、知识分子（即士人）的政治任务及政治机能等——这些本来都属于世界政治思想的核心内容。诸子百家的政治思想，无论是从其视野的广度、多元化及丰富程度，或从其对当时与后世的政治文化的影响上看，都明显地超越了世界上任何其他的传统政治思想。如果我们把中国跟其他所谓的“轴心时代（Axial age）”的文明相比较[1]，则可以得出以下结论：尽管中国传统思想从哲学理论角度或者从神学角度比不了古印度、希腊、波斯或者希伯来文明，但是从政治及社会思想的丰富角度则可以说超越了这些文明，足以跟现代欧洲多元化的政治思想相媲美。

然而为什么西方学者会忽略中国传统政治思想呢？为了回答这个问题我首先要集中阐述西方（主要是美国）的汉学家对中国古代思想的态度，此后将分析西方的政治学家为何会忽略中国古代的政治思想，最后要讨论为什么最近几年中国古代政治思想开始引起西方学者的注意，及其对西方政治学的潜在价值。

一　西方的汉学家及其“哲学偏见”

20 世纪 70 年代在中国大陆爆发的“批林批孔”运动对西方学术界具有相当大的影响。由于以江青为核心的“极左”派宣传“儒法斗争贯彻古今，也表现在共产党内”等思潮[2]，许多西方学者想要更深刻地了解中国传统思想的政治内涵，因此在那个时候西方汉学界开始对中国传统的思想比较关注。

例如，Sebastian de Grazia 把自己所出版的诸子百家文选叫《中国政治思想的诸子》（*Masters of Chinese Political Thought*），而牟复礼（Frederick W. Mote）则在同一时期翻译了萧公权的《中国政治思想史》第一卷[3]。对于中国古代思想史研究的政治化的最突出的代表是苏联的反共学者鲁宾（Vitaly Rubin）。鲁宾教授的《古代中国的个人与国家》（*Individual and State in Ancient China*）是“批林批孔”思潮的倒置：对他来说墨子和商鞅代表着左派及右派的全权主义，庄子代表着反

1　“轴心时代”是德国学者 Karl Jaspers（雅斯贝尔斯）所提出的概念，来解释公元前 800- 公元前 200 年间欧亚的大文明（古以色列、波斯、印度、中国及希腊文明）所发生过彻底的思想上变化。见 Karl Jaspers, *The Origin and Goal of History*, translated by Michael Bullock. New Haven, CT: Yale University Press, 1965；对后代学者所继承和修改雅斯贝尔斯的理论，见 Johann P. Arnason, Shmuel N. Eisenstadt and Björn Wittrock, eds., *Axial Civilization and World History*, Leiden: Brill, 2005.

2　刘泽华：《“文革”中的紧跟、错位与自主意识的萌生——研讨历史的思想自述之二》，《史学月刊》2012 年第 11 期，第 99 页。

3　Sebastian de Grazia, ed., *Masters of Chinese Political Thought*, New York: Viking 1973; Hsiao Kung-Chuan (Xiao Gongquan 萧公权), *A History of Chinese Political Thought*, Volume One: *From the Beginnings to the Sixth Century A.D.*, translated by Frede-rick W. Mote, Princeton: Princeton University Press, 1979.

自由派的无政府主义者，而孔子则代表着类似西方的自由与个人的精神[1]。鲁宾的书可以说是西方学者用“以古事今”方式来解释中国古代思想的顶峰，其后类似的学术方法基本上绝迹了。

中国改革开放以后，西方学者对中国政治思想研究失去了兴趣。例如，我们可以在金鹏程（Paul R. Goldin）编写的极为有用的《中国古代文明：西方语言著作目录》[2]中发现：从 20 世纪 80 年代一直到 21 世纪初，基本上没有西方学者在研究中国古代思想时用“政治”（political, politics）相关的词语或术语作为自己著作的标题。这个现象肯定不是偶然的。

西方汉学之所以避免讨论中国古代思想的政治内涵具有多重原因。一些学者对 20 世纪 70 年代中国思想史激烈的政治化深有反感，因此特别不想再涉及古代思想的政治问题。另外有些学者则受到后现代主义思潮的影响，对所有的政治与权威问题都不感兴趣。此外笔者认为更主要的原因来自西方学者的学科背景。欧美学者中研究诸子百家的，主要来自哲学系或是中文（即汉语言文学）系，从来没有来自政治学系的，甚至在历史系也极少有研究先秦思想的人。而哲学系的同事们习惯了从西方哲学的角度来分析诸子百家的著作，讨论其中的知识论、逻辑、伦理、审美观等。而由于政治哲学在许多哲学系并不受欢迎，因而从政治哲学的角度来分析诸子百家作品的学者基本上不存在。

此外，值得注意的是，对有西方哲学背景的汉学家还存在着另外一个隐性因素增加了其对政治思想的疏离，我称这一因素为“哲学偏见”。中国思想是否属于西方所定义的哲学的范畴在很长一段时期里都是学术争论的一个焦点问题[3]。西方的汉学家经过长久争论以证明中国思想属于“哲学”范畴而不属于“宗教”或是“神秘学”，他们担心具有较高实践性的政治思想会被其他同事们认为是“缺乏哲学特质的”。这一担心并非空穴来风。早在 19 世纪初著名的德国哲学家黑格尔（Hegel）就这样批评了孔子：

1 鲁宾的书原来将在苏联出版，但是由于作者是反共分子，并且要移民到以色列去，该书被禁止；1976 年英文版在美国出版（见 Vitaly A. Rubin, *Individual and State in Ancient China: Essays on Four Chinese Philosophers*, translated by Steven I. Levine. New York: Columbia University Press, 1976)。1999 年该书俄文版在俄罗斯出版（见 Rubin, *Lichnost'i vlast'v drevnem Kitae: Sobranie Trudov*, Moscow: “Vostochnaia literatura” RAN, 1999, pp.8-76)。

2 Paul R. Goldin, “Ancient Chinese Civilization: Bibliography of Materials in Western Languages,” http://www.sas.upenn.edu/ealc/paul-r-goldin.

3 Carine Defoort, “Is There Such a Thing as Chinese Philosophy: Arguments of an Implicit Debate,” *Philosophy East and West*, 51（3）, 2001，pp.393-413.

> 孔子只是一个实际的世间智者，在他那里思辨的哲学（speculative philosophy）完全不存在……为了保持孔子的名声，假使他的书从来不曾被翻译过，那倒是更好的事。[1]

黑格尔的这句话对西方汉学家具有极大的影响。为了证明中国古代的思想是真的“哲学”，他们的研究集中于具有“思辨的哲学”色彩的思想，如名家等，而具有“实际的世间智者”色彩的思想，如法家等的政治思想则被忽略[2]。我曾按照金鹏程的《目录》作过统计，1980—2010年间用西方语言讨论公孙龙的文章要比讨论商鞅的文章多五倍。这与二位思想家的实际影响成反比，但是由于《公孙龙子》的“思辨的哲学”色彩要比《商君书》大，因此它对属于哲学系的汉学家具有极大的吸引力。另一个例子是西方的荀子学，最近几乎每年都有新出版的西方学者关于《荀子》研究的学术书籍，但从内容来看，绝大多数是集中在讨论荀子的人性论及其对心、名、天等态度，而几乎没有人讨论荀子的君主观，或是讨论其关于君臣关系的理论、对国家体制的看法，以及经济理论等。除了少数学者以外，荀子极为丰富和系统并具有长远影响的政治思想在西方学术界极少被讨论[3]。

---

1 Georg W.F. Hegel, *Lectures on the History of Philosophy, 1825-6*, Volume 1, *Introduction and Oriental Philosophy*, Edited by Robert F. Brown; translated by Robert F. Brown and J.M. Stewart with the Assistance of H.S. Harris, Oxford : Clarendon Press, 2009, p.107.

2 这个趋向早在胡适先生的《中国哲学史大纲》（1919年）中就可以看出来。中国现代的思想家及西方汉学家为何急于让中国古代思想被承认为“哲学”，见 Carine Defoort（戴卡琳）教授的上述文章。

3 最近的有关荀子的学术讨论是很多的，具有代表性的见 David S. Nivison, “The Classical Philosophical Writings,” In: Michael Loewe and Edward L. Shaughnessy, eds., *The Cambridge History of Ancient China*, Cambridge: Cambridge University Press, 1999, pp. 790-799; cf. Angus C. Graham, *Disputers of the Tao: Philosophical Argument in Ancient China*, La Salle: Open Court, 1989, pp.235-267；另外见有关荀子的书和论文集，如 Edward J. Machle, *Nature and Heaven in the Xunzi: A Study of the Tian lun*, Albany NY: State University of New York Press, 1993; Kline, T.C., III, and Philip J. Ivanhoe, eds., *Virtue, Nature, and Moral Agency in the* Xunzi.,Indianapolis and Cambridge, Mass.: Hackett, 2000; Antonio S. Cua, *Human Nature, Ritual, and History: Studies in Xunzi and Chinese Philosophy*, Washington, D.C.: Catholic University of America Press, 2005 等。在西方学术界讨论 荀子政治思想的人很少，例如见 Paul R. Goldin, *Rituals of the Way: The Philosophy of Xunzi.*,Chicago and La Salle, Ill.: Open Court 1999，并且很重要的 Sato Masayuki（佐藤将之）的 *The Confucian Quest for Order: The Origin and Formation of the Political Thought of Xun Zi*, Leiden: Brill，2003。佐藤的著作修订本最近有中文版本：佐藤将之：《荀子礼治思想的渊源与战国诸子之研究》（台北：台大出版中心，2003年）。

二 西方的政治学与中国政治思想的缺乏

2014 年初我跟一位希伯来大学政治系的老师讨论我们两系之间的合作时，曾问他：“为什么在贵系所教的世界政治思想史课程中，从来不讨论中国的政治思想？”他非常惊讶，问我：“中国也有政治思想吗？”我回答：“当然有，而且比西方古代政治思想要丰富得多。”他惊讶更甚，但片刻之后他说：“如此则意味着中国的政治思想完全不具备现实的价值。否则在我们专业的著作中怎么可能不引用中国古代思想家的看法呢？”上述对话恰恰反映目前大多数西方政治学家所持的极端“欧洲中心论”（Eurocentrism, 严格地说是“西方中心论”）。

西方政治学界激进的“西方中心论”表现在诸多方面。例如，大部分欧美大学政治系所讲授的“古代政治思想史”课程都只讨论纯西方的思想家们：柏拉图（Plato）、亚里士多德（Aristotle）、奥古斯丁（St. Augustine）、托马斯·阿奎纳（Thomas Aquinas）、马基雅维里（Machiavelli）等，中国思想家则全部被忽略。四十年前 John Schrecker 曾哀叹“西方思想生活极大地被空间与时间的狭隘主义所影响（parochialism in space and time which deeply infects Western intellectual life）”[1]。可惜，西方同事们至今还没能走出这种狭隘主义。因而大部分西方政治学的主流作品，包括书籍、杂志、辞典及大百科全书等都忽略了中国政治思想（只有少数简略地讨论儒家而已）。这类例子举不胜举，我在这里只提出一些很有权威性的作品，如《剑桥政治思想史》（*Cambridge History of Political Thought*），《政治思想史》（*History of Political Thought*）杂志，《布莱克威尔政治学辞典》（*The Blackwell Dictionary of Political Science*），1986 年的《布莱克威尔政治思想大百科》（*The Blackwell Encyclopedia of Political Thought*），Mark Bevir 2010 年主编的《政治理论的大百科》（*Encyclopedia of Political Theory*）等。尽管曾有一些学者企图摆脱“西方中心论”的束缚，例如 Anthony Black 2009 年的《世界政治思想史》（*A World History of Ancient Political Thought*），但是类似的例子凤毛麟角。

西方政治学的狭隘主义有许多原因。最根本的是西方人对自己的政治制度过于自信。对许多西方的政治学家而言，欧美的政治模式是唯一正确、独一无二的，是世界历史上的“之最”；其他的政治模式或政治思想方式，都属于“古代史”或

---

1 见其 “Review *of Masters of Chinese Political Thought*, edited by Sebastian de Grazia,” *Political Theory*, 2（4），1974, p.462。

是“人类学”范畴，但对政治学而言没有任何价值。此外，20 世纪末期之后兴盛的“理性选择理论”（rational choice theory）等思潮又增强了对非西方文化及学术的忽略。由于当代许多学者认为所有的人类都是理性的历史参与者，因而个人或是个别国家具体的文化背景并不是重要的决定政治行为的因素。受此观点的影响，许多年轻的政治学家已经不要再浪费时间研究外国的语言、历史、文化等，对他们来说整个世界都可以由统一的模式来进行解释。对于这些学者，了解中国古代（乃至当代）的政治思想及政治文化完全不重要。

三　中国传统政治思想对西方政治学的价值

进入 21 世纪，中国崛起成为世界上最突出的现象，它对国际的政治、经济、媒体、舆论等影响是极大的。学术界对此也无法忽视。最近几年出版了许多书都从不同角度来讨论“中国的模式”或者未来“中国统治世界之时”其独特的文化将如何影响世界[1]。另外，中国国内的“国学热”以及“孔子热”也引起了国外学术界的关注，而在西方学术界对中国政治思想及政治文化的态度也逐渐发生了变化。看金鹏程的《目录》会很容易发现：2009—2013 年的四年中，新出版的西方语言的有关中国先秦政治思想的著作比之前四十年的总和还多。那这一现象是否会对西方的政治学家产生一定影响呢？中国传统的政治思想是否会进入西方大学的“政治思想史”课程呢？

为了回答以上问题我们首先要问：传统中国政治思想对西方的政治学会有何种影响呢？之前，在讨论中国哲学对西方哲学的潜在价值时，美国的汉学家万白安（Bryan Van Norden）已提出：外来的文明对本文明的研究者会有两种意义：第一是认知上（notional）的意义，即外来的思想会扩大自己视野，但是对本文明没有直接影响；第二是事实上（real）的意义，即个人可以通过学习外来的思想来影响自己及本文明的生活[2]。这样的话，中国传统的政治思想对当代西方政治思想和政治学会有什么样的意义呢？ 我认为会有两方面的意义：第一，是中国古代思想的一些根本特征——尤其是其现实性及灵活性——会让我们更深刻地了解世界上

1　例如看 Daniel Bell（贝淡宁）教授的即将出版的 *The China Model: Political Meritocracy and the Limits of Democracy*（Princeton: Princeton University Press，2015）; Martin Jacques（马丁·雅克）的 *When China Rules the World*（《中国统治世界之时》）(London: Penguin, 2012)。

2　见万白安先生的 “What Should Western Philosophy Learn from Chinese Philosophy?” In: Philip J. Ivanhoe, ed., *Chinese Language, Thought, and Culture: Nivison and His Critics.*，Chicago and La Salle, Ill：Open Court, 1996，p.226。

政治思想的得失。第二，从内容来说，中国传统的思想也许不足以弥补西方政治文化的不足，但起码会挑战西方的主流政治文化并让西方学者重新考虑自己的文化的缺陷。

1. 思想与实践

一些学者指出中国思想家的理论无法比拟柏拉图及亚里士多德类似理论的系统性。假如我们接受这一观点，那是否意味着中国的政治思想比西方的政治思想要落后呢？笔者认为不能这么评价。尽管中国的政治思想在理论上也许会有这样那样的缺陷，但它也具有明显的好处，这就是其现实性。马克思曾说过：“哲学家们只是用不同的方式解释世界，而关键问题在于改变世界。”[1] 无论我们是否同意马克思对哲学家们的评价，但起码对政治思想而言，其现实性和实用性应该是它的最重要的好处之一。中国古代哲人对该问题了解得很清楚，荀子曾说：“知之不若行之；学至于行之而止矣。”[2] 从战国时代一直到毛泽东的“实践论”，中国思想家都知道：辩论本身的魅力是不够的，理论的实用性才能决定该理论的价值。这可能是中国政治思想最重要的特征。

值得提醒读者的是：战国时代的思想家想的不仅仅是“解释世界”而已，相反，他们有明显的现实任务——改善自己的世界，走出“战国”状况、进入“大一统”、增强政治秩序和社会稳定等。中华帝国的产生与帝国之前的思想方向具有密切的关系，它可以说是代表着战国时代的主流政治思想的理想[3]。类似的成功无论是柏拉图还是亚里士多德都是无法想象的。然而，需要注意的是，中华帝国并没有全面地实现诸子百家的理想，也不是按照系统的规划而建立的。在实现帝国的理想时，其建筑师们不得不改变许多具体的政策进而调整自己的规划[4]。这是一个非常珍贵的历史经验。通过比较先秦思想家的理想与中华帝国的具体政治情况，我们可以更深刻地了解其他的政治理论与政治实践之间的关系（比如说马克思的理想与以马克思主义为主导思想的国家的具体的政策之间的关系）。这可以丰富整个政治学的学术方法。

1 引自《关于费尔巴哈提纲》。

2 《荀子·儒效》，《荀子集解》，中华书局 1992 年年版。

3 笔者关于这个问题的讨论，见拙著《展望永恒帝国：战国时代的中国政治思想》（上海古籍出版社，2013 年）。

4 笔者关于这个问题的讨论，见拙著 *The Everlasting Empire: Traditional Chinese Political Culture and Its Enduring Legacy*, Princeton NJ: Princeton University Press, 2012。

2. 政治理论、以史为鉴及理论的灵活性

有学者指出：与希腊思想比较，中国传统思想的弱点在于其逻辑结构，即三段论（syllogism）方法的缺乏；中国思想家更倾向于历史性论证。这个意见是正确的：中国的历史学与政治思想之间存在着密切的关系。许多先秦的史学作品（例如《国语》、《战国策》等）都具有浓厚的政治思想价值，而所谓“经”与“子”之类的作品则有明显的史学价值（《春秋》及其三传是最明显的例子，但是许多其他的作品，像《晏子春秋》、《韩非子》的一部分、《吕氏春秋》等也有半个史学本质）。我们要问：

这种史学色彩是中国古代政治思想的缺陷还是优点呢？

笔者认为这是优点。跟“纯哲学”不一样，对政治思想而言历史经验是极为重要的。通过历史性的论证，中国的思想家认识到了理论的局限性与实践的重要性。如上面所论述的，历史经验证明——在现实情况中任何理论都需要经过不断地调整。而中国的思想对这个必然性是非常清楚的。例如，具有比较刚性的政治原则的《公羊传》同时也承认在某些历史条件之下，政治家需要放弃那些主导的原则，而要按照所谓“权”来调整自己的行为[1]。又如，韩非子表面上是绝对的君权主义者，其书中常常主张君主万能的重要性，警告君主要保护自己的地位，不让大臣执政等，又警告君主，大臣们会像老虎一样要谋害自己的君主。但是《韩非子》中的许多历史逸事（historical anecdotes）又暗示着相反的看法：在这些故事中的国君一般来说都是昏君，由于不听忠臣的话会危害自身及自己的国家[2]。这些故事劝诫读者：绝对的国君的权利也要有限制，即使这个至高无上的原则也必须经过调整。

中国政治思想的内在灵活性深刻地影响了中国的历史经验。例如，众所周知“王权主义”是中国传统文化的“一贯”原则[3]，在理论上皇帝要支配一切，他是万能完美的“圣王”。但从过往的历史经验来看，大臣们知道：皇帝常常从知识、道

1 见《公羊传·桓公十一年》,《春秋公羊传译注》，中华书局，2011 年版；并见 Joachim Gentz, “Long Live the King! The Ideology of Power between Ritual and Morality in the *Gongyang zhuan*,” in: *Ideology of Power and Power of Ideology in Early China*, ed. by Yuri Pines, Paul R. Goldin and Martin Kern.，Leiden: Brill ，2015.

2 Romain Graziani, “Monarch and Minister: The Problematic Partnership in the Building of Absolute Monarchy in the Han Feizi 韓非子,” in: Yuri Pines, Paul R. Goldin, and Martin Kern, eds., *Ideology of Power and Power of Ideology in Early China* (Leiden: Brill, 2015).

3 见刘泽华《中国的王权主义》，上海人民出版社，2000 年版。

德、个人的成熟等角度来说，都比不了自己的大臣。因而他们采取了许多措施来控制平庸的皇帝对具体政治的影响，把具体的政治职责从君主手中转到大臣群体身上。因而，尽管中国历来有许多有名无实的君主（包括东汉、明朝常常有幼年的皇帝执政），但这种情况对国家的危害不大，因为官员能够在名义上的君主之下进行正常的行政工作。类似的激进王权主义的文化能够进行自我调整是非常了不起的。世界上有许多以君主为核心的政治文化（比如草原的政治文化就是一个很好的例子），然而这些文化常常因为国君的个人弱点而进入大的危机。中国的政治文化表面上更强调君主的权力，但同时也会控制君主个人的政治影响。

类似的灵活性是中华帝国获得独一无二的长寿的原因之一[1]。

3. 中国政治思想的内容：为西方文化服务还是提出挑战？

我们最后要问的是：从内容来说中国传统的政治思想对当今世界，主要是对当代西方的政治文明会不会有“事实上的意义”呢？一部分新儒家毫无疑问地做出正面回答。例如2004年的“甲申文化宣言”就宣布：

> 我们确信，中华文化注重人格、注重伦理、注重利他、注重和谐的东方品格和释放着和平信息的人文精神，对于思考和消解当今世界个人至上、物欲至上、恶性竞争、掠夺性开发以及种种令人忧虑的现象，对于追求人类的安宁与幸福，必将提供重要的思想启示。[2]

笔者认为该宣言具有误导性。中华文化中确实不乏美丽的理想，但是西方及其他的政治文化（如伊斯兰、印度、草原政治文化等）也都具有许多美丽的理想；可惜它们的实践常常跟该理想是相反的。而中国文化也不例外，理想与实践之间也有巨大的区别。纵观两千多年的中华帝国史（或者三千多年中国有文字以来的历史），很难发现存在着长久的“注重人格、注重伦理、注重利他、注重和谐”的时代，因此用中国的理想来批评西方的现实情况在方法上就是错误的。此外，理想并不代表着文化的全貌。为了分析中国政治思想和政治文化及其当代价值，我们要集中在该思想和文化的根本原则方面，并探讨该原则与当代西方政治文化的根本原则（如民主、人权、平等）会有何种对话。

这一问题涉及面非常广泛，企图用一篇文章来回答将难以避免陷入简单化。尽管如此，笔者还是想按照本人与老师及同事们的研究来尝试着指出：中国政治

1　详见 Pines, *The Everlasting Empire*，pp.44-75。

2　见 http://www.people.com.cn/GB/paper81/13119/1176605.html。

文化的主导原则包括“大一统”思想、王权主义、尚贤任能、知识分子（士人）的政治参与、君子与小人的对抗基础上的社会等级性、所谓“民本”思想等。这些原则属于战国时代的诸子百家的主流理念，也是中华帝国政治文化的最根本的特征。那它们具有怎样的现代价值呢？

众所周知，从 20 世纪初叶以后中国（无论是“中华民国”、中华人民共和国还是海外华裔）基本上放弃了自己传统的政治文化主导的原则，或者对其进行了彻底的重新诠释。例如今天的中国所主张的“大一统”是以中华民族为核心的“一统”（即台湾海峡两边的一统），这与之前的“天下一家”的理想基本上无关[1]。而王权主义，这个传统政治文化的“一贯”原则，则完全被抛弃了，到今天已经基本上被忘掉了。因而，甚至当代保守派的代表在宣传“国学”、“孔学”及“东方文化”的好处时，也从来不敢提出要复活中华帝国制度[2]。更广泛地说，在一些方面中国传统政治文化的影响已经基本上消失了。由于当代中国的政治话语深刻地吸收了西方政治话语的基本概念（如民主、人权、平等等），这也反映出传统政治文化在近现代中国政治中的弱化。

然而，笔者认为我们还是可以找到中国传统思想和文化中的一些积极方面，来挑战西方的主流政治文化。在这里我简略地举一个例子：即把西方的政治平等观与中国传统政治等级观进行比较。前者是西方文化的近代化最重要的产物之一。众所周知，欧洲的旧社会具有硬性的等级：即个人的社会地位由其出身、性别、种族、宗教等决定，而其个人的能力、知识及道德基本上影响不了他的地位。由于这一制度极不公平，法国大革命（1789）前后法国及其他欧洲思想家都对以出身为核心的旧社会制度进行了挑战，为了打破该制度而提出了“平等”的原则[3]。经过一百多年的长期过程，该原则成为西方政治文化的核心原则之一。这个“平

1 中华帝国历史上“大一统”的具体的地理范围也发生过许多变化，对一些王朝（如北宋、明等）它主要地意味着“塞内”一统，即华夏地区一统而已。然而“天下一家”的理想并不是空虚的：某些王朝（汉、唐、元、清等）起码理论上（而有的时候实际上）要扩大自己的领土，实现“天下一家”的理想。详见拙著 *The Everlasting Empire* 第一章。

2 蒋庆先生建议恢复“象征性”的皇帝（与当代英国、日本类似的）（见其 *A Confucian Constitutional Order: How China's Ancient Past Can Shape its Political Future*，Translated by Edmund Ryden.，Edited by Daniel A.，Bell and Ruiping Fan，Princeton: Princeton University Press, 2013）。但是值得注意的是，“象征”皇帝是跟中国传统的政治制度无关，因而蒋先生的建议不会被算“帝国复活”的现象。

3 有关平等观在法国革命的作用，详见 Jonathan Israel, *Revolutionary Ideas: An Intellectual History of the French Revolution from The Rights of Man to Robespierre.*，Princeton, NJ: Princeton University Press, 2014。

等”首先意味着政治上的平等，即任何公民都具有投票和被选举的权利，这就是欧美的“一人一票”制度的基础。然而，尽管“一人一票”制度是公平的，但却有着明显的弱点。人在政治上的绝对平等，意味着人们在知识、道德、能力上的区别都要被忽略。因而被选的人在思想上或者文化上没有任何优势：他们的素质跟普通老百姓一样，而有的时候甚至比一般老百姓还低。目前西方的民主制度所面对的危机之一就是其产物——即大部分政客——没有之前的政治领袖的声望及文化上的影响。例如，据以色列在 2014 年 12 月份所举行的民意调查发现，只有不到十分之一的人会尊重国内的政治家[1]。类似的情况从长远看，会威胁政治制度的合法性及其有效性[2]。

而传统中国的例子则不一样。尽管中国的旧社会中也存在过明显的等级性，但该等级性是相当灵活的，在一定程度上允许有较大的社会变动。这个等级上的变动性是战国时代的产物。当时大部分诸子百家都主张“君子”与“小人”之间应该存在着明显区分：只有“君子”才能执政，而“小人”永远是被统治者。这就是孟子的名言：“或劳心，或劳力。劳心者治人，劳力者治于人；治于人者食人，治人者食于人。天下之通义也。”[3]孟子也说过：“无君子，莫治野人；无野人，莫养君子。”[4]但是在主张政治上区分等级的同时，中国的思想家也认为：个人的“君子”属性是由其知识和道德水平来决定的，出身并不是唯一的——也不必是最重要的——决定其地位的因素。即使是一个非常强调社会等级的重要性的思想家——荀子，也明显地说明：“君子”与“小人”之间的区别并不是天生的：

> 故小人可以为君子，而不肯为君子。君子可以为小人，而不肯为小人。小人君子者，未尝不可以相为也，然而不相为者，可以而不可使也。[5]

荀子的结论非常清楚：小人可以变成君子，但是不想变成君子。因为他们不愿意转变自身，所以他们对政治的参与显然也是不受欢迎的。这一点也为中华帝国长远的社会实践所证明。由于“尚贤任能”的原则受到较广泛的认可，则起码在理论上大部分男人都有潜在的可能改善自己或者自己子孙的身份地位，无论是

1 见以色列《国土报》(*Haaretz*) 的文章“סכנה לדמוקרטיה - לבוחרים כבר נמאס ממה שקורה”（对民主制度的威胁：投票者已经接受不了目前的情况）(http://www.themarker.com/markerweek/1.2504435，2014 年 12 月 5 日下载)。

2 对“一人一票”的民主制度的批评并见贝淡宁的 *The China Model*（《中国模式》)。

3《孟子·滕文公上》，杨伯峻：《孟子译注》，北京：中华书局，1992 年。

4《孟子·滕文公上》。孟子用“野人”这一概念，最初是指那些居住在都城外乡野的被统治者。

5《荀子·性恶》。

经过军功制度、科举制度，还是发财以后买官，有许多途径可以让有雄心的社会成员在社会阶层的阶梯上上升。因而跟在欧洲不同，中国旧社会的等级制度在一定程度受到了老百姓的认可。此外中国的“尚贤任能”制度后果之一是统治阶层拥有了一定的合法性。由于——起码在表面上——中国历来的统治者都是“君子”，即有较高的知识和道德水平，他们的社会声望较高，在社会与文化上对下层民众的影响比较大。无论曾有多少假的君子参政，帝国长远的历史可以证明：统治阶层的知识与道德水平常常会比被统治者高，这与目前西方社会是大不一样的。从这个角度来看，中国灵活的等级性好像会比西方当代的绝对平等要更有效。

四 结语

西方政治学家忽略中国的政治思想是错误的，这局限了他们的视野，是“空间与时间的狭隘主义”的表现。然而他们对其的忽略并不是偶然的：首要的原因是西方汉学家在 20 世纪 80 年代以后的“非政治化”的研究趋向，在长达 30 多年中连汉学家自己都没有重视对中国古代政治思想的研究，因而其他的西方学者更没有机会注意到中国古代政治思想是多么的丰富；另一个原因是西方政治学自身的问题，即在对各特定国家的文化的研究中，忽略了这些国家在文化上和历史上各自的特征，这个问题是西方政治学家需要自行解决的；还有第三个原因，即中国的政治学家自己都不够重视中国传统的政治思想，没有系统地把它介绍给外国的同事们。

以上所提出的一个例子，即中国传统的以“尚贤任能”为核心的等级制度会挑战西方的政治平等观只是一个推测而已，还没有形成成熟的理论。目前我们无法预测中国的经验会不会影响外国（西方或者亚非拉美的发展中国家）的政治文化，但是笔者认为：通过研究，深刻了解传统中国政治思想和政治文化的得失，中国学者——尤其是中国政治学家——要把这些得失介绍、分享给西方的同事们。这样不仅会扩大西方政治学家的视野，进一步丰富世界的政治学，而且会挑战西方学者的一些一成不变的原则。中国传统政治思想终将进入西方政治学课程！

[本文的写作受到以色列科学基金 (grant No. 511/11) 和 Michael William Lipson Chair in Chinese Studies 的资助]

Western Political Sciences and Traditional Chinese Political Thought: from Indifference toward Recognition

Yuri Pines / Israel

Vice Dean of the Faculty of Humanities at the Hebrew University of Jerusalem

I started studying the history of Chinese thought in the early 1990s; however, I had been very confused for a very long time about the following question: What is the academic specialty I am engaged in? In the opinion of Western academic circles, the history of the thought during the pre-Qin period (the 21st century B.C.-221 B.C.) basically falls within the scope of "Chinese philosophy", and scholars analyze it mainly from the perspective of Western philosophy, and I am not interested in Western philosophy, so I am less willing to regard myself as a person involved in studying "the history of Chinese philosophy". In 1994, I met with Mr. Liu Zehua and his disciples while I was studying at Nankai University and there I heard of the topic "the history of Chinese political thought" for the first time, and I was enlightened; afterwards, I took "the history of Chinese political thought" as my academic specialty. In 1996, I studied at the University of California, Los Angeles; later, I attended many academic meetings held in Europe and in the USA and established very close relations with my European and American colleagues; through my collaboration with them, I found that most of them were not interested in "traditional Chinese political thought" and "traditional Chinese political culture"; these concepts were very rare in the European and US academic circles at that time.

It is incomprehensible that Western scholars ignore the political connotation of ancient Chinese thought. In fact, no matter what understanding we have of ancient Chinese thought, its obvious political complexity can hardly be denied. The topics discussed by ancient Chinese intellectuals—such as the essence of the monarchical power, the origin of the state and its authoritativeness, the monarch-subject relationship, the relationship between the governor and the people, the political tasks and political functions of intellectuals—are the core contents of world political thought. The political thought of various schools of thought during the Spring and Autumn Period and the Warring States Period (770 B.C.-221 B.C.) apparently surpassed any other traditional political thought in the world in terms of breadth of vision, diversity, richness or its impact on contemporary and subsequent political cultures. If we compare China with the other civilizations of the so-called Axial Age,[1] we can conclude that from the perspective of philosophical theory or theology, traditional Chinese thought lags behind the ancient Indian, Greek, Persian or Hebrew civilizations; however, Chinese civilization transcends those civilizations and can be on a par with the diverse political thoughts in modern Europe with respect to the richness of its political and social thought.

However, why do Western scholars ignore traditional Chinese political thought? In order to answer this question, I will first explain the attitudes of Western, mainly American, sinologists, towards ancient Chinese thought, and then analyze the reason

1 Axial Age is a concept put forward by the German scholar Karl Jaspers to explain the thorough thought changes in the great civilizations of Europe and Asia—ancient Israeli, Persian, Indian, Chinese and Greek civilizations—from 800 B.C.-200 B.C. See Karl Jaspers, *The Origin and Goal of History*, translated by Michael Bullock. New Haven, CT: Yale University Press, 1965. The Jaspers theory has been inherited and revised by descendant scholars, see Johann P. Arnason, Shmuel N. Eisenstadt and Björn Wittrock, eds., *Axial Civilization and World History*, Leiden: Brill, 2005.

why Western politicians ignore it; finally, I will discuss the reason why ancient Chinese thought has drawn the attention of Western scholars in recent years and its potential value for Western political science.

1. Western Sinologists and Their "Philosophical Prejudice"

The campaign of condemning Lin Biao and Confucius, which broke out on the Chinese Mainland in the 1970s exerted a great impact on Western academic circles. The ultra-leftists, with Jiang Qing as the central figure, openly suggested that the struggle between Confucianism and legalism had existed in all ages and was also present within the Communist Party of China[1]; many Western scholars wanted to understand the political connotation of traditional Chinese thought more profoundly, so Western sinological circles started to become somewhat interested in it at that time; for example, Sebastian de Grazia gave the name *Masters of Chinese Political Thought* to the selected works, published by him, involving various schools of thought during the Spring and Autumn Period and the Warring States Period, while Frederick W. Mote translated *The History of Chinese Political Thought* Vol.1 written by Xiao Gongquan during the same period.[2] The most prominent representative which politicized the studies of the history of ancient Chinese thought was Vitaly Rubin, an anti-communist scholar from the former Soviet Union. The *Individual and State in Ancient China* written by professor Rubin inverted the campaign of condemning Lin Biao and Confucius: He held that Mo Zi (A Chinese intellectual, politician, circa 468 B.C.-376 B.C.) and Shang Yang (A Chinese politician, reformer and intellectual, circa 395 B.C.-338 B.C.) represented the totalitarianism of leftists and rightists; Zhuang Zi (A Chinese intellectual and philosopher, circa 369 B.C.-286 B.C.) represented the anti-liberalist anarchists,

1 Liu Zehua, Catching-up, Misplacement, Emergence of Independent Consciousness in the Great Cultural Revolution—Self-narration of Thoughts in Studies and Discussions of the History Vol.2, *Journal of Historical Science*, 2012(11), p.99.

2 Sebastian de Grazia, ed., *Masters of Chinese Political Thought*, New York: Viking 1973; Hsiao Kung-Chuan (Xiao Gongquan 萧公权), *A History of Chinese Political Thought*, Volume One: *From the Beginnings to the Sixth Century A.D.*, translated by Frede-rick W. Mote, Princeton: Princeton University Press, 1979.

while Confucius (A famous Chinese philosopher, educator, circa 551 B.C.-479 B.C.) represented the spirit of freedom and the individual, which was similar to what was found in the Western world.[1] Rubin's book represented the peak of adoption by Western scholars of the way of describing today's affairs in terms of ancient affairs while explaining ancient Chinese thought; after his book, a similar academic method basically disappeared.

After China's reform and opening up, Western scholars lost interest in studying Chinese political thought; for example, we can find in the extremely useful *Ancient Chinese Civilization: Bibliography of Materials in Western Languages*[2] complied by Paul R. Goldin, that from the 1980s to the early 21st century, basically no Western scholar used "politics"-related words or terms as the titles of their works when referring to ancient Chinese thought. This phenomenon was certainly not accidental.

There are many reasons why Western sinologists avoid discussions about the political connotation of ancient Chinese thought. Some scholars are disgusted with the drastic politicization in the history of Chinese thought in the 1970s, thus they particularly dislike dealing with political issues. Moreover, with the impact of postmodernist thought, some scholars are not interested in all issues concerning politics and authority. In addition, the author believes that the most important reason comes from the disciplined background of Western scholars. The European and US scholars who study the various schools of thought during the Spring and Autumn Period and the Warring States Period mainly come from the department of philosophy or the department of Chinese language and literature, while nobody comes from the department of political science, even only very few people study

1 Rubin's book was originally scheduled to be published in the Soviet Union, but the author was an anti-communist and immigrated to Israel, so this book was prohibited; it was published in English in the USA in 1976 (see Vitaly A. Rubin, *Individual and State in Ancient China: Essays on Four Chinese Philosophers*, translated by Steven I. Levine. New York: Columbia University Press, 1976). It was published in Russian in Russia in 1999 (see Rubin, *Lichnost'i vlast'v drevnem Kitae: Sobranie Trudov*, Moscow: "Vostochnaia literatura" RAN, 1999, pp.8-76).

2 Paul R. Goldin, "Ancient Chinese Civilization: Bibliography of Materials in Western Languages," http://www.sas.upenn.edu/ealc/paul-r-goldin.

the thought during the pre-Qin period in the department of history. The colleagues in the department of philosophy get used to taking the perspective of Western philosophy in analyzing the works of the various schools of thought of the Spring and Autumn Period and the Warring States Period, and they discuss their theories of knowledge, logics, ethics and aesthetics. Political philosophy is not very popular in many departments of philosophy, so the scholars who study the above-mentioned works from the perspective of political philosophy are basically non-existent.

Furthermore, it is worth noting that another hidden factor further estranges the sinologists with the background of Western philosophy from political thought, and I call this factor a "philosophical prejudice". Whether the Chinese thought falls within the scope of philosophy defined by the Western world has been a focus of academic debate for a very long time.[1] Western sinologists have carried out long-term debates to prove that Chinese thought falls within the scope of "philosophy" rather than "religion" or "occultism"; they worried that the political thought with a relatively high state of practicality would be considered by other colleagues as "lacking in the characteristics of philosophy". This worry was not a groundless rumor. As early as the beginning of the 19th century, the famous German philosopher Hegel (1770-1831) criticized Confucius as follows: Confucius was nothing but a practical, wise man in the world and believed that the speculative philosophy was completely nonexistent... in order to preserve the reputation of Confucius, it would have been better not to translate his books.[2] This sentence exerted a huge impact on Western sinologists. In order to prove that ancient Chinese thought was real "philosophy", they focused their studies on the thought with a speculative philosophy such as the school of logicians, but ignored the thought with the characteristics of a practical

1 Carine Defoort, "Is There Such a Thing as Chinese Philosophy: Arguments of an Implicit Debate," *Philosophy East and West*, 51(3), 2001, pp.393-413.

2 Georg W.F. Hegel, *Lectures on the History of Philosophy, 1825-6*, Volume 1, *Introduction and Oriental Philosophy*, Edited by Robert F. Brown; translated by Robert F. Brown and J.M. Stewart with the Assistance of H.S. Harris, Oxford: Clarendon Press, 2009, p.107.

wise man in the world, such as the political thought of legalists.[1] I once compiled statistical data according to the *Bibliography* written by Jin Pengcheng: The number of articles which discussed Gong Sunlong (A Chinese philosopher, circa 320 B.C.-250 B.C.) in Western languages were five times more than those which discussed Shang Yang (A Chinese politician, reformer and intellectual, circa 395 B.C.-338 B.C.) from 1980 to 2010. This was in inverse proportion to the the actual impact of both intellectuals; however, the speculative philosophy in *Master Gong Sunlong* was stronger than that in *The Book of Lord Shang*, thus *Master Gong Sunlong* is highly attractive to the sinologists in the department of philosophy. Another example is the Xun Zi Theory in the Western world; Western scholars publish new academic books concerning the studies of *Xun Zi* almost every year; however, most of them discuss the humanity of Xun Zi and his attitudes towards the mind, fame and heaven, while hardly anyone discusses his views on the monarch or his theory of the monarch-subject relationship, his views on the state system and his economic theory. The extremely abundant systematic political thought of Xun Zi with a far-reaching impact is seldom discussed in the Western academic circles, except for a few scholars.[2]

1 This tendency can be found in the *Outline of the History of Chinese Philosophy* (1919) written by Mr. Hu Shi (A famous Chinese thinker, philosopher, 1891-1962). Why are modern Chinese thinkers and western sinologists eager to make the ancient Chinese thought recognized as a "philosophy" ? See the above article written by Prof. Carine Defoort.

2 Recently, there have been many academic discussions about Xun Zi, see David S. Nivison, "The Classical Philosophical Writings," In: Michael Loewe and Edward L. Shaughnessy, eds., *The Cambridge History of Ancient China*, Cambridge: Cambridge University Press, 1999, pp. 790-799; cf. Angus C. Graham, *Disputers of the Tao: Philosophical Argument in Ancient China*, La Salle: Open Court, 1989, pp.235-267; regarding the books and collected papers concerning Xun Zi, see Edward J. Machle, *Nature and Heaven in the Xunzi: A Study of the Tian lun*, Albany NY: State University of New York Press, 1993; Kline, T.C., III, and Philip J. Ivanhoe, eds., *Virtue, Nature, and Moral Agency in the Xunzi*, Indianapolis and Cambridge, Mass: Hackett, 2000; Antonio S. Cua, *Human Nature, Ritual, and History: Studies in Xunzi and Chinese Philosophy*, Washington, D.C.: Catholic University of America Press, 2005. Very few people in the Western academic circles discuss Xun Zi's political thought, see Paul R. Goldin, *Rituals of the Way: The Philosophy of Xunzi*, Chicago and La Salle, Ill: Open Court 1999; Sato Masayuki (佐藤将之), *The Confucian Quest for Order: The Origin and Formation of the Political Thought of Xun Zi*, Leiden: Brill, 2003. The revised works of Masayuki Sato have been recently translated into Chinese: *Masayuki Sato: A Study of the Origin of Xun Zi's Thought of Governing by Rites and Philosophers in the Warring States Period*, Taipei: National Taiwan University Press, 2003.

2. Western Political Science and a Lack of Chinese Political Thought

In early 2014, I had a discussion with a teacher in the Department of Political Science at the Hebrew University of Jerusalem about the cooperation among our departments, and I asked a question: "Why is Chinese political thought never discussed in the courses concerning the history of world political thought and taught at your department?" He was very surprised and asked me: "Is there political thought in China?" I answered: "Yes, Chinese political thought is more abundant than ancient Western political thought." He was more surprised, but after a moment, he said: "If there is any political thought in China, this means that it is of no practical value; otherwise, it would be impossible for the views of the ancient Chinese intellectuals not to be cited in our professional works." The above conversation reflects extreme Eurocentrism precisely—strictly speaking, Western-centrism—upheld by most of the Western politicians at the present time.

Radical Western-centrism in Western political science circles can be seen in many aspects; for example, the courses concerning the history of ancient political thought taught at the departments of political science at most of the European and US universities only touch upon Western intellectuals, including Plato, Aristotle, St. Augustine, Thomas Aquinas and Machiavelli, but they completely exclude Chinese intellectuals. Forty years ago, John Schrecker complained about "parochialism in space and time, which deeply infects Western intellectual life".[1] Unfortunately, so far Western colleagues have not yet abandoned this parochialism. Therefore, most of the mainstream Western works involving political science, including books, magazines and encyclopedias, do not deal with Chinese political thought—only a few works provide brief discussions about the Confucian school. The examples are too numerous to enumerate; I only mention some authoritative works here such as the *Cambridge History of Political Thought,* the *History of Political Thought, The Blackwell Dictionary of Political Science, The Blackwell Encyclopedia of*

1 See John Schrecker, "Review of Masters of Chinese Political Thought, edited by Sebastian de Grazia," *Political Theory*, 2(4), 1974, p.462.

Political Thought in 1986, the *Encyclopedia of Political Theory*, principally edited by Mark Bevir in 2010. Although some scholars tried to break away from the tether of Western-centrism, such as *A World History of Ancient Political Thought* by Anthony Black in 2009, similar examples are extremely rare.

There are many causes regarding parochialism in Western political science. The most fundamental cause is that Westerners are excessively confident about their political system. For many Western politicians, the European and US political pattern is the only one which is correct and unique, and represents the "epitome" in world history, while all of the other political patterns or political thought modes fall within the scope of "ancient history" or "anthropology" and are of no value to political science. Furthermore, the thoughts which thrived after the late 20th century, such as the Rational Choice Theory, further contribute to the disregard of non-Western cultures and academics. Many contemporary scholars believe that all human beings are rational historical participants, thus the cultural backgrounds of individuals or countries are not the important factors affecting political behaviors. With the impact of this view, many young politicians no longer waste time in studying foreign languages, history and cultures, and they think that the whole world can be explained by a unified pattern. For these scholars, understanding ancient (even contemporary) Chinese political thought and political cultures is absolutely unimportant.

3. The Value of Traditional Chinese Political Thought for Western Political Science

Since the 21st century, China's rise has become the most prominent phenomenon in the world and it has exerted an enormous impact on international politics, economy, media and public opinion. The academic circles cannot ignore this fact. Many books which have been published in recent years take different perspectives in discussing China's Model or how China's unique culture will influence the world when China rules the world in the future.[1] Moreover, the craze for traditional

1 See Daniel Bell, *The China Model: Political Meritocracy and the Limits of Democracy*, Princeton: Princeton University Press, 2015; Martin Jacques, *When China Rules the World*, London: Penguin, 2012.

Chinese culture and Confucius in China has also attracted the attention of foreign academic circles, while Western academic circles have also gradually changed their attitudes towards Chinese political thought and political culture. It is very easy to find in the *Bibliography* written by Jin Pengcheng that the works concerning Chinese political thought in the pre-Qin period recently published in Western languages, from 2009 to 2013, are more numerous than the total number published in the previous forty years. Does this phenomenon exert a certain impact on Western politicians? Will traditional Chinese political thought be included in the courses concerning the history of political thought at Western universities?

In order to answer the above questions, first we should ask this question: What impact will be exerted by Chinese political thought on Western political science? Previously, when the potential value of Chinese philosophy for Western philosophy was discussed, the American sinologist Bryan Van Norden stressed that there were two types of significance of external civilizations for the researchers engaged in local civilization: The first one was the notional significance—external thoughts would broaden their horizon but would have no direct impact on local civilization; the second one was the real significance—individuals can influence their lives and the life within the local civilization by learning about thoughts coming from civilizations outside their own.[1] So what is the significance of traditional Chinese political thought for contemporary Western political thought and political science? I believe that there will be a significance at two levels: First, some fundamental characteristics of ancient Chinese thought—especially its realism and flexibility—will make us more thoroughly understand the success and failure of world political thoughts. Second, in terms of contents, traditional Chinese thought may not be enough to make up for the deficiency of Western political culture, but it will at least challenge mainstream Western political cultures and make Western scholars reconsider the drawbacks of Western cultures.

1 See Wan Bai' an, "What Should Western Philosophy Learn from Chinese Philosophy?" In: Philip J. Ivanhoe, ed., *Chinese Language, Thought, and Culture: Nivison and His Critics*, Chicago and La Salle, Ill: Open Court, 1996, p.226.

1) Thought and practice

Some scholars point out that the theories of Chinese intellectuals are not as systematic as the similar theories of Plato and Aristotle. If we accept this view, does this mean that Chinese political thought lags behind Western political thought? The author does not think so. Although theoretically, Chinese political thought may have such a drawback, it presents an apparent advantage: its realism. Karl Marx said: "The philosophers have only interpreted the world, in various ways. The point, however, is to change it."[1] No matter whether we agree with Karl Marx's evaluation of philosophers, the realism and practicability of political thought should be one of its most important advantages. Ancient Chinese philosophers clearly understood this issue. Xun Zi said that taking action was better than understanding; practice ended when something was learned.[2] From the Warring States Period to Mao Zedong's Theory of Practice, Chinese intellectuals knew that the charm of debating was not enough, only the practicability of theories determined their value. This may be the most important feature of Chinese political thought.

It is worth noting that the intellectuals in the Warring States Period did not merely interpret the world; on the contrary, they carried out an obvious realistic task—improving their world to end the situation of warring states and thus achieve grand unification, and enhance the political order and social stability. The emergence of the Chinese Empire was closely associated with the direction of intellectual thought before the Chinese Empire, it represented the ideal of mainstream political thoughts in the Warring States Period.[3] Similar successes were unimaginable in either Plato or Aristotle. However, it should be noted that the Chinese Empire did not fully realize the ideal of the various schools of thought and was not built according to a systematic plan. In the process of realizing the ideal of the Chinese Empire, its

1 Quoted from *The Outline of Feuerbach.*

2 *Xun Zi—Usefulness of Confucianism, Xunzi Commentaries*, Beijing: Zhonghua Book Company, 1992.

3 The author's discussions about this issue are shown in the author's work *Outlook for the Everlasting Empire: Chinese Political Thought in the Warring States Period*, Shanghai: Shanghai Chinese Classics Publishing House, 2013.

architects had to change many concrete policies and thus adjust their plans.[1] This is a very valuable historical experience. By comparing the thought of the intellectuals in the pre-Qin period and the specific political situation of the Chinese Empire, we can profoundly understand the relationships between other political theories and political practice such as the relationship between the ideal of Karl Marx and the concrete policies adopted in the countries governed by the thought dominated by Marxism. This enriches the academic methods of all political science.

2) Political theories, taking history as a mirror, the flexibility of theories

Some scholars have pointed out that compared with Greek thought, the weakness of traditional Chinese thought consisted in its logical structure—a lack of a method of syllogism; Chinese intellectuals favored a more historical argumentation. This opinion is correct: China's historical science is closely related to political thought. Many works concerning historical science in the pre-Qin period, such as the *Commentaries of the Spring and Autumn Period*, the *Strategies of the Warring States*, are of high value within political thought. Such works as the books which epitomized something and the classics of the ancient Chinese philosophers are of significant historical value—*The Spring and Autumn Annals* and its three commentaries are the most striking examples, but many other works, such as *Yanzi' s Spring and Autumn Annals*, *Han Feizi* (partial), *Mister Lv's Spring and Autumn Annals*, also have a partial nature of historical science. Is the nature of historical science a defect or an advantage of ancient Chinese political thought?

The author believes that this is an advantage. Unlike "pure philosophy", historical experience is extremely important for political thought. The historical argumentation of Chinese intellectuals helps understand the limitations of theories and the importance of practice. As mentioned above, historical experience proves

1 The author's discussions about this issue are shown in the author's work *The Everlasting Empire: Traditional Chinese Political Culture and Its Enduring Legacy*, Princeton NJ: Princeton University Press, 2012.

that, in reality, any theory needs to be constantly adjusted. Chinese thought is very clear regarding this inevitability. For example, the *Commentaries of Gongyang*, governed by relatively rigid political principles, also recognized that, under certain historical conditions, politicians needed to abandon the leading principles and adopt the so-called "powers" to adjust their behaviors.[1] Han Feizi was seemingly an absolute monarchist, and in his books, he often upheld the importance of the conception that the monarch was almighty, warned the monarch to protect his status and not let ministers hold power, and also warned that the ministers would conspire to harm their monarch just like tigers do. However, many historical anecdotes in *Han Feizi* suggested the opposite view: In these stories, monarchs were generally fatuous, they would endanger themselves and their countries because they did not listen to their loyal ministers.[2] These stories admonish readers that the absolute power of a monarch should also be restricted, and even this supreme principle also must be adjusted.

The inner flexibility of Chinese political thought has profoundly influenced China's historical experience. For example, as we know, the doctrine of kingship is a constant principle in traditional Chinese culture;[3] theoretically, the emperor can control everything and is an almighty and perfect sage. However, in past historical experience, ministers knew that the emperor lagged behind his ministers in terms of knowledge, morality and personal maturity, thus they took numerous measures to control the political influence of a mediocre emperor, and transfer the specific political responsibility from the emperor to his ministers. Therefore, although there

1 See the *Commentaries of Gongyang—the 11th Year of Duke Huan*, *Translation and Annotation of the Commentaries of Gongyang*, Beijing: Zhonghua Book Company, 2011; Joachim Gentz, "Long Live the King! The Ideology of Power between Ritual and Morality in the Gongyang zhuan," in: Yuri Pines, Paul R. Goldin, and Martin Kern, eds., *Ideology of Power and Power of Ideology in Early China*, Leiden: Brill, 2015.

2 Romain Graziani, "Monarch and Minister: The Problematic Partnership in the Building of Absolute Monarchy in the Han Feizi 韓非子," in: Yuri Pines, Paul R. Goldin, and Martin Kern, eds., *Ideology of Power and Power of Ideology in Early China*, Leiden: Brill, 2015.

3 See Liu Zehua, *China's Doctrine of Kingship*, Shanghai: Shanghai People's Publishing House, 2000.

were many nominal monarchs in ancient China, including juvenile emperors in power in the Eastern Han Dynasty (25-220) and the Ming Dynasty (1368-1644), the country was less harmed because officials managed to carry out the administrative work normally under nominal monarchs. It was amazing that the cultures similar to the radical doctrine of kingship can be self-adjusted. There were many political cultures with a monarch as the core in the world; for example, the political culture on the prairie was an excellent example; however, these cultures were often vulnerable to great crises due to the personal weaknesses of monarchs. Chinese political culture seemed to place more emphasis on the powers of the monarch, but also controlled the political influence of the monarch. Similar flexibility is one of the causes for the unique long life of the Chinese Empire.[1]

3. Contents of Chinese political thought: Do they serve or challenge Western cultures?

In the end, we want to ask: In terms of content, does traditional Chinese political thought have "practical significance" for today's world, mainly for the contemporary Western political civilization? Some new Confucianists undoubtedly give a positive answer to this question. For example, the *Jia Shen Cultural Declaration* in 2004 reads: We believe that Chinese culture shows the oriental character which stresses personality, ethics, altruism and harmony, and the humanistic spirit which releases the information of peace, and Chinese culture provides some important inspirations for thought-creation regarding the ways of thinking and dispelling personal supremacy, the supremacy of material desire, cutthroat competition, predatory exploitation and various worrying phenomena, as well as pursuing the peace and happiness of human beings.[2]

The author thinks that this declaration is misleading. Chinese culture really presents many wonderful ideals, so do Western and other political cultures such as

1 See Yuri Pines, *The Everlasting Empire: Traditional Chinese Political Culture and Its Enduring Legacy*, Princeton NJ: Princeton University Press, 2012.

2 See http://www.people.com.cn/GB/paper81/13119/1176605.html.

Islamic, Indian and prairie political cultures; unfortunately, their practice often runs counter to their ideals. There is no exception for Chinese culture: There is a huge gap between ideals and practice. Given the history of the Chinese Empire spanning more than 2,000 years or the history of more than 3,000 years since the appearance of characters in China, it is not difficult to find a long-term era of stressing personality, ethics, altruism and harmony, so methodologically, it is wrong to use China's ideals to criticize the reality of the Western world. Furthermore, ideals do not represent the whole picture of a culture. In order to analyze Chinese political thought and political culture and their contemporary value, we should focus on the fundamental principle of thought and culture, and discuss the dialogue between this principle and those fundamental principles of contemporary Western political cultures such as democracy, human rights and equality.

This issue involves very extensive fields, so it is oversimplified to give an answer in one article. Nevertheless, based on the studies conducted by himself, teachers and colleagues, the author tries to point out that the leading principles in Chinese political culture include the thought of great unification, the doctrine of kingship, reverence for and appointment of able people, participation of intellectuals in politics, social hierarchy based on confrontation between gentlemen and villains, the so-called "people-based" thought. These principles were part of the mainstream philosophies from various schools of thought during the Warring States Period and the most basic feature of the political culture during the Chinese Empire. What is their modern value?

As we know, after the early part of the 20th century, China—the Republic of China, the People's Republic of China and overseas Chinese—basically abandoned the principles dominated by its traditional political culture, or thoroughly reinterpreted them. For example, the great unification upheld by China at present is the unification with the Chinese nation as the core—the reunification of the two sides of the Taiwan Strait, it basically has nothing to do with the previous ideal that “everyone under heaven belongs to one family”.[1] The doctrine of kingship—a constant principle in traditional political culture—was completely discarded and has been basically forgotten now. Therefore, even the representatives of the contemporary conservatives never vow to restore the system of the Chinese Empire when publicizing the advantages of the studies of ancient Chinese civilization, Confucianism and oriental culture.[2] More broadly, the influence of traditional Chinese political culture on some aspects has basically disappeared. The political discourse of contemporary China very deeply incorporates the basic concepts of Western political discourse, such as democracy, human rights and equality. This also reflects the decreasing influence of traditional political culture on contemporary Chinese politics.

However, in the author’s opinion, we can also find some positive aspects in traditional Chinese thought and culture to challenge the mainstream political cultures in the Western world. Here is an example I can make: Western outlook on political equality is compared with the traditional Chinese outlook on political hierarchy. The former is one of the important results of Western cultures in modern times. As everyone knows, the old European society had a rigid hierarchy: The social status of an individual was determined by that individual’s family background, gender, race and religion, while the ability, knowledge and morality of an individual basically did not influence his status. This system was extremely

1 Many changes have also taken place in the specific geographical scope of the great unification in the history of the Chinese Empire; for some dynasties, such as the Northern Song Dynasty (960-1127) and the Ming Dynasty (1368-1644), it mainly meant the unification within the Great Wall—the unification of the Huaxia region. However, the ideal that “everyone under heaven belongs to one family” was not empty talk: at least theoretically (sometimes actually), some dynasties, such as the Han Dynasty (202 B.C.-220), the Tang Dynasty (618-907), the Yuan Dynasty (1271-1368) and the Qing Dynasty (1644-1912), expanded their territories to achieve the ideal. For details, see the first chapter of *The Everlasting Empire* written by the author.

2 Mr. Jiang Qing suggested that the “symbolic” emperor (similar to contemporary UK and Japan) should be restored, see Jiang Qing, *A Confucian Constitutional Order: How China’s Ancient Past Can Shape its Political Future*, Translated by Edmund Ryden, Edited by Daniel A., Bell and Ruiping Fan, Princeton: Princeton University Press, 2013. However, it’s worth noting that the “symbolic” emperor has nothing to do with the traditional Chinese political system, thus this suggestion is not considered as restoration of the empire.

unfair, so before and after the French Revolution (1789), French intellectuals and other European intellectuals challenged the old social system that was mainly based on family background and put forward the principle of equality in order to break this system down.[1] Through a long, more than 100-year process, this principle has become one of the core principles in Western political cultures. This "equality" first means political equality—every citizen has the right to vote and be elected; this is the foundation for the one-man-one-vote system in Europe and in the USA. However, although the one-man-one-vote system is fair, it has obvious weaknesses. The absolute political equality of people means that the distinction of people who possess knowledge, morality and ability is ignored. Therefore, the elected people have no advantages in thought or culture: Their quality is the same as—even sometimes lower than—that of the ordinary people. One of the crises of the current Western democratic system is that its result—most politicians—lag behind previous political leaders in reputation and cultural influence. For example, according to the public opinion poll conducted by Israel in December, 2014, fewer than 1/10 of the people respected domestic politicians at the time the poll was taken.[2] Similarly, from a long-term perspective, this will threaten the legitimacy and effectiveness of the political system.[3]

The situation was different in traditional China. Although the old Chinese society also had an obvious hierarchy, this hierarchy was very flexible—to some extent, it allowed great social changes. The variability of this hierarchy was the result in the Warring States Period, during which most schools of thought held that there should be an obvious distinction between "gentlemen" and "villains": Only "gentlemen" can hold power, while "villains" were always to be ruled. Mencius had a celebrated dictum: "Some people carry out brain work, some people carry out manual work;

1 The role of the equality outlook in the French Revolution, see Jonathan Israel, *Revolutionary Ideas: An Intellectual History of the French Revolution from The Rights of Man to Robespierre*, Princeton, NJ: Princeton University Press, 2014.

2 See "סכנה לדמוקרטיה - לבוחרים בכר נמאס ממה שקורה" , http://www.themarker.com/markerweek/1.2504435, downloaded on 2014-12-0 5.

3 For the criticism of the one-man-one-vote democratic system, see Bei Tanning's *The China Model*.

brain workers rule people, while manual workers are ruled by people; the ruled people support others, while the ruler is supported by the people; this is a universal principle."[1] Mencius also said: "If there are no gentlemen, countrified people cannot be ruled; if there are no countrified people, gentlemen cannot be supported.[2]

However, while Chinese intellectuals upheld the political hierarchy, they also believed that the attributes of "gentlemen" were determined by their knowledge and moral levels, while the family background was not the only—not necessarily the most important—factor determining their status. Even Xun Zi, an ancient Chinese intellectual who highly stressed the importance of social hierarchy, clearly stated: "The distinction between gentlemen and villains is not inborn, thus villains can become gentlemen, but refuse to do so; gentlemen can become villains, but refuse to do so; villains and gentlemen can exchange their identities with each other, but they refrain from doing so because they cannot be forced to do so even though they can do so."[3]

Xun Zi's conclusion is very clear: Villains can become gentlemen, but refuse to do so because they are unwilling to transform themselves, thus they are not welcome to participate in politics. This has also been proved by the long-term social practice in the Chinese Empire. The principle of showing reverence for and appointing the able people is widely recognized, at least theoretically; most men may have the desire to improve their identity and status and that of their descendants, and the ambitious members of the society can climb the social strata in various ways, including through the military reward system, the imperial examination system and the purchase of official positions after making a fortune. Therefore, unlike Europe, the hierarchy in the old Chinese society was recognized by the people to some extent. Moreover, one of the consequences of China's system of showing reverence

1 *Mencius-Duke Tengwen,* Vol.1, Yang Bojun: *Mencius' Translation and Annotation*, Beijing: Zhonghua Book Company, 1992.

2 *Mencius-Duke Tengwen,* Vol.1, the concept of countrified people used by Mencius initially referred to the ruled people who lived in the countryside outside cities.

3 *Xun Zi-Evil Human Nature.*

for and appointing the able people was that the ruling class had a certain legitimacy. The rulers in China were—or at least they seemed to be—"gentlemen", they had a relatively high amount of knowledge and levels of morality and enjoyed a relatively high reputation in the society, so they exerted a strong social and cultural influence on the people of the lower class. No matter how many false gentlemen participated in politics, the long history of the Chinese Empire can prove that the ruling class often surpassed the ruled people with regard to knowledge and levels of morality. This is different from the current Western society. From this perspective, the flexible hierarchy in China appeared to be more effective than the absolute equality advocated in the contemporary Western world.

4. Conclusions

It was wrong for Western politicians to disregard Chinese political thoughts. Such disregard restricted their horizon and reflected parochialism in space and time. However, such disregard was not accidental: The first cause for it was that Western sinologists conducted studies which featured de-politicization after the 1980s, and sinologists did not even attach importance to studying ancient Chinese political thought for over 30 years, so other Western scholars had no opportunities to know that ancient Chinese political thoughts were very rich; another cause consisted in Western political science—their studies of the cultures in particular countries did not take into account the cultural and historical characteristics of those countries; this problem should be solved by Western politicians themselves; the third cause was that Chinese politicians did not pay attention to traditional Chinese political thought and did not systematically introduce it to their foreign colleagues.

The above example—that the traditional hierarchy of showing reverence for and appointing the able people in China will challenge Western political equality—is merely a conjecture and has not yet been supported by a well-proven theory. At present, we cannot make a forecast about whether China's experience will influence the political culture in foreign countries—the developing countries in the Western world or Asia, Africa and Latin America. However, the author believes that it is necessary to carry out studies to deeply understand the losses and gains in traditional Chinese political thought and political culture, and that Chinese scholars—especially Chinese politicians—should introduce these losses and gains to and share them with their Western colleagues. This will not only broaden the horizon of Western politicians and further enrich the world's political science, but it will also challenge some unchanged principles of Western scholars. Traditional Chinese political thought will ultimately become part of Western political science courses!

(This paper is funded by the Israel Science Foundation (grant No. 511/11) and Michael William Lipson Chair in Chinese Studies)

道路不同，价值共享

黄平　【中国】
中国社会科学院欧洲研究所　所长

东西、中外交流最大的问题当属一方面是各国的道路不同，另一方面是有没有可以共享的（shared, 不是共同的）价值？

这些年，中国的改革开放发展已经取得了举世皆知的惊人成就，成就的背后也有一些应该总结和提炼的东西。这些年很多人做了一个很重要的工作，就是提炼出一些让大家至少可以听明白的经验、特点、特性，我自己对中国道路也有一些提炼，比如说，除了人们说得很多的高速度增长、大规模脱贫外，还有广泛的参与、公平的分配、高度的共识、共同的愿景。

这些背后如果要讲理论其实就涉及中西、中外之别了，道路不同，有没有可以供人类共享的价值？我自己想到这样几个概念：

1. 大道之行，天下为公。要为私、小道，就永远有战争、冲突、误解、傲慢，所以，人类可以共享的中国价值，首先就是大道之行，天下为公。

2. 人间正道、共同富裕。虽然共同富裕程度不同，有些人快些，有些人慢些，有些人多些，有些人少些，但我们不是排他性的发展，而是包容性的发展，所以是人间正道，共同富裕。

3. 天下无外，互利共赢。人有差异，但不分内外，“四海之内皆兄弟”，这样才有“和合”，所以能互利共赢。

就中西文化之别来说，中西之别本来没有那么大，刚才刘梦溪先生讲的先秦诸子，我们的思想和苏格拉底、柏拉图、穆罕默德思想比，古典时期先哲们的伟大思想是很近的。举例来说，一些人老说中国是强调集体，西方是强调个人。其实在古希腊的时候，主张原子论的是极少数的，亚里士多德最著名的命题之一是“人天生是社会动物”。即使近代以来，启蒙大师卢梭也讲，人生而自由却无所不在枷锁之中，为了摆脱枷锁，就需要合作，所以他写了《社会契约论》。马克思最著名的命题是人的本质是社会关系的总和。鲁滨逊似的离群索居，是不可能的。后来西方的社会学、政治学、国际关系学，无不是在处理人际关系、社会关系乃至国与国的关系。

中西方交流、对话，从中国方面来看，晚清西学东渐以来就开始了，但没有在一个平等对话的基础上。80 年代以来，我们实行对外开放，西方的学术和思想大量引进，从介绍到学习，从对话到交流，今天不仅越来越多，而且也越来越深。我原来给今天发言定的题目是“从文化间的对话到跨越文化边界的互惠”，这个跨文化的互惠，一开始是由已故的汤一介老先生和他的夫人、现在还健在的乐黛云老师与意大利也是最近去世的艾科先生和法国仍健在的阿兰李比雄等一起推动的。这个跨文化对话（transcultural, 不是文化间 intercultural）从启动到今天已经 30 年了，其中最重要的一个概念是互惠性的知识（reciprocal knowledge），而不是强调我有一个中国文化，你有一个西方文化，各自只强调差异，看不到刚才刘梦溪先生说的“和合”。我们这个跨文化对话现在已经提升到了中欧国家和欧盟的层面，双方领导人也参加，甚至一些教会也参加了对话。记得最近在纽约的一次对话中，美国的一位主教就说，两百年前的启蒙运动，乃至于再早的文艺复兴，其实西方错过了与中国或东方平等对话的机会。当时中西本来是完全可能互利共享的。

现在，几百年后，随着中国经济社会发展，包括文化也重新繁荣起来，中外思想 / 中西思想的平等交流交融交汇是否又成为可能？乃至于还可以通过这样的平等交流交融交汇实现互利共享（sharing），包括价值层面的共享，是否可能？

中国提出的“一带一路”倡议确实不只是基础设施、投资、贸易、修路、架桥，而可以是通过这些基础设施和经济贸易合作，成为是一个载体，使我们真正回归到古典、回到本源。其实，中外 / 中西本来并没有那么多的边界和差异，更不必一定要非此即彼、你死我活，很多边界是被傲慢与偏见筑起来的，阻碍了文化、思想和价值的交流、交汇，并因此无法共享、共赢。

我自己曾在江南农村做过田野研究，为什么一方面如此严重的人多地少，另一方面会有琴棋书画、雕刻刺绣、诗书礼乐，有如此发达的江南文化？如果按照个人的投入产出、成本效益来计算，江南农村经济早就应该破产了，而不会发展成“上有天堂下有苏杭”这样的发达文明形态。但是如果我们不是以个人为单位，而是以家庭为单位，仍然按照投入产出、成本效益来计算，则边际效益就不是递减的，相反，随着家庭农业的增产，还有了发展副业甚至乡村轻工业的条件，也有了农耕文明下孕育诗书画的条件。这种江南模式（“中国模式”之一例）下也有自我，但这样的自我是复数的，是家、族、群、团、社、队、组、村，等等，而且，是由近及远、由己及人，逐渐推移却并无边界更无你我乃至无敌我的过程，它是包容的，也是普惠的，尽管在这种模式下，参与和受益、受惠程度有所不同，而不是简单的平均。

回到中外/中西文化对话，我的主要论点是：不论西方人认为自己的文化多么优越，也不论我们认为自己的文化多么悠久，不论各自都是多么伟大的文明的延续，各自有多么不同于别人的发展道路，我们能不能抛下各种傲慢与偏见，来共同面对我们共同的难题、挑战、风险和危机？

刚才刘梦溪先生也提到战争、大自然的退化，还有现在讲得很多的气候变化所带来的问题。至少，这已经不仅是愿景，例如，“一带一路”提供一种很重要的途径是通过利益共同体建造责任共同体，再建成命运共同体。这就可能产生出一种互补互惠性的知识和新的共享价值。随着“一带一路”的逐步推进，不只是中国，也不只是沿线国家和地区，而是整个世界，有可能成为我们走出这几百年来的丛林法则和零和游戏的抓手和途径。

今天，我们在知识层面、文化层面、价值层面讨论这种可能性的时机也到来了。

谢谢大家！

Is There a Shared Value behind Different Paths?

Huang Ping / China

Director of the Institute of European Studies, CASS

The biggest question in the exchanges between the west and the east, between China and the foreign countries is, on the one hand, different countries have chosen different paths; on the other hand, is there a value which is not common, but that can be shared?

As we know, China has made tremendous achievements through reform and opening up over the years. A bit of a summary should be made regarding how these achievements were reached. In these years, many people have carried out very important work on summing up some experience, characteristics and features which are understandable. I have summarized some of the knowledge about China's path; for example, besides the often-mentioned high-speed growth and massive alleviation of the poverty, I have also proposed extensive participation, fair distribution, a high degree of consensus and a shared vision regarding China's path.

Theoretically, in fact, this involves the differences between the west and the east, between China and foreign countries. Is there a value which can be shared by mankind in general since different countries have chosen different paths? I have considered several concepts:

1. A great path should be pursued for the whole world. Selfishness and small paths always beget wars, conflicts, misunderstandings and arrogance. Therefore, the Chinese value which can be shared by the whole of mankind should first be that a great path is pursued for the whole world.

2. The right way should be followed in order to achieve common prosperity. The degrees of common prosperity are different; some people move fast, while some go slowly; some people enjoy a lot of wealth, while some only get access to little wealth. However, we should not seek an exclusive development; on the contrary, we should pursue inclusive development, so the right path should be followed to achieve common prosperity.

3. There are no outsiders in the world, and mutual benefit and win-win results should be sought. There are differences among people, and no one should be treated as an outsider. All of the people in the world are brothers. In this way, there are harmony and unity, and mutual benefit and win-win results can be achieved.

The differences between the Chinese and western cultures are not large. The ways of thinking of Chinese thinkers before the Qin Dynasty (221 B.C.-207 B.C.), as just mentioned by Mr. Liu Mengxi, were very similar to those of Socrates, Plato, Mohammed and the great thoughts of the sages of the classical period. For example, some people often say that China stresses the collective, while Western countries place emphasis on individuals. In fact, in ancient Greece, only a very few people upheld atomism. One of Aristotle's most famous propositions is that "man is by nature a social animal". Since modern times, Rousseau, the master of enlightenment, said that man was born free, but he was everywhere in chains; in order to keep out of chains, cooperation is needed, so he wrote his theory in *The Social Contract*. Karl Marx's most famous proposition is that man is essentially the total sum of his social relations. Living in solitude like Robinson Crusoe is impossible. All of Sociology, Political Science, and the Science of International Relations in the Western world deal with interpersonal relationships, social relations, even relations among countries.

In our opinion, communication and dialogue between the East and the West started from the eastward transmission of western sciences during the late Qing Dynasty, but there was no equal footing regarding dialogue. Since the 1980s, China has been open to the outside world, and western sciences and ways of thinking have been massively introduced to China. The cases from an introduction to actual learning, from a dialogue to real communication are on the increase and will be intensified. Originally, the title of my speech today was "From the intercultural dialogue to mutual benefit beyond the cultural boundary". The transcultural mutual benefit was initially promoted by the late Mr. Tang Yijieand his wife, the teacher Le Daiyun who is still alive, the Italian Umberto Eco who died recently, and the French Alain Le Pichon who is still alive. This transcultural (not intercultural) dialogue has lasted for 30 years since its launch. One of its most important concepts is reciprocal knowledge rather than a mere emphasis on the differences between the Chinese culture and Western culture. Otherwise, harmony and unity as just mentioned by Mr. Liu Mengxi cannot be seen. This transcultural dialogue has been upgraded to the China-EU level. The leaders of both sides have also participated in this dialogue, even some churches have participated in it. In a recent conference in New York, a U.S. bishop said that, in fact, in the Enlightenment of two hundred years ago, even the earlier Renaissance, the Western world had already missed the opportunity for engaging in a dialogue with China and the Eastern world on an equal footing. At that time, it was completely possible that the West and the East would be able to deliver mutual benefits and share something.

Several hundred years later, with China's economic and social development, including also cultural prosperity, is it possible that Chinese and foreign thoughts/ Chinese and Western thoughts will be exchanged and integrated on an equal footing? Can mutual benefits and sharing, including value sharing, be achieved through equal exchange and integration?

The Belt and Road Initiative put forward by China not only involves infrastructures, investments, trade, roads and bridges, but it also gives birth to a carrier enabling us to really return to those of the classical age, through these infrastructures and economic and trade cooperation. Actually, there are not that many boundaries and differences between China and foreign countries/China and the West; it is not necessary to make them incompatible. Many boundaries are built by pride and prejudice. Boundaries hinder the exchanges and integration of cultures, thoughts and values, making it impossible to share and achieve a win-win outcome.

I once conducted field studies in the rural areas south of the Yangtze River. Why is there lyre-playing, chess, calligraphy and painting, sculpture, embroidery, poetry, literature, rites and music and a highly-developed Jiangnan culture amidst severe shortage of land in terms of such a huge population? From the perspective of the per capita input-output and cost-effectiveness, the rural economy in the regions south of the Yangtze River (Jiangnan) might go bankrupt earlier, and so a highly-developed civilization would not emerge. However, from the perspective of input-output and cost-effectiveness per household, the marginal benefits do not diminish; on the contrary, with the households' increasing agricultural output, there are the conditions for developing auxiliary businesses, even rural light industry, and for working on poetry, calligraphy and painting within an agricultural civilization. Under this Jiangnan mode (one of China's modes), self exists, but this self is plural and refers to family, clan, group, body, commune, team, village, etc. Moreover, there is a gradual shift from the near to the distant, from self to others, without boundaries and even distinction among people, between friends and foes. It is inclusive and also universal. Under this mode, the degrees of participation and benefits are different; there is no simple average.

Regarding the cultural dialogue between China and foreign countries/China and the West, my main argument is as follows: No matter how superior the Western culture is in the opinion of the Western people, no matter how long-standing our culture is in our opinion, whether China and the West are the continuation of the great civilizations, whether China and the West adopt paths different from those of others, can we eliminate pride and prejudice to jointly cope with our common difficulties, challenges, risks and crises?

Just now Mr. Liu Mengxi mentioned wars, natural degradation and the many problems caused by climate change. At least, this has not been a mere vision; for example, the Belt and Road Initiative offers a very important route: A community of shared responsibilities is built through a community of shared interests and then a community of a common destiny can be built. This may generate reciprocal knowledge and a new shared value. With the gradual development of the Belt and Road, not only China, but also the countries and territories along the Belt and Road and the whole world may serve as the means and ways for us to move out of the law of the jungle and a zero-sum game.

Today, we are discussing this possible opportunity at the levels of knowledge, cultural elements and value levels.

Thank you!

讲好中国发展的“两个故事”

贺文萍 【中国】
中国社会科学院西亚非洲研究所 研究员

1985 年 8 月，中国改革开放的总设计师邓小平在会见坦桑尼亚时任总统朱丽叶·K. 尼雷尔时曾说：“我们的改革不仅在中国，而且在国际范围内也是一种试验。如果成功了，可以为世界上的社会主义事业和不发达国家的发展提供某些经验。”自 1978 年末开始改革开放进程以来，中国在过去的 30 多年里取得了举世瞩目的发展成就。在这一发展的过程中，通过“摸着石头过河”和不断探索适合自身国情的发展战略，中国在经济改革和政治治理方面均摸索和积累了许多宝贵的发展经验，可以和包括非洲国家在内的广大发展中国家进行知识和经验的分享。而在这一知识和经验分享的过程中，笔者认为讲好中国发展的“两个故事”又至为重要。

“中国睡狮是如何醒的”：中国自身的发展故事

2014 年 3 月，习近平主席在出访法国及参加中法建交 50 周年纪念大会时曾说：“中国人民正在为实现中华民族伟大复兴的中国梦而奋斗。中国梦是追求和平的梦，拿破仑说过，中国是一头沉睡的狮子，当这头睡狮醒来时，世界都会为之发抖。中国这头狮子已经醒了，但这是一只和平的、可亲的、文明的狮子。”习主席的讲话当然针对的是国际上那些描黑中国和高喊“狼来了”的势力及声音。

的确，在中国走向复兴和融入世界的过程中，我们常常听到所谓的“中国威胁论”和“中国新殖民主义论”等这些让自古以来一直崇尚仁爱、和谐和宽厚待人的中国人感到莫名其妙、无法理解的“指控”。从国际传播的角度看，姑且不论那些从骨子里就看不惯中国人和以冷战思维铁定想遏制中国发展的极少部分人，世界上绝大多数公民的价值判断和思维定式形成还很大程度上取决于其日常接触的报刊书籍、媒体资讯、政府宣示、名人演讲，甚至包括影视作品以及口口相传的故事分享，等等。因此，要想在国际受众中树立一个“强大而可亲”绝非“强大但可畏”的中国形象（即中国这头狮子虽然已经醒了并强大，但这是一只和平的、可亲的、文明的狮子），就必须在对外传播中讲好“中国这头睡狮是如何醒的”（中国的发展故事）以及“中国醒狮的和平性、可亲感及文明性”（中国如何帮助相对滞后的非洲实现发展的故事）。这两个故事，一个是改变自己，即中国自身是如何发展的，一个是帮助别人，即中国是如何帮助非洲等其他发展中国家发展的。这看似简单的两个“发展故事”及命题，却蕴含着广博和深厚的内涵。要“讲清楚”（当然在行动中更要“做明白”）这两个“发展”故事，就必须在故事的内容和讲故事的方式上（包括讲故事的主体、故事载体）下大功夫。

仅仅 30 年以前，中国的人均 GDP 甚至低于非洲的马拉维和布基纳法索。但在过去的 30 多年中，中国成功使 3 亿人脱离了绝对贫困，GDP 以年均超过 9% 的增长率上升到了 5 万亿美元，成为仅次于美国的世界第二大经济体。纵观历史，放眼全球，人类历史上还从未有过一个国家在如此短时间内、如此大规模地发展得如此迅速。更重要的是，从未有过一个国家在这么短的时间跨度内，使数量如此众多的人口摆脱了贫困并改善了人们的生活水平。也正因经济发展的成果是硬碰硬的数字和在中国大地上实际发生的变化，因此中国过去 30 年所取得的减贫和经济发展成就，得到了包括西方国家在内的世界各国的广泛欣赏和赞誉，取得哪怕那些最挑剔的西方政界、学界和媒体人士都一致公认的巨大成绩。

然而，对中国睡狮苏醒过程的国际解读也存在诸多盲点，比如：中国经济发展是靠牺牲政治自由实现的，中国的人权和民主出现了倒退，经济自由化和政治集权化是一种奇怪的嫁接并且不可持续，等等。因此，这就要求我们在对外传播过程中要针对这些认识误区讲清楚至少以下三个问题：

第一，中国的改革开放是一个综合系统工程，30 多年来所取得的经济改革成就与我们所进行的政治和社会改革是同步进行且密不可分的。我们在对外传播中要着重讲清楚，中国的改革绝不仅仅限于单一的经济领域（尽管这一领域发生的变化最显著，也最直观），而是涉及经济体制、政治体制、文化体制以及社会体制等各个方面的全方位的改革。30 多年来，正是通过对领导体制、干部用人体制、选举体制（包括党内选举和基层选举）、立法和司法体制、决策体制等诸多权力的监督与制衡方面的渐进性改革，才得以确保经济改革不断向纵深推进以及在剧烈的社会和经济转型过程中各民族之间以及社会各阶层之间利益的兼容与和谐共处。尽管在发展的过程中，中国也面临贫富分化、地区发展失衡等诸多挑战，但从历史的纵向发展坐标看，中国人民正享受着历史上前所未有并且是越来越多的经济、社会和政治权利。这正是为什么在以发展为导向的“北京共识”在与以自由化为导向的“华盛顿共识”同场竞技中能被越来越多的发展中国家所追捧的原因所在。

另外，世界历史发展到今天，特别是通过近年来跌宕起伏的北非中东国家的社会转型，人们已经越来越清楚地认识到，“选举”并不是“民主”的代名词，更不是政治变革的唯一标签。各国选择通往民主、自由和发展之路的政治经济发展模式必须与自身的历史、文化、社会环境与背景相适应。中国发展成就的取得并不是照搬或照抄任何西方的政治或经济发展模式而得来的。相反，正是反对西方的干涉，走适合自己国情的发展道路，才保持了中国的社会和政治稳定以及在此基础上的经济发展。

第二，作为一个发展中的转型国家，中国正确处理和摆正了改革（reform）、发展（development）与稳定（stability）这三者间的关系。中国的改革与发展之路是秉着社会稳定优先的原则，采取先稳定后发展，以发展促稳定，以改革促发展，实现改革、发展与稳定之间的协调和平衡。我们在经济领域“以一种先易后难、循序渐进、摸索与积累的方式，从易到难地进行改革，并吸取中外一切优秀的思想和经验”。在改革推进的方式方法上，中国采取的是先搞试点再根据效果逐步扩大直至大面积推广的“不断试错并及时纠正”（the trial and error method）的“软着陆”方针。从农村联产承包责任制、乡镇企业发展、国有企业改革到金融领域改革，再从计划经济到市场经济过渡的过程中伴随着的是就业体制、社会保障体制、收入分配体制、户籍体制等各方面的改革，目的是减缓改革带来的震动对弱势群体的冲击，规避和分散改革的代价和风险。在政治领域的改革也同样是在稳定的大前提下逐步扩大政治参与，自下而上地积极推进基层民主选举和党内民主的探索，以最终实现政治平等的目标。因此，当我们回望过去的 30 年，可以自豪地说，中国人民在中国政府的领导下，至少完成了两件人类历史上罕见的大事：一是在短时间内人民的生活水平得到显著提高，国家综合实力显著增强；二是中国确保了人类历史上如此巨大的一个经济和社会转型是在一个相对稳定与和谐的状态下进行并且顺利完成的。在过去的30年里，中国没有大的内战和社会冲突，社会稳定和和平发展环境得以维护。

第三，中国的发展经验还表明，拥有一个强有力的、致力于发展的政府以及富有远见卓识的领导人和正确的政策同样是实现发展必不可少的因素。对于转型中的发展中国家来说，这些要素是凝聚全民对于实现现代化的共识、保持稳定并推进改革的重要保证。自1949年新中国成立以来，中国在国家安全方面经历过朝鲜战争和越南战争的洗礼，在内政方面经历过“文化大革命”十年动乱的浩劫，在外交方面经受过与西方世界几起几落的对抗与缓和，在金融领域也经受过亚洲金融危机以及华尔街金融动荡带给我们的冲击。而中国政府和人民正是在这些冲击和苦痛中历练自己，不断成长。自新中国成立60多年来，中国在相对稳定的四代领导人的领导下一步步走到今天。开国之父毛泽东对于中国作为一个民族国家的统一和团结做出了巨大贡献。改革开放总设计师邓小平不仅带领中国走向了发展的康庄大道，而且打破了领导干部的终身制，引入了集体决策机制。邓小平之后的江泽民、胡锦涛等第三代和第四代中国领导人同样引领着中国人民战胜了若干新挑战，使中国走向了科学发展、和谐发展的现代化之路。在过去的30年，中国政府制定并坚持贯彻了一整套正确的方针政策，如长期坚持低生育率政策、重视基础设施建设、建设经济特区、出口导向型的工业化政策，积极参与经济全球化，坚持科学发展观，建设和谐社会，等等。由于大政方针的正确和发展方向的始终不动摇，虽然中国经济在此期间受全球局势的影响也经历过几次大起大落，政治发展也经历过动荡和风险，但每次都是在政府强有力的干预和宏观调控下走出阴霾，使国家回到发展的正确轨道。

当然，我们在传播和宣讲成功的中国发展故事和经验时，也不能回避问题，如中国当前仍面临经济持续快速发展所带来的诸如贫富分化、城乡差距、地区发展不平衡、环境污染以及社会保障体制不完善等各方面的挑战。但这些挑战并不是中国所独有，而是很多发展中国家在发展和转型的过程中所共同面对、无法回避的问题。因此，中国在继续深化改革的过程中如何应对这些挑战的经验与教训同样可对其他发展中国家提供借鉴。

“中国醒狮的和平性、可亲感及文明性”：中国如何帮助非洲发展的故事

2013年4月，习近平主席在参加博鳌亚洲论坛2013年年会时曾指出，世界各国联系紧密、利益交融，要互通有无、优势互补，在追求本国利益时兼顾他国合理关切，在谋求自身发展中促进各国共同发展，不断扩大共同利益汇合点。他还引用诗词说：“一花独放不是春，百花齐放春满园。”的确，要打破“中国威胁论”和“中国新殖民主义”所秉持的所谓“国强必霸”和“损人利己”的立论依据，中国就不能仅对自身的发展“孤芳自赏”，而是要用中国自身发展的故事、经验和能力，来帮助和带动仍然发展滞后的发展中国家共同发展。

其实，“乐善好施”和“宽以待人”历来是中国人的传统美德，即便在中国仍然处于贫穷落后境况的时候也坚持对亚非拉人民施以援手。如早在20世纪50年代，当新中国自身还处于百废待兴和西方战略围堵的困难时期时，中国就对非洲国家反帝反殖的民族解放运动和南部非洲人民的反种族主义斗争提供了大量真诚无私的政治、经济和军事支持。早在20世纪60年代初周恩来总理访非期间提出的《中国对外援助八项原则》中，就明确提出：中国政府在对外提供援助的时候，严格尊重受援国的主权，绝不附带任何条件，绝不要求任何特权；中国政府以无息或低息贷款的方式提供经济援助，在需要的时候延长还款期限，以尽量减少受援国的负担；中国政府对外提供援助的目的，不是造成受援国对中国的依赖，而是帮助受援国逐步走上自力更生、经济上独立发展的道路；中国政府对外提供任何一种技术援助的时候，保证做到使受援国的人员充分掌握这种技术；中国政府提供自己所能生产的、质量最好的设备和物资；中国援助专家同受援国自己的专家享受同样的物质待遇，不容许有任何特殊要求和享受。在这一贯彻至今的原则指导下，中国已帮助非洲国家援建了包括纺织厂、水电站、体育场、医院、学校等在内的近千个各类项目。著名的坦赞铁路就是中国在自身经济十分困难的情况下为非洲援建的。这条友谊之路全长1860公里，中国曾先后有5万工程技术人员在坦赞苦战酷热和疾病，其中64人献出了宝贵生命，在中非关系中具有丰碑性的历史意义。近十多年来，随着中国国力的增强以及2000年“中非合作论坛”机制的建立，中国的对非援助和经贸合作更是得到突飞猛进的发展。迄今，中国对非洲的援助项目已遍及全非的50多个国家。中国在非洲已经援建了2000多公里的铁路，3000多公里的公路，建了100多所学校，60多所医院，还减免了200

多亿人民币的债务，等等。

另外，中国的对非政策践行的是“真、实、亲、诚”的四字箴言。2013年3月中国两会甫一结束，习主席即出访坦桑尼亚、南非和刚果（布）等非洲三国。在访非演讲时，习主席用“真、实、亲、诚”四个字高度概括中国的对非政策，指出对待非洲朋友，我们讲一个“真”字；开展对非合作，我们讲一个“实”字；加强中非友好，我们讲一个“亲”字；解决合作中的问题我们讲一个“诚”字，引起非洲领导人和民众的强烈共鸣。2014年1月，外交部部长王毅访问非洲时，再次强调“正确义利观是新时期中国外交的一面旗帜”。他在与塞内加尔外长恩迪亚耶会谈后共同会见记者时指出，“义”是指“道义”。中国在同非洲国家交往时应以道义为先，坚持与非洲兄弟平等相待，真诚友好，重诺守信，更要为维护非洲的正当权利和合理诉求仗义执言。“利”是指“互利”。中国在与非洲国家交往时决不走殖民者的掠夺老路，决不效仿资本家的唯利是图做法，也不会像有的国家只是为实现自己的一己私利，而是志在与非洲兄弟共同发展，共同繁荣。在此过程中，中方会更多考虑非洲国家的合理需求，力争通过合作让非洲早得利、多得利。在需要的时候，我们还要重义让利，甚至舍利取义。当年的坦赞铁路就是正确义利观的一个典范，今天屹立在亚的斯亚贝巴的非盟会议中心是另一个例证。

“真、实、亲、诚”的对非政策不是挂在嘴上的动听词汇，而是体现在实实在在的推动非洲发展的各项措施及其取得的成效上。不容抹杀的事实是，中非关系在过去的十余年里依托“中非合作论坛”这一强劲的机制化平台，在贸易、投资、承包合作、发展援助等各个领域均取得了骄人的成绩，实现了跨越性的大发展。如今，中国已自2009年超越美国连续5年成为非洲第一大贸易伙伴国。2013年中非贸易额达2100多亿美元，是1960年贸易额的2000多倍。另外，非洲还是中国第三大海外投资市场和第二大海外工程承包市场。截止到2013年底，中国在非洲直接投资的存量已达到250亿美元，在非投资的中国企业则超过了2500家。这样的成绩单既是中非共同努力的成果，也同样有利于中国与非洲双方的发展。

事实上，同非洲的西方传统合作伙伴相比，中国在同非洲合作中给非洲带来的好处要多得多。中非贸易和物美价廉的中国日用工业品为非洲人提供了买得起的商品，客观上提高了当地民众的生活水平。我认识的一位来华进修的尼日利亚军官曾激动地对我说，感谢中国，尼日利亚普通百姓现在不必再穿来自欧美的二手旧衣服，而买得起来自中国的新衣服了。穿新、旧衣服的区别，体现出的是一种期盼已久的自尊。另外，也正是得益于与中国贸易的大幅增加，撒哈拉以南的非洲国家近十年来取得了近6%的年均经济增长，成为全世界经济增长速度最快的地区之一（仅中非贸易一项近年来对非洲经济增长的贡献率就达20%）。就连英国著名的《经济学家》周刊，也把贴在非洲头上的标签从十年前的“无望的大陆”（hopeless）换成了如今的“崛起的大陆”（uprising）（该周刊在2001年和2011年关于非洲发展的封面文章标题）。中国对非援助、投资和经贸活动的加强不仅使非洲受援国实现了外援和外资来源的多元化，增强了非洲自主选择的能力和自主决定自身发展道路的自主性，而且还增加了非洲国家的就业和税收，培养了大批非洲人才和带来了适合发展阶段的适用技术。研究中非关系的著名南非学者马丁•戴维斯早就指出，“非洲的发展已经和中国在非洲投资贸易活动的开展呈现出一种紧密的正相关和共生共荣关系”。可见，中非合作的共同发展绝非一句“漂亮话”和空话，而是活生生的现实。

2015年12月，在中非合作论坛约翰内斯堡峰会上，习近平主席代表中国政府推出了未来三年推进中非关系、主要以投资带动并且总额达600亿美元的超强度升级版“十大合作计划”，将在工业、农业、基础设施、金融、绿色发展、贸易和投资便利化、减贫惠民、公共卫生、人文交流、和平与安全等十大领域开展合作。中国在自身经济发展呈现增长率下降态势的情况下仍然逆势而上，继续加大对非合作力度，充分表明了中国推动非洲发展以及中非团结共度时艰的决心。这种态度和勇气理应受到国际社会的高度赞赏，而不是相反。

Aptly Tell "Two Stories" of China's Development

He Wenping / China

Chief Research Fellow at the Institute of West-Asian and African Studies, CASS

In August, 1985, when meeting with Julius Kambarage Nyerere, President of Tanzania, Deng Xiaoping, Chief Architect of China's reform and opening up, said: "Our reform is an experiment not only in China but also at the international level. If it becomes successful, it can provide some experience for the development of the socialist cause and the underdeveloped countries in the world." Since the reform and opening up in late 1978, remarkable development achievements have been made in China over the past 30 years. In this developmental process, through "crossing the river by feeling the stones" and continuous exploration of the developmental strategy consistent with China's national conditions, China has explored and gathered a lot of valuable experience in development in both economic reform and political governance, and can share knowledge and experience with the developing countries, including African countries. The author believes that aptly telling "two stories" of China's development well is of great importance in the process of sharing knowledge and experience.

1. "How China, a Sleeping Lion, Awakes": Stories of China's Development

In March, 2014, when visiting France and attending the meeting commemorating the 50th anniversary of the establishment of diplomatic relations between China and France, Chinese President Xi Jinping said: "The Chinese people are striving to realize the Chinese dream of achieving a great rejuvenation of the Chinese nation. The Chinese dream is a dream of pursuing peace.Napoleon Bonaparte said that China was a sleeping lion; when this sleeping lion awakes, it will shake the world. The sleeping Chinese lion has awoken, but it is a peaceful, pleasant and civilized lion." President Xi Jinping's speech responded to the forces and voice which defamed China describing it as a wolf in the international community.

Indeed, when China revives and strives to become part of the world, we are often subject to the so-called "China Threat Theory", "China Neocolonialism Theory" and other "allegations" which are baffling and incomprehensible for the Chinese people who have always upheld benevolence, harmony and have treated others generously since ancient times. From the perspective of international communication, the value judgments and mindsets of most citizens in the world, except a few people who disdain the Chinese people in their bones and unalterably strive to contain China's development with aCold War mentality, largely depend upon newspapers, periodicals, books, media information, government announcements, celebrity speeches, even films, television programs and stories shared from mouth to mouth to which they get access in their daily lives. Therefore, in order to build the image of China as a powerful and pleasant country rather than a powerful but formidable China—although the sleeping Chinese lion has awoken and become powerful, it is a peaceful, pleasant and civilized lion—among the international audiences, it is essential to aptly tell, in communication to the outside world, two stories: "How China, a sleeping lion, awakes"—the story of China's development—and "How peaceful, pleasant and civilized the awakened Chinese lion is"—the story of how China helps the relatively underdeveloped Africa. One of the stories shows how

China changes itself—how China develops, while the other one explains how China helps others—how China helps other developing countries,including the developing countries in Africa. Both "development stories" and propositions seem to be simple, but they have extensive and profound connotations. In order to clearly tell both "development stories"—of course, let people understand through actions, it is necessary to make great efforts in the contents of the stories and in the way of telling them,includingstorytellers and story carriers.

Thirty years ago, China's per capita GDP was lower than that of African Malawi and Burkina Faso. However, over the past 30 years, China has successfully lifted 300 million people out of absolute poverty, the GDP has increased to 5 trillion USD at an average annual rate of above 9%, making China the second largest economy in the world, only second to the USA. Historically and globally, no country has ever developed so rapidly on such a large scale within such a short time in human history. More importantly, previously, no country has lifted such a huge population out of poverty and improved the people's living standard within such a short time. The achievements in economic development, evidenced by solid data and changes, have actually occurred across China, thus the achievements in poverty reduction and economic development made in China in the past 30 years have been widely appreciated and acclaimed by the countries around the world, including Western countries. These achievements are even universally recognized by the most critical people in the Western political, educational and media circles.

However, there are many misunderstandings in the international community about the process during which the sleeping Chinese lion awakens. For example, China's economy develops at the expense of political freedom; regression occurs in China's human rights and democracy; liberalization of the economy and political centralization is a strange kind of grafting and it is unsustainable. Therefore, this requires us to explicitly explain the following three issues in response to these misunderstandingswhen communicating abroad.

First, China's reform and opening up is a comprehensive systematic project. The achievements in economic reform made over the past 30 years have synchronized with and are closely related to our political and social reforms. We should clearly make the following explanations when communicating abroad: China's reform is not limited to the single field of the economy—although the changes in this field are the most significant and visible—but it is an all-round reform involving various aspects, including the economic system, the political system, the cultural system and the social system. Over the past 30 years, gradual reforms have been carried out in power supervision, checks and balances in the leadership system, in the cadre appointment system, in the election system, including intra-Party elections and grass-roots elections, in the legislative and judicial systems, so that the economic reform can be continuously intensified; in this way a compatible and harmonious coexistence of interests can be achieved among nationalities and among social strata during drastic social and economictransformations. Many challenges, such as the polarization between the rich and the poor, the regional developmentalimbalance, have occurred in China during its development, but from a historical perspective, the Chinese people are enjoying unprecedented, increasing economic, social and political rights. This is exactly the reason why the development-oriented Beijing Consensus can compete with the liberalization-oriented Washington Consensus which is becoming popular among an increasing number of developing countries.

Moreover, given the historical development of the world up until now, especially the turbulent social transformation of the countries in North Africa and the Middle East in recent years, the people have increasingly realized that "election" is not synonymous with "democracy" and not the only label for political changes. The political and economic patterns of development for achieving democracy, freedom and development as chosen by various countries must tally with their own historical, cultural and social environments and backgrounds. China's developmental achievements have not been made by copying any Western political or economic developmental pattern. On the contrary, thanks to China's opposition toWesternintervention and the adoption of a developmental path suited to China's national conditions, China has maintained social and political stability and it has developed its economy on this basis.

Second, as a developing country in transition, China has correctly handled and rationalized the relations among reform, development and stability. China's path towards reform and development is being pursued under the principle of putting social stability first—China has put stability before reform, and has improved stability through development and promoted development through reform in order to achieve coordination and balance among reform, development and stability. We have advanced in the economic field first by solving the easy-to-solve problems and then the hard-to-solve problems, proceeding in a gradual way, making explorations and accumulation, carrying out reforms in the order of increasing difficulty, and drawing upon all excellent domestic and foreign lines of thought and experiences. Regarding the way of pushing forward reforms, China has first carried out pilot work and then it has gradually extended that work into a wide range according to their effects, which is the soft landing policy based on the trial and error method. The process from adoption of the rural contract system with remuneration linked to output, the development of township enterprises, the reform of state-owned enterprises, to the financial reform, and the transition process from a planned economy to a market economy were accompanied by reforms in the employment system, the social security system, the income distribution system and the household registration system, which have been designed to mitigate the impact of reform-induced shock on the disadvantaged groups, to avert and spread the reform price and risks. The reform in the political field has also been conducted by gradually expanding political participation under the condition of maintaining stability, actively pushing forward the exploration of grassroots democratic reforms and intra-Party democracy from bottom to top to ultimately achieve political equality. Therefore, looking back on the past 30 years, all of the Chinese people can proudly say that, under the leadership of the Chinese Government, the Chinese people have accomplished at least two great things which are rare in human history: (1) significantly improving the people's living standard and remarkably enhancing the national comprehensive strength within a short time; (2) ensuring that the tremendous economic and social transformation in human history is smoothly completed in a relatively stable and harmonious state. Over the past 30 years, there have been no large civil wars or social conflicts in China so that an environment of social stability and peacefuldevelopmenthas been maintained. Third, China's developmentalexperience shows that a strong government dedicated to development, farsighted leaders and correct policies are the essential factors for development. For a developing country in transition, these factors are the important guarantee for building consensus on modernization among all of the people, keeping stability and pushing ahead with reforms. Since 1949 when new China was founded, China has undergone the Korean War and the Vietnam War in the national security field, the decade-long Great Cultural Revolution in domestic affairs, several confrontations and détentes with the Western world in foreign affairs, and the impact of the Asian Financial Crisis and the financial turmoil on Wall Street in the financial field. The Chinese Government and the people have improved the country's capability and have continuously grown amidst these impacts and hardships. In more than 60 years, since the founding of new China, China has moved ahead step by step under the leadership of four relatively stable generations of leaders. The founding father Mao Zedong made tremendous contributions to the national unity of China as a national country. Deng Xiaoping, Chief Architect of the reform and opening up, led China to embark on the broad road to development, broke the lifelong tenure of leading cadres and introduced the collective decision-making mechanism. The third and fourth generations of Chinese leaders with Jiang Zemin and Hu Jintao as the focal point,respectively, after Deng Xiaoping led the Chinese people to overcome a number of new challenges so that China embarked on the road towards modernization characterized by scientific and harmonious development. Over the past 30 years, the Chinese Government has developed and implemented a complete set of correct policies and guidelines, such as upholding the low birth rate policy for a long time, attaching importance to the construction of infrastructures, establishing special economic zones, adopting anexport-orientedindustrial policy, actively participating in economic globalization, carrying out the Scientific Outlook on Development, building a harmonious society, etc. China's economy has experienced ups and downs due to the impact of the global situation during this period, and political development has undergoneturbulences and risks; however, China, thanks to the adoption of major appropriate policies and guidelines and its perseverance in the direction of development, has successfully come out of gloom and has returned to the right track of development thanks to the government's strong intervention and macro control.

Of course, when disseminating and telling the successful stories and experiences of China's development, we cannot sidestep problems such as the challenges resulting from the sustained and rapid economic development in China at the present stage, including the polarization between the rich and the poor, the urban-rural gap, the regional development imbalance, environmental pollution and the underdevelopment of the social security system. However, these challenges do not merely occur in China; they are the common problems that many developing countries cannot avoid during their development and transformation. Therefore, China's experience and lessons in coping with these challenges in the process of continuing to intensify the reforms can also serve as reference for other developing countries.

2. "How peaceful, pleasant and civilized the awakened Chinese lion is": The story of how China helps Africa develop

In April, 2013, when attending the 2013 Annual Meeting of the Boao Forum for Asia, Chinese President Xi Jinping said that the countries in the world were closely interconnected with intertwined interests and that it was necessary to make up what others lack and complement each other's advantages, consider the reasonable concerns of other countries while pursuing one's own interests, promote the common development of various countries while seeking one's own development, and continuously expand the points where the common interests converge. He also quoted a poem: "A single blossoming flower does not make a spring, while all the flowers in full blossom bring a spring to the garden." In order to break the basis of the argumentation, according to the "China Threat Theory" and the "China Neocolonialism Theory", that "a powerful country is bound to seek hegemony" and "a powerful country certainly harms the interests of other countries to benefit itself", China cannot indulge in its own development and should help, with its stories, experience and capability in development, the developing countries with backward development achieve common development.

In fact, being happy in doing good and treating others generously are the traditional virtues of the Chinese people; the Chinese people provided assistance to the people in Asia, Africa and Latin America even when the Chinese people were still poor and backward. For example, in the 1950s, when new China still needed to rebuild itself in various aspects and was subject to strategic containment from Western countries, it provided much sincere and selfless political, economic and military support to the national liberation movements for combating imperialism and colonialism in African countries and the struggle against racism in southern Africa. The *China's Eight Principles for Foreign Assistance*,put forward by Chinese Premier Zhou Enlai when visiting Africa in the early 1960s,explicitly pointed out that when the Chinese Government provided foreign assistance, it strictly respected the sovereignty of the recipient countries, imposed no conditions and required no privilege; the Chinese Government provided economic assistance in the form of interest-free loans or loans with low interest, and when necessary, extended the loan term to minimize the burden on the recipient countries; provision of foreign assistance by the Chinese Government was designed to help the recipient countries gradually embark on a road with self-reliance for an economically independent development rather than cause recipient countries' dependence upon China; in the case of providing any technical assistance to foreign countries, the Chinese Government ensured that the personnel of the recipient countries could fully master the technology involved; the Chinese Government provided the highest quality of equipment and materials produced by China; Chinese experts in assistance enjoyed material treatment which was the same as that available to the experts of the recipient countries, and no special requirements and enjoyments were allowed. Under the guidance of these principles implemented up until now, China has assisted African countries in carrying out nearly 1,000 projects,including textile mills, hydropower stations, stadiums, hospitals and schools. The famous Tanzania-Zambia Railway was built for Africa with assistance from China when China had great economic difficulties. This friendship road was 1,860km long. Fifty thousand Chinese technical engineering personnel bitterly struggled with severe heat and diseases in Tanzania and Zambia, 64 of whom lost their precious lives. This railway is of monumental historical significance in Sino-African relations. In recent decades, with the enhancement of China's national strength and the establishment of the mechanism of the Forum on China-Africa Cooperation in 2000, China's assistance to and economic and trade cooperation with Africa have soared. So far, the projects carried out with assistance from China to Africa have been available in more than 50 countries across Africa. China has assisted Africa in building 2,000-plus-km of railways, 3,000-plus-km of roads, more than 100 schools, more than 60 hospitals, and it has reduced and cancelled 20-plus-billion RMB in debts.

In addition, China carries out policies towards Africa in a genuine, pragmatic, amiable and sincere way. In March, 2013, shortly after China's two sessions (CPC and CPPCC), Chinese President Xi Jinping visited Tanzania, South Africa and the Republic of the Congo. During his visit to Africa, President Xi used the four words "genuine, pragmatic, amiable and sincere" to summarize China's policies toward Africa extraordinarily well and pointed out that China treated African friends in a genuine way, engaged in cooperation with Africa in a pragmatic manner, enhanced friendly Sino-African relations in an amiable way and solved problems in cooperation in a sincere way. This remark had aroused a strong resonance among African leaders and people. In January, 2014, Foreign Minister Wang Yi visited

Africa and emphasized again that the correct righteousness and beneficial view was a flag in China’s diplomacy in the new period. When attending a press conference together with Senegal Foreign Minister Mankeur Ndiaye, after talks, Wang Yi stressed that righteousness meant that China put moral goodness first when dealing with African countries, treated African brothers on an equal footing, in a sincere and friendly way, honored commitments and kept faith, and more importantly, spoke out from a sense of justice to safeguard Africa’s legitimate rights and rational appeals; benefit referred to mutual benefit and meant that, when dealing with African countries, China would by no means follow in the footsteps of colonists, emulate the capitalists’ act of placing excessive emphasis on profits, or only deliberately seek its own selfish interests like some countries; China was willing to work with African brothers for joint development and common prosperity. In this process, China would give more consideration to the reasonable needs of African countries, and strive to make Africa soon obtain more benefits through cooperation. In case of need, we would also value righteousness and surrender part of the benefits, even give up righteousness to benefits. The Tanzania-Zambia Railway is a model of the correct view of righteousness and benefits. The Conference Center of African Union in Addis Ababa is another good example.

“Genuine, pragmatic, amiable and sincere” embodied in China’s policy toward Africa are not merely fair-sounding words, but these words are reflected in the measures for realistically promoting Africa’s development and the results obtained. The following facts cannot be denied: Based on the Forum on China-Africa Cooperation as a strong institutional platform, in more than a decade, the Sino-African relations have been enhanced by making spectacularachievements in trade, investment, contractedcooperation, development assistance and other fields, and achieving a great leap in development. China has surpassed the USA and has become the largest trading partner for Africa for five consecutive years since 2009. The China-Africa trade volume exceeded 210 billion USD in 2013, more than 2,000 times what it was in 1960. Furthermore, Africa is the third largest overseas investment market and the second largest overseas project contracting market for China. As of the end of 2013, China's direct foreign investment stock in Africa reached 25 billion USD, and more than 2,500 Chinese enterprises have invested in Africa. Such an impressive track record is the result of concerted efforts from China and Africa and is beneficial for the development of both China and Africa.

In fact, compared with traditional Western partners in Africa, China delivers many more benefits to Africa in cooperation with Africa.Sino-African trade and inexpensive and fine industrial goods for daily use from China provide African people with affordable goods, improving the living standards of the local people. A Nigerian military officer who pursues further education in China and with whom I am familiar excitedly said to me: "Thanks to China, now the ordinary people in Nigeria no longer wear the second-hand clothes from Europe and the USA and they can afford to buy new clothes from China. The difference in wearing new and old clothes is seen in a person's long-awaited self-esteem. In addition, thanks to a sharp increase in trade with China, the Sub-Saharan African countries achieved economic growth at an average annual rate of nearly 6% in almost ten years and have become one of the regions with the fastest economic growth in the world—Sino-African trade alone has contributed 20% to Africa's economic growth in recent years. The well-known UK weekly *The Economist* no longer labels Africa as a hopeless land and instead, regards it as a uprising land—the titles of cover stories about Africa's development in this weekly magazine in 2001 and 2011. China's intensified assistance, investment, economic and trade activities in Africa have diversified the sources of foreign assistance and foreign capital for African recipient countries and have enhanced Africa's capability for making independent choices and Africa's autonomy for deciding on the developmental path at its own discretion; these activities have also increased employment and taxes in African countries, and have helped cultivate a large number of African talents and brought appropriate technologies suited to the stages of development. The well-known South African scholar Martyn Davies, who is engaged in studying Sino-African relations, pointed out early on that Africa's development had a close positive relationship of correlation, co-existence and co-prosperity with China's investment and trade activities in Africa. As shown, joint development based on Sino-African cooperation is anything but fine words and empty talk, and it has become a reality.

In December, 2015, in the Johannesburg Summit of the Forum on China-Africa Cooperation, Chinese President Xi Jinping unveiled, on behalf of the Chinese Government, ten highly upgraded cooperation plans for promoting Sino-African relations, focusing on investment-driven activities with a total amount of 60 billion USD in the next three years, under which China and Africa would engage in cooperation in ten fields including industry, agriculture, infrastructure, finance, green development, trade and investmentfacilitation, poverty reduction for benefiting the people, public health, people-to-people exchanges, peace and security. China continues to intensify its cooperation with Africa amidst its own economic slowdown; this fully demonstrates China's determination to boost Africa's development and ensure that China and Africa work together to overcome hard times. This attitude and courage deserves to be highly commended by the international community and should not be treated differently.

对今后中国经济的几点看法

西川博史　【日本】
北海商科大学　代校长

一　“一带一路”建设与世界战略

1. 在东亚地区新动向

（1）亚洲基础设施投资银行（AIIB）

• 在最初的5—6年间，提供的贷款规模为100—150亿美元；

• 贷款对象国家为“一带一路”地区的国家（东盟）；

• 资金循环以美元为基础，那么现状将不会发生改变；

国际贸易决算中所占比重（2014.4—2015.3）：人民币1%，日元3%，美元41.6%，欧元36.6%，各国政府和中央银行的外汇储备都是美元。由此说明，AIIB对“地区一体化”可以起到一定的作用，但是对人民币的国际化还不能抱有太大的期待。

（2）东盟（ASEAN）地区

• 人口：6亿，经济规模：GDP 2万5700亿美元，相当于中国GDP的1/4，日本的1/2；

• “东盟经济共同体”已完成近8成，已被吸纳到世界经济体系之中，世界经济的动向将变得更加复杂。

2. 关于“另一个中国”的含义需要做说明

• 经历改革开放之后，中国的经济高速发展，人民生活的富裕化，与世界的交流在不断扩大，这些都受到很高的评价。

• 但是，也存在与此相反的一面，那就是资本主义世界存在的诸多弊端，对中国也产生了强烈的影响。这些弊端，可以说无论是发达国家和发展中国家，都存在同样的问题，特别是农业问题和贫富差距问题。

• 如果东盟实现了 7% 增长率，其经济规模在十年内将达到现在的日本规模。届时上述弊端的发生将不可避免。

• 这些问题到底由谁来负责？在更加复杂世界经济的动向之中，寻求解决方案将更困难。

3. 农业问题面临的困难

（1）东亚的农业生产形态

• 在美国，与数百公顷的土地规模的农业经营方式相适应的农业政策，在东亚是行不通的。如果在亚洲的以外出务工为补充的“小农经营”生产方式下，以市场机制为前提条件，照搬美国的农业政策，那么毫无疑问结果将会很悲惨。

• 换言之，不能在市场机制下进行农业的调节。

（2）农业受到工业化和城市化侵蚀的问题

• 工业的发展和耕地减少存在一种相对应的比例关系。耕地的减少导致粮食产量的减少，而解决粮食产量减少的问题一般有两种办法，一个是提高农业生产率，另一个是增加国外进口。

• 前者存在一定的限度，所以依靠进口是无法避免的，这样将会导致农地的进一步减少。

• 另一方面，如果只是单纯的扩张农业生产能力，后果很可能出现环境污染问题，或者热衷于生产一些质量粗劣的农产品（包括转基因农产品）和无视食品安全。

（3）如何对待环境的问题

• 中国有大片的沙漠，无论是从改善生存环境的角度来看，还是从农业发展的角度来看，把沙漠改造成农田牧场是人们极为迫切的希望，对于国家的持续发展具有巨大的意义。

• 以“沙漠的农田牧场化”为基础来构建农村共同体的话，将会为具有中国特色的社会主义市场经济提供一个样板和模式。

二　中国式发展的独特性

• 有关建立“一带一路”伙伴关系的设想和以东盟统一为前提的亚投行的构想，都与自由贸易带动经济增长这样的期待有关。

• 这个问题在于对世界经济危机缺乏正确的认识。当前的经济危机，正如马克思主义经济学曾经指出的那样，它是资本主义内在的基本矛盾，即世界性“生产过剩”的必然反映。

• 因此，大量的廉价产品和劳动力通过贸易自由化的方式涌入“经济增长地区”，必然会进一步造成世界规模供给过剩。依赖于外需的“出口主导型”增长只不过使过剩产品的所在地区发生了转移。

• 强逼东盟国家进行自由贸易，与曾标榜“互惠”“共存共赢”的欧美强国向东亚特别是中国索求自由平等权利的行为有什么不同？

• 贫富差距的问题对于资本主义来说是必然的，而哪些强国总是站在“富人”一方，他们主张的理论也只不过就是“自由贸易”的意识形态化而已。

• 但是，主张贸易保护主义也是行不通的。现在正处于一个能否从资本主义机制下彻底摆脱出来的关键时刻。

• 在这种情况下，应该选择的道路是“自由贸易”，还是“非市场化自给”呢？完全的自由贸易和完全的自给都是不可取的。

• 应该追求的是，提出一种对于贸易和自给进行管理的“构想”。问题在于，应该把国家管理这一概念从那种以市场经济为前提的“非效率”观念的束缚中解放出来。这就需要对

国家管理，也就是对“国有”概念重新进行讨论。

三　中国的改革深化与将来展望

1. 中国经济改革或体制改革的目标，就在于确立一个具有中国特色的社会主义市场经济体制模型

• 实现这个目标，就需要改变经济成长的类型，即由出口型为主导的经济增长转变为以内需为主导的经济增长，换言之，为经济的持续增长必须要找出“增长的新引擎”。

• 但是，单纯学习经济发达国家的经验，不能实现中国特色的改革。

• 中国要建立“有中国特色”的“社会主义”“市场经济”，那么“有中国特色”的这一形容词，究竟是形容什么呢？是“社会主义”呢？还是“市场经济”呢？

• 20世纪80年代以后，中国对社会主义计划经济体制作了改革，开始导入“社会主义市场经济体制”。

• 然而，对于以往的社会主义计划经济体制与社会主义市场经济体制之间的区别和不同特点做过哪些讨论呢？

• 虽然有许多论述就改革作了一些说明，但是，对于为什么要做这些改革这一个重要的问题却没有进行充分的说明

• 关于“开放”问题的讨论也存在同样的问题，例如“自由贸易”对于社会主义市场体制来说为什么是必要的?

2. 在中国，有必要进行彻底的“改革”

• 腐败是非法占有劳动者剩余价值，使之的私有化，所以应该考虑的问题是怎样才能建立起一个与有中国特色的社会主义的原则相符合的社会主义所有制。

• 现在，国家所有制或全民所有制，在所谓的“效率化”的名义下，被具体化为“国有控股公司”，只有那些在国家资产管理委员会的账簿上登记资产，才能转为归政府各机关所有，通过“利改税”，政府机关也变成了需要缴纳税金的机关，应该说这正是产生腐败的一个温床。

• 其原因在于尽管各机关并没占有国家资产及其收益的权利，只要缴纳税金，实际上就意味着它本身不过就是一个普通的公司。

以上所说的多种问题，都需要我们对资本主义经济再做讨论。资本主义的弊端是多方面的，把这些弊端单纯的归结为“企业社会责任”的问题是毫无意义的。即使企业不去实现它所应该担负的社会责任，资本主义也完全不会因此而改变它的机制。

把资本主义体制看作发展的最高形式，其最后的堡垒就是那些曾经的社会主义国家对于现状的批判。但是，那种主张资本主义能做到而社会主义做不到的观点是毫无根据的。

迄今为止，社会主义经济究竟错在哪里，还不能说已经得到了充分的论证。中国社会主义经济的错误，是社会主义经济本身不可避免的错误，还是中国自己造成的错误，并没有讨论清楚。因此，应该说现在已到了需要我们对社会主义究竟是什么重新讨论的时候。

Views on China's Future Economy

Hiroshi Nishikawa / Japan

Acting President of Hokkai School of Commerce

I. Construction of the Belt and Road and World Strategy

1. New developments in East Asia

(1) Asian Infrastructure Investment Bank (AIIB)

• The loan scale will be 10-15 billion USD in the first 5-6 years

• Loans will be extended to the countries in the Belt and Road region (ASEAN)

• Fund circulation is based on the USD, so the status quo will not be changed.

Proportions in international trade settlement (April, 2014-March, 2015): RMB 1%, Yen 3%, USD 41.6%, EUR 36.6%. All foreign exchange reserves of national governments and central banks are in USD.

This indicates that the AIIB can play a certain role in regional integration, but too much cannot be expected from the internationalization of the RMB.

(2) ASEAN

• Population: 600 million, economic scale: GDP 2.57 trillion USD, equivalent to

1/4 of China's GDP and 1/2 of Japan's GDP

• The ASEAN Economic Community is nearly 80% completed and has been integrated into the world's economic system, the developments in the world's economy will become more complicated; it will become another China that has experienced "reform and opening up".

2. Explanations of the definition of "another China"

• With the reform and opening up, China's economy has rapidly developed, the Chinese people have become well off, and China's communication with the world has continuously expanded. These achievements deserve to be highly commended.

• However, another aspect also exists that is contrary to this—there are many drawbacks to the capitalist world; these drawbacks have also exerted a strong impact on China. They can be found in both developed and developing countries; agricultural problems and the gap between the rich and the poor are particularly salient.

• If ASEAN achieves a growth rate of 7%, its economy will reach Japan's current scale within ten years. Once it reaches such a scale, the above will be unavoidable.

• Who should be responsible for these problems? It is more difficult to seek solutions amidst more complicated developments in the world's economy.

3. Difficulties in agriculture

(1) The form of agricultural production in East Asia

• The agricultural policy suited to the mode of agricultural operations on the land covering hundreds of hectares in the USA is unfeasible in East Asia. If the US agricultural policy is copied on the basis of a market mechanism in Asia where the mode of small-scale agricultural operations supplemented by non-local work is adopted, it will certainly be quite miserable.

• In other words, agricultural regulation cannot be conducted under a market mechanism.

(2) Problems concerning the erosion of agriculture by industrialization and urbanization

• Industrial development has a corresponding proportional relationship with the decrease in the amount of cultivated land. The decrease in cultivated land leads to a reduction of grain output, while such a reduction is generally addressed in the following two ways: First, improve the agricultural productivity; second, increase foreign importation.

• The latter is subject to a certain limit, so it is unavoidable to rely on importation, thus further decreasing agricultural land.

• On the other hand, if the capacity for agricultural production is merely expanded, the consequence may be environmental pollution or enthusiasm about making some agricultural products with inferior quality (including genetically modified agricultural products) and ignorance of food safety.

(3) Issues concerning how to treat the environment

• As there is a vast desert in China, from the perspective of improving the survival environment or developing agriculture, turning desert into farmland and pasture is an extremely urgent hope for the people, and is of enormous significance for the sustainable development of the country.

• If a rural community is built on the basis of turning desert into farmland and pasture, a sample and model will be provided for the socialist market economy with Chinese characteristics.

II. Unique Characteristics of Chinese-style Development

• The conception concerning the establishment of the Belt and Road partnership and the AIIB conception based on ASEAN's unification are associated with the unrealistic expectation that free trade stimulates economic growth.

• This problem lies in the lack of a correct understanding of the world's economic crisis. As mentioned in Marxist economics, the current economic crisis is the inevitable reflection of the basic contradiction within capitalism—global overproduction.

• Therefore, a large quantity of cheap products and labor flock to the areas with economic growth through trade liberalization, and the global excess supply will certainly be exacerbated. The export-oriented growth based on external demand is nothing but a regional shift of surplus products.

• What are the differences between the act of forcing the ASEAN countries to engage in free trade and the acts committed by the great European powers and the USA which flaunt reciprocity, coexistence and win-win outcomes to seek freedom and equal rights from East Asia, especially China?

• The gap between the rich and the poor is inevitable in capitalism, while the great powers always stand by "the rich", the theories upheld by them merely embody the ideologicalization of "free trade".

• However, upholding trade protectionism is also unfeasible. Now is the critical moment for thoroughly breaking away from the capitalist mechanism.

• In such a circumstance, should the path be "free trade" or "non-market-oriented self-sufficiency"? Neither complete free trade nor complete self-sufficiency is feasible.

• The pursuit should be the "conception" for managing trade and self-sufficiency. The concept of state-performed management should be freed from the shackles of the "non-efficiency" notion based on a market economy. It is necessary to discuss again the concept of state-performed management, namely "state-owned".

III. The Intensification of China's Reform and Outlook

1. The goal of China's economic reform or institutional reform consists in establishing a model of a system of a social market economy with Chinese characteristics

• In order to achieve this goal, it is essential to change the type of economic growth—shift from export-oriented economic growth to domestic demand-oriented economic growth—in other words, in order to ensure sustained economic growth, it is necessary to find a new engine of growth.

• However, merely learning the experience from the economically-developed countries cannot achieve the reform with Chinese characteristics.

• China vows to establish a socialist market economy with Chinese characteristics, so what are Chinese characteristics? Socialism or a market economy?

• After the 1980s, China reformed the socialist planned economic system and started to introduce a socialist market economic system.

• However, what are the discussions about the differences between the previous socialist planned economic system and the socialist market economic system and their different characteristics?

• A lot of material has provided some explanations of these reforms, but an important issue concerning the reason why these reforms should be conducted has not been fully explained.

• The same issues also exist in the discussions about opening up; for example, why is "free trade" necessary for a socialist market system?

2. It is necessary to carry out thorough "reforms" in China

• Corruption means illegal possession of the surplus value of workers and privatization of it, thus considerations should focus on how to establish a socialist ownership system that is consistent with socialism with Chinese characteristics.

• Now state ownership or ownership by all of the people is concretized into state-controlled companies in the name of so-called "efficiency"; only the assets registered in the account books of a state-owned assets administration commission can be owned by government agencies; replacement of profit delivery by taxes enables government agencies to become taxpayers, thus this is precisely a hotbed which breeds corruption.

• The cause is that although government agencies do not possess state-owned assets and the right to obtain their income, tax payment actually means that they are nothing but general companies.

The above issues require us to discuss capitalist economy again. The drawbacks of capitalism are multi-faceted, while merely considering that these drawbacks fall within corporate social responsibility makes no sense. Even if enterprises do not assume the social responsibility which they should bear, capitalism will by no means change its mechanism.

The last fortress for treating the capitalist system as the highest form of development is criticism of the status quo by the countries which were socialist ones. However, the view that capitalism can do it but socialism cannot do it is groundless.

So far, the errors in the socialist economy have not been fully demonstrated. Are the errors in China's socialist economy unavoidable in a socialist economy or have they been caused by China? The answer has not yet been found through discussions. Therefore, it is time for us to discuss the problems in socialism again.

《易经》的和同论

刘梦溪　【中国】
中国艺术研究院　终身研究员 / 中国文化研究所　所长

本文通过对《易经》《同人》卦的解析，探讨如何追寻人类的共同价值。

一

“和”“同”两个字，是中国文化的关键词，也可以说是中国文化的最基本的价值理念。

古代思想家有很多关于和、同的阐释。

和、同可以分阐，也可以合释。

和、同、和同，是三组概念，三重含义。

“和”由不同构成。不同而能共生，是为和。

人性的弱点，喜同而不喜异。权力者的弱点，不喜欢听不同声音。

但世界如果没有不同，这个世界就窒息了。

古代智者汤伯认为，周朝衰败的原因，是由于“去和而取同”(《国语·郑语》)。

他的哲学依据是：“和实生物，同则不继。”(同上)

汤伯说：“以它平它谓之和，故能丰长而物生之；若以同裨同，尽乃弃矣。”

“以它平它”，指两个不同物的和平相处，就是和。“和”则能长治久安，众望所归。

如果“以同裨同”，即狭小卑微和狭小卑微抱团在一起，结果将一无所有（“尽弃”）。

汤伯说，经验告诉我们：“和五味以调口，刚四支以卫体，和六律以聪耳”。好吃的食物，美丽的音乐，强健的身体，都是不同物的“合体”，所以“声一无听，物一无文，味一无果，物一不讲”。

汤伯在阐述这一义理的时候，用了一个特殊的语词，曰“剸同。“剸”字的读音作“团 tuan”，是割而断之的意思。“剸同”即专擅，强制为同。其结果便走向了“和同”义理的反面。

人类应追寻和同，反对“剸同”，记取古代衰周的教训。

二

现在回到《易经》的《同人》卦。

《同人》是《周易》“上经”的第十三卦。（易学家的习惯，把《易经》的前 30 卦，称为上经，后 34 卦称为下经。）

《同人》卦所演绎的核心题旨，正是“与人和同”的精神义理。

此卦的卦辞是：“同人于野，亨。利涉大川。利君子贞。”

当同人们以扩大的胸怀在一起的时候，有利于克服艰难险阻。

此卦给出了种种复杂情况。包括第一，《同人》之始，是不是心地单纯而无狭窄鄙吝。大而言之，行为是否符合正义，而不是谋一己之私。第二，有没有“同宗之吝”，即是不是拉帮结伙搞宗派。第三，遇到强敌，需要不需要按兵不动（“伏戎”）；第四，面对的险阻是不是无法克服（“不克之困”）；第五，如果遇到难以战胜的强大敌体（“大师”之患）怎么办。

孔颖达《五经正义》解释此卦，结论是：“同人，谓和同於人。”亦认为这是追求与人和同之卦。

该卦的《彖辞》云：“文明以健，中正而应，君子正也。”

王弼注写道：“行健不以武，而以文明用之，相应不以邪，而以中正应之，君子正也，故曰‘利君子贞’。”王的意思，要尽量不用武。

虽然自身刚健，也应该用文明的手段（“文明用之”）；即使对方不正，也应以中正来回应（“以中正应之”）

为什么要采取此种态度呢？王弼引用了楚昭王丢失弓的典故。

故事来源于《孔子家语》一书。其中记载，一次楚昭王出游，把他最心爱的弓（乌号弓）丢失了，左右的人要立刻寻找。楚昭王说：“不必找了，反正丢失弓的是楚国人，拾到弓的也是楚国人，何必费力去寻找。”说明楚王的宽怀大度。有此大度的心态，任何疑难都容易解决。

问题是孔子听说此事之后，表示颇不以为然。

孔子说：“太可惜了，原来楚王的志量如此之小。为什么不说：是人丢失了弓，人拾到了弓。何必仅仅局限于楚国呢。”

孔子把故事彰显的价值伦理，推至整个人类。

王弼对此有引申一步的论述。他说：如果心胸过于狭隘，爱自己的国家爱得神魂颠倒，不讲分寸，失去理性，也会导致对自己国家的不利。

他的原话是：“楚人亡弓，不能亡楚。爱国愈甚，益为它灾。”

史载，果然在楚哀王六年，吴国攻打陈国，楚国轻举妄动去援救，结果楚哀王死在了陈国。这个故事证实，“爱国愈甚”也可以导致其他的灾祸。

孔颖达的义疏说，王弼引用这个典故，是想证明，“同人不弘皆至用师”。

人类如何对待面临的问题、危机、困境？《同人》卦告诉我们：最主要的是要有“大通之志”。

“大通”的概念是王弼提出来的。他说：“不能大通，则各私其党而求利焉。”大通，即大同。兵戎，乃万不得已的手段，需要慎之又慎。争战、杀戮归根结底是反文明的野蛮行为。因此养成“大通之志”，具备“和同于人”的智慧，应该是第一位的。

是不是也有完全无法实现和同的情况？有。此种情况，《同人》卦也有回答。就是《象辞》讲的：“大师相遇，言相克也。”遇到大师（重兵），又无法和同，则需要用压倒对方的“大师”（重兵）克之。但这是万不得已之事，是没有其他选择的选择。而且必须占有有利条件，怀有正义，实力超过对手。

王弼注：“居中处尊，战必克胜。”

结果是：“先号咷而后笑。”

三

《同人》卦所演，就是《易·系辞》说的：“天下何思何虑？天下同归而殊途，一致而百虑。”人类的不同，主要是思考方式和所选择的途径不同，人们终归要走到一起。

如何认识、理解、把握“同”“和”“和同”这三组概念义理，对人类至关重要。

“和”是人人都乐于接受而向往的境界。但不要忘记，“不同”是“和”的条件。承认不同，容许不同，欣赏不同，才能走向和同。

如果一切都相同，声音相同，味道相同，穿衣相同，走路相同，思维相同，说话相同，这个世界就令人窒息了。孟子说：“充实之谓美，充实而有光辉之谓大”（《尽心下》）。试想，能够使之充实起来的东西，能够都是完全相同的东西吗？不同物的组合，才能称之为“充实”。不同的合乎审美规则的组合，才能创造美。

孔子的两句话：一句是“和而不同”，一句是“己所不欲勿施于人”。

这是中国文化给出的人类麻烦解决之道。

The Theory of Harmony and Similarity in *The Book of Changes*

Liu Mengxi / China

Tenured Fellow and Director of the Institute of Chinese Culture at the Chinese National Academy of Arts

In this paper, the hexagram entitled *Getting Along with Others by Seeking Harmony amid Differences* as specified in *The Book of Changes* is analyzed to explore how to pursue the common value of human beings.

1

"Harmony" and "similarity" are key words in Chinese culture and represent the most basic value philosophies.

Ancient thinkers had many explanations of harmony and similarity.

Harmony and similarity can be explained in either a separate or a combined way.

Harmony, similarity, a combination of harmony and similarity are three concepts and have three meanings.

Harmony consists of differences. Once differences can coexist, harmony can be achieved.

Human weakness is that people like similarities, but dislike differences and hate listening to different voices.

However, if there are no differences in the world, suffocation will prevail.

The ancient sage Tang Bo believed that the cause for the decline of the Zhou Dynasty (1046 B.C.-256 B.C.) consisted in accepting similarity while abandoning harmony (*Vol. The State of Zheng in The History of Vassal States*).

His philosophical basis is that "harmony actually fosters new things, while similarity does not sustain development." (ditto)

Tang Bo said: "If two different things peacefully coexist, materials can become rich and grow; if similarities are brought together, there will be nothing."

The aforesaid peaceful coexistence means harmony. As long as harmony is achieved, a lasting stability will be maintained, and public respect and support will be obtained.

If those characterized by narrowness and lowliness huddle together as mentioned above, nothing can be achieved.

Tang Bo said that experience tells us: "Five flavors produce deliciousness, four limbs guard the body and six pitches are pleasant to the ears." Delicious food, wonderful music and a strong body are a combination of different things.

Therefore, merely one voice is not pleasant to the ears; merely one color cannot create a beautiful world; merely one flavor cannot make delicious food; merely one thing cannot be compared.

When expounding this meaning, Tang Bo used a group of special words: severance of differences.

Severance of differences means an assumption of arbitrary power and a forced realization of similarities. The result is opposite to the meaning of a combination of harmony and similarity.

Human beings should pursue a combination of harmony and similarity and oppose a severance of differences. Please bear in mind the lesson concerning the decline of the Zhou Dynasty.

2

Now let us return to the hexagram entitled *Getting Along with Others by Seeking Harmony amid Differences* as specified in *The Book of Changes.*

Getting Along with Others by Seeking Harmony amid Differences is the 13th hexagram in the upper part of *The Changes of Zhou*. (Experts in *The Book of Changes* usually consider the first 30 hexagrams and the subsequent 34 hexagrams of *The Book of Changes* as the upper part and the lower part, respectively.)

The core theme under the hexagram entitled *Getting Along with Others by Seeking Harmony amid Differences* reflects precisely the meaning of getting along with others with differences.

The words explaining the hexagram are "once people get along with each other in vast areas, things will go smoothly; it is conducive to crossing the rivers with torrents and ensuring that gentlemen keep to the righteous path."

When the like-minded people work together in an open-minded way, it is beneficial to overcoming difficulties.

This hexagram deals with various complicated situations. First, as mentioned at the beginning of the hexagram entitled *Getting Along with Others by Seeking Harmony amid Differences*, are people pure in thought without narrowness? Generally speaking, are behaviors righteous rather than selfish? Second, do people gang up to form cliques and factions? Third, is it necessary to take no action before a formidable enemy? Fourth, is it impossible to overcome dangers and obstacles?

Fifth, what can be done before a difficult-to-overcome powerful enemy?

Kong Yingda explained the hexagram in *The Annotations to the Five Classics* and concluded: "Getting along with others means a combination of harmony and similarity in people." He also believed that it was a hexagram which stressed the pursuit of getting along with others with differences.

The words summarizing the meaning of the hexagram read: "It is the right way for gentlemen to become civilized, strong and sturdy, act righteously and work in concert with others."

Wang Bi's Annotations read: "Once people become strong, people should also act in a civilized way rather than resort to arms, and should take actions in a righteous rather than an evil way, which is the right way for gentlemen and it is beneficial for gentlemen to keep to the righteous path."

Wang Bi wanted to stress that arms should be avoided as much as possible.

Although people become powerful, they should also act in a civilized manner; even though the other party is not righteous, it is nonetheless necessary to respond in a righteous way.

Why is it necessary to assume such an attitude? Wang Bi quoted a classical story: King Zhao of Chu State lost his bow.

The story comes from *The Analects of Confucius*. As recorded, once King Zhao (523 B.C.-489 B.C.) of Chu State went on a tour, lost the bow which he loved most, his attendants wanted to find it immediately, but the King said: "It is not necessary to do so, since the man who loses his bow is a citizen of Chu State, and the man who picks it up is also a citizen of Chu State, so there is no need to make great efforts to find it." This suggests that King Zhao of Chu was magnanimous; he was so broad-minded that it was easy for him to overcome any difficulty.

After Confucius heard of this story, he thought otherwise.

Confucius said: “What a pity, the King of Chu State is so narrow-minded. Why did he not say: A man loses his bow, another man picks it up? It is not necessary to limit the area to Chu State.”

Confucius presented the value ethics demonstrated by this story to the whole of mankind.

Wang Bi expounded it further. He said that if someone was excessively narrow-minded and was too patriotic to lose his mind, his act would also be harmful to his country.

Wang Bi’s original words are as follows: “If the people of Chu State lose their bow, Chu State cannot perish. If the people are too patriotic, it will be a disaster for Chu State.”

According to historical records, during the sixth year after King Ai (266 B.C.-228 B.C.) of Chu State ascended the throne, Wu State attacked Chen State, and Chu State rashly assisted Chen State; as a result, King Ai of Chu State died in Chen State. This story proves that it is too patriotic to beget other disasters.

Kong Yingda’s annotations and Wang Bi’s quotation of this classical story are designed to prove that if people are not broad-minded, they will resort to arms.

How should human beings cope with problems, crises and dilemmas? The hexagram entitled *Getting Along with Others by Seeking Harmony amid Differences* tells us that the most important aspect of dealing with these events is the ambition of broad-mindedness.

The concept of broad-mindedness was put forward by Wang Bi. He said: “If people are not broad-minded, they will become selfish and will seek private interests.”

Broad-mindedness means great harmony. Arms should be taken as the last resort and should be carefully used. In the final analysis, war is a brutal anti-civilization act. Therefore, top priority should be given to fostering broad-mindedness and developing the wisdom of getting along with others.

Is there a case where it is impossible to achieve a combination of harmony and similarity? Yes. To find this case, one must look in the hexagram entitled *Getting Along with Others by Seeking Harmony amid Differences.*

The words summarizing the meaning of the hexagram read: "When the main forces meet, the mission is to win a victory by defeating the enemy."

In case of a massive force, it is impossible to achieve a combination of harmony and similarity, so it is essential to send a formidable force to conquer it. However, there is no alternative. There must be favorable conditions, righteousness and strength to defeat the enemy.

Wang Bi's Annotations read: "Those who occupy a commanding position are bound to win."

As a result: "First burst into loud sobs and then laugh."

3

As specified in the hexagram entitled *Getting Along with Others by Seeking Harmony amid Differences*, also mentioned in the *Interpretation of the Changes of Zhou*, human beings are different mainly because their ways of thinking and their chosen paths are different, but human beings ultimately come together.

Understanding and grasping the meanings of three concepts, which are similarity, harmony and a combination of harmony and similarity, is of great importance for human beings.

Harmony is a realm that everyone is willing to accept and yearn for. However, do not forget: differences are the conditions for harmony. Only when people acknowledge, allow and appreciate differences can a combination of harmony and similarity be achieved.

If all things, such as voices, flavors, clothes, paths, lines of thought and words are the same, it means that the world is suffocating. Mencius (a famous Chinese philosopher, politician, educator, who lived from 372 B.C.-289 B.C.) said: "Once someone becomes substantial, he will be handsome; once something is substantial and splendid, it will be magnificent (*Go All Out*). Are the things which can become substantial the same? Only when different things are combined can they become substantial. Only when there are different combinations consistent with aesthetic principles can beauty be created.

Two sentences from Confucius: First, harmony in diversity; second, do not do to others what you do not want others to do to you.

This is the solution proposed by the Chinese culture for dealing with the troubles of human beings.

“一带一路”与中国理念

张维为 【中国】
复旦大学中国研究院 院长

三年前，习近平主席提出了“丝绸之路经济带”和“21 世纪海上丝绸之路”，即“一带一路”的设想，这是中国在过去数十年中提出的最具雄心的全球发展倡议。

西方对此却很是怀疑，不大相信这一设想的可行性。他们强调中国这样做是为了化解自己的过剩产能，是为了扩展中国地缘政治的影响力。确实，中国有经济方面的需求，包括化解自己的过剩产能。此外，今天世界上 120 多个国家（包括几乎所有的邻国）的最大贸易伙伴都是中国。地缘政治方面的影响力也是可以理解的，毕竟无论是在陆地还是在海上，这个倡议所覆盖的地域之广前所未有。

然而，这样看“一带一路”也是偏颇的。这一宏大的设想的背后有着更为重要的理念。只有了解这些理念，我们才能更为全面地理解“一带一路”的意义，毕竟理念规范了一个蓝图及其世界影响的基调和框架。

下面五个理念特别值得注意：

首先是一个直白简单的理念，就消除贫困而言，筑路（发展基础设施）比西方倡导的一人一票更有意义。改革开放以来，中国建成了世界上最大规模的公路网、高速网和高铁网，实现了村庄道路的硬化，这帮助了超过 6 亿贫困人口脱贫。考虑到中国幅员辽阔的国土面积和复杂多样的地理状况，这种成就实属不易。中国愿与其他国家分享中国减贫的理念与经验。“一带一路”沿线的国家大都是发展中国家，他们基础设施改造的需求巨大，他们也往往乐于接受“一带一路”倡议。

第二，与筑路相关的是互联互通的理念：物质的流通、服务的流通、思想的交流、人员的流动。中国已从自己的互联互通中受益良多，现在又努力通过“一带一路”，在亚、欧、东非和北非等地区，把互联互通推进到一个新的高度。“一带一路”推进的互联互通包括政策沟通、设施联通、贸易畅通、资金融通、民心相通五个层面；更具体地说说，它涉及海陆空运输、能源设施联通、光纤通信、资本流通、进出口通关便利、电子商务与“信息丝路”、人际交流以及政策沟通和协调等许多领域。

第三，互联互通的意义将更加彰显，如果有关各方之间可以建立某种伙伴关系。中国是“一带一路”的倡议国，但这一计划的实施却不是中国一家的事，它离不开与“一带一路”国家之间建立一种合作共赢的伙伴关系。长期以来，美国一直批评中国在当今的国际秩序中“搭便车”，其实中国非常乐于让世界各国分享中国快速发展所提供的机会。中国把“一带一路”构想看作是中国向世界提供的国际“公共产品”，这种伙伴关系需要兼顾所有参与国的利益，寻求各国利益的“最大公约数”。中国不强迫任何国家参与这项计划，“一带一路”倡议中，每个国家都是独立的伙伴，他们出于自己的利益而选择加入这个计划。

第四，不同文明之间需要对话与合作。“一带一路”所涉的国家之多、文化传统之复杂使各国间的合作面临各种挑战，为此，中国倡导尊重主权，并推进不同文明体之间的对话与合作，以消弭差异，提升互信，探索实现共同繁荣的途径。在历史上，“丝绸之路”也不只是贸易，它也是文化和思想交流的渠道。欧洲和中亚的马匹、玻璃、舞乐经由“丝绸之路”传入中国，而中国的丝绸、茶叶、瓷器及儒家思想也传到了欧洲。在这种意义上，“一带一路”旨在振兴古代丝绸之路所体现的那种合作交流的精神。

第五，上述内容综合在一起就是要实现一个更重要的理想，即使全球化变得更为包容，从而有利于缩小世界范围内的贫富差距，推动根治极端主义和恐怖主义，最终创造一个全球的“利益、命运和责任共同体”。“一带一路”的实现过程将不断体现这种包容性的全球化，它将使占全球财富三分之一（即 2.1 万亿美元 GDP）的地区和 44 亿人（即全球人口的 63%）受益。

有人质疑这些理念是否真诚，有人认为其过于崇高而无法实现，然而他们忘记了一个事实：这些理念其实根植于改革开放以来中国人自己的集体体验，他们是中国迅速崛起的主要原因。中国自己就是一个世界，中国是一个“百国之合”，是历史上成百上千的国家慢慢整合而成的超大型大国，其人口规模大约等于100个欧洲国家之合。

改革开放以来，中国成功地通过修筑公路铁路来推动贫困，效果显著。在互联互通，特别是道路连通、政策协调、电子商务的推动下，中国形成了世界上最大的国内市场。中国各省市之间也形成了合作共赢的伙伴关系，中央与地方以及各地方之间不断地通过对话来解决各种分歧乃至争议。此外，尽管全球化迄今为止损害了许多国家的利益，甚至带来了灾难，如2008年全球性金融危机使世界上多数国家受到了巨大伤害，但中国却从全球化中受益良多，因为中国坚定捍卫了自己的主权，并对外来资金与技术进行了最大化地利用，在外国投资者获益的同时，也使绝大多数的普通百姓成为全球化的受益者。换言之，中国使全球化至少在中国境内变得更具“包容性”而非“排他性”。

当然，中国国内成功的东西走出国门并不一定就能成功，但中国还是乐于与世界分享这些理念。中国哲学中有一个概念叫作“势”，这意味着要推动一些不可逆转的大趋势，而许多中国人都认为“一带一路”背后的这些理念反映了当今世界发展的“势”。比方说，英国等诸多西方国家不顾美国的反对而选择加入亚洲基础设施投资银行（亚投行）就是一个例子，说明这些国家看到了这个不可阻挡之“势”及其背后的无穷机遇，而亚投行本身也是“一带一路”构想的一个组成部分。正是在这个意义上，笔者对于“一带一路”的前景持谨慎乐观的态度。“一带一路”有可能成为21世纪重塑全球化的伟大力量，那种只有少数人可以获利的“排他性”全球化可能会被改变，一个更加包容的、人性化的全球化趋势将会深刻地影响世界未来发展的轨迹。

Five Ideas behind China's Global Initiative

Zhang Weiwei / China

Director of China Institute at Fudan University

Three years ago, Chinese President Xi Jinping put forward the conception of building the "Silk Road Economic Belt" and "21st Century Maritime Silk Road" or the Belt and Road initiative, which is China's most ambitious global initiative over the past few decades.

The Western reaction is generally skeptical, with little confidence in its feasibility, focusing either on China's attempt to export its excessive industrial capacity or China's geopolitical intention or both.

There are obviously domestic economic imperatives for the initiative, as China indeed has excessive industrial capacity. Furthermore, the country is already the largest trading partner with over 120 countries globally, including almost all its neighbors. Geopolitical fallout from this initiative is also understandable as it reaches so vast a distance in both land and sea.

Yet, this may not be the whole picture, and to this author at least, the ideas behind the initiative should merit more attention as they offer a holistic reading of the initiative, and after all, it's the ideas that will set the tone and the framework for the whole undertaking and its global fallout. Five ideas are particularly noteworthy here:

The first is simple and straightforward: poverty eradication starts more with road construction and infrastructural development than with one person one vote (as advocated by the West). China has lifted over 600 million people out of poverty over the past three decades while having completed the world's largest networks of highways, express ways and bullet trains, with all villages linked now by paved roads, a remarkable achievement for a country of China's size and geographical diversity. China is promoting this down-to-earth idea to the Belt and Road countries, most of which are developing ones with a huge demand for infrastructural transformation, and the initiative is thus well received by many.

Second, following the above is the idea of connectivity. Infrastructural development facilitates connectivity, which in turn facilitates exchanges of goods, ideas, services and people. Gained so much from China's extensive connectivity within the country and without, the initiative promotes a "five-way" connectivity in policy, trade, transportation, currency and people-to-people in the Belt and Road countries across the vast regions of Asia, Europe, Eastern Africa and North Africa, more specifically, a connectivity of roads, sea and air traffic, energy infrastructure, optical cables, capital flows, improved customs clearance, e-commerce and "information silk road", people-to-people exchanges as well as policy coordination.

Third, the significance of connectivity will be multiplied by a mutually beneficial partnership. True, the Belt and Road is a Chinese initiative, but China will not do it alone, rather it endeavors to forge a win-win partnership with all the Belt and Road participants. Long criticized by Washington as a free rider in the existing world order, Beijing openly welcomes other countries to share China's development opportunities and Beijing in fact regards the Belt and Road initiative as a public good that China offers to the world. This partnership endeavors to accommodate the interests and concerns of all parties involved, seeking the "biggest common denominator" for cooperation. No country will be forced to join in, and it will join in only out of its own interest and share its benefits as an independent partner.

Fourth, partnership among so many countries with diverse culture and traditions is bound to be challenging, so Beijing put forward the idea of respecting sovereignty and promoting dialogues and cooperation among civilizations as a way to reduce difference, enhance mutual understanding and jointly explore the best way to realize this visionary prospect of common prosperity. Historically, it's also true that the concept of the "Silk Road" was not only about trade links, but also about cultural and civilization exchanges, about bringing European and Central Asian horses, glass, music and dance to China while introducing Chinese silk, tea, porcelain and Confucian ideas to Europe. In this sense, the initiative tries to revive the cooperative spirit of the ancient Silk Road.

Lastly, all these ideas put together mean a new type of globalization, a more inclusive globalization, which will contribute meaningfully to closing up the gap between the world's poor and rich, tackling the root cause of extremism and terrorism and paving the way for creating a "community of shared interests, destiny and responsibility." Indeed, if the initiative can be fully realized, it will benefit a population of 4.4 billion people or 63 percent of the global population, with a collective GDP of 2.1 trillion U.S. dollars that account for nearly one third of the world's wealth. Nothing could be more exciting than this prospect.

Cynics may question the sincerity of these ideas, or they are simply too good to be true, but this misses the point, as these ideas are part of China's collective experience over the past three decades or part of the reasons why China has risen so fast. China itself is a universe, and it is an amalgamation of hundreds of states into one over its long history, and it is the size of about 100 average European states in terms of population.

Over the past three decades, China has built roads and railways across the country as a most effective way to conquer poverty; China has established the world's largest domestic market through connectivity of all sorts, from road connection to policy coordination to e-commerce; Chinese cities and provinces have evolved win-win partnerships on all fronts; and dialogues between center and provinces and among provinces are the most commonly used means to solve their disputes which are many; and China is one of the few beneficiaries of globalization, which has, as a contrast, caused harms or even havoc to many others, with the fallout of the 2008 financial crisis still being felt today. In other words, globalization has been made more"inclusive" than "exclusive" within China, when the country has safeguarded its sovereignty and harnessed foreign capital and technologies to the best of its ability to serve the interests of most Chinese rather than merely foreign investors.

Of course, what's working within China may not necessarily work outside China, but the Chinese are tempted to introduce these ideas abroad, and furthermore, Chinese philosophy contains a concept called *shi* or overall trend, and these ideas, as many in China believe, represent part of the overall and irresistible trends in the world today. If an overall trend takes shape, few can resist and succeed, just as shown in the case of Britain and other Western countries joining the Asian Infrastructure Investment Bank (AIIB)one after another despite the opposition from the United States, as these countries find unparalleled opportunities in the AIIB undertaking, which is in fact part and parcel of the Belt and Road initiative. In this sense, this author is cautiously optimistic about the future of the initiative, which may eventually reshape the trajectory of globalization in the 21st century, which should be made more inclusive, humane and beneficial to all, rather than a tiny minority of people.

知识分享与共同家园

Knowledge Sharing and Common Home

关于中外对鲁迅早期文言论文的反应

寇志明 【澳大利亚】
悉尼新南威尔士大学中文系　系主任

鲁迅的早期文言论文有五篇，是他离开仙台专门医学院回到东京以后写的。也就是说这五篇冗长的学术论文是他“弃医从文”以后重要的研究成果。写作时间是在1907—1908年间。原来想发表在鲁迅和周作人、许寿裳等打算出版一个叫《新生》的文学期刊上。因为《新生》未能办成，所以他投稿给同盟会在日本办的期刊《河南》杂志。这五篇是：

《人[間]之历史》用笔名令飞发表在《河南》1号（1907年12月），第85—96页。

《摩罗诗力说》笔名令飞，分期发表在《河南》2号（1908年2月），70—90页及《河南》3号1908年3月），45—74页。

《科学史教篇》笔名令飞，发表在《河南》5号（1908年6月），76—89页。

《文化偏至論》笔名迅行，发表在《河南》7号（1908年8月），1—18页。

《破恶声论》笔名迅行，发表在《河南》8号（1908年12月），16—31页。

日本学者竹内好没有重视鲁迅的早期文言论文。他说这是因为这些论文属于鲁迅不成熟的时期，因此不用重视它。但我假设：如果竹内好没有这样说，那会全面否定他自己的那套“鲁迅是文学家而不是思想家”说法。

在西方的学者对鲁迅的早期文言论文是怎么看的呢？1941年美国纽约哥伦比亚大学中文系华人教授王际真在他为《阿Q及其他中国短篇小说》（Ah Q and Others）英译本写的序言里说“没有几个人看过”这几篇文章，所以当时没什么反应。但这里也有矛盾，因为他还补充说没有多少人注意的“真正的原因是因为它们代表的是异己分子的看法，哪怕在目前 [的中国]，[鲁迅的文章] 也要算是离心分子的观点”。

第二次世界大战后的美国有芝加哥大学陈夏珠 1953 年的博士论文《鲁迅的社会思想》(The Social Thought of Lu Xun)。她认为清末对西方的反应有三派：(1) 荣禄 (2) 张之洞 (3) 鲁迅。鲁迅已经应该算是“激进改革派最敢于直率地发表意见的领导人物”(“the most outspoken leader of the radical reformers”) (p. 41)。

两年后，舒尔茨 (William Rudolph Schultz) 在他 1955 年西雅图华盛顿大学博士论文《鲁迅在创造年间》(Lu Hsun: The Creative Years) 反驳了她：“He [Lu Xun] was not in any sense of the word a leader during those years, and there is even much question as to whether he really questioned the ‘basic’ soundness of Chinese institutions and ideas, as is stated, during this period of his life.” (pp. 124—5) 舒尔茨认为鲁迅当年该算是一位文化保守主义者。舒尔茨认为鲁迅的早期论文当时没有受到重视是因为它们太保守，不合时宜。舒尔茨说达尔文的进化论用了科学的框框作为鲁迅的人道主义的靠山。因此鲁迅的人道主义可以肯定有一部分来自西方。舒尔茨说：当时鲁迅没有顾虑到中国社会和经济上的若干问题，他只要从西方拿来中国需要的东西。鲁迅并不反对发展工业、国会；但他认为现代化需要些其他的因素。国会和工业不过是表面上的东西。在这点上舒尔茨认为鲁迅比当时别的思想家还先进：“It was not his intent to argue that a modern industrial structure and parliamentarian rule necessarily were undesirable in themselves, rather that other factors were more essential to modernization than the outward symbols with which the above-mentioned individuals concerned themselves. In this respect his reasoning perhaps went deeper than his contemporaries.” (p. 90)

当时鲁迅推荐约翰·斯图尔特·密尔 (John Stuart Mill) 的著作给周作人看，可以说明鲁迅接近西方自由主义，不过那是因为他本来相信“人之初，性本善”，而对 19 世纪的自由主义及浪漫主义产生认同。因此他认为人类和国家的进步要看精神上和个人自由的发展程度。鲁迅痛恨压迫、伪善、以众欺寡，是因为他自己的经验和个人背景。他接受的欧洲思想自然也就是接近他自己本来的人道主义。

可惜，舒尔茨没讨论“破恶声论”。关于“摩罗诗力说”他写得不多，但强调这篇涉及的范围很广，自古代印度到 19 世纪欧洲。虽说鲁迅强调了文学的社会角色，他也认为文学的美学因素很重要。但舒尔茨并没有提到鲁迅在"摩罗诗力说"的反抗精神，没说明鲁迅如何脱离民族主义而走向国际精神，笔者估计这是因为鲁迅受到自己所处的时代背景的限制：当时在美国是冷战和麦卡锡时期（McCarthy Era）。

莱尔（William A. Lyell）在 1971 年在芝加哥大学完成了博士论文《鲁迅的现实观》Lu Hsun's Vision of Reality。他认为从"文化偏至论"里可以看出鲁迅思想中很重要的一面——就是"怀疑"。在这篇论文里，鲁迅怀疑了洋务派、维新派以及其他启蒙运动的动机。莱尔认为鲁迅的"文化偏至论"主要是反对全盘西化。在"文化偏至论"中，可以看到鲁迅成熟期所创造的思想构造。"个人"的解放是中国人民作为一个全体的解放的前提。"Here we have the concrete expression of the intellectual framework that would inform most of Lu Hsun' s mature literature; the spiritual (psychological) liberation of the individual is a precondition for the liberation of the collective energy of the Chinese people and the eventual establishment of a new, strong and vigorous society." (p. 90)

莱尔并没有讨论鲁迅的"立人"概念，也不提西方的自由主义的影响，像舒尔茨（或复旦大学教授郜元宝）那样。从莱尔的语气中可以感觉他对鲁迅、对旧中国的批判觉得尴尬，想要在翻译过程中把它给柔化。说到"摩罗诗力说"，莱尔重视它的反抗精神、它的不符合主流（non-conformity），后者是 20 世纪 60 年代的用语，也可见莱尔如何受到当时的思想的影响。不错，摩罗诗人是反抗者，但同时也是复兴者。那么，怎么理解鲁迅讲的"心声"？莱尔认为摩罗诗人的著作是"心声"，也就是能够讲出全国全民心里的感受以及他们的希望、痛苦和恐惧。(p.91). 莱尔认为鲁迅像果戈里，并不像高尔基。果戈里有黑暗的一面，但也有他的幽默，因此他比较像鲁迅。

莱尔把鲁迅曾经用的"心声"翻译成"voices of the mind"，没有直译成"voices of the heart"。我认为这样对英文读者比较强调鲁迅的理性（rationality）。但日本学者北冈正子（Kitaoka Masako）则认为"心声"来自日本滨田佳澄（Hamada Yoshizumi）对英国诗人雪莱的形容词"赤心"（sekishin）—— 英文翻译包括 sincerity, one's inmost heart, true heart, the faithful mind。而 19 世纪末英国评论家约翰·阿丁顿·西蒙兹（John Addington Symonds）的书《雪莱》（*Shelley*），我认为可能是滨田佳澄的主要的来源之一则谈到"Shelley' s vivid logical sincerity"，"雪

莱的那种活跃的、合乎逻辑的诚心”（Symonds, p.39）。

莱尔提到鲁迅佩服德国爱国诗人阿恩特（Arndt）和克尔纳（Körner），但没注意到鲁迅的更显著的民主主义、国际主义精神。鲁迅在“摩罗诗力说”写道：“败拿破仑者，不为国家，不为皇帝，不为兵刃，国民而已。”这点在鲁迅的早期思想中很重要。

从“破恶声论”中，我们能看到鲁迅关于小说对社会的任务已经离梁启超多远。鲁迅积极地反对绅士的反迷信运动，这是值得赞扬的。鲁迅对中国文化和西方文化的理解是独一无二的。在1908年（就是写“破恶声论”那年），鲁迅在中国知识分子还没接触马克思主义的时候已经有一定程度的阶级意识。因为他对宗教敬佩，所以他一直对“赛先生”和“德先生”（“Mr Science and Mr Democracy”）这个流行于五四时期的口号，保持距离。其实，当时西方知识分子也是如此，因为是建立在第一次世界大战的经验之上的。

莱尔认为鲁迅在当时是一位先觉者（就是在他那一代知识分子里面）。莱尔说鲁迅对中国和西方的理解是理性的，它经过了学习、反省还加上了“恩爱”，鲁迅的这种独一无二的理解是下了很大的功夫而得到的。作为一个“摩罗诗人”，鲁迅才能打破中国的“无声”，打破自己的寂寞。莱尔认为鲁迅之所以重视翻译是因为它能够打破中国在世界里的孤独。莱尔认为鲁迅通过他的创作和翻译变为一个“文化哲学家”（a philosopher of culture）。因为他用他的文笔写出中国人民的无声的痛苦，鲁迅自己也变成了一位“摩罗诗人”。

后来美国学者胡志德（Theodore Huters）于2005年出版的《把世界带回家》（Bringing the World Back Home），最后一章写道鲁迅早期四篇论文。他一开头就说是“非常杰出的四篇”“a remarkable series of four early essays”，但又说“语气过分悲观”“the early essays already give voice to an exceedingly pessimistic mood”。但他认为鲁迅早期论文中的矛盾很明显：

> For all the rhetorical flourish that Lu Xun brings to bear in this essay, however, a number of obvious contradictions protrude from the deceptively smooth surface of the discourse. The most glaring reveals itself in his conclusion that, should the reformist attitudes he advocates be adopted in China, “the people of our nation will attain self-awareness, their individuality will flourish, and this country that is now a heap of loose sand will become

a nation of true human beings." [1] What could have been the source of this sudden ability of the entire population to gain the sort of awareness that Lu Xun had previously viewed as the exclusive property of the discerning few? There seems to be a slippage here between what Wang Hui (汪 晖) has identified as two quite distinct strains of individualism: that which regards all individuals as equal and that which stresses the rights of particular persons. At the end of his essay Lu Xun appears to conflate the two, evidently generalizing the Nietzs chean notion of rights pertaining to the superior individual to the whole population of a reimagined China. In the final analysis, perhaps, Lu Xun seems unable to bring himself to limit possession of the liberated subjectivities he describes in such fine detail to a specific subset of Uebermenschen.[2]

如果概括地翻译他的意思，胡志德认为鲁迅最后不肯把人权的要求限制到“超人”而似乎要扩大到广大群众。但是我并不认为这是一个矛盾。鲁迅之所以希望“超人”出现，是为了救国救民，没有别的目的。胡志德认为另一个矛盾是鲁迅强调主体性和个人的声音的重要，但在他的早期文言论文里从来不写一个“我”字，从来不说什么是他个人的看法。我认为鲁迅之所以这样写是因为他要客观一点。他引用西方权威的目的也是说明他自己的看法。

关于竹内好对鲁迅最基本的理解，胡志德引用了日裔美国学者 Naoki Sakai 的话：

“Naoki Sakai has summarized Takeuchi Yoshimi’s fundamental realization about Lu Xun: ‘[R]esistance has to be likened to a negativity, as distinct from a negation, which continues to disturb a putative stasis in which the subject is made to be adequate to himself.” [3]（试译：反抗一定要被比喻为一个消极的东西，但它并不是一个否定；它一直在扰乱主体所谓不变的形态，而这主体由是会变得足够完成自己。）

---

1 The original reads 则国人之自觉至，个性张，沙聚之邦，由是辅为人国 . *Lu XunQuanji* (1991) 1: 56.

2 Theodore Huters, *Bringing the World Home: Appropriating the West in Late Qing and Early Republican China* (Honolulu: University of Hawaii Press, 2005), p. 256.

3 Sakai, “Modernity and Its Critique,” p. 501. As quoted in Huters, *Bringing the World Home: Appropriating the West in Late Qing and Early Republican China*, p. 258. Note that Sakai writes in English.

邓腾克（Kirk Denton）评论胡志德而认为鲁迅的矛盾是一面要求极端主体性，但一面要求推崇科学主义式发展的必然性：

> I do not agree with Huters that the absence of a subjective voice in Lu Xun's 1908 essay "On Cultural Extremities" ("Wenhuapianzhilun") was done self-consciously as a way of problematizing the very subjectivism promoted in the essay. Rather, and more simply, it is a product of the medium in which the essay was written – classical Chinese, which suppresses the subjective voice – as well as of a need, in a time of "semicolonialism," to seek the voice of authority from Western masters.[1] In deconstructing the early Lu Xun in this way, Huters seems to want to forge a consistent skepticism toward subjectivity that runs throughout Lu Xun's writing from the late Qing period to May Fourth period. Rather, I would suggest seeing Lu Xun's late Qing writing as fundamentally torn between an extreme subjectivism, on the one hand, and a determinist scientism, on the other.[2]

这点我在鲁迅的早期论文看不出来。他推崇的是科学的精神，所以也就是提倡主体性。

在日本，北冈正子从 1972 到 1982 写过“摩罗诗力说材源考”。1983 年何乃英出版了一本很好的中文节译本，但不是全译。在中国有的学者以为北冈正子的结论是鲁迅的早期文言论文基本上是抄袭别人的作品，但我认为北冈并不是这个意思。中国学者李震最近写道：

> ……将《摩罗诗力说》当做一部翻译，甚至剽窃之作。此见出自日本学者北冈正子。她认为《摩罗诗力说》是鲁迅在日本期间转译别人的文字，全文的九个部分中，第四部分到第九部分的前半部分可以算译文，

---

1 I would question the use of this term. Brandes was not a "master," nor Byron, nor Shelley nor Lermontov, nor Petofi. The brothers Zhou chose Brandes because of his sympathy for the rebel poets and the fact that he was an outsider to the "establishment," according to Zhou Zuoren who wrote: "Brandes, it seems, was a Dane of Jewish descent, so he was a bit unconventional / subversive in his approach and sympathized with those revolutionary poets, but this made him even more useful to us" 勃兰兑斯大概是犹太系的丹麦人，所以有点离经畔道，同情那些革命的诗人，但这于我们却是很有用的 . See Zhou, *Zhitang Huixianglu*, 1:210.

2 See Denton's review of *Bringing the World Home*. In *The Journal of Asian Studies* 65, no. 1 (Feb. 2006): 166-168.

而前三部分是译序，第九部分的后半部分是译跋。这种误读显然是偏狭的。[1]

可是北冈早在1975年的"笔记"里把她的立场写得很清楚：

我想补充一点，在《摩罗诗力说》，关于"恶魔派"的发展，我们现在几乎可以找到每一个部分的材料来源。但《摩罗诗力说》这篇文章不是可以通过确定材料来源是如何使用的等等让我们能够看清楚它的大意。如果我们用现在流行的话语来讨论，"抄袭"可能也会在这种情况里出现，但我觉得我在上面引用的例子会澄清这一点。再说，鲁迅有关斯拉夫和匈牙利民族所写的，所构成的，我能果断而明确地强调这不是"抄袭"。要了解鲁迅写《摩罗诗力说》的真实意图，我认为我们必须准确地按照它的结构来解释。另外一点是，我们必须分清楚鲁迅怎么样选用材料来回答他自己提出来的问题跟他怎么用其他人的贡献来阐明他正在讨论的事项。[2]

北冈现在有新书叫《鲁迅文学渊源的探讨》，2015年出版的，厚650页。也是写这个题目，她修改了原来的文章和一些看法，并加了很多新的内容，我正在读。

我的结论是，海外的学者虽说对鲁迅早期文言论文有不同的分析，但都认为是非常重要的文献，并认为鲁迅不仅是一位作家也是一位思想家。我认为他的早期文言论文形成了一个蓝图，从中可以看出鲁迅一生中的事业、情怀，也可以知道他希望中国要走的方向。

1 See Li Zhen 李震, "Moluoshi li shuoyuZhongguoshixue de xiandaizhuanxing" 摩罗诗力说与中国诗学的现代转型 (On the Power of Mara Poetry and the modern transformation of Chinese poetics) in *Yan shuobujin de Lu XunyuWusi*, 181.Li Zhen cites He Naiying's1983 Chinese translation of *Nōto*, but does not give a page number.Kitaoka's position is that "the sources used" in that segment of "On the Power of Mara Poetry" can now be determined, not that it is a translation. See Kitaoka, *Rojinbungaku no engen wo saguru: "Mara Shi Ryoku Setsu" zaigenkō*,xiii-ix.

2 北冈正子：《摩罗诗力说材源考笔记》其7，出版单位 2015年版，第75-76页。

On the Reception of Lu Xun's Classical-style Essays

Jon von Kowallis / Australia

Head of the Department of Chinese Studies at the University of New South Wales, Sydney

In 1906, after withdrawing from medical school, Lu Xun 魯迅 (1881-1936), who came to be widely regarded as the founder of modern Chinese literature, returned to Tokyo and began to research and write five lengthy treatises in an archaistic classical prose style influenced by that of the eccentric anti-Manchu philologist Zhang Taiyan 章太炎 (i.e. Zhang Binglin 章炳麟 [1868-1936]) in his publication *Minbao* 民報 (The People's Journal),[1] for whom Lu Xun still professed in 1936 a life-long admiration, mainly due to Zhang's uncompromising oppositional stance vis-a-vis the powers that be in China.[2]

---

1 As he put it in his preface to *Jiwai ji* 集外集 (Collection of the Uncollected): "Later (i.e. after Yan Fu) I was influenced by Mr Zhang Taiyan's and got 'ancient'" 以後又受了章太炎先生的影響，古了起來. See *Lu Xun quanji*, 7:4, published in 1991. Hereafter cited as *LXQJ*(1991).

2 See his moving "recollections" of Zhang Taiyan—two essays in *LXQJ* (1991) 6:545-551; 556-561. These are available in English translations by Yang Xianyi and Gladys Yang under the titles "Some Recollections of Zhang Taiyan" and "A Few Matters Concerned with Zhang Taiyan," see *Lu Xun Selected Works*, 4:322-326; 327-334. Hereafter *LXSW*. For an extended discussion of their relationship, see Chan, "Zhang Taiyan yu Lu Xun de shitu jiaoyi chongtan." Chan concludes that the

Zhang Taiyan edited *Minbao* from July 1906 to October 1908. This choice of style was in itself a major statement. By so doing Lu Xun rejected the ornate, Qing-identified *pian wen* 駢文 (parallel prose) but also bucked the popular trend toward a modernized, simple *wenyan wen* 文言文 (classical prose) used by Liang Qichao 梁啟超 (1873-1929) in his journal *Xinmin Bao* 新民報 (The New People), which came to be referred to as *Xinmin ti* 新民體 (the style of the “New People”). I have argued elsewhere that Lu Xun was trying to create a style that was at once more authentically “Chinese” by reverting to the *guwen* 古 文 (classical-style essay) of the Han 漢 (206 BCE-220 CE), Wei 魏 (220-265) and Jin 晉 (265-420) eras, while at the same time attempting to develop a discursive style that could accommodate modern concepts and also resonate with a moral and intellectual authority akin aurally and linguistically to that of the classics.[1]

Lu Xun published five essays and one translation in *Henan* 河南 (Ho-nan) magazine under the pseudonyms of Ling Fei 令飛 (Let Fly) and Xun Xing 迅行 (Swift Travel/ Action). They came out in the following order:

“Ren [jian] zhi lishi” 人 [間] 之歷史 (History of [(the Evolution of) Humankind], published under the pen name Ling Fei 令飛 , *Henan*, no. (*hao* 號) 1 (December 1907): 85-96.[2]

“Moluo shi li shuo” 摩羅詩力說 (On the Power of Mara Poetry) by Ling Fei, serially in two parts, *Henan*, no. 2 (February 1908): 70-90; and *Henan*, issue (*qi* 期)

Zhang Taiyan Lu Xun admired was the late-Qing anti-Manchu revolutionist-scholar and that they later grew apart due to opposing positions regarding the New Culture Movement and vernacular literature. Although this may be the case, I would argue that there is actually a degree of self-identification between the Zhang Lu Xun described in 1936 and himself. In some ways Zhang Taiyan is a foil in Lu Xun’s 1936 essays, but in others he becomes an alter-ego. In those essays, Lu Xun concludes his own life by harking back to the idealism of his youth.

1 See my chapter titled “Lu Xun’s Han Linguistic Project: the use of *wenyan* to create an ‘authentic’ Han vocabulary for literary terminology in his early essays.”

2 The original title of the essay *Ren zhi lishi* 人之歷史 was *Renjian zhi lishi* 人間之歷史 when it was published in Henan magazine in 1907. Lu Xun revised the title to *Ren zhi lishi* 人之歷史 (History of Humankind) for publication in 1926 in his anthology *Fen*.

3 (March 1908):45-74; [1]

"Kexueshi jiaopian" 科學史教篇 (Lessons from the History of Science) by Ling Fei, *Henan*, issue 5 (June 1908): 76-89;

"Wenhua pianzhi lun" 文化偏至論 (On Imbalanced Cultural Development), under the pen name Xun Xing 迅行 , *Henan*, issue 7 (August 1908): 1-18;

"Pei-tuan-fei shi lun" 裴彖飛詩論 (On Petöfi's Poetry), a translation published under the name Xun Xing, *Henan*, issue 7 (August 1908): 65-72;

"Po e'sheng lun" 破惡聲論 (Toward a Refutation of Malevolent Voices), by Xun Xing, *Henan,* issue 8 (December 1908): 16-31.

These essays have been considered to have continuing relevance by Chinese readers in part because Lu Xun himself included the majority of them (the first four from the above list) when he edited and compiled the first collection of his essays under the title *Fen* 坟 (The Grave)in 1926. In his preface to *Fen*, written in Xiamen and dated October 30, 1926 "on a night of great winds" 大風之夜 [2] (probably symbolic of the threatening political situation in China, which in part was responsible for his leaving warlord-governed Beijing) he noted:

The poets I talked about [in "On the Power of Mara Poetry"] no one has mentioned again until now, and this is another minor reason that I have not been able to bring myself to discard this old manuscript. How excited I used to get at the mere mention of their names! After the proclamation of the Republic I forgot all about them, but how could I have imagined that they would surprisingly begin to appear nowadays time and again before my eyes.

其中所說的幾個詩人，至今沒有人再提起，也是使我不忍拋棄舊稿的一個

1 The journal *Henan* itself used the terms *hao* 號 (number) and *qi* 期 (issue) alternately. In the list here I used the terms as they stood on the original copies of the journals, which I have seen. This is at variance with the reprinted set, which uses *qi* on the newly-designed front covers, but preserves the original numbering nomenclature inside.

2 *LXQJ* (1991) 1:5.

小原因。他們的名，先前是怎樣地使我激昂呵，民國告成以後，我便將他們忘卻了，而不料現在他們竟又時時在我的眼前出現 .[1]

Lu Xun seems to be alluding to what he saw as the quashing of the May Fourth spirit and the demise of the New Culture Movement. Further on in the preface he talks about the need to continue to protest the warlord government's massacre of unarmed demonstrators, most of them students, in front of Government House on March 18, 1926 as well as his desire to continue to offend their apologists by publishing this anthology. Indeed, my suspicion after re-reading his preface is that the name of this anthology, *Fen* has nothing to do with "burying" his earlier works, as some have thought, and may actually allude to the deaths of the protestors.[2]

The archaic style of classical Chinese in which the early essays were written proved an impediment to readers, so much so that they were eventually translated into *baihua wen* 白話文 (vernacular Chinese), first by a group at Nanjing Normal University, including Hong Qiao 洪橋 and others in 1976,[3] an edition that was never officially published (perhaps because Hong Qiao had been labeled one of Hu Feng's 胡風 (1902-1985)"Rightist" [*youpai* 右派]

1 Ibid.

2 Although the preface is dated October 30, 1926, the volume was first published in March 1927 in Beijing by his literary associates in the Unnamed Society 未名社 . Eileen J. Cheng discusses Lu Xun's preoccupation with ensuring martyrs will be remembered in her monograph *Literary Remains: Death, Trauma, and Lu Xun's Refusal to Mourn*, which I think tends to confirm my theory regarding the hidden meaning of this title.

3 A *neibu* 内部 (internal circulation) book with no author accreditation treating six of the early essays came out under the *Lu Xun wenyan lunwen shiyi* 魯迅文言論文試譯 (A Draft Vernacular Translation of Lu Xun's Early Theses in the Classical Style) in 1976. It also contains an appendix (pp. 260-285) of remarks about the early essays from Lu Xun, Xu Guangping 許廣平 (1898-1968), Tang Tao 唐弢 (1913-1992), Li Jiye 李霽野 (1904-1997), Wang Yeqiu 王冶秋 (1909-1987), Li Helin 李何林 (1904-1988), Sun Yong 孙用 (1902-1983) etc. and a two page bibliography (pp. 286-287) of journal articles about them from 1946-1970s. The last page (p. 288) contains an afterword that is refreshingly unapologetic regarding the content of the essays, saying that they "are a thorough manifestation of Lu Xun's revolutionary democratic fighting spirit."

co-conspirators).[1] In 1978 they were again translated by Lu Xun scholar Wang Shijing 王士菁,[2] whom C.T. Hsia once praised as one of Lu Xun's most capable biographers. The next year the longest of these, "Moluo shi li shuo" was again translated into *baihua wen* by Zhao Ruihong 趙瑞蕻 (1915-1999), then Professor of Chinese and Comparative literature at Nanjing University.[3] William A. Lyell, perhaps the foremost American Lu Xun scholar at the time, said a whole book could be devoted to that essay alone, and indeed Zhao Ruihong did precisely that in 1982. Zhao's book contains an extensive afterword in which he presents his views on "Moluo shi li shuo." There he proposes that it constitutes a manifesto for a romantic literary movement.

But I would argue that there is more to it than that. In "Moluo shi li shuo," Lu Xun reassesses the Chinese literary legacy, offers a sweeping view of Western and Eastern European poetry in the 19th century, assesses Byron (1788-1824), Shelley (1792-1822), and Pushkin (1799-1837), champions Lermontov (1814-1841) and Mickiewicz (1798-1855), lionizes Petőfi (1823-1849), explains at least one version of "terrorism,"[4] and posits a new poetics for China in the 20th century." Over the years since they were written, the content and style of these essays have been the subject of considerable scholarly scrutiny and this has drawn out divergent views. Scholars in Japan have done an admirable job of tracing down the sources of some of the essays, although their interpretation was not without controversy

---

1 Professors Hu Zhu 胡鑄 and Fu Xiao 符哮 argue that the mid-1950s campaign against Lu Xun's erstwhile protégé the Marxist literary theoretician Hu Feng was in reality just an extension of a purge by Mao directed at associates of Premier Zhou Enlai 周恩來 (1898-1976), which also saw General He Long 賀龍 (1893-1969) and erstwhile Communist intelligence chief Pan Hannian 潘漢年 (1906-1977) as casualties. See "Mao Zedong qiaoda Zhou Enlai bao yijian zhi chou: Hu Feng yuan' an tanyuan."

2 See Wang Shijing's *Lu Xun zaoqi wupian lunwen zhuyi*. This book contains an afterword by the translator assessing the significance of the essays from a Marxian perspective. The afterword, completed in June 1977 was slightly revised in August 1980 (pp. 248-267 of the 1981 edition). Notable in this volume is the exclusion of the 1908 essay "Po e'shen lun," which must still have been deemed too controversial.

3 See Zhao Ruihong, *Lu Xun Moluo shi li shuo zhushi, jinyi, jieshuo*.

4 See my article, "Lu Xun and Terrorism: a Study of Revenge and Violence in Mara and Beyond."

there. Chinese scholars have first discounted, then eschewed, then annotated, and finally extolled them as harbingers of a new poetics or a profound meditation on unresolved issues still facing China. Westerners, by and large, give them a degree of primacy, but from different perspectives and to different degrees. The full version of this article critically examines the reception of these essays internationally, re-contextualizing it within the historical factors that have contributed to and molded it.

With this article I intend to give an indication of how seriously Lu Xun's early essays have come to be taken by scholars both within and outside China. This is in part, as I have argued, because these essays constitute a blueprint for Lu Xun's future career. It is also because they give an indication of the formative influences on the young Lu Xun. As such, they are a key to understanding the development of his thought, even if they are considered a product of his youth and an immature period, as Takeuchi Yoshimi 竹内好 (1908-1977)viewed them. Elsewhere I have speculated on the reasons for their neglect in China up until the late 1970s (and actually a good deal later). This had in part to do with their arcane language, but it has more to do with the controversial ideas in the texts and some of the thinkers he refers to, such as Nietzsche, who until recently was regarded as a proto-fascist (not just in China), and Lu Xun's condemnation of the suppression of the rights of the individual and the minority by the majority or, still worse, those who claim to rule on behalf of the majority. In term of literature and thought, they strike out in a bold, new direction that is critical of elements in China's literary, cultural and political past without being iconoclastic, and although they champion intellectual freedom, they decline to posit the West as the ultimate model. As such, they make a mature attempt at mapping a path for China then and now: one that prizes internationalism, cultural self-reflection, and gives precedence to *jingshen* 精神 (Geist, spirit, intellect, ideals) over *wuzhi* 物质 (materialistic culture / materialism).

从“开而不放”到主动开放
——以敦煌石窟的过去与未来为例

葛剑雄　【中国】
复旦大学　教授 / 中央文史研究馆　馆员

长期流行一种说法，汉朝与唐朝是对外开放的，特别是唐朝，经常被称为中国对外最开放的时代。其实，汉唐的开放是相对于其他开放度更低或完全不开放的阶段而言，即使在盛唐也只是“开而不放”，即有条件地允许外国、外族的人员和文化进来，却并不允许本国、本族人员外出，更没有主动对外传播自己的文化。近代以前走出中国、走向世界的中国人如凤毛麟角，中国文化在外界的影响远低于我们以往的想象。

如在张骞通西域以后，一批西域（泛指今新疆与以西地区）的使者、商人进入中原，有的还长期居留。东汉以后更有大批移民迁入，还有不少佛教徒来内地传经弘法，魏晋南北朝迁入并定居的更多。但这几个世纪中，仅汉武帝时曾派出大批使者往西域各国招引对方来朝，其他就找不到史料记载，连西行取经的僧人也屈指可数。迁入唐朝的外国人、外族人更多，动辄以万数，大批人长期居留，或最终融入汉族。胡人、胡商、胡姬、胡乐、胡旋（舞蹈）在各大城市普遍存在，长安、洛阳、扬州、广州、泉州等城市中聚居着大批外国侨民，甚至形成“蕃坊”，有自己的“蕃长”。但唐朝仍不许国民外出，见于记载的，主要只有战争中被外国、外族军队俘虏的人员，如公元751年怛罗斯（今哈萨克斯坦江布尔）之战被阿拉伯军队所俘的士兵、工匠，被吐蕃军队掠往青藏高原的唐朝军民等。

在文化主要只能通过人传播的时代，移民与流动人口是文化传播的主要手段。大量外国、外族的文化包括宗教随着传带它们的人口被传入中国，只有这些人回迁时才有可能将他们在中国的感受或接受的中国文化自觉或不自觉地传播出去。但除了朝鲜、日本等主动派遣专人来中国学习并积极传播、仿效的以外，有限的迁回者不自觉的传播产生的影响相当有限。直到近代以前，中国都视外国、外族为蛮夷，绝不会主动去传播华夏文明，连国内少数民族聚居地区，也要到改土归流设置州县后才设学校、开科举。而迁入东南亚等地的中国侨民一般都是底层贫民，又大多聚居，既不可能自觉传播中国文化，即便有不自觉的传播，其能力也很低。

敦煌石窟被称为世界罕见的文化瑰宝和艺术宝库，是当之无愧的。但将它当作古代中国长期开放、对外来文化艺术兼收并蓄的产物，并不符合历史事实。实际上，敦煌石窟的形成、发展和保存主要得益于其特殊的历史人文地理环境，而不是中国主动开放的结果。

尽管从公元前 2 世纪开始，敦煌一带就已成为西汉的郡县，但直到清代，始终处于中原政权的边疆或边缘，甚至经常游离于中原政权之外，成为独立或半独立的地方政权。

从公元前 60 年西汉在今新疆和中亚设置西域都护府起，敦煌不再处于西汉疆域的边缘，并成了连接西域的枢纽。但这种状况只延续了数十年。到东汉时，朝廷三次放弃对西域的控制，中原与西域的联系“三通三绝”，敦煌一次次重新处于汉朝疆域的边缘。西晋后期，敦煌所在的河西就脱离了朝廷控制，十六国期间长期为割据政权所有，一百多年后才为北魏所统一。到安史之乱爆发后，河西走廊又陷于吐蕃，大中二年（848 年）虽由张议潮收复，并在三年后重归唐朝，但不久又与唐朝分离，敦煌所在的沙州先后为张氏、曹氏所有，孤悬于中原之外，直到北宋时灭于西夏，到 1227 年随着西夏的覆灭归入元朝。明朝初年曾在敦煌一带设立卫所，但到嘉靖年间已退守嘉峪关，敦煌成为吐鲁番的辖地，直到清康熙中叶才归入清朝版图，到乾隆初才得到安定。

所以当地的行政制度从来就不是完整的专制集权制度，更多是多元的、混杂的、实用性、地域性的制度，介于政教合一与政教分离之间，客观上给宗教、文化、思想、艺术的保存与发展提供了很大的空间与自由度。

由于远离政治中心，甚至完全脱离中原政权的统治或控制，敦煌一带往往成为战乱或分裂时期的世外桃源，并由于高素质移民的迁入而出现经济、文化的超常繁荣，成为中原“礼失求诸野”的资源。统治者和民众更关注本土利益和日常生活，也给宗教艺术注入不少世俗成分和民间特色。

敦煌处于农业文化与牧业文化、农业民族与牧业民族、华夏（汉族）与其他民族、各种宗教及其不同流派、不同层次的文化、不同形式的艺术等交汇的地方，但各种方式的消长和融合不断发生。相对隔绝的环境和远离各种因素的中心或发达地区，导致一些独特的因素形成积淀。

从公元前 2 世纪至公元 8 世纪中叶，尽管丝绸之路基本通行，但不时出现不同时间的中断。作为丝绸之路上一个重要枢纽和集散地，敦煌经常滞留一批人员和物资，有些人不得不长期居留或就此定居，一些物资不得不就地交换或消费。因此敦煌一度积聚的人员和物资，远超其东、西两边。由此产生的物质和精神文化，往往既不同于其原产生，又不同于其最终目的地。

近二千年来，敦煌的自然条件没有太大的变化。石窟周围地质构造稳定，没有发生过破坏性地震和其他重大自然灾害。流经敦煌绿洲的河流没有重大改道，水源一直充足，满足了居民和流动人口的生活生产用水，也保证了石窟的开凿和维护、造像和壁画的创作和更新、建筑和维修的用水。

应该指出，这些特殊的人文地理和自然地理因素造就的环境，并非都有利于敦煌石窟艺术和敦煌文化的发展和保存，其积极成果往往不是人类主观努力的结果。面向未来，人类应该共同给敦煌这一世界文化遗产的保护和合理利用提供最有利的人文地理环境，通过全面保护生态环境，并用科学的理念和先进的技术加以修复和维护。这需要全人类的共同努力，也离不开中国主动的、全方位的对外开放。

From Partial Opening-Up with Restrictions to the Outside World to Active Opening-Up

——Take the Past and Future of the Dunhuang Grottoes as an Example

Ge Jianxiong / China

Senior Professor of Fudan University /Member of the Central Research Institute of Culture and History

It has long been believed that China was open to the outside world during the Han Dynasty (202 B.C.-A.D.220) and the Tang Dynasty (A.D.618-A.D.907); in particular, the Tang Dynasty is often considered as the era during which China was most open to the outside world. In fact, the level of openness during both dynasties was high only in comparison with other stages with lower levels of openness or without any opening up at all. Even in the glorious age of the Tang Dynasty, China was partially open to the world, and it imposed restrictions on access to it—China conditionallyallowed the entry of people and cultures from foreign countries and other clans, but did not allow the outflow of Chinese people and the people of the same clan and so China did not actively disseminate its culture to the outside world. Before modern times, very few Chinese people went to the world outside China, so the influence of Chinese culture on the outside world was much lower than we imagine.

After Zhang Qian (164 B.C.-114 B.C.), an envoy, an outstanding diplomat during the Han Dynasty, was sent to the western regions on friendly exchanges, a large number of envoys and merchants from the western regions (broadly referred to as Xinjiang and the regions to the west of Xinjiang) flocked to the Central Plains and some of them even stayed there permanently. After the Eastern Han Dynasty (A.D.25-A.D.220), there was a massive inflow of immigrants, and even not a few Buddhists went to the inland to do missionary work. The Wei,Jin,Northern and Southern Dynasties (A.D.220-A.D.589) witnessed more inflows and inhabitants. However, during these several centuries, only Emperor Wu of the Han Dynasty sent a large number of envoys to the countries in the western regions so that the people of these countries made a pilgrimage to the areas under his governance. No historical records have shown other similar actions. Even the number of Buddhists who made a pilgrimage to the west to obtain Buddhist scriptures was very small. Many—tens of thousands of—foreigners and the people of other clans migrated to the Tang Dynasty; a multitude of people permanently resided in the Tang Dynasty or finally became part of the Han nationality. The Northern barbarian tribes in ancient China, the merchants, women, musicians and dancers from the tribes were very numerous in large cities. Such cities as Changan, Luoyang, Yangzhou, Guangzhou and Quanzhou were inhabited by a large number of foreign nationals, and they even formed their own compact communities where there was a chieftain. However, no nationals were allowed to go to the outside world during the Tang Dynasty. The recorded occasions where nationals went to the outside world were mainly wars in which people were captured by the troops of foreign countries and other clans; for example, in the Battle of Talas (currently Zhamby l, Kazakhstan) in A.D.751, soldiers and craftsmen were captured by Arab troops; the soldiers and civilians of the Tang Dynasty were plundered by the troops of the Tibetan regime in ancient China on the Qinghai-Tibet Plateau.

In an era during which culture was disseminated only by people, immigrants and floating populations were the main means for cultural dissemination. A lot of cultures from foreign countries and people not of the same clan including religions were transmitted to China by the people who carried and spread them. Only when these people returned to their native places could their experience in China or their knowledge of the Chinese culture accepted by them be consciously or unconsciously disseminated to the outside world. However, except for Korea, Japan and other countries that actively sent people to China for learning and vigorously disseminating and imitating Chinese culture, the impact from the unconscious dissemination by a small number of people who returned to their native places was very limited. Before modern times, China treated foreign countries and the people not of the same clan as barbarians and never actively spread the Chinese civilization; even in the domestic areas inhabited by ethnic minorities, schools could not be run and imperial examinations could not be conducted unless native officers were bureaucratized, and prefectures and counties were established. The Chinese nationals who migrated to such areas as Southeast Asia were generally poor lower-class people who, for the most part, lived in compact communities, so it was impossible for them to consciously disseminate the Chinese culture, and their capability for unconscious dissemination was very low.

The Dunhuang Grottoes are regarded as rare cultural treasures and art treasure houses in the world. They are worthy of such a title. However, thinking that the Dunhuang Grottoes are the result of ancient China's long-term opening up and absorption of external cultural arts does not tally with historical facts. In fact, the formation, development and preservation of the Dunhuang Grottoes mainly results from their special historical, cultural and geographical environments rather than from China's active opening up.

The Dunhuang area became a county of the Western Han Dynasty (206 B.C.-A. D.24) from the 2nd century B.C. However, the Dunhuang area was a border area or on the edge of the Central Plains Regime until the Qing Dynasty (A.D.1636-A. D.1912), and it even often fell outside the Central Plains Regime and was an independent or semi-independent local regime.

From 60 B.C. when the supervisory military organizations for the western regions were established in today's Xinjiang and Central Asia during the Western Han Dynasty, Dunhuang was no longer on the edge of Western Han Dynasty's territory and it became the hub which connected the western regions. However, this situation only lasted for several decades. During the Eastern Han Dynasty, the Imperial Court gave up control over the western regions three times; the connection between the Central Plains and the western regions was set up and discontinued three times, and Dunhuang was placed on the edge of the Han Dynasty's territory time and time again. In the later period of the Western Jin Dynasty (A.D.265-A.D.316), Hexi, where Dunhuang was situated,got out of the Imperial Court's control. During the period of the Sixteen States (A.D.301-A.D.460), Dunhuang was owned by a local separatist power for a long time. More than 100 years later, Dunhuang was unified by the Northern Wei Dynasty (A.D.368-A.D.534). After the An Lushan Rebellion broke out, the Hexi Corridor again became part of the Tibetan regime in ancient China (A.D.618-A.D.842). The Hexi Corridor was regained by Zhang Yichao in the Dazhong Second Year (A.D.848), and three years later, it returned to the Tang Dynasty; shortly afterwards, it was again separated from the Tang Dynasty. Shazhou, where Dunhuang was located, was successively owned by the Zhang Clan and the Cao Clan and was isolated from the Central Plains; in the Northern Song Dynasty (A.D.960-A.D.1127),it was owned by the Western Xia Regime (A.D.1038-A.D.1227). In 1227, with the collapse of the Western Xia Regime, it was merged into the Yuan Dynasty (A.D.1271-A.D.1368). During the early years of the Ming Dynasty (A.D.1368-A.D.1644), garrisons were established in the Dunhuang area;however, the Qing retreated and stood on the defensive at Jiayuguan during the Jiajing period (A.D.1522-A.D.1566), and then Dunhuang became part of Turpan. It was not part of the Qing Dynasty until the middle of the Kangxi period (A.D.1654-A.D.1722),and it was not at peace until the early years of the Qianlong period (A.D.1736-A.D.1795).

Therefore, the local administrative system was never a complete centralized autocratic system but a diversified, mixed, practical and regional system. It fell in between the unification of the state and the church and the separation of the church from the state. Objectively, it provided a large space and freedom for preserving and developing religions, cultures, thoughts and the arts.

The Dunhuang area was far away from the political center and was even completely isolated from the governance or control of the Central Plains Regime, so it often became a retreat, a place that was far away from the turmoil of the world during periods of war or secession. Thanks to the inflow of high-caliber immigrants and the resulting extraordinary economic and cultural prosperity, it became a resource for those "seeking a system of etiquette based on the folklore after its disappearance elsewhere" in the Central Plains. The governor and the general public paid more attention to local interests and daily life, and so many secular elements and folk characteristics were injected into the religions and the arts.

Dunhuang was the intersection between farming and animal husbandry cultures, between farming and animal husbandry nations, between Huaxia (the Han nationality) and other nationalities, and among various religions and other different schools, different levels of cultures and various arts forms. However, various forms of growth, decline and integration constantly occurred. The relatively isolated environment and the center or developed areas free from various factors led to the formation and accumulation of some unique characteristics in Dunhuang.

From the 2nd century B.C. to mid-8th century A.D., the Silk Road was basically open, but it was often interrupted during different periods of time. As an important hub and center of distribution on the Silk Road, Dunhuang often witnessed the fact that large numbers of people and large quantities of materials remained there; some people had to live in Dunhuang permanently or settle there, and some materials had to be exchanged or consumed there. Therefore, the people and materials in Dunhuang greatly exceeded those to the east and west of it, and the resulting material and spiritual cultures were different from the original places and their destinations.

For nearly two thousand years, Dunhuang's natural conditions did not change greatly. The geological structure around Dunhuang was stable, and no destructive earthquakes or other major natural disasters occurred. The rivers passing through Dunhuang oasis were not greatly diverted; the water sources were ample and could meet the residents' and the floating population's water needs for their daily lives and their productive activities; the water sources also guaranteed enough water for the making and maintenance of the grottoes, the fabrication of statues and the creation and renewal of frescoes, buildings and repairs.

It should be noted that the environment resulting from these special cultural, geographical and natural factors was not all beneficial for the development and preservation of Dunhuang's grotto art and culture. Its positive results were not achieved by subjective human efforts in most cases. In the future, the human beings should jointly provide the most favorable cultural and geographical environment for the protection and rational utilization of Dunhuang, a world cultural heritage; it should be repaired and maintained by fully protecting the ecological environment, adopting scientific philosophies and advanced technologies. This requires the concerted efforts of all human beings, as well as China's policy of active and all-round opening up.

尼日利亚与中国的治理伦理与社会秩序

奥什塔　【尼日利亚】
尼日利亚和平与冲突解决研究所　所长

一　引言

全球化的政治逻辑对当代世界国家与国家之间的关系进行了定义，但这种政治逻辑正变得更加复杂化，且不断引起争议。对于政治、经济、技术等方面较为弱势的国家而言，跨国的社会交流、政治交流、文化交流以及经济交流等，正愈发严重地剥削乃至毁坏着这些国家固有价值观的本质要素。从中国和尼日利亚两国的历史来看，决定两国社会政治格局、文化格局、经济格局的传统秩序都或多或少地受到外部因素的影响。例如，前殖民时期“尼日尔地区”的国家——后来在弗罗拉·肖的提议下改称尼日利亚——便曾受到阿拉伯人的跨撒哈拉奴隶贸易、欧洲人的跨大西洋奴隶贸易、殖民主义、帝国主义以及当代的新自由主义全球秩序等多重历史因素的影响。由于受到这些历史因素的影响，当地民众传统价值观和传统秩序的重要特征变得最小化、边缘化甚至完全丧失。同样，中国的原生价值观也曾受到欧洲、日本等国殖民主义的影响，致使后殖民时期，中国的传统伦理、价值观、社会秩序等变得面目全非。这些外部影响对于定义以及重新定义尼中两国与国际社会其他成员的关系时，扮演了重要的角色。在某些情况下，这些经历扭曲了经济和发展的取向，改变了国内群体间的内部权力动态。尽管在奴隶贸易时期、殖民主义和帝国主义时期，尼中两国传统社会与外部文化的交流很大程度上改变了两国社会的原生秩序，但一些重要的伦理准则却得以代代相传，这些准则可以用于强化良政，有助于在愈发不稳定的国际社会中和平共存。

毋庸置疑的是，尼中两国均遭受着全球化带来的剥离与摧残，因国际社会秩序功能失调而面临着安全上的挑战。这些顽疾往往以恐怖主义、暴力极端主义、贪污腐败等形式表现出来，尼中两国正各自采取不同的措施来应对这些顽疾，取得的效果也不尽相同。因此，基地组织、伊斯兰国、博科圣地、青年党、真主党等极端伊斯兰势力才会在中国和尼日利亚有所抬头。

阿拉伯商人进入中国北部后，与当地人通婚，形成了中国新疆地区的穆斯林群体。据统计数据显示，1949 至 2013 年间，新疆维吾尔自治区发生恐怖袭击案件 500 余起，造成数千人死亡、数十亿人民币的财产损失。2014 年发生恐怖袭击案件 5 起，造成 100 人死亡，300 人受伤，财产损失严重。2014 年 1 月，中国西南边陲城市昆明火车站发生的恐怖事件给许多人留下了永久的伤痛，短短十分钟内，蒙面持刀的恐怖分子杀害了 29 名平民，更造成 149 人受伤。 2014 年 4 月 30 日，乌鲁木齐火车南站出口发生恐怖事件，造成 1 人死亡，79 人受伤。2014 年 7 月 30 日，一所清真寺发生恐怖袭击事件，艾提尕尔清真寺居的伊玛目居玛 · 塔伊尔在主持晨礼后被杀，导致穆斯林的斋月中途结束。

同样，伊斯兰教和基督教也是随着商人和传教士从南北两路传入尼日利亚。自 20 世纪 80 年代“麦塔特斯尼暴动”以来，尼日利亚某些群体中的伊斯兰极端主义有所抬头，由此造成的暴力冲突时有反复，一直持续至今。最近一段时期，特别是 2009 年，博科圣地组织的恐怖活动一直占据着新闻头条。的确，博科圣地组织在博尔诺、约贝、阿达马瓦等北方地区发起的猛烈袭击严重破坏了尼日利亚在国际社会中的形象。该组织还曾对尼日利亚联邦首都区阿布贾的警察总部、联合国机构大楼、商场、停车场等地发起攻击。博科圣地组织在东北地区的恐怖活动十分猖獗，在恐怖活动最严重的的时期，东北地死亡、受伤、流离失所的人数达到上百万人。此外还有多人遭到绑架，包括奇博克镇政府女子学校的 270 名女学生。叛乱分子甚至占领了面积为 20000 平方千米的地区（相当于比利时国土面积）其中包括 11 处地方政府机构，并在果扎建立了哈里发总部。在乍得湖流域委员会成员国的多国联合部队的支持下，尼日利亚军队重新夺回了这些地区。据 201 年全球恐怖主义指数报告显示，随着这些致命的恐怖袭击不断发生，尼日利亚恐怖主义在全球排名第四，仅次于伊拉克、阿富汗、巴基斯坦，2015 年跃居首位，当然这点并不令人感到羡慕。这里需要强调的一点是，所有此类极端势力都不是尼日利亚和中国传统社会的产物。两国的传统社会均注重善、忍等美德，崇尚集体利益。

除了恐怖主义和极端势力，贪污腐败也对国家治理、尼中两国的内外关系造成了消极影响。中国曾先后逮捕、起诉、并判处了一批参与贪污腐败的官员和商人。2009 年，上海浦东新区的副区长康慧军因收受贿赂被判处无期徒刑。据称，2013 至 2016 年间，在中国的反腐败行动中，有一百多万人因贪污腐败遭到惩处。就在中国的反腐行动不断取得成就时，尼日利亚仍在因官员的腐败问题而犹豫不决，许多腐败分子并未得到有力的惩处。不久前，英国前任首相卡梅伦将尼日拉描述成腐败重地，而透明国际则连续七年将尼日利亚的腐败程度定位高危级别。为开展强有力的反腐行动，尼日利亚经济金融犯罪委员会最近逮捕了行政及司法部门多名涉嫌贪污的官员，在国内民众间引发了不同程度的反响。欧沃拉比认为，尼日利亚每年因洗钱造成的财产损失达到 6000 万美元，20 世纪 80 年代中期至 1999 年，尼日利亚因洗钱造成的损失高达 1000 亿美元。在所谓的民主时期，即 2001 至 2004 年间，尼日利亚因洗钱造成的财产损失达到 2500 亿美元。从事国际货币转账业务的尼日利亚人涉嫌海外诈骗金额达到 357，147，857 美元。这种非法的巨额财产流入、流出造成了尼日利亚经济的困境。

本文认为，前殖民时代尼日利亚与中国的传统伦理中的原生价值观有助于治理国家、维持社会秩序、促进民族团结以及基础设施建设。如今，这些伦理准则在经过一定的调整后，有助于两国应对治理危机和维护社会秩序，有助于缩小尼中双边关系中存在的伦理差距，增进互信，为两国发展过程中遇到的挑战提供解决方案。

二　概念解释

所谓伦理是关于人类行为的一门科学，其研究主题在于探索人类行为最恰当的表现形式，特别是判别促成人类行为正误的因素。伦理与道德两个概念经常发生混淆。道德仅仅与人类行为相关，只能影响人类行为，而伦理则是研究道德的科学。一些思想家认为，所有人类行为都是具有缺陷的，而另外一些人则认为，并非所有人类行为都是不完善的，因为人类行为有善恶之分，两者常常混杂一处。从广义上讲，治理是指人类社会中用来协调行为的所有模式。在国家层面，治理涉及主权行为（政府实施治理）或通过公私网络开展治理（与政府一道实施治理），以及非国家参与者的管控行为、民间社会的自我管控行为（无政府治理）。

布林克霍夫认为，治理体系可以分为多个子系统，分别为安全治理、行政–经济治理和政治治理。

（1）安全治理：通过国家机器确保安全，包括使用专断或强制性措施来确保领土完整、维护法律权威和社会规范。安全治理的理想效果为：维持国家与公民之间的社会契约，国家有义务保护人民，保障繁荣。安全治理措施包括对内打击犯罪和不法行为，对外抵抗他国侵略。为达到这些效果，国家必须对安全力量进行监管，确保强制性力量的合法性、防止权力滥用、维护依法治国。

（2）行政–经济治理：将提供有效和高效服务作为国家的一项职责，其理想效果为：国家根据大多数公民的意愿提供服务，服务的质量和数量应能够满足大多数公民要求。服务内容在某种程度上需要国家参与，通过实施规章制度、制定透明政策、制定法律法规、制定财政协议、构建伙伴关系以及行政体系等方式，提供经济机遇。

（3）政治治理：通过权力制衡确保合法性，建设反应迅速、负责制政府，代表人民利益，具有包容性，保障所有公民的基本权利。合法性的构建涉及扩大参与机会、减少社会–经济或部族群体的不平等现象，实现信息透明，出台反腐措施，施行依法治国，定期施行权利竞赛（选举）。

非洲学者历来对全球治理格局持批判态度，特别是对西方国家与南方国家的关系层面。马佛杰认为，非洲关于治理问题的争论最开始起源于对“良政”展开的论辩。所谓良政是世界银行针对非洲政府的不善管理而提出的一个概念，很显然，世界银行所关心的重点在于技术官僚而不是在社会层面。为确保“结构调整计划”的顺利实施，世界银行需要高效、透明、清廉的非洲政府，需要非洲政府以按部就班而非极端的形式实现转型。这就要求非洲国家一方面在发展问题上保持落后的位置，同时需要“强有力的国家”或独裁政府来推行不得民心的计划。在这个背景下，非洲学者对世界银行所谓“良政”的概念提出批判，并最终进行抵制。一些学者坚持认为，根本不存在所谓的“良政”与“劣政”，因为劣政意味着不治理。从对于“良政”的争辩中演化出“民主治理”的理念，这一理念认为，“政府和民间社会之间的定期交流、民间社会通过政府机制、机构自由参与治理，其重要性应高于理论上的效率和清廉”。当然，这一理念是基于民主获得广泛青睐这一前提。

本文中所指的治理是指查赞提出的治理概念，是指“对整体结构进行有意识而广泛的管理，治理的目的是提高公共领域的合法性”。所谓的社会秩序是指对相通相连的社会结构、体制机制、关系、习惯、价值观以及行为进行系统化、有组织的管理，为确保社会的良性发展构建相互关联模式以及行为模式，确保这种模式得到保持和贯彻。

三　尼日利亚与中国的传统伦理

传统尼日利亚社会并非同质，而是由多元的部落和宗教群体构成，包含多种文化和传统准则。然而这种本质上的异质特征并不意味着不和谐。相反，这种多元特征被看作是广阔而丰富的互补资源，能够为发展提供独特的动力。这种多元性之中蕴藏着包容的伦理准则，而这种准则可以追溯到非洲传统中的社群主义理念，这种理念强调相互关系，以社群而非个体为导向。拉丹对这种社群及其司法行政做出了十分贴切的描述：

（1）在以面对面交流为主的社群中，问题不仅仅关乎个人，而且关乎整个集体

（2）强调恢复社会的和谐，而不是单纯的非判断有罪或清白

（3）司法行政过程中，公众参与度很高

（4）主政者通常为社群中具有威望的酋长、长辈和具有影响力的人物

（5）从本质上看，决议是一种折中方案，综合考虑了惯例法以及可能引发纠纷或有助于协调各方利益的因素

（6）在针对纠纷举行听证时，传统法官既会证据为基础，又不会将证言、证词等因素排除在外。但在做出决议时，会严格区分直接证据和间接证据。

（7）传统司法体系中并不存在专业法律代表

（8）司法程序以自愿为基础，决议的形成以意见的一致为基础

（9）“惩处”措施强调的是“修复”而非“索偿”

（10）执行是通过社会压力而非人身强制来实现

以上论述清晰地展示出尼日利亚传统社会社群主义的本质，而民众对传统社会保持忠诚是有着必然道理的。社群是推动发展的动力，是与治理和社会秩序最为相近的一种机制。正是通过社群，民众才能实现对语言的共同理解和共同记忆。在这种以阐释为主的社群中，人们生活在同一政治框架下，分享着彼此的价值观，分享着目标、模式、现实感知、效用感等概念所隐含的意义。

艾柯曾指出，对于大多数传承至今的传统文化——如西非农村地区的沿袭至今的文化——法律不仅仅是一种保障便宜性的规则，更是价值观和行为模式的综合体，它决定着善与恶、物质与精神的判定，决定着社群的道德健康程度。哪怕是最轻微的侵越行为，如触碰禁忌、不尊奉习俗等，都可能对整个群体造成致命的影响，因此需要一系列复杂的仪式来进行复原。社会整体的规章制度具有道德和精神两个层面的意义，这促使每个个体尊重法律、抵抗谋私行为。在某种程度上来说，这些情形正是依法治国更为具体、更为严格的表现。

传统伦理与乌班图的理念一致，认为人之所以为人主要在于与“他者”的关系。个体的人性来源于承认“他者”的独特性和差异性，因此“他者”变为反映某一个体“存在”的一面镜子。这一理念在向我们暗示：人性并不仅仅在于个体，更在于他者和个体之间的相互关系。人性是个体间相互给予的一种品质，我们彼此塑造、并有必要将这种具有他者性的塑造持续下去。若彼此间能够建立一种相互的所属关系，我们便能够参与到自身的塑造中来：此方的存在取决于彼方的存在，因为彼方存在，才有我的存在。因此，“我的存在”并非一个死板的话题，而是一个动态的自我构建过程，这种构建依赖于他者对关系和距离的构建，与西方的个人主义形成鲜明对比。西方的个人主义最明显地体现在笛卡尔“我思故我在”的哲学思想中。这种思想将个体与其思想剥离开来（并不考虑具体语境），认为两者是构成“个人”的基本要素。因此，笛卡尔所指的“我”既是出发点，又是归结点，社群在“我”的定义中没有占据任何位置，因此才会引发社会秩序危机。

儒家思想，特别是和、善、义、礼、智、诚、忠、孝等传统价值观都深深地影响着中国社会。这些价值观的核心是和谐。和谐是指“事物所处的一种平衡而协调的状态”，其内涵包括理、礼以及兼容性。所谓的理是指根据客观法则和客观真理调节个人行为。礼是指恰当性和合理性。和谐的价值观倡导“和而不同”，即对不同的事物进行协调，用恰当的方式引导这些事物从不协调的状态发展为协调状态，从不对称走向对称，从不平衡走向平衡。现代中国社会努力在人类与自然之间、人类与社会之间、不同的群体成员之间、身心之间寻求平衡。

从以上论述中可以看出，影响尼日利亚和中国社会的传统价值观分别为非洲的“社群主义”和中国的儒家思想，前者以“ubuntu”为基础，后者以“和谐”为基础。这些价值观在很多方面都决定着公众对于治理和社会秩序的态度，这些理念之间的相互交汇能够增强凝聚力，在尼中双边关系的语境下为“一代一路倡议”提供支持。一带一路倡议需要整个非洲的支持。

但目前还有一个问题没有得到解释：为何在尼中两国，贪污腐败都会对治理造成困扰，而恐怖主义都会对社会秩序造成威胁？传统社会价值观的扭曲、殖民主义和帝国主义对民众的排斥以及全球化带来的粗鲁行径等，都是滋生腐败的因素。事实上，尼日利亚打击博科圣地组织的事实证明，针对恐怖主义的行动，始终将人民的和平与安全置于核心地位，始终争取群体的力量来支持反恐。目前，尼日利亚政府在反腐过程中也运用了这一战略，鼓励公民、社群领导者指认和举报腐败分子。

四　全球治理、治理伦理以及社会秩序

自 2000 年纽约全球治理会议以来，全世界各国政府均承认了非国家行为者在治理、和平、安全等问题上所发挥的作用。然而在实践中，国家行为者仍然是治理和维护社会秩序的主体。

随着各种新安全问题和新犯罪问题的出现，国际社会亟须向社会伦理而不是自由主义范式寻求解决方案。联合国通过 1325 和 2550 号决议，将妇女儿童等关键群体纳入到和平问题和安全问题中来，并提供了一些参数，以此应对世界所面临的威胁。然而，联合国也希望扩大国际社会在安理会中的参与度，特别是对亚洲和拉丁美洲国家而言——这些国家正不断地面临气候变化、新国际经济秩序（NIEO）造成的不平等、跨国组织犯罪等严峻挑战。

从区域的角度来看，西非国家经济共同体（ECOWAS）正通过“预防冲突框架”等方式，实现从国家到人民的再平衡。非洲联盟规定了公民的义务、扩大了民间社会在非洲联盟活动中的参与度，包括在提高透明度、实行领导人责任制等方面的参与度。

五　结论

本文指出了当代发展中出现的一些问题，特别是威胁到尼中两国的治理和社会秩序的腐败问题和恐怖主义问题，这两个问题正日益对世界秩序造成威胁。同时，文本指出，尼中两国的原生价值观分别建立在社群主义和和谐理念基础上，这些原生价值观有助于保持社会秩序，治理社会混乱。随着尼日利亚东北部群体不断与尼日利亚政府军展开合作，激进的伊斯兰恐怖分子正逐渐遭到驱逐。从世

界各国文化中汲取经验，能够为尼中两国的反腐运动和反恐运动带来诸多利益。

我的建议是，中国在实施“一代一路”倡议的过程中，不应过于注重“喜好问题”，如“谁喜欢中国、谁不喜欢中国”。用尼日利亚著名女作家奇玛曼达·恩戈兹·阿迪契的一句话来说：“（中国）的任务不是讨取各国喜欢，而是做一个完全的自我，这个自我是真实不欺的，对他者身上的人性具有觉察力。”这就是我们所说的真诚与虚伪。

本文对于“民众参与治理”持赞成态度，认为联合国、非洲联盟、西非国家经济共同体等组织，应增强民众在治理方面的参与度，认为联合国安理会应给予非洲、拉丁美洲、尼日利亚、非洲、埃及、巴西、阿根廷、印度尼西亚等国家和地区在治理问题上的参与权。

Ethics in Governance and Social Order in Nigerian and Chinese Societies

Oshita Oshita / Nigeria

Director-General of the Institute for Peace and Conflict Resolution in Nigeria

Introduction

The politics of globalization, which defines interstate relations in the contemporary world, is getting more complicated as it is also contested. Transnational social, political, cultural and economic interactions are increasingly exploitative and even destructive of some essential elements of the indigenous values of states that are politically, economically and technologically less endowed. Historically, in both Nigeria and China, the traditional order that determines the socio-political, cultural and economic structures has been impacted in varying degrees by exogenous influences. For example, the pre-colonial states in the 'Niger area', which later became Nigeria, courtesy of Flora Shaw's coinage, were altered by the multiple historical forces of the Arabian trans-Saharan slave trade, European trans-Atlantic slave trade, colonialism, imperialism and the contemporary neo-liberal global order. These have successfully minimised, marginalised and dispossessed the people of vital features of their traditional value projections and order. In a similar way, the Chinese autochthonous values were impacted by the colonial adventurism of European and Japanese, tinkering with aspects of traditional ethics, values and social order in post-colonial China. These exogenous influences play a role in defining and redefining the relationships of both Nigeria and China with other members of the international community.[6] In some cases, these experiences distorted traditional economy and development orientations and altered the internal power dynamics of constituent groups in the country. Although, the interactions of traditional Nigerian and Chinese societies with exogenous cultures during slave trade, colonialism and imperialism significantly altered aspects of the autochthonous order of these societies, yet some significant ethical principles have endured from generation to generation, which can be harnessed to strengthen good governance and peaceful coexistence in an increasingly volatile global community.

Undoubtedly, Nigeria and China are both impacted by the disarticulations of globalization and the security challenges accompanying the prevailing dysfunction resulting in the international social (dis)order. Some of these maladies manifest in the form of terrorism, violent extremism and corruption, which Nigeria and China are confronting in different ways, with varying degrees of successes. The intolerant activities of radical Islamic groups such as Al-Qaida, Islamic State (IS), Boko Haram, Al-Shaabab, Hezbollah, etc., have thus found expressions in both China and Nigeria. The arrival of the Arab merchants into northern China resulted into intermarriages and the existence of indigenous Muslims in the Xinjiang Province. One account of the statistics of terror attacks in China indicates that between 1949 and 2013, more than 500 terrorist attacks happened in the Xinjiang Autonomous Province resulting in the death of thousands of innocent people and the destruction of properties worth billions of RMB. In 2014, five terrorist attacks took place resulting in the death of 100, injury of 300 people and the destruction of many properties. The March 1, 2014 incident occurred at a railway station in the south-western city of Kunming that left several people traumatised because the Mask knife wielding terrorist killed 29 civilian and injured 149 people within 10 minutes. While in April 30, 2014, the incident occurred at the exit of the South Railway Station of Urumqi leaving 1 dead and 79 injured. On July 30, 2014 terrorists attacked a Mosque and murdered Jume Tahir, the Imam of the Id Kah Mosque during the ceremony to mark the end of the Islamic Holy Month of Ramadan.

In a similar way, Islam and Christianity came to Nigeria through the activities of traders and missionaries from the northern and southern parts respectively. With the emergence of the Maitatsine group in 1980s, Islamic radicalism has buoyed in some communities in Nigeria resulting in recurring violent conflict since then, and more recently in 2009, the activities of Boko Haram continue to dominate the headlines. [8] Indeed, the activities of the Boko Haram Islamic terrorists have dented the image of Nigeria in the international community with their deadly onslaughts in the North-Eastern states of Borno, Yobe, and Adamawa. The group also carried out fatal attacks on the Nigeria Police Headquarters, United Nations Building, a Shopping Mall and Motor Parks, all in the Federal Capital Territory, Abuja.

At the height of their violent atrocities in the North-East, the Boko Haram insurgents had killed, injured, and displaced millions of people from their communities, and abducted several others, including the over 270 schoolgirls of the Government Girls School, Chibok. The insurgents captured an area of about 20,000 square kilometres covering about 11 Local Government Councils (an area about the size of Belgium), with Gwoza as their Caliphate headquarters. These areas have since been recaptured by the Nigerian Military with the support of the Multinational Joint Task Force of the member-states of the Lake Chad Basin Commission. On the heels of these deadly attacks, the global terrorism ranking placed Nigeria 4th after Iraq, Afghanistan and Pakistan on the Global Terrorism Index in 2013, climbing to the unenviable position of 1st in the 2015 ranking. It is important to underscore the point that these radical tendencies are alien to both traditional Nigerian and Chinese societies, aspects of which demonstrate love, tolerance and the common good as integral parts.

Apart from terrorism and radicalization, corruption has negatively impacted governance, inter and intra community relations in Nigeria and China. The Government of the Peoples Republic of China has severally arrested, prosecuted and convicted public officers and captains of industries for involvement in corrupt practices. In 2009, Kang Huijun, former deputy of Shanghai's Pudong New Area District, was sentenced to life imprisonment for taking bribes. Over one Million people were said to have been convicted for corruption in Chinese anti-corruption drive between 2013 and October 2016. While the Chinese solution appears to be yielding positive results, Nigeria has continued to wallow under the burden of corrupt practices by mainly state officials without clear-cut convictions. The former British Prime Minister, Cameron recently described Nigeria as fantastically corrupt while Transparency International has rated Nigeria very high on corruption for 7 consecutive years. In the efforts to implement a robust anti-corruption regime, the Nigerian Economic and Financial Crimes Commission (EFCC), recently arrested public officials in the legislative and judicial arms on allegations of corruption, attracting diverse responses from the public. According to Owolabi,

Nigeria loses US$600 Million annually to money laundering. Between the mid-1980s and 1999, Nigeria lost US$ 100 Billion to money laundering. In the so acclaimed democratic era, between 2001 and 2004, the country lost an estimated US$ 25 Billion to money laundering. Nigerians who specialise in international money transfer have also exhorted about US$ 357,147,857 from overseas victims. However, such illicit inflow and outflow of huge amount of money…has contributed to the impoverishment of the Nigerian economy.

In this paper we argue that pre-colonial Nigeria and China had autochthonous values ingrained in the traditional ethics that can be leveraged for governance, social order and community solidarity for infrastructural development in both societies. Today, these ethical principles, with some tinkering, are capable of responding to the contemporary crises of governance and social disorder in both societies. Doing so will narrow the existing ethical gap in Nigeria-China bilateral relations, increase trust and contribute to sustainable solutions to the development challenges in China and Nigeria.

Conceptual Clarification

Ethics is the science of human behaviour whose subject matter is the discovery of the appropriate manner of conducting human actions.[14] The point there is in the determination of what constitutes rightness or wrongness in human action. Ethics is often confused with morality. Morality is about human actions, exclusively, while ethics is the science of the study of morality. Only human actions can be subjected to the canons of morality. Some thinkers argue that all human actions are imperfect, while others believe that not all human actions are imperfect as they could be mixture of good and bad.

The term governance, in its broad sense, refers to all modes of coordinating action in human society. It could also cover sovereign action on the part of the state ('governance by government') or governance via networks of public and private actors ('governance with government'), as well as regulation by non-state actors or self-regulation by civil society ('governance without government'). According to Brinkerhoff, governance system can be divided into sub-systems namely security, administrative-economic and political governance.

(i) Security Governance provides security by use of the instruments of the state, including ultimately its monopoly or force to maintain border integrity and to uphold the laws and norms of the society. The desired end result of the security governance function is upholding the social contract between state and citizen, in which the state is responsible for protecting people and prosperity. This includes dealing internally with crime and illegal activity and externally with cross-border intrusions. In achieving these results, the state also exercise oversight of security forces to ensure the application of coercive force is legitimate, to curb abuses and to maintain the rule of law.

(ii) Administrative-economic governance provides effective and efficient service delivery. The desired end result of administrative-economic governance is that the state produces and/or provides the types of services at the level of quality and quantity that are generally agreed upon by at least a majority of citizens as a state responsibility. Service provision meets basic needs that require some degree of state involvement and provides economic opportunity through rules-driven and transparent policy-making, regulation, fiscal arrangements, partnerships and civil service systems.

(iii) Political governance generates and sustains legitimacy through separation of powers, responsive and accountable government, representation and inclusiveness, and protection of basic rights for all citizens. Creating legitimacy involves expanded opportunities for participation, reduced inequities across socioeconomic and/or ethnic groups, information transparency and anti-corruption measures, rule of law, and periodic and formal contestation for power (elections).

African scholars have been critical of the deployment of the word governance especially by the Western countries in their relationships with the global south. Mafeje argues that the debate on governance in Africa started off as a debate on "good governance", a concept first introduced by the World Bank as a response to what was seen as gross mismanagement by African governments. It is obvious that the concerns of the World Bank were more technocratic than social. For the success of its Structural Adjustment Programmes it needed efficient, transparent, and incorrupt African governments. It did not want a radical transformation of African governments but rather conformist ones. While demanding for African states to take a back seat in development, it wanted "strong states" or authoritarian governments to implement its unpopular programmes. It was in this context that African intellectuals became critical of the World Bank's concept of "good governance" and ultimately rejected it. Some scholars have insisted that there could there be "bad governance" as against "good governance". The verdict was that there could be no such a thing as "bad governance"; bad governance is no governance. From the debate of 'good governance' emerged the notion of "democratic governance", which implies, 'over and above technical efficiency and probity, regular interaction between government and civil society and free participation by the latter through its institutions and popular organs.' In turn, this presupposes that democracy prevails in general.

In this paper, we adopt Chazan's view that governance is "the conscious [and inclusive] management of regime structures with a view to enhancing the legitimacy of [the] public realm." By social order we mean an organized and systematic arrangement of interlinked social structures, institutions, relations, customs, values and practices that ensure the consistent maintenance and enforcement of certain patterns of relating and behaving for the good of society.

Nigerian and Chinese Traditional Ethics

Traditional Nigerian society is not homogenous but consists of diverse ethnic and religious groups with various cultural and traditional principles. This essentially heterogeneous character of Nigeria does not portend disharmony. Rather, the diversity is viewed in terms of a rich network of complementary resources, which provides unique stimuli for development. Within this diversity is found a cross-cutting ethics of accommodation traceable to the ontology of traditional African Communalism, which emphasizes mutuality, is community-oriented and looks beyond the individual. Ladan aptly describes the community and justice administration in this community:

a) That it is located in face-to-face communities where the problem is viewed as not only that of individuals, but also that of the whole community.

b) It emphasised on the restoration of social harmony rather than the determination of guilt or innocence:

c) The process involves a high degree of public participation

d) The administrators are usually chiefs, elders or influential persons from the community and known to the community.

e) A decision is more in the nature of a compromise which takes into account not only customary rules of law but also the underlying factors which led to the dispute and factors which may have a bearing on successful reconciliation.

f) During the hearing of a dispute, traditional judges will not rule out testimony on the basis of strict rule of evidence. They do, nevertheless, distinguish sharply between primary and circumstantial evidence in reaching a decision.

g) Professional legal representation is not a feature of the traditional justice system.

h) The process is voluntary and the "decision" based on agreement.

i) "Penalties" emphasise restoration as opposed to retribution.

j) Enforcement is secured through social pressure rather than physical coercion.

The foregoing clearly demonstrates the communalistic nature of Nigerian traditional society, to which the ordinary people give their primary loyalty for very good reasons. The community is the engine of development and the closest mechanism in existence for governance and social order. It is also through the community that the people share common understanding of speech markers and the memory of language. By virtue of being an interpretative community, people are operating within the same political framework of shared values and meanings about goals, modalities, perceptions of reality, sense of efficacy, etc.

Ake notes that, for most of the traditional cultures which survive in rural West Africa for instance, laws are not just rules of convenience but the structuration of the values and behavioural modes which determine for good or ill, the material, moral and spiritual well-being of the community. A seemingly minor transgression, the violation of a taboo, a careless disregard of a custom, may be life-threatening to the entire community and may call for elaborate rituals of restitution. The moral and spiritual significance of the regulation for the entire society induces everyone to respect the law and to resist its corrupt exploitation for private benefit These circumstances operationalize the rule of the law in a manner that is at once more rigorous and more concrete.

This traditional ethics is consistent with the notion of Ubuntu, summarised as, a person is a person through ‘other people’. An affirmation of one’s humanity derives from recognition of an ‘other’ in his or her uniqueness and difference. It is a demand for a creative inter-subjective formation in which the ‘other’ becomes a mirror for my own ‘being’ or existence. This idealism suggests to us that humanity is not embedded in my person solely as an individual; my humanity is co-substantively bestowed upon the other and me. Humanity is a quality we owe to each other. We create each other and need to sustain this otherness creation. And if we belong to each other, we participate in our creations: we are because you are, and since you are, definitely I am. The ‘I am’ is not a rigid subject, but a dynamic self-constitution dependent on this otherness creation of relation and distance.

The above is a contrast to the western notion of individualism characterised in the Cogito Ergo Sum philosophy of Rene Descartes as ‘I think therefore I am’, which isolates the person and his thoughts (not minding the context), as essence of personhood. Here, the ‘I’ is beginning and end and community has no place, hence the crisis of social order.

Confucianism greatly influenced the Chinese society especially the traditional cultural values of harmony, benevolence, righteousness, courtesy, wisdom, honesty, loyalty, and filial piety. Of these, the core value is harmony. Harmony means “proper and balanced coordination between things” and encompasses rationale, propriety, and compatibility. Rationale refers to acting according to objective laws and truths. Propriety indicates suitability and appropriateness. The value of harmony advocates “harmony but not uniformity.” Properly coordinating different things by bringing them together in the appropriate manner allows them to develop from an uncoordinated state to one of coordination; from asymmetry to symmetry; and from imbalance to balance. Modern Chinese society tries to maintain harmony between humankind and nature; between people and society; between members of different communities; and between mind and body.

It is expedient to note that the two outstanding traditional ethics that influenced both Nigerian and Chinese societies are African communalism and Confucianism, based on 'ubuntu' and 'harmony' respectively. These have in many respects determined public attitudes towards governance and social order. An intersection of ideas such as this can strengthen ontological solidarity in support of the 'one belt and one road' initiative in the context of Nigeria-China bilateral engagements and indeed of the continent of Africa as a whole. Despite the foregoing, the question still lingers why is corruption bedevilling governance in both Nigeria and China and terrorism threatening social order? The distortion of the traditional social values, exclusion of the people by colonialism and imperialism, and the brutality of the forces of globalization are some of the drivers of corruption. In fact, Nigeria's counterterrorism campaign proves the centrality of people in peace and security by the game changer in the fight against the deadly Boko Haram terrorists, which was the inclusion of the community in counter-terrorism operation. This strategy is being employed in the ongoing fight against corruption by the Government where the ordinary citizens and community leaders are being encouraged to name and shame corrupt individuals.

Ethics, Governance and Social Order in the Global Space

Since the global governance conference in New York in 2000, governments all over the world acknowledge the role of non-state actors in governance, peace and security. However, in practice, state actors continue to dominate avenues for governance and the maintenance of social order. As the international community is challenged by new forms of insecurity and criminality, there is the urgency for alternative social ethics other than the liberal paradigms and the inclusion of both the open and formal civil society in governance, peace and security. The United Nations, through resolutions 1325 and 2250, is providing some of the parameters for the inclusion of critical populations like women and youth in peace and security as a response to the menaces confronting the world. However, the United Nations is also expected to broaden participation in the Security Council to the international community, especially countries of Africa and Latin America that are increasingly confronted by existential challenges relating to climate change, transnational organised crimes and the pangs of the unfair regimes of the New International Economic Order (NIEO).

At the regional level, the Economic Community of West African States (ECOWAS), through the instrumentality of the ECOWAS Conflict Prevention Framework (ECPF), is repositioning from the ECOWAS of States to ECOWAS of Peoples. In a similar manner, the African Union (AU) prescribes the obligations of citizens and broadens the participation of the civil society in the activities of the Union. This includes the participation in holding leaders accountable in ensuring transparency in the discharge of the functions of public office.

Conclusion

The paper highlighted the contemporary problems of development, especially corruption and terrorism, as threats not only to governance and social order in Nigeria and China, but also to the emerging borderless world. It argued that some autochthonous values of Nigeria and China, founded in the political and cultural philosophies of communalism and harmony, have the potentials for effectively responding to the problems of social (dis)order. Just as communities in the North-East of Nigeria have successfully expelled radical Islamic terrorists in their midst through collaboration with the Nigerian military, anti-corruption and counterterrorism endeavours in both countries have a lot to gain from understanding the cultures and worldviews of the people. My advice is that in pursuit of the belt and Road initiative China should focus less on the project of likeability: 'who likes China and who does not.' To appropriate the words of Chimamanda Ngozi Adichie, a fellow Nigerian, "[China's] job is not to make herself likeable, her job is to be her full self, a self that is honest and aware of the equal humanity of other people." This is what we refer to as being authentic as opposed to inauthenticity in the existentialist sense of this rendition. Others may describe this phenomenon in other ways.

The paper noted as positive steps, the emerging paradigm shifts by supranational institutions in favour of 'people participation and inclusion' in governance. In particular, that the UN, AU and the ECOWAS, must give back the organisations to the peoples by enlarging people-to-people participation in these organisations. It noted the urgency and propriety of enlarging the United Nations Security Council (UNSC) to include participation of some countries in Africa and Latin America, especially Nigeria, South Africa, Egypt, Brazil, Argentina, Indonesia, among others.

我所了解的梁漱溟

艾恺 【美国】
芝加哥大学历史系 教授

对绝大多数有记录的历史而言，中华文明毫无疑问是世界上最成功的文明，而且最不受外来文化的影响。绵延不断是中华文明最显著的特色。当其他文明遭到外族侵入或者陷入混乱的时候，常常就崩溃灭亡，不能重新建立起来，只有中华文明能承受得住这些困难的时期，继续用同一套基本的原则重新建立自身的文明体系。

可是进入 20 世纪，情况完全改变了，因为中国思想的主流开始对传统文化抱持敌视与批判的态度。在 20 世纪，只有一位中国的思想家既有系统又有说服力地展现了文化绵延不断的特质：这就是梁漱溟。他在历史上或许以哲学家闻名，你要是找一位知识分子来问“梁漱溟是谁？”八成会回答他是“一位哲学家”。因此，当我写他的传记的时候，将书名定为《最后的儒家》，同样认为他主要是一位思想家。

这么多年以来，我不断对他生涯的总体进行反省思考与重新检讨，最近我得出一个结论，他人生的另外一面，或许是最重要的一面，是他的“行动主义”，或者说是他在历史上所扮演的“实践者”的角色。

梁漱溟从 11 岁开始，一直到至少 1953 年 9 月为止，他人生的大部分都致力于领导与推进实际的社会与政治活动，并且始终不偏离他自己在智识上与精神上的许诺与原则。他的人生体现了他自己的两个座右铭：“独立思考”与“表里如一”。

梁漱溟 11 岁就走上街头参与 1905 年的抵制美国商品运动，后来他参加过同盟会与国民革命，撰写过反军阀的政治小册，更是中国乡村建设运动最早的发起者。抗战期间他为了团结全国，在国、共两党之外，筹组了后来的民主同盟，战后他又对避免中国内战做过努力。梁漱溟一直是毛泽东的朋友与顾问，可是他所坚持的“独立思考”与“表里如一”导致 1953 年 9 月他与毛泽东的公开冲突。在 1950 到 20 世纪 80 年代，他是唯一胆敢对政策公开表示反对意见的重要知识分子。

由于时间有限，我无法详细叙述梁漱溟的行动家生涯。但我们可以说他大部分的人生都奉献给了社会的各种运动，在书斋中读书与写作只是他人生中的一小部分。

现在对我而言似乎很清楚了，梁漱溟跟他的朋友熊十力不一样，他并非主要是一位新儒家的哲学家。梁漱溟曾对亲口我说过好几次：“我常常对人表示我不是一个学者。我承认自己是一个有思想的人，并且是本着自己思想而去实行、实践的人”。

梁漱溟并非中国的海德格尔或伯格森，而是像印度的甘地那样主要是一位行动家，基于他自己的思想而采取行动。甘地也是一位思想家，但他在历史上主要是以行动家闻名。在梁漱溟过世前几个月，他对自己的人生是这么看待的，他说：“我不单纯是思想家，我是一个实践者。我是一个要拼命干的人。我一生是拼命干的”。

因此，我预测一个世纪之后，梁漱溟会被大家视为是“中国的甘地”。

What I Know about Liang Shuming

Guy Alitto / United States of America

Professor of the Department of History at the University of Chicago

For most of the history on record, Chinese civilization is undoubtedly the most successful civilization in the world and is the most immune to the cultures of other countries. Continuity is the most striking feature of Chinese civilization. When other civilizations were invaded by aliens or fell into disorder, they often collapsed and perished, and could not be rebuilt. Only the Chinese civilization can survive the difficult times and continue to rebuild its own system of civilization under the same basic principle.

However, the situation totally changed in the 20th century because China's mainstream thoughts started to show hostile and critical attitudes towards traditional culture. In the 20th century, only one Chinese thinker systematically and convincingly demonstrated the trait of culture: continuity; this thinker was Liang Shuming. He may be famous as a philosopher in history. When asked the question: who is Liang Shuming, an intellectual will most likely answer: a philosopher. Therefore, when I wrote his biography, I named it *The Last Confucian*, and I also thought that he was a thinker.

Over the years, I constantly reflected on, thought and reviewed his whole life, and finally, I concluded that another aspect, or the most important aspect, of his life was his activism or his role as a practitioner in history.

From the time when Liang Shuming was 11 years old to at least September, 1953, most of his life was dedicated to leading and pushing forward practical, social and political activities, and he always kept to his promise and principles at the intellectual and spiritual levels. His life embodied his two mottos: one should develop an independent line of thought; deeds should be in agreement with words.

When Liang Shuming was 11 years old, he participated in the campaign for boycotting American goods on streets; later, he joined the Chinese Revolutionary League and the national revolution, and he wrote political pamphlets against warlords; moreover, he was one of the first to initiate China's rural construction movement. During the Anti-Japanese War, he prepared and organized the subsequent Democratic League outside the Kuomintang and the Communist Party of China in order to unite the people nationwide. After the Anti-Japanese War, he also made efforts to prevent the Chinese civil war. Liang Shuming had been the friend and advisor of Mao Zedong. However, his mottos—one should develop an independent line of thought; deeds should be in agreement with words—led to his open conflicts with Mao Zedong in September, 1953. From the 1950s to the 1980s, he was the only important intellectual who was bold enough to openly raise objections to policies.

Because of limitations on time, I cannot give a detailed description of his life activist career. Suffice it to say that he spent the bulk of his life in activities in society, and only a small portion of it in a study reading and writing books.

Now I seem to clearly know that Liang Shuming was different from his friend Xiong Shili and he was not mainly a neo-Confucian philosopher. Liang Shuming said to me several times, "I often stress before others that I am not a scholar. However, I admit that I am a thoughtful person and I act according to my thoughts."

Liang Shuming was not China's Martin Heidegger or Henri Bergson; he was mainly an actionist like the Indian Gandhi and took actions according to his thoughts. Gandhi was also a thinker, but he was mainly well-known as an actionist in history. Several months before his death, Liang Shuming viewed his life as follows: "I am not merely a thinker, I am an actionist; I am a person who works very hard; I have never stopped working during my life."

Therefore, I have predicted that Liang Shuming will be generally recognized as the Chinese Gandhi after a century.

论知识分享与共同家园在“一带一路”建设中的历史传承

李国强　【中国】
中国社会科学院中国边疆研究所　副所长

距今2100年前，我们的先人在极为艰难的条件下，开启了东西方国家相互交往的大门，在中国与世界之间形成了多条重要的国际通道，这就是时至今日仍为人们称道的陆地丝绸之路和海上丝绸之路。

文献记载和考古发现表明，早在公元前10世纪至公元前3世纪，东西方之间已经有了零星的物质和文化交流。而在公元前2世纪丝绸之路开通前，中国中原至西域，乃至黑海北岸之间，的确存在往来之路，尽管不那么连贯，但东西方已经开始接近。在西汉王朝和古希腊两大帝国的共同作用下，连接东西方的丝绸之路得以贯通，并就此拉开沿线国家和地区知识分享和共同家园塑造的历史大幕。

古代丝绸之路之所以能够形成，是因为它顺应了沿线国家不同历史时期对商品贸易、人员交往和人文交流的多种需求。古代丝绸之路之所以能够持续繁荣，是因为它构建起了东西方经贸和文化交流平台，集中反映了古代历史时期沿线各国先进的理念、发展的方向和文明的互动。

古代丝绸之路在沿线国家经济发展的利益诉求下应运而生，在沿线国家的互通有无中日渐兴盛。它聚合了沿线国家的商贸、产业和资源配置，成为各方利益交汇的经济走廊。而古代丝绸之路在多领域多层面的物质与精神的相互交流中，进一步促成沿线国家商品结构、生产方式、市场行为以及政策机制、社会组织、思想观念重新建构的连锁反应。可以说，古代丝绸之路不仅实现了商品大交流，贸易大流通，科学技术大传播，而且首开人类文明交流之先河，是不同国家、不同民族和平交往的典范，持续的跨文明交流对话和知识分享，记录了也见证了沿线不同国家、众多民族成长的历程，从而成为全人类的集体记忆。

古代丝绸之路不仅是贸易之路，更是把中华、印度、埃及、巴比伦、伊斯兰等多种古代文明广泛联结起来的知识分享之路，不同民族的文化、宗教、艺术以及各种生产技艺百花争艳，相互浸染，实现了人类历史上史无前例的大交融。

中国的儒学在1世纪初传入朝鲜，5世纪传入日本，10世纪进入越南，明清之际往来于海上丝绸之路的耶稣会士将儒学带入欧洲，对欧洲启蒙运动产生了重大影响。法国启蒙运动泰斗伏尔泰对孔子极为推崇，被誉为“欧洲孔门第一弟子”。

源于唐朝的中国律令体制沿丝路散播至东亚诸国，8至10世纪日本、朝鲜、越南纷纷引入中国科举制。至17世纪，英、法、德等国效仿科举制建立了文官制度。科举制被西方人誉为“中国的第五大发明”。此外，汉字、汉服、建筑等相继传播，对丝路沿线许多国家的文学艺术、生活习惯、社会风俗等产生了重要影响。

佛教经由西北、南方、海上多条丝绸之路传入中国，公元前1世纪末佛教已传遍西域各地。佛教传入是外部文化第一次大规模输入中国，并迅速被中国本土文化改造和吸收，形成汉传、藏传和南传佛教三大派别。经过与儒、道等本土文化的不断磨合，佛教最终融入中华传统文化。而印度佛教艺术，经过中国艺术家和民间工匠的再创造，形成富有浓郁中国特点的佛教艺术，感染了整个世界佛教。

随着阿拉伯帝国的兴起，伊斯兰教迅速向东传播。651年大食首次遣使至唐，伊斯兰教由此传入中国。从哈里发时代起，穆斯林在丝绸之路往来中，展现了伊斯兰文明在哲学、伦理学、逻辑学、建筑学、科学、医学和艺术领域的魅力，对中国多民族社会文化生活影响至深。

曾经活跃在丝路之上的不同民族、不同信仰的人们，历史无法一一记录他们的名字，但仍然有不少文化使者名垂千古。627年，玄奘历时17年西行5万里，游历110余国，带回657部佛经，翻译经论75部，堪称继承印度正统佛教学说的集大成者。753年，六次东渡终获成功的鉴真，在日本弘传佛法，开创门派，被日本人民誉为“文化之父”“律宗之祖”“天平之甍”。13 世纪意大利旅行家和商人马可·波罗经中东到达蒙古，历时四年多，于 1275 年到达元朝大都即今天的北京。他在中国游历 17 年后写下的《马可·波罗游记》，激起欧洲人对古老中国的热烈向往。14 世纪初，阿拉伯伟大的旅行家伊本·白图泰从非洲之角摩洛哥来到中国，开辟了中阿文化交流的新时代。1405 年至 1433 年，郑和七下西洋，扬帆 9 万里，足迹遍及印度洋、阿拉伯海、红海和非洲东海岸 30 多个国家和地区，使中华文明远播四海。

历史表明，不同地区的文明发展有各自的内在逻辑，不同文明之间没有高低优劣之分。古代丝绸之路沿线不同国家不同民族在文明的交流、交融甚至交锋中，跨越语言、意识形态、宗教等种种差异，相互尊重、相互学习、相互理解，哲学思想、人文精神、教化思想、道德理念得到最充分展示、最深入交流。沿线各国各民族在交往交流中以开放的心态，尊重彼此文明形态；以包容的观念，善待各自文化差异，从而实现了商品互补和知识分享，技术互鉴和文明互动。

回顾古代丝绸之路的历史，可以清楚地看到：从道路畅通到经贸繁荣，从物质文明到精神文化，无一不是沿线各国人民共同创造，无一不是沿线各国人民智慧的结晶。四通八达的道路由沿线国家共同开辟；频繁的经贸交流和人文互动，由沿线国家共同参与；持续的繁荣发展，由沿线国家共同推动。显而易见的是，丝绸之路从来不是中国一个国家的利益独享地带，而是沿线各国的共有财富，是沿线各国人民的共同家园。

古代丝绸之路之所以富有生命力和感召力，正是因为它对推动东西方文明交流与对话乃至整个人类文明的发展做出了无与伦比的贡献。其最重要的价值和意义就在于，历经两千多年所凝练而成的“团结互信、平等互利、包容互鉴、合作共赢”的丝路精神，而“知识分享与共同家园”无疑是古代丝绸之路留给我们最宝贵的财富之一。

“一带一路”一端连着历史，一端指向未来；一端连着中国，一端通向世界。“一带一路”倡议不是简单地借用古代丝绸之路这个名称，也不是简单地运用古代丝绸之路这个符号；它不是古代丝绸之路的复兴，更不是古代丝绸之路的翻版，而是一次伟大的超越。“一带一路”汲取的是古代丝绸之路文明的精髓，传承的是古代丝路文明的精神，致力于打造的是互利共赢人类命运共同体的光明未来。

知识分享既是“一带一路”倡议的内涵属性之一，也是“一带一路”建设的必然结果，更是“一带一路”可持续发展的重要依托。“一带一路”倡议是中国给世界提供的公共产品，就如同古代丝绸之路的繁荣发展，不是仅仅依靠中国所能成就的一样，“一带一路”建设也不是中国一个国家的事，而是沿线各国共同的事业。当今国际社会诸多全球性传统和非传统安全问题层出不穷，对国际秩序和人类生存都构成严峻挑战，在越来越多的传统与非传统安全问题面前，任何一个国家都难以独善其身。不论人们身处何国、信仰如何、是否愿意，实际上都已经处在一个命运相关的共同体当中。丝绸之路原本就是沿线各国共同的家园，无论政治、经济还是安全层面，丝路沿线国家一荣俱荣、一损俱损，因此，只有携手共建、同舟共济，才能最终实现互利共赢。

“一带一路”倡议从提出至今，已经走过 3 个年头。在三年多的时间里，“一带一路”建设取得列令人瞩目的成就，有 70 多个国家和组织表达了支持和参与“一带一路”建设，中国同 56 个国家和区域组织发表了对接“一带一路”倡议的联合声明，超出了传统“一带一路”范围，形成了具有广泛影响的国际合作框架。可以说，“和平友好、互学互鉴、开放包容、互利共赢”的丝路精神，正在成为沿线国家区域合作的价值理念；在政策沟通、道路联通、贸易畅通、货币流通、民心相通的每一个环节中，“知识分享”得到良好体现；共商、共建、共享的原则，得到沿线国家普遍认同，携手打造绿色、健康、智力、和平丝绸之路，成为塑造“一带一路”共同家园的必由之路。

古代丝绸之路的辉煌历史，不只是记忆，更是我们继往开来的底蕴所在。“一带一路”建设是一项伟大的事业，要实现“一带一路”建设的宏大目标，必须在沿线国家人民中传承好古代丝绸之路知识分享和共同家园的历史传统，形成一个相互欣赏、相互理解、相互尊重的人文格局。只有建构起这样一个格局，才能给“一带一路”建设提供强大的精神动力，才能给“一带一路”建设营造和谐融洽的人文环境，才能确保“一带一路”建设生生不息、永续发展。

随着“一带一路”建设的逐步深入，我们要更加注重政治互信、经济合作和人文交流“三位一体”的同步推进，更加注重在人文领域的精耕细作，更加注重知识的分享，更加注重共同家园从理念到现实的升华。通过知识分享，最大程度把沿线国家地缘相连、文化相通、人文交流基础好的优势发挥出来，进一步密切沿线各国和地区多领域宽层面的合作。通过构建共同家园，最终打造沿线各国休戚与共、互利共赢的利益共同体、责任共同体和命运共同体。

在“一带一路”建设和发展中，我们要坚持钉钉子精神，持之以恒，久久为功，分享更多先进的知识，共建我们和谐的家园，“一带一路”建设的愿景必将实现。

Historical Inheritance of Knowledge-Sharing and Common Homeland in the Construction of the Belt and Road

Li Guoqiang / China

Deputy Director of the Institute of Chinese Borderland Studies, CASS

Two thousand and one hundred years ago, our ancestors opened the door for contacts between eastern and western countries under extremely difficult conditions, and built a number of important international channels between China and the world. They are the Land Silk Road and the Maritime Silk Road which are still commended by people today.

According to documentary records and archaeological discoveries, as early as the 10th century B.C. – the 3rd century B.C., sporadic material and cultural exchanges occurred between the east and the west. Before the Silk Road was open in the 2nd century B.C., there were roads for contacts from China's Central Plains to the western regions, even the north bank of the Black Sea; although the roads were not so distinct, the east and the west started to meet. With the combined actions of two great empires, including the Western Han Dynasty (202 B.C-A.D. 8) and ancient Greece, the Silk Road connecting the east and the west was opened and began to share knowledge and to build a common homeland in the countries and territories along it.

The building of the ancient Silk Road is attributable to the fact that it catered to various needs of the countries along it for merchandise trade, personnel and cultural exchanges in different historical periods. The ancient Silk Road was continuously prosperous because it offered a platform for economic, trade and cultural exchanges between the east and the west and epitomized the advanced philosophies of the countries along it, the directions of their development and the interactions of the civilizations among them during the ancient historical periods.

The ancient Silk Road emerged amidst the interest appeals of the countries along it for economic development; it increasingly flourished together with exchanges among these countries. It gathered commerce, trade, industry and resource allocation in the countries along it; and it became the economic corridor for the convergence of the interests of the relevant parties. With material and spiritual interactions in multiple fields and at various levels, the ancient Silk Road triggered chain reactions involving the reconstruction of commodity structures, production modes, market behaviors, policy mechanisms, social organizations and mindsets in the countries along it. The ancient Silk Road enabled extensive exchanges of commodities, great trade circulation, wide dissemination of science and technology; it pioneered exchanges of human civilizations of ancient cultures and was the model of peaceful contacts among different countries and different nationalities. The sustained cross-civilization exchanges and dialogues, as well as knowledge sharing, recorded and witnessed the course of the growth of different countries and many nationalities along it, thus it became the collective memory of the whole of mankind.

The ancient Silk Road was not only a road for trade, but also a road towards knowledge sharing with an extensive connection of multiple ancient civilizations including Chinese, Indian, Egyptian, Babylonian and Islamic civilizations; thanks to the ancient Silk Road, the cultures, religions, arts and techniques of production of different nationalities bloomed and interacted, resulting in an unprecedented integration during the history of humankind.

Chinese Confucianism was introduced to Korea in the early 1st century, to Japan in the 5th century and to Vietnam in the 10th century. During the Ming and Qing Dynasties (A.D. 1368-A.D. 1912), Jesuit missionaries who travelled along the Maritime Silk Road introduced Confucianism to Europe, exerting a great impact on European Enlightenment. Voltaire, the leading authority of the French Enlightenment, highly adored Confucius, and was regarded as the first disciple of Confucianism in Europe.

China's system of laws and decrees originated from the Tang Dynasty (A.D. 618-A.D. 907) was spread to East Asian countries along the Silk Road. During the span of the 8th – 10th centuries, Japan, Korea and Vietnam introduced China's imperial examination system. In the 17th century, such countries as the UK, France and Germany emulated the imperial examination system to establish the system of civil servants. The imperial examination system was hailed by westerners as China's 5th great invention. Moreover, Chinese characters, Han Chinese clothing and architecture were successively disseminated, exerting a great influence on literature, art, living habits and social customs in many countries along the Silk Road.

Buddhism was introduced to China through several northwestern, southern and maritime silk roads. At the end of the 1st century B.C., Buddhism had been disseminated to various parts of western regions. The introduction of Buddhism was a large-scale input of external culture into China for the first time; Buddhism was rapidly transformed and assimilated by local Chinese culture so that three large schools, including Chinese Buddhism, Tibetan Buddhism and Southern Buddhism came into being. By means of continuous interactions with local cultures, including Confucianism and Taoism, Buddhism was ultimately integrated into Chinese traditional culture. Indian Buddhist art was recreated by Chinese artists and folk craftsmen to form Buddhist art with Chinese characteristics, which influenced

Buddhism all over the world.

With the rise of the Arab Empire, Islam was rapidly disseminated eastward. In A.D. 651, Tazi sent envoys to the Tang Dynasty for the first time, thus Islam was introduced to China. Since the era of the Caliph, Muslims demonstrated, amidst contacts via the Silk Road, the charms of Islamic civilization in philosophy, ethics, logic, architecture, science, medical science and art, exerting a far-reaching impact on the multi-ethnic, social cultural life in China.

For different nationalities and people with different religions once active on the Silk Road, their names have not been historically recorded. However, many cultural envoys went down in history. In A.D. 627, Xuanzang, a Chinese Buddhist monk (A.D. 602-A.D. 664), took 17 years to complete a 2,500km westward journey crossing more than 110 countries; he brought back 657 Buddhist scriptures and translated 75 Sutta and Abhidhamma texts, which epitomized the Indian orthodox Buddhist doctrine. In A.D. 753, Jianzhen, a monk (A.D.688-A.D.763) during the Tang Dynasty, took six sea voyages eastward ; he carried forward the Buddhist doctrine in Japan, created schools, and was hailed by the Japanese as the Father of Culture, the Father of the Ritsu School and the Roof of Tenpyō. In the 13th century, the Italian traveler and merchant Marco Polo arrived in Mongolia via the Middle East, and it took him more than four years to arrive at the Great Capital of the Yuan Dynasty (A.D. 1271-A.D. 1368), currently Beijing, in 1275. He travelled across China for 17 years and then wrote his *Travels of Marco Polo*, which made Europeans yearn for ancient China. In the early 14th century, the great Arab traveler Ibn Battuta came to China from Morocco, the Horn of Africa, and opened the new era of Sino-Arab cultural exchanges. From 1405 to 1433, the famous Chinese navigator Zheng He led seven maritime expeditions to the Western Seas covering 45,000km and reaching more than 30 countries and territories of the Indian Ocean, the Arabian Sea, the Red Sea and the East Coast of Africa, spreading the Chinese civilization around the world.

History has proven that the developments of civilization in different regions are governed by the respective internal logics, and there is no distinction—high or low, good or bad—among different civilizations. Different countries and nationalities along the ancient Silk Road overcame the differences in language, ideology and religion through exchanges, integration, even confrontation of civilizations; they respected, learnt from and understood each other, and fully demonstrated philosophical thoughts, humanistic spirits, moralizing thoughts and moral conceptions, and engaged in the deepest exchanges. The countries and nationalities along the ancient Silk Road respected the different forms of civilization through contacts and exchanges in an open-minded way, and properly treated the cultural differences in an all-inclusive manner, so that commodities complemented each other, knowledge was shared, technologies were mutually learnt and civilizations interacted with each other.

As shown by a review of the history of the ancient Silk Road, various things, from smooth roads to economic and trade prosperity, from material civilization to spiritual culture, were jointly created by the people of the countries along the ancient Silk Road and resulted from the crystallization of the wisdom of these peoples. The roads which extended in all directions were jointly opened by the countries along the ancient Silk Road; frequent economic and trade exchanges, people-to-people interactions were the result of a joint participation of the countries along the ancient Silk Road; sustained prosperity and development were jointly promoted by the countries along it. Obviously, the Silk Road was never a road where only China enjoyed interests; on the contrary, it was the common wealth shared by the countries along it and the common homeland for the people of the countries along it.

The ancient Silk Road was vibrant and appealing because it made unmatched contributions to pushing forward the exchanges and dialogues between the eastern and western civilizations, even the development of the entire human civilization. Its most important value and significance lies in the spirit of the Silk Road—unity and mutual trust, equality and mutual benefit, inclusiveness and mutual learning, win-win cooperation—developed during a period of more than 2,000 years, while knowledge sharing and common homeland is undoubtedly one of the most valuable forms of wealth left to us by the ancient Silk Road.

The Belt and Road connects history at one end and directs it towards the future at another end; it connects China at one end and provides access to the world at the other end. The Belt and Road Initiative does neither simply adopt the name of the ancient Silk Road nor simply apply the symbol of the ancient Silk Road; it is neither the revival of the ancient Silk Road nor the refurbished version of it; on the contrary, it represents a great transcendence. The Belt and Road absorbs the quintessence of the civilizations along the ancient Silk Road and inherits the spirit of those civilizations; it is dedicated to creating a bright future for the community with a common human destiny with mutual benefit and win-win results.

Knowledge sharing is one of the connotative attributes of the Belt and Road Initiative; it is the inevitable result of the construction of the Belt and Road and serves as an important support for its sustainable development. The Belt and Road Initiative is the public goods supplied by China to the world. Like the ancient Silk Road, whose prosperity and development did not merely rely on China, the Belt and Road is not merely built by China, and its construction is the common cause of the countries along it. Today's international community is fraught with many global traditional and non-traditional security issues which pose severe challenges to the international order and to the survival of humankind. No country can independently act amidst increasing traditional and non-traditional issues of security. All people have actually become part of the same community with a common destiny, regardless of their country, faith and willingness. The Silk Road is the common homeland for the countries along it, and the countries along it share weal and woe at the political, economic and security levels. Therefore, only when all of the people work together to jointly overcome their difficulties can mutual benefit and win-win results be ultimately achieved.

Three years have elapsed since the Belt and Road Initiative was put forward. Over the past three years, remarkable achievements have been made in the construction of the Belt and Road; more than 70 countries and organizations have expressed support for and participated in its construction. China and 56 countries and regional organizations issued joint declarations for the Belt and Road Initiative, exceeding the scope of the traditional Belt and Road and developing an extensively influential framework for international cooperation. The Silk Road spirit—peace and friendship, mutual learning, openness and inclusiveness, mutual benefit and win-win results—is becoming the philosophy of values for regional cooperation among the countries along the Belt and Road. Knowledge sharing is well reflected in policy communication, road connectivity, trade, currency circulation and people-to-people contacts. The principle of consultation, joint construction and sharing is universally recognized by the countries along the Belt and Road, while these countries join hands to create a green, healthy, intelligent and peaceful Silk Road, which is indispensable for shaping the common homeland on the Belt and Road.

The glorious history of the ancient Silk Road is not only a memory but also a depository for us to keep going. The construction of the Belt and Road is a great cause. In order to achieve the ambitious goal of its construction, it is necessary to better inherit the historical tradition of knowledge sharing and common homeland created among the people of the countries along the ancient Silk Road, and to form a humanistic pattern in which the people appreciate, understand and respect each other. Only when such a pattern is built can a strong spiritual impetus be provided for the construction of the Belt and Road, can a harmonious humanistic environment be created for its construction, and can its construction proceed endlessly and sustainably.

By intensifying the construction of the Belt and Road, we should place more emphasis on concurrently promoting mutual political trust, economic cooperation and people-to-people exchanges, and pay more attention to an intensive cultivation in the humanistic field, knowledge sharing and upgrading the idea of a common homeland from merely a philosophy to a reality. With knowledge sharing, we maximize the efforts to fully utilize the advantages of the countries along the Belt and Road in geographical and cultural connections and the foundations for people-to-people exchanges, and further enhance cooperation in multiple fields and at many levels among the countries and territories along the Belt and Road. The common homeland is built to shape a community with common interests, a community with shared responsibilities and a community with a common destiny for the countries along the Belt and Road in order to share weal and woe and achieve mutual benefits and win-win results.

In the construction and development of the Belt and Road, we should persevere in our actions in a down-to-earth manner, share more advanced knowledge and jointly build our harmonious homeland, so that the vision of the construction of the Belt and Road is bound to be achieved.

互联互通与共同发展

Interconnection and Mutual Development

中国国内变化对中欧经济关系再分配中的影响

傅立门　【欧盟】

欧洲学院　研究员 / 布鲁塞尔中欧研究院　高级研究员

随着中国在全球经济中的重要性不断增加，其国内经济的变化对欧盟的影响也在不断增加。中国经济的崛起导致了中国与欧盟、欧盟成员国之间的经济关系、中国对待欧盟各国的态度上的差异。

然而，关键问题已不在于中国崛起这样一个简单的事实，而是中国经济不仅经历着快速的变化（如增长速度放缓）同时也正经历着结构性的转型。许多学者指出，政治与经济层面的互动，是中过与欧盟成员国之间经济利益分配中的一个重要因素。然而，中国经济结构的变化使局势变得越来越复杂，促使中国与欧盟及欧盟成员国之间的关系发生再分配。中国崛起过程中的“新常态”阶段将促使欧盟成员国或成为赢家，或成为输家。

引言

中国与欧盟之间的关系十分复杂，涵盖各个层面，但经济向来是双方关系的核心，这点不论是在欧盟还是在中国都已经得到广泛的接受。20 世纪 80 年代，欧盟与中国的经济关系发展迅速，双方之间的贸易额及投资额均在不断增长。特别是从 21 世纪之初以来，双方的贸易量或对外直接投资量来衡量均不断增长。2000 至 2015 年间，欧盟对华进口额从 746 欧元元增长至 3500 亿欧元，欧盟对华出口从 258 亿欧元增长至 1703 亿欧元。在同一时期内，中国占欧盟外部出口的比重从 3.0% 增长至 9.5%。欧盟在中国的对外直接投资额从 2014 年的 213 亿欧元增长至 2014 年的 1442 亿欧元，同期内，中国对欧盟直接投资较少，但总额仍然从 17 亿欧元增长到 207 亿欧元。

从官方角度来讲，欧洲方面对华经济关系主要受到欧盟各组织机构的管辖。欧盟负责贸易谈判、投资协定以及相关政策的实施。因此，欧盟与中国各机构间的官方互动大多由欧盟委委员会、欧盟议会及欧盟理事会主管。欧盟委员会负责中欧之间于 2014 年开启的《全面投资协定》的谈判工作、贸易防卫措施的实施，包括根据《中国入世议定书》第十五条规定，对中国市场经济地位进行认定，负责欧盟最终与中国签订的所有贸易协定。

从理论上讲，欧盟在对华经济关系方面实施的政策，是在欧盟各成员国达成一致的基础上，制定出的整体性的统一政策。这些政策的实施主要是为了保障欧盟各成员国企业的整体商业利益，为了更好地应对贸易和投资中出现的问题，比如市场准入、知识产权保护、反倾销或防止钢铁行业面临的产能过剩等问题。（欧盟委员会 2016）

另外，自 1975 年欧共体成员国与中国建立正式外交关系以来，欧盟相继出台了多份对华文件，从理论上讲，这些文件的目的在于构建一个更为广阔的对华政策框架，不仅包括对华经济，也包括对华政治关系。最近出台的一份对华统一政策为 2016 年 7 月颁布实施的《欧盟对华新战略要素》。

但事实上，对于中欧关系的分析更多地集中在欧盟内部的政策分歧及利益分歧上，特别是在经济领域的分析，很少涉及欧盟的整体目标。不少学者将欧盟描述为一个多层级的体系，这一观点通常在讨论中欧关系时得到引用。在中欧关系方面，欧盟表面看是一个整体，但内部各成员国与中国之间的经济关系存在很大差异。福克斯及歌德蒙特等学者指出，中欧关系的经济和政治层面往往是决定欧盟对华政策的基础，因而不仅在经贸和投资方面，更在各个领域都造成了欧盟成员国对华关系上的差异。这些学者得出这样一个结论：造成欧盟成员国之间利益分歧的核心要素是经济问题，这也造成了欧盟各机构之间的分歧，影响了对华经贸政策和投资政策。与此同时，经济因素也影响了中欧关系的其他层面，比如，欧盟就中国的很多问题，特别是人权问题，无法达成统一，立场不够坚定。经济问题不仅是中欧摩擦的来源，更是造成欧盟内部分歧的主要原因。尽管欧盟一直宣称，与世界各国的关系核心在于价值观，但如果从对华关系的角度来看，经济因素的重要性已经超过了所谓的价值观的重要性。《欧盟对华新战略要素》中甚至提到了欧盟成员国之间发生冲突的可能，指出“欧盟在对待中国的立场上，必须坚定、明确、统一，各成员在构建对华双边关系的过程中 ...... 应与欧盟委员会、欧盟对外事务部以及其他成员国相互协作，贯彻欧盟法律、法规以及政策，确保欧盟的整体利益。”（欧盟委员会 2016）

对于那些以福克斯和歌德蒙特的观点为基础来制定对华政策的欧盟成员国而言，经济利益和政治利益的紧密联系决定着中国在这些国家中的地位。（福克斯，歌德蒙特 2009）根据两位学者的分析显示，欧盟成员国在政策优先程度上的冲突导致了对华立场上的不统一，而中国可以利用这些分歧来提高自身优势。福克斯和歌德蒙特指出，“中国已经学会利用欧盟成员国之间的分歧，把对欧关系当作一场博弈，而与之对弈者，正是 27 个彼此争论不休的对手。”在两位学者的分析研究中，一个关键的因素在于欧盟成员国能在多大程度上从对华关系中获取经济利益，这种经济利益又如何与各国的优先政策、欧盟的整体利益进行平衡，因而，根据对华政治、经济的不同态度，欧盟成员国分化为不同的派别。相比之下，中国的对欧政策更为统一和连贯，能够轻而易举地对内部松散的欧盟施加影响。中国、欧盟、欧盟成员国三者间，各个级别的双边关系中存在着经济利益与政治利益的交叠，而这种交叠正是决定三者关系的中心要素。

这种观点一直持续至今。2015 年霍泰利 · 艾特 · 奥尔提出了一个类似的观点，他指出欧盟和中国的政治关系和经济关系中存在分歧，这导致了欧洲在整体上缺乏一个统一的声音（霍泰利 · 艾特 · 奥尔 2015）。有学者发现，“在处理对华关系问题上，欧盟内部分歧较大，且各国间常常存在竞争”，认为中欧关系的中心问题在于经济利益的分歧，“多数欧盟成员制定的对华国家战略均受到经济逻辑的支配，许多成员国在面临政治理想——如在中国推广民主和人权、推广自身的经济战略时，往往要做出两难的选择。”其他学者的分析也主要集中在这个层面。福斯发现，中国与其他国家的关系主要受到达拉喇嘛来访的影响（福斯 2016）。福斯与柯兰的统计数据表明，凡是接待达赖喇嘛的国家，其对华关系都会受到影响，尽管这种影响不会持续很久（福斯，柯兰 2013）

这些关注欧盟成员国及其经济利益的观点，是以这样一种假设为支撑依据的：决定中欧关系的关键因素在于欧盟内部的政治状况，认为欧盟成员国之间的利益竞争以及为获得利益而做出的努力，最终决定了对华经济关系和利益分配的模式。

即便在经贸关系和投资关系不断扩展的领域内，欧盟成员国之间的竞争仍然决定着利益如何分配。这种博弈的结局或许不是“零和”，但各国始终会将经济利益放在首位，从而会引发各国竞相从对华关系中获取利益。

另一方面，此类分析还做出这样一种假设：利益分配至少在某种程度上受到中国对欧盟以及欧盟成员国的政治决策的影响。流行的看法认为，中国正利用欧盟成员国之间的差异以及经济利益的分配模式，对欧盟政府软硬兼施，从而获得政治上的利益。欧盟成员国政府生怕因对中国的人权问题妄加批判、官员会见达赖喇嘛、对中国采取贸易防卫措施等政治决策而招致中国报复，从而损害其商业利益。在这种分析中，中国能够在政治层面恩威并施，从而对分化、控制欧盟成员国政府。

这种分析框架偏重于中欧双边关系中的经济和政治层面，承认中国作为重要的经济和政治大国，能够对欧盟造成越发广泛的影响，而导致这种局面的主要原因在于欧盟成员国内部之间的利益分化。因此，欧盟内部的经济竞争和政治竞争在如何构建中欧双边关系的过程中，是最具解释力的因素。尽管基于种种假设，但最终结论仍然为：双方的政治和经济层面是决定如何构建中欧关系的唯一因素。文本认为，即便上述结论存在一定的合理性，但关于经济关系以及利益分配方式的看法已经过时，除了欧盟成员国之间的政治经竞争外，还有诸多要素能够对中欧双边关系造成影响。

中欧双边关系的发展不仅仅在于经贸投资和对外直接投资。欧盟和中国本身都属于复杂经济体，同时又处于复杂的全球语境，特别是自 2007 年美国和欧盟遭遇的金融危机和经济危机以来，全球形式更加复杂，一方的经济结构发生变化必然会造成双边关系的改变。首先，欧盟成员国经济的改变能够引起经济关系的改变。国际货币基金组织曾指出，对于欧元区而言，国内改革和外部平衡微调是摆脱经济危机的关键政策（国际货币基金组织 2016）。欧盟成员国采取了一些政策来应对危机，从而引起了国内需求的下降，进而影响到进口和外部出口以及经常账目平衡。欧盟成员国中，许多国家的对华进口额也在经济危机后的这段时间有所下降。同样，中国的国内政策也会影响中欧经济关系。

文本旨在分析中国经济的国内变化以及对欧盟造成的影响，指出中国经济的变化对欧盟以及中欧关系造成了影响，使中国与欧盟和欧盟成员国之间的关系以及各成员国的国家利益发生了一系列复杂的变化，从而使中欧关系不能单纯以商品交易额和对外直接投资额来定义。在中国与欧盟成员国之间的关系格局中，双边政治、经济的交叠在重要性上有所下降，中国经济的变化是创造和分配双边利益的重要因素。这不仅仅是中国经济规模的问题，而是结构问题。对于欧盟成员国而言，其利益分配会随着中国经济结构的演化而发生变化。这点不能仅仅通过商品出口的交易量、贸易差额或对外直接投资额的增长来衡量。其他因素，如服务，特别是金融服务，包括旅游业、间接投资等，重要性都在增长。

中国的变化

按照中国政府的说法，中国经济正在经历一场向“新常态”的转变过程。中国经济需要通过改革和结构的调整来实现向新的发展模式的转变，这在中国的发展议程中已经存在多年。在习近平主席的领导下，新的改革议程出炉。尽管改革的路径和终点尚不明朗，但中国目前正在发生的变化已经对中欧关系产生了重大影响。受到影响的不仅是与欧盟成员国之间的经济关系，还有与欧盟间的经济关系。后经济危机时期，中国经济的几次发展都对中国与欧盟成员国之间的关系以及成员国之间的利益分配造成了影响。最重要的结构性变化在于由投资向消费的转变，以及中国国内服务业重要性的提升。这造成了中国商品交易的变化，导致了服务交易的迅速增长。2005 年以来，中国境外直接投资迅猛增长，这在改变中欧经济关系中成为关键因素。与此同时，来自中国的间接投资不断增长，在这个方面，金融业的投资一直在不断增加，因而中国在欧盟的地位正不断上升。

在后金融危机期间，中国经济对于欧盟及欧盟成员国而言变得愈发重要。这一方面是由于中国自 2008 年后，GDP 的强劲增长导致了经济规模的绝对扩大，另一方面是由于欧盟的政策制定者未能为欧盟的经济增长带来复兴。因此，中国对于欧盟的经济增长做出了巨大贡献。例如，为应对金融危机，中国出台刺激政策，增加了对欧进口，不仅欧盟对华绝对出口额有所增长，在欧盟出口总额中的比重也有所增长。然而，一些欧盟成员国与中国的经济关系要比其他成员国更为重要，不仅仅是因为这些成员国需要增加对华出口，更因为这些国家的对华出口在其出口总额中的比重有所增加。欧盟及其成员越来越依赖通过出口拉动经济增长，而中国则恰好相反。这种变化在暗示我们，中国经济的结构变化，正使中国与欧盟的关系、欧盟成员国的关系变得复杂化、差异化。

商品贸易的变化

尽管全球化进程导致中国和欧盟深度融入全球生产，但关于中欧贸易关系的讨论通常局限于简单的双边视角，由于中国对欧盟的贸易持续顺差，中欧贸易关系似乎明显有利于中国。商品交易领域的摩擦在中欧关系中表现最为明显，通过欧盟频繁对华采取贸易防卫措施这一事实便能看出。对华进口额的快速增加导致了欧盟不断采取反倾销、贸易防卫措施，这点最主要地体现在纺织品和太阳能电池的对华进口上。根据世贸组织协定规定，中国的“市场经济待遇”于 2016 年 12 月到期，关于是否继续承认中国市场经济地位的争论，其争论的核心恰好是商品贸易。正如福克斯和歌德蒙特所说，欧盟成员国的利益分化正是围绕着这些争论进入大众事业。

欧盟与中国的外部商品交易关系主要受到德国影响。2014 年，德国占欧盟对华出口总额的46%，进口总额的20.1%。后金融危机期间，德国对华贸易持续顺差，尽管在 2015 年有所下降，但很大程度上是因为德国工资在中国国内的汽车生产量的增加。近年来，欧盟国家很少对华出口顺差，2015 年芬兰除外。在后金融危机期间，德国对华出口迅速增长，这主要是由于中国经济的增长，而中国的刺激政策对双方的投资和消费都起到了鼓励作用。与此同时，尽管在后金融危机期间，德国对华出口增长迅速，但由于进口量始终未能增长，德国对华贸易出现最终出现顺差。单纯从商品交易来看，德国是中欧经济关系中的获胜者，这也能够解释，为何中国和德国在政治上关系紧密。

在金融危机前期，多数欧盟成员国的贸易模式都十分相似，而在 2009 年金融危机最严重的的时期，欧洲对华进口有所下降，但很快在 2010 年复苏，而出口则继续增加。但正是在这一时期，欧盟成员国开始发生路线上的分歧。在金融危机之前，欧盟对华贸易逆差是一种常态，但与德国不同，其他成员国成功地逆转了这一不利形势，并实现了对华贸易的持续顺差。这些国家与德国的不同之处在于——后金融危机期间贸易逆差的减轻主要是由于进口量的缩减，而不是出口量的大幅增加。世界货币基金组织曾指出，当时欧元区的许多债务国都面临这种状况，意大利便是绝佳的例证，该国至今尚未从对华贸易中获得丰厚利益。法国的贸易逆差已经稳定，尽管离实现顺差还有很远的距离，因为法国自金融危机后，进出口均有增长。自 2009 年起，英国的进出口迅速增长，不过对华出口的增长属于特例，最近几年，对英国贡献最大者要数黄金出口。

自金融危机以来，德国一直是对华贸易关系中的主要受益国，因此中国对于德国而言，具有十分重要的意义。德国的经济高度依赖口口，而中国对于进口的需求增长也十分迅速。欧盟金融危机后，德国对华出口已经超过那些消费遭受遏制的欧元区成员国。德国施行的政策对中国具有很强的政治容纳性。在所有欧盟成员国中，德国与中国的政治关系最为紧密。欧盟对于中国这个贸易伙伴的依赖性越发增强，欧盟对华进口在其进口总额中的比率从 2002 年的 9.6% 增长至 2015 年的 20.3%。同一时期内，中国对欧盟进口所占进口总额的比重从 4.0% 增长至 9.5%，但中国与欧盟各成员国之间的贸易状况存在极大差别。在德国占据的欧盟外部出口份额中，对华出口占比率从 6.1% 增长至 14.2%，远远高于欧盟的平均水平。其他成员国对于中国出口市场的依赖相对较轻。在法国所占的欧盟外部出口份额中，对华出口所占比重由 2002 年的 3.0% 增长至 2015 年的 9.5%，在英国的比重由 2.1% 增长至 10.8%，但所占意大利的出口额比重仅仅从 3.9% 增长至 5.6%。欧盟越发依赖出口拉动增长，在后金融危机期间，欧盟内部增长势头较弱，因此对中国的依赖仅仅是一个缩影。2008 年，欧盟商品出口和服务出口所占 GDP 的比率达到 39%，2009 年这一数字有所回落，但在 2015 年继续增长至 42.9%，远远高于 29.3% 的全球平均比率。2015 年，德国商品出口和服务出口所占 GDP 比率达到 46.9%，经常账户盈余占 GDP 的 8.5%。相比之下，2006 年中国的商品出口和服务出口所占 GDP 比率达到顶点——35.7%，随后于 2015 年回落至 22.4%。

服务贸易

近年来，中国经济的主要变化在于——服务贸易相对于其他行业有所增长，其影响不仅表现在国内，更日益明显的体现在中国的国际经济关系上。中国的服务贸易逆差增长迅速，从 2008 年的 120 亿美元增长至 2014 年的 1920 亿美元。中国的交通服务逆差于 2014 年达到 579 亿美元，旅游业贸易逆差达到 1079 亿美元。

由于中国的服务进口持续增长，欧盟对华服务出口从 2010 年的 195 亿欧元增长至 2010 年的 360 亿欧元，欧盟同期贸易顺差从 23 亿欧元增长至 103 亿欧元。事实上，对华服务出口的增长速度要比欧盟服务出口总量的增速快。在中欧经济关系的其他方面，欧盟成员国获利并不相等。从 2010 至 2015 年，德国对华服务出口额由 40 亿欧元增长至 115 亿欧元，而英国的对华服务出口额则增幅较小，从 25 亿欧元增长至 44 亿欧元。2011 年到 2015 年间，法国对华服务出口额由 32 亿欧元增长至 49 亿欧元，但同一时期内，意大利的增幅较小，从 6.957 亿欧元增长至 11 亿欧元。从总体上看，德国从对华服务出口贸易中获利最多，而欧盟各个成员国之间的获利并不均等。欧盟对华旅游服务收益从 2010 年的 28 亿欧元增长至 2015 年的 75 亿欧元，但英国在对华旅游业中获益最大，2015 年的对华旅游服务收益达到 3.67 亿欧元。同一时期内，欧盟对华金融服务收益从 2010 年的 5.335 亿欧元增长至 2015 年的 9.605 亿欧元，其中英国获益最大，收益为 3.167 亿欧元。

直接投资

自 20 世纪 80 年代以来，除商品交易外，外商投资流入量一直是全球化的重要组成部分。自 20 世纪 90 年代起，中国已经成为世界上最大的外商投资目的地，欧洲企业在中国注入了大量的投资，据欧盟国际收支统计数据显示，截至 2014 年，欧盟对华投资累积达到 1442 亿欧元。更近一段时期内，自 2005 年后，中国企业开始对欧盟进行投资，且投资额持续增长。然而，中国对欧盟的投资在 2014 年的累积量仅为 207 亿欧元。与贸易量相比，中国对欧盟投资额相对较小。目前进行的《全面投资协定》谈判的主要目的在于增加中欧彼此间的投资流入量。对于欧盟而言，中心目标在于促进中国放宽欧盟对华投资的市场准入，同时促进中国对欧盟成员国的投资。

欧盟对华投资分配与对华贸易相似，在欧盟成员国中，德国是对华投资的主力。2014 年，德国在华投资额累积达到 612 亿欧元，所占欧盟投资总额的 42.4%。荷兰位居其次，占 15.0%，法国占 14.0%，英国与意大利份额较小，分别占 5.8% 及 4.9%。中国对外投资量的增长近期内大于外商投资流入量，这主要是由于中国政府最初于 2001 年启动的“走出去”的政策发生了根本转向。政策的转向有助于放宽之前在对外投资方面的限制，鼓励对外投资。2005 年之后，中国对外投资额增长迅速，但对欧盟的投资分配并不均匀。根据 2014 年国际收支统计数据显示，中国对荷兰投资额累积达到 142 亿欧元，在所有欧盟成员国中位居首位，其次为对法投资，投资额达到 21 亿欧元，对英国投资额达到 18 亿欧元。但由于投资规模相对较小，每年的投资额变化较大。中国企业利用一些欧盟成员国来尽可能降低税务负担，这会严重影响中国在对外投资目的国的选择上。欧盟成员国政府竞相吸引中国投资，因而中国对欧投资额不断增加。这些投资主要来自私有企业，且流向的目的地存在极大差别。中国投资者考虑的因素主要是投资目的国的经济吸引力。2013 年，自“一带一路”倡议提出后，中国在对外投资政策方面打开了一个新的维度。这一战略的宗旨在于，通过海陆线路实现中欧间的互通和互联，但目前为止，中国对欧投资受到的影响很小。中国政府已经就加入欧洲战略投资基金问题与欧盟委员会展开谈判，双方虽然在中国加入问题上达成一致，但并没有就如何实施达成一致。“一带一路”倡议在欧洲得到广泛的推广，但在重大投资方面取得的成果较为有限，然而不论是欧盟还是欧盟成员国，都对这一倡议表示出高度的关注，多国政府都表示出参加“一带一路”倡议的意愿。中国政府以400亿美元的资本成立了丝路基金，为“一带一路”倡议的实施提供支持。该基金最大的一笔投资用在了支持2015年中国化工对倍耐力股份的收购上。

金融

间接投资与商品贸易和外商直接投资类似，向来是全球化经济中的一个主要因素。20世纪80年代以来，间接投资流入量经历了快速增长期，随后在金融危机期间经历了波动阶段。从总体上来看，流入的间接投资主要集中在发达国家的金融市场，中国尚未成为间接投资的重要目的国。中国资本账户逐渐而有限度的开放，开始允许间接投资对内流入和对外流出。中国对外间接投资有所增加，但与发达国家相比，投资规模仍然较小。中国的对外间接投资额于2006年达到峰值——1113亿美元，随后在后金融危机时期急剧下降，2015年年底达到后金融危机时期顶峰——723亿美元，正是在这一年，中国对外间接投资总额累计达到2808亿美元。中国对外间接投资最重要的目的国为美国，2015年，中国对美间接投资额累计达到1111亿美元，远远超过对其他国家和地区的投资，但欧盟同样是中国对外间接投资的重要目的地。中国对欧盟的间接投资在规模上与对欧直接投资相近，然而其分配却与直接投资大相径庭，间接投资主要集中在英国，2015年中国对英间接投资总额累计达到124亿美元。在同一年，中国对德间接投资总额累计达到50亿美元，对法间接投资额为49亿美元，对意大利间接投资额为11亿美元。

中国金融体系的不断国际化以及与欧盟的关系的变化主要体现在中国银行国际地位的提升以及人民币的国际化上。目前，除中国外，世界各地已经建立多个人民币交易中心，伦敦便是其中最重要的一个。从英国金融体系的其他层面也能看出，英国在金融方面占据欧盟成员国的首位，从国际清算银行的图表中便能看出中国与欧盟银行业之间的关系。2016年第一季度，中国金融机构可以从英国银行提取14240亿美元，这一数额远比世界其他国家要高。中国银行在美国的提款额为796亿美元，相比之下，欧盟其他成员国与中国银行的关系显得微不足道：在法国提款额仅仅为390亿美元，德国为257亿美元，意大利为27亿美元。英国在这一方面的优势仅仅从2008年美国和欧盟经济危机开始后不久才开始提高，在金融危机之前，即2007年年底，中国对英国银行的提款额为606亿美元，而德国为214亿美元，法国为216亿美元。

结论

中国与欧盟之间的经济关系正在经历迅速的变化过程中，不能仅仅以国内的商品交易和外商直接投资额来定义，这种关系是多层面的。中国和欧盟的关系之所以愈发复杂化，最重要的原因在于，中国经济正发生着变化，特别是在2008年之后的后金融危机期间。这些变化为中国与欧盟、欧盟成员国的经济关系打开了新的维度。这些变化表明，欧盟与欧盟成员国之间政治和经济的交叠或许仍然是影响对华关系的一个因素，但在衡量经济利益分配模式方面，其重要性远远不足。中国本身的变化也促成了新的经济关系，带来了新的经济利益，促进了经济关系的多样化，从而创造出诸多新要素。政治控制往往无法对这些要素造成直接影响。在中国与欧盟的经济关系中，受益最大的国家更可能是那些拥有潜在经济优势的国家，而不是那些仅仅在政治关系上与中国最紧密的国家。

Redistributing the EU-China Economic Relationship: The Role of Domestic Change in China

Duncan Freeman / European Union

Research Fellow at the College of Europe /Senior Research Fellow of the Brussels Institute of Contemporary China Studies

As the importance of China in the global economy has grown, changes in its domestic economy have increasing impact in the EU. China's economic rise is already established, and it has resulted in differentiated economic relationships with the EU and its member states, and in their responses to China. However, a key factor is no longer the simple fact of China's rise, but that the economy is undergoing rapid change not only in terms of a slower rate of growth, but also structural transition. Many scholars argue that the interaction of political and economic dimensions is a significant factor in the distribution of economic benefits of the EU's relations with China among Member States. However, the increasing complexity resulting from structural change in China is likely to create a redistribution in the relationship with the EU, notably among Member States. This "new normal" stage in China's rise will create winners and losers in the EU.

Introduction

The EU-China relationship is complex and has multiple dimensions, but the assertion that economics has been and remains at its core is widely accepted in both the EU and China. Since the 1980s, the EU's economic relationship with China has developed enormously as both trade and investment between them have grown. Measured in simple terms of trade in goods and foreign direct investment (FDI) flows, this has been especially the case since the beginning of the 21st century. Between 2000 and 2015, EU imports from China grew from €74.6 billion to €350 billion and EU exports to China rose from €25.8 billion to €170.3 billion. China's share of the EU's extra-EU imports increased from 7.5% to 20.2% and its share of extra-EU exports from 3.0% to 9.5% in the same period. The EU's stock of FDI in China increased from €21.3 billion in 2004 to €144.2 billion in 2014 and China's much smaller stock of FDI in the EU rose from €1.7 billion to €20.7 billion over the same period.[1]

In formal terms, on the European side much of the economic relationship with China falls under the jurisdiction of the EU institutions. The EU is responsible for negotiation of trade and investment agreements, and implementation of policies in this area. Thus the European Commission, but also the Parliament and Council, are the focus of much of the formal institutional interaction between the EU and China. The European Commission is responsible for the negotiations on a Comprehensive Agreement on Investment (CAI) with China launched in 2014, the implementation of trade defence, including adoption of measures to resolve the status of China under Article 15 of its accession to the World Trade Organization (WTO) and any trade agreement that the EU may eventually sign with China. In theory, the policies adopted by the EU are based on a single, unified policy agreed by Member States in regard to its economic relationship with China. The implementation of these policies is in general directed toward the advancement of the collective business interests of European companies, and deal with trade and investment issues such as market

1 Eurostat.

access, protection of intellectual property, anti-dumping or overcapacity like that in the steel industry (Commission 2016).[1]

In addition, over the years, since the foundation of formal diplomatic relations by the European Economic Community in 1975, the EU has adopted numerous documents that have been in theory intended to define a wider policy framework on China including not only economics but also the political relationship. The most recent example of such a document intended to commit the EU and its Member States to a common policy approach to China is the Elements for a New EU Strategy on China adopted in June 2016 (Commission 2016).[2] Nevertheless, in practice, analysis of the EU's relationship with China relationship frequently focuses more the divergent policies and interests within the EU, especially those in the area of economics, than on unity of purpose. Scholars describe the EU as a multi-level system and this view has been incorporated into discussion of its relations with China. Underlying the aggregate EU-China relationship are disaggregated relationships that embody considerable differences between EU Member States in the nature of their economic ties with China. Besides the formal EU statements, scholars such as Fox and Godemont have noted the interaction of economics and politics in the EU-China relationship that is frequently said to underlie the formulation of policy in the EU toward China and create divergences relating not only directly to trade and investment but in other fields as well. Such scholars conclude that economics is at the core of divided interests amongst Member States and also between them and EU institutions in their approach to trade and investment with China. At the same time economics is said to impact other aspects of the relationship, such as the failure to achieve strong, unified positions in the EU with regard to China across numerous issues, notably human rights. Economics is not only a source of friction between the EU and China, but also of conflict

1 Elements for a New EU Strategy on China, Joint Communication to The European Parliament and The Council, European Commission, High Representative of The Union for Foreign Affairs and Security Policy, June 22, 2016.

2 Ibid.

within the EU itself, and in this respect, economic interests trump the values that the EU proclaims are a core part of its relationship with the rest of the world. The potential for such conflicts is implicitly recognised even in the Elements for a New EU Strategy on China, which states that, "The EU must project a strong, clear and unified voice in its approach to China. When Member States conduct their bilateral relations with China...they should cooperate with the Commission, the EEAS and other Member States to help ensure that aspects relevant to the EU are in line with EU law, rules and policies, and that the overall outcome is beneficial for the EU as a whole" (Commission 2016).[1]

The close link between economic and political interests underlies the categorization of EU member states based on their policy toward China undertaken by Fox and Godemont (Fox and Godement 2009).[2] In their analysis conflicting policy priorities of EU member states led to lack of unity in dealing with China. But, more than this, these differences can be exploited by China to its advantage. According to Fox and Godement, "China has learned to exploit the divisions among EU Member States. It treats its relationship with the EU as a game of chess, with 27 opponents crowding the other side of the board and squabbling about which piece to move". A key element in their analysis is the degree to which Member States seek economic benefit in their relationship with China, and how this is balanced against other policy priorities, or the wider EU interest and go so far as to categorise Members States on a graph with axes based on their political and economic attitudes toward China. By contrast, Chinese policy toward the EU is portrayed as being coherent and unified, and thus easily able to impose itself on the divided EU. The conjuncture of economic and political interests in the multilevel bilateral relationship between China, the EU and Member States is given the central role in determining the nature of relationship.

This view has persisted, and was similarly made in 2015 by Huotari et al, who

1 Ibid.

2 Fox, J and Godemont, F, A Power Audit Of EU-China Relations, European Council on Foreign Relations, April, 2009.

point to divergent economic and political relationships between EU Member States and China, and the resulting lack of a unified European voice (Huotari et al 2015).[1] They find that, "in dealing with China, Europe is divided and competes with itself" and argue that divided economic interests are at the heart of the EU-China relationship, in which, "most, if not all European national strategies towards China are dominated by the logic of economics", and where "many European states are continuing to make hard choices between political ideals, such as the promotion of democracy and human rights in China, and their economic strategy". Other scholars similarly focus on this dimension. Fuchs finds that relationships between China and other states are impacted by visits of the Dalai Lama (Fuchs 2016).[2] Fuchs and Klann find statistical evidence that visits of the Dalia Lama have an impact on trade flows between China and the countries where he is received, although the effect is not long lasting (Fuchs and Klann 2013) .[3]

Underlying this influential view focusing on EU Member States and their interests is the assumption that a key factor determining the European economic relationship with China lies in the political realm within the EU. The analysis implicitly relies on the assumption that competing interests among the EU member states and their efforts to access benefits are a determinant of the patterns of the economic relationship and the distribution of its benefits. Even in an expanding relationship where trade and investment flows are increasing, the competition between member states will determine how the benefits are distributed. While the game may not be quite zero sum, the primacy of these interests leads to competition to benefit from the relationship with China.

On the other hand, the analysis similarly assumes that the distribution of benefits at least in some degree is the result of political decisions on the Chinese side

1 Mikko Huotari, Miguel Otero-Iglesias, John Seaman and Alice Ekman, Mapping Europe-China Relations: A Bottom-Up Approach, European Think-tank Network on China, October 2015.

2 Fuchs, A, China's Economic Diplomacy and the Politics-Trade Nexus, University of Heidelberg Department of Economics, Discussion Paper Series No. 609, March 2016.

3 Fuchs, A and Klann, N-H, Paying a Visit: The Dalai Lama Effect on International Trade. Journal of International Economics 91(1), 2013.

with regard to its relations with the EU and Member States. The view of China as exploiting differences and distributing economic benefits like gifts to supplicant EU governments or threatening their withdrawal, normally in order to achieve political gains, is a prevalent one. Governments may fear removal of benefits through retaliation that damages their commercial interests for political decisions concerning issues such as criticism of the Chinese government for human rights record or meeting of government leaders with Dalai Lama or support for economic policies such as adoption of TDMs against China that would damage its interests. In this analysis China provides rewards and punishments on political grounds, with which it is able to divide and rule supplicant European governments.

The framework of this analysis focuses on the interaction of the economic and political dimensions of the EU-China bilateral relationship. It recognizes that China has become an important economic and political actor and that its impact is growing in the EU, partly as a result of the fact that Member States have competing interests. The intra-EU economic and political competition at this bilateral level of the relationship with China is considered to be a key explanatory factor in the how the bilateral and the wider EU relationships are constituted.

Despite these widespread assumptions, the bilateral political and economic dimension is only one factor in determining how the EU-China relationship is constituted. This paper argues that even if it was ever accurate, such a view of the economic relationship and how its benefits are distributed is increasingly out of date. The relationship is determined by other factors that lie outside the nexus economic and political competition of EU member states in the bilateral relationship with China.

The development of the relationship is not only a matter of the bilateral exchanges between EU and China shown by trade and FDI flows. The EU and China are two complex economies that are evolving in the global context, notably since the financial and economic crisis in the US and EU that began in 2007. Structural change in the economy of one party changes the relationship. On one side, the economic relationship is determined by the changing structures of EU member state economies. For instance, as the IMF has pointed out in relation to the Eurozone, domestic reform and readjustment of external balances are key policies that have been adopted to recover from the crisis (IMF 2016).[1] Policies adopted in some EU member states to address causes of the crisis led to reduction of domestic demand which in turn impacts imports and thus the external trade and current account balances, including those with China. Imports of several member states from China were reduced in this in the period following the crisis. Similarly, domestic policies adopted in China may affect the economic relationship with the EU.

This paper focuses on domestic changes in the Chinese economy and their impacts in the EU. The paper argues that changes in the Chinese economy have impacts in the EU and the relationship between the two. It also argues that such changes in China create an increasing complex set of relationships with EU Member States and interests in them, and these are no longer simply defined by trade in goods and FDI flows. The bilateral political and economic conjuncture is declining in importance in determining the pattern of relationships between Member States and China. Changes in China's economy are an important element in both in the creation and distribution of benefits. This is not just a question of size of Chinese economy, but also its structure. For the EU member states, the distribution of the relationships their benefits will evolve as China evolves. This will not just be measured in trade in goods expressed by exports or the trade balance, or the increasing FDI flows. Other elements such as services, especially finance but also others including tourism, and portfolio investment will rise in importance.

Change in China

According to China's government, the Chinese economy is undergoing a process of transition to a "new normal". Reform and restructuring of the Chinese economy and the need to shift to a new model of development has been on the agenda in

1 Euro Area Policies: Staff Report For The 2016 Article IV Consultation, IMF, June 2016.

China for many years and under President Xi Jinping, a reform agenda was set out. The progress on the path of reform and its end point is not yet clear, but regardless of this, changes are occurring that already have a significant impact on the EU-China relationship. This has impacts on economic relations with the EU, not just at the aggregate EU level. There are several post-crisis developments in China's economy that impact on relations with Member States, and the distribution of benefits between them. Among the most important structural changes are the shifts from investment to consumption, and also the rising importance of services in China. This has led to changes in China's trade in goods while at the same time its trade in services has been rising rapidly. The dramatic growth in outward direct investment (ODI) from China since 2005 has been a key element in the changing economic relationship between the EU and China, but so also has been emerging portfolio investment from China. One key rising sector has been the financial sector, where China plays an increasing role, especially in the EU.

In the post-crisis period, the Chinese economy has become increasingly important to the EU and its Member States. This is in part a function of absolute size resulting from strong GDP growth in China since 2008 and the failure of policymakers to revive growth in the EU. China thus made a significant contribution to growth in the EU, for instance, through increased imports from the EU following China's policy of stimulus in response to the crisis. Not only did the absolute amount of exports from the EU to China increase, but also their size relative to total EU exports. However, the economic relationship with China is more important for some member states than others not just because they export more, but because they export relatively more as a share of their total exports. The EU and its Member States are becoming increasingly export-dependent for growth, while China is becoming less so. Such shifts suggest structural changes in China in particular are creating more complex differentiated relationships with the EU and its member states.

Merchandise Trade

Despite the fact that the process of globalization has led both the EU and China to be deeply integrated into global production chains, the discussion of their trading relationship is usually framed in simple bilateral terms, with the relationship apparently tilted in China's favour as result of its persistent trade surplus with the EU. Goods trade is also the area where friction between the two has traditionally been greatest, as evidenced by the frequency of trade defence measures adopted in the EU against China. Rapidly increasing imports from China brought a growing number of anti-dumping actions and other trade defence measures by the EU, notably in the major cases of textiles and solar panels. The debate over the granting of Market Economy Status (MES) for China in relation to expiry in December 2016 of provisions in its World Trade Organization (WTO) accession typify the centrality of trade in goods to public debate. As Fox and Godemont argue, it is around these disputes that the differences in interests between Member States often come into focus.

The EU's external goods trade relationship with China is dominated by Germany. In 2014 Germany accounted for 46% of EU exports of goods to China, and 20.1% of imports. In the post-crisis period Germany has enjoyed a consistent trade surplus with China, although in 2015 it declined, in large part because of a shift to German companies increasing production of cars in China. No other EU member state has enjoyed a trade surplus with China in recent years, with the minor exception of Finland in 2015. In the post-crisis period German exports to China grew rapidly, largely as a result of growth in the Chinese economy, driven by a stimulus policy that encouraged both investment and consumption. At the same time, although they increased rapidly in the immediate post-crisis period, German imports from China subsequently fell back, and their lack of growth has contributed to the Germany's trade surplus with China. Based purely on goods trade Germany has been the winner of the EU's economic relationship with China, which could help explain the close political ties between Berlin and Beijing.

In the immediate crisis period, the patterns of trade of most EU Member States were similar. At the height of the crisis in Europe in 2009 imports of EU from

China fell, but recovered rapidly in 2010, and exports continued to grow as they had done even at the height of the crisis, but since then the paths of Member States have diverged. In the pre-crisis period growing trade deficits with China were the norm, but unlike Germany, no other Member State has managed to reverse this and achieve a sustained trade surplus with China. Unlike Germany, for many member states any reduction of their trade deficits with China in the post crisis period has been the result of suppression of imports rather than a significant increase in exports. As the IMF notes, this has generally been the case across many debtor Member States in the Eurozone. Italy is one such example which until now has not benefitted significantly from demand from China. The trade deficit of France has stabilised, although it is far from being a surplus, as both imports and exports increased after the crisis. Since 2009 both the UK's imports and exports have risen rapidly, although the rise in exports to China is a special case, as in recent years the most significant contributor has been sales of gold.

Germany has been the primary trading beneficiary of the trading relationship with China since the crisis. Indeed China has been a necessity for Germany. Germany's economy is highly export-dependent and China has a rapidly growing demand for imports. Following the EU crisis, Germany's exports to China replaced those to Eurozone member states where consumption has been suppressed. Germany has adopted a policy of close political accommodation with China. Indeed, it has arguably the closest political relations with China of any EU member state.

The EU is increasingly dependent on China as a trading partner. China's share of EU imports from outside its borders increased from 9.6% in 2002 to 20.3% in 2015. In the same period, China's share of extra-EU exports increased from 4.0% to 9.5%, but there major differences between Member States in this regard. The share of China in Germany's extra-EU exports increased from 6.1% to 14.2%, well above the EU average. Other Member States are less reliant on China for export markets. The increase in China's share of the extra-EU exports of France was from 3.0% to 9.5% between 2002 and 2015, and for the UK the increase was from 2.1% to 10.8%, but for Italy it was only from 3.9% to 5.6%. The EU is increasingly dependent on exports to sustain growth. The increasing reliance on China is part of a wider dependence on exports as a source of growth in the EU in the face of weak internal growth in the post crisis period. Exports of goods and services as a percentage of the EU's GDP reached 39% of GDP in 2008. The figure fell in 2009, but increased subsequently to 42.9% in 2015, well above the global average of 29.3%. In the case of Germany, its exports of goods and services were equivalent to 46.9% of GDP in 2015 while its current account surplus was 8.5% of GDP. By contrast, China's exports of goods and services as a percentage of GDP reached a peak of 35.7% in 2006, and have since declined to 22.4% in 2015.

Service trade

One of the key shifts in China's economy in recent years has been the growth in services relative to other sectors. This is not only domestic in impact as the role of services is increasingly evident in China's international economic relations. China has a rapidly growing service trade deficit, which increased from US$12 billiion in 2008 to US$192 billion in 2014. China's deficit on transport services reached US$57.9 billion in 2014, and the deficit on tourism US$107.9 billion.

As a result of China's growing service imports, the EU's service exports to China have increased from €19.5 billion in 2010 to €36 billion in 2015, with the EU's surplus rising from €2.3 billion to €10.3 billion in the same period. In fact, the growth rate in service exports to China has been faster than the EU's total service exports. As is the case in other aspects of the EU-China economic relationship, not all member states are benefiting equally. Germany's service exports to China increased from €4.0 billion in 2010 to €11.5 billion in 2015, but the UK's exports rose by much less from €2.5 billion to €4.4 billion. Service exports from France to China increased from €3.2 billion in 2011 to €4.9 billion in 2015, but those from Italy only rose from €695.7 million to €1.1 billion. While it may appear that Germany once again has the most beneficial relationship with China in the services sector as a whole, the benefits are not equally distributed. The EU's income from

China in travel services rose from €2.8 billion in 2010 to €7.5 billion in 2015, but it was the UK which was the greatest beneficiary in this sector. In 2015, UK earnings from travel services from China were €2.1 billion, while for France the amount as €966 million and Italy it was €367 million. In the same period, EU income from the financial services sector increased from €533.5 million in 2010 to €960.5 million in 2015 when they were dominated by the UK with earning of €316.7 million.

Direct Investment

In addition to trade in goods, FDI flows have been a major constituent of globalization since the 1980s. China has been one of the largest destinations for FDI in the world and since the 1990s, it has received significant investment for European companies so that by 2014 the total stock of EU FDI China had reached €144.2 billion according to EU balance of payments statistics. More recently, the emergence after 2005 of Chinese enterprises as major investors has been followed by increasing investment in the EU. However, the stock of Chinese FDI in the EU was only €20.7 billion in 2014. The FDI flows, especially from China to the EU, are small, especially when compared to the trade flows. One key aim of the current CAI negotiation is to increase investment flows between the EU and China in both directions. For the EU a central goal is to push an agenda of market access in China for European investment, but member states also seek to attract increasing investment from China.

The distribution of FDI from the EU to China is similar to that for trade. Germany is the main EU investor in China. In 2014 Germany's stock of FDI in China was €61.2 billion, or 42.4% of the total. This was followed by the Netherlands, with 15.0% and France with 14.0%. The UK had a much smaller share with 5.8% and Italy 4.9%. The growth in FDI outflows from China is more recent than its inflows, and is the result of a fundamental shift in Chinese government policy originating with the initiation of the "go global" strategy in 2001. This policy shift involved the removal of the previously tight restrictions on ODI and later increasing encouragement of outflows. In the period after 2005, ODI from China grew rapidly, including to the EU. Chinese ODI in the EU is nevertheless unevenly distributed. Based on balance of payments statistics, in 2014, the Netherlands, with €14.2 billion had the largest stock of Chinese ODI in the EU. This was followed by France €2.1 billion and the UK €1.8 billion. However, given the relatively small size of the investment, the amounts tend to be volatile and vary considerably from one year to the other. The destinations of China's investment also tend to be heavily influenced by the fact that some EU Member States are primarily used by Chinese companies as conduits to keep their tax burdens as low as possible. The governments of Member States compete to attract Chinese investment, but the increasing amount of investment, notably from private companies, has greatly diversified the destinations in the EU. Chinese investors make their investments for different reasons that are determined by the economic attractions of destination countries. One new dimension since 2013 has been the initiation of the One Belt, One Road strategy or Belt and Road Initiative (BRI), is a new evolution of policy on outward invest. The policy is directed to building connectivity between China and Europe through land and maritime routes, but so far has had little effect on investment flows to EU. . At the EU level the Chinese government has negotiated with the European Commission to participate in the EFSI. While there has been agreement in principle on China's participation, there has been no agreement on how it should be implemented. Despite the promotion of the BRI in Europe, the actual results in terms of significant investment have been limited, either at the EU or member state level, despite expressions of interest from many governments in participation. The single largest investment undertaken by the Silk Road Fund, a fund with US$40 billion in capital established by the Chinese government to support the BRI, was to support the acquisition of shares in Pirelli by ChemChina in 2015.

Finance

Like trade in goods and FDI, portfolio investment flows have been a major factor in the globalized economy. Since the 1980s these flows have undergone periods of rapid increase, followed by volatility in times of crisis. In general these flows have been concentrated in the financial markets of the major developed economies and China has not been a significant source or destination of portfolio investment. The gradual and limited opening of China's capital account has begun to permit both inward and outward portfolio investment flows. Portfolio investment from China has increased although it remains small compared to the developed economies. Outward portfolio investment flows from China reached a peak of US$111.3 billion in 2006, before sharply declining in the post-crisis period. Portfolio investment outward flows reached a post-crisis peak of US$72.3 billion at the end of 2015, and in that year China's total stock of outward portfolio investment was US$280.8 billion. The most important destination for China's portfolio investment is the US with a stock of US$111.1 billion in 2015, which far outweighs any other, but the EU also receives significant portfolio investment from China. Indeed China's portfolio investment in the EU is similar in scale to its FDI. Nevertheless, the distribution of portfolio investment is very different from FDI, and is concentrated in the UK where China had a stock US$12.4 billion of portfolio investment in 2015. In the same year, the stock of Chinese portfolio investment in Germany was US$5.0 billion, while in France it was US$4.9 billion and in Italy it was only US$1.1 billion.

The increasing internationalization of China's financial system and its relationship with the EU is also demonstrated by the growing international role of Chinese banks. The internationalization of the RMB is one aspect of this. There are now several centres for trading of RMB outside China of which London is the most important. Other aspects of the financial system demonstrate the dominance of the UK among EU member states. Figures from the Bank of International Settlements (BIS) illustrate the banking relationship between China and the EU. In the first quarter of 2016 Chinese financial institution had claims of US$142.4 billion on banks in the UK, the largest amount of any country in the world. At the same time, the claim of Chinese banks on the US was US$79.6 billion. Other EU Member States had much less important relationships with Chinese banks. The claims of Chinese banks on France were only US$ 39.0 billion, while for Germany they were

US$25.7 billion and US$2.7 billion for Italy. The dominance of the UK in this regard has only increased in the period after the commencement of the crisis in the EU and US in 2008. Prior to crisis at the end 2007, China's claims on UK banks were US$60.6 billion, compared to US$21.4 billion for Germany and US$21.6 billion for France.

Conclusion

The economic relationship between the EU and China is undergoing rapid change and is no longer defined within the boundaries of trade in goods and FDI flows, but is increasingly multi-faceted. One of the most important reasons for emergence of this increasingly complex relationship is the changes that are occurring in the Chinese economy, especially in the post crisis period since 2008. These changes are creating new dimensions in the economic relationships at the EU and Member State level. The changes suggest that while the conjunction of politics and economics between the EU and its Member States may continue to be one element in the relationship with China, it is far from being significant in determining how economic benefits are distributed. Changes in China itself create new economic relationships and benefits. The increasingly diversified relationship resulting from these changes in China creates new elements that are often beyond direct political control. The beneficiaries in the EU are more likely to be those that have underlying economic advantages rather than those that simply have the best political relationship with China.

References

European Commission (2016), Elements for a New EU Strategy on China, Joint Communication to The European Parliament and The Council, European Commission, High Representative of The Union for Foreign Affairs and Security Policy, June 22, 2016.

Fox, J and Godemont, F (2009), A Power Audit Of EU-China Relations, European Council on Foreign Relations, April, 2009.

Fuchs, A (2016), China's Economic Diplomacy and the Politics-Trade Nexus, University of Heidelberg Department of Economics, Discussion Paper Series No. 609, March 2016

Fuchs, A and Klann, N-H (2013), Paying a Visit: The Dalai Lama Effect on International Trade. Journal of International Economics 91(1), 2013.

Huotari, M, Otero-Iglesias, M, Seaman, J and Ekman, J (2015), Mapping Europe-China Relations: A Bottom-Up Approach, European Think-tank Network on China, October 2015.

International Monetary Fund (IMF) (2016), Euro Area Policies: Staff Report For The 2016 Article IV Consultation, IMF, June 2016.

中国的“一带一路”倡议与欧盟的基础设施政策：欧亚一体化的绝佳机遇

马歌德 【德国】

德国全球和区域研究中心 副主任

在以下讨论中，我会把重点放在这样一个问题上：“一带一路”倡议是否能够为欧亚一体化带来新的机遇。我最终得出的结论是，“一带一路”倡议的确有足够的潜力来支持欧亚经济一体化的实现，但同时也面临着诸多问题，其具体原因在于——针对如何就基础设施建设开展合作的问题，各方存在利益上的分歧。

首先，我要阐明我的主要论点：

1）欧盟委员会正计划构建“欧盟–中国互联互通平台”，在中国的“一带一路倡议”和欧盟的交通运输政策之间寻求合作的可能。

2）欧盟希望中方能够在欧盟的政策框架下，积极参与成员国及周边国家的基础设施建设及基础设施融资。

3）欧盟成员国及周边国家热诚欢迎中国为其基础设施建设进行融资。

4）相比之下，中国企业参与基础设施建设会遇到诸多困难。

5）中国建筑企业必将面对欧盟标准的严格要求。同时，欧洲企业在建筑领域具有很强的竞争力。

2015 年 9 月，中欧双方签署《关于欧盟–中国互联互通平台的谅解备忘录》，签字仪式由中国国家发改委和欧盟交通运输部专员共同主持。互联互通平台旨在推进中欧双方在交通运输的战略合作、计划、战略、项目等方面加强信息共享，促进双方的投资互动，加强双方在交通运输管理、基础设施投资、融资等方面进行经验交流。

欧盟建立互联互通平台的意义，在于鼓励中国在欧盟同行的交通运输政策框架下，参与到基础设计建设的投资和融资中来。自 2012 年中国提出“16+1 合作”框架以来，欧盟委员会便一直对中东欧国家的投资活动给予紧密关注，因为中东欧 16 国在欧盟中扮演重要角色，是连接中国、中亚以及欧盟共同市场的物流走廊。

目前，中国已经与塞尔维亚、马其顿、匈牙利等国家进行接触，当中国宣布在希腊的 比雷埃夫斯港口、贝尔格莱德以及布达佩斯之间修建一条高速铁路的计划时，公众的反响十分强烈。随着“16+1 合作”的不断推进，欧盟也以观察着的身份参加了 2015 年 11 月在苏州召开的会议。《苏州纲要》指出，与会成员国对“欧盟–中国互联互通平台”表示欢迎和支持。

然而欧盟对于如何发展基础设施建设有着自己的观点，这一点早已反映在“全欧交通政策”（TEN-T）中。该政策着重打造 9 条主干走廊，预计到 2030 年竣工，其中波罗的海–亚德里亚海走廊 连接波兰、斯洛伐克等沿线国家；东欧–地中海走廊联通波罗的海、黑海以及地中海。

综上所述，中东欧国家与中亚国家亟须发展基础设施建设，但却缺乏足够的资金，因而这些国家非常欢迎中国为其提供资金支持。在这个问题上，中欧双方已经取得了一些进展：欧洲投资银行及丝路基金的代表将于今年年底与一家出口集团举行会谈。

但中国企业在参与基础设施建设的过程中，必然遇到更大的挑战。中国政府及企业需要了解欧盟运输业的法规要求，同时要遵守欧盟关于政府采购、竞争、环保标准和技术标准等方面的要求。

China's Belt and Road Initiative and the EU's Infrastructure Policy: New Opportunities for Europe–Asia Integration

Margot Schüller / Germany

Deputy Director of the German Institute of Global and Area Studies

In my contribution I focus on the question of the Belt and Road Initiative can bring about new opportunities for Europe–Asia integration. I argue ultimately that the Belt and Road initiative does, indeed, have the potential to support the economic integration of Europe and Asia. There are some challenges to be faced however, due specifically to diverging interests regarding how cooperation in the building of infrastructure should take place exactly.

I start my contribution by presenting my main arguments:

1) The EU Commission has proposed the establishment of an EU–China Connectivity Platform that should explore the potential for cooperation between Belt and Road and the EU's own transport policies.

2) The EU expects the Chinese side to be active in the financing and building of infrastructure in Europe and neighboring countries within the EU regulatory framework.

3) Participation in the financing of infrastructure in EU member states and neighboring countries is highly welcome.

4) In contrast, Chinese companies' involvement in the building of infrastructure will be difficult.

5) Chinese construction companies will face strong EU regulatory requirements. Besides, European companies are already highly competitive in this field.

In September 2015 a Memorandum of Understanding on the EU–China Connectivity Platform was signed. It is co-chaired by the National Development and Reform Commission (NDRC) and the EU Commissioner for Transport. The Platform is expected to support the exchange of information on plans, strategies, and projects for strategic transport-related cooperation between the Chinese government and the EU Commission. Investment opportunities in both directions will be promoted, meaning Chinese investment in the EU's infrastructure as well as vice versa. In addition the Platform aims at fostering the exchange of best practices and experience in transport management, infrastructure investment, and the financing thereof.

The interest of the EU in setting up the Platform lies in engaging China in the financing of infrastructure building based on the existing EU common transport policy. Since China set up the 16+1 Initiative in 2012, investment activities in the Central and Eastern European countries (CEEC) has been looked on by the EU Commission with suspicion. The CEEC play an important role herein: they represent a logistics corridor that bridges China, Central Asia, and the EU Common Market.

So far, China has approached individual CEEC such as Serbia, Macedonia, and Hungary. Public attention was strong when China announced the plan for a transport corridor connecting the Greek port of Piraeus with Belgrade and Budapest through a high-speed train network. With the 16+1 Initiative gaining speed, the EU became involved as an observer at the last meeting in Suzhou, held in November 2015.

The "Suzhou Guidelines" note that the participants of the meeting "welcomed and supported" the EU–China Connectivity Platform.

That the EU has its own specific idea on how to develop infrastructure is reflected in the Trans-European Transport Policy (TEN-T). Nine network corridors should be forerunners, and their construction should be completed by 2030. Among the TEN-T corridors, some stretch for example across the Baltic–Adriatic Corridor, including such countries as Poland and Slovakia, through the Orient–East Mediterranean Corridor, including the Baltic, Black, and Mediterranean Seas.

In my conclusion, I underline the fact that the CEEC and Central Asia are in urgent need of funds to develop local infrastructure but lack the financial means for that. Therefore, China's interest in providing financial support is very welcome in those locations. Some progress on this side has already been made: an Export Group (including representatives from the European Investment Bank and the Silk Road Fund) on financing and investment will meet by the end of the year.

When it comes to the involvement of Chinese companies in the building of infrastructure, the challenges faced are much greater. Chinese government officials and companies need to understand the regulatory requirements in place for the EU transport sector. In addition, EU regulations on government procurement, competition, and environmental and technical standards also need to be observed.

“一带一路”背景下的中国担当与国际产能合作

田丰 【中国】
中国社会科学院世界经济与政治研究所 研究员 /《国际经济评论》编辑部 主任

“一带一路”倡议彰显中国作为一个大国对时代和世界的担当。当前，世界经济复苏乏力，各类风险和不确定性仍然比较突出，如何直面问题综合施策、标本兼治，推动世界经济走上强劲、可持续、平衡、包容增长之路，这是世界各国的一致关切。“一带一路”地区覆盖总人口约 46 亿（超过世界人口 60%），GDP 总量达 20 万亿美元（约占全球 1/3）。通过“一带一路”战略，有望构筑全球经济贸易新的大循环，成为继大西洋、太平洋之后的第三大经济发展空间，更加深入推动世界经济发展以及区域合作进程。

中国担当的客观基础是中国在国际社会具有的举足轻重且还在不断提升、日益广泛的影响力。“天行健，君子以自强不息。”正如国家主席习近平在 G20 杭州峰会上的系列讲话所指出的，经过长期的建设，中国已经发展成为世界第二大经济体、最大的发展中国家、最大货物贸易国、第三大对外直接投资国，人均国内生产总值接近 8000 美元。我们奉行独立自主的和平外交政策，坚持对外开放的基本国策，敞开大门搞建设，从大规模引进来到大踏步走出去，积极推动建设更加公正合理的国际秩序，中国同外部世界的互动持续加深。强劲的发展与世界经济的深度融合使得中国已经成为全球经济增长的主要引擎，国际形象不断提升。《中国国家形象全球调查报告 2015》显示，中国经济的国际影响力位居世界第二，中国整体形象稳定提升，科技创新能力广受好评，高铁被认为是最突出的科技成就。一个国家强盛才能充满信心地开放，而开放促进一个国家强盛。随着我国经济发展进入新常态，我们要保持经济持续健康发展，就必须树立全球视野，通过“一带一路”等战略更加自觉地统筹国内国际两个大局，全面谋划全方位对外开放大战略，以更加积极主动的姿态走向世界。

中国担当的现实华彩是明确务实、标本兼治的中国方案。解决问题靠的不是空谈，而是实实在在有效的方案。中共十八大以后，党中央着眼于我国“十三五”时期和更长时期的发展，逐步明确了“一带一路”建设、京津冀协同发展、长江经济带发展3个大的发展战略，先后于2014年和2015年发布了《丝绸之路经济带和21世纪海上丝绸之路建设战略规划》以及《推动共建丝绸之路经济带和21世纪海上丝绸之路的愿景与行动》，有关地方和部门也出台了配套规划，在国际上引起较大反响。目前，已经有100多个国家和国际组织参与其中，我们同30多个沿线国家签署了共建“一带一路”合作协议、同20多个国家开展国际产能合作，联合国等国际组织也态度积极，以亚投行、丝路基金为代表的金融合作不断深入，一批有影响力的标志性项目逐步落地。“一带一路”建设从无到有、由点及面，进度和成果超出预期。

国际产能合作是“一带一路”建设的重要抓手。国际产能合作是指两个存在意愿和需要的国家或地区之间进行产能供求跨国或者跨地区配置的联合行动。产能合作可通过两个渠道进行：既可以通过产品输出方式进行产能位移，也可以通过产业转移的方式进行产能位移。以“一带一路”建设为契机，开展跨国互联互通，提高贸易和投资合作水平，推动国际产能和装备制造合作，本质上是通过提高有效供给来催生新的需求，实现世界经济再平衡。特别是在当前世界经济持续低迷的情况下，如果能够使顺周期下形成的巨大产能和建设能力走出去，支持“一带一路”沿线国家推进工业化、现代化和提高基础设施水平的迫切需要，有利于稳定当前世界经济形势。

“一带一路”背景下的国际产能合作是优势产能合作。所谓“优势产能合作”意味着“一带一路”背景下的国际产能合作具有深厚的产业、市场以及合作基础。从产业领域看，中国已经是一个世界性工业大国，诸多产业具有较强的国际竞争力。联合国工业发展组织发布的数据显示，2012年，中国在22个制造业二位数行业中，有12个行业的增加值居世界第一位，9个行业的增加值居世界第二。从市场领域看，2008 年国际金融危机发生以后，欧美日等发达经济体把重振工业作为应对危机的一个重要选项，下力气部署再工业化战略，强化制造业创新，重塑制造业竞争优势。同时，非洲、西亚、南亚和东南亚等城镇化水平较低、全球人口分布比较集中地区的发展中国家将迎来城镇化与工业化加速推进的高潮。从合作领域看，中国正在积极构建全方位开放新格局。近年来，中国在“一带一路”建设旗帜的引领下，坚持“亲、诚、惠、容”的外交理念，加强与沿线国家合作，中印缅孟经济走廊、中巴经济走廊、中俄蒙经济走廊等倡议得到周边国家的积极回应并签订了双边合作协议，与东盟、非盟、阿盟和中东欧等建立了良好的往来关系，达成产能合作的共识。展望未来，“一带一路”背景下国际产能合作将迅速发展，合作形式、主体、产业和区域将更为多样化。为在“一带一路”背景下推进国际产能合作，中国政策的重点应放在增强企业国际竞争能力、完善配套支持政策、加强国际政策协调、做好组织服务保障和风险防控等方面。

“一带一路”背景下国际产能合作的实质是构建以合作共赢为核心的新型国际关系。无论是在 G20 工商峰会开幕式上发表演讲，还是在 G20 领导人峰会上致开幕和闭幕词，“合作”“共赢”“共同”都是习近平主席提到的关键词。在这些场合，习近平主席也都谈到了“伙伴精神”。“我们要继续加强宏观政策沟通和协调，发扬同舟共济、合作共赢的伙伴精神，凝聚共识，形成合力，促进世界经济强劲、可持续、平衡、包容增长”，习近平主席的话语，为峰会取得丰硕成果定下基调。所谓人类命运共同体的深刻内涵在于，政治上要建立平等相待、互商互谅的伙伴关系；安全上要营造公道正义、共建共享的安全格局；经济上要谋求开放创新、包容互惠的发展前景；文化上要促进和而不同、兼收并蓄的文明交流；环境上要构筑尊崇自然、绿色发展的生态体系，要以“人与自然和谐相处”为目标，实现世界的可持续发展和人的全面发展。可以看出，打造“人类命运共同体”的宏伟愿景实质上是中国“五大发展理念”的扩展版、国际版，是中国处理与他国关系的顶层设计，是中国构建国际秩序的根本引领。

“一带一路”背景下国际产能合作是基于新发展理念的全面系统合作。习近平用 G20 各方的五大“决心”介绍了杭州峰会达成的共识和取得的主要成果：决心为世界经济指明方向，规划路径；决心创新增长方式，为世界经济注入新动力；

决心完善全球经济金融治理，提高世界经济抗风险能力；决心重振国际贸易和投资这两大引擎的作用，构建开放型世界经济；决心推动包容和联动式发展，让二十国集团合作成果惠及全球。尤为关键的是，杭州峰会在推动可持续发展议程、气候变化和结构性改革等问题上取得了历史性的突破。G20 第一次将发展问题置于全球宏观政策框架突出位置，第一次就落实联合国 2030 年可持续发展议程制定行动计划，发起《二十国集团支持非洲和最不发达国家工业化倡议》和《全球基础设施互联互通联盟倡议》，通过了《二十国集团创新增长蓝图》，共同制定《二十国集团全球贸易增长战略》和全球首个多边投资规则框架《二十国集团全球投资指导原则》。G20 历史上首次就气候变化问题专门发表声明，一致同意推动《巴黎协定》尽早生效。杭州峰会首次提出综合运用货币政策、财政政策和结构性改革来促进经济增长，是 G20 从侧重短期政策向短中长期政策并重转型的重要表征。“一带一路”背景下国际产能合作不是马歇尔计划的更新版，而是基于新发展理念的全面系统合作。

抓住重点行业、扎实推进国际产能合作。《国务院关于推进国际产能和装备制造合作的指导意见》（国发〔2015〕30 号）将钢铁、有色、建材、铁路、电力、化工、轻纺、汽车、通信、工程机械、航空航天、船舶和海洋工程等作为重点行业。以铁路为例，我国铁路生产能力位居全球第一。在国内客运和货运市场增长的带动下，我国铁路产业规模发展迅速。以铁路车辆为例，2011 年产量一度超过 7 万辆，近几年虽然有所下降但年产量也在 4 万量左右，稳居全球第一。受高速铁路系统建设的影响，我国铁路客车产量自 2008 年之后增速加快，2014 年客车产量是 1998 年的 2.18 倍，铁路货车车辆在 2011 年达到顶峰，受全球经济疲软、大宗货运量下降的影响产量，在 2011 年之后有所下降，但 2014 年产量仍然是 1998 年的 1.46 倍。

根据商务部的统计，目前我国的铁路产品已经出口到 30 多个国家和地区，2014 年，我国参与境外铁路建设项目 348 个，同比增加 113 个，累计签订合同金额 247 亿美元，同比增长 3 倍多，完成营业额 76 亿美元，同比增长 31.3%。加入世贸组织以来，我国机车车辆出口由 2001 年的不到 8000 万美元增长到 2014 年的 37.4 亿美元，年均增速 34.7%，高于同期的全国外贸出口增速 16.5 个百分点。2014 年，机车车辆出口同期增长 19.3%，也是我国同期外贸出口增速的 3 倍。

铁路属于基础设施建设相关的产业，其市场发展或产业增长除受一国的基本经济和社会发展水平影响外，还要重点考察基础设施的发展现状与发展趋势，所以需要分析东道国相应城镇化率、铁路里程、公路里程等数据。铁路包括路网建设和装备制造两大子行业，高度依赖于东道国的客货运市场需求大小。在铁路网建设方面，美国、欧盟等发达经济体对老旧铁路改造升级、城市轨道交通有较大的市场需求，中东欧、拉美、南亚、东南亚等地区对普通铁路、高速铁路、城际和城市轨道交通等方面需求比较迫切，非洲地区对普通铁路有较大的需求，以上地区适合采取对外直接投资（含对外工程承包）和装备出口相结合的方式。在铁路装备制造方面，受工程建设、技术标准等因素影响较大，城市轨道交通装备"走出去"相对容易，适合采取装备出口的合作方式。

中国铁路产业"走出去"面临的主要障碍包括：首先，由于目标国政治局势的不稳定性，造成对外铁路项目建设的不确定性。例如，在合同签署期间、签署之后和在施工期间，目标国因为政府换届、甚至军事冲突，已经确定或者正在实施的项目被搁浅。例如，泰国高铁项目推进缓慢与政府换届有直接关系。其次，由于文化习俗的不同，在境外铁路项目的谈判和建设过程中会收到很制约。例如，中铁铁建公司在中东地区的铁路建设工程进度缓慢，原因之一是中方施工人员对高温、缺水的作业环境非常不适应。再次，中国铁路系统的走出去面临越来严重的知识产权壁垒，发达国家在技术转让中制定了越来越苛刻的知识产权使用范围规定，在很多时候，即便我们已经掌握成套技术和工艺也不能实现出口。第四，无论是在发达国家还是发展中国家，都不断出现用工纠纷。发达国家对劳动者的保护力度大，经常会影响到工期进度；很多发展中国家没有产业工人储备，工人的纪律性和技能水平都难以满足要求。第五，别有用心的人和组织无事生非、散布谣言，"中国威胁论"弥漫于世界各地。相比较而言，我国对外舆论宣传能力和手段存在差距，还不能对中国铁路系统的"走出去"创造良好的舆论环境。

为了务实、高效、精准地推动"一带一路"背景下国际产能合作，我国应该从增强企业"走出去"能力、促进境外园区健康发展、完善配套支持政策、加强国际政策协调、做好组织服务保障和风险防控等方面制定或完善相关的支持政策。要以企业为主体，在支持企业开展对外投资活动的同时探索新的商业模式。依托地方商会、行业协会等行业中介服务组织，探索"协会 + 企业 + 境外园区"合作模式，抱团赴外投资，形成地方优势产能向国外延伸，促进国内外产业互动发展。

加强对国外行业领军企业的战略性投资，促进优势产能与行业领先技术的优势结合，积极开拓第三方市场。支持一批有实力的企业承揽国际大型工程项目，大踏步地走进工程总承包商之列，带动相关优势产能对外输出。

China's Role and International Cooperation on Production Capacity under the Background of the Belt and Road Initiative

Tian Feng / China

Fellow of the Institute of World Economy and Politics, CASS / Director of the Editorial Department of *International Economic Review*

At present, the world's economy is sluggishly recovering; various risks and uncertainties remain striking. How to squarely face the problems, take comprehensive measures, carry out both temporary and permanent solutions to make the world's economy embark on the road to vigorous, sustainable, balanced and inclusive growth is the common concern of the countries around the world. The Belt and Road regions cover a population of about 4.6 billion—more than 60% of the world's population, and have a total GDP of 20 trillion USD, accounting for about 1/3 of the global GDP. With the Belt and Road Initiative, it is expected that a new large cycle of global economy and trade will take shape and it will become the third-largest area of economic development following those of the Atlantic and the Pacific Ocean; moreover, the development of the world's economy as well as regional cooperation will be further intensified.

The objective foundation for China's sharing of responsibilities is China's crucial role in the international community and China's continuously heightened and increasingly extensive influence. While the universe keeps rolling on orbit, a superior man should make untiring endeavors for advancement. As mentioned by Chinese President Xi Jinping in a series of speeches during the G20 Hangzhou Summit in 2016, with long-term construction, China has developed into the second-largest economy in the world, the largest developing country, the largest country of trade in goods and the third-largest outward foreign direct investment country; China's per capita GDP approaches 8,000 USD. China has been committed to an independent foreign policy of peace, it upholds the basic national policy of opening up to the outside world, and has opened the door to carrying out construction projects; China is going global in big strides after a large-scale introduction, and is actively promoting the building of a more just and rational international order. China's interaction with the outside world is intensifying. Thanks to robust development and a profound integration into the world's economy, China has become the main engine for the growth of that economy and enjoys an increasing improvement of its image within the international community. According to the *Global Survey Report on China's National Image 2015*, the international influence of China's economy ranked No.2 in the world, China's overall image steadily improved, China's capacity for scientific and technological innovation was highly commended, and its high-speed railway was regarded as the most prominent scientific and technological achievement. Only when a country becomes powerful and prosperous can it have full confidence in opening up, while opening up stimulates a country to becoming powerful and prosperous. As China's economy enters the new normal of development, in order to keep the development of its economy sustained and healthy, China must foster a global view, more consciously consider the overall domestic and international situations through such strategies as the Belt and Road Initiative, comprehensively plan a great strategy for an all-round opening up and more actively approach the world.

The realistic assurance for China's sharing of responsibilities is China's clear, pragmatic plan which addresses both the symptoms and the root causes. Problems are solved by a feasible plan rather than by empty talk. After the 18th National Congress of the Communist Party of China, with a focus on China's development during the period of the 13th Five-Year Plan and beyond that period, the Central Committee of the Communist Party of China gradually developed three great development strategies covering the construction of the Belt and Road, the coordinated development of Beijing-Tianjin-Hebei and the development of the Yangtze River Economic Zone; moreover, it released the *Plan for the Construction of the Silk Road Economic Belt and the 21st Century Maritime Silk Road*, the *Vision and Actions on Jointly Building the Silk Road Economic Belt and the 21st-Century Maritime Silk Road* in 2014 and 2015 respectively, while relevant local authorities and departments also unveiled supporting plans. These plans had aroused strong repercussions on the international scene. Currently, more than 100 countries and international organizations have participated in the action; China has signed a cooperation agreement for the joint construction of the Belt and Road with over 30 countries along it, and has engaged in cooperation on international production capacity with more than 20 countries, while such international organizations as the United Nations have also taken positive attitudes; the financial cooperation represented by the Asian Infrastructure Investment Bank and the Silk Road Fund has been continuously intensified; a number of influential iconic projects have been gradually carried out. The construction of the Belt and Road started from scratch and proceeds from points to areas; its progress and results have exceeded the expectations.

International cooperation on production capacity serves as an important means for the construction of the Belt and Road. This cooperation refers to the joint actions for the transnational or transregional allocation of production capacity demand and supply between two countries or territories with willingness and needs. The cooperation on production capacity can be conducted via two channels: Production capacity can be displaced through product output and industrial transfer. With the construction of the Belt and Road as the opportunity, actions can be taken to build transnational connectivity, increase the level of trade and investment cooperation, and it can promote cooperation on international production capacity and equipment manufacturing; essentially, this generates new demand by increasing the effective supply to rebalance the world's economy. In particular, as the world's economy is experiencing a sustained downturn, if the huge production capacity and construction capacity, which was formed on a pro-cyclical basis, can be delivered to the outside world in order to meet the urgent needs of supporting the countries along the Belt and Road to push forward industrialization and modernization and increase the infrastructure level, this will be conducive to stabilizing the current situation of the world's economy.

International cooperation on production capacity against the background of the Belt and Road Initiative is cooperation in advantageous production capacity. The cooperation in advantageous production capacity means that there is a solid industrial, market and cooperation foundation for international cooperation on production capacity against the background of the Belt and Road Initiative. From the perspective of industry, China has become a large global industrial country, which enjoys an international competitive edge in many industries. According to the data released by the United Nations Industrial Development Organization, in 2012, China ranked No.1 in the world in terms of added value in 12 sectors and No.2 in the world in terms of added value in 9 sectors among 22 double-digit sectors of the manufacturing industry. Regarding the markets, after the global financial crisis in 2008, the developed economies, including Europe, the USA and Japan, took the revival of industry as an important option for coping with the crisis, made great efforts to deploy a strategy of re-industrialization, and strengthened innovation in the manufacturing industry to shape a competitive edge on the manufacturing industry. Meanwhile, those developing countries in Africa, West Asia, South Asia and Southeast Asia, with relatively low levels of urbanization and relatively concentrated global population, will embrace the upsurge of accelerated urbanization and industrialization. Regarding the areas of cooperation, China is striving to actively build up a new pattern for all-round opening up. In recent years, under the guidance of the flag of the Belt and Road construction, China upholds the diplomatic philosophy of "amicable, sincere, beneficial and inclusive" to intensify cooperation with the countries along the Belt and Road; such China-proposed initiatives as the China-India-Myanmar-Bangladesh Economic Corridor, the China-Pakistan Economic Corridor and the China-Russia-Mongolia Economic Corridor have received positive responses from the surrounding countries, and bilateral cooperation agreements have been signed; China has established a good relationship with ASEAN, the African Union, the Arab League and Central and Eastern Europe, and it has reached a consensus on cooperating with them on production capacity. Looking towards the future, the international cooperation on production capacity against the background of the Belt and Road Initiative will rapidly develop; cooperation modes, cooperators, industries and regions will become more diverse. In the case of promoting international cooperation on production capacity against the background of the Belt and Road Initiative, China's policy should focus on enhancing the enterprises' international competiveness, on improving the supporting policies, on strengthening international policy coordination, and on organizing efforts for the guarantee of services as well as risk prevention and control.

The essence of international cooperation on production capacity against the background of the Belt and Road Initiative is the building of a new type of international relations that focuses on win-win cooperation. In the speech delivered during the G20 Summit, the opening and closing speeches at the G20 Leaders' Summit, "cooperation", "win-win outcome" and "joint" were the keywords used by Chinese President Xi Jinping. On these occasions, President Xi also talked about a "partnership spirit". "We should continue to strengthen macro policy communication and coordination, carry forward the partnership spirit of working together and engaging in win-win cooperation, build consensus and make concerted efforts at promoting vigorous, sustainable, balanced and inclusive growth of the world's economy". This remark made by President Xi Jinping set the tone for making fruitful achievements at this Summit. The profound connotation of the community with a common destiny for human beings is as follows: At the political level, establish a partnership of dealing with each other on an equal footing, holding consultations and gaining mutual understanding; at the security level, create a security pattern characterized by righteousness, joint construction and sharing; at the economic level, seek the developmental prospect of open innovation, inclusiveness and mutual benefit; at the cultural level, promote civilization exchanges focusing on fostering harmony in diversity and discriminately absorbing all good things; at the environmental level, build an ecosystem which favors nature and green development, ensure that people and nature coexist in harmony, and achieve sustainable development of the world and all-round development of the people. As indicated, the ambitious vision for building a community with a common destiny for human beings is essentially an expanded version and international version of China's five developmental philosophies, and the top-level design for China's handling of its relations with other countries as well as China's fundamental guide for establishing an international order.

International cooperation on production capacity against the background of the Belt and Road Initiative is a comprehensive and systematic kind of cooperation based on new philosophies of development. President Xi Jinping used the five "determinations" of the G20 parties to introduce the consensus reached and the main achievements made during the Hangzhou Summit: Be determined to identify the direction of the world's economy and plan routes; be determined to innovate the manner of growth so as to inject new impetus into the world's economy; be determined to improve the global economy and economic governance so as to enhance the capability of the world's economy for withstanding risks; be determined to re-invigorate two engines, which are international trade and investment, so as to build an open world economy; be determined to promote inclusive and interdependent development, and render the cooperation achievements made by the G20 beneficial to the whole world. In particular, historical breakthroughs were made during the Hangzhou Summit in promoting the agenda for sustainable development, addressing climate change and pushing ahead with structural reform. The G20 put the issue of development in a conspicuous position within the global macro policy framework for the first time, and developed an action plan for implementing the *United Nations 2030 Agenda for Sustainable Development* for the first time; it initiated the *G20 Initiative on Supporting Industrialization in Africa and in the Least Developed Countries* and the *Global Infrastructure Connectivity Alliance Initiative*, adopted the *G20 Blueprint on Innovative Growth*, and it jointly developed the *G20 Strategy for Global Trade Growth* and the first multilateral investment rule framework in the world, the *G20 Guiding Principles for Global Investment*. The G20 issued a special statement on the issue of climate change for the first time, and agreed to ensure that the *Paris Agreement* went into force as early as possible. The Hangzhou Summit vowed, for the first time, to comprehensively utilize monetary policy, fiscal policy and structural reform to promote economic growth, which was an important sign that the G20 had been transformed from putting an emphasis on short-term policies to putting equal emphasis on short, medium and long-term policies. The international cooperation on production capacity against the background of the Belt and Road Initiative is not the updated version of the Marshall Plan, but comprehensive and systematic cooperation based on the new philosophy of development.

Emphasis is placed on key industries, and actions are taken to solidly boost international cooperation on production capacity. The *Guiding Opinions of the State Council on Promoting International Cooperation on Production Capacity and Equipment Manufacturing* (Guo Fa (2015) No.30) regards the steel, nonferrous, building material, railway, electric power, chemical, light textile, automobile, communication, engineering machinery, aviation and aerospace, shipping and ocean engineering industries as key industries. Take railways as an example: China ranks

No.1 in the world in terms of railway production capacity. Thanks to the growth of the domestic market for passenger and cargo transportation, the scale of China's railway industry has rapidly developed. Take railway vehicles as an example: The output exceeded 70,000 railway vehicles in 2011; in recent years, it has decreased to some extent but has been about 40,000 railway vehicles, and has ranked No.1 in the world. With the impact of the construction of the high-speed railway system, the output of passenger trains in China has rapidly increased after 2008; the output of passenger trains in 2014 was 2.18 times what it was in 1998; the output of freight trains peaked in 2011 and declined to some extent after 2011 due to global economic downturn and a decrease in bulk cargo volume, but the output in 2014 was 1.46 times what it was in 1998.

According to the statistics from the Ministry of Commerce, at present, China's railway products have been exported to more than 30 countries and territories. In 2014, China participated in 348 overseas railway construction projects, up 113 on a year-on-year basis; the cumulative amount of signed contracts was 24.7 billion USD, up more than three times on a year-on-year basis; turnover was 7.6 billion USD, up 31.3% on a year-on-year basis. After China's accession to the WTO, the exportation of China's rolling stock grew from less than 80 million USD in 2001 to 3.74 billion USD in 2014, an average annual growth rate of 34.7%, up 16.5 percentage points compared with the national foreign trade exportation growth rate in the same period. In 2014, the exportation of rolling stock grew by 19.3% in the same period, three times China's foreign trade export in the same period.

The railway industry is an industry that relates to infrastructure construction. Its market development or industrial growth is affected by the levels of the basic economic and social development of a country; besides, it is necessary to intensively examine the current situation and trend in infrastructure development, so it is essential to analyze the rate of urbanization, rail and highway mileage and other data involving the host country. The railway industry covers two large sub-industries, which are railway network construction and equipment manufacturing.

The railway industry is highly dependent upon the demand within the passenger and cargo transportation market of the host country. Regarding railway network construction, the developed economies, including the USA and the EU, have a huge market demand for renovating and upgrading their old railways and urban rail transit; Central and Eastern Europe, Latin America, South Asia and Southeast Asia have an urgent demand for ordinary railways, high-speed railways, intercity and urban rail transit; Africa has a brisk demand for ordinary railways. A combination of outward foreign direct investment (including overseas project contracting) and equipment exportation is appropriate for the above regions. Regarding railway equipment manufacturing, there is a great impact from such factors as project construction and technical standards; moreover, it is relatively easy to make urban rail transit equipment go global, so it is appropriate to adopt the following method of cooperation: equipment exportation.

China's railway industry is mainly subject to the following barriers when going global: First, the political situation in the target country is not stable, causing a certain amount of uncertainties in the construction of overseas railway projects; for example, when and after contracts are signed and during construction, the projects which have been determined or are being implemented run aground due to the change of the government, or even military conflicts in the target country; for example, slow progress in Thailand's high-speed rail project is directly related to the change of the government. Second, cultural customs are different, thus many restrictions may occur in the negotiation and construction of overseas railway projects; for example, the progress in the railway construction project carried out by China Railway Construction Corporation in the Middle East is slow partially because Chinese construction personnel are highly unable to adapt to the operating environment where temperatures are high and there is little water. Third, China's railway system is subject to increasing intellectual property barriers when going global—the developed countries have developed increasingly harsh regulations on the scope of the application of intellectual properties in technology transfer; in many cases, even if we have mastered complete technologies and processes, we cannot achieve exportation of them. Fourth, labor disputes occur in both developed and developing countries. In the developed countries, great protection is provided for workers and this often affects construction progress; in many developing countries, there are no reserves of industrial workers, and it is difficult for workers to meet the needs in terms of discipline and level of skills. Finally, the people and organizations with ulterior motives make trouble out of nothing and spread rumors, the "China Threat Theory" is extensive around the world, while China still lags behind in external publicity capability and means and therefore cannot create a good environment of public opinion that will help China's railway systems go global.

In order to pragmatically, efficiently and precisely promote international cooperation on production capacity against the background of the Belt and Road Initiative, China should develop or improve its relevant support policies so as to enhance the capability of enterprises for going global, it should boost the healthy development of overseas parks, improve its auxiliary support policies, strengthen the coordination of international policies, and organize efforts for the guarantee of services, risk prevention and control. It is necessary to focus on enterprises, and support them in exploring new business models when carrying out overseas investment activities. It is essential to rely on local chambers of commerce, industrial associations and other industrial intermediary service organizations to explore the "association + enterprise + overseas park" cooperation mode, jointly make overseas investments, create local advantageous production capacity to be extended to foreign countries, and promote the interactive development of domestic and foreign industries. Steps should be taken to strengthen strategic investments in the leading enterprises in foreign industries, combine the advantageous production capacity with the leading industrial technologies, and actively exploit the third-party market. Actions should be taken to support a number of powerful enterprises in undertaking large international projects, in becoming general project contractors and stimulating the exportation of the relevant advantageous production capacity.

中国与阿拉伯国家之间的共同发展

萨米尔　　【约旦】
约旦安曼市文化局　局长

引言

中国在开拓未来的同时，也为当代世界提供了一个全新的发展模式，在这种模式下构建文明关系，无疑对整个人类都有所裨益。因此，阿拉伯国家需要做出种种努力，以促进阿拉伯国家与中国建立更加紧密的友好关系、借鉴中国的成功经验与中国文化，从而为创建全人类共有的美好未来做出贡献。

中阿友好关系已经持续千年之久，阿拉伯国家应以这段友谊为依托，以习近平主席提出的“一带一路倡议”为契机，为当下乃至今后中阿之间全新文明关系的构建做出努力。

本文 主要从两个层面来考虑中国与阿拉伯国家之间的关系：

第一，中国作为世界大国在当代取得了举世瞩目的成就，我们应学习中国的成功之处，借鉴中华文明之所以在世界范围内取得成功的经验。

第二，从文明关系角度出发，探讨如何在知识一体化、经济一体化的基础上——而非仅仅在贸易交易的基础上——构建中阿之间的未来关系。

阿拉伯国家民众的未来会与中国的未来紧密联系在一起，因为他们相信，中国在未来几年、几十年内，将取得更多的成就，他们相信，中国有能力对未来进行合理的规划，并通过实施这些规划来取得一项又一项伟大的成就。多年来，中国取得的成就已经向全世界展示出一幅光辉而亮丽的中国形象。

有鉴于此，本文将以“文明的追随”为题，探讨阿拉伯国家与中国的未来关系。

何谓“文明的追随”

18世纪中叶爆发于英格兰的“工业革命”是人类历史上的一个重大转折点，随着物质财富的不断累积，人类的知识财富与精神财富也在不断地增长。21世纪之初，世界分化为发达世界与落后世界两个极端，前者的国家发展水平、社会发展水平、个人发展水平，均直接受益于“工业革命”，此类发展对人类生产能力的历史产生了重大影响；而后者则很难通过借鉴这些发展经验来实现命运的自主或影响他国或他国人民的生产能力。遗憾的是，阿拉伯世界便属于后者。

第二次世界大战后的几十年时间内可谓前景光明，人们普遍认为物质文明成果的创造、政治成就和社会成就的取得，会带来人类历史上的“最佳发展机遇”。然而，在这“世纪大发展”的后期阶段，促成工业达到如此成就的一个重要因素却是军工业的发展，特别是非常规武器制造业的发展。通讯与信息技术仍是一片广阔而有待开发的领域，为了促进这一领域的开放与开发，必须打下一定的基础才能确保优势地位。

亚洲的一些国家恰好赶上了这趟“最佳机遇”号列车，从此对人类发展的轨迹产生了深远而广泛的影响。中国便是此类范例中的杰出代表，目前，她已然具备了世界大国所拥有的实力。

相比之下，许多国家却错失了这一“最佳机遇”，其中的原因是多方面的，或因未能制定有效的发展战略，或因缺乏有效的战略思想，最终导致国家丧失对主权和自然资源的控制。阿拉伯世界便一直处于这种状态中。从目前的状况来看，阿拉伯国家想要实现发展或是摆脱束缚、重新起步，都是不大现实的。这一点，在19世纪末至20世纪期之间的这段历史经历中已经得到了很好的诠释。

阿拉伯世界与美国之间存在巨大的文明差异，因而美国拥有诸多借口来控制和利用阿拉伯人民，趁机打压异已，这导致阿拉伯国家的民众只能单纯倚靠本国国力和资源进行发展。尽管美国发展势头强劲，但若想彻底抹杀文化差异也无异于天方夜谭。

发展相对落后的国家可采取一种独特而可行的方式，与发达国家共同构建“利益共同体”，从而实现互利合作，而非单纯期待获利。欠发达国家可以从中参考发达国家的成功经验，借鉴其文明中的成功范例。这种关系的建立也能为发达国家的长期发展带来利益。

中国与德、法等欧洲发达国家间便建立过类似的合作关系，本章中将对这一点进行详细论述。中国的发展进程曾一度受到美国的限制和阻挠，但中国通过转变思维，从欧洲国家吸引投资和先进技术，为彼此创造巨大的投资机遇。中国的“技术引进”为自身发展带来了利益，通过积极鼓励高新产业投资科技领域，中国实现了从“探索、摸索”到“自主研发”的飞跃。我们从中国经验中总结出这样一条规律：当国家之间存在巨大的政治差异、社会差异和文化差异时，“利益共同体”的构建 可以为彼此间的交流提供渠道，而“信息革命”恰好为各个文明的融合交汇提供了更进一步的可能性。

但与此同时，我们要意识到这样一个现实问题：“利益共同体”只适合于发展水平相当的国家，对于发展落后的国家而言，我们首先应迎头赶上，然后才谈得上“文明追随”，因为“文明追随”的前提在于——追随方渴望拥有与领导方同等的地位，故而不宜将“文明追随”的内涵描述为“寻求共同利益”，因为发达国家不会帮助欠发达国家，而后者也无法满足前者的要求，在发达国家的控制、剥削和掠夺面前，毫无抵抗之力。

在真正实现“文明追随”之前，民族意志的铸造极其重要。若没有民族意志，任何规划或布局都会沦为空谈，而盲目追随发达国家或发展中国家更非明智之举。中国之所以能够一飞冲天、博得世界关注，主要在于自由而坚定的民族意志。中国作为一个独立自主的现代化国家，历经改革开放 30 多年的探索和实践，最终摸索出一套符合国情、行之有效的发展方案，从而在人文和物质两方面均取得了令人瞩目的成就。

坚定的民族意志可以转化为可行性计划，但富有远见、果断的领导力是不可或缺的。民族复兴计划除了布局、参与外，更需要执行力、监督力以及评估机制，唯其如此，才能有效应对和解决问题，才能更好地适应变幻莫测的国际环境。可以说，中国正是因为拥有如此强劲的领导力，才能在新中国时期，特别是在改革开放后取得如此巨大的进步。

阿拉伯世界若具有这种渴望自由的民族意志，则足以团结一致，摆脱对他国的依附。凭借民族意志的凝聚力，阿拉伯国家能够共同参与、共同制定民族进步与民族复兴的战略，不论这种合作以何种方式开展、能够达到何种程度，哪怕最初的合作只是从某些阿拉伯国家开始，而并非整个阿拉伯世界的大联盟。除了自由的民族意志，还需要自觉而持续的文明领导力，这种领导力的性质如何、形式如何都不重要，只要不追求乌托邦便可。如果满足了上述两个条件，是否会有国家愿意帮助阿拉伯国家开展“文明追随”的战略呢？

事实上，很少有国家愿意这样做，其中的原因是多方面的。这里需要强调的是，西方国家仅仅希望从阿拉伯世界获取资源，并不愿意为阿拉伯世界的发展和进步提供支持，因为此举无利可图。因此，阿拉伯世界应该寄希望于逐渐强大的中国，与中国一道寻求复兴之路，阿拉伯国家既能发展自身文明，又能凭借自身发展为中国提供支持。

中国之所以成为阿拉伯世界实施“文明追随”的首选对象，不仅因为中国的文明复兴取得了显著的成果，更因为中国将会对世界政治产生巨大的影响力。在世界舞台上，阿拉伯文明原本具有取代西方文明的潜力，至少有能力与之竞争，但西方国家操控下的全球格局却造成了阿拉伯文明衰落。

中国能够帮助阿拉伯人民从外部压力造成的束缚中解脱出来，使之摆脱被剥削压榨的困境，在双方互利合作的基础上，实现现代阿拉伯文明的繁荣复兴。值得指出的是，中国的发展前景无可限量，这会吸引全世界的国家，包括阿拉伯国家，不断向其靠拢。在这样的背景下，阿拉伯世界应尽早投入到“合作机遇”的竞争之中。

综上所述，“文明追随”这一理念可以总结为“寻求复兴的落后民族在具备坚定的民族意志、自觉、忠诚、前瞻的领导力之后，渴望与发达国家建立以下两方面的紧密关系”：

1. 先进民族应捍卫落后民族的利益，满足其迫切需求，为其提供保护，使之免于外界的压力和干涉，为其民族复兴计划的实施创造适宜的环境。

2. 先进民族应向落后民族给予帮助，对于落后民族凭借自身能力暂时无法发现、理解或创造的物质文明成果，先进民族应给予支持，加快落后民族实施复兴计划的步伐。通过弥合国家之间的发展鸿沟，先进民族将从双方合作中受益。

当然，目前为止仍有以下几个问题需要探讨：

“追随”中国的前提条件

经贸合作是世界各国与中国建立紧密联系的关键，而中国发展对外关系是以国家利益为出发点，而并非套用教条的原则。

考虑到中国的对外关系，若想以中国为对象开展“文明追随”，则必须要关注两条路径：

第一，要认识到——为中国经济发展提供支持、特别是石油供给的重要性。随着中国的经济发展，其石油需求必然增长。2004 年，中国超越日本成为仅次于美国的世界第二大石油消费国。2014 年，全球石油消耗总量为四十六亿三千万吨，其中美国消耗占九亿六千七百万吨，中国占五亿两千一百万吨，日本占两亿一千五百万吨。由此可见，中国对自然资源的需求正不断增长，而当前中国的石油储备及石油产生率无法满足这一需求。据统计，中国目前的石油消耗正以每年 7% 的比率增长，相比之下，石油生产的年增长比率仅为 2%。因此，为保持经济增长，中国必然要进口大量石油。2014 年，中国进口汽油占全国汽油总量的 59.5%。[2] 从能源安全角度出发，中国必然紧密关注与石油生产国之间的关系。一方面，中国的石油企业会采用先进技术开发国内的潜在油田，但另一方面，中国会出台相关政策，鼓励海外石油业投资，特别是在中东及非洲地区的投资。除石油外，中国还需近一步吸引投资和先进技术，从而确保经济的稳定发展。改革开放三十年以来，中国在外资利用方面，实现了由“量”到“质”的转变。在 2007 年中国国务院发布的《外商投资产业指导目录》中，对于国家鼓励投资的产业和国家限制、禁止进行投资的产业进做出了明确规定。《目录》规定，中国的国家经济安全一部分是由战略性产业和敏感性产业构成，因而在管理中既要做到开放，又要做到小心谨慎。中国在对国内发展和对外开放进行布局和规划的同时，政策上会进行适当的调整。鼓励外商投资会促使制造业扩展到新技术、新设备制造等非传统产业，但传统制造业中生产率较高的国内企业即便没有外商投资也能够接触到先进技术。针对贸易顺差过大、外汇储备迅速增加等形势，中国对单纯鼓励出口的导向政策进行了调整，不再单纯鼓励出口。对于中国稀缺或不可再生的重要矿产资源不再鼓励外商投资。对于不可再生的重要矿产资源不再允许外商投资勘察开采，限制或禁止高物耗、高能耗、高污染外资项目准入。尽管出台了种种限制政策，大量外次仍然不断涌入。2015 年，中国吸引外资总额一千二百九十亿，位居世界第一。

第二，满足中国在世界各个地区、特别是在发展中国家扩大政治影响力的需要。中国在扩大政治影响力时，往往会从已经建立历史友好关系的国家开始，其中便包括阿拉伯国家，然后在和平共处、互谅互助的基础上将双方的紧密关系保持下去。20 世纪 90 年代以来，中国的防御型外交政策正在发生改变，中国正根据实际需求积极扩大在世界各地的政治影响力。由于中国的繁荣发展需要一个和平稳定的周边环境和商品出口市场，因此，东南亚国家作为中国的邻邦，在中国的外交格局中占有突出的地位。中国与泰国、菲律宾、孟加拉国、柬埔寨、老挝等东南亚国家的友好关系，有助于限制日本的影响力、赢得在台湾问题上的支持，并遏制美国在亚太地区的势力。值得指出的是，对于苏联与委内瑞拉等与美国关系紧张的国家，中国同样加强了彼此间的联系，这些国家在石油出口和自然资源出口方面拥有极大的潜力，能够为中国带来直接利益。中国此举并非针对美国，相反，中国尽量避免与美国发生冲突，特别是在地理上与中国相隔较远的国家和地区。中国既与美国的盟友发展关系，也与反美国家发展关系，这正是中国全方位外交政策的体现。此外，中国与本地区以外国家的关系并非仅仅着眼于军事问题和安全问题，一般以相互访问和人员培训等内容为主。然而，中国与邻国的军事合作却极为紧密，特别是与俄罗斯的合作。自俄罗斯独立以来，中国一直是该国最大的武器采购商。此外，中国与上海合作组织的成员国也保持着紧密的合作，尽管该组织只是一个区域性而非世界性的国际组织，但它却显示出中国扩大自身影响力的雄心壮志。当然，正如《中国的和平发展道路》白皮书中所说，中国不和任何国家、国家集团结盟，始终和平共处五项原则，互相尊重主权和领土完整，始终坚持走和平发展的道路。

中国主要通过以下三个基本途径来加强对外关系：

经济方面：通过兴建投资项目、无偿援助、贷款等形式提供经济援助。从统计数据上来看，中国直接对外投资额已经从 2002 年的 27 亿美元增长至 2014 年的 1231.2 亿美元[4]，这些投资主要集中在金融、材料及石油等领域。此外，中国已经同多个国家签署自由贸易协定、双边贸易协定以及区域贸易协定。

政治方面：通过签署双边合作协议、加入区域组织、全球组织、国际组织来增强与各国之间的关系、促进相互交流、构建相互信任。

文化方面：文化是最具活力的一条路径。中国向多国青年提供政府奖学金、在全世界范围内设立孔子学院，开办文化节、艺术展，同时通过中国国际广播电台、新华社、中央电视台、《今日中国》等国际媒体、刊物，使用多种语言，甚至包括阿拉伯语，来讲述中国故事。中国的文化影响力正不断扩大，这点可以在来华留学生的数量上得到体现。在中国各大学学习的留学生数量已经从 20 世纪 80 年代末的 8000 人左右增长至 2012 年的 32 万人。

很显然，中国发展对外关系不只是为了满足经济需求。从这点可以看出，中国需在各世界各国的人民中间，特别是那些希望与中国建立紧密联系的国家中，树立良好的国家形象，为维护自身国家利营造良好的氛围与环境，最终实现国家统一、扩大在世界范围内的影响力。

阿拉伯国家需要考虑的因素

中国对于阿拉伯世界的需求主要体现在三方面：石油、投资、政治支持。虽然在经贸方面，中国每年都会向阿拉伯世界出口大量的商品，但与其他地区相比，阿拉伯世界在这个方面，并没有让中国取得实质性的优势，双方的贸易方式也并无任何独特之处。事实上，世界上很多国家或地区在中国的对外贸易格局中占据更重要的战略地位，比如美国、欧洲等地，这些国家和地区的人口相对较多、生活水平较高、消费能力更强，因而市场也更为广阔。　石油方面：阿拉伯世界占有全世界石油总储量的 57.5%，其中沙特阿拉伯的石油储量位居第一，伊拉克位居第三，科威特位居第四，阿拉伯联合酋长国位居第四，非阿拉伯国家伊朗位居第二。需要强调的是，此处统计的石油储量，并不包括大量的油砂在内。油砂实质上是沥青、沙、高质黏土和水的混合物，但由于生产成本较高、萃取程序复杂，油砂目前尚未被列入石油总储量之中。21 世纪初以来，由于石油淬炼技术的发展，油砂得以在大范围内进行开采，这将为经济带来极大的利益。目前，阿拉伯产油国的石油产量约占世界石油总产量的 30%，其中沙特阿拉伯在这一份额中占 42%，阿联酋和科威特各占 11% 左右。除石油资源外，阿拉伯国家还蕴藏着丰富的天然气资源，天然气储量占世界总储量的 29%。需要指出的是，对于产油国而言，提取微量石油的能力如何，其重要性并不低于石油储量。长期以来，阿拉伯国家一直依赖拥有先进勘探技术和开采技术的国外企业开发本国石油资源。尽管自 20 世纪 70 年代以来，阿拉伯世界各国均各自成立了从事石油勘探、开发、开采业务的企业，但核心技术始终掌握在美国、欧洲及日本等国的大企业的手中。阿拉伯石油企业无法接触到此类先进技术，更无法通过从国外企业手中购买设备和技术的方式来发展本国石油业。2008 年石油价格飙升（每桶价格在 100—150 美元之间）后，针对阿拉伯石油出口国的对外投资大幅增加，当地也出现不少私人石油公司，其中包括阿联酋的 18 家，科威特 10 家，巴林 8 家，沙特阿拉伯 6 家，卡塔尔 1 家。这些新成立的私人石油公司均从事油田的勘探及开发业务，但均无一例外地使用着国外的技术。

投资方面：一些阿拉伯国家主要倚靠石油出口带来的丰厚收益，主权财富大幅增加时，政府负责对主权财富基金进行管控，对基金的规模进行限制。这些阿拉伯国家与其他地区一样，因政府体制原因，需要大量投资。尽管阿拉伯世界并不缺乏财力雄厚、极具影响力的投资者，但这些投资者大多在海外进行投资。阿拉伯世界对外投资者的数量大约为 20 万，其中 27% 来自沙特阿拉伯，28% 来自阿联酋，17% 来自科威特。尽管阿拉伯国家对外投资的详细数据尚不清楚，但据相关机构估算，截至 2002 年，阿拉伯国家对外投资总额便已达到 1 万亿至 3 万亿美元，而到 2015 年时，这一数字已经达到 14 万亿美元，[5] 其中 70% 左右投向美国，其余较小的份额则主要集中在欧洲、东南亚等地区的国家。需要说明的是，由于阿拉伯国家的技术创新能力薄弱，其海外投资并没有像中国一样，流入高新技术产业、设备制造等行业，而是流向了证券、股票、房地产等领域。尽管如此，阿拉伯国家仍然可以利用官方和民间的准备金，为开展大规模对华投资提供支持，投资的导向和质量可以由中阿双方企业联合管控。简言之，通过投资，中阿双方能够为彼此创造盈利的条件。以 2011 年为例，据阿拉伯货币基金组织统计数据显示，阿拉伯国家石油收入占财政总收入的 70%，部分国家甚至超过了 90%。

政治支持：目前，阿拉伯世界在文明的各个层面均相对落后，这也导致了阿拉伯世界在世界政治格局中地位较低的局面。不过，阿拉伯世界凭借其国家数量上的优势，在国际组织，特别是联合国中占据着举足轻重的地位。在中阿关系方面，阿拉伯国家的政治价值在于——作为一个政治团体，阿拉伯国家与中国建立紧密联系的能力如何，能够在国际组织的外交活动中为中国提供政治支持。如果阿拉伯世界想要实施“文明追随”，则各国必须作为阿拉伯国家联盟的一个独立实体进行运作，相互沟通协调，不能各自采取不同的外交政策。这一点是不容忽视的。此外，一个国家或地区在世界政治中的作用往往与其军事实力密切相关，而阿拉伯国家军事实力的薄弱，极大地限制了其自身的政治影响力。总之，阿拉伯世界能够为包括中国在内的世界其他国家提供的政治支持还很有限，受到很多因素的影响。

综上所述，阿拉伯世界若想与中国建立紧密关系、对中国实现文明追随，其关键在于尽快形成统一的行动计划，把中心放到经济合作、特别是能源合作为上。至于政治方面，阿拉伯国家能够发挥的作用还十分有限。

阿拉伯国家、中国以及未来

目前，中国发展势头良好，与阿拉伯世界的关系前景光明，自进入21世纪以来，中阿关系不论在官方还是民间层面，都已经取得了显著的成就。随着经济实力的提升，中国在国际社会的影响力与日俱增。尽管阿拉伯国家的出发点有所不同，但都无一例外地对中国的号召予以积极的回应。

有些人希望中国强大的国力能与当今世界唯一的超级大国——美国的势力形成平衡，从而减少美国对阿拉伯世界，特别是对巴勒斯坦问题上造成的伤害；而有些人则意识到，中国的外交政策更加务实，其出发点是保护国家利益，避免与其他大国之间发生紧张局面，如此才能确保发展以及互利合作，特别是经济合作；还有些人认为，中国与阿拉伯国家向来关系友好，因而从情感角度来讲，更加尊重中国的崛起。当西方媒体恶意中伤中国，对中国的人权问题、产品质量问题等大肆炒作时，许多阿拉伯人感到深恶痛绝，认为中国与阿拉伯国家正面临着相似的境遇，因此理应与中国站在一起，共同应对西方国家。

从中阿关系的发展现历程中可以看出，未来中阿关系可以在以下领域实现更大的发展：

经贸、投资及石油

（1）经贸方面

阿拉伯国家作为一个整体已经成为中国第七大贸易伙伴，而中国则是阿拉伯国家的第二大贸易伙伴。近年来，中阿经贸关系发展迅速，2006年双方贸易额已达到655亿美元。阿拉伯国家对华出口额达到340亿美元，中国对阿出口达到320亿美元，到2011年，两国经贸总额增长至1959亿美元，2012年增长至2224亿美元，2014年增长至2510亿美元。[6]需要指出的是，阿拉伯国家每年从中国进口的商品大多为纺织品、机电产品和电子产品，而阿拉伯国家对华出口的商品则以石油为主，石油已经成为维系中阿经贸关系平衡的关键因素。尽管自进入21世纪以来，中阿经贸关系发展迅速，但与中国高达3.6万亿美元的贸易总额相比，中阿贸易份额仍然较低。自2000以来，中阿贸易值在中国贸易总额中所占份额一直保持着平稳态势，这主要是因为中国积极扩展全球贸易的结果，阿拉伯国家对中国贸易总额的贡献仍然十分微薄。中国的贸易伙伴，如阿联酋、沙特阿拉伯、阿曼、苏丹及也门等国，与中国的经贸往来主要集中在对华石油出口或吸引中国企业参与石油勘探两个方面。尽管如此，中阿经济存在较强的互补性，中阿贸易还有十分巨大的潜力可以挖掘。

（2）投资方面

进入21世纪以来，中国对阿拉伯国家的投资迅速增长，截止到2010年，中国在阿投资总额累计达到150亿美元，这些投资主要集中在轻工、建筑、石油勘探等领域，但在同一时期内，各国对阿投资的总额为680亿美元，相比之下，中国对阿投资规模较小。与此同时，阿拉伯国家对中国的投资规模更小，2010年累计数字仅仅为25.8亿美元。然而，中阿双方在加强相互投资方面还存在巨大的发展空间，因为双方都拥有大量资本需要投资到海外。2010年，中国非金融类对外直接投资额为601亿美元，而股票投资却高达3000亿美元。与此同时，阿拉伯国家对美国、欧洲的投资额超过1万亿美元。这说明，相互投资可以作为加强中阿关系的一条重要途径。

（3）石油方面

中国的石油储量正日益减少，这便要求中国提高对阿石油进口量。统计数据显示，2010年，中国对进口石油的依赖超度过55%，在高达2400万吨的石油进口总额中，半数石油来自中东地区。近年来，中国能源消费每年都保持着两位数的增长速度，中国石油进口总量的70%均来自中东地区。在这一背景下，中国希望与沙特阿拉伯、阿联酋、苏丹以及也门等国继续开展大规模的石油勘探开发合作，从而在政治、经贸、投资等三个方面建立紧密联系。如此一来，中国可以提高在阿地区石油项目的直接对外投资额，与科威特等产油国的石油企业、石化企业合作，组建合资企业。与此同时，中国也可以利用阿拉伯国家提供的优惠贷款，参与港口建设、公路建设等各类基础设施工程。上述措施能够确保中国与阿拉伯国家之间建立紧密的联系。目前，中国主要从沙特、安哥拉、伊朗、阿曼、俄罗斯、苏丹、委内瑞拉、哈萨克斯坦、利比亚以及刚果等国进口石油，其中只有四国属于阿拉伯世界。鉴于阿拉伯国家巨大的石油储量以及中国日益增长的石油需求，阿拉伯国家与中国在石油领域的合作前景十分广阔。

政治和文化领域

1955年万隆会议后，阿拉伯国家与新中国的外交关系发展一直较为平稳。

1956 年，中国最早与埃及、叙利亚、也门三国建交，随后与其他阿拉伯国家也开启了外交关系。1990 年，中国最终与沙特阿拉伯确立外交关系，这标志着中国与阿盟 22 个成员国全部确立外交关系。值得注意的是，近年来中阿友好关系发展迅速，双方在能源资源和经济贸易等领域不断开展合作，但与中欧、中美关系相比，中阿间的高层对话尚且有待加强，中国领导人与阿拉伯国家领导人之间的正式会晤多局限于合作协议的签订和伙伴关系的建立，比如 2004 年中国与阿盟共同举办的中阿合作论坛等。尽管这增强了双方在政府和民间各个领域内的公开互动和交流，但重点仍然局限于经贸合作和投资合作。而且还有一点不容忽视的是：尽管在目前中阿关系框架下，双方已经连续举办了四届“中阿友好大会”和五届“中阿关系暨中阿文明对话研讨会”，中阿双方的专家学者和各界精英也对国际政治互动、文明间的互动等话题进行了探讨，并掀起了一场思想风潮，但目前为止，还缺少实质性的重要成果。长期以来，中阿关系的“精英化”特点也体现在双方的文化交流上。近年来，教育成为中阿双方加强民间交流的突破口，越来越多的阿拉伯学生来到中国求学。统计数据显示，在 2003 年，中国国内的阿拉伯留学生数量大约在 300 人左右，而到 2015 年，这一数字则增长至 14000 人。[7] 此外，中国不仅在国内多个高校开设了阿拉伯语院系，加强人才储备和对阿拉伯世界的研究，还在埃及、突尼斯等地开设了孔子学院，向阿拉伯民众传授汉语和中国文化。然而，从中阿书籍互译的角度来看，双方的合作仍有待扩展。尽管双方政府签署了多项出版协议，但实际付诸行动的项目却十分有限，双方精英阶层的文化交流也因此受到了限制。信息革命正在把世界变成一个地球村，然而无论在信息革命之前还是之后，中国与阿拉伯世界在彼此民众的眼中似乎都更像是一个遥远而未知的世界。中阿之间缺乏文化交流，这里面既有语言差异的原因，也有西方国家对阿拉伯世界进行文化控制的因素，因此阿拉伯文化很少在其他国家留下印记。由于中阿双方在文化上存在一定距离，两国民众往往只能通过西方媒体这一影响力较大的第三方媒介进行相互了解、实现相互理解。随着中阿在各个领域内的合作日益加强，未来中阿文化交流方面存在极大的发展空间，双方应努力推动文化交流，增进双方人民之间的相互理解。

阿拉伯世界的“文明追随”为何望向中国

“文明追随”的根本目的是推动自身社会的进步，因此，阿拉伯世界的出发点是寻求自身文明的全面发展，而非仅仅建立“非经济”合作关系，而中国恰恰是建立这种紧密关系的绝佳对象，尽管目前中阿关系的中心仍然停留在经济层面。需要指出的是，能否建立“文明追随”关系的决定权在于中阿双方。一方面，中阿建立这种关系必须符合中国的国家利益，特别是在保障石油供应和产品出口两个方面。另一方面，阿拉伯国家必须在与中国建立经济关系的同时，考虑到阿拉伯文明的复兴计划，争取开展中阿之间的全方位合作。在寻求构建“文明追随”关系的过程中，阿拉伯国家首先必须能够掌控自然资源，能够独自制定经济政策，这也是把握未来中阿关系的根本所在。高效发展和创建发达文明像是硬币的正反两面，前者是基础，后者创造条件。在此基础上，阿拉伯世界所寻求的“文明追随”必须同时能够给中国带来利益。如果中国在未来需要石油进口，阿拉伯国家可以列出自身尚未掌握的先进技术，邀请中国共同开发，如此一来，便能够推动内部发展、进步、创新，迅速缩小与发达国家的差距。阿拉伯国家需要勘探和采油技术，此类技术能够提高对本国自然资源的掌控能力。当然，如果摆脱对他国的依赖、自主开发石油，这意味着阿拉伯国家必须从根本上实现独立，而且要能够抵挡海外国家的压力。在国际角逐的赛场上，阿拉伯国家在政治上需要中国的支持，只有得到中国的支持，阿拉伯国家的政治态势才能有所转变，才能开启发展进程。如果向强权霸权屈服，阿拉伯民众的利益便会遭到伤害。这也是向世界的新兴大国——中国寻求支持的根本出发点。这不仅有助于解决阿拉伯世界面临的种种难题，更有助于营造公平的氛围，有助于阿拉伯世界摆脱外界压力，在更加宽松的环境下开启自身的发展进程。此外，国际地位的全面提高对于阿拉伯文明而言也是一次伟大的飞跃。加强各领域的交流合作、实现民族复兴是中阿双方共同追求的梦想，不过从目前状况来看，这种追求尚未取得实质性的成果，目前仍然只是一种美好的愿景。阿拉伯国家和中国都没有做好十足的准备。中国已经取得了重大的发展成就，但在工业上，中国虽然致力于引进欧美国家的前沿项目，但仍然无法接触到其中敏感、先进的技术。尽管中国的科技成就引发世界瞩目，尽管中国拥有很多大规模企业，但目前为止仍然缺乏能够享誉全球的世界级品牌。虽然近年来中国的经济发展十分迅速、民众的生活水平有了显著的提高，但仍面临着1亿人口的贫困问题。目前为止，中国还未能在国际政治事务上发挥全部实力和影响力，也正是为此，作为联合国安理会常任理事国之一，中国在大量敏感问题上、甚至是涉及国家利益的敏感问题上，从未行使过否决权，而且在某种程度上为美国提供了支持。当然，这符合中国“韬光养晦、有所作为”的务实外交政策。中国已经开始着手解决在全面复兴道路上遇到的种种问题。在科技领域，改革开放后，中国不断鼓励发明创造，并于 1980 年设立国家专利局，1985 年颁布专利法。在这个背景下，中国的专利数量迅猛增长，截至 2004 年，中国的专利总数已经超过 125 万，其中 87% 的专利持有者为中国人，13% 为外国人；2007 年，中国专利数量增长至 208 万，其中 17% 为发明创造，47.3% 属于实用新型，25.3% 为设计专利。据联合国世界知识产权组织发布的数据显示，2007 年中国已经成为仅次于美日的世界第三大专利申请国，2012 年已经赶超日本，专利申请数量达到 40000。中国在技术方面的不足主要在于缺少通用技术领域的发明创造，如发动机和网络技术等能够在全世界范围内广泛运用、并足以成为人类发展标志的重大发明。文明追随于中国是一个未来的愿景，其条件尚未成熟，在各自的有限条件下，尚无法全面开启文明追随的历程。

因此，当我们回答“为什么选择中国？”这个问题时，必须考虑到以下三个因素：

第一，阿拉伯国家尚未做好准备。阿拉伯人民期待着开启“文明追随”的进程，但首先应团结一致，实现独立发展，为文明复兴制定统一的行动方案。开启“文明”追随进程不仅需要极富远见、坚定且锲而不舍的领导力，同时需要借鉴中国的“特色”发展模式，如此才能在实施行动方案的过程中，针对失误随时进行调整，在出现问题时，及时找到解决方案。

第二，中阿友好合作关系为开启“文明追随”奠定了现实基础。自古以来，中国和阿拉伯世界都保持着友好交流，如今更在一系列政治问题上拥有共同的追求，这无疑能够加强双方的合作关系。例如，中阿双方均反对冷战后美国推行的霸权主义，双方在经济、能源资源能领域的互补性强，且中阿友好关系的不断发展为双方带来了机遇。

第三：对于阿拉伯国家的“文明追随”，中国尚未做好准备。正如前文所述，目前中国掌握的先进技术尚不足以满足阿拉伯文明复兴的需要，但却能够对国际政治产生足够影响。但是，从中国的经济数据和中国制定的未来发展规划中可以看出，中国必然会在 21 世纪的某一历史时刻做好准备。在此期间，阿拉伯人民会争取做好准备。尽管与中国建立“文明追随”关系并非易事，但这个千载难逢的机会是不容错过的。如果阿拉伯人不够努力，中国又有什么理由去帮助他们呢？

从"特色"发展到"文明追随"

在整个殖民时代，西方国家不断对阿拉伯世界的现代化进程和民族复兴大业进行阻挠，极尽肇事之能事，最终导致阿拉伯国家愈发落后。为了实现这一企图，西方国家或开动国家机器进行直接干预，或对阿拉伯国家进行内部渗透，扶植独裁势力，对阿盟进行挑唆分化，特别是引发周边国家对于色列的强烈偏见，这一切都对阿拉伯文化复兴造成了极为消极的影响。西方国家对于第三世界的剥削从未停止，特别是处心积虑、妄图使阿拉伯世界依附于彼。对于西方国家而言，推行帝国主义政策是再自然不过的事情：阿拉伯国家拥有丰富的石油储量，占据着重要的地理位置，这些都与西方国家的国家利益息息相关。当然，不能够将阿拉伯文明面临的危机全部归咎于外部因素，但外部因素的确是导致阿拉伯国家落后的根本原因，这一点已经是公认的事实，尽管文化因素也在其中扮演了重要的角色。即便如此，需要强调的是，各种外部因素，特别是殖民主义，已经给阿拉伯国家带来了灾难性的后果。如今，殖民主义的余毒尚存，而阿拉伯国家也始终在两条道路前徘徊不定：要么倒退回过去，要么走西方国家的道路。这也是造成阿拉伯复兴缓慢的最重要的原因。冷战之后，西方发展模式似乎偏重于"促进人类社会进步"、"由人类决定其最终命运"，作为世界上唯一的超级大国，美国控制着国际政治，极大地影响着全球的文化、科学、技术。美国企图凭借全球化（或资本全球化）推行西方的自由经济、社会发展模式以及生活方式。在此背景下，阿拉伯国家的思想界出现了两种声音：

第一："复古模式"。持此种观点者，大多沉浸在历史的辉煌之中，坚信通过走历史发展的老路能够医治阿拉伯世界的诸般疾症。这一主张在殖民时代早期便已出现，是对阿拉伯国家衰落而做出的极其情绪化的回应，认为复古更加符合历史的发展规律，能够增加解决问题的概率。这种主张背后的逻辑仅仅是复制过去的社会制度、政治体制、思想体系，但却没有考虑到，古代模式仅仅适用于古代的人类行为、生活方式以及语言使用。

第二，仿照美国模式。自冷战后，美国鼓吹自由主义是实现人民、政府、经济现代化最有力、也最可行的途径，宣称西方国家的发展路线可以解决一切难题，能够帮助阿拉伯国家达到西方国家的发展水平。必须指出的是，照搬美国模式已经成为一种世界范围内的普遍现象，对此，阿拉伯国家并不感到陌生。美国处处插手国际政治，特别是巴勒斯坦地区问题，这给阿拉伯国家民众造成了严重的伤害。但阿拉伯国家并没有放弃寻找解决问题的途径。美国模式与其自身的政治体制、经济体制、社会体制紧密匹配，但不应推广到国际政治中来。但思想界的一些人士不仅主张照搬美国模式，甚至认为应把美国模式作为“阿拉伯国家现代化思想指南”来信奉受行。

必须强调的一点是，上述两种主张并非阿拉伯世界所独有，而阿拉伯世界也并非仅仅存在这两种声音，只是相比之下，这两种主张的影响力更大。面对思想界如此大相径庭的分歧，关键问题在于：我们应该选择哪一条路？复古，还是仿照美国模式？事实上，以上两条道路都与19世纪上半叶的阿拉伯文明复兴毫无共同之处，只不过从客观角度来看，这两条路更加可行，更适合作为复兴的开端。

若西方国家将阿拉伯世界视作殖民地，阿拉伯民众却仍然选择美国模式，那么阿拉伯文明会在两个方面受到严重影响。从当前状况来看，阿拉伯世界实现复兴的机会十分渺茫，因为帝国主义国家仍然对阿拉伯地区抱有强烈的兴趣，不会轻易放弃，至少在21世纪上半叶不会放弃。尽管西方文明取得了伟大的成就，值得研究学习，但西方模式不能给阿拉伯人民带来帮助，也无法为阿拉伯文明复兴创造环境。阿拉伯国家实现独立的时间并不长，如果西方国家继续掠夺其自然资源，实现复兴大业的可能几乎为零。

通过西方模式实现复兴面临着重重困难。之前，阿拉伯思想界一直以西方为典范，从西方寻求改革和现代化的理念。然而，历史证明走西方路线对阿拉伯人民没有任何好处。尽管西方国家已经取得了重大进步，但殖民主义势力早就在阿拉伯世界买下了深重的祸根，使阿拉伯世界陷入了恶性循环。

在西方道路陷入困境时，东方国家却实现了发展，特别是东亚国家。她们的崛起值得阿拉伯国家学习。20世纪中期之前，东亚与阿拉伯一样，都曾遭受殖民主义的影响、受到西方国家的剥削，在发展水平上存在着诸多共性。因此，紧密关注东方国家的发展对阿拉伯国家而言，具有重大意义，能够帮助阿拉伯国家了解东亚国家，特别是中国之所以崛起的原因。

中国改革开放最显著的特点在于其“中国特色”，这一政策使得中国城乡社会在短期内发生巨大变化，因此，中国“特色”发展的成功经验值得阿拉伯人学习和借鉴。

如果阿拉伯世界在20世纪40年代提出经济一体化思想之初，通过努力实现了独立发展，那么阿拉伯人就能够在20世纪90年代更好的应对全球化，并像中国一样，利用全球化带来的机遇实现复兴，凭借经济改革成果成跻身世界大国之林。

遗憾的是，在过去的几十年中，阿拉伯人并没有做到这一点。但中国的特色发展经验能够帮助阿拉伯人摆脱依赖、实现发展。

阿拉伯人需要满足两个条件：第一，实现经济一体化；第二，提高对自然资源的控制能力。若无法满足这两个条件，阿拉伯人则无法利用本国资源，而本国资源的利用则是阿拉伯世界复兴和发展的根本所在。

中国为世界提供的“特色”发展经验并非适用于所有发展中国家，特别是那些在面积、人口、地理位置、资源、社会融合度等方面与中国国情相距甚远的国家。然而，可以肯定的是，中国的发展经验可以为阿拉伯人提供参照。不过，尽管阿拉伯世界与中国在资源方面存在诸多共性，阿拉伯国家却缺乏可行的计划或方案。

我们时常听到有关阿拉伯世界与欧洲的比较。阿盟成立后，阿拉伯世界在经济一体化方面，具备了追赶欧洲的条件。欧洲的经济体化进程始于1951年，比利时、法国、联邦德国、意大利、卢森堡和荷兰六国共同签署建立了欧洲煤钢共同体条约，1957年欧洲共同市场宣布成立，1991年欧盟宣告成立。尽管欧盟国家内部分歧不断，但欧盟一直在阶段性地发展壮大。

阿拉伯国家与欧盟之间存在着许多共同点，经济一体化的实现，将有助于阿拉伯各国在达成一致的基础上，促进文明进步、实现共同发展。然而由于政治分歧、贫富分化等原因，阿拉伯世界一直未能出台具体的行动方案。

综上所述，中国的经验、特色发展有助于“文明追随”关系的建立，有助于阿拉伯世界取得发展、实现民族复兴。19世纪上半叶，阿拉伯人开始寻求复兴之路，随后历经了帝国入侵、掀起抵抗殖民主义的运动。这条道路与中国务实的特色发展极为相似。当然，阿拉伯人从未放弃过阿拉伯文明复兴的理念。真理建立在行动的基础上，因此，阿拉伯国家若能向中国一样务实进取，用实干取代幻想，则一定能够实现文明复兴。

里发阿·拉斐阿·塔哈塔维是阿拉伯复兴事业的启蒙思想家，他的哲学思想与中国领导人邓小平的哲学思想存在相似之处。塔哈塔目睹了法国社会与政治的发展，认为其发展方式有利于伊斯兰世界实现文明与进步，值得重视和借鉴，并主张效仿其中不违背伊斯兰教义的成功经验。这些思想有助于民族复兴，法国的经验将在适合阿拉伯国家国情和文化的方面带来巨大的变化。这与邓小平现实、务实的思想是一致的。邓小平承认西方资本主义经济取得的成就，并以之为鉴，选用其中适合中国发展的成分，最终摸索出一条适合中国国情的发展道路。不论何种经验、何种意识形态，是改变还是改革，最终目的永远是实现民族复兴。

中国已经向全世界证明，从国家利益出发的、务实的发展计划是中国取得成功的重要保障。

阿拉伯人之前的复兴之路已经抛弃了务实思想，正是思想上的局限导致了发展的失败。阿拉伯人应该从中国的经验中看到：伟大的民族复兴要求阿拉伯人重拾最初的务实思想，这一思想的核心在于务实求真，既要与民族复兴大业时刻保持一致，又要通过不断取得成就来振奋人心。阿拉伯世界渴望重振复兴事业，而中国为其提供的不仅仅是可供学习和借鉴的经验，更有未来的机遇，我们必须珍视并牢牢把握。

自拿破仑的军队攻克阿拉伯世界的大门以来，西方列强（英法美等国）便一直对阿拉伯世界进行着剥削和压迫。我们希望，中国作为世界大国，不会向西方国家一样对待阿拉伯世界，中国会与我们一道，为创造一个公平的国际环境而努力，双方携手，克服困难，最终消除阿拉伯国家发展道路上的障碍。

为此，我们要发展好同中国的关系。当然，这并不意味着谄媚，因为谄媚并非国家利益之所在。中阿双方开展紧密的经济合作，不仅能为双方带来财富，更能够实现更高意义上的战略利益。

我们需要从文明的视角出发，处理好同中国的关系，在互利共赢的基础上，实现我们在物质与非物质层面的文明复兴。

阿拉伯人渴望更加美好的未来，中国提供的种种机遇不容忽视。从中国的“特色”发展路线到“文明追随”，我们可以看到，与中国建立积极友好的关系是至关重要的。在友好关系的框架下，阿拉伯世界能够为中国实现中国梦做出贡献，也能够抓住机遇，让阿拉伯梦尽快变为现实。

Mutual Development between China and the Arab Countries

Samer Khair Ahmad Khrino / Jordan

Director of Cultural Affairs of the Municipality of Amman in Jordan

Introduction

China is proceeding to the future providing a new contemporary model for humanity. Therefore, building the civilization relations therewith would be so beneficial to humanity. Thus, many efforts are needed to be provided from arab countries, to make them closer to China and to introduce them to China's success and culture for better future to humanity everywhere.

the Arab countries can take advantage from the history of friendship with China going on for thousands of years; building on the initiative of the Chinese President Xi Jinping : "the Belt and Road" for the construction of a renewable space of robust civilization relations now and tomorrow between the Arabs and China.

the relationship between the Arabs and China could be addressed in two dimensions:

the first is the study of the Chinese contemporary success in progress being an important country of value and worldwide presence, to conclude lessons that are applicable to the Arab Countries highlighting the civilization success worldwide;

the second is how to build future relations between the Arabs and China in line with civilization relations based on the knowledge and economic integration not only on the transactions basis.

Arab people are to be concerned with the China's future simply because they trust that China will definitely achieve more successes during the coming years and decades. they give credit to the successes of China and its ability to undertake the sound planning and implementation as well as the materialization of more consecutive great successes that have portrayed an outstanding character before the whole world.

In order to achieve that, this research will propose a thesis entitled "Civilisational Repositioning" for the future relations between arab countries and china.

The "Civilisational Repositioning"

In the mid-18th century, the industrial revolution in England brought about one of the biggest turning points in human history. Along with material development came an unceasing accumulation of intellectual and spiritual wealth which divided the world in two by the start of the 21st century; the developed and the undeveloped world. The former's levels of state, society and individuality are all a direct result of the industrial revolution, and these advances had a tremendous impact on the history of human productivity. The latter has had no way of drawing on this experience, gaining autonomy for its destiny, influencing other nations or their people's productivity. Regrettably, the Arab World falls into the latter category.

The ten years following the Second World War were bright, and it was believed that realising a material civilisation and the creation of politics and society would result in 'optimum opportunities'. However, a crucial element which contributed to such industrial success in the later stages of this vast development was the military industry, in particular the production of non-traditional weapons. Finally, so as to open up and develop this vast space of communication and information technology, a foundation was safeguarded so as to ensure favourable conditions.

Some Asian countries have stepped on to the train of optimum opportunities, and have had far reaching and significant influences on the course of human development. China is an outstanding example of this, and already enjoys the strength of a major world power.

However, many countries have become uncertain about the notion of optimum opportunities for a number of reasons. Either it hasn't formulated an effective development strategy or strategic thought, leading to the state losing control of its sovereignty and of natural resources. The Arab World is in such a condition. It is at present unrealistic that Arab countries are in a position to advance, or at least liberated enough to start over. The late 19th until the mid-20th century was considered to have been a good period for Arab people.

There is an enormous disparity between the civilisations of the Arab World and the US. The US has various reasons for controlling and using the Arab people, such as fighting dissidents which has resulted in Arab people merely relying on their national power and resources. The US's powerful developmental momentum would like to diminish cultural disparities, as in Arabian Nights.

For lagging nations, a unique and viable approach would be to establish a 'community of interests' with developed countries which could facilitate mutually beneficial cooperation rather than purely expecting to benefit. Lagging nations have referenced the successes of advanced countries, and drawn upon their various fields of civilisation. Such a relationship would also be beneficial for the long term growth of advanced countries.

China has a similar history cooperating with advanced European countries like Germany and France, and there are examples which this chapter will expand upon.

China's developmental process has been contained and obstructed by the US, so China has steered toward attracting investment and advanced technology from European countries which have created enormous bilateral investment opportunities. China's 'technology import' has benefited its development, and actively encouraged new high-tech enterprises to invest into science and technology fields. This has enabled enormous progress allowing China to leap from the 'exploring and understanding' stages to conducting 'autonomous research'. We have found that when there is a massive disparity between countries in terms of politics, society and culture, establishing a 'community of interests' can create a means to communicate. The information revolution has further brought about the possibility for civilisations to converge.

However, we must also be aware that the term 'community of interests' is realistically suited to comparable countries. To serve lagging nations, we must firstly follow the road to advancing them, and implement the principle of 'civilisational repositioning'. Such a concept involves a follower wishing to develop into an equal partner. Describing civilisational repositioning as the aims or pursuit of common interests creates contradiction for the lagging country. Advanced nations will not help less developed nations, and less developed nations often cannot comply with the requests of developed nations thus leaving them powerless to resist the control, exploitation and lootings.

Before civilisational repositioning can even take place, establishing a national willpower is extremely important. Without it, any plan or scheme will fail to materialise, and blindly following a developed or developing country is also not wise. The reason China has spread its wings and attracted the world's attention is due to its free and steadfast national will. China is an independent and sovereign modernising country, and more than thirty years has passed since the Reform and Opening Up Policy. It has concerned itself with a practical exploration to achieving fitting national conditions and effective development projects which have resulted in notable humanitarian and material achievements.

A strong national will can transform into a workable plan with a long term vision, but cannot lack decisive leadership. In addition to drawing up and participating in a plan, or developing projects for a national revival, no effort can be spared during the implementation, supervision and evaluation of such schemes. Doing so would thoroughly resolve problems as they arise, and actively responded to unrelenting changes in global conditions. It could be said that it is on account of New China's powerful leadership that such enormous advances be realised, especially since opening up.

If the Arab World has the will to liberate itself, this solidarity would be enough to function independently from other countries. This will enable them to participate in formulating a scheme to improve and rejuvenate their nations. The form and degree of cooperation doesn't matter, even if it emerges in some countries initially rather than as a unified Arab utopia. Another possibility is to form a civilised leadership which is conscious and consistent. The nature and form of the leadership is unimportant as long as it isn't in pursuit of utopia. If this is the case, will any country help Arabic nations adopt civilisational repositioning?

In truth, many possible factors have led to why these countries are few and far between. What needs to be emphasised is that western countries only require resources from the Arab World, and are unwilling to support development and advancement in which they would not benefit. However, China is an emerging nation the Arab World ought to aim towards. By pursuing China's path to revival, the Arab World can advance their own civilisation, and also support China with their development.

The reason that China is a first choice for the Arab World's implementation of civilisational repositioning is that its revival has seen some outstanding results, and also because they will become extremely influential in world politics. The global structure controlled by western countries is the main reason the Arab civilisation has fallen behind, however they should be powerful enough to supersede the west on the world stage or at least contend with them.

China can help liberate Arab people currently being exploited by external pressures so that they create a flourishing modern Arab civilisation built on mutually beneficial cooperation. What is worth pointing out is that China's development has boundless prospects which will attract all countries of the world, among which are Arab, to be drawn closer. In this context, the Arab World should engage in this competition as early as possible.

In conclusion, the concept of 'civilisational repositioning' can be summed up as lagging nation's pursuit of revival prepared with an engaged national will, and a conscientious, loyal, and visionary leadership wishing to establish tight relations with other advanced nations in two aspects:

1. The advanced nation should defend the interest of the lagging nation, meet their active demands, protect them from the pressures and interferences of the outside world, and create an adaptive environment in which they can implement plans for a national revival.
2. Advanced nations can help lagging countries by providing them with the fruits of their material advancement that they are unable to discover, understand, or create for themselves. This will expedite the implementation of plans for a national revival. Advanced nations will also benefit from this cooperation as removing the development chasms between nations.

There are however questions that require response. Should China adopt the Arab countries as they undergo civilisational repositioning?

"Civilisational Repositioning" on China's Terms

Economic and trade cooperation with various countries across the world is the key to establishing tight relations with China, and developing foreign relations rather than applying dogmatic principles should be the main starting point and is in the nation's interest.

In view of China's foreign relations, there are two different paths to be aware of when undergoing civilizational repositioning:

Firstly, the importance of supporting China's economic development, especially with oil supply. As China's economy develops, their need for oil is going to increase. In 2004, China surpassed Japan to become the world's second largest consumer of oil following the US. In 2014, global consumption amounted to 4.63 billion metric tonnes of which the US consumed 967 million, followed by China with 521 million, and Japan with 215 million[(1)]. Thus, China's oil reserves and productivity cannot satisfy its growing demand for natural resources. Their consumption is growing annually at a rate of 7% compared with its annual production increase of 2%. Therefore, China must import large quantities of oil to ensure their economic development. In 2014, China imported 59.5% of its petrolium[(2)]. So as to safeguard energy security, China must play close attention to strengthening their relations with developing oil producing countries. Their oil enterprises should use advanced technology for potential domestic drilling, but also formulate policies for the future which will increase overseas investment in the oil industry, especially in the Middle East and Africa.

In addition to oil, China also needs to further attract investment and advanced technology so as to ensure its stable economic development. In the thirty years following the open door reforms, foreign investment has enabled China to make the transition from quantity to quality. In 2007, China's State Council issued the 'Catalogue of Industries for Guiding Foreign Investment' which listed the investment they wished to encourage as well as the investment they wished to restrict or prohibit. The catalogue stipulated that a portion of the state's economic security should be composed of strategic and sensitive industries which should be managed in both a cautious and open manner. Clauses can be adjusted as appropriate when planning domestic development and opening up to the outside world. Encouraging foreign investment will enable an expansion of the manufacturing industry into new technologies, equipment manufacturing and various other non-traditional industries. Meanwhile, some domestic companies with strong production capacities in traditional manufacturing industries were able to access advanced technology without foreign investment.

Adjustments were made to the orientation of the policy to simply encourage exports. Foreign exchange reserves increased rapidly aimed at dealing with the oversized trade surplus, so there was no longer any need to continue to encourage exports. China's scarce or important non-renewable mineral resources did not further encourage foreign investment. Some important non-renewable raw materials stopped allowing foreign investment for exploration and mining. They also either limited or prohibited the admittance of foreign investment projects which produced high material and energy consumption, or high levels of pollution. In spite of various limitations, a large amount of foreign investment continued to flow into China. In 2015, China's ability to attract foreign investment became the largest worldwide, amounted $129 billion.(3)

Secondly, so as to meet China's requirements in various regions in the world, especially in expanding political influence to developing countries. China's process of expanding political influence began with countries in which there had already been friendly exchanges through history, among which are Arab countries. It was then hoped that close relations could be established with China of peaceful coexistence, and mutual understanding and support. Since the 1990's, China's legacy of protective foreign policy underwent a process of change in accordance with practical needs to actively expand political influence across the world.

China's neighbours in Southeast Asia had established patterns of foreign exchange, and thus enjoyed a prominent position. China's development and prosperity requires peaceful and stable surroundings, and a commodity export market. Development with Southeast Asian countries including Thailand, the Philippines, Bengal, Cambodia, and Laos was also conducive to limiting Japans influence, winning over support with regards to Taiwan, and containing the US in the Asia-Pacific region. What is worth noting is that China also strengthened its contact with countries in which the US had tense relations, such as the Soviet Union and Venezuela. These countries generally had great potential for exporting oil and natural resources which would directly benefit China. These measures weren't aimed at opposing the US and were in fact aimed at avoiding a clash, especially for countries and regions which are geographically far away from China. China has developed friendly as well as opposing relations with the US, which embodies China's comprehensive foreign relations.

China's regional relations with foreign countries aren't focused on military and security, and generally more about reciprocal visits and personnel training. However, China's militarily cooperation with these neighbouring countries is extremely tight, especially Russia from whom China has always been their largest buyer of arms since its independence. China and the SCO's members have also maintained close cooperation. Although this is a regional rather than global international organisation, it demonstrates China's ambitions to expand influence. Of course, just as the White Paper 'China's Road to Peaceful Development' points out, China cannot create a group alliance with any other country, as one of the main principles of the Five Principles of Peaceful Coexistence is state sovereignty, and an adherence to a peaceful development path.

China has used these three fundamental measures to strengthen foreign relations:

Economy: China provides economic aid in the form of non-reimbursable assistance, loans, and by establishing investment projects. Statistically, the scale of China's FDI has already grown from $2.7 billion in 2002 to $123.12 billion in 2014 [(4)], and is mainly focused on finance, minerals, and oil. In addition, China has signed free trade, bilateral trade and regional trade agreements with a number of countries.

Politics: Signing bilateral cooperative agreements and entering into regional or global international organisations has strengthened relations and interactions with various countries, as well as built up mutual trust.

Culture: Culture is the most dynamic path. China has offered the youth from other countries government scholarships, and established Confucius Institutes across the world which holds cultural festivals and art exhibitions. China also has various international media such as China Radio International, the Xinhua News Agency, China Central Television (CCTV), and China Today. They have also included an Arab language recording for their foreign audiences so as to narrate China's story. China's increased cultural influence can be attested for by the numbers of foreign students in China's many universities, which has risen from 8000 students in the late 1980's to 320,000 in 2012.

It is clear that China's aim to develop foreign relations has more than satisfied their economic requirements. It therefore needs people from across the world, especially those wishing to establish tight relations with China, to create a favourable national image. For this reason, China's national interests to protect itself has created a favourable atmosphere and environment, finally realising unity between countries and becoming an important influence on the world.

Factors for Arab People to take into Consideration

China's main requests of the Arab World are embodied in three aspects; oil, investment and political support.

Foreign trade: China exports a large amount of commodities to the Arab World, but the Arab World doesn't offer up any real advantage over other regions in the world in this regard, and the way in which they trade is nothing unique. In fact, there are many other countries of more strategic importance to China, for example the US and Europe with their larger populations and higher standards of living which make for a stronger consumer base and market.

Oil: The Arab World occupies 57.5% of the world's total oil reserves, among which Saudi Arabia is first, Iraq is third, Kuwait is fourth, United Arab Emirates is fifth, and the non-Arab country Iran coming second. What needs to be emphasised, is that when compiling statistics relating to Arab oil reserves, oil sands have not been accounted for although their reserves are enormous. Oil sands in essence are a compound of bitumen, sand, high grade clay and water. On account of its high production costs and complicated extraction, it has not been included in total oil reserves. Since the beginning of the 21st century, the development of oil extraction refining technology has enabled oil sands to be extracted on a large scale which would be extremely beneficial for the economy. At present, Arab oil producing countries amounts to 30% of the world’s total among which Saudi Arabia occupies 42% and the United Arab Emirates and Kuwait occupy around 11%.In addition to oil resources, Arab countries hold 29% of the world’s natural gas reserves.

What should be mentioned is that for oil producing countries, the importance of being able to extract the smallest amount should be worth no less than oil reserves. For quite some time, Arab states have relied on capital from foreign enterprises for advanced exploration and extraction technology. Since the 1970’s, Arab states have established enterprises to explore, develop, and exploited, but the main technology has always been in the hands of large enterprises from US, Europe and Japan. Arab oil companies cannot access such advanced technology and so have no choice to go through oil companies from other countries to purchases assets and technology as a means to developing their industries. Along with the 2008 soar in oil prices (when a barrel cost between \$100-\$150), investment in Arab oil exporting countries was plentiful, but many private oil companies also began to spring up; 18 in the United Arab Emirates, 10 in Kuwait, 8 in Bahrain, 6 in Saudi Arabia, and 1 in Qatar. These newly established privately owned companies were engaged in the exploration and development of oil fields and without exception used technology from overseas.

Investment: Some Arab states rely on the substantial earnings generated form oil exports, and their governments control their increasingly enormous sovereign wealth and scale of funds. The government systems of these various Arab countries as well as other regions all require enormous investment. In addition, the Arab World has a host of rich and powerful people whom hold large amounts of capital which they invest overseas. There are around 200,000 Arab investors occupied in overseas investment of which 27% are from Saudi Arabia, 28% are from United Arab Emirates, and 17% are from Kuwait. Although there isn't any detailed data relating to overseas Arab investment, a related organisation estimates that in 2002, total Arab foreign investment amounted to between $1 trillion and $3 trillion which had already reached about $14 trillion by 2015.(5) Around 70% of this investment has gone to the US, with residual amounts concentrated in European countries, and a small portion to Southeast Asian countries. What needs to be explained is given the weak technological and innovative capabilities of Arab countries, it is clear that foreign investment in Arab countries doesn't resemble China's investment into the high technology and equipment manufacturing industries. It instead flows into securities, stocks, and real estate. Even so, official and civil capital reserves can be used by Arab states to strengthen the enormous potential and capability for investment in China. Even the orientation and quality of investment can be controlled in cooperation with Chinese companies. In short, Chinese-Arab bilateral relations can create mutually profitable conditions through investment.

In 2011 for example, statistics from The Arab Monetary Fund (AMF) revealed that oil accounted for 70% of their total revenue and more than 90% in some countries.

Political Support: At present the Arab World is lagging in all fields of civilisation which has resulted in it holding a correspondingly weak position in world politics. However, the Arab World has taken advantage of its number of individual states and enjoys a decisive position in international organisations, especially the United Nations. With regards to Chinese-Arab relations, the political values of Arab people lies in the ability for Arab countries to act as a political group thus enabling them to establish tight relations with China, and support them politically (for instance with votes in elections) during diplomatic activities in international organisations. It cannot be disregarded that if the Arab World expects to implement civilizational repositioning, each country will need to apply different foreign policies if it cannot coordinate as a single entity as part of the League of Arab States. In addition, the impact of a country or region in world politics often goes hand in hand with their military power, thus the weak military power of Arab countries vastly limits its influence. In short, the Arab World has a limited ability to support China and other countries in the world, which will impact them in many ways.

In conclusion, in order to establish tight relations between China and the Arab World, the starting point for undertaking civilisational repositions should be to construct a unified action plan centred on economic cooperation in the field of energy. Politically, the Arab states individually exert relatively little influence.

The Arab Countries, China and the Future

China's momentum of development and prospects for relations with the Arab World are favourable, and have already made remarkable developments from official to civil capacities in the 21st century. With growing economic strength, China's impact on international society grows day by day. In spite of having different starting off points, the Arab people have all responded positively. Some people hope that China's strength is enough to create a world balance with the US, currently the only superpower, which would lessen damage caused by the US, especially with regards to Palestine. Some recognise that China's pragmatic diplomacy protects national interests and avoids tensions with other major nations so as to enable development and mutually beneficial cooperation, especially in terms of the economy. Others believe that China and Arab countries have always enjoyed friendly relations, and on an emotional level respect their rise to power. Many see how the western media viciously attacks China on issues such as human rights and product quality. These are detested, as they believe they face similar conditions, and thus should stand by China against Western countries.

Observing their development, the future of bilateral relations with enable further developments in the following fields:

1. Trade, Investment and Oil

Trade

If considered as a single entity, the Arab states are China's seventh largest trading partner, and the China is their second. In recent years, Chinese-Arab trade has developed rapidly, and amounted to $65.5 billion in 2006. The Arab States exports to China were worth $34 billion, and China's exports to Arab states were worth $32 billion. By 2011, this total figure had already reached $195.9 billion and rose again to $222.4 billion by 2012 and to $251 billion by 2014.[(6)] What needs to be mentioned is that every year, the majority of imports from China are textiles, mechanical and electrical products, whereas China mainly imports oil. Oil has been the key factor for holding together balanced Chinese-Arab trade relations. Although these developed rapidly in the 21st century, it pales into insignificance when compared with China's total foreign trade of $3.6 trillion. Since 2000, the value of Chinese-Arab trade as a portion of China's total trade has remained stable, which has mainly been a product of China's progressive policies in expanding global trade, with very little contribution from the Arab side. China's main Arab trading partners are United Arab Emirates, Saudi Arabia, Oman, Sudan, Yemen, which are engages in either exporting oil to China, or attracting Chinese industry for oil exploration. Even so, Chinese-Arab economic complementarity means that there is still a great deal of potential in terms of trade.

Investment

In the 21st century, China's investment in Arab states has grown rapidly. Until 2010, it had invested a total of $15 billion into Arab countries focused mainly on light industry, construction, and oil exploration. However, by 2010 there was $68 billion foreign investment alone. Meanwhile, the scale of Arab investment into China has also been minimal amounting to a total of $2.58 billion by 2010. Chinese-Arab mutual investment has strengthened but still has enormous capacity for development, as both have large amounts of capital to invest abroad. In 2010,

China's non-financial industry OFDI (outward foreign direct investment) reached $60.1 billion, and over $300 billion was invested in stock. Arab countries have invested over $1 trillion in the US and Europe which means that investment could be used as an important path for enhancing relations between Arab countries and China.

Oil

China's depleting oil reserves has resulted in them requiring increasing amounts of oil from Arab countries. According to statistics, in 2010 China's dependence on imported oil exceeded 55% with 240 million tonnes being imported, half of which was from the Middle East. In recent years, China's energy use has maintained double figure growth rates, more than 70% of its total oil is imported from the Middle East. In this context, China hopes that Arab countries Saudi Arabia and the United Arab Emirates in particular and also other oil producing countries such as Sudan will proceed with large scale oil exploration so that political, trade and investment relations can be established. Therefore, China could increase its FDI into oil projects in Arab states and shares in foreign oil companies, and form joint ventures with petrochemical companies in oil producing countries such as Kuwait. They could also use concessional loans provided by Arab countries to engage in various infrastructure projects such as building ports and roads. Such measures would establish intimate relations with Arab countries. At present, China imports oil (ranked in order) from Saudi Arabia, Angola, Iran, Oman, Russia, Sudan Venezuela, Kazakhstan, Libya and the Congo. Only four are Arab states. In view of the fact that Arab states have enormous oil reserves, and China requirements are increasing day by day, the prospects for cooperation in this field are vast.

2. Politics and Culture

Arab countries have enjoyed smooth diplomatic relations with New China since the 1955 Bandung Conference. In 1956, China initially established diplomatic relations with Egypt, Syria and Yemen, and later with other states. In 1990 relations were finally established with Saudi Arabia which marked the completion of established relations with all 22 Arab states. What is worth noting is that although in recent years, relations between China and Arab states have quickened in pace and tightened, cooperation is driven by energy resources and trade. High level interaction is extremely limited compared China's relations with Europe and the US. For example, Chinese leaders have conducted official meetings with Arab leaders so as to sign cooperative agreements and establish partnerships for example. In addition, China and the League of Arab States came together in 2004 to establish the China-Arab States Cooperation Forum. Although this strengthened prospects for open interaction of various fields within political and civil levels, focus was still placed on cooperation in terms of trade and investment. What also shouldn't be disregarded is that within this framework, four China-Arab Friendship Conferences and five China-Arab Relations Inter-Civilization Dialogue Seminars have been held, in which authoritive academics from various disciplines come together to discuss the interactions of international politics and civilisations, and to lift away any ideological storms. Although such work continues, it is lacking in any important achievements.

For a long time, the 'elitist' characteristics of Chinese-Arab relations are reflected in the degree of cultural exchange. In recent years, education has enabled breakthroughs strengthening non-governmental Chinese-Arab relations, as an increasing number of Arab students study in China. According to statistics, in 2003 only around 300 Arab students studied in China, which increased to 14000 students in 2015.[(7)] In addition, China has established a number of Arab language departments in higher education institutions and strengthened its reserve of talents researching the Arab World. By 2016, 11 Confucius Institutes have also opened in Egypt, Tunisia, Jordan and other arab countries to teach the masses about Chinese culture and language. However, from the perspective of intertranslation, Chinese-Arab cooperation has been extremely limited. Although authorities on both sides have signed a number of publishing agreements, very little is actually available thus limiting cultural exchange to elite levels.

The information revolution has turned the world into a global village, but regardless of this, China and the Arab World still regard each other as being from a remote and unknown world. There is very little Chinese-Arab cultural exchange, which in part is due to language, and also to the fact that Western countries control culture in the Arab World and so has been unable to leave its mark on other countries. This distance between the Arab World and China has led to its people turning to western media, an extremely influential third party, as a means to understanding each other. Chinese-Arab cooperation has strengthened in various fields, but there is still vast room for improving cultural exchange in the future as this will help further strengthen mutual understanding.

Why is the Arab World looking to China for Civilisational Repositioning?

The fundamental objective of civilisational repositioning is to advance one's own society. Based on this, the Arab World's perspective is to aim for the overall advancement of their civilisation rather than simply build 'non-economic' cooperation. China has enough to justify establishing tight relations, although at present the Chinese-Arab centre of gravity is still economic.

What needs to be mentioned is whether the decision to undertake a process of civilisational repositioning should be decided by China or the Arab World. Chinese-Arab relations must firstly be in China's interests, especially in terms of safeguarding oil supply and guaranteeing that its products can be exported. Arab people must develop economic relations with China, but in the context of an Arab revival set out a plan which enables all round cooperation.

By seeking to establish a process which can bring about civilisational repositioning, the Arab World must first be capable of seizing control of their natural resources and independently formulating economic policies. Doing so is also essential for managing Chinese-Arab relations in the future. Efficient development and the creation of an advanced civilisation like a coin has two inseparable sides. The former serves as the underlay, and the latter enables the possibilities.

On this basis, the Arab World's civilisational repositioning must also benefit China. Should China require oil in the future, Arab people can plan out what advanced technology they are lacking, and invite China to bring theirs which would promote internal development, advancement, innovation, and quickly lessen the disparity with developed countries. Arab people require technology for oil exploration and extraction, and access to such would allow them to strengthen sovereignty over their own natural resources. Of course, unlocking the processes of development without dependence requires that Arab people are fundamentally independent, and able to withstand the impact of overseas pressures. Arab people need China's support in the international arena with regards to its political affairs, so as to allow Arab political affairs and development processes to undergo transformation. Succumbing to powerful imperialists harmed the interests of Arab people, and was the starting point for seeking a renewed strength in the world - support from China. This can resolve a lot of Arab problems, and create a more just atmosphere. Doing so would enable the Arab World to rid themselves of external pressures and kick-start their development in a more favourable environment. Finally, an improved overall international position would be a great leap for their civilisation.

China and Arab countries have exchanges and cooperation in various fields, and realising a national revival is a great dream they both share. However, such pursuit has resulted in little, and remains a hope for the future. Arab people are not sufficiently prepared, and the same is true for China.

China has made tremendous achievements in development. In industry, they have been applied to bringing leading European and US projects with sensitive and advanced technologies. China's technological achievements haven't been the focus of the world's attention, and although they have a number of large scale enterprises, they have yet to create a global brand. Although China's economic development has been rapid and living standards have improved markedly in recent years, the most important task China faces is the 100 million people on the poverty line. They cannot yet exert their full potential and influence in international political affairs. This could account for why China hasn't exercised its veto power as a permanent member state of the United Nations on a number of sensitive issues, even those involving national interests. They have adopted positions which are neutral, abstain, or sometimes even to a degree support the US. Of course, this is in accordance with China's pragmatic diplomatic policy to 'keep a low profile and bid time, while getting something accomplished.'

China has already started working to resolve the various problems it has encountered on its road to revival. In the fields of science and technology following the reform period, invention and innovation was encouraged which led to the National Patent Office being established in 1980, and the Patent Law in 1985. The number of Chinese patents rapidly increased and exceeded 1.25 million by 2004, of which 87% were by Chinese, and 13% foreign. In 2007, Chinese patents had already increased to 2.08 million, of which 17% were inventions, 47.3% were patents for utility models, and 25.3% were design patents. In accordance with data from the UN's World Intellectual Property Organisation (WIPO), China followed the US and Japan as the third largest country for patent applications in 2007, and had surpassed Japan with 40,000 patent applications by 2012. China's technological deficiencies lie in the lack of invention and innovation of general purpose technologies (GPTs). Engines and network technology for example has already been developed extensively across the world, and are considered to be inventions of great significance.

Civilisational repositioning with reference to China is a vision for the future, but the conditions are not yet mature enough for such a process to begin.

What is our response to "Why choose China?" With this question, it is important to consider three factors:

Firstly, Arab people aren't prepared. Arab people wish to implement civilisational repositioning, but firstly wish to unite so as to realise development without dependence, and to formulate a unified action plan for revival. In addition, launching a process for civilisational repositioning requires a firm and tenacious level of leadership with foresight. They must strive to take reference from China's non-conformist development, and apply themselves to implementing an action plan that can be changed when necessary in response to mistakes made, and solutions found.

Secondly, Chinese-Arab friendly cooperation is a realistic basis to undergo civilisational repositioning. Firstly, China and the Arab World have enjoyed friendly exchanges throughout history, and now share common interests in a number of political issues which can strengthen cooperation. For example, both opposed US hegemony following the Cold War. Secondly, there is a strong complementarity in terms of the economy and energy resources. Both have real requirements and the development of relations provides opportunities.

Thirdly, China is not prepared for the Arab people to engage them in civilisational repositioning. As previously stated, China has not yet grasped enough advanced technology to satisfy an Arab revival, but it does have enough influence in international politics. However, based on China's economic data and their plan for future development, we can be sure that this point will inevitably come in the 21st century. In the interim period, Arab people should do their level best. As Arab people say, realising civilisational repositioning with China and an Arab revival is not going to be easy, but such a chance should not be missed as may only come once. If Arab people don't work themselves, why would China is interested in helping them?!

From Non-Conformist Development to Civilisational Repositioning

Western countries obstructed the Arab World's course to modernization and renaissance through the colonial period. Even after troops were withdrawn however, they spared no effort in continuing to cause problems which resulted in them falling behind even further. They either made direct use of state owned machinery, or worked from the inside by stealthily supporting dictators for example. When the Arab states were in the process of diverging, intense bias towards Israel in particular had a serious negative impact in the Arab renaissance. Western countries have always exploited the third world; especially Arab states in which they have attempted to foster a dependence they had no choice but to pursue.

Imperialism comes extremely naturally to Western countries, and the Arab states with their abundant oil reserves occupy an important geographical position thus holding enormous interest. Certainly, it cannot be said that the Arab civilisational crisis is due completely to external factors. Anyone would agree that it is definitely the root to its falling behind, however perhaps cultural factors play a major role also. Even so, it must still be stressed that various external factors, colonialism in particular, have been disastrous for Arab people.

Just as the residual effects of colonialism continue to remain, so do the two paths which define the Arab World's ideological response: either regress to the past, or follow their example. This is the most significant reason why an Arab revival is so stifled in its development.

Following the cold war, the Western development model was deemed to be the "the formation of human societal advancement" and that "humans will determine its final form". The US was seen as the only superpower in the world that controlled international politics as well as wielding a deep influence on all fields of development such as global culture, science and technology. The US hoped that globalisation (or 'capitalist' globalisation) would promote Western liberal economic and societal development models, and way of life. In the face of these trends, Arab people have responded with two main approaches:

The first is to "restore ancient ways". Supporting this ideology were those deeply immersed in history, and devoted to the notion that by repeating Arab approaches to development through history was the remedy for reforming the Arab World. This ideology was generated during the early stages of colonization, and was an extremely emotional response to what was considered the beginning of the regions decline in development. Those holding these ideas believed that restoring ancient ways to be more consistent with history, and would improve the possibility of resolving this problem. The logic that merely duplicating a departed social, political, and ideological system, doesn't take into account that they were applied to the behaviour, lifestyle and even language customs of the ancients.

The second direction was following the US example. After the US won the Cold war; liberalism was advocated as a beneficial and realizable path to modernization for people, governments, and the economy. It promised to overcome all manner of difficulties, and enable states to reach a level of Western development by following their efficient path. It should be said that following the US was a worldwide phenomenon, and not unique to Arabs. US involvement in international politics, especially in Palestine, severely harmed the interests of Arab people, but yet they are still looked to for solutions. The US model is closely related to its political, economic and social systems, and shouldn't be involved in international politics. More than just merely referring to US models, these thinkers proposed that they should serve as "guidance for modern Arab ideology", and complied with in all aspects.

It must be stressed that the above mentioned ideologies do not fall into the field of Arab though, or are indeed the only ones. They just happen to be the most influential. With such obvious divides, the critical question is: What ideology should we adopt? Is it restore to ancient ways, or follow the US? In truth, these two ideologies bear no resemblance to the Arab renaissance of the first half of the 19th century, but are perceived objectively as a practical starting point.

If Western countries regard the Arab World as a colony, Arab people response to this ideology would impact on the Arab renaissance in two crucial ways. Looking at the current situation, the Arab World's opportunity to realise a revival is remote, as imperialist countries still have enormous interest which they won't give up, at least for the first half of the 21st century.

Although the West's civilisation has achieved a great deal and deserves to be studied, the West cannot help Arab people, or create an environment in which they can realize a revival. As the Arab World has only been independent for a short time, a revival is impossible if the West continues to exploit its natural resources.

An Arab revival which follows the path of the West is already loaded with obstacles. The West is continuously followed as an example, and the fountain from which Arab ideologists seek out ideas on reform and modernisation. However, history has proved that following the West is in no way beneficial to Arab people. Although Western states have realised enormous advances, the force of colonialism had brought about a deep crisis in the Arab World. It is a vicious circle.

The Western path is blocked, but it is in fact mainly Eastern states that are developing, East Asian states in particular. Their emergence should be an example for the Arab revival to learn from. Prior to the mid-20th century, East Asian and Arab states suffered equally from the effects of colonization and exploitation at the hands of Western countries, and hence have similarities in terms of development. Therefore, paying close attention to their development is extremely beneficial. It can help us understand the aspects in which East Asian countries have fallen behind, especially China.

Non-conformity is the most remarkable feature of China's 1978 reforms, as this policy allowed enormous changes in a very short space of time. The successful experiences of non-conformist development are something that Arab people can learn and take reference from. If the Arab World had devised an ideology for economic integration in the 1940's and strived to implement development without dependence, then they would have been in a better position to respond to globalisation in the 1990's, and like China used it to bring about a revival. China has used its economic development achievements to become an important world figure.

It is regrettable that over the past decades, Arab people just haven't done this. However, following these non-conformist development experiences could help Arabs feasibly develop without dependence.

Arab people need to meet with two conditions. Firstly, make economic integration happen, and secondly strengthen control of natural resources. Without these two conditions, Arab people have no way of making use of their resources which are essential for bringing about development and a revival of the Arab World.

China has given the world experience of non-conformist development. However, it won't necessarily fit all developing countries, especially if their national conditions are a far cry from China's in terms of land area, population, geographical location, natural resources, and degree of societal integration. It is certain however that China's developmental experiences can be referenced by Arab people. Although the Arab World has many similarities with China in terms of resources, it is lacking a feasible plan or scheme.

We often hear the Arab World and Europe being compared. With the establishment of the League of Arab States, the Arab World preceded Europe in terms of proposing economic integration. Europe's process began in 1945 firstly in Belgium, France, Federal Germany, Italy, Luxembourg, and the Netherlands whom signed a treaty to establish the European Coal and Steel Community (ESCS). In 1957, the European Common Market (ECM) was established, and the European Union (EU) in 1991. In spite of various disputes and divergences between EU countries, they have always continued to grow. Although Arab states have a number of similarities, economic integration would be conducive to realising advancements in civilisation and a common development with consensus. However this has never been realised and is extremely significant. Political divergences and disparities between rich and poor are the main issues impeding the Arab World from formulating a concrete action plan.

This paper concludes that by looking at China's experiences, of non-conformist development which led to civilisational repositioning, can help the Arab World develop enough to drive a revival. In the first half of the 19th century, Arab people began seeking a path to revival. Since then the invasion and abandonment of colonialism, this path has been similar to China's practical approach to Non-Conformist development. Of course, Arab people have never abandoned the notion of an Arab renaissance. Truth lies on actions, and by Arab countries replacing fantasy with practical action like China will inevitably lead to revival.

Rifa'a al-Tahtawi was the enlightened thinker of the Arab renaissance, and his philosophies are similar to that of Deng Xiaoping. Tahtawi witnessed France's societal and political development, and believed that their mode would benefit the Islamic world and enable them to advance as a civilisation. What worth attaching importance to and taking reference from is that they sought to follow the example of their successes without rebelling against Islamic teachings. Such thoughts have stemmed from a national revival, and their experiences brought about transformation which conformed to Arab national conditions and culture. This is identical to Deng Xiaoping's realistic and practical ideology. Deng Xiaoping recognised the West's capitalist economic achievements, sublated them for reference, and cheery picked the parts he believed would be used for China's advancement. Finally, it was moulded to fit China's national conditions. Regardless of any experiences, or how ideologies transformed or reformed, the ultimate objective to realise a national revival always remained.

China has proved to the world that prioritising national interests combined with pragmatic development planning is what has brought about and ensured its successes. Arab people's pursuit of a road to revival has abandoned pragmatic ideologies, and has confined their ideologies thus resulting in repeated failures to develop. Arab people ought to realise from China's experiences that: A great national revival required that Arab people recover their initial pragmatic ideology, and the core of such ideology is an everything work, and all must comply with serving the high objective of a national revival whilst without overlooking the successes necessary for a moral code.

The Arab World longs for a revival, and China can provide it with experience to learn from and reference, and future opportunities, so we should treasure and firmly grasp. If you say that since Napoleon's military force opened the door to the Arab World, western powers (Britain, France, and the US etc.) from which stemmed exploitation which oppressed the Arab world, then it is hoped that China will become important in the world and won't behave like the west towards the Arab World, but stand with us, and hand in hand create a just global environment, and resolve the various problems obstructing Arab advancement.

We want to develop a positive relationship with China. Of course, this doesn't involve flattery, as this wouldn't be in the national interest. Tight Chinese-Arab economic cooperation could bring wealth to both sides, but high levels strategic interests alone aren't enough to bring about an Arab revival. We need to look at civilisation as a starting point when forging positive relations, and build a foundation which is mutually beneficial to our material and immaterial revival of civilisation.

Arab people long for a brighter future, and the various opportunities China can provide should not be overlooked. By paying attention to China's course from non-conformist development to civilization repositioning, it is clear that establishing positive relations with China is vital. It will enable the Arab World to contribute to the realisation of the Chinese dream whilst also seizing the opportunity as early as possible to make the Arab dream come true.

References

1. http://www.argaam.com/ar, 25/11/2015.
2. http://www.alarabiya.net/ar/aswaq/oil-and-gas, 28/6/2015.

3. http://www.bna.bh/portal/news, 9/9/2015.

4. http://arabic.cntv.cn, 17/9/2015.

5. http://www.aidmo.org/beta/index.php

6. http://www.alkhaleej.ae/economics, 11/9/2015.

7. http://arabic.news.cn, 28/1/2016.

“一带一路”与中国经济思想领导力

罗思义 【英国】

前英国伦敦经济与商业政策署 署长 / 中国人民大学重阳金融研究院 高级研究员

“一带一路”倡议除本身具有重要意义之外，更彰显出中国战略思想在全球经济讨论中所扮演的愈发重要的角色。本文认为，在审视“一带一路”倡议时，应考虑中国的“思想领导力”在全球经济讨论中日益上升这一背景。

中国关于国际发展的全球对话不断深入

2016 年，中国与各国之间就全球经济政策展开的对话大幅加深，但中国的角色却发生了变化：随着西方经济“新平庸化”的不断持续，中国，确切地说是共产党领导下的中国开展的分析、制定的议程正逐步获得国际信赖。在国际讨论中，这种趋势明显地表现在最近的三件大事上：

2016 年 9 月 4 日至 5 日期间举办的“G20 杭州峰会”；

2016 年 10 月 13 日至 15 日期间“2016 中国共产党与世界对话大会”；

2016 年 10 月 15 至 16 日期间，在印度果阿举办的“金砖国家峰会”。

因此，“一带一路”倡议的发展应考虑中国在全球经济中“思想领导力”不断增强这一事实。

最近的这些发展并非偶然间实现，而是由于过去三十多年中，中国采取的不同于西方的经济战略取所得的成果，更是由于中国的社会主义发展战略促成的重大增长所致。这种发展战略与世界银行与国际国币基金组织达成的华盛顿共识可谓截然不同。在这一期间，中国经济路线的正确性在事实中得到了验证，极大地提高了中国在世界经济中的地位。同一时期内，西方经济所处的地位大幅下降。经济形势发生的新变化意味着世界经济正在发生客观的转向，而这种转向正主观地体现在国际经济讨论中——如今，许多国家都表示渴望向中国学习。

有一点必须要注意，那边是中国自身的经济发展同时也会部分地受到这种国际讨论的支配。借鉴中国经济政策的国家越多，中国在国际经济增长中的获益越多。总之，中国与中国共产党的国际“思想领导力”正逐步提升，这不仅会对全球经济发展产生影响，也会对中国本身的发展带来影响。

本文旨在分析国际经济讨论过程中主观因素与客观因素的交互关系，分析这些因素如何在中国的经济发展中得到体现。

1978 至 1980 年间的关键转折点

1978—1980 年间，中国与西方经济体几乎同时踏上了全新的经济路线。1978 年，中国开始实施邓小平提出的“改革开放”政策，而在 1980 年，西方国家则开始施行国际上奉行的“华盛顿共识”，当时撒切尔夫人就任英国首相，而更重要的是，里根随后也就任美国总统。这位当前的经济讨论提供了一个长期的语境，因为这两种截然不同的政策所处的基本框架一直持续至今。

三十五年后，这两条经济路线所产生的资产负债表上出现了明显的对比。中国的 GDP 年平均值从 1950 至 1997 年间的低于 5% 增长至 1978 年至 2015 年间的 9.8%。而美国的增速则从 1950 至 1980 年间（里根上台的前一年）的 3.7% 下降至 1980 至 2015 年的 2.7%。因此，自 1978 年，中国实施“改革开放”政策以来，中国经济经历了人类历史上所有大国均未曾经历的最快速的增长，而美国在 1980 年后，由于受到里根经济学——后来国际上奉行的华盛顿共识——的影响，经济增长的速度一直在下降。

政治上的“资产负债表”也存在明显差异。截止到 2016 年，随着特朗普上台和英国脱欧，英美两个以“盎格鲁—撒克逊”族裔为主的大国均经历了最严重的的政治动荡。伴随“里根主义”政策而来的，是经济放缓，以及英美两国的严重政治动荡。尽管英美两国在政治和经济上均遭遇失败、中国的政策却取得了成功，但为何负责全球经济治理的机构，如国际货币基金组织和世界银行等，仍然在 20 世纪 80 年代继续施行"华盛顿共识"？答案很明显，尽管新自由主义经济理论翻了严重的错误，但在 1989 年，华盛顿共识出台时，美国占据世界 GDP 的 28%，其他发达经济体占据 84%，而中国所占份额则不足 2%。

尽管在 1978 至 1989 年间，中国的年平均增长率达到 9.5% 的世界最高水平，但中国经济总体规模仍然十分有限。正如英语中的俗语所说，"强权就是公理"，尽管华盛顿共识如今已经证明遭遇失败，但在 20 世纪 80 年代，世界银行和国际货币基金组织仍然实行着这些政策，不管中国的政策是否更为成功。

中国逐渐改变世界经济格局

时间已经过去近四十年，现在也是时候用事实检验中国的"社会主义发展模式"和"华盛顿共识"这两种不同的政策了。1978 年后中国经济连续数十年取得成功，1980 年发达经济体经济持续放缓，世界经济形势因此发生质变，世界经济讨论的格局也因此发生改变。因为中国经济发展战略是中国共产党智慧的结晶，这必然也意味着中国共产党在世界经济讨论中的重要性已经稳步或者大幅提升。

按照当前汇率计算，从 1989 年至 2015 年，美国占世界 GDP 比重从 28% 降至 24%，中国则从 2% 升至 15%。与此同时，发展中经济体占世界经济比重也从 16% 升至 35%。中国从占世界经济中的边缘地位，到成为世界第二大经济体。

按照西方经济机构认为更能反映世界经济长期趋势的购买力平价（PPP）计算，这种变化更引人注目。2015 年，中国占世界经济比重为 17%，超过美国的 16%，这让中国成为世界最大经济体。发展中经济体占世界经济比重现已超过半数，为 53%。总之，从 1980 年里根当选，以及 1989 年"华盛顿共识"正式生效以来，中国和发展中经济体已完全改变了世界经济格局。但中国 1978 年后的经济政策没受到国际广泛研究也存在一个主观原因：中国在某种意义上过于低调。当时的中国在国际上遵循邓小平所主张的"韬光养晦"政策。中国强调"中国特色发展道路"——虽然邓小平也谨慎指出"我们努力按照客观经济规律办事"、"经济规律具有普遍性"。在这种情况下，中国选择低调行事，坚持中国特色发展道路。只有那些对国际经济趋势抱有极大兴趣的人，才会对引人注目的中国经济发展速度给予足够的重视。

印度支那以及印度

虽然中国没有要求别国认真研究其经济政策，但其也没有阻止别国这样做。其三个邻国——越南、老挝、柬埔寨就深受中国经济模式影响，他们同样成绩斐然。除人口低于五百万的小国或者石油生产占主导地位的国家外，拙文《世行数据中隐藏着一个秘密》对"华盛顿共识"问世以来的人均 GDP 增长率进行了详细的国际比较，四个国家取得了世界最快的人均 GDP 增速，他们的排名按递减顺序分别为：中国、柬埔寨、越南和老挝。现实再次证明，中国的"社会主义发展模式"远比新自由主义的"华盛顿共识"表现优越。这项政策在其他国家而非中国取得同类结果证明，中国的"社会主义发展模式"确实符合邓小平所说的"经济规律具有普遍性"，而不仅仅只适用于中国。

中国的成功吸引了中南半岛诸国，如越南、老挝、柬埔寨等国的关注，他们效仿中国经济发展模式取得成功后，导致中国的经济战略影响进一步蔓延到一个举足轻重的国家——印度。印度现任总理莫迪在其先前担任印度古吉拉特邦首席部长时就经常访问中国。莫迪政府任命研究中国经济的专家、彼得森国际经济研究所前研究员、《黯然失色：生活在中国经济统治的阴影下》一书的作者阿文德萨勃拉曼尼亚（Arvind Subramanian），为首席经济顾问。在莫迪的领导下，印度新经济政策呈现三方面较为明显的特点，首先是强调加大政府对基础设施投资，其次是强调发展制造业，三是吸引投资，让卢比汇率更具竞争力。可以明显看出，这些政策是效仿中国模式。正如中南半岛那些国家一样，印度经济增长成绩斐然，帮助其与中国一道，成为世界上增长最快的主要经济体。

除了印度这个典型例子外，中国的经济政策，尤其是政府投资所发挥的作用，也开始在一些非洲和拉美国家产生重大影响。正如哈佛大学国际政治经济学教授丹尼·罗德里克指出：

> 在非洲，埃塞俄比亚是过去十年中最引人注目的成功故事。自2004 年以来，该国经济年均增长率超过了 10%，并因此实现了贫困状况和医疗卫生条件的显著改善。该国资源较为贫乏，并未像其他许多非洲国家那样从大宗商品繁荣中获益，其经济自由化进程和体制改革也并未像世界银行和其他捐助者一贯建议的那样扮演主要角色。
>
> 这一快速增长实际上是大幅增加公共投资的结果——20 世纪 90 年

代占 GDP 的 5%，到 2011 年的 19%，增速全球排名第三。埃塞俄比亚政府发动了一场预算支出高潮，修建公路、铁路、电站，以及一项令大部分贫困农村地区生产力显著提升的农业技术推广体系。

他谈到拉美的情况时指出：

至于拉丁美洲，玻利维亚是稀有矿产出口国，在当前商品价格低迷时期还不至于爆发危机。在拉美总产出萎缩（约 0.3%，根据国际货币基金组织的最新预测）的背景下，该国 2015 年全年 GDP 增长预计保持在 4% 以上。其中很大一部分源自于公共投资，而总统莫拉莱斯也将此认定为本国经济的增长引擎。从 2005 年到 2014 年，玻利维亚的公共投资总额相对于国民收入的比率增加了一倍多，从 6% 提升到 13%，而政府则计划在未来几年进一步提高该比例。

综上所述，1978 年或者 1989 年时国际上极少数寻求借鉴中国经济政策的国家，现已成为非常重要的势力。显然，这是中国的思想领导力近来在世界经济中的作用增加的原因之一。

中国的思想领导力在不同论坛上的作用

当然，中国 / 中国共产党的思想领导力日益提升，在近来召开的不同性质的论坛上以不同的方式得到了体现。

- 杭州 G20 峰会汇聚了世界政治经济界最有影响力的角色——美国、中国、欧盟、日本和世界其他主要国家的领导人。虽然中国作为 G20 主办国，具有设置议程、提出倡议的最大权利和引领作用，但 G20 成员国涵盖世界上所有最具影响力的国家，任何倡议的达成必须得到这些国家的同意。这意味着，中国、美国和其他一些国家都拥有否决 G20 倡议的权利。而这同时又是 G20 的典型特征：规模大、代表性强。因此，G20 无法快速推进任何一项倡议的达成，其潜在作用主要是推动全球经济治理战略，而这会限制 G20 发展进程。
- 金砖国家峰会任何倡议也是如此，它必须是拥有实际否决权的所有与会成员国达成共识才能生效。但由于其中四个成员国（巴西、印度、中国、南非）均是发展中国家，俄罗斯是一个半发达国家，使得金砖国家的共同利益清晰明确，因此金砖国家比 G20 在思想和行动上做出决策时要快得多。比如最近在果阿举行的金砖国家峰会，明确强调了发达经济体呈缓慢增长的趋势，并提出了超越 G20 共识的解决方案，比如加大基础设施投资，注重消除贫困，促进并强化发展中国家利益。

- 在重庆召开的“2016 中国共产党与世界对话会”则展现了不同的特点，与会代表是来自 50 多个国家的 70 多个主要政党和政治组织领导人。这轮对话会是中国共产党充分发挥其思想领导力作用的一个很明显的例子。当然，这并不是说，其他政党就应效仿中国共产党。事实上，从讨论可以明显看出，中国共产党也希望借鉴其他政党经验。但在某种意义上，对话议程明显深受中国共产党的影响。许多会议报道和讲话也反映了这一点。中国方面的出席代表包括中共中央政治局常委、中央书记处书记刘云山，重庆市委书记孙政才，重庆市长黄奇帆，中国人民大学校长刘伟，前世界银行高级副行长林毅夫和其他许多嘉宾。与会的还有许多外国嘉宾，包括上文概述全球经济趋势时所特别提及的印度的人民党执委会委员、发言人戈帕尔·克里希纳·阿加瓦尔等。值得赞扬的是，就思想深度而言，这次对话会所设置的框架超过 G20 共识——但当然，重庆对话会是一个供讨论的论坛，而非一个决策机构。

当前趋势带来的影响

总结当前的趋势和事件，有必要对中国思想领导力做出客观中肯的评价，它正在全球范围内发挥着作用，但这些作用受重视的程度与其对全球发展的贡献相比，还有差距。中国已在全球金融倡议方面比如亚投行（AIIB）发挥着决定性的作用，在此不赘述。

- 就世界经济增长而言，深受中国影响的国家已起着决定性的作用—— 2007 年至 2015 ，单单中国和印度的 GDP 增量加起来就高达 8.2 万亿美元，美国的这一数据为 3.5 万亿美元。
- 就当前世界经济总体权重而言，按照当前汇率计算，2015 年金砖国家占世界 GDP 比重为 22%，欧盟为 22%，美国则为 24%；按照购买力平价计算，金砖国家现在的领先优势引人注目，美国占世界 GDP 比重为 16%，欧盟为 17%，金砖国家则为 31%。但金砖国家的政策连贯性和机构实力不仅远不如美国，而且也远不如欧盟——就世界经济权重而言，发达经济中心仍然处于主导地位。

- 正如上文分析所示，中国的国际权重和中国共产党的政策，不仅已经在中国之外最重要的发展中国家——印度产生相当大的影响，而且已经在中南半岛诸国和其他一些发展中国家也产生了极大的影响。但在发达国家，由于其宣传机构的意识形态原因，数十年来“中国即将崩溃”、“中国即将轰然坍塌”、“中国将遭遇硬着陆”等类似的报道一直占据主导地位——尽管事实是，这样的预测早已破产。中国之外的“中国通”对中国经济的分析则客观得多，越来越多的经济界人士现在也开始客观认识中国，拙文《美国经济学家开始客观认识中国》对此过程有详细的分析，这里就不再赘述。

趋势变化

上述分析的关键点是，这不仅仅事关思想领域斗争，而是决定中国在国际经济论战当中的分量不断上升。受中国发展战略影响的国家的增长表现，优于那些效仿新自由主义的“华盛顿共识”的国家，这是决定性因素。受中国发展战略影响的国家，在世界经济中的权重正逐步增加，而效仿新自由主义“华盛顿共识”的国家在世界经济中的权重，则正逐步下降。对其他国家来说，实际的经济成就当然比设想的经济理论更具说服力。

但这种经济现实也证明，中国共产党政策的国际影响力将进一步增加。由于“华盛顿共识”政策和里根经济学的影响，西方国家陷入低速增长，年增长率约为 2%。相比之下，受中国的经济政策影响的国家则继续保持着经济快速发展的模式。正如上述分析所示，这意味着，中国 / 中国共产党在国际经济讨论中的重要性将继续增加。也即是说，国际经济讨论中的“资产负债表”不是静止不变的，而是将继续对中国有利。

但这种发展态势不仅有利于世界经济，而且也有利于中国自身。世界经济增长放缓主要是受发达经济体缓慢增长所拖累，造成了更不利于中国的国际背景，因为这种情况导致全球贸易缓慢增长，进而连累中国出口缓慢增长。中国政策的国际影响力越大将推动世界经济增长加速，中国自身亦可从中受益。因此，中国积极参与国际经济讨论不仅有利于其他国家，也有利于中国自身。

当代中国的讨论

最后，当代中国的讨论在国际语境中可以得到很好地理解。正如前文所述，因里根经济学及《华盛顿共识》而造成的西方经济放缓已经达到十分严重的地步，甚至已经威胁到西方经济在全球经济中的总体地位。西方国家无法加快自身的经济增长，但为了保持其国际经济地位，只有处心积虑地阻止中国经济发展——这一点我在《一盘大棋？中国新命运解析》中进行了详细的剖析。

“一带一路”倡议除本身具有重要意义之外，更彰显出中国战略思想在全球经济讨论中所扮演的愈发重要的角色。

结论

综上所述，在中国共产党的领导下，中国在国际经济讨论中扮演的角色愈发重要，这与中国经济在实践中取得的成就直接相关。这不仅为中国，更对其他处于“良性循环”中的国家带来了利益。

- 中国经济政策在理论层面的正确性吸引了许多经济学专家，但促使中国经济迅速赶超西方国家，对国际舆论产生重要影响的，是中国经济政策在实践上取得的成就。因此，中国共产党在引领本国经济发展上做出的贡献是中国在国际经济讨论中地位提升的关键因素。
- 与此同时，中国和中国共产的经济政策国际影响力的提升，对其他国家也是十分有力的。由于《华盛顿共识》导致了西方经济增长放缓，发展中国家也不可避免的受到影响，中国和中国共产党的经济政策影响力度越大，其他国家的经济发展速度便越快，这返回来会为中国创造一个有力的国际环境。

众所周知，加强各国经济合作对中国和对其他国家都是一种“双赢”，但正如本文所述，中国共产党源自邓小平的经济政策在国际“思想领导力”上不断提升，这对于中国和其他国家而言，也是一种“双赢”的局面。

因此，“一带一路”应该在这样的国际框架内进行审视。

China's Economic Thought Leadership and the Belt and Road

John Ross / United Kingdom of Great Britain and Northern Ireland

Former Director of Economic and Business Policy for Mayor of London /Senior Fellow of the Chongyang Institute for Financial Studies at Renmin University of China

The Belt and Road (OBOR) Initiative is not merely important itself but it illustrates the way in which China's strategic concepts are playing an increasingly key role in discussion on the global economy. The aim of this paper is to therefore to place the Belt and Road within the context of China's developing 'thought leadership' in global economic discussion.

China's deepening global dialogue on international development

The dialogue between China and a wide range of other countries on policy for the global economy considerably deepened in 2016 but its character is changing: China's, more specifically the CPC's, analysis and agenda is steadily gaining international credibility the longer the 'new mediocre' in the Western economies continues. This trend in international discussion was shown clearly at three recent significant events:

- The G20 summit conference in Hangzhou on 4-5th September,
- ‘The CPC in Dialogue with the World 2016’ conference in Chongqing on 13-15th October,
- The BRICS summit in Goa India on 15-16 October.

The development of the Belt and Road Initiative should therefore be seen within this wider context of China’s increasing role in ‘thought leadership’ regarding the global economy.

These recent developments have not come ‘from out of the blue’. They are the culmination of the different results of more than three decades of divergent economic strategies between China and the West and the superior growth results of China’s ‘socialist development strategy’ compared to the World Bank/IMF Washington Consensus. During this period China’s economic course was vindicated by the facts, producing a major increase in China’s weight within the world economy. In the same period the weight of Western economies fell significantly. The new change in the situation is that these objective shifts in the world economy are now being reflected subjectively in international economic discussion - an increasing number of countries now want to learn from China.

It is important to note that China’s own economic developmentin turn will also be partially determinedby this international discussion. The more other countries learn from China’s successful economic policies the more rapid will be the international economic growth in which China can develop. In summary China’s and the CPC’s increasing international ‘thought leadership’ will have an impact not only on global economic developments but on China itself.

This article analyses the interrelation of these objective and subjective processes in international economic discussion and how they are reflected in China.

The key turning point of 1978-1980

In 1978-80 almost simultaneously fundamentally new courses were embarked on by both China and the Western economies. In 1978 China commenced Deng Xiaoping's 'reform and opening up': In 1980 the West embarked on the policies which would be internationally codified as the 'Washington consensus' with the coming to office of Thatcher and then most importantly Reagan. This provides the long term context for current economic discussion as the fundamental framework of these two fundamentally different policies has continued to the present.

Three and a half decades later the balance sheet of these two economic courses is clear.China's annual average GDP growth accelerated from under 5% in 1950-1977 to 9.8% in 1978-2015. US growth slowed from an annual average of 3.7% in 1950 to 1980, the last year before Reagan came to office, to 2.7% in 1980-2015. Therefore, after 1978 China with the policy of 'reform and opening up' underwent the most rapid economic growth in any major country in human history, while after 1980 the US under Reaganomics, later codified internationally as the Washington Consensus, experienced economic deceleration.

Politically the balance sheet is equally clear. By 2016 the two major 'Anglo-Saxon' countries were undergoing the most serious political destabilisation of any major economies with the rise of Trump in the US and the economically irrational vote for Brexit in the UK. 'Reaganite' policies were accompanied by economic slowdown and culminated in serious political instability in both the UK and US.

Nevertheless, the reasons why, despite their economic and political failure, the policies of the 'Washington Consensus,' and not China's successful policies,were adopted by institutions responsible for global economic governance, above all the IMF and World Bank, in the 1980sis obvious. Much more powerful than the errors in neo-liberal economic theory was the fact that in 1989, the year the Washington Consensus was codified, the US accounted for 28% of world GDP, and the advanced economies for 84%, while China accounted for less than 2%.

China might have undergone 9.5% annual average growth from 1978-89, the fastest in the world, but the total size of China's economy was still small. In the

English phrase 'might is right' so despite its by now proven failure the Washington Consensus was adopted in the 1980s by the IMF/World Bank and China's far more successful policies were not.

Cumulative trends in the world economy by 2016

But there has now been nearly four decades of testing out in reality the different economic policies of China's 'socialist development model' and the Washington Consensus. The decades long success of China's economy after 1978, and the simultaneous slowdown of the advanced economies after 1980, has by now qualitatively changed the situation in the world economy which in turn has now begun to alter the terms of international economic debate.As China's economic development strategy is clearly a product of the CPC this necessarily also means that the CPC's weight in international economic discussion has also steadily and greatly increased.

From 1989-2015 the US share of world GDP at current exchange rates declined from 28% to 24%, while China's share rose from 2% to 15%. By the same measure the total share of developing economies in the world economy rose from 16% to 35%. China, from a marginal position in the global economy, had become by this measure the world's second largest economy.

Even more dramatic are the changes measured in purchasing power parities (PPPs) which are considered by Western economic institutions to provide a better guide to long term trends in the global economy. By 2015, on this measure, China's economy accounted for 17% of the global total, making it the world's largest economy ahead of the US's 16%. Developing economies now account for the majority, 53%, of the world total. In short since 1980, the election of Reagan, and 1989, the official adoption of the 'Washington Consensus', China and developing economies have completely changed the shape of the world economy.

But there was also a subjective reason why immediately after 1978 China's economic policies were not strongly studied internationally: China in a sense discouraged it. China at that time followed the international policy advocated by

Deng Xiaoping of 'hide brilliance, cherish obscurity'. China laid great emphasis on the specifically 'Chinese characteristics' of its development – although Deng Xiaping was also careful to state 'we have tried to act in accordance with objective economic laws' and laws by their nature are universal. Under conditions in which China was 'hiding brilliance', and insisting on the specifically Chinese character of its development, only those with great interest in international economic trends paid sufficient attention to China's dramatic economic development.

Indo-China then India

But if China did not urge others to carefully study its economic policies that did not prevent others from doing so. Three neighbouring countries – Vietnam, Laos and Cambodia – were hugely influenced by China's economic model. Their economic results were almost equally spectacular. As analysed in detail in my "The Secret in the Data of World Bank" taking international comparisons since the putting forward of the Washington Consensus, and leaving aside very small countries with populations of less than five million or oil producers, then the four countries with the fastest growing per capita GDPs in the world were in descending order China, Cambodia, Vietnam and Laos. China's 'socialist development model' was therefore once again proven in the real world to far outperform the neo-liberal Washington Consensus. The fact that that this policy yielded comparable results in other countries than China showed it did indeed correspond, as Deng Xiaoping had stated, to universal 'economic laws' and not merely 'Chinese characteristics'.

China's success, however, and its replication in strong economic development in Indochina has now led to the influence of its economic strategy spreading further, indeed to a decisive country - India.India's current Prime Minister Modi himself, in his former position as Chief Minister of Gujurat, was a regular visitor to China. The Modi government appointed as its chief economic adviser a specialist on China's economy - Arvind Subramanian, formerly of the Peterson Institute for International Economics and author of *Eclipse: Living in the Shadow of China's Economic Dominance*.Key aspects of India's new economic policies under Modi, in particular strong state infrastructure investment, a shift into manufacturing industry, a competitive exchange rate, are clearly based on China. The result, as in Indochina, has been than spectacular growth – with India joining China as the world's most rapidly growing major economy.

In addition to the decisive example of India China's economic policies, in particular the role of state investment, are also beginning to have significant influence in some African and Latin American countries.As Professor of International Political Economy at Harvard University Dani Rodrik noted:

> 'In Africa, Ethiopia is the most astounding success story of the last decade. Its economy has grown at an average annual rate exceeding 10% since 2004, which has translated into significant poverty reduction and improved health outcomes. The country is resource-poor and did not benefit from commodity booms, unlike many of its continental peers. Nor did economic liberalization and structural reforms of the type typically recommended by the World Bank and other donors play much of a role.
>
> 'Rapid growth was the result, instead, of a massive increase in public investment, from 5% of GDP in the early 1990s to 19% in 2011 – the third highest rate in the world. The Ethiopian government went on a spending spree, building roads, railways, power plants, and an agricultural extension system that significantly enhanced productivity in rural areas, where most of the poor reside.'

And regarding Latin America:

> 'Turning to Latin America, Bolivia is one of the rare mineral exporters that has managed to avoid others' fate in the current commodity-price downturn. Annual GDP growth is expected to remain above 4% in 2015, in a region where overall output is shrinking (by 0.3%, according to the International Monetary Fund' s latest projections). Much of that has to do with public investment, which President Evo Morales regards as the engine of the

Bolivian economy. From 2005 to 2014, total public investment has more than doubled relative to national income, from 6% to 13%, and the government intends to push the ratio even higher in coming years.'

In short if in 1978 or 1989 very few countries internationally were seeking to learn from China's economic policies now very significant forces are. It is this which is reflected in China's recent emergence as a clear 'thought leader' in the global economy.

Forums for China's thought leadership

Such increasing China/CPC 'thought leadership' is of course expressed in different ways in the different recent forums depending on their nature.

- The Hangzhou G20 summit brought together the most powerful players in the world economy and politics – the leaders of the US, China, the EU, Japan and the other major world states. Although China was the G20 host, and therefore the country with the greatest ability to take initiatives and give leadership, nevertheless the G20 cannot proceed more rapidly than the pace at which the most powerful states within it will agree to. This means, to be practical, that China, the US and some other states all possess effective vetoes on G20 initiatives. This simultaneous determines the powerful nature of the G20, and therefore its potential role in global economic strategy and governance, but limits the speed of its advance.
- The BRICS summit must also proceed by consensus with each constituent country possessing an effective veto.However, the BRICS in ideas and certain actions are able to go further and faster than the G20 in terms of initiative dues to the fact that four of its members are developing countries and the other, Russia, is a relatively underdeveloped advanced economy. This gives the BRICS countries clear common interests. The BRICs summit in Goa was therefore rather clear in terms of highlighting the slow growth in the advanced economies and pushing forward solutions, such as infrastructure investment, attention to

poverty reduction, and promotion of the interests of developing countries, which went beyond the G20 consensus.

- 'The CPC in Dialogue with the World' in Chongqing had a different character. It was a meeting of representatives from more than 70 political parties and experts from more than 50 countries.As its explicit frame of reference was dialogue with the CPC it was a rather clear example of the ability of the CPC to play a role 'thought leadership'. This, naturally, does not mean that other parties copy the CPC, and indeed it was clear from the discussion that the CPC also wanted to draw lessons from others, but in the sense that the agenda for discussion was obviously highly influenced by the CPC. This was reflected in the numerous reports and speeches to the conference. On the Chinese side these included by Liu Yunshan, member of the Standing Committee of the Political Bureau of the CPC Central Committee;both Chongqing's Party Secretary and Mayor; Liu Wei, President of Renmin University of China, Lin Yifu, former Senior Vice President of the World Bank and many others.There were numerous foreign guests including, and particularly significant in terms of the global economic trends already outlined, the attendance of the National Spokesperson on Economic Affairs for India's BJP, Gopal Krishna Agarwal. These all set a framework of discussion which was complimentary to but in terms of ideas went beyond the type of consensus that must necessarily exist in the G20 – but of course the Chongqing conference was a forum for discussion,not a decision making body.

Balance sheet of recent trends

Summarising these trends and events, it necessary to have a balanced assessment. There are three process underway – in addition to a rather different but interrelated one by which China has already become a decisive player in terms of global finance with initiatives such as the AIIB.Taking overall trends:

- In terms of world economic growth countries heavily influenced by China already play a decisive role – in 2007-15 China and India alone accounted for \$8.2 trillion in GDP increases compared to \$3.5 trillion for the US.

- In terms of current overall weight in the world economy measured in current exchange rates in 2015 the BRICS accounted for 22% of world GDP - roughly comparable to the 22% for the EU and 24% for the US. In PPPs the lead of the BRICS is now striking - in 2015 in PPPs the US accounted for 16% of the world economy, the EU 17% and the BRICS 31% of world GDP. However, the coherence and institutional strength of the BRICS is far less not merely than the US but also of the EU – so in terms of weight in the world economy the advanced economic centres still dominate.
- The international weight of China's and therefore the CPC's policy, as already analysed, already has great influence in India, which after China is the most important developing country, in Indochina, and in some other developing countries. But in developed countries the propaganda 'industry' of 'the coming collapse of China', the 'coming crash of China', the China 'hard landing' etc has been dominant for several decades - despite the fact that none of these predictions has ever actually occurred! Outside of 'China specialists' more objective analyses of China's economy are therefore only now beginning to receive the attention of much wider circles of economists – a process analysed in "American Economists Beginto know China Objectively".

The dynamics

The key point that flows from the analysis given above is that it is not simply the 'battle in the realm of ideas' that is determining the increasing weight of China in international economic debate. The decisive factor is the proven superior growth of economies influenced by China's socialist development strategy compared to those following the neo-liberal Washington Consensus. This progressively increases the weight in the global economy of countries influenced by China's economic development strategy and reduces the weight of those following the Washington Consensus. Practical economic successes are naturally much more convincing to other countries than any theoretical economic argument!

But this economic reality also determines that the international weight of the

CPC's policies is going to increase further. Due to the policies of the Washington Consensus and the impact of Reaganomics the Western economies are locked into low growth – around 2%. In contrast economies influenced by China's economic policies are continuing to undergo much more rapid economic development. Due to the processes outlined above this means that the weight of the China/CPC position in the international economic discussion will continue to increase. Therefore, the balance sheet of the international discussion given above is not static but will continue to evolve in China's favour.

It should also be understood, however, that this development is not only in the interests of the global economy but also of China itself. The very slow growth of the global economy, primarily produced by very slow growth in the advanced Western economies, creates a more unfavourable context for China – in particular because it leads to slow growth of world trade and therefore a slow growth of China's exports. Greater international influence of China's policies influence will lead to speeding up of the global economy and therefore be of benefit to China itself. China's vigorous participation in the international economic discussion is therefore not merely in the interest of other economies but of China itself.

Contemporary discussions in China

Finally, recent discussions in China itself may be clearly understood in this international context. The slowdown in the Western economies produced by Reaganomics/Washington Consensus has become so severe that, as noted in the data above, it now threatens to progressively undermine the overall position of the Western economies within the global economy. As the failure of the Washington Consensus makes it impossible for the Western economies to accelerate their own growth instead they have to seek to maintain their position compared to China by slowing down China's economic development - by means analysed in detail in *You Don't Know China.*

The Belt and Road Initiative must therefore be seen not only as important itself but as part of this increasing role of China's 'thought leadership' in the world economy.

Conclusion

As was analysed above the increasing weight of China's and the CPC within international economic discussion is directly connected to the practical success of China's economy compared to the Washington Consensus. But this increasing weight corresponds both to the interests of China and other countries in a 'virtuous circle'.

- The theoretical correctness of China's economic policies is of interest to economic specialists. But it is the practical effects of these in more rapid growth of China's economy than Western strategies which influences political leaders and the international public opinion. The CPC's success in guiding China's own domestic economic development is therefore also the key to China's position in international economic discussion.
- This in turn means that the increasing international influence of China's and the CPC's economic policies are in the interests of other countries. As the policies of the Washington Consensus have brought economic slowdown to the Western economies, and developing countries influenced by it, the greater the influence of China and the CPCs economic policies the more rapid will be economic development in other countries – in turn creating a more favourable international context for China.

It is already well known that increased economic cooperation between countries is a 'win-win' not only for China but for others. But, for reasons analysed in this article, it should also be increasingly understood that the increased international 'thought leadership' of the CPC, of the economic policies which originated with Deng Xiaoping, is also a win-win both for China and for other countries.

This is the overall international framework in which the Belt and Road should be seen.

中国的东亚互联互通战略：多维内涵与时代价值

赵江林　【中国】

中国社会科学院亚太与全球战略研究院国际经济关系室　主任、研究员

自中共十八大提出“推动同周边国家互联互通”以来，在3年的时间里，中国已经完成有关互联互通战略从理念到体系，再到具体部署的构建工作，作为中国全新对外经济开放格局塑造的重要战略支点，东亚互联互通的成功推进将成为实现中国梦、亚太梦关键性的第一步。

中国的东亚互联互通战略出台的背景

中国的东亚互联互通战略是新时期中国对外开放战略调整的反映，是中国从关注自身到关注周边、亚洲乃至世界经济增长的结果，是中国经济实力提升之后愿意与周边国家共同改写东亚未来发展命运的战略举措。

首先，中国经济实力的提升使中国有能力支持其他东亚国家实现经济的快速增长与繁荣。如果翻阅中国改革开放之后的对外交往历史，可以发现，无论是在双边场合还是多边场合，中国提倡议较多，对地区提供大规模、实质性的支持却相对较少。随着中国经济实力的快速提升，当前中国不仅提倡议，更重要的是能够将倡议转化为具体的行动，金砖国家开发银行、丝路基金、亚洲基础设施投资银行等创意就是中国经济实力提升之后对外战略调整的典型性反映。

其次，周边发展中国家的高度认同增强了中国推行东亚互联互通战略的便捷性。在2014年11月8日中国倡议召开的“加强互联互通伙伴关系”东道主伙伴

对话会上，中国提出的有关加强亚洲互联互通伙伴关系建设的想法得到了与会者的高度认同，并写入了《加强互联互通伙伴关系对话会联合新闻公报》中，该公报也因此成为亚洲加强互联互通的第一份“宣言”。在双边层面上，近两年中国也与周边国家就加强双边互联互通达成共识。

再次，中国已有的合作基础为互联互通的推进创造了条件。截至目前，中国已经同周边国家开展涉及贸易、投资、产业、金融、文化、教育、科技、旅游等多领域的合作，签署了大量的双边合作协议，如货币互换、经贸未来5年发展规划、产业园区建设、人员交流、学历相互认证等，这些已有的合作为未来的互联互通建设奠定了基础，同时也构成互联互通推进的重要组成部分。

中国的东亚互联互通战略的多维内涵

中国有关互联互通战略的具体内容是在综合已有的多边互联互通框架和中国自己提出的战略构想基础之上确立的，并通过东道主伙伴对话会向外宣布的。

由于互联互通至少是两个及两个以上国家之间在硬件、软件和人文建设上进行的“链接”，且加入互联互通建设的国家越多，获得的效果也越理想，因而互联互通往往最先由多边合作机构提出。在亚太地区，较早提出互联互通建设的有东盟和亚太经合组织（APEC）等国际性合作机构。中国较完整地阐述互联互通战略体系是在“加强互联互通伙伴关系”东道主伙伴对话会上，习近平主席再次将互联互通战略的具体内容、实施的优先领域和重点国家进行了全面说明，且其主体思想被纳入到中国与亚洲7国领导人共同发表的《加强互联互通伙伴关系对话会联合新闻公报》中，即：“21世纪亚洲互联互通是‘三位一体’的联通，包括交通基础设施的硬件联通，规章制度、标准、政策的软件联通，以及增进民间友好互信和文化交流的人文联通，涵盖政策沟通、设施联通、贸易畅通、资金融通和民心相通五大领域。”“基础设施建设是互联互通的基础和优先。”

与此同时，中国不仅形成了自己的东亚互联互通战略体系，同时也发出倡议，希望东亚各国能够参与到东亚互联互通建设中来。在2014年“10+3”领导人峰会上，李克强总理提出探讨制定“东亚互联互通总体规划”的建议，目的是促使东亚互联互通能够尽快提到建设日程上来，以尽快服务于东亚地区经济增长。

从以上来看，中国的东亚互联互通战略具有开放包容、交往便捷、利益共享等多重内涵，目的是真切地服务于东亚的经济增长，谋求的是如何增进东亚人的幸福。所谓开放包容即指东亚各国应以最小的壁垒促进商品、资本、人员等流动，并将开放的领域向第三方延伸，在尊重各国主权和领土完整基础上，不强人所难，最终实现跨界的自由流动。所谓交往便捷是指尽可能消除东亚各国交往之间存在的物理、规则、人文方面的障碍，促进东亚各国在商品、资本、人员等往来方面采用统一的规则，减少用于交往的时间和费用等成本，最大限度地提高通行效率。所谓利益共享是指互联互通能够为东亚各国带来好处，且有利于实现东亚人的共同梦想。

中国的东亚互联互通战略是集全方位、高水平、高标准于一身的对外合作战略。由于互联互通涉及的范围之大、领域之广、国家之多、问题之复杂多样，可以称得上是亚洲历史上新一代的大交融。在互联互通稳步推进的过程中，无论是项目规划还是资金使用上都必须要有所侧重，通过结点问题的解决，以保证互联互通战略的顺利实施。“加强互联互通伙伴关系”东道主对话会上已经明确提出了中国的互联互通战略的优先关注领域，即以亚洲国家为重点方向，优先关注和实现亚洲的互联互通；以陆路经济走廊和海上经济合作为依托，建立亚洲互联互通基本框架；以交通基础设施为突破，实现亚洲互联互通早期收获；以人文交流为纽带，夯实亚洲互联互通的社会根基。与此同时，中国业已为东亚互联互通建设提供示范性做法，前不久中国已经同韩国和澳大利亚结束了高标准、多领域的实质性自贸区谈判，同时中国也在加紧同 RCEP 成员进入实质性的谈判阶段；另外，中国倡议筹建的亚洲基础设施投资银行也将以“绿色”和“廉洁”为原则进行运作。[1]

中国的东亚互联互通战略的时代价值

中国虽然不是互联互通倡议提出的第一家，但中国却是东亚互联互通战略的最积极推进者。中国的东亚互联互通战略回应了东亚地区客观发展的要求，体现了时代的精神。

第一，有利于稳定和拓展东亚地区经济增长的物质基础，改变“亚洲”在世界中的位置。习近平主席在 2013 年 APEC 工商领导人峰会上曾谈及，增长动力只能从改革中来，从调整中来，从创新中来。互联互通涵盖了中国与东亚国家合作的所有方面，阻碍商品、资本和人员自由流动的即为经济增长的瓶颈，消除这些障碍即为经济增长的动力。中国的东亚互联互通战略即是赋予东亚地区经济增长新动力的纲领性做法。不仅如此，中国的互联互通战略还有利于改变亚洲传统形象，提升亚洲在世界经济发展中的位置。正如习近平主席在“加强互联互通伙伴关系”东道主伙伴对话会上所说：“亚洲国家必须积极作为，在亚洲资源、亚洲制造、亚洲储蓄、亚洲工厂的基础上，致力发展亚洲价值、亚洲创造、亚洲投资、亚洲市场，联手培育新的经济增长点和竞争优势。实现这些目标，互联互通是其中一个关键环节。”

第二，为未来的东亚合作设计了新的发展方向和新的合作思维模式。无论是时代背景，还是东亚自身的经济增长需要，客观上都要求东亚摆脱传统的发达国家狭隘的合作范围和路径，进入一个全新的合作阶段。中国的互联互通战略正是上述现实的反映和下一个合作阶段推进的践行者。一直以来，东亚国家试图通过“遵循”欧美等发达国家的传统合作路径，促进自身的经济增长，例如，在合作领域，东亚国家一直在努力尝试以规章制度、标准、政策等软件联通为主，自 1997 年亚洲金融危机以来，东亚成员参与并签署的自贸区协议多达上百个。不过，这种过多偏重于“规则”的统一显然不能满足东亚发展中成员实现经济发展的客观要求。毕竟，东亚在经济发展水平、人文环境等诸多方面不同于欧美等发达国家，所面临的国际环境更是不同于当时欧美国家发展时所面临的国际环境，单一“联通”已不能满足东亚各国之间未来交往的需要，包含有全方位的“五通”才是题中之意。也正因此，建立包括硬件的基础设施、软件的政策制度和人文交流在内的联通才能真正反映诸多东亚发展中成员的利益诉求，也才能顺应东亚地区的未来发展需要。

当然，要实现东亚的全方位发展需要在思想与行动上的创新。中国的东亚互联互通战略正在努力引领东亚国家实践一种全新的合作模式。完成互联互通战略的目标不仅需要东亚各国改变传统封闭的思维理念，同时在具体行动上也要突破传统经济发展路径的思维，如中国倡议设立的亚洲基础设施投资银行就是一种创新，通过整合亚洲资源，树立亚洲资金为亚洲人服务的理念，发挥亚洲基础设施投资银行的杠杆效应，以撬动亚洲基础设施建设资金不足的难题，改变基础设施长期滞后于经济增长和民众生活水平提高的现实。

第三，有利于展示中国作为新一代大国的形象。互联互通在某种意义上是一种公共产品，公共产品的投入往往在一国国内需要政府出面，在地区层面上则需要地区领导者出面。历史上，任何大国在实施对外战略、提供地区公共产品时，都会附加某些政治条款，例如1997年美欧主导的国际货币基金组织在援助遭遇金融危机重创的部分东盟国家时即如此，由日美长期主导的亚洲国家开发银行在帮助亚洲国家减贫过程中也是如此。当今东亚发展中国家硬件基础设施资金严重缺乏，而传统上依靠发达国家资助也显得力不从心，一方面发达国家国家在经历2008年全球金融危机之后普遍陷入增长的困境，自然对周边发展中国家的“援助”能力有所下降，另一方面，发达国家对周边发展中国家援助方向也在调整，从过去重基础设施等硬件建设的投入转为向人力资源开发等软件建设的投入上。另外，像亚洲开发银行、世界银行等多边机构限于目标定位和业务方向，也难以满足庞大的互联互通建设的资金需求，例如，亚洲开发银行在2013年仅向亚洲基础设施提供了210亿美元的资助。

随着中国经济实力的增强，中国正在以新一代大国形象出现在地区乃至世界上，中国提出的东亚互联互通战略正是新一代大国对地区发展的责任意识的体现。在亚洲基础设施投资银行创设和丝路基金使用，以及中国向东盟国家提供的优惠贷款等方面，中国打破传统发达国家的做法，在积极出资支持地区经济增长的同时，不附加任何政治条款。中国不仅成为当今东亚地区基础设施的最大出资人之一，而且也是最大的智慧贡献者之一。向东亚地区输出中国的发展经验，与东亚国家分享经济增长经验，以便相互借鉴和学习正在成为中国关注地区经济增长的另一做法。中国是亚洲最大的发展中国家，在经济发展过程中，中国需要解决的基础设施问题难度之大超过亚洲任何一个国家，但是中国经济发展并没有为基础设施所制约，反而在短时期迅速完成了基础设施的建设工作，在这期间，中国在长期的基础设施建设过程中积累了宝贵的经验和教训，无疑对亚洲基础设施提供了“软”贡献。亚洲基础设施投资银行和丝路基金一旦走上正式运作轨道，不仅可以借鉴其他多边机构的有益经验和做法，也可以将中国的经验和做法传播给东亚，加快东亚国家建设基础设施的速度，以便在尽可能短的时间内解决基础设施瓶颈问题。

China's East Asian Connectivity Program: Multi-dimensional Connotation and the Value of Times

Zhao Jianglin / China

Director of International Economic Relations Studies of the National Institute of International Strategy, CASS

Over the three years since the idea of "promoting connectivity with the surrounding countries" was put forward at the 18th National Congress of the Communist Party of China, China has completed the construction of its connectivity strategy from its philosophy to a system to its concrete arrangement. East Asian connectivity is an important strategic pivot for China's new pattern of economic opening up, while successfully pushing forward the East Asian connectivity is the critical and first step in realizing the Chinese and Asia Pacific dream.

Background of China's East Asian Connectivity Program

China's East Asian Connectivity Strategy reflects the adjustments of China's opening up in the new period; it is the result of the shift of China's focus from China itself to the surrounding countries, Asia and even to the growth of the world's economy; it is the strategic move arising out of China's willingness to work, after the improvement of China's economic strength, with the surrounding countries in order to change the destiny of East Asia for future development.

First, the improvement of China’s economic strength enables China to support other East Asian countries in achieving rapid economic growth and prosperity. As shown by the history of foreign contacts after China’s reform and opening up, there have been more bilateral and multilateral occasions where China has put forward initiatives than the bilateral and multilateral occasions where China has provided large-scale substantial support to regions. With the rapid improvement of China’s economic strength, at present, China not only puts forward initiatives, but it can also turn initiatives into concrete actions. Such ideas as the BRICS Development Bank, the Silk Road Fund and the Asian Infrastructure Investment Bank typically reflect the adjustments of China’s foreign strategy after the improvement of its own economic strength.

Second, high recognition by the surrounding developing countries increases the advantages for China in carrying out its East Asian connectivity strategy. At the Dialogue on Strengthening Connectivity Partnership held, as advocated by China, on November 8, 2014, China’s idea of strengthening the Asian connectivity partnership was highly applauded by the participants. This idea was written into the *Joint Press Communiqué of the Dialogue on Strengthening Connectivity Partnership*. This communiqué is the first manifesto on the strengthening of Asian connectivity. At the bilateral level, China and the surrounding countries have reached a consensus on strengthening bilateral connectivity in the past two years.

Third, China’s existing foundation of cooperation has created the conditions for promoting connectivity. So far, China has engaged in cooperation with the surrounding countries in trade, investment, industry, finance, culture, education, science, technology, tourism and other fields, and has signed a number of bilateral cooperation agreements with them, involving currency swaps, a future 5-year trade development plan, industrial park construction, personnel exchanges and mutual authentication of diplomas. This existing cooperation lays the foundation for the development of future connectivity and also forms an important part of its efforts at connectivity.

Multi-dimensional connotation of China's East Asian Connectivity Program

The specific contents of China's Connectivity Program are based on the existing framework for multilateral connectivity and on the China-proposed strategic conception, which were announced at the Dialogue on Strengthening Connectivity Partnership.

Connectivity entails the connection between and among at least two or more countries in the development of hardware, software and humanistic elements, and the effects will be more ideal if more countries participate in its development, thus connectivity has often been proposed by multilateral cooperation agencies early on. In the Asia-Pacific Region, the multilateral cooperation agencies which early on put forward the idea of the development of connectivity include ASEAN and APEC. China set forth the system of a connectivity strategy in a relatively complete way at the Dialogue on Strengthening Connectivity Partnership. During this meeting, Chinese President Xi Jinping once again fully explained the specific contents of the connectivity strategy, the priorities for its implementation and the key countries involved in it, while its main ideas were expressed in the *Joint Press Communiqué of the Dialogue on Strengthening Connectivity Partnership* jointly issued by the leaders of China and seven Asian countries. Its main ideals are as follows: Asian connectivity in the 21st century involves three-in-one connections, including a hardware connection concerning transportation infrastructures, a software connection involving rules, regulations, standards and policies, and people-to-people connections for enhancing friendly, non-governmental mutual trust and cultural exchanges; it covers five main fields, which are policy communication, infrastructure connectivity, trade links, capital flow, and understanding among peoples; the building of infrastructures is the foundation for and priority of the connectivity.

Meanwhile, China has not only established its own system of an East Asian Connectivity Program, but it has also put forward an initiative showing that China hopes that the East Asian countries can participate in the development of East Asian connectivity. At the "10+3" Leaders' Summit in 2014, Chinese Premier Li Keqiang suggested exploring and developing the *Overall Plan for East Asian Connectivity* with the aim of helping to put East Asian connectivity on the construction agenda as soon as possible in order to serve the economic growth of East Asia as early as possible.

As indicated above, China's East Asian Connectivity Program has multiple connotations—open, inclusive, convenient for contacts, sharing of interests—and it aims at really serving the economic growth of East Asia and seeks to improve the well-being of the East Asian people. "Open and inclusive" means that the East Asian countries should minimize barriers in order to promote the flow of goods, capital and people, and extend the opening-up fields to third parties; the sovereignty and territorial integrity of the various countries should be respected and no country should be forced to participate in this process, ultimately a cross-border free flow will be achieved. "Convenient for contacts" means that actions are taken to remove the barriers among the East Asian countries regarding physical contacts, rules and people-to-people contacts; they stimulate the East Asian countries to adopt unified rules concerning contacts in goods, capital and people, and they reduce the time and costs for those contacts to come about so as to improve the efficiency of access as much as possible. "Sharing of interests" means that connectivity can deliver benefits to the East Asian countries and is conducive to realizing the common dream of the East Asian people.

China's East Asian Connectivity Program is an all-round foreign cooperation strategy characterized by a high level and a high standard. Connectivity involves a wide scope, extensive fields, many countries, and complicated and diverse problems, so it is hailed as the new generation of a great integration in the history of Asia. During the steady development of connectivity, project planning and the use of funds must focus on key points, and the problems at the nodes must be solved in order to guarantee the smooth implementation of the connectivity strategy. The Dialogue on Strengthening Connectivity Partnership spelled out the priorities of China's Connectivity Program—focus on Asian countries, give priority to and achieve Asian connectivity; rely on land-based economic corridors and maritime economic cooperation to build the basic framework for Asian connectivity; make breakthroughs in transportation infrastructures to realize the rapid achievement of Asian connectivity; strengthen the social foundation for Asian connectivity by promoting people-to-people exchanges. China has provided a model for the development of East Asian connectivity. Not long ago, China concluded high-standard, multi-field substantive free trade zone negotiations with South Korea and Australia. Meanwhile, China has been losing no time in conducting substantive negotiations with the RCEP (Regional Comprehensive Economic Partnership) members. In addition, the Asian Infrastructure Investment Bank, advocated by China, will be operated in a green and clean way.[1]

The Value of the Times in China's East Asian Connectivity Program

Although China is not the first to put forward the connectivity initiative, it has been very active in pushing forward the East Asian connectivity strategy. China's East Asian Connectivity Strategy responds to the objective developmental needs of East Asia and embodies the spirit of the times.

First, be conducive to stabilizing and expanding the material foundation for the economic growth of East Asia, and change Asia's status in the world. At the 2013 APEC CEO Summit, Chinese President Xi Jinping said that the growth impetus only comes from reforms, adjustments and innovations. Connectivity covers all aspects of the cooperation between China and the East Asian countries. The barriers to the free flow of goods, capital and people are the bottlenecks in economic growth, while the removal of these barriers gives birth to the growth impetus. China's East Asian Connectivity Strategy is the programmatic practice for providing new impetus for the economic growth of East Asia. Moreover, China's Connectivity Strategy is also beneficial to changing the traditional image of Asia and improving Asia's status in the world economic development. At the Dialogue on Strengthening Connectivity Partnership, Chinese President Xi Jinping stressed: "Asian countries ought to redouble their efforts at building on their traditional strengths in resources, manufacturing capacity, savings and as the world's workshop and acquire new strengths in added value, innovation, investment and markets, with a view to cultivating new growth areas and new competitive edges together. In achieving all these goals, connectivity holds a key link."

Second, design a new direction for development and a new way of conceiving of cooperation for the future East Asian cooperation. The background of the times and the economic growth needs of East Asia objectively require East Asia to break away from the narrow scope and routes of cooperation of the traditional developed countries, and enter a new stage of cooperation. China's Connectivity Strategy reflects precisely the above-mentioned reality and helps move into the next stage of cooperation. For a long time, the East Asian countries have tried to boost their economic growth by "following" the traditional routes of cooperation of the developed countries including those of the European countries and of the USA; for example, the East Asian countries tried to concentrate cooperation on software connectivity including rules, regulations, standards and policies. Since the Asian financial crisis in 1997, the East Asian members have participated in and signed about 100 free trade zone agreements. However, this excessive emphasis on unifying the "rules" obviously fails to meet the objective needs of the developing members of East Asia for their economic development. After all, East Asia is different from the developed countries, including the European countries and the USA regarding the level of economic development, the humanistic environment and other fields; the international environment of the East Asian countries differs from that of the previous development of European countries and the USA, so a single connectivity cannot meet the needs of the East Asian countries for future contacts; so, an all-round "five-way connectivity" is appropriate. Therefore, only the connectivity covering hardware—infrastructures—and software—policies, institutions and people-to-people exchanges – really reflects the interest appeals of the developing members of East Asia and caters to its future developmental needs.

Of course, in order to achieve an all-round development of East Asia, it is necessary to innovate in ways of thinking and activities. China's East Asian Connectivity Strategy is leading the East Asian countries towards practicing a new manner of cooperation. In order to achieve the goals under the connectivity strategy, the East Asian countries should change their traditional closed lines of thought and philosophies, and break away from the traditional ideas of an economic developmental path in concrete actions; for example, the Asian Infrastructure Investment Bank, advocated by China, is an innovation because Asian resources are integrated, and the philosophy that Asian funds serve Asian people is fostered, and scope is given to the leverage effect of the Asian Infrastructure Investment Bank to address the shortage of funds for the development of Asian infrastructures, change the reality that infrastructure has lagged behind economic growth and the improvement of the people's living standard for a long time.

Third, be beneficial for demonstrating the image of China as the new generation of large country. In a sense, connectivity is public goods, while the input of public goods in a country is often achieved by the government and its input at the regional level is enabled by regional leaders. Historically, any large country imposed some additional political terms during implementation of foreign strategies and provision of regional public goods; for example, additional political terms were imposed when the International Monetary Fund led by Europe and the USA assisted some ASEAN countries devastated by financial crisis in 1997, when the Asian Development Bank led by Japan and the USA helped Asian countries reduce poverty for a long period of time. At present, the developing countries in East Asia are suffering from severe shortage of funds for their hardware infrastructures, while traditional financial assistance from the developed countries is highly unable to address such a severe shortage—on the one hand, generally, the developed countries got into a growth dilemma after the global financial crisis in 2008, so their ability to "assist" the surrounding developing countries decreased to some extent; on the other hand, the developed countries have adjusted the direction of their assistance to the surrounding developing countries by shifting their focus from input in hardware development, such as infrastructures, to that in software development, such as the development of human resources. In addition, it is difficult for multilateral agencies, including the Asian Development Bank and the World Bank, to meet the huge fund needs of the development of connectivity due to the goals, positioning and business directions of multilateral agencies; for example, the Asian Development Bank provided assistance worth only 21 billion USD for Asian infrastructures in 2013.

With the improvement of China's economic strength, China is showcasing its image as the new generation of large country in regions, and even all over the world; the East Asian Connectivity Strategy proposed by China embodies precisely that sense of responsibility which the new generation of large countries have regarding regional development. In the case of the Asian Infrastructure Investment Bank, the Silk Road Fund and concessional loans extended to ASEAN countries by China, China breaks away from the practice adopted by traditional developed countries and actively funds regional economic growth while imposing no additional political terms. China is not only one of the largest fund contributors to current East Asian infrastructures, but it is also one of the largest "wisdom" contributors. Another way in which China pays attention to regional economic growth is that China provides its experience in development to the East Asian countries and shares its experience in economic growth with them so as to learn from each other. As China is the largest developing country in Asia, China's difficulties in solving problems regarding infrastructures during its economic development greatly exceed those for any other Asian country; however, China's economic development has not been restricted by infrastructures; instead, China completed its building of infrastructures within a short period of time and has acquired valuable experience and learned many lessons during its long-term building of infrastructures; undoubtedly, China has made "soft" contributions to Asian infrastructures. Once officially in operation, the Asian Infrastructure Investment Bank and the Silk Road Fund can be operated by drawing upon the beneficial experience and practices of other multilateral agencies and spreading China's experience and practices to East Asia so that the East Asian countries can speed up their construction of infrastructures and solve the infrastructure bottlenecks in the shortest period of time possible.

新背景下提高东盟—中国合作的效果

杜进森　【越南】

越中友好协会　常务委员 / 前越南社科翰林院中国研究所　所长

前言

2016 年是纪念东盟—中国建立对话关系 25 周年，回顾东盟—中国的合作历程、合作机制，发现其成功和不足之处，由此吸取经验，这不仅具有科学性，而且具有深刻的实践价值。

自 21 世纪初以来，尤其全球金融危机之后，世界形势出现许多深刻、甚至前所未有的变化。其中，中国和东盟的局势也受其影响也发生了明显的变化。因此，提出措施以提高新背景下东盟—中国合作的效果是一件既必要又重要的事情。

本文分析、评价东盟和中国的形势、东盟—中国双方合作的现状，由此提出旨在提高今后双方合作效果的一些建议。

一　世界、东盟和中国形势概况

（一）世界形势

尽管和平、合作和发展依然是大的趋势，但是仍然存在着难以确定、难以预测的因素。宗教、种族紧张冲突，分离主义，局部战争，领土战争，政治暴乱，干涉、颠覆、恐怖仍然尖锐；威胁非传统安全因素譬如财政金融、电子电信、生物学、环境等领域的高科技犯罪继续增加。世界经济在金融危机后虽然有复苏的迹象但仍存在许多困难和不稳定；保护主义以多种形式发展；各国大力进行体制、部门和经济领域重组。全球性的问题譬如财政安全、能源安全、粮食安全、气候变化、海平面上升、天灾、疫病继续发生复杂变化。

中国和东盟在内的亚太依然是发展充满活力的地区，在世界上具有日益重要的地缘经济政治战略地位。同时，这里也是一些大国的战略竞争区域，存在许多不稳定的因素。本地区和南海上的领土、海洋和岛屿主权争端依然尖锐、复杂。

（二）东盟形势

在过去的几年里，尽管地区、国际形势连续发生变化并出现与东南亚地区直接相关的新挑战，譬如：大国间的战略竞争增加、国际恐怖主义、自然灾害以及南海的不稳定危机等，但是东盟仍然在和平中繁荣发展。这充分体现了东盟政治安全合作对于保障地区和平、安全和稳定的贡献。实际上，2009—2015 年，东盟开展并完成 146 项具体的合作行动，集中于 14 个优先领域和 3 个主要问题。3 个主要问题是：按照共同规则活动；具有全面保障安全的共同责任；扩大与外部的合作。至今，几乎所有的合作行动都已完成并发挥作用，对维护地区的和平、安全、稳定、合作发展做出重要贡献[1]。

在新的情势下，东盟成为共同体，继续在维护地区和平稳定、促进经济合作联结发挥主导作用，但是也面对着许多来自内部和外部的困难和挑战[2]。值得注意的是，各大国譬如中国支持东盟在不断演变的区域架构中发挥主导作用[3]。

（三）中国形势

经历 30 多年的改革开放，中国取得了诸多成就：经济平稳较快发展，成为世界第二大经济体；改革开放取得重大进展，人民生活水平显著提高，民主法制建设迈出新步伐，文化建设迈上新台阶，社会建设取得新进步；中国在国际上的地位得到增强[4]。中共十八大以后，中国在对内和对外方面都出现重大调整，其中，可以说，“一带一路”战略倡议是这种调整的集中体现。这一新的战略倡议营造了帮助中国扩大与世界其他各地区、各大洲联结的基石。

---

1 越南外交部副部长黎怀忠：《政治安全合作：东盟共同体的发展基石》，《全民国防杂志》2016 年 4 月 15 日。

2 越南中央宣教部：《越共十二大文件学习材料》，国家政治出版社 2016 年版，第 116 页。

3 《纪念中国—东盟建立战略伙伴关系 10 周年联合声明》。

4 胡锦涛：《坚定不移沿着中国特色社会主义道路前进为全面建成小康社会而奋斗》，在中国共产党第十八次全国代表大会上的报告（2012 年 11 月 8 日），人民出版社 2012 年版。

二 东盟—中国合作现状

（一）政治安全合作

经过 20 年共同努力合作，东盟与中国之间的政治互信明显增强。2003 年，中国成为首个参加《东南亚友好合作条约》（TAC）的区域外成员国，与东盟形成面向地区和平与繁荣目标的战略伙伴关系。双方建立了较为完善的对话合作机制，包括东盟—中国领导人会议、部长级会议机制和 5 个工作层对话合作机制。2002 年，中国和东盟签署《南海各方行为宣言》（DOC），达成通过和平方式解决争端，共同维护地区稳定，在南海开展合作。与此同时，中国与东盟各国的双边合作也得到大力发展。

在中国与东盟发表关于非传统安全领域合作联合宣言之后，东盟各国与各个对话国，尤其是与中国、日本、韩国、美国、欧盟及各国际组织开展合作打击非传统安全领域跨国犯罪。其中有 2000 年《东盟和中国禁毒合作行动计划》，东盟和中国禁毒合作国际会议《北京宣言》，《东盟联合反恐行动宣言》，2002 年 8 月《东盟—美国合作打击恐怖主义联合宣言》，2003 年 1 月《东盟—欧盟合作打击恐怖主义联合宣言》，2003 年 10 月关于建立东盟共同体的《第二巴厘宣言》和东盟地区安全论坛（ARF）等。只在 10 年多的时间里，中国和东盟就建立了战略伙伴关系，共同合作应对非传统安全危机。

但是，目前东盟与中国的安全合作关系仍然存在一些引发矛盾、分歧的重要因素，例如中国与东盟一些国家之间关于领土争端的有关问题。这些争端仍然是潜在的不稳定因素，如果处理不好、不彻底将影响到中国与东盟的关系。

（二）经济合作

在东盟—中国合作框架内，经贸领域合作成为一个亮点，不仅有助于推动东盟与东北亚各国的经济、贸易、投资合作，而且还创造了亚洲经济增长的动力。其中，东盟和中国相互成为对方首要的贸易和投资伙伴。

根据统计资料，中国现在是东盟的第一大贸易伙伴，东盟是中国的第三大贸易伙伴。中国—东盟建立了经济贸易和投资合作基础的战略伙伴关系，创造双方合作联结的新架构，使中国和东盟的合作成为东盟与各战略伙伴间合作的成功模式之一；双方连续举办各种会议、论坛、博览会，譬如中国—东盟金融合作与发展领袖论坛、中国—东盟文化论坛、中国—东盟中小企业跨境投资与贸易合作洽谈会、中国—东盟博览会（CAEXPO）等，以交流和促进经济合作。在第18次中国—东盟领导人会议上，双方一致同意继续推动战略伙伴关系，集中到共同关心的领域如贸易、投资、金融、互联互通、缩小发展差距、环境、医疗和教育；努力到2020年将双边贸易提高到1万亿美元、双向投资提高到1500亿美元的水平。现今中国出资400亿美元成立“丝绸之路基金”，发展亚太各国的基础设施互联互通；中国和东盟签署中国—东盟自贸区升级版（2015年11月22日）。

以上数据和事件表明，东盟—中国经济贸易合作在过去的很长时间里得到大力发展并成为战略伙伴关系的重要支柱。

在取得上述成就的同时，双方仍存在一些不足之处。一是，东盟各国对中国的贸易逆差继续增加，2010年东盟—中国自贸区全面建成后，东盟各国对中国的货物贸易已由顺差变成2013年逆差450亿美元。其中，制造类产品尤其是机械和电子设备仍为双方贸易的主力。二是，中国对东盟的直接投资与经济潜力不相称。根据《2015年东盟投资报告：基础设施和互联互通》的统计，2014年，进入东盟的直接投资增长26%，大部分来自对话伙伴国的投资。尤其是，美国对东盟的直接投资增长165%，澳大利亚的投资增长63%，欧盟增长31%，而中国只增长31%。2014年，香港特别行政区成为对东盟直接投资的第五大外资来源地（排在欧盟、东盟、日本和美国之后），投资额大约95亿美元[1]。2015年，中国对东盟的投资达81.55亿美元，位居第四（排在欧盟、日本和美国之后）[2]。三是，中国的投资通常集中在东盟国家的自然资源开发项目，引起打乱部门、区域规划的危机，影响各国的生存环境和可持续发展。四是，中国的直接投资在技术转让方面薄弱，大部分是技术落后或引发环境污染的行业。五是，加强中国—东盟经济合作将使得大量的中国商品“涌入”东南亚和国际市场，对东盟各国的商品生产产生强大影响。此外，东盟各国都正在集中发展劳动密集型产业，出口市场主要是美国、日本、欧盟，因此，争夺销售市场的商业竞争，甚至中国—东盟内部市场的竞争也将变得尖锐[3]。

1 ASEAN Secretariat (November 2015), ASEAN Investment Report, Jakarta pp. 3-5.

2 ASEAN Statistics (2016), Foreign direct investment net inflows in ASEAN from selected partner countries/regions, Table 26.

3 越南计划投资部外国投资局：《中国与东盟各国间投资、贸易的一些特点》，2015年版。

（三）其他领域

除了上述政治、安全和经济领域的合作，东盟和中国也加强了许多其他领域的合作。双方确定了农业、信息通信技术、人力资源开发、投资、湄公河流域开发、交通、能源、文化、旅游、公共卫生和环境为 11 个重点合作领域。中国与东盟签署了农业、信息通信、湄公河信息高速公路、交通、文化、新闻媒体、知识版权等十余个合作谅解备忘录和合作框架。

教育培训方面，每年东盟有上千名大学生到中国学习。2003 年，只有 7.7628 万名外国大学生在中国留学，其中近 80% 来自亚洲，到 2015 年，在中国学习的东南亚大学生已有大约 3.1 万名，其中越南大学生大约 1.3 万名[1]。

2006 年 7 月 20 日在南宁举办的泛北部湾经济合作论坛上，中国提出了“一轴两翼”的合作构想。“一轴两翼”的形成进一步推动和深化中国与东盟的全面合作关系。以北部湾、南海和从华南到新加坡的沿海公路、铁路作为“一轴两翼”的载体，以及湄公河次区域合作载体的泛亚铁路、公路，中国与东盟的合作涵盖了陆地和海上空间。

东盟与中国也加强在解决国际事务上的配合和合作，中国一贯支持东盟在东亚合作进程中发挥主导作用，共同推动通过东盟 +3、东亚峰会（EAS）、东盟国防部长扩大会议（ADMM+）、亚洲合作对话（ACD）、亚太经合组织（APEC）会议等机制加强合作。2013 年，中国国家主席习近平在出访东南亚国家时提出共同建设更为紧密的中国—东盟命运共同体，同时提出签署《中国—东盟睦邻友好合作条约》，推动成立亚洲基础设施投资银行（AIIB）。中国与东盟各国也建立了“2+7”合作框架，包括两点政治共识即“深化战略互信”、“聚焦经济发展”和 7 个领域包括政治、经济贸易、金融、海上合作、互联互通基础设施建设、安全、人文等方面的合作。

三　提高东盟—中国合作效果的建议

（一）认识方面

我们认为，双方首先要在认识上达成一致：要加强双方的政治信任，若出现争端、分歧，则按照国际法通过和平的方式解决争端、分歧，管控好分歧，不影响到地区和世界安全。要在切实有效和平衡的基础上维持经济、文化、社会领域

1　[越] 刘越河：《冷战后至今中国—东盟关系》，《政治理论杂志》2015 年第 8 期。

的关系。首先，双方要在维持双边贸易额长期稳定增长的同时，解决双方贸易不平衡的问题。各种合作机制要走向实质，在相关经济利益关系上，给各参与方带来切实、平衡的经济成果。

（二）一些具体的措施

政治合作方面。坚持不懈地巩固和增强双方的政治互信。双方高层通过各种灵活的访问、会晤和接触，经常见面真诚坦率和切实地交换意见，寻求促进合作、解决存在或产生问题的措施。双方也要加强分享经验，有效开展已经商定的交流合作项目和机制；发挥已有的调节促进双方合作领域的各种合作机制、论坛的作用；加强外交、国防、安全、经济、文化等重要领域的合作。注重推进双方人民尤其是年青一代的交流活动。

经济合作方面。推动经济合作走向实质、平衡、有效发展。双方领导人要重视指导各部门严格执行高层已经达成的协议和共识，同时积极通过的有效措施，扩大和促进各领域合作共赢。建议双方采取切实措施，推动东盟与中国之间以及东盟内部之间的双边贸易稳定、平衡和可持续发展；通过具体的合作计划、项目，推动中国与东盟各国的互联互通合作项目，如通过“两廊一圈”战略推进越南与中国的互联互通，通过老挝从“陆锁国”转变为“陆联国”项目推进中老互联互通，所有依照符合中国提出的“一带一路”倡议内容的双方和多方互联互通，要在尊重相互正当利益、平等互利的基础上进行；加强符合双方水平和需求之领域的产能合作。与此同时，也要提高贸易和投资的自由化和便利化水平，努力实现到2020年贸易总额达到1万亿美元的目标；加强金融合作，扩大双边货币互换的规模和范围，加强试点以推进实施各国间的贸易使用本币结算。

安全合作。东盟—中国要管控好领土纠纷方面的分歧、冲突，避免导致不稳定的危机发生。管控好中国与一些东盟国家之间的海洋争端、东盟各国内部的领土冲突，不让该问题影响到双方正常发展关系。双方要紧密配合有效监管存在纠纷区域的情势；尊重相互的正当利益；严格实施双方高层已经达成的共识和协议；在争端区域维持现状，不采取使争端复杂化、扩大化、导致局势紧张的行动。建议中国与各相关国严格和充分地执行《南海各方行为宣言》(DOC)，并尽早有效制定《南海行为准则》(COC)；增强树立信心以顺利开展双方达成的合作项目。建议双方有效和实质性地开展关于争端问题的谈判机制，积极交流寻求双方均能接受的基本和长久解决办法。与此同时，双方也要注意重视保障共同的安全，积极推动合作来保障地区共同安全、总体安全，以应对非传统安全威胁如恐怖主义、跨境犯罪、网络犯罪、气候变化带来的挑战和影响。

结论

新的背景对东盟和中国提出了新的要求，需要双方作出新的行动来维持和确保双方关系稳定健康发展。东盟应该成为中国对外关系的优先方向。中国的“一带一路”倡议与东盟各国的战略对接过程应该面向可持续、切实和有效发展的目标，确保利益平衡——不仅是东盟与中国之间的利益平衡，而且是东盟各国之间的利益平衡。另外，双方在发展经济贸易的同时要确保生态环境安全，确保社会福利。

我们认为，东盟—中国的友好合作关系会日益美好发展，满足双方领导人和人民的愿望和长久根本的利益，为维护地区乃至世界的和平稳定作出重要贡献。

参考文献

越南外交部副部长黎怀忠：《政治安全合作：东盟共同体的发展基石》，越南《全民国防杂志》2016 年 4 月 15 日。

越南中央宣教部：《越共十二大文件学习材料》，国家政治出版社 2016 年版，第 116 页。

《纪念中国—东盟建立战略伙伴关系 10 周年联合声明》。

胡锦涛：《坚定不移沿着中国特色社会主义道路前进　为全面建成小康社会而奋斗》，在中国共产党第十八次全国代表大会上的报告（2012 年 11 月 8 日），人民出版社 2012 年版。

ASEAN Secretariat (November 2015), ASEAN Investment Report, Jakarta pp. 3-5.

ASEAN Statistics (2016), Foreign direct investment net inflows in ASEAN from selected partner countries/regions, Table 26.

越南计划投资部外国投资局：《中国与东盟各国间投资、贸易的一些特点》，2015 年。

［越］刘越河：《冷战后至今中国—东盟关系》，越南《政治理论杂志》2015 年第 8 期。

Improve the Effects of ASEAN-China Cooperation under the New Situation

Do Tien Sam / Vietnam

Standing Committee Member of the Vietnam-China Friendship Association / Former Director of the Institute of Chinese Studies at the Vietnam Academy of Social Sciences

Introduction

The year 2016 marked the 25th anniversary of the establishment of relations in the form of dialogue between ASEAN and China. The course and mechanism of ASEAN-China cooperation are reviewed in order to analyze its success and drawbacks and thus draw upon the experience. This is not only of scientific value but also of profound practical value.

Since the early 21st century, especially after the global financial crisis, many profound, even unprecedented, changes have taken place in the world. Obvious changes have also occurred in the relationship between China and the ASEAN countries due to impact of that crisis. Therefore, it is necessary and important to put forward measures to improve the effects of ASEAN-China cooperation in the new situation.

This paper analyzes and evaluates the situation of China and the ASEAN countries and the current situation of their cooperation, and it gives some suggestions on how to enhance the effects of future cooperation between the two parties.

1. Overview of the World, the Situation in the ASEAN Countries and in China

1.1 World situation

Peace, cooperation and development remain the general trends, but unpredictable, difficult-to-determine factors still exist. Religious and racial tensions and conflicts, separatism, local wars, territorial wars, political unrest, intervention, subversion and terrorism are still acute. Non-traditional security-threatening factors, such as high-tech crimes in such fields as fiscal and financial, electronic, telecommunications, biological as well as environmental fields are on the rise. The world's economy has shown a sign of recovery after the financial crisis, but many difficulties and uncertainties are still lingering. Protectionism is developing in various ways. Various countries are stepping up efforts in institutional, sectoral and economic reorganizations. Complicated changes are occurring in global issues such as financial security, energy security, food security, climate change, sea level rise, acts of God and diseases.

The Asian-Pacific region, including China and the ASEAN countries, remains vibrant and enjoys an increasingly important strategic geo-economic and political position in the world. However, it is also a region where some great powers strategically compete with each other, so it is fraught with many unstable factors. The sovereignty disputes over the territory, sea and islands in the region and the South China Sea remain acute and complicated.

1.2 The situation of the ASEAN countries

Over the past years, continuous changes have taken place in regional and international situations and new challenges directly related to Southeast Asia—such as an increasing strategic competition among the great powers, international terrorism, natural disasters and an instability crisis in the South China Sea—have popped up, but despite this, the ASEAN have achieved peaceful prosperity and development. This fully reflects the contributions of the cooperation on political security by the ASEAN countries to safeguarding regional peace, security and stability. In fact, from 2009 to 2015, the ASEAN countries undertook and completed 146 concrete cooperative actions focusing on 14 priority fields and 3 major issues. The three major issues are as follows: carry out activities according to common rules; assume the shared responsibility for safeguarding security in an all-round way; expand external cooperation. So far, almost all of the cooperative actions have been completed and have played their roles, making important contributions to safeguarding regional peace, security and stability and cooperative development.[1]

Under the new situation, the ASEAN has become a community and continues to play the leading role in safeguarding regional peace and stability and in promoting economic cooperation; however, the ASEAN community is also subject to many internal and external difficulties and challenges.[2] It is worth noting that the great powers, such as China, support ASEAN and play a leading role in the evolving regional framework.[3]

1.3 China's situation

After more than 30 years of reform and opening up, China has made many achievements: the economy is steadily and rapidly developing and China has become the second-largest economy in the world; significant progress has been made in reform and opening up; the people's living standard has significantly

1 Vietnamese Deputy Foreign Minister Le Hoai Trung, Political Security Cooperation: the Cornerstone for the Development of the ASEAN Community, *Tạp chí Quốc phòng toàn dân*, April 15, 2016.

2 Vietnam Ministry of Central Publicity and Education, Document Learning Materials of the 12th National Congress of the Communist Party of Vietnam, National Political Press, 2016, p.116.

3 Joint Declaration on Commemorating the 10th Anniversary of the Establishment of a Strategic Partnership between China and ASEAN.

improved; new steps have been taken in the development of democracy and law; cultural development has reached a new height; new progress has been made in social construction; China's status in the international community has been enhanced.[1] After the 18th National Congress of the Communist Party of China, China made great adjustments in its domestic and foreign affairs, and The Belt and Road Strategic Initiative epitomizes these adjustments. This new strategic initiative will create the cornerstone for helping China expand connections with the rest of the world.

2. The Current Situation of ASEAN-China Cooperation

2.1 Cooperation on Political Security

With concerted efforts and 20 years of cooperation, the mutual political trust between the ASEAN countries and China has been significantly enhanced. In 2003, China became the first country outside of ASEAN to join the *Treaty of Amity and Cooperation in Southeast Asia* (TAC), making it possible for China to establish a strategic partnership towards regional peace and prosperity with the ASEAN community. Both sides have built relatively perfect mechanisms of cooperation through dialogue, including the ASEAN-China Leaders' Meeting, a ministerial meeting mechanism and five working-level dialogue cooperation mechanisms. In 2002, China and the ASEAN countries signed the *Declaration on the Conduct of Parties in the South China Sea* (DOC) and reached a consensus on settling disputes in a peaceful way, jointly safeguarding regional stability and cooperating in the South China Sea. Meanwhile, a bilateral cooperation between China and the ASEAN countries has also vigorously developed.

After China and the ASEAN community issued their joint declaration on the cooperation in non-traditional security fields, the ASEAN countries and the dialogue countries, especially China, Japan, South Korea, the USA, the EU and

1 Hu Jintao, Unswervingly Follow the Path of Socialism with Chinese Characteristics and Strive to Build a Moderately Prosperous Society in All Respects, Report in the 18th National Congress of the Communist Party of China (November 8, 2012), People's Publishing House, Beijing, 2012.

the international organizations, engaged in cooperation to combat transnational crimes in non-traditional security fields, as evidenced by the *Action Plan for Anti-drug Cooperation between China and the ASEAN Community* in 2000, the *Beijing Declaration* at the international meeting on anti-drug cooperation between China and the ASEAN countries, the *ASEAN Declaration on Joint Anti-terrorism Action*, the *Joint Declaration on Anti-terrorism Cooperation between the ASEAN Community and the USA* in August, 2002, THE *Joint Declaration on Anti-terrorism Cooperation between the ASEAN Community and the EU* in January, 2003, *The Second Bali Declaration* on the establishment of the ASEAN community in October, 2003, the ASEAN Regional Forum, etc. Over ten years, China and the ASEAN countries have established a strategic partnership and jointly coped with non-traditional security crises.

However, currently the relationship of security cooperation between the ASEAN community and China are still subject to some important factors that contribute to contradictions and disagreements—specifically, the issues concerning territorial disputes between China and some ASEAN countries. These disputes remain some potential destabilizing factors; if not properly and thoroughly handled, they will affect China-ASEAN relations.

2.2 Economic cooperation

The cooperation in the fields of the economy and trade is a bright spot within the ASEAN-China cooperation framework; it not only helps boost ASEAN's cooperation with the Northeast Asian countries on economy, trade and investment, but it also creates the impetus for Asia's economic growth. The ASEAN countries and China have become each other's primary trade and investment partner.

According to statistical data, China is currently the largest trading partner of the ASEAN community, while the ASEAN community is China's third-largest trading partner. China and the ASEAN community have established a strategic partnership based on cooperation on the economy, trade and investments and have created a new framework for cooperation and connection between the two parties, making China-ASEAN cooperation one of the successful cooperation modes between the ASEAN community and their strategic partners. Both sides have continuously held various meetings, forums and expos—such as the China-ASEAN Summit Forum on Financial Cooperation and Development, the China-ASEAN Cultural Forum, the China-ASEAN Small and Medium-Sized Enterprise Cross-border Investment & Trade Cooperation Fair, the China-ASEAN Expo (CAEXPO) —to communicate and promote economic cooperation. At the 18th China-ASEAN Leaders' Meeting, the two sides agreed to continue to push forward the strategic partnership focusing on the fields of common concern, such as trade, investment, finance, connectivity, the narrowing of the development gap, the environment, medical treatment and education; to strive to increase bilateral trade and bilateral investment to 1 trillion USD and 150 billion USD by 2020, respectively. Now China contributes 40 billion USD to the establishment of the Silk Road Fund for developing the infrastructure connectivity in Asia-Pacific countries; China and the ASEAN community signed the updated version of the China-ASEAN free trade zone (November 22, 2015); both sides have undertaken to conclude the negotiations concerning the *Regional Comprehensive Economic Partnership* (RCEP) as early as possible in 2016.

The above data and events show that the economic and trade cooperation between China and the ASEAN community has vigorously developed and become an important pillar for strategic partnerships for a very long time in the past.

In spite of the above achievements, some drawbacks still exist between the two parties. First, the trade deficit of the ASEAN countries with China has been on the increase; after the ASEAN-China Free Trade Zone was fully completed in 2010, the trade in goods from the ASEAN countries to China changed from a surplus to a deficit of 45 billion USD in 2013. The manufactured products, especially machinery and electronic devices, still dominated the bilateral trade. Second, China's direct investments in the ASEAN community were not commensurate with their economic potential. According to the statistics, in the *2015 ASEAN*

Investment Report: Infrastructure and Connectivity, in 2014, the direct investments in ASEAN countries grew by 26% and mostly came from their dialogue countries. In particular, the direct investments from the USA, Australia and the EU to the ASEAN community grew by 165%, 63% and 31% respectively, while those from China grew by only 31%. In 2014, the Hong Kong Special Administrative Region became the fifth-largest foreign capital source of direct investments in the ASEAN community following the EU, the ASEAN countries, Japan and the USA ; the investments from the Hong Kong Special Administrative Region to the ASEAN countries was about 9.5 billion USD.[1] In 2015, China's investments in the ASEAN community reached 8,155 million USD, making China No.4 following the EU, Japan and the USA.[2] Third, China's investments were generally concentrated in the natural resource development projects in the ASEAN countries, thus posing the risk of disturbing sectoral and regional plans and affecting the survival environment and sustainable development of the ASEAN countries. Fourth, China's direct investments were weak in technology transfer and mostly involved the technologically backward or industries provoking the pollution of the environment. Fifth, intensified economic cooperation between China and the ASEAN community will result in a great quantity of Chinese goods "flooding" the Southeast Asian and international markets, exerting a huge impact on the production of goods in the ASEAN countries. In addition, the ASEAN countries are focusing on developing the labor-intensive industries with products mainly exported to the USA, Japan and the EU, thus the business competition on the sales market, and even the competition within the China-ASEAN domestic markets, will become acute.[3]

2.3 Other fields

Besides the above-mentioned cooperation in the fields of politics, security and

1 ASEAN Secretariat (November 2015), ASEAN Investment Report, Jakarta pp. 3-5.

2 ASEAN Statistics (2016), Foreign direct investment net inflows in ASEAN from selected partner countries/regions, Table 26.

3 Foreign Investment Bureau of the Vietnam Ministry of Planning and Investment, Some Characteristics of Investments and Trade in China and ASEAN Countries, 2015.

the economy, the ASEAN countries and China have also enhanced their cooperation in other fields. The two sides have determined the following 11 fields as priorities in their cooperation: agriculture, information communications technology (ICT), human resources development, investments, the development of the Mekong River basin, transportation, energy, culture, tourism, public health and the environment. China and the ASEAN countries have signed more than ten memoranda of understanding on cooperation and cooperation frameworks involving agriculture, information communications, the Mekong River information superhighway, transportation, culture, news media and intellectual property.

Regarding education and training, each year about 1,000 university students from ASEAN countries come to China to study. In 2003, only 77,628 foreign university students studied in China, nearly 80% of whom came from Asia; in 2015, about 31,000 Southeast Asian university students studied in China, including about 13,000 Vietnamese university students.[1]

During the Pan-Beibu Gulf Economic Cooperation Forum held in Nanning on July 20, 2006, China envisioned the "one-axis two-wing" cooperation. The formation of "one axis and two wings" has further pushed forward and intensified the relationship of comprehensive cooperative between China and the ASEAN community. As the Beibu Gulf, the South China Sea, the coastal highways and railways from South China to Singapore serve as the carriers for "one axis and two wings", and pan-Asian railways and highways act as the carriers for the cooperation in the Mekong Sub-region, the cooperation between China and the ASEAN community covers land and sea areas.

The ASEAN countries and China have also reinforced their coordination and cooperation in dealing with international affairs. China has always supported the ASEAN community in playing the leading role in the East Asian cooperation process, and has worked with them to strengthen their cooperation through such

1 (Vietnam), Master Liu Yuehe, China-ASEAN Relations after the Cold War up until Now, *Journal of Political Theory*, 2015(8).

mechanisms as ASEAN+3, the East Asia Summit (EAS), the ASEAN Defense Ministers Meeting Plus (ADMM+), the Asia Cooperation Dialogue (ACD) and the Asia-Pacific Economic Cooperation (APEC). In 2013, when visiting the Southeast Asian countries, Chinese President Xi Jinping proposed jointly building a closer China-ASEAN community of common destiny and signed the *China-ASEAN Treaty on Good Neighbourliness and Friendly Cooperation*; he also encouraged the establishment of the Asian Infrastructure Investment Bank (AIIB). China and the ASEAN countries have also developed the "2+7" cooperation framework covering two political consensuses—deepening their strategic mutual trust, focusing on economic development—and seven fields including politics, the economy and trade, finance, maritime cooperation, the construction of connectivity infrastructures, security and people-to-people contacts.

3. Suggestions on Improving the Effects of ASEAN-China Cooperation

3.1 Consensus

We believe that the two sides should first reach a consensus: It is necessary to enhance the political trust between the two sides; in case of disputes and differences, they should be settled in a peaceful way according to international laws, they should be properly controlled so as not to affect regional and world security. It is essential to maintain the relations in the economic, cultural and social fields in a practical, effective and balanced way. The two sides should address the trade imbalance between them while maintaining the long-term stable growth of bilateral trade. Various cooperation mechanisms should be substantive and be able to deliver tangible and balanced economic achievements to various participants in relevant relationships of economic interest.

3.2 Some concrete measures

Regarding political cooperation, the mutual political trust between the two sides should be unremittingly consolidated and enhanced. Both sides should have flexible high-level visits, meetings and engagements, and frequently meet to sincerely, frankly and practically exchange views, seek and boost cooperation, and solve the existing problems. The two sides should also share experiences, and effectively carry out the agreed exchange cooperation projects and mechanisms; moreover, they should give play to the roles of the existing cooperation mechanisms and forums in regulating and enhancing the cooperation between the two sides and strengthen the cooperation in such important fields as foreign affairs, national defense, security, the economy and culture. Finally, attention should be paid to promoting the exchange activities between the people, especially young people on both sides.

Concerning economic cooperation, economic cooperation should be stimulated and carried out in a substantive, balanced and effective way. The leaders of both sides should attach importance to guiding various ministries and departments to strictly carry out the agreements and consensuses reached at a high level while actively taking effective measures, expanding and promoting win-win cooperation in various fields. It is suggested that both sides should adopt feasible measures to boost the sound, balanced and sustainable development of bilateral trade between the ASEAN community and China and within ASEAN; it is also suggested that concrete cooperation plans and projects be carried out in order to push forward the connectivity cooperation projects between China and the ASEAN countries; for example, implementing the "two-corridor one-circle" strategy to enhance the connectivity between Vietnam and China, carrying out the project for turning Laos into a land-connected country from a land-locked country so as to push forward the connectivity between China and Laos, and impel the bilateral and multilateral connectivity based on and consistent with the China-proposed Belt and Road Initiative by respecting the legitimate interests with each other, ensuring equality and mutual benefit as well as reinforcing the cooperation on production capacity in the fields consistent with the levels and needs of the two sides. Meanwhile, it is also necessary to increase the levels of trade and investment liberalization and facilitation, strive to make total trade volume reach 1 trillion USD by 2020; and finally, financial cooperation should be strengthened, the scale and scope of bilateral currency swaps should be expanded, and pilot implementation of local currency-based settlements in the trade among various countries should be intensified.

Regarding security cooperation, the ASEAN countries and China should properly control their differences and conflicts in territorial disputes to prevent the crises leading to instability. It is necessary to properly manage maritime disputes between China and some ASEAN countries, and territorial conflicts among the ASEAN countries, and prevent them from affecting the normal development of bilateral relations. Both sides should closely and effectively supervise the situation of the areas in dispute, respect each other's legitimate interests , strictly implement the consensuses and agreements reached by the two sides at a high level, maintain the status quo of the areas in dispute, and refrain from taking actions which complicate and magnify disputes and lead to tensions. It is suggested that China and relevant countries should strictly and fully implement the *Declaration on the Conduct of Parties in the South China Sea* (DOC) and effectively develop the *Code of Conduct in the South China Sea* (COC) as early as possible; other suggestions include building up and enhancing confidence in smoothly carrying out the cooperation projects agreed upon by the two sides. Finally, it is suggested that the two sides should effectively and substantively carry out the negotiation mechanism concerning disputes and actively communicate and seek the basic and long-term solutions acceptable to both sides. Meanwhile, the two sides should also attach importance to safeguarding common security, energetically promote cooperation and safeguard common regional security and overall security, cope with non-traditional security threats such as terrorism, cross-border crimes, cyber crimes, and the challenges and impact from climate change.

Conclusions

A new background presents new requirements to the ASEAN community and China and requires both sides to take new actions to maintain and ensure the steady and healthy development of bilateral relations. The ASEAN countries should become the priority of China's foreign relations. The alignment of the Belt and Road Initiative put forward by China with the strategies of the ASEAN countries should focus on the goal of sustainable, practical and effective development, and ensure an interest balance between the ASEAN community and China and among the ASEAN countries. Moreover, both sides should ensure the safety of the ecological environment and social welfare while developing their economies and trade.

We believe that the friendly cooperative relationship between the ASEAN community and China will become increasingly good and that this relationship will meet the expectations of the leaders, the people and the fundamental interests of both sides, making important contributions to the peace and stability of the region, and even of the world.

文化认同与共同遗产

Cultural Identity and Common Heritage

从中文化层面看“一带一路”倡议

黄吉利 【缅甸】
缅甸仰光大学历史系　主任

在第一次世界大战之前，两国或多国结盟的趋势已经表现得十分明显，尽管第一次世界大战后成立了国际联盟，但在第一次世界大战后、第二次世界大战结束之前，这种趋势并未停止。后来受到冷战影响，区域间的联盟变得比国家间的联盟更为普遍，区域性的军事联盟、经济联盟纷纷涌现。各国在区域安全、区域经济交流等问题上扩大合作的同时，也转向各自的经济利益。欧洲出现了北约、华约、欧盟、经济互助委员会等组织，而亚洲则出现了东南亚条约组织、中央条约组织以及东南亚国家联盟。20 世纪后期，随着东南亚国家联盟的影响力不断增强并获得高度的国际认可，许多国家纷纷加入东南亚联盟。20 世纪末叶，由于受到世界政治格局影响，联盟的缔结方式也发生了重大变化。21 世纪初，联盟的缔结模式重大变化，从互惠互利的区域合作转向划区域合作，致力于经济发展和国家安全的联盟数量远远超过军事联盟。在诸如此类的联盟之中，中国主席习近平勾画出“一带一路”倡议这一致力于发展的战略框架。可以说，这一倡议是对 21 世纪广泛的国际合作而做出的最卓越的规划和布局。

“一带一路”旨在促进亚非欧 65 国之间的互联、互通、相互理解，在促成双赢局面的同时确保区域安全，通过国家合作确保世界和平。多数国家对于“一带一路”倡议表现出积极热情的态度，但同时也有部分国家表现出担忧和疑虑。“一带一路”正是在这一背景下开始实施。

现代丝绸之路（或）21世纪丝绸之路的五大目标如下：

（1）政策沟通；

（2）设施联通；

（3）贸易畅通；

（4）资金融通；

（5）民心相通。

从上述五大目标中可看出，“一带一路”是中国为促进沿线国家在经济上实现合作互惠而勾勒的伟大战略。

中国领导人向来强调“三个共同”和“三个绝不”的理念。所谓三个共同是指：（1）与相关方共同磋商，确定合作项目和互利项目，（2）共同协作，在共同利益的基础上开展合作项目，（3）共同分享互利合作带来的成果。所谓“三个绝不”是指：中国绝不干涉别国内政、绝不搞所谓的“势力范围”、绝不寻求霸权地位。上述目标具有十分积极的意义，但在实现互利的同时也会遇到重重挑战：可见的挑战主要包括政治稳定、安全、电信网络、交通运输以及投资，而不可见的挑战，如文化差异、传统差异、观念差异、相互理解过程中的优势与劣势等，对于合作双方均具有重要意义。

被誉为“卓越的全球性规划”的“一带一路”倡议提出后，许多国家均高度关注着这一战略的实施情况。因为对于合作项目如何开展、如何分享成果和利益、如何划分权利与义务等，不同国家均持有不同的观点。特别是发展中国家，占绝大多数人口的中产阶级始终把各自的生活放在首位，很少有机会去理解“一带一路”倡议或对其产生兴趣。因此，“一带一路”倡议在实施过程中，必须得到各国人民的支持，人民才是确保“一带一路”取得成功的中坚力量。相互理解、彼此尊重对方的文化和传统是促进民众互信、互敬的主要因素，各国能否认同彼此的文化身份、将彼此的文化身份视作共同的文化遗产，对于保证各国的国家利益同样重要。在“一带一路”倡议实施的过程中，相互理解、相互尊重扮演着重要角色，这与21世纪丝绸之路“民心相通”的宗旨是相吻合。参与“一带一路”的各国除了要面对贫富分化、社会稳定、民主体制差异等问题外，还要面临各国之间存在的冲突、强国寻求政治霸权、经济霸权等意想不到的困难和障碍。因而，“一带一路”倡议应视作一项长期规划，在实施过程中要倚靠各国乃至各级政府之间的磋商，在各国相互理解的基础上创造共同利益，在和平的基础上开展经济合作，这也是“一带一路”倡议的目标之一。可以说，这种和平发展不仅是各国的利益所在，更是中国发展规划的题中之意。

中国领导人曾指出，由于地理位置上相近、环境上相连、政治上接触、商业上友好，因此，邻邦具有重要的战略地位，中国应与邻邦一道，共同构建利益共同体。东盟成员国不仅属于陆上丝绸经济带沿线国家，更属于21世纪海上丝绸之路的沿线国家。自从公元前时代开始，中国古代的帝王便开辟了这条通往中亚、用于丝绸贸易的道路。蒙古帝国衰落后，欧洲海上商贸航线的影响力不断增强，古丝绸之路的地位逐渐遭到蚕食，后于15世纪的明朝，郑和率领船队到达印度洋沿岸国家。不论是陆上丝绸之路还是海上丝绸之路，都起到了沟通东西方的纽带作用，使中国自古以来便与东盟在经济上、社会上、文化上发生接触。

而在这条连接世界东西方的丝绸之路上，缅甸恰恰占据着战略要冲地位。有着两千多年历史的古丝绸之路正是穿过缅甸，将东方与西方连接在一起，对缅甸的政治、经济、社会经济生活以及文化产生了巨大的影响。彼时，东西方的商旅在丝绸之路上往来穿行，随之而来的，是东方与西方之间的商业交流，是经济的发展，是文化的交流，是各国之间的相互理解。而从那时起，东西各国文化开始相互融通，各国文化也彼此间相互影响和支配。

除了自身的商业纽带作用之外，丝绸之路还曾为第二次世界大战期间的军事行动做出过巨大贡献。当时为增援中国的反日本法西斯战争，同盟国重新打通了这条丝绸之路，举世闻名的利多公路（即史迪威公路）由此而来。利多公路沿线的欣贝延、德乃、帕敢、莫冈、密支那及八莫等地，均是中缅关系史上极具历史意义的城镇。这些城镇同时也因出产琥珀、玉石以及林产品而闻名。利多公路在当地的政治、经济、战事等方面扮演了重要的角色。因此，这条丝绸之路可以说是在中国、印度、缅甸三国的历史上恪尽职守的一条道路。目前，利多公路的修缮工程已经在中缅边境开工，克钦邦境内的路段施工大体已经完工，靠近印度的实皆市路段仍待修缮。一方面，根据印度的“东向政策”来看，与中国开展贸易活动能够促进印度北部区域的经济发展。但与此同时，民众也表示出忧虑，担心中国产品会沿着 利多公路源源不断地流入缅甸。利多公路与中缅公路的连通为南亚、东南亚以及东亚的内部互联铺平了道路，在保证区域安全的前提下，这条公路会在经济战略上扮演至关重要的角色。“一带一路倡议”致力于世界范围内的沟通互联，而利多公路与中缅公路相接而形成的长达1900英里的通路将全面促进贸易活动的繁荣，带来丰厚的利益。随着经济的发展，利多公路沿线居民的生计将变得更加容易，社会经济生活将得到极大改善，利多公路沿线国家人民之间的接触将更加频繁，这一切将对实现 21 世纪丝绸之路的目标提供强有力的支持。

除利多公路外，孟加拉–中国–印度–缅甸经济走廊（BCIM）也是 21 世纪丝绸之路的主要分支线路之一。这条连接中缅两国的经济走廊已经被纳入到“一带一路倡议”的版图之中。孟加拉–中国–印度–缅甸经济走廊穿过印度、孟加拉国、缅甸，将西南方诸国与印度洋连接在一起。这条经济走廊长 165 万千米，通过公路、铁路、水路、航线，连通中国的云南、孟加拉共和国、缅甸以及印度北部，穿过中国的昆明、印度的加尔各答、缅甸的曼德勒、孟加拉国的达卡、吉大港等重要城市。目前，中印加缅等四国已经达成一致，将在教育、体育、科技等领域扩大合作范围。

关于“一带一路”倡议的评估

一些分析人士将“一带一路倡议”视作中国自实行经济开放政策以来的第二次对外开放，而一些批评人士则认为，中国试图通过经济实力积累政治影响力。

然而在笔者看来，“一带一路倡议”是中国为对外投资创造绝佳机遇的重大战略。这一战略要求实现公路、铁路、港口互联，并在此基础上扩大联通范围，这不仅会为经营建筑业务的企业以及国内外投资带来利益，“一带一路”沿线国家也能从中分享利益。亚洲基础设施投资银行（AIIB）的建立与成功运营（目前拥有 57 个成员国），特别是人民币“入篮”等事例，均反映出“一带一路”倡议所取得的成就。可以说，这一倡议已经取得了世界各国的支持。

东南亚区域已被纳入“一带一路倡议”的重点项目。自 2009 年以来，中国已经成为东盟国家的最大贸易伙伴，而自 2011 年起，东盟则成为中国最大的贸易伙伴。因此，东南亚地区的基础设施建设无疑将极大地促进双方的贸易交流。“一带一路倡议”在实施过程中，始终以基础设施建设、经济发展政策、程序标准化、技术标准统一化为重，致力于消除贸易壁垒、建立自贸区、开展金融合作、促进各国人民友好关系、在文化、教育、媒体等领域、在青少年和女性群体间开展交流。

由于“一带一路”倡议能够消除全球差异、促进各国间的商业接触、鼓励各国人民之间进行社会接触，因此许多分析人士认为，这一倡议将促成新的政治格局的形成。由于中国始终奉行着和平发展战略，因此在“一带一路”倡议实施的过程中始终表现出十足的自信。东盟国家，包括缅甸在内，应对这一倡议所带来的互惠互利给予认真考虑。

可以说，“一带一路”倡议已经取得了重大成就，虽然仍在实施阶段，却已然获得多数分析人士的好评，因为该倡议的宗旨便是在互惠互利的基础上开展经济合作、构建利益共同体。

继贸易交易、贸易交流而来的，将会是各国人民之间的相互理解、对彼此文化的相互最终，种种有利的形式将促进利益共同体地顺利形成。由于“一带一路”倡议的目标之一便是构建这样一个共同体，因此，在“一带一路”倡议取得成功的过程中，文化无疑扮演着至关重要的角色。

Cultural Aspects in the Belt and Road Initiative

Margaret Wong / Myanmar

Head of the Department of History at the University of Yangon

Forging alliance between and among nations become distinct before World War I and between two world wars although the League of Nations existed. Later, allies between regions become more widespread than allies between nations. That is the consequence of the cold war. Numerous regional military allies and economic allies emerged. While expanding co-operations for regional security and regional economy transactions, each nation had turned to their own profits. In Europe there are organizations such as NATO, Warsaw, European Union (EU), Council for Mutual Economic Assistance and so on while in Asia there are South East Asian Treaty Organization (SEATO), Central Treaty Organization (CENTO), especially the Association of Southeast Asian Nations (ASEAN) that gained more strength in the late 20th century and has stood as an organization well recognized by the international community and these many nations has allied with ASEAN. When it approached the late 20th Century, the formation of allies changed significantly in accordance with political situations all over the world. The turn of the 21st Century witnessed the significant change in the pattern of the formation of allies, shifting from regional co-operation for mutual interests to cross-region co-operations. There have been more allies that aim at co-operating for economic development and national security than allies for military co-operations. Among these co-operations, "the Belt and Road Initiative", a development strategy and framework, proposed by Chinese President Xi Jinping, can be said to be a paramount planning of the 21st Century for extraordinary and wide-reaching international cooperation.

With the connectivity among 65 nations through Asia, Europe and Africa, it aims at promoting mutual understanding and win-win situation as well as safeguarding regional security and world peace by co-operating among these nations. Many nations responded with a warm welcome to "the Belt and Road Initiative" whereas some nations showed their concern about and remained skeptical of it. Under these circumstances this Initiative is being implemented.

The five main goals of Modern Silk Road (or) the 21st Century Silk Road are as follows:-

(1) Policy coordination
(2) Facilities connectivity
(3) Unimpeded trade
(4) Financial integration and
(5) People-to-people bond.

Considering these aims, this can be said to be China's great strategy for economic cooperation on mutual benefit basis with the nations along this Silk Road. The Chinese leaders emphasize the concept of the "Three Together's" and "Three No's". Three Together's are (1) Discussion among the parties concerned to identify projects of co-operation and mutual benefit, (2) Working together to realize the projects on the basis of common interest and (3) Enjoying the benefits together from the fruits of this common endeavor. While Three No's are that China does not interfere in the internal affairs of other nations, that China does not seek to increase so-called "sphere of influence" and that China does not strive for hegemony or dominance. However positive these aims are, challenges will arise together with garnering profits: Tangible elements such as political stability, security, telecommunication networks, transportations, and investments are essential whereas intangible elements such as different cultures and traditions, diverse notions, reciprocal understanding strengths and weaknesses between two sides are important necessities.

After the proposal of modern Silk Road that can be dubbed as Extraordinary Global Plan has been raised, it is clear that many nations are observing with a keen interest how the proposed initiative is being implemented. It is true that as nations differ, notions differ concerning operations, sharing profits, benefits, rights, liabilities and so forth. In developing countries in particular as the majority are middle-class who have to give priority to their living, they have a little chance to take interest in and understand "the Belt and Road Initiative" proposal. Hence, "the Belt and Road Initiative" should be a plan to be implemented with support of peoples from respective nations as they are the supporting force who will contribute to make "the Belt and Road Initiative" a success. The mutual understanding and respect of cultures and customs is the main factor in building trust and esteem among the peoples of these countries. The reciprocal recognition of cultural identity of each and every nation and acceptance of each cultural in identity as cultural heritage related to all is similar to safeguarding the interests of these nations. Hence, mutual understanding and respect plays an important role in implementing the Belt and Road Initiative and it will correspond with the fifth goal People-to-People Bond from the five main goals of the 21st century Silk Road. Apart from the gap between the rich and the poor, social unrest of the nations involved in the Initiative, different domestic situations in respective nations, conflicts between respective nations, and superpowers vying for political and economic dominance, unexpected hardships and barriers may arise. Thus, "One Belt One Road Initiative" is a long term plan that should be implemented by negotiating with respective nations at different levels. If it is implemented, by negotiating with nations, and creating mutual benefits with friendship based on mutual understanding among respective nations, peaceful economic co-operation, one of the aims of "One Belt One Road Initiative", will be realized. It can be said that such peaceful development is not only the interests of related nations but also China's own development plan.

The Chinese Leader has mentioned that neighbouring countries are in a strategically important position due to their geographically close locations, environmental connections, political contacts and economically and commercially good conditions and China is striving for setting up a community of shared interests with these nations. ASEAN countries are included not only in One Belt (or) the Silk Road Economic Belt but also in One Road (or) 21st Century Maritime Silk Road. Since the time B.C., the Chinese Emperors christened trade route to Central Asia that emerged from trying to trade"the Silk Road". After the fall of Mongol Empire, this ancient Silk Road was eclipsed by the emergence of European maritime mercantile route that gained increasing strength. In Ming Dynasty of 15th Century, Chinese ships under the command of Admiral Zheng He reached the countries on the coasts of the Indian Ocean. In fact, the Silk Road and Maritime Silk Road connecting the East and West of the world are routes that have brought China into contact with ASEAN countries economically, socially and culturally since ancient times.

Myanmar is found to be an unavoidable strategic region on the Silk Road that connects the East and West of the world. This thousands-years-old Silk Road connecting the East and West via Myanmar has tremendous impact on politics, economy, socio-economic life and culture of Myanmar. At that time people who roamed on the Silk Road were merchants. Thanks to the merchants who came from the eastern and western parts of the world there were commercial transactions between the orient and the occident and economies developed. Together with those merchants came their cultures and they had a chance to exchange their cultures and raised mutual understanding among them. From then on cultures have intermingled with one another and there have been mutualities of cultural dominance.

Utilized for commerce, the Silk Road played an important role for military operations during World War II. In order to send in reinforcements to China repelling the invasion of Japanese fascists, allied forces rebuilt a road along this Silk Road and world famous Ledo Road (or) Stillwell Road came into being. Along Ledo Road stand well-known towns and cities such as Shinbweyan, Tanaing, Hpakant, Moekaung, Myitkyina and Bhamo and they have been the important towns and cities throughout the history of Sino-Myanmar relations until today. These towns are also related with jade and amber mines and forest products. This Road played an important part in politics, warfare and economy of the region. Thus, this Silk Road can be said to be a historic road that has served dutifully in the histories of China, India and Myanmar. The maintenance of Ledo Road has started from the border of Myanmar and China and almost all the sections of Ledo Road in Kachin State have been finished roughly. There are sections to maintain on the side of Sagaing adjacent to India. On the one hand, according to India's Look East Policy, trading with China can boost the economy of regions in northern India. On the other hand, there are concerns that Chinese products will roll in along this Road. The connection of Ledo Road and China-Myanmar Road has paved the way to the interconnection of between South Asia and Southeast Asia and East Asia, and if there is regional security, it will play a vital part in economic strategy. While "the Belt and One Road Initiative" is inter connecting businesses all over the world, Ledo Road has joined China-Myanmar Road, making 1900 mile-route along which all round businesses will flourish and bring many benefits. With economic development local people along Ledo Road will find it convenient to make a living and their socio-economic lives will enjoy a change for the better. There will be increasing contacts among the citizens of the nations depending on Ledo Road and this situation will support much to the aims of the 21st Century Silk Road.

Like Ledo Road, one of the main routes of the 21st Century Silk Road that connecting Myanmar and China (or) Silk Road Economic Belt is Bangladesh-China-India-Myanmar (BCIM) Economic Corridor. It is included in Regional Cooperation

Plan of "the Belt and Road Initiative." Bangladesh-China-India-Myanmar Economic Corridor crosses India, Bangladesh and Myanmar to connect southwestern states with the Indian Ocean. This economic corridor is 1.65 million kilometer long, connecting Yunnan of China, Bangladesh, Myanmar and northern India by road, by rail, by water and by air. This corridor is a route crossing from Kunming of China to Kolkata of India and Mandalay of Myanmar, Dakka and Chittagong of Bangladesh. These four nations have agreed to expand mutual co-operations in the sectors of education, sport, science and technology.

Evaluation

Some political analysts considered that "the Belt and Road Initiative" is China's second steps to the outside world after China adopted open economic door policy. There are other critics who thought that China is gathering political forces through its economic power. However, this initiative is a strategy that generates opportunities for China to invest in foreign countries. As "the Belt and Road Initiative" demands the extension of interconnecting motor roads, rail roads and ports, this can bring benefits to construction enterprises and domestic and foreign investments. Countries in connection with this route will enjoy these benefits. The establishment and successful operation of Asia Infrastructure Investment Bank (AIIB) with 57 member nations, in particular and the inclusion of China's *Yuan* in the basket of IMF's special drawing rights, or SDR has reflected the success of "the Belt and Road Initiative". It can be said that this initiative has gained the support of world countries.

Southeast Asian region is included in an important programme of the Belt and Road Initiative". China has become the biggest trading partner with ASEAN since 2009 and ASEAN has become China's biggest trading region since 2011. Accordingly infrastructural development in Southeast Asia will boost trade transactions between both sides. "the Belt and Road Initiative" is implemented with the aim of bringing about infrastructural development as well as economic development policies, standardization of procedures, the uniformity of technological standards, the removal of trade barriers, the establishment of free trade zones, co-operation in financial sector, promoting friendship among peoples and exchanges in cultural, education and media sectors and youth and women sectors.

Hence, some political analysts believed that a new political landscape will emerge since "the Belt and Road Initiative" will narrow down the globe and create a community of peoples not only with commercial contacts but also with social contacts. Holding peaceful development policy, China continues to implement this Initiative with complete confidence. ASEAN countries, including Myanmar, should consider the mutual benefits that they will gain from this Initiative.

"the Belt and Road Initiative" can be said to have achieved considerable success as many political analysts made favourable comments on it although it is now in the stage of implementation. Together with implementation of economic co-operation on mutual benefit basis, founding a community of shared interests is included in the aims of this Initiative. After experiencing business transactions and exchanges, there will be mutual understanding among peoples and mutual respect for one another's culture. These favourable conditions will head to a success of building a community of shared interests. Since building such community is the goal of "the Belt and Road Initiative", it cannot be denied that culture plays a vital role for achieving success of "the Belt and Road Initiative", the 21st Century Silk Road.

References

1. *Banglasesh-China-India-Myanmar Forum for Regional Cooperation*, www.bicm-forum.com/en/article.aspx?aid=60

2. National Development & Reform Commission, *Vision and Action on Jointly Building Silk Road Economic Belt and 21st Century Maritime Silk Road*, Beijing, Foreign Languages Press Co. Ltd., 2015.

3. Prof. Shi Ze, *"One Road & One Belt" & New Thinking with Regard to Concepts and Practice*, The International Schiller Institute, Forum for a New Paradigm, www.ciis.org.cn., Nov 25, 2014.

4. One Belt One Road- Wikipedia, the free encyclopedia
5. Kyaw Win, *Dragonomist's 21st Century Silk Road*, ('&*kdaemrpf&JU 21 &mpkykd;vrf;r), Yangon, Voice Journal, October, 2016.
6. Thetkatho Han SoeOo, *One Region One Road*, (&yf0ef;wpfckvrf;aMumif;wpfck), (series 1 to 16), Kyemon Daily News Paper, 29-2-2016 to 4-7-2016, Yangon.

中国元素之所在：移植海外的中国园林设计与功用

邓肯　【新西兰】
新西兰惠灵顿维多利亚大学　研究员

“一带一路”为审视全球化主义的未来提供了另外一个视角（也可能是多元视角），正如本次座谈会上的诸位学者所说，开展“一带一路”有一个必要的前提，即海陆丝绸之路沿线国家之间应在各个层面增强文化上（精神层面）的相互的理解。目前各种误解（甚至是互不信任）会损害“一带一路”倡议所带来的经济效益。

从这个角度来讲，我认为中国与世界各国应共同努力，为促进文化上的相互理解打下基础。那么有哪一所文化机构最适合承担这样的使命呢？或许各位立刻会想到博物馆和艺术馆。然而在跨文化语境中，博物馆和艺术馆面临着诸多困境，很难打破场馆的限制，将馆内展出的“过去”与当下的文化（和人民）联系在一起，而且展览往往会陷入这样一个陷阱：不仅不能够增进新的理解，反而会增强文化定势和文化偏见，或被用来宣传某个国家所特有的宏大叙事。那么，该如何以简洁的表达（如博物馆展览、大学课程等）来捕捉我们所谓的“中国文化”（这一名称过于简化且不够恰当）的恢宏与丰富，来再现它的整体性和文化嵌入性呢？

正如本文的标题和摘要所示，我今天要讨论的内容是，在促进各国文化与中国文化相交融的过程中，中式园林可能扮演什么样的角色。作为园林艺术的研究者，我曾发表过一些关于园林艺术在中国历史地位的文章，翻译过一些晚晴时期重要的园林著作，同时与詹姆士·比蒂合著并出版过一本关于达尼丁阑园的作品《灵悟的园林》；此外，作为流芳园（位于加州圣玛丽诺地区杭廷顿图书馆）的园长，以及新西兰惠灵顿滨海园林——惠园的设计团队成员，我今天的讨论既带有批判性，既带有批判的性质，也带有趣闻的性质。

由于文本的副标题为“文化认同与共同遗产”，因此，我会在具体的语境中讨论：所谓“中国的崛起”（尽管这一说法不够准确，而且已被反复使用）对于太平洋地区——21 世纪海上丝绸之路南线的最南端——的国家而言，究竟具有什么意义？仅在三十年前，我们还无法预料中国的“崛起”，但现在我们已经认识到，中国经济的快速发展、中国逐步恢复对亚太政治的主导地位，将对这一地区造成重大且永久地影响。

文化（艺术，特别是文学）的互联是一个复杂、微妙且往往比较隐秘的过程。这一过程常常具有潜伏性，它带来的成果是永久性的，这与国家之间开展的官方文化交流形成鲜明的对比，因为官方文化交流往往流于表面和琐碎，时常贴有“文化外交”的醒目标签（我把中国的文化外交命名为“饺子与书法”模式），但事实上，大凡能够漂洋过海、到达异国彼岸的，通常是一国文化中最轻浮的部分，而且即便能够上岸，大多已褪去本色，面目全非。

以下，我将简要地讨论——移植海外的“中国”园林是如何在设计和功能上与博物馆和艺术馆进行互补、甚至在某种程度上对其进行颠覆的。毕竟园林欣赏既带有参与性又带有创造性，与参观博物馆或艺术馆截然不同。

通常情况下，“移植”海外的“中国”园林仅仅被视作一种典雅（且常常是仿制的）而刻板的文化符号、一名“文化大使”（中国最近出版的一本作品便是以此为标题），将其视为中国政府采取的一种文化政策。那么对于这些“中国”园林，人们的误解究竟达到了什么样的程度？

以下，我将结合具体实例，从功能和设计的角度来探讨这个问题。

杭廷顿图书馆的流芳园是海外最大的中式园林。它的设计一丝不苟地遵照中国历史上特定时代、特定地域（特别是 17、18 世纪江南地区）的园林构造理念。流芳园第一期工程于 2008 年向公众开放，但距离竣工日期尚有数年的之遥。该园采用借景的手法与南加州风光（远山、园中的加州橡树、牧场冰雪融水形成的映芳湖等）巧妙地构成辉映，极大地提升了这片园林的内涵，且随着时间的流逝定会更见风致。流芳园的建立旨在保存、推广、营造中华文明中隽永、微妙、艺术以及风雅的传统，特别是关于园林建造和花木栽培的传统。一方面，流芳园可以为居住在南加州的华人群体保存故乡记忆，另一方面，由于人口流动较为迅速，该园可以为非华裔族群提供理解乃至欣赏中国文化各个层面的绝佳机会。但一座园林要如何才能完成这两项使命？在我担任流芳园园长期间，还参加了前任园长李关德霞（June Li）开展的一系列项目，在园区内定期举办了一系列活动，比如，每周星期三下午在“爱莲榭”举办的音乐活动，每月举办关于中国园林史讲座，以及在“清越台”开展戏曲表演、组织学生参观（有些学生甚至试着用英语写中国风格的诗歌）、举办团体节日活动，如庆祝昔年、中秋节、艺术家驻留活动等等。与此同时，园林的最初设计、构建以及后期的维护等，都是与苏州的合作伙伴共同开展。流芳园同时也是探索（复兴乃至革新）中国百年园林艺术史的绝佳场所。最重要的是，多数访客（不论经常来访还是偶尔造访）都从各自不同的角度来解读中国园林建造的内涵和意义。

相比之下，由维特联合有限公司、阿斯费尔德建筑公司以及邓肯·坎贝尔联合设计、拟在惠灵顿弗兰克·基茨公园中修建的“惠园”，则为探索园林设计的新方法提供了绝佳的机会。流芳园的设计目的是将园林建造、园林设计的悠久传统与当代元素相结合，而威灵顿惠园的设计说明中却要求建造“一座独特的当代中国园林，以此象征威灵顿的华人群体、中国移民经验、华人群体对丰富文化体验和城市的构建发展所作出的贡献”。为了突出“当代感”、表现“此地、当下”等意蕴，将惠园的园址选在了海边，这给设计团队造成了一系列的困难，特别是设计说明中关于多种象征意义的要求。相比之下，中国古代园林，以及其他地区的园林，往往都在寻求与当下环境的隔绝，比如流芳园的设计中便采用隔墙来达到这一效果。而惠园却遵循“远借”原则，明确地选择将园景与海景相结合，以此凸显“早期中国移民经由海路来到惠灵顿”的含义，同时突出中国移民的后裔所生活居住的这座城市。在惠园的园区中，具体的“中国元素”更多是通过对称、轴对称、分层、悬顶等微妙的建筑手段来唤起对“中国风”感受。这些设计都符合典型的中国设计理念。例如，在飞檐的设计和结构中可以感受到中国元素，从园中的小径、水景、岩石、亭台、墙壁的设计中也能感受到这一主题。这些细节都在《设计说明》中做出了明确规定。可以说，惠园的设计并没有生搬硬套中国传统园林建造的规则，传统的建造规则往往中规中矩，很少融入不同地区的多样化风格。

总之，惠园并不寻求原封不动地复制中国古代园林的形式或意义，不论这些园林能够多么有效地代表中国古代的多种传统。相反，惠园用一种独具特色和创意的方式，十分有效地将园址的地理位置、惠园象征意义，以及世界上最悠久的园林设计传统融合在一起。通过这种方式，惠灵顿的中式园林能够帮助人们更好的理解中国园林的特质，理解中国园林的各种可能性。

走进流芳园时，首先映入眼帘的是一副牌匾，匾额是一副风格特异的书法题词（台湾书法家罗青所做）：别有洞天。这里是一个截然不同的世界，也是一个能够让我们慢下来、让我们偶尔驻足沉思的世界。而当我们停下脚步开始思索时，我们便开始发现真我，对我们的念头观察的更为清楚，对物质世界的经验进行反思。在这个空间里，我们能够瞬间从平凡而世俗的生活中解脱出来，以更好的精神面貌，以更加深刻的体悟再次回到“真实”的世界中去。当透过我们中式园林特有的格窗向外张望时，我们瞥见的，正是人类普遍而共有的特性，这也恰恰是本文副标题的含义之所在。

Transplanted Gardens as Sites of Chineseness: Design & Function Cultural Identity and Common Heritage

Duncan Campbell / New Zealand

Researcher at Victoria University of Wellington in New Zealand

If the "Belt and Road" initiative offers something by way of an alternative (and hopefully pluralistic) vision of the globalism of the future, then, as numerous participants in this symposium have already pointed out, an essential precondition will be increased levels of cultural (indeed, spiritual) understanding along and across both the land and the maritime routes it is to take. Present levels of misunderstanding (even mistrust) will serve to undermine whatever economic benefits might flow from the initiative.

In this vein, I believe that a greater effort needs to be given to the issue of the infrastructure of cultural understanding between China and the rest of the world. What are the cultural institutions that are best designed to serve this purpose? One thinks immediately of museums and galleries, of course. In an intercultural context, museums and galleries face certain difficulties in trying to reach beyond the museum walls to establish connections between the past as exhibited and the living cultures (and peoples) that that past derived from, and avoiding the ever-present pit-falls of exhibitions that, far from generating new understandings, serve simply either to confirm existing (largely unchanging and historical) cultural stereotypes and preconceptions, or to promote a particular state-inflected master narrative of one sort or another. That is, specifically, how does one in brief compass (in a museum exhibition, a university course and so on) capture something of the scale and richness, the wholeness and embeddedness, of something (for brevity's sake and anachronistically) we may call Chinese culture?

As you may have gathered from my title and abstract, today, in brief, my contribution to this symposium seeks to argue the role of the Chinese-style garden as the possible site for enhanced cultural engagements with aspects of Chinese culture. I will do so, both somewhat polemically and anecdotally, on the basis of a variety of engagements with such gardens: as researcher (with articles on the historical role of the garden in China, translations of some of a number of important late imperial Chinese accounts of gardens, and (with James Beattie) a book on Dunedin's Lan Yuan 蘭園 : Garden of Enlightenment); as curator (of the Huntington Library's Garden of Flowing Fragrance or Liu Fang Yuan 流芳園 in San Marino); and as member of a design team (as in the case of Wellington's proposed harbour-side garden, the Garden of Beneficence or Hui Yuan 惠園). That is, a professional concern with the pasts, presents, and futures of such sites.

The title of this sub-topic is "Cultural Identity and Common Heritage" and I address it in the very specific context of what (somewhat tiresomely and largely inaccurately) tends still to be referred to as the "Rise of China", with all the implcations for someone situated in the Pacific (at the very southernmost end of the 21st Century Maritime Silk Road) of a circumstance that, a short three decades ago, was quite unanticipated. We now understand that the rapid economic and (increasingly) political return of China to a position of pre-dominance in our Asia-Pacific world, in particular, is both fundamental and permanent.

And yet cultural (and artistic and, especially, literary) interconnections are complicated, subtle, often hidden processes. They are, more often than not, latent, and their abiding outcomes contrast starkly with the usual flotsam and jetsam of official cultural exchange between nations covered by the rubric cultural diplomacy (in the case of China, what I call the "Dumplings and Calligraphy" approach to such things), where the rule seems to be that it is only the lightest products of the one culture that travel furthest across the oceans before beaching themselves upon the distant shores of another, bleached of colour and distorted of shape.

In brief, then, I hope to suggest ways in which in their functioning and their design, the displaced "Chinese" garden (as an all-encompassing and ever changing simulacrum) plays a role in this domain that both supplements and to some extent subverts that played by the museum or the gallery. The experience of strolling through a garden, after all, is both participatory and generative is a way often different to that offered by museums and galleries.

To what extent can the "displaced" and "Chinese" garden be understood as being something more than just an elegant (if always inauthentic) stereotype, and/or a"Cultural Envoy" (as the title of a recent Chinese book has it)[1] for party-state cultural policy decided in Beijing?

I will discuss two case studies, in terms, respectively, of function and design.

The Huntington Library's Garden of Flowing Fragrance is amongst the largest Chinese-style gardens outside China. It is designed, explicitly and in detail,in accordance with ideas of garden making that derive from a very particular time and place: the late imperial period of Chinese history (the seventeenth and eighteenth centuries, especially) and the Lower Yangtze Delta region known in Chinese as Jiangnan 江南, that which lies south of the Yangtze River. At the same time, however, the

1 *Wenhuashijie—Zhongguoyuanlinzaihaiwai* 文化使節—中國園林在海外 [Cultural Envoy—Chinese Gardens Built Overseas] (Beijing: Zhongguojianzhugongyechubanshe, 2000)

garden, which opened in 2008 but the completion of which is still a number of years away, also both responds powerfully to its Southern California site (the hills beyond, by way of "Borrowed Scenery" (借景), the garden's elderly Californian oaks, its Lake of Reflected Fragrance (映 芳 湖), where once the ranch's winter run-off would gather), and lends to this site additional levels of meaning, as it will doubtless continue to do so as the years pass by.[1] The garden's purpose is to serve towards the maintenance, promotion, and engendering of the rich and sophisticated artistic and scholarly traditions of Chinese civilization, especially as they pertain to gardens and to plants. As such, on the one hand, the intention is that Flowing Fragrance will continue to be something of a storehouse of memory for members of the various diasporic Chinese communities resident here in Southern California.[2] At the same time, in a context of rapidly shifting demographic trends, the garden also provides a site where non-Chinese people are given opportunities to understand,

1 Toward the end of his article "Approaches (New and Old) to Garden History," in Michel Conan, ed., *Perspectives on Garden Histories* (Washington, D.C.: Dumbarton Oaks Research Library & Collection, 1999),John Dixon Hunt sets out a series of "guidelines or principles" upon which histories of gardens will need to be constructed. As his 5th principle, he argues that: "We need, above all, a history of the reception or consumption of gardens that acknowledges that they yield as much a dramatic as a discursive experience. There is a virtual dimension to the designed landscape: despite its palpable objectivity, it needs an addressee, as it were, to receive it—a spectator, visitor, or inhabitant, somebody to feel, to sense its existence and understand its qualities. To use or to inhabit a landscape may be regarded as a response to its design, and to study such responses will bring us to a better understanding of design history. So we need to track how people have responded to sites in word and image" (p. 89). This is the concern of his book, *The Afterlife of Gardens* (London: Reaktion Books, 2004). "The history of landscape architecture is narrated almost exclusively from the point of view of the original designs and their designers," he argues (p. 17), "The new history would obviously depend on verbal and visual representations of sites after the fact of their creation, and particularly precious here would be sketches, maps or other records in which visitors obviously tried to encode their impressions; we also have imagery (and indeed verbal reports) that were in some sense commissioned to represent a required or official point of view…." (p. 20). In the Chinese case, historiographically, as I argue below, the problem would seem to be the converse of that identified by Hunt; there exists a vast bulk of responses (verbal and pictorial) to gardens, most of which have since disappeared, but virtual silence on the part of the actual designers (rather than owners) of these gardens.

2 For a moving and highly relevant treatment of issues of cultural nostalgia at play amongst the various diasporic Chinese communities of Southern California, particularly as they relate to cuisine, see Hua Hsu, "Wokking the Suburbs," *Lucky Peach*, January 9, 2015.

the better to appreciate, aspects of Chinese culture.[1] How does the garden seek to do this? During my period as curator of this garden, and picking up on a number of programs initiated by my predecessor June Li, the garden hosted a regular series of events (music in the Love of the Lotus Pavilion on Wednesday afternoons, monthly lectures on aspects of the history garden making in China, opera and other concert performances in the Clear and Transcendent Terrace, school tours (some of which involved students in trying to write Chinese-style poems in English), community festivals to celebrate the New Year of the Mid-Autumn Festival, an artist in residence program, and so on). At the same time, in terms of both the initial design and construction of the garden, and for the purposes of on-going maintenance, in conjunction with the Huntington's Suzhou partners, the garden was also a site for the exploration (in some cases, revival and renewal) of certain aspects of the detailed age-old Chinese craft of garden making. Most importantly, the many visitors to the garden (both frequent and one-off) engaged in making of the garden their own variety of meanings.

In terms of design and by way of contrast, the Chinese garden intended as the centerpiece of the revitalization of Frank Kitts Park that has been proposed for Wellington, designed by Wraight + Associates Ltd, in conjunction with Athfield Architects and Duncan Campbell, offers exciting opportunity to explore alternative approaches to the design of such gardens. Whereas Flowing Fragrance seeks to lend contemporary relevance to long-standing traditions of design and garden making, the Design Brief for Wellington Garden of Beneficence asked for "…a unique, contemporary Chinese Garden that will symbolize the history of the Chinese people in Wellington, the Chinese migrant experience and the contribution of the Chinese

1 In this respect, perhaps we can think about gardens in China (and now Chinese gardens elsewhere) as constituting a particular kind of "contact zone;" this term, coined by Mary Louise Pratt in her 1991 essay "Arts of the Contact Zone," refers to "social spaces where cultures meet, clash, and grapple with each other, often in contexts of highly asymmetrical relations of power." One important (and under-researched) dimension of late imperial Chinese history is the extent to which the gardens of Jiangnan played a vital role in the acculturation of the new ruling Manchu elite during the second half of the seventeenth-century in China.

community in the enrichment of the cultural experience and fabric of the city". This emphasis on the "contemporary", upon the here and nowness of the garden to be designed and built beside the sea, posed a series of particular difficulties for all those involved in its design, as did the various levels of representational meaning expected of the garden once it is built. Whereas the gardens of the past in China, and many of those built elsewhere, seek to remove themselves from their immediate surroundings by means of walls, like Flowing Fragrance, Beneficence seeks explicitly, by means of the principle of "distant borrowing" (遠借), to embrace the sight of the sea, in the one direction, as constituting, historically anyway, the route by which the bulk of the early Chinese community here would have arrived, and the city where many of their descendants work, in the other. And within the garden itself, the specific "Chineseness" of the garden will expressed more through the subtle evocation of motifs such as symmetry, axiality, hierarchy, suspension and disclosure, all of which seem quintessential to Chinese conceptions of design, as can be captured in the design and texture of the up-turned edges of the roofs that might soar above the garden, for instance, or in the details of the pathways, water feature, rocks, pavilion and walls, as also stipulated in the Design Brief, rather than through the rigid imposition of a set of inherited (and frequently misapprehended) laws that never, in any case, held universal sway over the variety of regional styles of Chinese garden making.

What is proposed, in short, is not a garden that seeks to replicate the form and meaning of a garden built long ago and elsewhere and for other purposes, however well such a garden may embody the quintessence of aspects of past Chinese traditions, but rather one that engages, creatively and productively and in a manner quite unique to itself, with its particular site, its specific representational purposes, and with aspects of one of the word's longest continuous traditions of garden design. In this way, the design of Wellington's Chinese garden may serve also to extend understandings of the nature of the Chinese garden and its evolving possibilities.

As one enters the Garden of Flowing Fragrance, the first plaque that meets your eyes, just inside the gate and brushed in strikingly unusual calligraphy (by the Taiwanese calligrapher Luo Qing 羅青) read: "Another World Lies Beyond" (*Bie you dongtian* 別有洞天). A world set apart, then, but a world that is designed to slow us down, to give us pause, occasionally to stop us in our steps in wonder, and, in so doing, to have us discover within ourselves a heightened awareness of our own senses and the manner in which they mediate our experience of the material world. And if it is a space that momentarily frees us from the quotidian concerns of our day-to-day lives, it is also one that might occasionally allow us to re-engage with that "real" world with renewed energy and enhanced understanding. In keeping with the theme of this sub-topic, therefore, through the framed windows of the particularly Chinese space of such gardens, then, we may be permitted a glimpse of that which is common and universal and shared among mankind.

一代人的“国际视野”

陈平原　【中国】
北京大学中文系　教授 / 中央文史研究馆　馆员

假如你热爱足球，他关心科技，我对美食更有兴趣，那么，我们之间并不拥有“同一个地球”。个人如此，群体也不例外——晚清之关注富国强兵，“五四”之时谈论被压迫民族，抗战之时瞩目战争与和平，都深刻影响那个时代普通人的“国际视野”。今天也不例外，全世界 230 个国家和地区，你不可能面面俱到，关注这些，忽略那些，其实大有讲究，隐含着很多潜台词。上一代人激动不已的，下一代很可能毫无感觉，这背后是时势推移以及思潮变化。某种意义上，一代人“国际视野”的形成，并非自然而然，而是世界局势、国家战略与个人教养相互激荡的结果。

远的不说，就说近在眼前的，20 世纪五六十年代对于俄苏及东欧文化的向往，七八十年代向欧美及日本文化致敬，九十年代小幅震荡，随着 2001 年中国加入世界贸易组织（WTO），更是自觉地卷入全球化浪潮。此后，中国人确实可以站在家门口，“胸怀全世界”了。即便如此，国人对于世界的想象，依旧是有所发现、有所凸显，同时也有所遮蔽。

比如当下中国，谈及国际政治、文化及学术，除了专门家，一般民众还是有意无意地以经济发展水平为标尺。大学里的学术交流，自然也不例外，我曾感叹：“真希望有一天，我们不只跟‘美国的中国学’对话，也跟西欧的、中欧的、俄国的、日本的、韩国的、印度的中国学家对话。那样的话，所谓‘国际学术交流’，才能名副其实。”（《国际视野与本土情怀——如何与汉学家对话》，初刊《上海师范大学学报》2011 年第 6 期，收入《读书的“风景”——大学生活之春花秋月》，北京大学出版社，2012 年）这里有语言方面的问题，毕竟懂英文的人多，对话容易展开，好书一下子就译介进来；但这不是主要原因，关键还是心态。若真的想了解，无论哪个国家的政治、思想、文学、艺术，我们都能找到合适的译者。

举个现成的例子，今日中国，接受过高等教育的，到底有多少人真正了解非洲的地理与历史，关心其现状及未来？没有做过统计，但我知道比例很低。这么说，不是炫耀自己先知，恰恰相反，是过去一年多受到若干刺激，促使我认真反省这个问题。

2015 年 4 月 10 日，笔者有幸出席在华盛顿召开的“第四届中美文化论坛”，与我同台发表演的美国历史学家，长期关注中非关系，谈的是 20 世纪 70 年代中国如何援助非洲建设坦赞铁路。这条东起坦桑尼亚首都达累斯萨拉姆，西迄赞比亚中北部城镇卡皮里姆波希的东非交通大动脉，全长 1860.5 公里，1968 年开始勘测设计，1970 年 10 月正式开工，1976 年 7 月全部建成移交，在新中国外交史上意义重大，当年曾被广泛宣传，我辈耳熟能详。因此，关于这个话题，没有事先准备，我也能说上几句。

2016 年国庆期间，亚吉铁路正式通车，媒体有大量的报道。从文明古国埃塞俄比亚首都亚的斯亚贝巴，到亚丁湾西岸、扼红海进入印度洋要冲的吉布提，非洲这第一条电气化铁路，全长 752.7 公里，设计时速 120 公里。更重要的是，整个项目的运作方式不再是援建，而是中方负责融资、承包建设和运营，如此互利合作，开创了中非关系的新模式。国庆节后，当我兴致勃勃地谈论这两条铁路的差异时，发现我的学生既不知情，也不关心。开始有点抱怨，后来想想，不是他们的问题，而是时代变了——我有 20 世纪 70 年代援建坦赞铁路的深刻记忆，所以关心亚吉铁路从技术到运作的巨大变化；他们则没有接收这方面信息的愿望与热情，因为他们学的是中国文学。

这就说到我们的文学教育。还是在第四届“中美文化论坛”上，一位美国教授问我，中国人如何讲授非洲文学。我是中文系教授，本可以此为由，完全推开。之所以愿意说几句，因我了解中文系课程的变化。作为 1977 级大学生，我在中山大学读书时，教“外国文学”的老师受此前十几年“亚非拉人民要解放”思潮的影响，在课上介绍了好些亚洲、非洲、拉丁美洲的文学作品——可惜只是人名和书名，绝大部分没有译本，更谈不上认真阅读。这与1980年代以后大学生的知识贮备与阅读兴趣，明显有很大差异。

借助于诺贝尔文学奖巨大的新闻效应，中国人起码关注1986年获奖的尼日利亚作家沃莱·索因卡、1988年获奖的埃及作家纳吉布·马哈富兹、1991年获奖的南非作家纳丁·戈迪默，以及2003年获奖的南非作家约翰·马克斯韦尔·库切。除此之外，普通读者很少关心“非洲文学”。这怪不得他们，今天中国大学，不要说中文系不教，即便外国语学院，除相关专业，也都不怎么阅读非洲文学作品。

2016年夏天，我接受某欧洲学者的专访，谈及中国大学问题，我滔滔不绝；聊到欧美及日本的大学，我也能应付自如。没想到人家话锋一转，问我对非洲大学有什么看法。说实话，那一瞬间我愣住了，从没想过这方面的问题。事后恶补，方才对这拥有54个国家的非洲大陆的高等教育有大致的了解。读塔费拉与阿特巴赫的《非洲高等教育面临的挑战与发展前景》(《高等教育研究》2003年第2期)，明白财政资源短缺、殖民主义影响、长期社会动荡以及艾滋病的严重威胁，使得非洲的高等教育相当落后，尼日利亚、苏丹、南非和埃及分别拥有45、26、21和17所大学，这已经算是其中最好的了。

即便如此，以中国的经验，我坚信学术实力不太雄厚的非洲各国大学，在其追求民族独立以及战后重建方面，肯定发挥了重要作用。果不其然，近期读《非洲大学：关照现实还是追求卓越——穆罕默德·马姆达尼在上海大学的讲演》(2016年8月19日《文汇报·文汇学人》)，让我大开眼界。若做历史溯源，你会读到非洲教育史上不少重要机构的名字，比如始建于公元前280年左右的亚历山大图书馆、公元737年建立的突尼斯的齐图纳(Ez-Zitouna)大学、公元970年创立的埃及的艾资哈尔(Al-Azhar)大学等，可实际上今日非洲各国大学，其起源大都带有殖民主义色彩，与上述古代机构关联极少。单就起步阶段模仿欧洲大学这一点而言，中国的情况与非洲很相像——所谓“上法三代，旁采泰西”，上半句是门面话，根本无法落实。我多次谈及：“20世纪中国思想文化潮流中，‘西化’最为彻底的，当推教育。……这其实正是20世纪中国大学教育的困境所在：成功地移植了西洋的教育制度，却谈不上很好地继承中国人古老的‘大学之道’”(《中国大学百年？》,《学人》第十三辑，江苏文艺出版社，1998年3月)。这个大判断，得到中国学界的普遍认可。我相信，这也是非洲弟兄们创办现代大学所面临的最大困境。

上述穆罕默德·马姆达尼的讲演，以20世纪90年代的南非开普敦大学为例，讨论学术自由与社会责任之间的巨大张力——“白人大学将自我定义为卓越中心，而黑人大学的师生员工运动都强调大学的现实意义。两者的竞争逐渐演变为不同的定位，前者是一种眼光在全球的话语，其中多是追求自我实现的白人学者；后者成为公共知识分子的话语，其中黑人白人都有。”因为夹杂种族问题，两种不同话语的冲撞显得格外刺眼；如果撇开具体时空，作为现代大学，其主要责任到底是“关照现实”还是“追求卓越”，这其实是中非大学共同面临的两难处境。我注意到，此次演讲的原题是《游走于公共知识分子与学者之间——非洲高校在独立后的一些行动方案》，整理稿改了题目，着重点从学者选择变成大学策略，明显包含了当下中国大学的困惑。

说实话，要不是受采访的刺激，我不会关注《文汇报》上这篇文章。因为，按照QS世界大学排名（2016），非洲大陆的学术研究中心、成立于1829年的南非开普敦大学，也不过排第171位，远不及北大和清华；至于埃及和整个阿拉伯世界最古老的高等教育机构、创建于1908年的开罗大学，排名507，更是不在话下了。可我也在认真反省，教育界这种深受排行榜影响的“国际视野”，是否过于势利了？即便这些排名全都公正无误，最多也只能说明其学术水准；而我们都知道，大学对于所在国的贡献，远不只论文与专利，更包括深刻影响所在国的政治、社会及经济发展进程。

记得20世纪80年代，北大中文系曾派教授到与开罗大学齐名的埃及著名高等学府艾因·夏姆斯大学教古代汉语及中国文学。这所创办于1950年的大学，在非洲地区率先开设中文系，至今仍有中国教师任教，只不过来自不同高校，且最好懂阿拉伯语。截至2016年年底，中国在非洲32个国家建立了46所孔子学院，虽说主要任务是教汉语，不讲专业课，但规模相当可观。说起来有点“动机不纯”，对于青年教师来说，到非洲教一两年书，交流加旅游，其实是很有诱惑力的。

作为“一带一路”倡议的重要区域，非洲得到中国人前所未有的关注。维和部队去了，企业家去了，工程技术人员去了，做小生意的人去了，大批旅游者也去了，假以时日，国人对非洲的了解将越来越深入，那片广袤的黑土地，也将逐渐撩开神秘的面纱。在这个意义上，新一代中国学者、政治家、企业家乃至普通民众，他们的“国际视野”，必须包含这日渐崛起的黑非洲。

我当然知道，中国社会科学院、北京大学、南京大学、浙江师范大学等都有很好的专门从事非洲教学和研究的机构。但我讨论的并非博雅精深的“非洲学”，而是非洲能否成为大学里的通识课程或社会上的公共知识。恕我直言，相对于欧美学界及民众，中国人在这方面是落后的。不说玄妙的殖民遗产或后殖民反思，就说坚硬的摆在面前的政治、军事、外交、经济、贸易等，非洲都是巨大的存在，且有良好的发展势头。我不仅情感上亲近这块大陆，且坚信中国的非洲研究正迅速崛起，若干年后很可能成为显学。可惜的是，因精力及学养限制，我没有能力参与其中，只能乐观其成。

"International Perspective" of One Generation

Chen Pingyuan / China

Professor of the Department of Chinese Language and Literature / Member of the Central Research Institute of Culture and History

If you love football, he is interested in science and technology, while I show more interest in delicious food, we do not share "the same planet". This situation occurs among individuals, and there is no exception for groups—people paid attention to making the country prosperous and the military force powerful during the late Qing Dynasty; people talked about the oppressed nations during the May 4th Movement; people fixed their eyes upon war and peace during the Chinese People's War of Resistance against the Japanese Aggression; all of these phenomena exerted a profound impact on the "international view" of the ordinary people in the relevant times. There is no exception today. There are 230 countries and territories in the world; you cannot attend to every aspect of matters; you may overlook other aspects while focusing on some particular aspects. In fact, this entails careful consideration and many hidden rules. Something may be exciting for the current generation, but may not be interesting for the next generation. The causes are the changes in the situation and the changes in the trends of thought. In a sense, the "international view" of one generation does not take shape naturally; it results from the interaction among the world's situation, national strategies and personal qualities.

The Chinese people adored Russian, Soviet Union and East European cultures in the 1950s-1960s, saluted the American, European and Japanese cultures in the 1970s-1980s; there was a slight fluctuation in the 1990s. With China's accession to the WTO in 2001, the Chinese people more consciously followed the wave of globalization. In the future, the Chinese people might really "have the whole world in mind" domestically. Nevertheless, the Chinese people's imaginationregarding the world still results from a mix of some discoveries, a certain notoriousness and a certain concealment.

For example, in today's China, when it comes to international politics, culture and the arts, except for the experts, the ordinary people still consciously and unconsciously take the level of economic development as the yardstick. There is also no exception for the academic exchanges in universities. I once realized: "I really hope that we can engage in some kind of a dialogue with not only US scholars specializing in Chinese studies, but also with sinologists from Western Europe, Central Europe, Russia, Japan, South Korea and India. This would bea true 'international academic exchange'"(International View and Local Feelings—How to Engage in Dialogue with Sinologists, first published in the *Journal of Shanghai Normal University*, 2011(6), included in *"Landscape" in Attending School—Beautiful Scenery in University Life*, Peking University Press, 2012). However, there are language problems. After all, many people understand English, it is easy to carry on a conversation and good books can be quickly translated and introduced; but, this is not the main cause, the key lies in mentality. If there is a real desire to gain an understanding, we can find appropriate translators, no matter which country is involved in terms of politics, thought, literature and the arts.

For example, how many highly educated people in today's China really understand the geography and history of Africa, and care about its current situation and its future? No statistical data is available; however, I know that the proportion of these people is very small. Such a view is not designed to display my knowledge; on the contrary, I was irritated several times in the past year, making me seriously reflect on this issue.

On April 10,2015, I had the honor of attending the Fourth Sino-US Cultural Forum held in Washington;at that Forum, an American historian who shared the same stage with me and has been attentive to Sino-Africa relations for a long time, talked about how China assisted Africa in building the Tanzania-Zambia Railway in the 1970s. This railway is the main artery of transportation in East Africa starting from Dar-es-Salaam, the Capital of Tanzania, in the east, to Kapiri Mposhi, a town in North Central Zambia, in the west. It is 1,860.5km long. Its design and surveying for it started in 1968. Its construction officially began in October, 1970 and it was completed and handed over in July, 1976. It was of great significance in the diplomatic history of the new China and was widely publicized at that time. The people of my generation were familiar with it. Thus, I can say a lot on this topic even if I made no preparations regarding it.

During the National Day this year, the Addis Ababa-Djibouti Railway was officially opened to traffic. It was extensively reported by the media. It starts from Addis Ababa, the Capital of Ethiopia, a country with an ancient civilization, to Djibouti City on the west bank of the Aden Gulf in the Red Sea; Djibouti City is a gateway to the Indian Ocean. It is the first electrified railway in Africa. It is 752.7km long. Its designed speed is 120km per hour. More importantly, the operational mode of the entire project is not a matter of assistance; on the contrary, China is responsible for financing, construction and operation. With such a mutually beneficial cooperation, it initiates a new method of Sino-Africa relations. After the National Day, when I enthusiastically talked about the differences between both railways, I found that my students knew nothing about them and were not interested in them. I complained some what at first, but later, I realized that this was not their problem, the times had changed—I had a profound memory of the assistance in building the Tanzania-Zambia Railway in the 1970s, so I showed interest in the great changes in the Addis Ababa-Djibouti Railway project, from technology to operations, while they had no desire or enthusiasm to learn about these projects because they had studied Chinese literature.

The topics also involve our literature and education. At the Fourth Sino-US Cultural Forum, an American professor asked me to tell him about how to teach African literature. I am a professor at the Department of Chinese Language and Literature. Due to this, I could have completely refused to talk about this topic. I was willing to say something because I realized that there had been changes in the courses at the Department of Chinese Language and Literature. When I attended Sun Yat-Sen University as a student of the Class 1977, influenced by the decade-long trend of thought that “the people of Asia and Africa need to be liberated”, our foreign literature teacher introduced the literature of Asia, Africa and Latin America in the classroom—unfortunately, only the names of people and books were introduced; most of the books were not translated, let alone read carefully. There have been obvious differences between us and the university students after the 1980s in terms of reservoirs of knowledge and reading interests.

With the great effect of the news of the Nobel Prize in Literature, the Chinese people are at least interested in:Wole Soyinka, a Nigerian writer who won the Nobel Prize in Literature in 1986, Naguib Mahfouz, an Egyptian writer who won the Nobel Prize in Literature in 1988, Nadine Gordimer, a South African writer who won the Nobel Prize in Literature in 1991, and John Maxwell Coetzee, a South African writer who won the Nobel Prize in Literature in 2003. General readers show little interest in Black African literature, except for the above writers. We cannot blame them. African literature is not taught at the Department of Chinese Language and Literature in today’s Chinese universities; even in the colleges of foreign languages, African literature is seldom read, except at relevant courses of specialization in that subject.

When talking about issues concerning Chinese universities,in an exclusive interview conducted by a European scholar this summer, I eloquently spoke of the universities in Europe, the USA and Japan. Surprisingly, this scholar turned to another topic by asking: what are your opinions on the universities in Africa? To be quite frank, my jaw dropped in amazement at that moment, I had never thought about this issue. Afterwards, I looked up a lot of relevant information and got a rough idea of higher education on the African continent,which is made up of 54 countries. After reading the Challenges and Prospects of African Higher Education in the Early 21st Century written by Damtew Teferra and Philip G.Altbach (Journal of Higher Education, 2003(2)), I realized that higher education is highly underdeveloped in Africa due to the shortage of fiscal resources, the impact of colonialism, long-term social turbulence and the severe threat from AIDS; there are 45, 26, 21 and 17 universities in Nigeria, Sudan, South Africa and Egypt,respectively; these universities are the best of Africa's higher educational institutions.

Nevertheless, given China's experience, I strongly believe that the universities with less academic strength in Africa have certainly played an important role in pursuing national independence and carrying outpost-war reconstruction. Not unexpectedly, I recently read the *African Universities: Caring for the Reality or Pursuing Excellence—Mahmood Mamdani's Speech at Shanghai University*(Wenhui Xueren under Wen Hui Bao, August 19, 2016), and it greatly widened my horizon. If the historical sources are traced, you will learn about the names of many important organizations in African educational history, such as the Library of Alexandriaestablished in about 280 B.C., Ez-Zitouna University established in A.D.737, Al-Azhar University established in Egypt in A.D.970. However, actually the universities in today's Africa mostly originated from colonialism and have very little association with the above-mentioned ancient organizations. With respect to imitation of European universities at the initial stage, China is very similar to Africa—"derive models from three generations of Chinese sages in ancient times, learn advanced thoughts and technologies from the West": the first half of the sentence only serves the purpose of window-dressing and cannot be carried out. I repeatedly stated that the most westernized of China's thoughts and cultural tides in the 21st century was education… This is indeed the dilemma in China's university education in this century: China has successfullytransplanted the Western educational system, but has failed to better inherit the Goals of University Education defined by the Chinese people in ancient times (One Hundred Years of Chinese Universities?, *Xueren*, Vol.13, Jiangsu Literature and Art Publishing House, March, 1998). This general judgment is widely recognized by China's educational circles. I believe that this is also the biggest dilemma for our African brothers in running their modern universities.

In the above speech, Mahmood Mamdani took the University of Cape Town, South Africa, in the 1990s as an example in order to discuss the huge ramifications of academic freedom and social responsibility—"the universities for white people were self-defined as excellence centers, while teachers, staff members and students' campaigns in the universities for black people stressed the practical significance of universities. The competition between both gradually evolved into different positions—the former focused on how much say they could have in the world and was dominated by white scholars who pursued their own self-realization, while the latter became the voice for public intellectuals including both white and black people". Racial problems were involved, so the collision between two different voices was extremely striking; subject to giving no considerations to a specific time and area, how can we answer the following question? Does the main responsibility of a modern university consist in caring for reality or pursuing excellence? Actually, this is a common dilemma for the universities in both China and Africa. I note that the original title of this speech was *Go between Public Intellectuals and Scholars—Some Action Plans of African Higher Educational Institutions after Independence*. The original title was revised during the reorganization of the manuscript to shift the focus from scholar selection to university strategy, and obviously covers the bewilderments in the universities of today's China.

In fact, if I had not been irritated by the interview, I would not have paid attention to the article published in *Wen Hui Bao*. The reason is the following: According to QS World University Rankings (2016), the University of Cape Town, South Africa, established in 1829, the academic research center of the African Continent, only ranked No.171, much lower than Peking University and Tsinghua University, not to mention Cairo University, established in 1908, the oldest higher educational institution in Egypt and in the whole Arab World, ranked No.507. I also carefully reflected: Is the "international view" that is deeply affected by such rankings in the educational circles too snobbish? Even if all of these rankings are fair and correct, they indicate the academic level at the most. As we know, the contributions from universities to the countries where they are located are far from being limited to papers and patents, and they have a profound impact on the process of political, social and economic development in the countries where they are located.

In the 1980s, the Department of Chinese Language and Literature, Peking University, sent some professors to Ain Shams University, a famous higher educational institution in Egypt, on a par with Cairo University, to teach ancient Chinese and Chinese literature. Founded in 1950, this university was the first to set up the Department of Chinese Language and Literature in Africa. So far, Chinese professors are still available at this university; they come from different higher educational institutions, and it would be best for them to understand Arabic. As of the end of 2016, China had established 46 Confucius Institutes in 32 African countries. These Confucius Institutes are mainly responsible for teaching Chinese and do not touch upon professional courses, but their scale is considerable. It seems to have "impure motives", as a matter of fact, teaching in Africa for 1-2 years is highly attractive for young teachers because they can engage in communication and travel.

As an important region in the Belt and Road Initiative, Africa has drawn unprecedented attention from the Chinese people. China has sent peacekeeping forces to Africa; Chinese entrepreneurs, engineering technical personnel, small business owners and a large number of Chinese tourists go to Africa as well. Chinese people have gained an increasing amount of understanding of Africa;that vast black land, the mystery of Africa will be gradually unveiled. In this sense, the “international view” of the new generation of Chinese scholars, politicians, entrepreneurs, even the ordinary people, must cover the rise of black Africa.

As I know, the Chinese Academy of Social Sciences, Peking University, Nanjing University and Zhejiang Normal University have excellent institutions specializing in African teaching and research. However, instead of discussing the elegant and profound “African studies”, I discuss whether Africa can be included in the general educational curriculum of universities or become the public consensus in society. To be quite frank, compared with the educational circles and the general public in Europe and the USA, the Chinese people are way behind in this aspect. Without considering the abstruse colonial legacy or postcolonial reflection, Africa has an enormous presence in politics, military and foreign affairs, economy and trade, and it also enjoys a good momentum of development. I approach this land quite emotionally, and I strongly believe that China’s African studies are rapidly rising, and may become a famous discipline in several years. Unfortunately, I am unable to participate in this process due to the restrictions on my energy, learning and cultivation; the only thing I can do in this respect is express my optimism regarding its success.

汉学与当代中国座谈会

杨莫塔　【秘鲁】
中国秘鲁文化中心　主任 / 秘鲁卫生部　前部长

一带一路

新丝绸之路是一条惠及当今世界 30 多亿人口的经济带，其前身拥有坚定夯实的历史基础。早在 4000 多年以前，中华帝国就已经是各国热望和倾慕的对象，丝绸之路因而也成为一条古代文化间相互亲近、相互理解的渠道。它是人类史上影响最为深远、所得最为非凡的成就之一：蔚为壮观的商船队越洋渡海，开辟了从中国到欧洲的航路，文化交流由此而勃兴、琳琅满目的货物贸易由此展开，丝绸、锦缎、丝绒、珠宝、服饰、陶器、瓷器、宝石、金、银、种子、植物等是最受青睐的商品。

自 1613 年起，中国的影响便已出现在秘鲁，这样的历史史实使得我们既震惊不已又兴趣盎然。中秘民族文化上的接触得益于丝绸之路的发展，而彼时两国人民的亲近又使他们成为当前“一带一路”倡议的先行者和开拓者。从墨西哥到安第斯美洲，从太平洋沿岸的卡亚俄到大西洋畔的布宜诺斯艾利斯，来自中国的丝绸及其他贵重货品，因其质量上乘、用途广泛而备受追捧，秘鲁丝绸之路的悠久历史可见一斑。

自 1565 年至 1820 年，大宗的商品及丝绸陆续由中国运抵秘鲁。图一中，面值 8 雷亚尔的金币最早于 1720 年在利马铸造而成，在中国流通并被重铸后，最终返回秘鲁。上述种种俨然成为丝绸之路在秘鲁存在过的明证。

图一

考古出土的文物也是丝绸之路在秘鲁存在过的佐证。图二为重修利马古城墙时发掘出的中国明代（1368—1644）细瓷器残片（援引自 Fhon Bazan，图片经利马市政府 Bodega y Cuadra 博物馆授权）。这是自 1565 年起秘鲁就已经同中国进行商业交流的确切证据。

图二

中国谚语：百闻不如一见

1565 年的丝绸之路，主要运力为来自中国的大帆船（西方也称为马尼拉大帆船）。丝绸之路海上航线：中国—马尼拉（菲律宾）—阿卡普尔科（墨西哥）—卡亚俄（秘鲁）—布宜诺斯艾利斯（阿根廷）。

二十一世纪新丝绸之路（“一带一路”）

2013 年 9 月 7 日，习近平主席在视察陕西省时说“我们要建设丝绸之路经济带”；“我的家乡陕西，就位于古丝绸之路的起点。站在这里，回首历史，我仿佛听到了山间回荡的声声驼铃，看到了大漠飘飞的袅袅孤烟。”“古丝绸之路经过的地方，曾经为沟通东西方文明，促进不同民族、不同文化相互交流与合作做出过重要贡献。东西方使节、商队、游客、学者、工匠川流不息，沿途各国互通有无、互学互鉴，共同推动了人类文明进步。”这样的观点，今日的秘鲁也坚信不疑，古丝绸之路必将重生。

The Speech on the Symposium of China Studies

Eduardo Yong Motta / Peru

Director of Chinese-Peruvian Cultural Center /Former Peruvian Minister of Health

The Belt and Road

The new Silk Road is a new economic belt which will benefit 3 billion people in the world with the historical basis. Since 4000 years ago, China was a country people was eager to visit and the Silk Road also became a channel for the ancient culture communication and for people's mutual understanding. The Silk Road is one of the chievements which influenced people for so long and deep. The spectacular Merchant sailed throught the ocean and sea, made a new route from China to Europe, which brought the thriving of cultural exchange, the beginning of various prodcts and goods trade. The silk, brocade, velvet, jewelry, clothing, pottery, porcelain, gold, silver, precious stones, seeds and plants were the most popular commodities at that time.

Since 1613, the influnce of China appeared in Peru, so long a history that surprised us. Under the help of the Silk Road, the friendship and the culture exchange of China-Peru development while the closeness of the two nations made them the frontiors and pioneers of the Belt and Road nowadays. From Mexico to America, from the Pacific coast of Callao to the the Atlantic River in Buenos Aires, silk and other valuable goods from China, widely used and highly welcomed because of its superior quality, which shows that Silk Road's long history and remarkable effect in Peru.

Figure 1

From 1565 to 1820, large quantities of goods and silks were sent from China to Peru. The figure 1 shows that the par value of 8 reais of gold in the early 1720 in Lima was cast, circulated and be recoined in China, and returned to Peru eventually. All these things seem to be the evidence of the Silk Road in Peru.

Archaeological finds are also evidence of the Silk Road in Peru. Figure 2. Shows the Fragments of China's fine porcelain in Ming Dynasty (1368-1644) were excavated at the time of rebuilding the ancient city wall in Lima. This is the exact evidence that Peru has conducted commercial exchanges with China since 1565

the Fragments of China's fine porcelain in Ming Dynasty (1368-1644) were excavated at the time of rebuilding the ancient city wall in Lima (Quated from Fhon Bazan, the figure is copyrighted by the Lima government and Bodega y Cuadra Museum).

Figure 2.

Chinese Saying: It is better to see once than hear a hundred times

The big sailing ships from China were the major viechles (which is also known as the Manila galleon) since 1565. The Route of the Maritime Silk Road at that was: China—Manila (Philippines) —Acapulco (Mexico) — Callao (Peru) —Buenos Aires (Argentina).

21st Century Maritime Silk Road (the Belt and Road)

In September 7, 2013, President Xi Jinping inspected Shaanxi and said, “we will build the Silk Road Economic Belt”; “My hometown, Shaanxi, is the starting point of the ancient Silk Road. Standing here, looking back to the history, I like to hear the sound of bells echoed the mountain, saw a wisp of smoke rising from the desert.” “The ancient Silk Road has made important contributions to communicating Eastern and Western civilizations and promoting exchanges and cooperation between different ethnic groups and cultures. Envoys from East and West, caravans, tourists, scholars and craftsmen flowed continuously. The countries along the way exchanged, learned and studied each other, which jointly promoted the progress of human civilization.” Today’s Peru also firmly believe this view that the ancient Silk Road will be reborn.

汉代之前的丝绸之路

王巍　【中国】
中国社会科学院考古研究所　所长 / 中国考古学会　理事长 / 中国社会科学院学部　委员

丝绸之路是公元前 138 年张骞从西域开始的，但是我算了算，距今 2254 年。我要讲的是丝绸之路在张骞通西域之前已经有了很久远的通过这一条路线，古代的东方和西方的交流。而且我主要是从考古的发现来看。

丝绸之路这样一条路线从中国的洛阳、西安古都经过中亚、西亚、地中海到达古罗马。

首先讲一个故事，在中国的文献当中有一个《穆天子传》，记载大约是 2900 年前西周王朝一个很喜欢游历四方的王，他游历四方有这样的一个文献记载，记载他到了西方，这个西方相当于现在的中亚地区。见了当地的一个女王叫西王母，他们以礼相待，周天子给了很多的礼物，其中包括玉器，中国人自古以来就很喜欢玉器，重要的还给了很多丝绸，数百捆的丝绸，这个应该是中国最早的记载。公元前大约 900 年左右，比张骞通西域还要早。文献的记载是不是可信？有各种各样的说法。但是经过我们的考古发现来看，首先是粟和黍的产地，这是两种农作物，小米是黄颜色的，一种是不黏的，一种是黏的。在中国的自制餐里经常可以看到小米粥，那就是粟。

长江流域的水稻，北京粟和黍的发现。中国乃至世界上目前最早的小米，大约距今 10000 年，在北京的郊区，靠近香山的地方，是世界上已知发现最早的粟和黍。在欧洲和西亚也有小米的发现，这两者之间的关系一直是米，据说欧洲那边是7000年前，但最新的研究，都不早于4000多年，我们这边是10000年。即使早，有可能两地有不同的起源。最近几年，和剑桥大学和华盛顿大学的学者一起研究小米之间究竟有没有联系，形态上差不多，味道上也没有明确的区别。但是通过现在的测定，欧洲不早于4000年，当然我们这边更久远一些，有10000年、8000年。欧亚地区出土的早期的小米分成两个部分，有一种可能是它们之间各自有独立的起源，还有一种是它们之间有联系。我们从考古当中会不断地获取标本，中国各地出土炭化小米，埋藏了几千年都已经变成黑色的了，已经炭化。8000年前的中国已经很普遍了，我们对它进行了基因的研究。

结论来说，中国北方的小米粟和黍和欧洲的在遗传基因上有密切的关系，显然只有一个起源地，就是中国的北方地区。主要承担这个项目的是剑桥大学的马丁教授，如果是中国人，有些人说，是不是又想把你们国家的文化说得很早？但是是马丁教授组织的，而且有DNA的证据。所以我们现在可以说，至少4000年前，中国的粟和黍起源应该是通过丝绸之路传到了西方地区。

第二个是小麦的故事，今天吃的面包用的面粉明确无误是西亚的原产，大约也有9000年的历史。在中国没有这种野生种，所以显然是从西亚传过来的。但是是什么时候传过来的？迄今为止不清楚。从结论上来说，一系列的测年表明，大约4500年左右，小麦已经传到中国。

是什么路线传到中国的？我们现在认为应该就是通过丝绸之路这样的路线传过来的。值得注意的是，粟和黍虽然在中国出现很早，但是往那边传的年代大约是4000多年前，同样小麦传到东方也是4000多年，那就是4000多年前的时候，确实有两方面之间人员的交流。哈萨克斯坦和中国出的小麦路线大致是一样的，在甲骨文当中小麦的文字是象形字，传过来的路线总之是从西边传过来的。

同样是4000多年前，在中国4000多年前的遗址当中出土的绵羊和黄牛的遗传基因显示来自西亚地区。发现西亚起源的A世系、B世系的绵羊基因普遍存在，中国传统家族大约在9000—10000年前就开始养猪了，但是绵羊是4000多年前通过丝绸之路传过来的。黄牛也是一样的，跟绵羊的出现同样都是4000多年前，我们在各地有很多的发掘，都是通过DNA的方法来解决的。

正是有了DNA等最新的科学技术在考古上的应用，让我们知道原来丝绸之路并不出现在2000多年前，至少可以往上再追溯2000多年，在4000多年前已经有了。

比如说冶金术，同期的技术，在西亚地区也是有7000年的历史，在中国大约是5000年或者是4500年。有很多西方的技术以及小麦、黄牛、绵羊都是距今4500年左右传入到中国，中国的粟和黍也在这个时期传过去的。比丝绸之路早2000多年的4000多年前的时候，曾经有一个双方密切交流的时期。所以我们说，汉代之前有交流的路线。

最后我要讲，丝绸在中国的出现，距今不晚于6500年前。我最后讲蚕，蚕形状的固执品、石制品在中国6500年前就出土，有考古发现表明，那个时候在黄河流域也已经开始养蚕，所以丝绸的制造已有6500年的历史。而且往西传播也早于汉代，因为在古希腊时期的贵族已经能够以穿中国的丝绸作为高贵和优美。

还有马车的传来，马车大约在3300年前突然出现在中国，原来没有马车，也没有家马。在高加索西亚至少4000多年前已经有马车的使用。所以马车是随着丝绸之路突然出现在中国商代晚期的都城当中，是一个重要的交流方式。在此之前没有马车，恐怕也没有骑马的风俗在中国。远的距离应该是不断地经过中间环节，骑马的出现使这些交流大大加速了。

这是我从考古材料分析后大致可以看出的汉代以前的丝绸之路的交流，谢谢大家！

The Silk Road before the Han Dynasty

Wang Wei / China

Director of the Institute of Archaeology, CASS /President of the Chinese Society of Archaeology /CASS Member

The Silk Road started in 138 B.C. when Zhang Qian, an outstanding diplomat during the Han Dynasty, was sent as an envoy to the western regions. As calculated by me, it was 2,254 years ago. I want to point out that the exchange between the east and the west in ancient times had been carried out by means of the Silk Road for a very long time before Zhang Qian was sent as an envoy to the western regions. I mainly take the perspective of an archaeological discovery.

The Silk Road started from Luoyang and Xi'an,China, and went all the way to ancient Rome via Central Asia, Western Asia and the Mediterranean.

First, I will tell you a story. According to Chinese literature, in *The Story of King Mu*, about 2,900 years ago, Mu, a king of the Western Zhou Dynasty (1046 B.C.-771 B.C.) who was highly keen on travelling,used to travel to many places;among the places he went to was the west which was equivalent to today's Central Asia. He met with a local queen called Queen Mother of the West; the local people treated him with due respect, and in return, King Zhou gave them many gifts, including jade ware—the Chinese people have loved jade objects very much since ancient times—more importantly, King Zhou also gave them hundreds of silks. This is probably the earliest record of China's Silk Road and it happened around 900 B.C., before Zhang Qian was sent as an envoy to the western regions. Is this record reliable? Opinions vary. However, our archaeological discovery has revealed the places where millet and glutinous millet were produced;these are two types of yellow crops, one type is glutinous while the other type is not. Millet congee is often seen in homemade meals in China; millet congee is made of millet.

Paddy rice in the Yangtze River Basin, millet and glutinous millet in Beijing were found during our archeological discoveries. It was the earliest kind of millet in China, even in the world. That was about 10,000 years ago. The millet and the glutinous millet in Beijing's suburban areas, near Fragrant Hills,which were recently discovered, are the earliest kinds known in the world. Millet has also been discovered in Europe and in Central Asia. The relationship between the two has always been rice. It is reported that rice was present 7,000 years ago in Europe; however, the latest research indicates that it was there about 4,000 years ago, while it was present 10,000 years ago in China. Even though it was present earlier in China, its origins may be different in the two regions. In recent years, along with scholars from the University of Cambridge and the University of Washington, I have conducted studies on whether there is an association betweenthe two kinds of millet. They are almost similar in form and not clearly different in taste. However, according to current tests, millet was present in Europe more than 4,000 years ago; in China, it was a longer time, probably 10,000 or 8,000 years ago. The early kinds of millet unearthed in Eurasia are divided into two types:they may have their own, independent origins or there may be an association between them. We obtained specimens through archaeological studies. Carbonized millets have been unearthed all across China. They were carbonized and had turned black after they had been buried for several thousand years. The millet was very common in China 8,000 years ago. We have carried out gene research on them as well.

It was found that millet and glutinous millet in North China were closely associated with those in Europe in terms of genes. Obviously, their origins are only North China. Professor Martin from the University of Cambridge takes charge of this project. If a Chinese led this project, some people might wonder: Does China have the desire to state that Chinese culture came into being very early? However, this project is organized by Professor Martin and moreover, there is DNA evidence. Therefore, now we can be sure that, at least 4,000 years ago, millet and glutinous millet originated in China and were introduced to the West by means of the Silk Road.

The second story deals with wheat. The flour from which today's bread is made, definitely originated in Western Asia, about 9,000 years ago. There was no such wild species in China, so it was obviously introduced from Western Asia. When was it introduced into China? So far, the answer is unclear. A series of dates shows that wheat was introduced to China about 4,500 years ago.

What route did it take? We think it was introduced via the Silk Road. It is worth noting that millet and glutinous millet have been present since the earliest times in China, but they were introduced from China to the West about 4,000 years ago; also wheat was introduced to the East about 4,000 years ago; this suggests that exchange of people between the East and the West took place about 4,000 years ago. The route for introducing wheat into Kazakhstan was roughly the same as that for its introduction into China. Wheat was recorded with pictographic characters in the inscriptions on bones or tortoise shells. It was introduced from the West.

It has been shown that the genes of sheep and cattle unearthed in the 4,000-year-old ruins in China came from Western Asia. It has been discovered that the genes of sheep of pedigrees A and B, which originated from Western Asia, were prevalent.

Traditional Chinese families raised pigs about 9,000-10,000 years ago, but sheep were introduced via the Silk Road 4,000 years ago. Like sheep, cattle appeared 4,000 years ago. Many of our explorations in different areas have been made through DNA analysis.

Thanks to the application of DNA, the latest science and technology in archaeology, we know that the Silk Road does not date back to 2,000 years ago,but to 4,000 years ago.

Take metallurgy as an example. Metallurgy emerged in Western Asia 7,000 years ago, and in China about 4,500or 5,000 years ago. Many technologies, as well as wheat, cattle and sheep were introduced to China about 4,500 years ago from the west. China's millet and glutinous millet also date back to this period. Close exchanges were conducted between the West and the East more than 4,000 years ago, 2,000 years earlier than the existence of the Silk Road. Therefore, we believe that there were routes for exchanges before the Han Dynasty.

Finally, I want to stress that silk was present in China no later than6,500 years ago. The silkworm-shaped products and stoneware that were unearthed appeared in China 6,500 years ago. According to archaeological discoveries, silkworms started to be reared in the Yellow River Basin at that time, so the history of silk-making dates back to6,500 years ago. Its introduction to the West was earlier than the Han Dynasty because the nobles in ancient Greece wore Chinese silk clothes in order to enhance their beauty and emphasize their nobility.

Regarding the introduction of carriages, they appeared suddenly in China about3,300 years ago. Originally, there were no carriages or equus caballus in China. However, carriages had been used in Caucasus, West Asia at least 4,000 years ago. Therefore, carriages showed up in the capital of China during the late Shang Dynasty (1600 B.C.-1046 B.C.) along with the Silk Road; carriages were an important way of exchange. Previously, there were no carriages or the custom of horseback riding in China. A long distance might involve many intermediate links, so horseback riding greatly accelerated these exchanges.

These exchanges occurred by means of the Silk Road before the Han Dynasty as roughly observed by me from an archaeological perspective. Thank you!

文化认同和人文交流对“一带一路”倡议的重要意义

斯巴修　【阿尔巴尼亚】
阿中文化协会　会长

我一直从事中华文化研究与传播，尤其关注中国文学作品以及图书的翻译出版，另外在自己国家成立了阿中文化协会，目的是维持两国人民之间的传统友谊并把这一友谊传达给青年一代以及在新的形势下继续促进两国的人文交流。

我们都知道在全球化的世界历史潮流中，各个民族国家的文化，汇成了一个史无前例的差异性交融的广浩域场，使得文化认同成为非常敏感、极其重要的议题。

我认为中国文化认同的发展历程应该从两个方面来看。

中国在其历史上长期以来比较封闭，推行闭关锁国的政策。因此历史上的中国相对很少与其他文明，与其他文化所接触，所以在那个时期可以说不存在文化认同的问题。只有在被西方所入侵，中国国门被迫敞开，在西方文化开始涌入中国的时候，就出现了各种方式的保护本国文化、本国传统的努力和运动，而贯穿其中的主题都是中华民族的自我意识、自我张扬和自我富强。然而我想以我个人的身份和在不同时期的一些经历和体会谈谈中国人的文化认同，尤其是对外来文化价值的认同的转变。1974 年我第一次来中国留学。那是“文化大革命”末期，也算是中国与世隔绝之时。那个时候几乎完全缺乏对外交流，中国人对本国文明，对本国古老文化了解得很少或者是持批判态度。对外国文化就更不用说。众所周知 20 世纪六七十年代，阿尔巴尼亚与中国有着非同一般的特殊关系，虽然这一关系基于意识形态，艺术团、电影等频繁的文艺活动使两国人民之间建立了纯朴的友谊。直到现在，许多50岁以上的中国人都曾向我谈起那个时候。我谈到这一点是想证明人文交流的重要性。

2002年，中国实行改革开放政策以后，我第二次来中国工作并生活了较长时间。我来的时候，不仅北京全变了，连中国人本身也发生了很大的变化，有正面的也有负面的变化。西方文化，电影，音乐艺术，生活方式到处可见，特别是年轻人可以说已经西方化了。虽然中国已经很开放，国家在快速发展，生活在不断改善，但是我的感觉是，他们对自己的文化，对自己的文明还是和之前一样漠不关心，甚至有时候也可以听到对中国一些传统习惯的批评声音。 也就是说在21世纪初，中国人还在埋头苦干，很少或者说才刚刚开始认知文化认同的概念。 但是2008年，北京奥运会和世界金融危机爆发后，中国不仅自己没有受到危机的影响，而且还为克服危机做出了重要贡献，成了世界经济的发展动力。之后它成为世界第二大经济强国，人民的生活实现了小康水平，政府和人民的自信度大大提高了。 这个时候，中国开始面向本国的古老文明，开始谈起有中国特色的价值观。就在这个时候，我第三次注意到，在很多中国人看来，代表着现代性的所谓西方文明的输入，是对自身文化传统乃至意识形态的渗透、演化和颠覆。

毫无疑问，随着改革开放政策的实行，中国文明实现了由被动吸收向主动吸收和输出的成功转型。当前，中国市场经济对外的开放程度、孔子学院在世界各地的受邀落户等事实充分地见证了中国文明实现的这一成功转型。究其根源，就社会层面而言，它与中国近现代的文化启蒙以及当代改革开放所取得的伟大成就及其面向普世文明的文化自觉密切相关。中国经过数十年的摸索才正确地处理现代化与西方化、计划经济与市场经济之间的内在关系，迈出了改革开放这一关键步伐。但是，特别是2008年以后我又注意到有，改革开放给中国带来的繁荣，并没有进一步强化改革开放对西方文明所持有的开放姿态，有时候民族主义伴随着民族富强的过分自信悄然兴起。中国已经不仅仅从经济上和国际影响力方面，而且从价值观方面开始挑战西方。

2013年中国国家主席习近平提出了“一带一路”的倡议。这一倡议将使它不仅从经济、市场、政治方面，而且还从文化方面与世界更加接触，更加一体化，这将是中国的一个大挑战。中国将不仅带着自己的资金、技术、设备，而且还带着自己的文化、自己的价值观和发展模式融入世界。然而人家肯定很乐意得到你的投资，你的好处，但未必愿意接受你的文化和价值观，甚至有时候会出现反感和抵制。现在我想在中国可以说不存在文化认同问题或者被外来价值观所主导的危险。我认为要实现“一带一路”的宏伟目标就必须在文化认同的同时，需要更重视和尊重共同遗产，推动人文交流。我同意这两天一些外国学者的看法，中国在介绍自己的发展模式和价值观方面做得还不够，特别是这个任务很多时候是通过官方渠道。这里面除官方外，还要发挥民间的作用，要加强别人对中国文化的认同就必须增加人文交流，推动旅游，加深彼此文化的相互了解和互相借鉴。中国作为正在快速、全方位融入国际社会的国家需要在文化认同的同时还要着重于共同遗产。在全球化和“一带一路”倡议积极实行的今天，文化间相互理解、容忍和共存的问题是非常重要的，只有这样才能增进社会和谐和世界和谐。文化往往是最好的黏合剂和缓冲地带。

Cultural Identification and Communication Are of Important Significance for the Success of the Belt and Road Initiative

Iljaz Spahiu / Albania

Chairman of the China-Albania Cultural Association

I am engaged in the study and dissemination of the Chinese culture; in particular, I deal with the translation and publication of Chinese literary works and books. Moreover, I established the Albania-China Cultural Association in Albania with a view to maintaining the traditional friendship between the people of the two countries and conveying this friendship to the young people as well as continuing to promote the people-to-people exchanges between the two countries in the context of the new situation.

As we know, in the historical trend of globalization throughout the world, the cultures of various national countries constitute an unprecedentedly extensive field with different levels of integration, making cultural identification a very sensitive and extremely important topic.

In my opinion, the developmental course of China's cultural identification should be considered regarding two aspects.

Historically, China has been a relatively closed country and has adopted a policy of seclusion for a long time. Thus, it has seldom been exposed to other civilizations and other cultures; the issue of cultural identification did not exist in China in that period. After the Western countries invaded China, China was forced to open its doors. When the Western cultures penetrated China, there were various types of endeavors and campaigns designed to protect Chinese culture and traditions, which were mainly characterized by the self-awareness, self-demonstration and self-improvement of Chinese nationalism. However, I want to talk about the cultural identification of the Chinese people—especially the changes in the identification of the external cultural values—according to the experiences and personal understanding which I have had in different periods. I studied in China for the first time in1974. It was the latter period of the Cultural Revolution, a decade during which China was isolated from the outside world. At that time, China almost completely lacked exchanges with the outside world and the Chinese people knew little about or criticized the Chinese civilization and the ancient Chinese culture, let alone foreign cultures. As you know, there were extraordinarily special relations between Albania and China in the 1960s-1970s though these relations were based on ideology, and a pure friendship established between the people of the two countries through frequent literary and artistic activities, including art troupe and films. Nowadays, many Chinese people above 50 years of age still talk to me about that period. By telling you about this, I want to prove the importance of people-to-people exchanges.

I came to China in 2002 after China adopted the policy of reform and opening up, then I worked and lived in China for a relatively long time. When I arrived in Beijing, I noticed that it had totally changed, even great changes, both positive and negative, had occurred in the Chinese people. The Western culture, films, music, art and life style could be found everywhere; in particular, young people had been westernized. China has now become very open and is rapidly developing, life is improving, but I am aware that the Chinese people remain indifferent to Chinese culture and civilization just like before, sometimes there are even criticisms about some traditional Chinese customs. In the early 21st century, the Chinese people worked hard, they seldom knew or just started to understand the concept of cultural identification. However, in 2008, the Beijing Olympic Games were held, the global financial crisis broke out, and afterwards, China not only was free from the impact of the financial crisis, but it also made important contributions to coping with the financial crisis, and became the impetus for the development of the world's economy. Subsequently, China became the second-largest economic power in the world, the people became well-off, and the confidence of the government and the people was greatly enhanced. At that time, China started to shift its attention to the ancient Chinese civilization and talked about the value outlook with Chinese characteristics. At that time, I became aware for the third time that many Chinese people thought that the input of the so-called Western civilization representing modernity had penetrated, progressively affected and subverted the Chinese cultural traditions, even its ideology.

Undoubtedly, with the implementation of the policy of reform and opening up, the Chinese civilization has successfully been transformed from passive assimilation to active assimilation and output. At present, with the high level of openness of China's market economy and the establishment of the Confucius Institute, on an invitation basis, around the world, people have witnessed the successful transformation of the Chinese civilization. Socially, the root cause is closely related to China's cultural enlightenment in modern times, the great achievements made by the contemporary reform and opening up and the cultural self-consciousness regarding a universal civilization. It took decades for China to explore and investigate before it correctly dealt with the inner relations between modernization and Westernization, between a planned economy and a market economy and took the crucial step—reform and opening up. However, I also note, especially after 2008, that the prosperity brought to China by the reform and opening up does not further reinforce its openness, resulting from the reform and opening up, to the Western civilization; sometimes a narrow line of nationalism rises along with the over-confidence amidst the national prosperity and mightiness. China has started to challenge the Western world in economy, international influence and value outlook.

In 2013, Chinese President Xi Jinping put forward the Belt and Road Initiative. This will enable China to further interact with the world and become more integrated at the levels of the economy, markets, politics and culture. This will be a big challenge for China. China will introduce not only its capital, technologies and equipment, but also its culture, value outlook and developmental model to the world. However, the rest of the world is certainly willing to obtain China's investments and benefits, but not necessarily to accept the Chinese culture and value outlook; sometimes it even dislikes and boycotts those aspects. I believe that now China is not subject to the problems having to do with cultural identification or with the risk that it is led by a value outlook that comes from the outside world. In my view, in order to achieve the ambitious goal of the Belt and Road Initiative, it is necessary to pay more attention to and show more respect for common heritages and promote people-to-people exchanges while maintaining one's own cultural identity. I agree with the views expressed by some foreign scholars during these two days. China has not carried out enough work to introduce its developmental model and value outlook; in particular, this task is often completed through official channels. Besides the official channels, space should also be given to the role of non-governmental forces. In order to make others further recognize the Chinese culture, it is necessary to enhance people-to-people exchanges, boost tourism, and deepen mutual understanding and learning of the respective cultures. As China is rapidly becoming part of and interacting with the international community in an all-round way, it needs to focus on common heritages while addressing its cultural identity. Amidst today's globalization and active implementation of the Belt and Road Initiative, mutual understanding of cultures, tolerance and coexistence are very important; only the mutual understanding of cultures, tolerance and coexistence can promote harmony in society and in the world. Culture often serves as the best adhesive and buffer zone in achieving this.

古“丝绸之路”上的文化交流

沙曼 【印度】
德里大学甘地中心 主任 / 德里大学社科院 前院长

第二届加德满都文化论坛对于印度、中国、尼泊尔以及南亚诸国具有十分重要的意义。南亚区域合作联盟的宗旨在于“促进经济、社会、文化、科技领域的积极合作与互助”，因此，在牢记这一宗旨的同时，我们应通力合作，共同承担起保护、保存以及管理文化遗址的责任。

自古以来，印度与中国乃至邻国之间的文化接触和宗教接触都是通过佛教来实现，这也是印度在文化接触中最为显著的特点之一。文化交流促进了佛教在中国以及南亚诸国的传播，而在文化交流和宗教交流的过程中，古丝绸之路扮演了重要的角色。除南、北、中三条线路外，还存在着中国东海及南海两条丝绸之路，往来于丝绸之路各条干线上的僧人及商旅，促进了沿线国家国民间的交流。这些国家都拥有各自尊奉的信仰和传统，而正是由于丝绸之路的存在，各国的信仰和传统才得以相互借鉴、相互适应。

印度境内至今保留着多处丝绸之路的遗址，据 2010 年联合国教科文组织在印度开展的考古调查显示，最重要的遗址包括：古毗舍离城遗址、古印度超戒寺大学遗址、拘尸那罗、舍卫城、考夏姆比等地的佛教遗址、萨格尔的佛塔及佛教遗址、卡瓦里帕蒂纳姆考古遗址、哈尔万地区、克什米尔地区的佛寺及佛塔、马哈拉施特拉地区的那拉梭帕拉佛塔等。以上遗址均代表着佛教区的文学传统，这在当地出土的考古证据中便能得到印证。这些区域都与佛陀和佛教的历史紧密相连。

尽管其他地区（如庇浦拉瓦、阿马拉瓦蒂、纳迦耳君康达）均留有佛塔遗址，但目前公认的最古老的佛塔要属毗舍离市的佛塔遗址。同理，印度境内许多地区都留有阿育王柱，但毗舍离市的阿育王柱被认为是年代最久远且唯一未经雕饰的一根。此外，印度境内保留着大量的佛寺，但专供比丘尼（俗称尼姑）修行的卐形佛寺只有在毗舍离市才能见到。

超戒寺曾是古代著名的学术中心，兴盛于公元 8 世纪末叶至公元 13 世纪初。

拘尸那迦则被公认为佛祖释迦牟尼佛证悟涅槃之地，当地曾出土涅槃寺和涅槃塔的考古遗迹，经印度考古调查机构复原后保存至今。

舍卫城相传为佛陀说法及显演神通之地。据说，当年佛陀在舍卫城洒下树种，土地中便立刻长出一颗芒果树来。

考夏姆比是佛陀证悟之后，在第六年和第九年雨季的驻足之处。在佛陀所说的经文之中曾多次提到这里。目前，这里已经成为考古重地，受印度考古调查机构保护。

萨格尔位于旁遮普地区，是当时重要的佛教中心。中国的玄奘法师曾于公元 629 至 645 年间造访此地。在以此考古挖掘过程中，这里曾出土一尊古代的佛塔遗迹。

卡瓦里帕蒂纳姆出土的佛陀精舍、古玩、青铜佛像及石灰雕像均可证明，在早期的历史阶段，佛教便已然开始在这里盛行，并且得到诸国国王的支持。卡瓦里帕蒂纳姆作为当时佛教信仰的中心，在两部泰米尔史诗——《西拉巴提伽拉姆》及《摩尼梅伽拉依》中均有提及，而佛寺的发现更是证实了史诗中的记载。

哈尔万地区曾出土大量的陶瓦，因而被公认为是第四次佛教法会（迦腻色伽王一世统治期间）的举办地。当地出土的遗迹中有一尊三级基座的佛塔，周围铺有雕纹陶瓦，此外还有屋宇数间，出土文物包括陶土雕塑、佛陀画像残片以及数张刻有佛塔画像的泥土版。

马哈拉施特拉地区最重要的历史古迹要属当地出土的佛塔及文物堆，位于那拉梭帕拉镇以西四分之一英里处。在公元前 250 年至公元 1500 年间，这里曾是古阿波兰多迦（今康坎）地区一座重要的圣城和贸易中心，这在佛教、耆那教、婆罗门教的经典以及希腊罗马古典文学中均可以得到印证。这里是西海岸地区重要的佛教中心，相传佛陀曾亲自驾临此地。梭帕拉在不同的历史时期内，也是印度教、佛教、耆那教发生文化演进的区域。

除上述佛教遗址外，印度境内的古丝绸之路沿线还保留着大量的佛教石窟。这些石窟是当初僧侣敬用来礼拜和居住的场所，后于印度西部出土发掘。雄伟壮观的阿旃陀石窟和埃洛拉石窟群位于马哈拉施特拉，这些石窟群均是在岩石上开凿而成，堪称古印度建筑遗产中杰出的典范。此外，卡尔利、坎赫里、番达夫勒尼、帕扎、贝德萨、奥兰加巴德、乌达其里、瓮达瓦利以及皮塔尔考拉等地的石窟均具有重要意义。中国境内的敦煌石窟是古丝绸之路上主要的交汇点，对于中国与印度间的文化交流打下了坚实的基础。上百座石窟中的彩色石壁、雄伟的佛像等，都是中印文明交流最有力的见证。

与佛教相关的遗址，如蓝毗尼、菩提伽耶、鹿野苑、拘尸那迦、王舍城、瓦伊沙利、僧迦斯等地的佛教古迹，向来深受广大游客青睐，菩提伽耶寺甚至被联合国教科文组织列入世界遗产名录，而位于那烂陀的玄奘博物馆更是中印合作的见证。总理纳伦德拉·莫迪不仅对开发旅游业佛教遗址寄予厚望，更对发掘和保存印度境内的所有佛教遗产抱有兴趣。

此外，海上丝绸之路也对各国人民的交流起到了重要作用，泉州的开元寺便是一个绝佳的例证。该寺位于中国的福建省泉州市，以弘扬印度佛教而闻名，其浓厚的南印度建筑风格与13世纪古马德拉斯邦时期兴建的寺院极为相似。

诸如此类的文化接触构成了古文明长河中璀璨的篇章，对人类的精神、文化乃至社会都产生着强有力的影响。佛教遗址吸引着游客、学者、艺术家、历史学家、地质学家、考古学家以及各界学会的会员，在复兴古文化交流的同时，各国人民也因此拉近了关系。因此，我们需要通力合作，为保护和保存这些遗产而努力。相关领域内的艺术家、建筑师、博物馆学家、文物保护专家等，需要跨越国界，建立国际合作关系。印度考古调查机构、国家博物馆、邦博物馆、中心及邦立大学等机构，正在为保护工作、遗产管理、博物馆学培养生力军，我们要培养年轻一代、为他们提供实习机会、为这些领域内的研究提供奖学金。就我个人而言，我希望跨国合作项目能够被纳入到大学课堂中来。

第二届加德满都文化论坛将进一步促进中国与南亚诸国间的相互理解、加强双方的文化纽带。本届论坛将为我们提供一个交流的平台，为共同保护历史文化遗产搭建桥梁。

最后，预祝第二届加德满都文化论坛圆满成功！

Cultural Communication through Ancient Silk Road

Anita Sharma / India

Director of the Gandhi Bhawan at the University of Delhi /Former Dean of the Faculty of Social Sciences at the University of Delhi

The Second Kathmandu Cultural Forum is very significant for India, China, Nepal and other South Asian Countries. One of the main objectives of SAARC is *to promote active collaboration and mutual assistance in the economic, social, cultural, technical and scientific fields*. Keeping this in mind, we should have mutual commitment to cooperate for protection, conservation and management of cultural heritage sites. For achieving this, there is a need to have joint projects, seminars, workshops, conferences and field works.

As far as India is concerned, cultural and religious contacts between India, China and other neighbouring countries through Buddhism constitute one of the most outstanding factors since ancient times. It was through cultural exchanges that Buddhism travelled to China and other South Asian countries. The ancient Silk Road played an important role in Cultural and religious exchanges. In addition to Southern Route, Central Route and Northern Route, there are also East China Sea and South China Sea Silk Road. Buddhism had a deep impact on art and architecture on the sites along the Silk Road. Monks and traders who travelled through these different arteries of the Silk Road were the carriers who brought the people of these countries along the Silk Road closer. There were a lot of adaptations from each other’s cultures respecting their beliefs and traditions.

There are many Silk Road sites in India, some of the most significant sites suggested by the Archaeological Survey of India to UNESCO in 2010 are Ruins in Ancient Vaishali, Remains of Vikramshila ancient university, Buddhist Remains of Kushinagar, Sravasti, Kaushambi, Ancient site and Buddhist stupa at Sanghol, Excavated Remains of Kaveripattinam, Ancient monastery and Stupa together with adjacent land in Harwan, Kashmir and Nalla Sopara Stupa in Maharashtra. These Buddhist sites represent both literary tradition of famous Buddhist settlements and archaeological evidence corroborating them. These places are connected with the history of Buddha and Buddhism.

Though there are relic stupas elsewhere also (like Piprahwa, Amaravati, Nagarjunkonda etc.), the relic stupa at Vaishali is so far accepted to be the earliest stupa. Similarly, Asoka Pillars are there at many other places but the Vaishali pillar with a square abacus is regarded as the earliest and is the only one which is un-inscribed. Though there are a good number of monasteries scattered all over the country, presence of a swastika shaped monastery meant for nuns has been found only at Vaishali.

Vikramshila was a famous seat of learning. It flourished from the last quarter of the 8th Century CE to the beginning of the 13th Century CE.

Kushinagar is the identified place where Lord Buddha attained Mahaparinirvana. The archaeological remains of the Mahaparinirvana Temple and Mahaparinirvana Stupa have been found here which are restored and maintained by the Archaeological Survey of India.

It was at Sravasti that the Buddha is said to have performed great miracles. It is believed that a Mango tree instantly arose when he threw seeds in the ground.

Kaushambi is a place where Buddha passed his sixth and ninth rainy season after attaining enlightenment. It is also related to many sermons that were preached by Buddha. This archaeological is protected by the Archaeological Survey of India.

Sanghol in Punjab was an important centre of Buddhism. Chinese pilgrim Xuan Zang visited Sanghol during the period 629-645 CE. At Sanghol remains of an ancient Buddhist Stupa were found during an excavation.

The excavated structure of Buddha Vihara, Temple site at Pallavanesarm and antiquities like bronze Buddha and lime Buddha confirm that Buddhism was prevailing during early historic period in Kaveripattinam and it was also patronized by Kings. The discovery of a Buddhist monastery confirmed the literary evidence found in the Tamil epics - Silappatikaram and Manimekhalai which records that Kaveripattinam was a centre of Buddhist faith.

Harwan is identified with Terracotta Tiles that is said to be the centre of the fourth Buddhist Council held during the reign of Kanishka. Among the remains are three-step base of a stupa and a set of rooms. The area around the Stupa is paved with decorated terracotta tiles. The antiquities found include terracotta figures, and fragments of Buddha image and a few clay tablets bearing miniature stupa in relief.

The most significant monuments of Maharashtra is the Buddhist stupa or relic mound about a quarter mile west of Sopara town. It was an important holy city and trade point in Aparanta (Ancient name of Konkan) from 250 BCE to 1500 CE. This is evidenced by the different religious Buddhist, Jain and Brahminical old literature classical literature of Greek and Rome and also by the epigraphical records. It was an important Buddhist centre on the west coast where Buddha himself is said to have visited. Sopara remained the place for cultural evolution of Hinduism, Buddhism and Jainism in different periods.

Along with these Buddhist sites, there are many Buddhist caves on the ancient

Silk Road in India. These caves were used by Buddhist monks as places of worship and residence. Initially the caves were excavated in the western India. Maharashtra is home to the spectacular and amazing Ajanta and Ellora group of caves. The caves at Ajanta and Ellora were cut out of rock and rank amongst some of the most outstanding specimens of ancient Indian architectural heritage. Karle, Kanhery, Pandavleni, Bhaja, Bedse, Aurangabad, Udaigiri, Undavalli and Pitalkhora Caves are some other important caves. Dunhuang in China was a major point of inter section on the ancient Silk Road that had played a foundational role in bringing closer the India-China cultural connections. Hundreds of caves with painted walls and grand statues are exceptionally powerful cultural connections between Indian and Chinese civilizations.

Buddhist sector sites are very popular among the tourists. These are Lumbini, Bodhhgaya, Sarnath, Kushinagar, Rajgir, Vaishali, Sravasti, and Sankisa. UNESCO has declared Bodhhgaya Temple as World heritage monument. Xuanzang Museum in Nalanda is a result of collaboration between India and China. Aside from developing Buddhist sites for the tourism industry, P.M. Narender Modi has also shown interest to excavate and preserve Buddhist sites across Indian states.

Maritime Silk Road also connected people of various countries. A good example of connection there is Kaiyuan Temple in Quan Zhou, China that is known as Hindu-Buddhist temple. It was made in South Indian style and has close similarities with the 13th century temples constructed in Tamil Nadu.

Contacts of this type constitute a wonderful chapter in ancient civilization which had a strong influence on the mind, culture and society. Buddhist sites are an attraction among tourists, scholars, artists, historians, geologists, archaeologists and academicians from other fields. All these ancient cultural connections can be revived to bring the people of both the countries closer. Joint efforts are needed to protect and conserve these sites. Scholars working in the areas related to art, architecture, museology and conservation need to have International collaborations.

Archaeological Survey of India, National Museum, State Museums, various central and state universities are training youngsters for Conservation work, Heritage Management and Museology. It is very important to train young generation and give internships, scholarships in these areas of research. I hope that collaborative projects will become a part of academic courses.

The Second Kathmandu Cultural Forum will strengthen the mutual understanding and cultural ties between China and other South Asian countries. This Forum will give us a platform to exchange ideas and views to safeguard our historical and cultural heritage sites.

I wish success to the Second Kathmandu Cultural Forum!

历史上的全球化与中国文明的发展

稻畑耕一郎　【日本】
早稻田大学中国古籍文化研究所　所长/早稻田大学文学学术院　教授

这次座谈会的总主题是“汉学与当代中国”(Symposium on China Studies)。在我看来，以传统的观念来说，“中国研究(China Studies)”的含义仅限于政治、经济、社会等，主要是面临现代问题，而“汉学”(Sinology)则主要研究中国历史上的文史哲领域的学问。我的理解虽然与今天有些不同，但是因为个人的经历和近年从事的工作，略有体会，所以还是敢到北京来参加这次会议。

我本人从半个世纪之前上大学的时候开始对中国抱有兴趣，学习中文和中国古代典籍。1972 年日中邦交正常化，1974 年我第一次到中国，从此以后经常到中国来跟中国学者进行交流。1985 年至 1986 年间，曾以访问学者的身份驻留北京大学考古系，1986 到 1987 年在南开大学东方艺术系任教，并于 2005 年又到北大中国古文献研究中心进行客座研究。此外，目前还参加了北京大学《儒藏 · 日本编》的编纂工作。

从第一次来到中国直到今天，我一直抱持着“何以中国”的疑问从事着研究。简言之，我的一直抱持的问题是：究竟什么是中国？我们外国人怎样理解中国是最合适。中国的真面貌在哪里？

这似乎不仅是我一个人的问题。诸位可能都记得，半个世纪以前，英国有一位中国专家雷蒙 · 道森(Raymond Dawson)，他撰写了《中国变色龙——对于欧洲中国文明观的分析》(The Chinese Chameleon: An Analysis of European

Conceptions of Chinese Civilization）一书。欧洲人对中国的观念，在不同时期有着很大的变化。有趣的是，这些变化当然一定程度上反映着中国社会的变迁，但是更多的是反映了欧洲知识史的进展。对欧洲人来说，有时候中国是理想土地，有时候中国是落后国家，或强大或虚弱，或聪明或愚笨，或美丽或丑陋，往往是完全相反的两个极端。今天，我们究竟怎样来理解中国才是最好的呢？

这几年来我从事着一项工作是将北京大学出版社出版的《中华文明史》翻成日文版，最近才全部出版完成。《中华文明史》一书，是一部总字数 166 万字的巨著，由北京大学的文学、史学、哲学及考古学专业的朋友们，组织力量编纂。翻译此书的过程中，我也一直在思考着这个问题，“何以中国？”中国到底是什么？什么是中国？中国的意象很复杂，要回答这个问题，绝非易事。然而这次我通过对《中华文明史》的翻译，逐渐认识到，从“文明史”的角度进行考察，或许能够为我们理解中国提供重要的线索。

目前，在“全球化”的大势之下，人类正以前所未有的速度和规模，走向统合。从相对的观点来看，这是历史的趋势，同时也是无法阻挡的发展之路。然而，在全球化进展的过程中，各式各样的问题随之不断产生，也是无法否认的事实。各国和各地域的主张及利害盘根错节，相互影响，加上资源、粮食、信息、科技等领域的你争我夺，民族纠纷、宗教对立、环境污染、经济差距、贸易摩擦等课题，一跃成为人类发展的重大挑战。

当我们面对上述这些全人类的重要课题，其中不容小觑的是中国的影响。中国人口占了世界总人口的五分之一，同时有着欧盟两倍之广的版图。那些忽视中国之存在的论调，是毫无意义的。相信这一点任何人都不难理解。

跟过去相较，今天我们必须对中国有更进一步的认识。对中国缺乏理解，已经不为时代所容许。然而，中国幅员辽阔、人口众多，加上社会结构复杂，其历史也超乎想象的漫长。经过千变万化的历史演变，才发展至今的现代中国，要掌握其实情，绝非容易之事。

在人类文明史的发展历程中，中国文明在每个历史阶段带来的贡献，皆有无法取代的重要性，值得给予高度评价。举例来说，一般认为，起源于中国的吃茶风尚，很早就传播至日本，同时孕育了日本独特的茶道文化。进入 17 世纪以后，茶叶被引进到欧洲，很快便在上流社会间流行开来，成为广受欢迎的饮料。不久，随着饮茶习惯的大众化，茶叶的消费量增加，贸易摩擦也随之增加。17 世纪到十八世纪由此引发了英荷战争，进一步造成了19世纪东西文明冲突的鸦片战争，其后并发展为美国独立战争的远因。此外，丝绸、造纸、印刷术等诞生于中国的技术与文化，也给予人类文明深远的影响。

然而，文明间的影响绝非只是单向的。对全世界造成影响的“中华文明”，本身也受到众多地域的不同文明的启发。世界也对中国文明带来了重要影响这一点上，也是毋庸置疑的。

举例来说，如没有印度佛教的影响，今日中国文明的样态，应是难以想象的。当然，在为数众多的外在影响中，佛教不过是其中一个显著的例子而已。从有史以前的远古时代，直到近代的共产主义、社会主义等诸多外来影响，可以说不胜枚举。如果少了这些文明的要素的影响，“中华文明”恐怕不会有今天的深度与广度，甚至是否能够延绵不绝地持续至今，也是难以断言的。

进一步理解上述文化现象背后的意义，是理解今日中国最为直接而有效的方法。

“全球主义”这个词，是近几年才出现的。但我认为，实际在人类的文化史上，至少在中国文明发展过程中，全球化的现象早就有了，当然其规模和速度不如现在。

我们要想一想，20世纪中期，第二次世界大战之后，在“Nationalism”的主张下，很多殖民地都在争取独立，当时大家认为“Nationalism”或者民族独立是对的，有道理的，是正义的。但是后来各个国家、各个民族之间的主张不同，或者一个国家内的民族之间有了矛盾，因此出来了“Internationalism”的主张，以求跨国家，或者跨民族解决问题。现在国家间的矛盾越来越复杂化，人们想妥善处理国家、民族之间的各种矛盾，随着信息化的趋势，才逐渐进入了全球主义（globalism）的时代。

我的研究领域，不是政治，也不是经济，而是古代文化。从我的研究领域了解到，在中国广大的领土上，长久以来“文明”间的冲突与融合，在不断重复上演。我认为，这样的过程存在每一个历史时代环节中，实际上正相当于我们今天面临的全球化现象。中国文明从先史以来便不断地与其他文明接触，正是在这样的过程中，融合了对方的文明内涵，并扩充了自身，一路发展至今。

昨天，在这次会议上，中国社会科学院考古所的王巍所长给大家介绍《汉代以前的“丝绸之路”》，考古学的成果也很明显地证明，文明史上的全球化的趋向，是从远古时代早就有的。可以看出，这不仅仅是现代的问题。因此也可以说，没有全球化，就没有人类文明的进步。

Globalization in History and the Development of Chinese Civilization

Koichiro Inahata / Japan

Director of the Research Institute for Chinese Old Book Culture at Waseda University /Professor of the Faculty of Letters Arts and Sciences at Waseda University

The overall theme of this symposium is "Symposium on China Studies". In my view, from the perspective of the traditional concept, the meaning of "China Studies" is limited to politics, economy and society and "China Studies" mainly deals with modern issues, while "Sinology" focuses research on the knowledge concerning the cultural, literary and philosophical fields in Chinese history. My understanding is different from today's situation to some extent; I have gained a slight understanding thanks to my personal experience and recent work, so I have the courage to attend this symposium in Beijing.

I started showing interest in China, learning Chinese and reading ancient Chinese books and records when I attended university half a century ago. The diplomatic relations between China and Japan were normalized in 1972. I came to China for the first time in 1974. Afterwards, I have often come to China to communicate with Chinese scholars. From 1985 to 1986, I stayed as a visiting scholar at the

Department of Archaeology at Peking University. From 1986 to 1987, I taught at the Department of Oriental Art at Nankai University. In 2005, I served as a visiting research fellow at the Center for Ancient Chinese Classics &Archives at Peking University. In addition, I also participated in compiling the *Collections of Confucian Classics: Japan Volume* at Peking University.

Since I came to China for the first time, I have always been involved in doing research by focusing on the following questions: What is China? How do foreigners understand China in the most appropriate way? What is the true face of China?

These questions seem to not merely attract my attention. You may remember that, half a century ago, the British sinologist Raymond Dawson wrote a book entitled *The Chinese Chameleon: An Analysis of European Conceptions of Chinese Civilization*. The European conceptions of China have greatly changed throughout different periods. Interestingly, these changes reflect, to some extent, the changes that have occurred in Chinese society, but they give more expression to the progress in the history of European knowledge. For Europeans, sometimes China has been an ideal land, sometimes it has been a backward country, powerful or weak, smart or foolish, beautiful or ugly; the Europeans' views of China have been two completely opposite extremes. What is the best way for us to understand China today?

I have recently translated *The History of Chinese Civilization*, published by the Peking University Press, into Japanese, the publication of which was fully completed last month. The book *The History of Chinese Civilization*, a great work consisting of 1.66 million words, was compiled by friends from Peking University who are engaged in literature, historical science, philosophy and archaeology. During the translation of this book, I thought about this question: What is China? As the portrait of China is very complicated, it is not easy to answer this question. However, the translation of *The History of Chinese Civilization* has enabled me to gradually realize that by observing it from the perspective of the history of civilization, it may provide us with important clues for understanding China.

At present, under the general trend of globalization, human beings are moving towards integration at an unprecedented rate and on an unprecedented scale. Relatively speaking, this is a historical trend and also an unstoppable road towards development. However, globalization is accompanied by a great variety of problems, which is an undeniable fact. The claims and interests of various countries and territories are intricately intertwined and interact with each other; furthermore, the fights for resources, grain, information, science and technology, ethnic feuds, religious confrontations, environmental pollution, economic gaps and trade frictions have become great challenges for human development.

When we face the important issues above concerning all human beings, China's influence cannot be ignored. China's population accounts for 1/5 of the world's population and China's area is two times that of the EU. The views which disregard China make no sense. This is understandable for everyone.

Compared with the past, now we must understand China even more profoundly. Lack of an understanding of China is not tolerated by the times. As China has a vast territory and a huge population, its social structure is complicated and its history is incredibly long. China has undergone an ever-changing historical evolution before it became a modern country, so it is not easy to understand China's present situation.

The contributions made by the Chinese civilization at each historical stage in the history of human civilization are irreplaceably important and deserve to be highly commended. For example, it is generally believed that the tea-drinking custom originated in China and was spread to Japan very early, and that it also gave birth to Japan's unique culture of the tea ceremony. In the 17th century, tea was introduced to Europe and quickly became popular in the high society, and since then, it has developed into an immensely popular drink. Before long, with the popularization of the tea-drinking custom, tea consumption increased and trade frictions occurred. Thus the Anglo-Dutch Wars broke out during the 17thand 18thcenturies, further causing the Opium War which led to the clash of Eastern and Western civilizations in the 19th century, which was the remote cause for the American Revolution. In addition, silk, papermaking and printing are technologies and cultures that originated in China, and that have exerted a far-reaching impact on human civilization.

However, the impact of civilizations on one another is by no means a one-way impact. The Chinese civilization which has had an impact on the whole world has also been inspired by different civilizations from many regions. The important impact of the world on the Chinese civilization is also unquestionable.

For example, if there had been no impact from Indian Buddhism, the state of today's Chinese civilization would be unimaginable. Of course, Buddhism is nothing but a significant example among a large number of external influencing factors. The external influencing factors from ancient prehistoric times to communism and socialism in modern times are too numerous to enumerate. If the impact from these civilization factors had not been available, the Chinese civilization might not have the depth and breadth that it has today, and it might even be difficult to be certain that it would have lasted until now.

Further understanding the significance behind the above cultural phenomena is the most direct and effective way to understand today's China.

The word "globalism" did not appear until recent years. However, in my opinion, the phenomenon of globalization existed early on in the history of human culture, at least during the development of the Chinese civilization, though its scale and speed did not reach today's levels.

We should think: In the middle of the 20th century—after the Second World War, under the influence of nationalism, the people in many colonies sought independence, and it was generally believed at that time that nationalism or national independence was right, reasonable and righteous. However, afterwards, different countries and nationalities have different claims, or contradictions occurred among nationalities within a country, thus internationalism emerged with a view to solving problems across countries or across nationalities. Now the contradictions among countries have become increasingly complicated, the people want to handle various contradictions among countries and nationalities properly; with the development of information, the people have gradually entered the era of globalism.

My research touches upon ancient cultures rather than politics and economy. According to my field of research, the clashes and integration among civilizations have repeatedly taken place in China's vast territory throughout the ages. In my view, this process existed at each segment of the historical period; in fact, it was exactly equivalent to today's phenomenon of globalization. The Chinese civilization has been interacting with other civilizations since prehistoric times, through which the Chinese civilization has incorporated the connotations of other civilizations to expand itself and develop up until now.

In yesterday's meeting, Wang Wei, the Director of the Institute of Archaeology at the Chinese Academy of Social Sciences, introduced the *Silk Road before the Han Dynasty (202 B.C.-A.D.220)* to you. Archaeological achievements also apparently prove that globalization in the history of civilization existed as early as ancient times. As shown, it is not an issue which has merely emerged in modern times. Therefore, there is no progress in human civilization without globalization.

Thank you!